Determinants
of
Investment
Behavior

What determines the investments of
consumers and business firms has long
been a subject of controversy. By presenting new and sometimes surprising
information on the subject, the papers
in this volume provide additional fuel
for the current contoversies. These papers
were prepared for a conference sponsored by the Universities-National Bureau Committee for Economic Research
and held at the University of Wisconsin.
The purpose of the conference was to
bring together the work of people studying the investment decisions of different
economic units and to compare their
methods and results.

The volume is divided into five parts.
The first, dealing with the anatomy of
investment behavio.·, presents an empirical study of consumer investment and a
survey of the current theories of business
and consumer investment behavior.

Part II is devoted to the financial aspects of business investment. The costs of

(continued on back flap)

Determinants of Investment Behavior

UNIVERSITIES–NATIONAL BUREAU CONFERENCE SERIES

Determinants
of Investment Behavior

A CONFERENCE OF THE

UNIVERSITIES–NATIONAL BUREAU COMMITTEE

FOR ECONOMIC RESEARCH

Edited by
ROBERT FERBER
University of Illinois

NATIONAL BUREAU OF ECONOMIC RESEARCH
NEW YORK   1967
Distributed by COLUMBIA UNIVERSITY PRESS
NEW YORK AND LONDON

RELATION OF NATIONAL BUREAU DIRECTORS TO PUBLICATIONS REPORTING CONFERENCE PROCEEDINGS

Since the present volume is a record of conference proceedings, it has been exempted from the rules governing submission of manuscripts to, and critical review by, the Board of Directors of the National Bureau. It has, however, been reviewed and accepted for publication by the Director of Research.

(Resolution adopted July 6, 1948, as revised November 21, 1949)

Contents

Part III: Consumer Assets

Part IV: Producer Durables

Part V: Anticipations

Determinants of Investment Behavior

Introduction

ROBERT FERBER

UNIVERSITY OF ILLINOIS

This volume contains the papers presented at a conference sponsored by the Universities-National Bureau Committee for Economic Research on June 10–12, 1965, at the University of Wisconsin, together with much of the discussion of these papers. The purpose of this conference was to bring together the work of people studying the investment decisions of different economic units and to compare the methods employed and the nature of the results obtained. The conference was concerned with theoretical approaches to explaining investment as well as with behavioral relations. Consumer units and business firms were the subjects of study. (The original plans included a session on government investment behavior, but these plans could not be implemented because of the sparse analytical work on the subject.)

The conference was organized into five sessions, which served as the basis for the organization of this volume. The first session, reported in the first part of the book, was designed to explore some of the fundamental questions of consumer and business investment. The result is two papers that are very different, not only in subject matter but also in content. In the first of these papers, Jean Crockett and Irwin Friend take an empirical approach to the analysis of consumer investment behavior. After providing a concise review of the current literature on consumer saving and investment, they proceed to formulate a theory of the determinants of consumer holdings of different tangible as well as financial assets wherein the desired stock of assets depends primarily on the normal or permanent income of the household. Increments to this stock then depend on the difference between the desired stock and the actual stock, with normal income serving as a proxy for desired stock in the empirical tests.

Two sets of cross-section data are used for the empirical tests, carried out by a series of multiple regressions. The tests were designed partly to experiment with ways of separating normal from transitory income effects and partly to obtain improved estimates of the effect of initial asset holdings on consumer saving and investment by holding tastes constant in various ways. The most noteworthy feature of the results, the authors state, is the tendency for the long-run normal income elasticity of saving or of assets to exceed unity by substantial margins. The results also suggest that initial assets are necessary in explaining saving behavior, as is implied by a lagged adjustment model, though in a number of the regressions the assets effect is very weak.

In commenting on this paper, James Tobin feels that the formulation of the basic hypothesis is too static, that allowance should be made for changes in desired wealth and in its composition. He also questions whether sufficient allowance has been made for the effects of age, inheritances, and unrealized capital gains (though more complete allowances for age effects in the final draft of this paper does not alter the main results), and urges that better ways be sought to hold tastes constant. Tobin and Zvi Griliches feel that the speed-of-adjustment estimates are not too satisfactory, which may well be due to lack of sufficient data.

The second paper at the first session, by Dale Jorgenson, follows a highly theoretical bent in considering the investment behavior of business firms. In presenting a survey of some of the current theories of business investment behavior, it seeks to provide a framework for comparing alternative models of investment behavior. Such a framework is badly needed at this time, Jorgenson argues, as "a basis for evaluating evidence on the determinants of investment behavior." In seeking such a framework, Jorgenson contrasts the neoclassical theory of optimal capital accumulation with the current theory in the literature that business firms maximize utility in a broader sense than just profits. His basic point is that it is indeed possible to derive a demand function for investment goods on the basis of neoclassical assumptions and that the resulting theory provides a framework for the principal econometric models of investment behavior. The alternate theory based on utility maximization, he notes, conflicts with much of the literature on cost and production functions.

Jorgenson uses the neoclassical assumptions in conjunction with the premise that the firm maximizes the utility of a consumption stream subject to a fixed set of production possibilities and to fixed current and future prices, including interest rates. The production plan, which is then independent of the choice of a consumption stream, is selected by maximizing the present value of the firm subject to a production function relating output to flows of labor and of capital services. In addition, capital services as well as replacement are considered to be proportional to the stock of capital goods. The demand function for investment goods is then obtained as the sum of the rate of change in the flow of capital services and of replacement needs, the latter being proportional to capital stock. By assuming that changes in the rate of interest leave the price of capital services unchanged, the desired demand function is readily obtainable. This demand function has a negative slope with respect to changes in the rate of interest.

In his comments on Jorgenson's paper, Tobin agrees with the usefulness of the neoclassical theory of the firm and with the principle of maximization of the present value of the firm as a basis for a dynamic theory. Tobin feels, however, that the development of this principle "is only barely dynamic" because the "firm can maximize present value simply by maximizing profits at every point in time." Decisions about time paths of profits do not enter the picture. In addition, Tobin questions the continuity of such variables as prices, wages, and the rental cost of capital services, and argues that if these variables are subject to discontinuities, no demand schedule for net investment exists, only one for capital. The investment demand schedule obtained by Jorgenson, Tobin notes, is not the demand schedule considered by previous theorists because other variables are not held constant but are manipulated to compensate for the effect of a change in the interest rate.

In his reply Jorgenson distinguishes between whether present and *future* prices or present and *forward* prices are fixed in considering the existence of a demand schedule for investment goods. In the former case, he agrees with Tobin that no demand schedule can exist, but he notes that the latter case does support the existence of a demand schedule and is a point previously overlooked.

The second part of this volume is devoted to the financing of business investment. In the first of the two papers here, Merton Miller and Franco Modigliani develop further their approach for estimating the costs of capital applicable to investment decisions under uncertainty. This leads them to hypothesize that the cost of capital depends primarily on the market capitalization rate for pure equity streams of firms of that type, and not on the financial structure of the firm or on its dividend policy. This approach differs radically from the one usually followed in econometric models which relies upon some standard index of yields on high-grade corporate or government bonds as a measure of the cost of capital. The present approach means that the cost of capital has to be estimated from cross-section regressions between the market value of the firm, on the one hand, and its earnings and rate of growth, on the other. Miller and Modigliani apply such regressions to a cross-section sample of large electric utilities for the years 1954, 1956, and 1957. From these regressions, estimates of the cost of capital in each year are obtained and compared with capital costs estimated by the more usual approach. They note that in the present study the usual yield measures seriously understate the rise in capital costs that occurred during this period, a rise brought about by the increase in the market's evaluation of the growth potential of that industry.

In the second paper, John Lintner considers the role of financial behavior in investment policy. Like Miller and Modigliani, Lintner assumes that firms seek to act in such a way as to maximize the market value of their equity. Unlike them, however, he assumes that bonds as well as stock are risk assets, and comes to the diametrically opposite conclusion that investment outlays are related inversely to leverage. Also unlike Miller and Modigliani, Lintner places heavy stress on the priority of cash dividend payments in short-run financial investment policy, because of "the extraordinarily high 'information content' of changes in dividend payments in the eyes of shareholders as they form their expectations." Hence, dividend payments are introduced as a constraint on investment.

Lintner tests his model by attempting to explain quarterly capital expenditures of manufacturing companies during 1953–63. The equations, incorporating accelerator, financial, and risk variables, yield highly favorable results by the usual statistical criteria. In particular, Lintner notes that the coefficients of interest rates, their smoothed rate of change and leverage all turned out to be highly and very consistently significant and negatively related to investment.

The comments on these papers raise questions about the theoretical bases of the papers and discuss alternative means of dealing with the same problem. Thus, Irwin Friend suggests "estimating the cost of equity . . . as the sum of a dividend yield plus an estimated growth rate in earnings and dividends, and obtaining the over-all cost of capital as the market-value weighted sum of the costs of equity and senior capital (adjusted for tax effects)." This approach does not require assuming the irrelevance of capital structure, though the difficulty of estimating growth rates still remains. J. Fred Weston questions the validity of many of the basic assumptions in both papers. In the Miller-Modigliani paper, he questions the irrelevance of capital structure, the continuity and independence of investment decisions, and the reliance on an assets variable to measure growth; and in the Lintner paper, he questions the greater role of uncertainty in financing than in capital budgeting, the rise in the marginal cost of capital with leverage, and other statements which do not seem to have empirical support.

The third part of this volume contains four papers on consumer investment. The first of these, by Richard Muth, deals with housing and focuses on *where* such investment is likely to take place rather than on how much. From this study of the spatial aspects of urban housing, Muth concludes that the urban decentralization that took place up to 1950 "is far from haphazard and only in small part a 'flight from blight.'" The basis for this conclusion is his finding that the "distribution of population between the central city and its suburbs and the total land occupied by an urban area can be explained to a considerable extent, though not solely, by the same forces that affect the spread of population within the central city." Principal among these forces are car registrations per capita, the population of the urbanized area, and median income in the area. Interestingly enough, the changing racial composition of the central city is found to be of relatively small importance in accounting for suburbanization.

The paper by Gordon Sparks deals with a different aspect of residential construction; he develops and tests a model to link such activity with the monetary sector. The model contains a series of equations seeking to measure the effect on housing construction of the flow of funds through financial intermediaries. Accumulation of savings deposits in different types of financial institutions represents one set of equations with one equation for each type of institution. These deposits "together with interest rates and other variables then determine the volume of commitments made by financial institutions to supply residential mortgage funds"; and the resulting supply of funds is shown to affect housing starts and residential construction outlays. Postwar time series regressions provide strong support for this approach, serving to highlight the importance of interest rates, as well as of the ratio of rents to construction costs, in affecting housing starts.

The determinants of consumer investment in selected durables is the subject of the paper by Marvin Snowbarger and Daniel Suits. Their study applies a computer interaction search program developed by Sonquist and Morgan to cross-section reinterview data from the 1960–62 Surveys of Consumer Finances and attempts to identify the principal variables affecting the purchase of a television set, refrigerator, washer, furniture, and automobile, with multiple-car ownership as a separate facet. Among other things, the empirical results show that, for each of the products studied, "expressed intentions to buy are the first criterion for identifying eventual buyers," even though less than half of the intenders actually carried out their purchase plans. Debt position and income were also important discriminators, but attitudinal variables were not. There was no evidence of complementarity or substitutability of durable purchases. Multiple-car ownership was affected by number and age of children and by wife's work status as well as by income. The authors note that a number of interaction effects were uncovered in this study that might not have been obtained by the more usual multivariate methods.

The paper by Roger Miller and Harold Watts is concerned with the financial investment of consumers. Entirely theoretical, it presents a model designed to explain the dynamics of consumer choice of financial assets. The model contains two parts: one is concerned with the household's long-range decisions about such basic variables as time allocation, income, and the value of the portfolio; the other is a short-run suboptimizing model on the explanation of changes in the portfolio. Both parts of the model assume that the household seeks to maximize expected utility over its lifetime, and assign a major role to the subjective probability beliefs of the household. The measurement and incorporation of such probabilities within a general framework should serve as a key, it is felt, to explaining many different aspects of household financial behavior.

A number of technical points on the formulation of the models and the interpretation of data are clarified in the discussion of these papers, some of which are worthy of note. Louis Winnick comments on Muth's paper that the subject of housing investment requires the study of more than population movements and that results pertaining to consumption of housing may be different for households and in per capita terms. Vernon Lippitt notes that the computer interaction search program used by Snowbarger and Suits does not deal fully with interaction effects and is best regarded as a prior step to multiple regression or to analysis of variance. James Morgan finds that many more stocks than just the financial portfolio are involved in household decision-making and should be incorporated in the Miller-Watts model, along with means of allowing for learning and changes in tastes by the household over time.

The fourth part of this book contains two papers on the factors that affect investment behavior. In the first of these, Locke Anderson attempts to throw further light on the controversy about the relative importance of the acceleration principle and the profits principle in investment. From the results of multiple regressions fitted to annual time series in the postwar period, he concludes that "both capacity utilization and financial variables belong together in an adequate explanation of investment." Thus, his results support the findings of others that these two theories of investment behavior tend to complement rather than compete with each other.

Phoebus Dhrymes and Mordecai Kurz have undertaken a more extensive investigation of investment behavior, in which they focus on the extent to which the firm's investment, dividend payments, and use of external finance are interrelated. The analysis is based on the simultaneous estimation of the parameters of a three-equation model applied to data for 181 industrial and commercial firms year by year over the period 1951–60. Among their principal findings is a significant degree of interdependence between investment and dividend payments and between use of external finances and investment. They also find, as did Locke Anderson, that both the accelerator and the profits versions of investment theory are relevant to explaining investment behavior. In addition, their findings suggest that the influence of profits on investment is more complex than has previously been supposed, so that the effect of this variable may have been underestimated in past, mostly single-equation, studies.

Of major methodological interest is the finding of Dhrymes and Kurz that the single-equation approach tends to obscure the true relationships and that even limited information estimation is not fully satisfactory. A particularly striking example is the consistently positive relationship obtained by single-equation methods between investment and dividend payments, a relationship which turned out to be strongly negative once full information estimation was applied to a system of simultaneous equations.

The discussion of these papers revolves primarily around the specification of the models and the interpretation of the empirical results, particularly of the Dhrymes-Kurz model. R. W. Resek relates both of these papers to those of Miller-Modigliani and of Lintner, noting that both appear to adopt the view that the cost of funds is related to financial structure. Henry Latané, as well as Resek, questions the general omission of lagged variables in the two papers, though Dhrymes and Kurz argue that the results are perhaps more meaningful in their present form because of estimation difficulties when such variables are introduced. The instability of the same regression coefficients among years is highlighted by William Vickrey as a major reason for considering the Dhrymes-Kurz results to be inconclusive, to which the authors reply that for some of the key coefficients this instability is more apparent than real.

The last part of this volume provides new evidence on the relation of anticipations to investment behavior. The first of the two papers in this part, by Reynold Sachs and A. G. Hart, focuses on the effectiveness of capital appropriations in explaining investment outlays of large durable goods manufacturing firms. The study is based on capital appropriations and expenditures of 627 of the largest manufacturing corporations in the United States. On the basis of a number of multiple regressions involving capital appropriations, expenditures, and related variables over time, capital appropriations are found to embody much information relevant to the explanation of capital expenditures which is not contained in the usual *ex post* economic variables. In particular, an eclectic model incorporating both capital appropriations and financial and accelerator variables provides a much better explanation of fluctuations in capital expenditures than either a model based on accelerator variables, or on purely financial variables, or an autoregressive model.

An eclectic model also serves to explain fluctuations in capital appropriations much better than any of the other three types of models. Hence, Sachs and Hart conclude that both capital expenditures and capital appropriations are influenced partly by financial variables and partly by accelerator variables, but that, even when such variables are incorporated into a function seeking to explain variations in capital expenditures, appropriations variables continue to make a net contribution. Further investigation of the nature of capital appropriations suggests that "plans formulated as of the end of the third quarter before the expenditure may be taken as fairly firm, but that reactions to surprises of later dates are appreciable and significant."

In his paper, Michael Lovell explores the value of anticipations data in explaining fluctuations in the other principal component of investment, namely, inventories. Utilizing recently compiled data of the Office of Business Economics, Lovell explores once more the impact on inventory investment of errors made by firms in forecasting their sales volume and comes up with some rather surprising results. First, he finds that short-run sales forecasts of manufacturers are considerably more accurate than was indicated by earlier studies. Nevertheless (or perhaps because of this fact), "only a marginal improvement could be obtained by using observations on sales anticipations in a model describing the generation of finished goods inventories. . . ." Thus, information on anticipated sales volume does not turn out to be very useful in explaining variations in inventory investment.

A second surprising result is that "evidence suggests that production plans and schedules for the delivery of raw materials are sufficiently flexible to permit considerable adjustment within the quarter to what errors are made in forecasting sales volume." As Lovell notes, this finding may undermine one of the basic assumptions underlying the theory of the inventory cycle, namely, that businessmen do not immediately adapt their production plans to a change in sales. On the contrary, Lovell finds that inventory plans are subject to quick and substantial modification within a period of two to three months. If this is true, a drastic modification of inventory theory would seem to be indicated.

The discussion of this paper centers on the validity of the foregoing inferences. Robert Eisner suggests that the absence of the buffer stock mechanism may be due to the fact that the new sales anticipations data are released late enough to be closely equivalent to actual sales and do not truly reflect anticipations. Millard Hastay notes that the buffer stock theory is plausible primarily for stocks of finished goods whereas some of Lovell's results pertain to inventories of all types of goods. The contrary results for finished inventories Hastay ascribes to failure to separate inventory reactions to *ex post* stock disequilibrium from reactions to *ex ante* stock disequilibrium. In his rejoinder, however, Lovell raises doubt about the value of these explanations.

Both Hastay and Eisner raise some questions about the analytical approach in the Sachs-Hart paper—the significance of results obtained from a large-scale screening process and the means of utilizing such results in further research. In addition, Victor Zarnowitz suggests that the accelerator-type variable used in the analysis is in reality another form of anticipatory variable, which may explain why this variable makes little net contribution to equations already containing capital appropriations; and James Morgan urges study of the possible effect of the accounting and tax year on investment decisions.

To summarize, the papers that were presented at this conference and that are contained in this volume seem to have contributed to our knowledge of investment behavior in at least two ways. They have provided additional fuel for some of the principal controversies on investment behavior, and they have provided new information on the subject, some of a rather surprising nature. In the former category are the questions of whether an investment demand function can be derived from neoclassical theory and whether the cost of capital to the firm is indeed independent of its financial structure. The new findings include empirical evidence or interrelationships among investment expenditures, dividend payments, and the use of external financing by business firms, and on the determinants of consumer investment in both financial and non-financial assets. Not the least of the empirical findings is the apparent failure of the buffer stock theory of inventory investment to be supported by new, presumably more accurate, data. If this evidence is borne out after further scrutiny, a new theory of inventory accumulation will be needed.

Other implications for theory are contained in the papers in this book. This is apparent most directly in Jorgenson's work supporting the neo-classical theory of investment and the Miller-Watts report presenting a general model of household investment in financial assets. Such implications are also apparent, however, in many of the empirical papers, besides the study by Lovell on inventory investment. Two further examples are the finding in the Crockett-Friend paper that the income elasticity of net worth is greater than unity and the significance ascribed to interest rates in the paper by Sparks. The interested reader will undoubtedly find many other examples.

The members of the planning committee for the conference were Robert Ferber (chairman), Irwin Friend, Dale W. Jorgenson, Edwin Kuh, Harold Watts, and Victor Zarnowitz. The volume was edited by Marie-Christine MacAndrew and the charts were drawn by H. Irving Forman.

PART I

Anatomy of Investment Behavior

Consumer Investment Behavior

JEAN CROCKETT AND IRWIN FRIEND

UNIVERSITY OF PENNSYLVANIA

I. Determinants of Consumer Investment Decisions

A consumer's investment decision is based on much the same considerations for both real and financial assets and is closely related to if not equivalent to his savings decision. While saving is traditionally thought of as a device for achieving the preferred balance between current and future consumption, given the available opportunities for transforming current dollars into future dollars, it is also used to acquire assets to perform certain specific current and future services that are sufficiently valued by the household to compete with current consumption for the household's resources. For example, currency and demand deposits provide convenience, now and in the future, by bridging differences in the time patterns of receipts and expenditures; insurance provides (on a current and continuing basis) security against certain contingencies, while savings accounts provide security against other types of contingencies; owned homes provide housing, frequently of a sort not readily available otherwise; annuities and equity in private or governmental pension funds generate retirement income (providing for future consumption), while many other types of assets also perform this function.

As with consumption items, and perhaps to a greater extent, we find one type of asset performing more than one service, while a given service frequently may be performed by more than one type of asset. However, there do not appear to be close substitutes for currency and demand deposits in balancing transactions, for insurance in providing protection

NOTE: We wish to thank Edward W. Green for valuable statistical assistance. This paper is part of a Study of the Determinants of Consumption and Saving supported by the National Science Foundation.

against specific contingencies, or for consumer durables in providing the various services for which they are intended.

The desired stock of assets is derived from the household's demand for the services performed; and we expect, as for consumption, that the primary determinant (aside from tastes) will be the normal or permanent income of the household, defined in some appropriate way.[1] Rational consumer behavior means balancing the utility of an additional dollar's worth of current consumption in each time period against the current and discounted future value of the services of an additional dollar's worth of assets.

The evidence indicates that, particularly for relatively high incomes, the desired stock of assets is large compared to a single year's income. Hence, it is reasonable to suppose that the desired stock may be achieved only gradually over several years and that current saving will be related to the size of the gap between actual and desired assets. Further, it is reasonable to suppose that the gap will be closed more quickly for certain assets rendering important current services than for others rendering primarily future services. In some cases the desired stock of a particular asset may be accumulated quickly by introducing debt, which may be treated as a negative asset, into the portfolio. The negative asset is then gradually eliminated over time.

The simplest assumptions about the form of the relationship between the desired stock of assets, A^*, and normal income, Y_N, are

$$A^* = a + bY_N \tag{1}$$

$$A^* = \alpha Y^\beta_N. \tag{2}$$

The second form gives a somewhat better fit for actual income and asset holdings from cross-section data,[2] but the suggested logarithmic trans-

---

[1] For purposes of the present paper, normal income is defined as the expected value of annual household income over whatever time span is most relevant to the consumption decisions and asset goals of the household. The length of the time span will vary among households and may depend on the specific decision to be made. The span which is most relevant to the average American family for most decisions is an open question. In the present state of our knowledge, it may be no longer than a single year or as long as the entire working life of the head of the household.

For the retired, the desired stock of assets at the end of any year does not necessarily depend on normal income, but is more likely to depend on the actual stock at the beginning of the year, the expected retirement span, and the desired size of bequest. Of course, actual assets at the beginning of the retirement span should be closely correlated with normal income during working life. Furthermore, actual retirement income will be related to current asset holdings, particularly if these are so measured as to include the value of annuities and equity in pension funds.

[2] Based on Federal Reserve Board tabulations of grouped data for 1962 (*Federal Reserve Bulletin*, March 1964, p. 293).

formation is not generally convenient for ungrouped cross-section data because of the frequent occurrence of zero observations for particular types of assets. These relationships suggest, respectively, the following formulations for current saving or the current asset level as a function of normal income and lagged assets or net worth, disregarding capital gains:[3]

$$S_t = r(A^*_t - A_{t-1}) = ra + rbY_{Nt} - rA_{t-1} \tag{3}$$

$$\text{or } A_t = ra + rbY_{Nt} + (1 - r)A_{t-1};$$

$$\frac{A_t}{A_{t-1}} = \left(\frac{A^*_t}{A_{t-1}}\right)^\rho = \left(\frac{\alpha Y^\beta_{Nt}}{A_{t-1}}\right)^\rho \tag{4}$$

or $\log A_t = \rho \log \alpha + \rho\beta \log Y_{Nt} + (1 - \rho) \log A_{t-1}$.[4]

For purposes of this paper we have assumed that r or ρ is a constant, but it may in fact be a function of the size of the gap, of the level of normal income, or of other variables.

In addition, saving, particularly in certain forms, may serve as a buffer, partially absorbing transitory bumps and dips in income receipts or in consumption needs. In this capacity it behaves to some extent as a residual, and one of its primary determinants is expected to be transitory income. There is an implicit assumption here that temporary departures from the desired asset position based on normal income, or from the optimum time path for achieving that asset position, are resisted less strongly than departures from the preferred time pattern of consumption. In fact, one of the functions of the asset stock is to protect consumption against undue deviations from this pattern because of foreseen or unforseen variations in income. This is not to suggest that consumption is independent of transitory income but simply that saving presumably bears more than its share of the brunt of variations in such income. For this reason it is important to measure separately the normal and transi-

---

[3] Unanticipated capital gains (losses) early in the period presumably have almost the same effect on saving as higher (lower) initial assets, but progressively smaller effects the later they occur in the period. Where data on capital gains are available and savings decisions are assumed to be revised within a single time period, it would be desirable either to add some fraction of unanticipated gains to initial assets or to include such gains as a separate causal variable. To the extent that capital gains are anticipated, however, the average value of such gains should be incorporated in normal income, while positive or negative deviations from the average should be added to transitory income. In other words the expected value of anticipated gains should affect desired assets, while the actual gains affect actual assets.

[4] Another appealing formulation, $S_t = r(\alpha Y^\beta_{Nt} - A_{t-1})$ is not considered here because of the difficulty of fitting such a relationship.

tory components of income in saving regressions, and a number of devices for doing so are tested in the present paper.

In the explanation of individual components of saving (i.e., investment in specific types of real or financial assets), the question of portfolio balance assumes considerable importance. The optimum portfolio structure would be expected to depend on the size of the portfolio (and thus on normal income), on tastes (in particular attitudes toward risk), and on relative rates of return and risks of assets which are reasonably close substitutes in the services they perform. Because certain types of assets can only be purchased in rather large amounts and because some items are subject to substantial capital gains and losses, portfolio imbalances are continually created and only gradually eliminated. A significant proportion of the variation in individual components of savings reflects this process, rather than simple adjustments to current variations in income or total net worth. Therefore, we expect investment in a specific type of asset to show a considerably stronger negative correlation with initial holdings of that type of asset than with other assets. In fact, the effect on an individual savings component of total initial net worth may well be positive, when holdings of the relevant specific asset are held constant, since high values of initial net worth tend to be associated with situations where the portfolio is short in the specific asset or long in other assets, while low values of initial net worth tend to be associated with the reverse situation. Futhermore, the household's initial portfolio provides resources which, like income, may be used to build up the holdings of any particular asset to the extent that the household desires to do so.

The role of initial net worth with respect to investment in a specific asset is, in fact, ambiguous, for given initial holdings of the specific asset, unless tastes are also held constant. It is reasonable to suppose that investment in a specific asset varies directly with the gap between the actual and desired holdings of that asset, $(A_{it}{}^* - A_{i(t-1)})$ and inversely with the gap between actual and desired holdings of other assets. In a linear model

$$S_{it} = r_1(A_{it}{}^* - A_{i(t-1)}) - r_0(A_t{}^* - A_{it}{}^* - A_{t-1} + A_{i(t-1)}),$$

$$= (r_0 + r_1)(A_{it}{}^* - A_{i(t-1)}) - r_0(A_t{}^* - A_{t-1}).$$

Holding tastes constant, we expect low values of A_{t-1} to be associated with high values of $(A_t{}^* - A_{t-1})$ and thus with low values of S_{it}. The partial correlation of A_{t-1} with S_{it} will then be positive. However, if tastes are not held constant, then for given holdings of the ith asset, low values of A_{t-1} are likely to be associated with a stronger relative preference for that particular asset (a higher $A_{it}*$) than high values of A_{t-1} are. A negative partial correlation may then occur between S_{it} and A_{t-1}.

This paper, after reviewing the current literature on consumer saving and investment, attempts to make an integrated analysis of consumer decisions to invest in various types of real and financial assets, utilizing a number of variants of the stock adjustment model outlined above to investigate the influence of permanent income, transitory income, initial asset holdings, and other factors. Because of data difficulties, it has not been possible to complete all the analyses originally planned, and we are continuing this work.

Two serious statistical problems arise in attempting to measure income and asset effects on saving behavior. The first is obtaining separate estimates of the influence of normal and transitory income, since these components cannot be observed directly. The second is separating the effects of actual and desired assets, in view of the high correlation between the two. Thus in a cross-section much of the variance in initial asset positions, even when income is held constant, simply reflects variation in households' tastes for holding assets, rather than any asset disequilibrium, while in time series it is probable that most of the variance in assets (except in highly unusual periods) reflects a planned adjustment to rising levels of normal income. In meeting both problems, panel data, covering the same families over a period of years, are extremely advantageous; and, accordingly, the primary emphasis of our paper is on data of this type.

One method of separating the two income effects is to estimate normal income from information on the income history of the individual household. This has been attempted by others on the basis of time series data, but not systematically on the basis of cross-section panel data.[5] A number of the analyses presented here utilize this type of estimate of normal income in conjunction with a variable reflecting transitory income. However, the transitory income effect may be rather different in the aggregate (where transitory income primarily arises from cyclical variations in employment and profits) than in the cross-section (where a number of other factors may be responsible).

A second device which has been frequently advocated[6] for estimating

---

[5] Some interesting experiments by Paul Taubman are discussed later.

[6] Irwin Friend and Irving B. Kravis, "Consumption Patterns and Permanent Income," *American Economic Review,* May 1957; Robert Eisner, "The Permanent Income Hypothesis: Comment," *American Economic Review,* December 1958; and Franco Modigliani, Albert Ando, Milton Friedman, Margaret Reid, and Robert Eisner in *Consumption and Saving,* edited by Irwin Friend and Robert C. Jones, Philadelphia, 1960.

the normal income effect is to utilize regressions based on group means, on the theory that, for sufficiently large groups, mean transitory income will approach its expected value of zero, so that mean income for the group is in effect normal income. Some correlation must exist between normal income and the grouping variable for this procedure to be feasible, but transitory income should, of course, be uncorrelated with the grouping variable. There are two difficulties with this approach. First, it is not certain that in any given year mean transitory income approaches zero, though over a period of years it presumably does. In a recession year transitory income is expected to be negative on the average, and in a period of high prosperity it is expected to be positive. Furthermore, the incidence of negative transitory income in a recession (or of positive transitory income in prosperity) is not likely to be constant for groups. Certainly if we group by occupation, education, region, race, or age, it is to be expected that some groups will be affected more seriously than others. Other possible grouping variables are highly correlated with these characteristics, so that similar expectations apply.

Second, and perhaps more serious, it is difficult to find a grouping variable that has no independent effect on consumption or saving and is uncorrelated with any characteristic other than normal income which does have such an effect. Unless both conditions are met, the regression based on group means erroneously attributes to normal income part of the effect of the grouping variable or characteristics correlated with it.[7]

Several regressions of this general type are utilized in our paper, but an attempt is made to avoid the first problem by averaging group income over a five-year period and to avoid the second one by including variables which specifically take account of differences in group tastes or by considering changes in group saving over time. A variable representing deviations from normal income is also included to permit estimation of the transitory income effect.

Finally, normal income for the individual household may be estimated as a multivariate function of the mean income of the occupational, educational, age, and other groups to which the household head belongs, where all grouping variables are believed to be significantly correlated with normal income. Again, it is important to include a variable reflecting tastes to avoid absorbing the effect of group tastes into the estimate of the normal income effect. In future studies we plan to apply this type of normal income estimate to the data analyzed here, since it probably permits the most accurate estimate of transitory income and, therefore,

[7] Jean Crockett, "Technical Note" in *Consumption and Saving,* Vol. II, pp. 220–221.

of the effect on saving of such income. The estimate of the effect of normal income is presumably an average of those provided by single grouping variables.[8]

Separate analyses are carried out for the self-employed and for the retired since the savings behavior of each of these groups may differ significantly from that of the rest of the population. Also in some instances homeowners are studied separately from nonhomeowners. The self-employed may face somewhat greater variation in transitory income than others and certainly are faced with different transformation relationships between current and future income. The retired may well have standards of living based on preretirement income—i.e., income in the fairly distant past—and may in general be reducing rather than building up their asset positions. Homeowners may show quite a different portfolio structure from nonhomeowners, even though total net worth is much the same. For homeowners, larger expenditures for consumer durables, more debt, and perhaps smaller holdings of financial assets for given income levels are to be expected.

II. Prior Analysis

By far the most extensive earlier work on consumer investment decisions has been directed toward determining the over-all propensity to save (or consume), with particular emphasis on the long-run and short-run marginal saving propensities (or elasticities) with respect to personal disposable income. Considerably less work has been devoted to determining the components of saving, i.e., to the allocation of consumers' funds (earned or borrowed) to the major items of real and financial investment. However, in recent years there has been an increasing number of studies of consumer real investment in housing, automobiles, and other durables—with automobiles receiving most attention—and of financial "investment" in money and near-money. There have been fewer studies of consumer investment in other types of financial assets, and only very few have attempted to analyze the entire structure of consumer assets and saving to the extent the available data permitted. The comparative dearth of the latter type of study reflects in part the difficulties of isolating meaningful demand functions for many important items of financial assets (e.g., corporate stock) from time series data, which are

---

[8] While unbiased estimates of the normal income effect will be obtained from any of the grouping variables if mean transitory income is zero for all groups (see Part III of this paper), estimates may in fact differ depending on the grouping variable used, due to sampling error and to small deviations of group transitory income from zero.

even greater than the corresponding problems for total saving,[9] and in part the limitations of the available cross-section data, which are more serious for the financial than for the real components of saving.

In this prior analysis, both flow and stock relationships have been derived to explain the demand for individual items of saving or investment. It is interesting to note that basically only flow relationships explaining total saving have been used, to the virtual neglect of the demand for total assets or for net worth. To some extent, this neglect can be explained by the greater availability of data on total saving than those on net worth. However, it is probably also attributable to the greater interest in explaining income flows than asset levels and to the tendency in most saving analysis to overlook the close connection between the short-run marginal propensity to save and the long-run marginal propensity to hold assets.

Both time series and cross-section data have been mined intensively.[10] Cross-section data have been used to study the influence of all types of socioeconomic-demographic characteristics on saving and investment, and obviously much of such information could only be obtained in this manner. On the other hand, basically only time series data can be and have been used to study the influence of interest rates and prices. We do not propose to review here the scope and findings of prior analysis of the influence of sociodemographic characteristics (such as occupation, age, size of family, race, education, geographic location, etc.) and of interest rates and related variables on consumer expenditures and saving in view of the availability of earlier summaries, the absence of significant later findings in these areas, and the fact that we will have relatively little new to say in this paper about the influence of sociodemographic characteristics and even less about interest rates. However, it might be useful to point out that, while no one to our knowledge has had much success in isolating an interest rate effect on household saving and only limited success on household investment, this may reflect the concentration in most earlier analyses on the interest rate rather than more broadly on the rate of return on assets. Thus it is quite conceivable that, even though

---

[9] In addition to the difficulty of distinguishing demand from supply relationships, a further difficulty arises from substitutability among different components of saving.

[10] A very useful summary and bibliography may be found in Robert Ferber, "Research on Household Behavior," *The American Economic Review,* March 1962. One interesting set of studies not covered in that article is discussed in Arnold C. Harberger, ed., *The Demand for Durable Goods,* Chicago, 1963. Another recent summary of other results of research on saving is provided in Irwin Friend, "Determinants of the Volume and Composition of Saving," *Impacts of Monetary Policy,* Englewood Cliffs, 1963.

the interest rate may not play much of a role in influencing the household propensity to save, other types of returns—notably capital gains—may play such a role.[11] It might be also pointed out that there have been several recent analyses covering the postwar period which suggest that the rate of substitution between demand deposits and other types of deposits in response to changes in the structure of rates of return has not been very high, but that the rate of substitution between other types of deposits and between deposits and certain other types of financial investment has been somewhat higher.[12]

Both cross-section and time series data have been used to analyze perhaps the most interesting question relating to consumer saving and investment decisions, viz., the role played by income and assets, which is the problem with which we shall be primarily concerned in this paper. It is extremely difficult to identify the appropriate demand relations and the associated income and asset parameters from time series data because of the small number of independent observations and the difficulties of isolating income from correlated nonincome effects, of distinguishing among different types of income, of recognizing shifts in the demand relations, and of holding constant supply conditions. Hence it may appear surprising that in recent years relatively little effort has been made to integrate the income (or asset) parameters from cross-section data into time series models explaining either income and expenditures as a whole or specific areas of consumer outlay, in spite of the proliferation of such models and the wide range of estimates implied by different models.

There are several reasons why cross-section estimates of saving and investment propensities have been or might be regarded as inferior to the time series estimates, in spite of the very great intrinsic deficiencies

[11] In the related area of corporate investment, we have found that an over-all cost-of-capital variable adjusted for taxes (i.e., an adjusted market-value weighted average of the bond yield and the required rate of return on equity, which is estimated as the sum of the current dividend yield plus the anticipated future growth rate in earnings based on past growth) seems more useful in explaining the demand for plant and equipment than the more customary interest rate, which may at times be negatively correlated with the "cost of equity." However, the rate of capital gains like the interest rate may turn out to be a two-edged sword in its influence on the demand for saving.

[12] See Edgar L. Feige, *The Demand for Liquid Assets: A Temporal Cross-Section Analysis,* Englewood Cliffs, 1964; and Irwin Friend, "The Effects of Monetary Policies on Nonmonetary Financial Institutions and Capital Markets," *Private Capital Markets,* Englewood Cliffs, 1964. These analyses combine household and corporate accounts, though the Feige analysis introduces as an explanatory variable in the combined demand function for demand deposits the ratio of those held by individuals to the total of such deposits. Two other studies bearing on this point will be considered at the end of this section in a discussion of recent work on the determinants of the demand for money.

of the latter. First, and perhaps most difficult to correct, the basic cross-section data for saving, though not necessarily for investment, are subject to much larger statistical biases as well as larger random error than the time series data, especially for cash and deposits,[13] with the troublesome possibility that the known understatement of the average saving-income ratios in survey data might be associated with a similar, though presumably not so great, understatement of the marginal propensity to save. Second, in addition to the statistical inadequacies of consumer survey data, they pose the conceptual difficulties associated with their use for purposes to which they are not well adapted—i.e., inferring intrapersonal behavior over time from interpersonal comparisons at a point of time. One such difficulty is the separation of long-run or normal from short-run or transitory income effects on the basis of survey data which typically measure household income for one year only, though on occasion for a somewhat longer time perspective. As is by now well known, a cross-section observation of income of a household, particularly in the lowest brackets, is much more likely to be affected by transitory income than a time series observation of aggregate income. Assets as well as income may reflect transitory or disequilibrium conditions to a greater extent than is typically true of the time series data. Another conceptual difficulty associated with cross-section data is the need to hold tastes constant in attempting to infer intrapersonal behavior over time from interpersonal behavior.

Both of these conceptual limitations of cross-section data can be avoided in part by using continuous cross-section or panel data where the response of economic behavior to changes in relevant variables can be traced as these variables change over time. (The collection of survey data over a longer period than the customary year also has the potential advantage of cutting down on the impact of random influences on the variables analyzed.) As a result, the statistical analysis in this paper will be largely devoted to the new consumer panel data collected for the 1960, 1961, and 1962 Surveys of Consumer Finances.[14] Some earlier work along similar lines was carried out under our general guidance by Paul Taubman on the basis of a much smaller consumer panel in the

---

[13] See Irwin Friend and Stanley Schor, "Who Saves?" *Review of Economics and Statistics,* May 1959; and Robert Ferber, "The Reliability of Consumer Surveys of Financial Holdings: Time Deposits," *Journal of the American Statistical Association,* March 1965.

[14] See Richard F. Kosobud and James W. Morgan, eds., *Consumer Behavior of Individual Families Over Two and Three Years,* Ann Arbor, 1964, for a description of the basic data, including copies of the questionnaires used.

Philadelphia area conducted by the Consumer Expenditures Unit of the Wharton School.[15]

Before proceeding with our analysis, it may be useful to discuss briefly the wide range in the estimates of income and asset effects and the major internal inconsistencies which seem to characterize much of the earlier work in this area. To justify our preoccupation with cross-section data in this paper in spite of their substantial deficiencies, only some of which we were able to correct, we might point first to the extremely unsatisfactory nature of the estimates of the marginal propensity to save or to consume derived from time series data—a parameter which might be expected to be relatively stable and which has received an unusual amount of research. There have been as many different estimates of the long-run and short-run marginal propensities to consume obtained from different time series models of income determination as there have been models.[16] This is not surprising since there are virtually an infinite number of possible ways of combining different forms of each of a number of structural equations if the number of equations and the number of forms fitted or tested for each equation are at all large. In contrast, the number of time series observations available for distinguishing among these alternatives is extremely limited. Thus the short-run marginal propensity to consume out of personal disposable income is somewhat less than .55 according to the Klein-Goldberger annual model, .67 according to the Suits' annual model, and for transitory income about .30 according to Friedman, and the variations in the time period covered are hardly sufficient to explain these differences.[17] The long-run marginal propensities are also markedly

[15] See Paul Taubman, "A Synthesis of Saving Theory with Special Reference to the Components of Personal Saving," unpublished Ph.D. dissertation, University of Pennsylvania, 1964, Chapter VI. An earlier paper by Irwin Friend and Paul Taubman, "The Aggregate Propensity to Save: Some Concepts and their Application to International Data," *Review of Economics and Statistics,* May 1966, applied the same theoretical model and general framework of analysis to time series data where countries rather than households were the unit of observation.

[16] The short-run propensity to consume is usually defined as the current response of consumption to an additional dollar of income over a year, half-year, or quarter (with the time period depending on the analysis), irrespective of whether the income reflects normal or transitory influences, and so may be regarded as some average of short-run response to normal and transitory incomes. The long-run propensity to consume is usually defined as the ultimate response of consumption to an additional dollar of income if that income is maintained indefinitely and reflects the effect of normal income after full adjustment.

[17] L. R. Klein and A. S. Goldberger, *An Econometric Model of the United States,* Amsterdam, 1955, pp. 51 and 90; Daniel B. Suits, "Forecasting and Analysis with an Econometric Model," *American Economic Review,* March 1962, p. 113; and Milton Friedman, *A Theory of the Consumption Function,* Princeton for NBER, 1957, p. 147. The Friedman estimate has been adjusted to include durables in consumption for comparability.

different, amounting to .75, .82, and .90, respectively. The more recent Klein quarterly model implies a short-run (quarterly) marginal propensity to consume of .72 and a long-run propensity that is actually less, .60, while the current very large-scale S.S.R.C. quarterly model implies a corresponding short-run consumption propensity between .35 and .53 and a long-run propensity between .53 and .70, depending on which of two sets of equations is used.[18] All of these results other than Friedman's explicitly incorporate a liquid asset variable at least in part as a proxy for initial net worth. The semiannual Friend-Taubman relation of consumption to disposable income, which does not incorporate any asset variable, implies a short-run marginal propensity to consume of .41 and a long-run propensity of .82, while an earlier annual analysis by Friend which does not distinguish between short- and long-run propensities but does incorporate a liquid asset variable points to an income coefficient of .73 (and an assets coefficient of .11).[19] A recent annual analysis by Crockett devoted to consumption of nondurable goods and services pointed to a marginal propensity to consume of .75 out of normal income and .5 to .6 out of transitory income.[20] The latter estimates, which do not incorporate any asset variable, would of course be increased somewhat if durables were included. Not surprisingly in view of the interrelations of assets, income, and consumption, the estimates of the marginal propensity to consume out of normal income tend to be higher in analyses which do not include assets as well as income among the explanatory variables, so that the income effect on consumption includes the associated asset effect.

While there are significant conceptual differences among some of these estimates, the Klein annual and quarterly, the Suits annual, and the S.S.R.C. quarterly estimates are conceptually quite comparable, introducing liquid assets as well as long- and short-run income as explanatory variables. Ando and Modigliani have recently added a large number of new time series estimates to this already rich harvest, using annual current disposable labor income and net worth as their basic explanatory

[18] L. R. Klein, "A Postwar Quarterly Model: Description and Applications," *Models of Income Determination,* Studies in Income and Wealth 28, Princeton for NBER, 1964; and Robert Eisner, "Over-All View of the Model," *Proceedings of the Business and Economic Statistics Section,* American Statistical Association, 1963.

[19] Irwin Friend and Paul Taubman, "A Short-Term Forecasting Model," *The Review of Economics and Statistics,* August 1964, and Irwin Friend (with the assistance of Vito Natrella), *Individuals' Saving: Volume and Composition,* New York, 1954.

[20] Jean Crockett, "Income and Asset Effects on Consumption: Aggregate and Cross Section," *Models of Income Determination.*

variables, and they obtain marginal income propensities ranging from .55 to .79 though their preferred estimates vary only from .55 to .64.[21] The latter figures, like many of the others incorporating asset variables, are considerably lower than those obtained from cross-section data.[22] It might be noted that the much higher marginal than average propensity to save in these relations incorporating asset variables is not necessarily inconsistent with the comparative secular stability in the average propensity which has received so much attention, though according to our model such stability does require either a high degree of constancy of such variables as the desired asset-income ratio, the speed of adjustment to the desired ratio, and the growth rate of disposable income, or approximately offsetting tendencies among these variables.[23] However, if any of the time series estimates are correct, it would be nice to know which. It would appear desirable to explore further the potentialities of cross-section data in this area.

Similar statements might be made about the wide range and unsatisfactory nature of time series estimates of asset effects on consumption (varying from .02 for liquid assets in Klein-Goldberger to .55 in some relationships presented by Suits).[24] While most studies of this type have relied on liquid assets as a proxy for net worth because of their greater accessibility and reliability, the recent analysis by Ando and Modigliani used the more theoretically desirable figures for net worth. It is interest-

[21] Albert Ando and Franco Modigliani, "The Life Cycle Hypothesis of Saving," *American Economic Review,* March 1963, and "Correction" March 1964.

[22] Using the BLS-Wharton 1950 data, Watts and Tobin obtain a marginal propensity to save out of normal income of .23, excluding insurance, and Crockett and Friend a marginal propensity out of measured income of .28 including insurance. (See *Consumption and Saving,* Vols. I and II.) In both results, several initial asset (and liability) variables were held constant. However, tastes were not held constant and it can be shown that in such cross-section regressions of saving on income and initial assets, the absence of an explicit savings-tastes variable biases the income coefficient downward in view of the positive correlation between income and assets and between assets and tastes, assuming no positive correlation between income and tastes.

[23] In our linear model, disregarding capital gains, for a stable average propensity, the normal saving-income ratio $(S/Y) = rbg/(r + g - rg)$, where r is the speed of adjustment, b the desired asset-income coefficient, and g the growth rate in income. Ando and Modigliani, who use a somewhat different saving formulation predicating lifetime planning, implicitly assume that the product of the asset-income ratio and the growth rate has remained relatively constant since the latter part of the nineteenth century. Our normal saving-income ratio approximates bg only if g is small relative to r.

[24] Daniel Suits, "The Determinants of Consumer Expenditure," *Impacts of Monetary Policy,* pp. 30–33. Suits attributes the major part of this variation to the difference in time periods covered and a postwar upward shift in the impact of liquid assets on consumption.

ing to note that their estimates of the net worth coefficient, ranging from .040 to .082 with a narrower range of .072 to .08 for their preferred results, are substantially lower than the rough .12 figure which seems to be implied by their theoretical analysis.[25] Because of the tastes complication, single cross-section analysis is likely to be even less satisfactory than time series analysis for isolating the asset effect on consumption and saving. However, panel data are more promising.

Turning next to consumer real investment, we might review briefly the major results, especially those relating to income and asset effects on automobile demand. Automobile demand has not only received more attention than other areas of consumer investment, but it also illustrates the problems that arise in these other areas. A rather comprehensive summary of prior automobile demand studies[26] shows a range in short- and long-run time series income elasticities from somewhat over 1 to close to 4 (with a correspondingly wide range for price elasticities). Cross-section studies for postwar years generally implied estimates close to 1,[27] with somewhat larger figures for years of high automobile demand than for other periods. By using panel data which are available for automobiles, Houthakker and Haldi lowered somewhat but did not change significantly the customary cross-section income elasticities. However, the asset effects (for stock of automobiles) implied by the panel data were markedly different from those implied by single cross-section analysis, with the asset coefficient changing from $-.13$ and $-.16$ in the usual cross-section analysis to $-.36$ and $-.39$ for 1952 and 1955, respectively, once tastes were held constant.[28] One last result of some interest was the absence of any difference between the effects of nor-

[25] Similarly, their preferred estimates of the marginal propensity to consume (.55 to .64) seem to be considerably below the value implied by their theoretical analysis, assuming an aggregate income growth rate of about 3 per cent and an assets yield of over 4 per cent (*American Economic Review*, March 1963, p. 60).

[26] H. S. Houthakker and John Haldi, "Household Investment in Automobiles," *Consumption and Saving*, Vol. I.

[27] Houthakker and Haldi derived income elasticities of .87 and 1.02 for 1952 and 1955, respectively. Crockett and Friend obtained 1.18 for 1950 (*Consumption and Saving*, Vol. I), while the results by Watts and Tobin seem to imply a substantially lower result for the same year ("Consumer Expenditures and the Capital Account" in *ibid.*, Vol. II).

[28] Watts and Tobin obtain an even larger absolute value for the asset effect in 1950, but, as they point out, their auto stock variable seems substantially understated.

mal and transitory components of income on gross investment in automobiles.[29]

Perhaps the most comprehensive work on automobile demand based on time series data is that by Gregory C. Chow, whose earlier study was updated in *The Demand for Durable Goods,* which also contains interesting papers on the demand for nonfarm housing by Richard F. Muth and on the demand for refrigeration by M. L. Burstein. According to Chow's results, the long-run income elasticity of demand for automobile stock, which is also the long-run income elasticity of gross investment, is probably somewhere between 1.4 and 2.0, considerably higher than that indicated by either single or continuous (panel) cross-section analysis. The short-run (i.e., the current year's) income elasticity of gross investment implied by his analysis, though not given, seems to be over 2.5, while the S.S.R.C. quarterly model referred to earlier (which, unlike Chow's, does not include an initial auto stock variable) seems to imply a drastically lower figure in the neighborhood of one, with no distinction between short- and long-run effects. The asset or auto stock coefficient in Chow's gross auto investment equations ranges from −.23 to −.30. Though this is somewhat lower in absolute value than the corresponding coefficients in the Houthakker-Haldi panel analysis, the variations could be explained by the differences in measurement used as well as by the differences in time period. Chow shows that the asset coefficient in the auto investment regressions may be regarded as the difference between the depreciation rate (.25 per annum) and the speed of adjustment to the desired level of stock (.48 to .55 of the discrepancy in a year).

Chow's results indicate that, while the measure of normal income he uses performs somewhat better than current annual income in explaining variations in the level of the auto stock, current income performs appreciably better than normal income in explaining variations in auto investment. He points out that the somewhat better performance of normal than of current income in explaining the auto stock may simply reflect the fact that the stock, unlike the flow regressions, assumes complete adjustment of the stock within a year; since this is presumably incorrect, the results may be biased in favor of normal income which, in view of its definition, can (unlike current income) take into account a slow approach of stock to a new equilibrium level. When normal income and

---

[29] This confirmed an earlier finding by Friend and Kravis, "Permanent Income and Consumption Patterns," *American Economic Review,* May 1957. Watts and Tobin do obtain a higher normal than transitory income coefficient, but the device they use to separate normal from transitory effects seems quite questionable. (See Crockett, "Technical Note," in *Consumption and Saving,* Vol. II, pp. 213–216.)

transitory (current minus normal) income are introduced as separate variables in the stock regressions, the two coefficients are virtually identical.[30]

Largely on the basis of time series analysis, Muth concludes that the income elasticity of stock demand for housing is in the neighborhood of one, considerably higher than that obtained by some of his predecessors, and that the speed of adjustment of the housing stock per annum is around .32. (The housing stock coefficient is somewhat less than .32 in absolute value, reflecting a depreciation rate of about .035.) Burstein derives income elasticities for refrigeration ranging from 1.0 to 3.0 on the basis of time series data, and at the low end of the range on the basis of household cross-section data.[31] The estimates of the adjustment or asset coefficient for refrigeration range from .36 to .73. Muth finds that normal income is superior to current income in explaining variations in housing demand, though the difference does not seem large, while Burstein obtains the reverse results for refrigeration when trend, which is highly correlated with the measure of normal income used, is introduced into the analysis.[32]

Probably the most comprehensive analysis of the entire structure of consumer assets based on single cross-section data is the Watts-Tobin study referred to earlier, which estimated linear relationships of the stocks of automobiles, each of a large number of other consumer durables, mortgage debt, instalment debt, cash balances, and insurance to many socioeconomic-demographic characteristics of the household including disposable income and housing level, the latter providing a

[30] In a subsequent time series analysis using a small-scale complete model, Paul E. Smith derived a value of one for the marginal propensity to invest transitory income in automobiles, which is of course very much higher than the corresponding propensity for normal income (*The Journal of Political Economy,* October 1962). This unusually high value of the transitory propensity to invest in automobiles may reflect the incorporation in the model of an "investment equation," in which government expenditures as well as private investment are determined by gross national product in the current and preceding years.

[31] He concludes "somewhat less conclusively that the income elasticity is between 1.0 and 2.0" (*The Demand for Durable Goods,* p. 99).

[32] Though somewhat outside our main focus of interest in this paper, Chow, Muth, and Burstein all derive substantial and highly significant price elasticities, while Muth also obtains a substantial and significant interest rate elasticity. Any overstatement of the income elasticities in these studies, as suggested by cross-section data, would of course normally be associated with an error in the same direction in the estimates of price and interest rate effects.

basis for distinguishing between normal and transitory income effects. Flow regressions were also derived relating changes in assets or saving in each of the forms indicated to the same socioeconomic-demographic variables plus initial assets in that form and in each of the other forms. The authors' main conclusion is that "There is evidence that households tend to maintain some sort of balance in their capital accounts both between assets yielding direct services and financial assets, and between liquid assets and liabilities. . . . adjustments in capital account items tend to eliminate rather than perpetuate deviations from a basic or preferred portfolio pattern." They further conclude that "The differences between short- and long-run coefficients for saving are definitely in the direction, if not in the amount, predicted by the permanent income hypothesis."[33]

As noted earlier, the Watts-Tobin estimate of the marginal propensity to save out of normal income in 1950 seems reasonably consistent with other cross-section results, but their implicit estimate of the income elasticity of automobile investment seems substantially lower than other cross-section results and lower still than time series estimates. While the transitory income coefficient is higher than the normal coefficient for saving as a whole (which is defined to exclude consumer durables) and for changes in cash and debt, the reverse is true for investment in automobiles, in other consumer durables, and apparently in insurance. As would be expected, normal income generally has a much larger impact than transitory income on the stocks of assets. The greater influence of normal than of transitory income on automobile investment, which seems inconsistent with the results obtained in other studies, may reflect the deficiencies previously referred to in separating normal from transitory effects and in estimating the stock of automobiles.

It is possible to make an interesting comparison of the results from the Watts-Tobin stock and flow regressions which the authors do not discuss. It can be argued that dividing the normal income coefficients in a saving or flow regressions (p. 46) by the corresponding asset or adjustment coefficients in the same regression (pp. 41–44) should give an approximation to the long-run income coefficients in the stock or asset regressions (p. 34), except for automobiles and other durable goods where an adjustment should be made for depreciation. To the extent that the derived normal income coefficients from the flow regressions deviate from the corresponding coefficients in the stock regressions, the

---

[33] Watts and Tobin in *Consumption and Saving*, Vol. II, pp. 45, 48.

former would be expected to be lower.[34] Instead, the indicated divisions in the flow regressions, except for debt, give results substantially higher than the long-run income coefficients in the stock regressions. While this may be partly attributable to the fact that the relation of actual assets to normal income would be expected to give a somewhat lower income effect than the relation of desired assets to normal income, to which the former is an approximation, it probably reflects to a greater extent the bias in the asset or adjustment coefficients in the flow regressions because of the absence of a tastes variable.[35] Since tastes are not held constant in these regressions, the initial stock or asset variables in the flow regressions act as proxies for tastes and this reduces the magnitude of the stock coefficients.

One further limitation of the Watts-Tobin analysis is the absence of a net worth variable. Thus net worth does not appear in the over-all saving regression, though several individual items of assets and liabilities are included.

A more recent analysis of the structure of consumer assets based on single cross-section data appears in Henry J. Claycamp's *The Composition of Consumer Savings Portfolios*.[36] The two most interesting findings are that households "give far more consideration to the specific needs each asset fulfills than to the effect the asset has on the total portfolio" and that total assets but not income was a major determinant of the composition of the total portfolio as measured by the proportion of variable-dollar assets. The first of these conclusions is open to question

---

[34] If $A_i^* = j + kA^*$ where A_i represents a particular asset and A net worth, and as noted earlier we assume for simplicity $A^* = a + bY_N$, so that $A_i^* = j + ak + bkY_N$, then $S_i = r[A_i^* - A_{i(t-1)}] = (rj + rak) + rbkY_N - rA_{i(t-1)}$, where r is the speed of adjustment. Then bk, the long-run marginal propensity to hold A_i, may be estimated (not necessarily without bias) by dividing the coefficient of Y_N from the savings regression by the coefficient of $A_{i(t-1)}$.

However, with a somewhat more sophisticated model which allows for disequilibrium in assets generally, the interpretation of the savings regression coefficients must be changed. If $S_i = r_1(A_i^* - A_{i(t-1)}) - r_0[(A^* - A_i^*) - (A_{(t-1)} - A_{i(t-1)})] = (r_1 + r_0)(j + ka) - r_0a + [(r_1 + r_0)bk - r_0b]Y_N - (r_1 + r_0)A_{i(t-1)} + r_0A_{(t-1)}$, then the ratio of the two coefficients gives an estimate of $bk - r_0b/(r_1 + r_0)$, which is less than bk since all factors are positive.

In comparing this ratio with the normal income coefficient obtained using A_i as the dependent variable and omitting lagged stock variables, it should be noted that the latter is also presumably an underestimate of the desired long-run marginal propensity, if adjustment periods exceed one year and if households with rising income (for which A_i is expected to be less than A_i^*) are more frequent at the upper end than at the lower end of the income scale.

[35] As mentioned earlier, the adjustment coefficient in the automobile investment equation also seems affected by an understatement in the estimated stock.

[36] Urbana, Ill., 1963, p. 90.

since it is based largely on the findings of simple correlations, which are generally small and positive, between dollar amounts held of various assets, and may reflect common scale factors rather than any absence of substitutability among different asset items. This conclusion, moreover, is inconsistent with the findings of an earlier analysis which does hold income (both one year and a three-year average) constant and finds a fairly high degree of substitutability among most components of saving.[37] On the other hand, the Watts-Tobin analysis indicates less substitutability for asset items than for saving items. However, both the recent and earlier analyses (as well as others not considered here) are subject to the serious deficiency that substitutability among portfolio items cannot be adequately tested from a single cross section but requires panel data in view of the influence of tastes.[38]

It would be useful to check also against panel data the second major conclusion drawn by Claycamp, based on the relationship between the percentage of the portfolio invested in variable assets and a number of other household characteristics including total assets and current income, so that tastes which are so highly correlated with assets can again be held constant. Moreover, it would be desirable to test the effect of substituting for the year's income a normal or longer-run income variable.[39]

An attempt to correct the more significant deficiencies in cross-section analysis of consumer saving and investment behavior on the basis of panel data was made by Paul Taubman in *A Synthesis of Saving Theory,* using continuous cross-section information for a very small sample of families in the Philadelphia area (ranging from 157 to 78 families depending on the time span). We have considerably extended that earlier analysis and applied it to different and significantly larger samples, covering a somewhat longer time span for selected saving items and for income. However, the basic information in the smaller sample (saving

---

[37] Substitutability among saving items is used here in the sense that, for given income and other variables determining household saving, a lower value for a component of saving (S_i) among different households is more likely to be associated with a higher value of other items of saving ($S - S_i$) than with higher consumption. It is not a measure of the response of saving to changes in relative yields. For a more precise discussion of this concept, see Friend and Jones, "The Concept of Saving," in *Consumption and Saving,* Vol. II, pp. 336–359 and pp. 381–389.

[38] See *Consumption and Saving,* Vol. II, p. 388.

[39] Of the other socioeconomic-demographic characteristics Claycamp tested, he finds that homeownership in particular but also self-employment and age of head have a significant impact on the variable dollar asset share in household portfolios. Neither education nor psychological views (the latter as measured by the SCF indexes) seems to have a comparable impact.

in all forms for each of the two years covered, 1961 and 1962) did make it possible to test certain relationships not duplicated here. Moreover, Taubman's interesting experiments with the introduction of a rachet variable have no counterpart in our analysis. Taubman's main substantive conclusions are that the marginal propensity to save out of normal income (in forms other than consumer durables) was in the neighborhood of .17, while the corresponding marginal propensity to save out of transitory income was .23. Including gross investment in consumer durables, the propensities were .31 and .42, respectively. The only items of saving significantly affected by transitory income were consumer durables and indebtedness. Transitory income in this analysis was defined as the difference between current income and an average of three years' income. All of the results were derived from saving regressions in which several initial asset (and liability) variables were incorporated.

Another paper by Taubman, analyzing the 472 employees in the Survey Research Center Ford Panel Study for the years 1954 and 1955, points to somewhat higher marginal propensities to save including gross investment in consumer durables, amounting to from .37 to .40 for normal income and from .50 to .63 for transitory income.[40] While the fits are unusually good for cross-section data, these estimates may err on the high side, compared with other cross-section studies, since Taubman indicates the disposable income figures used are probably too small. Normal income is defined here both as two-year averages of income (which might tend to introduce a significant transitory component in the measurement of normal income) and by a Koyck transformation.

A relatively unique feature of this last paper is the presentation of the propensity to save out of normal (and transitory) income by the age of the head of the household. Though Taubman introduces these data for other purposes, they can be used to test, in an admittedly crude fashion, whether his normal income measures can be interpreted as implying too short a planning span. If a longer planning span than that implied in these measures is relevant to saving behavior, then the marginal propensity to save for the youngest age group (18–34), who are below their long-run incomes, would be expected to be strongly biased downward if the understatement of normal income is roughly proportional to the level of such income; and the constant term would be biased downward if the understatement is the same for different households in the group. For the oldest age group (55 and over excluding the retired),

[40] Paul Taubman, "Permanent and Transitory Income Effects," *Review of Economics and Statistics,* February 1965.

the bias might be expected to be in the same direction but (if it exists) should not be nearly as large. The results, interestingly enough, conform reasonably well to these expectations for normal income defined as an average for two years, which suggests that such a time span is too short for this purpose. The results derived through the Koyck transformation are more mixed. However, this test as a whole is quite inconclusive in view of the broad age groups used (so that, for example, household heads at the upper end of the 18–34 age range may have high incomes which are closer to their true normal incomes than are the lower incomes of younger heads) and because of the possibility of a strong saving tastes effect associated with age. To the extent that the data permit, we plan to analyze further the relevant planning span for explaining consumer saving and investment behavior.

Finally, some mention might be made of the numerous recent studies of the demand for money. The most intensive studies in this area have been based on time series analyses of data going back to the turn of the century and have combined corporate with household accounts. Milton Friedman, defining money to include time deposits in commercial banks, concluded several years ago that the demand for money (apart perhaps from very short time periods) is determined by permanent or normal rather than by transitory income, that interest rates do not affect the demand very significantly, and that either permanent income or wealth (net worth) can be regarded as the primary determinant of demand.[41] If the income interpretation is adopted, the permanent income elasticity for money including time deposits is estimated at 1.8. Friedman states that his findings cast doubt on the transactions and speculative motives for holding money.

More recently, Allan H. Meltzer concluded that interest rates do play an important role in the demand for money (which he prefers to define in the more traditional manner as currency plus demand deposits but which he also considers for comparative purposes to include time deposits) and that wealth is more important than income in determining

[41] Milton Friedman, "The Demand for Money: Some Theoretical and Empirical Results," *The Journal of Political Economy,* August 1959. For a criticism of Friedman's conclusions on the comparative unimportance of the interest rate and of transitory income on the demand for money, see James S. Duesenberry, "Discussion," *American Economic Review,* May 1959. It may be recalled that Watts-Tobin found, as might be expected, a lower transitory than normal income effect in the demand equation for the stock of cash (effectively defined as all types of deposits) but found a reverse effect for cash saving or changes in the stock of cash.

such demand.[42] His analysis does not seem to us to indicate any clear basis for a preference between permanent income and wealth as the major determinant of the demand for money defined to include time deposits; it does not provide any data to distinguish between the two effects for the narrower definition of money; and it does not measure the influence of transitory income in view of the long-run orientation of the analysis.[43] Both permanent income and asset effects on money (including time deposits) seem quite unstable from one decade to the next and point to much smaller elasticities in the last decade, with negative values indicated in two of the three regressions (one utilizing wealth and the other permanent income) for which he presents data, though not in the wealth regression he likes best.[44] Indeed there is some suggestion that current income alone has a more stable effect than wealth on money (excluding time deposits) as between the two periods for which such data are shown, 1900–29 and 1930–58.[45] The permanent income elasticity of money is estimated at about one excluding time deposits, but higher including time deposits. Wealth elasticities are of the same general order of magnitude. Meltzer's results suggesting a relatively strong interest rate effect are for the period as a whole since the beginning of the century. For the

[42] Allan H. Meltzer, "The Demand for Money: The Evidence from the Time Series," *The Journal of Political Economy,* June 1963. For a criticism of an earlier paper along similar lines coauthored by Meltzer (Karl Brunner and Allan H. Meltzer), "Predicting Velocity: Implications for Theory and Policy," *Journal of Finance,* May 1963), see "Discussion," by Albert Ando and Martin J. Bailey. Ando in particular questions the conclusion on the comparative unimportance of income both on theoretical and statistical grounds. It might be noted, however, that the empirical work Ando cites relates to the postwar period only. For further discussion of the June 1963 paper, see comments by T. J. Courchene and H. T. Shapiro and rejoinder by Meltzer in *The Journal of Political Economy,* October 1964.

[43] However, Meltzer does measure the influence of the ratio of transitory to permanent income on the demand for money in his rejoinder in *The Journal of Political Economy,* October 1964, and finds that for the period as a whole (1900–58) the effect was insignificant, with a negative impact in the first half of the period and a positive impact in the second half, regardless of which of the two definitions of money was used.

[44] *The Journal of Political Economy,* June 1963, p. 236.

[45] See equations (3) and (8) in *ibid.,* pp. 225, 229, and 232.

Since the stock regressions used by Meltzer assume complete adjustment of the stock of money within a year, the correlation results may be biased in favor of total assets (or permanent income) which can, unlike current income, take into account a slow approach of the stock of money to a new equilibrium level. It might be useful therefore, especially in time series analysis where the tastes problem is less serious, to experiment with flow as well as stock regressions. It can also be argued that the correlation of the stock of money with income may more properly be compared to the correlation of money with nonmonetary assets than to the correlation with total assets.

broader definition of money where he presents decade estimates, the interest rate effect is less evident in the postwar period and does not exist in one of the two wealth relationships for which he presents relevant data.[46] The interest rate effect would, of course, be expected to be more marked for the narrower definition of money.

Feige, using a combination of state income and deposit data for a number of postwar years, derived a permanent income elasticity of demand deposits not significantly different from one.[47] His permanent income elasticities of time deposits and of deposits in savings and loan associations were on the average significantly lower, though the value for time deposits varied substantially over time from a figure somewhat over that for demand deposits in 1949–53 to substantially lower in 1954–59.

While there do not appear to be any comparable estimates readily available from household cross-section data, the Watts-Tobin analysis for 1950 indicated a normal income coefficient of .20 in the demand for cash (including time and savings accounts and deposits in savings and loan associations) by homeowners and .12 for renters, which would seem to indicate an over-all mean elasticity well under one.[48] Such a value would appear to be much closer to that estimated by Feige, who essentially also used a cross-section analysis, though not of household data, than to the values estimated by Friedman and Meltzer.[49] While the household data are known to underestimate cash holdings, this would not be true of the state data used by Feige. Moreover, it is not clear that an understatement of the level of cash holdings should result in any understatement of the estimated income elasticity.

III. Plan of the Present Analysis

The new results presented in this paper are based on cross-section data. Our first analysis utilizes a Federal Reserve Board Survey for a single

[46] *Ibid.*, p. 236.

[47] *Demand for Liquid Assets.*

[48] The corresponding normal income coefficients implicit in the Watts-Tobin flow regressions are only moderately higher for homeowners, but impossibly high for renters.

[49] This presumably cannot be explained even in part by the inclusion of currency in the Friedman and Meltzer money demand functions since the available evidence indicates that the income elasticity of currency is less than that of demand deposits. See Philip Cagan, "The Demand for Money Relative to the Total Money Supply," *Quarterly Journal of Economics,* August 1958. It might be explained in part by Feige's results for the early 1950's compared with the late 1950's and perhaps also by Meltzer's results for the postwar period compared with the prewar period if we depart from his assumption of a stable demand for money function for the 1900–58 period as a whole.

year (1962) to investigate relationships between asset holdings and income, and between various types of assets and total net worth. This is presented in the first section of Part IV.

For the remaining analyses the data used are those collected from a continuous panel of families in the 1960, 1961, and 1962 Surveys of Consumer Finances. They cover the incomes, asset holdings, expenditures on consumer durables, total savings, and savings components of 567 families for the years 1959–61, with some information on incomes for additional years.

The dependent variables studied are net worth, net outlays on autos (i.e., purchases less sales) and on other durables, additions and repairs to owned homes, total saving (excluding durables expenditures), contractual saving, saving in the form of liquid assets, saving in the form of insurance, business saving, saving in corporate stock and other investments, changes in mortgage debt, and changes in instalment debt. The mortgage debt item overlaps contractual saving to the extent of debt repayment, but also includes new debt incurred. Contractual saving also includes life insurance premiums. No analysis of home purchase was possible, since families who moved during the three-year period were dropped from the sample. However, stock regressions, based on value of owned homes, will be fitted in future work. Two-year averages of durables expenditures and savings components for the years 1960–61 are available for all items. In addition, single-year figures are available in all three years for each of the three durable items, for insurance premiums in 1959 and 1961, and for liquid saving in 1959. Regressions are fitted for more than one time period where data permit, and several transformations of the dependent variables are tested. Regressions with asset stocks as the dependent variables are discussed in the second section of Part IV and flow regressions in Part V.

As indicated previously, one of the primary purposes of this paper is to test a number of devices for separating the effects of normal and transitory income. Accordingly, some estimate of normal income is used in each regression, and current income is ordinarily included as a second explanatory variable in linear forms. In such forms, the coefficient of current income measures the transitory income effect, while the sum of the two income coefficients measures the normal income effect.[50]

---

[50] An analogous result holds in logarithmic relationships, except that transitory income is defined there as the ratio of current income to normal income rather than the difference of the two, so that $\log Y_T = \log Y - \log Y_N$. When the logarithms of both current and normal income are included, the coefficient of the former provides an estimate of the elasticity with respect to transitory income thus defined.

In one group of regressions normal income is estimated by averaging the actual income of an individual household over several years. For regressions involving two-year savings items a five-year income average is used (covering 1958 through anticipated 1962 income), while for single-year items a three-year average is used, centered on the year to which the savings figure refers. In all cases the current income variable refers to the same time period as the savings variable. A third income measure, based on scattered information for still earlier years, is included in some regressions to test the hypothesis that incomes in the relatively distant past may contribute to the explanation of current consumer saving and portfolio decisions.

A second group of regressions takes normal income to be the mean income for the occupational group to which the household head belongs. If normal income is believed to be average lifetime income, a reasonable first approximation to this might be obtained from the average income of the appropriate occupational group. However, if the relevant time span for defining normal income is substantially shorter than the head's working life, a more appropriate estimate would be average income for the occupation-age group to which the head belongs, and we plan to make use of this measure in future work. In a further variant, we plan to estimate normal income for each household as a linear function of the income means for the occupational, educational, racial, regional, sex, and age groups to which the household head belongs, but these results are not yet available. Number of earners, another characteristic correlated with household income, is not utilized because it is not clear to what extent variation in number of earners may reflect differences in transitory income rather than in normal income.

We have noted earlier that some device for holding group tastes constant should be used, when normal income is approximated in this way, to prevent the effects of the grouping variables from being absorbed into the estimate of the normal income effect. If this is done and if mean transitory income is constant over all groups, an unbiased estimate of the normal income effect is obtained, regardless of the grouping variables used, even when transitory income, computed as the difference between actual household income and estimated normal income, is included as a second independent variable.[51] The accuracy with which the transitory

[51] Let us assume that, holding tastes and lagged assets constant, saving for the jth household in the kth group is given by

$$S_{kj} = bY_{Nkj} + cY_{Tkj} + u_{kj},$$

where saving and income are measured from their over-all means, Y_T is transitory income, and u is a random residual uncorrelated with Y_N or Y_T. If we approximate

Y_{Nkj} by Y_{Gk}, the mean income for the group to which the household belongs, and if mean transitory income is zero for all groups, then an unbiased estimate of b may be obtained by regressing S_{kj} against Y_{Gk}.

The least-squares estimate of b is then

$$\hat{b} = \frac{\sum_{k,j} S_{kj} Y_{Gk}}{\sum_{k,j} Y_{Gk}^2} = \frac{\sum_k N_k Y_{Gk} S_{Gk}}{\sum_k N_k Y_{Gk}^2},$$

where S_{Gk} is mean group saving, N_k is the number of households in the kth group and the summations in the last fraction are over groups. Since Y_{Tk} is assumed to be zero,

$$S_{Gk} = bY_{Gk} + u_{Gk},$$

and the expected value of $\sum_k N_k Y_{Gk} S_{Gk}$ is $b\sum_k N_k Y_{Gk}^2$ since Y_{Nkj} and u_{kj} are uncorrelated and Y_{Gk} and u_{Gk} are linear functions of the Y_{Nkj} and the u_{kj}, respectively. The expected value of b is therefore b. The estimate of b is not changed by including a second independent variable, $Y_{kj} - Y_{Gk}$, in the regression as an approximation to transitory income. While any error in Y_{Gk} as an approximation to Y_{Nkj} leads to an equal and opposite error in the approximation to transitory income, the two approximations are nevertheless uncorrelated. For their covariance

$$\frac{1}{N} \sum_{k,j} Y_{Gk} (Y_{kj} - Y_{Gk}) = \frac{1}{N} \sum_k Y_{Gk} \sum_j (Y_{kj} - Y_{Gk}) = 0,$$

since within each group the sum of the deviations from the mean must be zero. Thus, the addition of the second independent variable does not change the least-squares estimate of the coefficient of the first.

income effect is estimated will depend, however, on the closeness with which the household's normal income is approximated. With an imperfect approximation to normal income, the estimated transitory income effect will be biased downward for total savings and those components where this effect is larger than the normal income effect.

In fact, it seems highly unlikely that in any given year mean transitory income is constant for all the groups used, though it may be approximately so for longer time periods. We have, therefore, utilized a five-year average of group income and hope in this way to obtain estimates of the normal income effect which are relatively free of bias due to transitory income. However, some bias due to our imperfect ability to control tastes undoubtedly remains.[52] Furthermore, the understatement of savings, and particularly certain components of savings, which occurs in cross-section data is probably greater, in absolute if not relative terms,

[52] The omission of a variable reflecting the household's tastes for holding assets in general, or particular types of assets, probably leads to a downward bias in the coefficient of normal income because of the positive correlation between initial asset holdings and tastes and between asset holdings and income as well as the negative correlation between asset holdings and saving. This tendency may be reinforced (offset) by negative (positive) correlation of normal income with savings tastes.

at high income levels than at low ones; this leads to a downward bias in the income coefficients, at least for linear regressions.

A second major purpose of the paper is to obtain improved estimates of the effects of initial asset holdings, or net worth, on consumer saving and investment decisions by holding tastes constant in some fashion. Since some households (and groups) have stronger preferences than others for the services produced by real or financial assets, compared with alternative uses of their resources, we expect certain households to wish, and eventually acquire, more assets than others with the same normal income. In other words, in the cross section, there is a substantial correlation between asset holdings and savings tastes, which makes it difficult to estimate the inhibiting effect that assets already acquired exert on further asset acquisition, when tastes are given. In addition, there may be a correlation between normal income and saving tastes, both in the cross section, as already indicated, and in the aggregate over time. For example, as new consumer products become available, the effect is to introduce a negative time trend into the aggregate savings function, while aggregate normal income is characterized by a rising time trend, so that the normal income effect is biased downward. Failure to hold tastes constant may, therefore, bias estimates of income as well as asset parameters.[53]

Two devices are used for holding tastes constant in the cross-section analysis. One is to introduce a variable into the regression which serves to distinguish "high" savers from "low" savers. The variable used is the percentage of normal income saved, either by the individual household or the group to which it is assigned, in some time period other than that to which the dependent variable refers, or alternatively the ratio of net worth to normal income in some earlier or later period. Both taste proxies are subject to certain limitations: the first because savings in any relatively short period may be strongly influenced by transitory components of income or consumption, and the second because net worth may represent an incomplete adjustment to normal income or may fluctuate erratically because of capital gains. For 1959 savings and expenditure items, we use the ratio of total savings in 1960–61 to estimated normal income. For the two-year savings items, the situation is much less satisfactory, since a limited number of savings components are available for 1959. Two alternatives based on savings items were tried—the ratio of insurance premiums to estimated normal income in 1959 and the ratio of insurance premiums plus liquid saving to normal

---

[53] The bias in estimated income effects is not expected to be very large for ungrouped cross-section data.

income. Since liquid saving is highly erratic in view of its sensitivity to transitory elements of income and consumption, the former gave slightly more promising results. A third alternative, the ratio of 1959 net worth to a three-year average of income centered on 1959, seems somewhat preferable because of its more inclusive coverage and, while not appropriate for total saving, is used in a number of regressions involving savings components and related investment items.

The second device for holding tastes constant is to utilize regressions that relate changes in savings to changes in income and initial assets for the same families or the same groups of families in different time periods. This is more satisfactory in theory, but less so in practice with the limited data available. Changes in initial assets can be computed only for a couple of savings components, since full asset information is available only at the beginning of 1960 and at the end of 1961.

Change regressions are also used as a device for isolating the influence of normal income from that of the grouping variables, when income means for the groups to which the household belongs are used in estimating its normal income. A disadvantage of such regressions for estimating normal income effects, particularly when two adjacent and relatively brief time periods are used, is that the variance of change in normal income among groups is likely to be much smaller than the variance in level of normal income. Thus, if some transitory elements remain in the mean incomes for groups, the variance of these elements probably gains in importance relative to the variance of the normal components when we shift to regressions involving first differences.[54]

As indicated earlier, our savings model presupposes a desired asset level which is based on normal income, tastes, and possibly other considerations and which is perhaps achieved only gradually over time. As long as actual income is equal to normal income, the optimum time path for asset growth is assumed to depend only on the size of the gap between actual and desired assets and the preferred speed of adjustment. Thus, in a linear model, we have as one component of saving

$$S'_t = r(A_t^* - A_{t-1}).$$

When actual income deviates from normal income, adjustments are made both in consumption and in the time path of asset growth, with the latter presumably more flexible than the former. Thus we have a second savings component which in a linear model takes the form

$$S''_t = cY_{Tt},$$

[54] This problem is discussed in some detail by Jean Crockett in *Consumer Expenditures and Incomes in Greece,* Center of Economic Research, Athens (in press).

where Y_T is transitory income. This will very likely be considerably more important for certain forms of saving than for others. If deviations from normal income are for the most part unanticipated, we may think of the first component as the planned and the second as the unplanned component of saving. Total saving is the sum of the two components:

$$S_t = r(A_t{}^* - A_{t-1}) + cY_{Tt}.^{55}$$

For a specific form of saving, S_{it}, we must consider the gap between desired and actual assets not only for the ith asset but for other assets as well.

$$S_{it} = (r_0 + r_i)(A_{it}{}^* - A_{i(t-1)}) - r_0(A_t{}^* - A_{t-1})Y + c_{iTt}.$$

A number of regressions of this type are fitted under various assumptions about the determinants of A^* or $A_i{}^*$. Under the assumptions

$$A_t{}^* = a + bY_{Nt} + d\mu,$$

$$A_{it}{}^* = j_i + k_iY_{Nt} + m_i\mu,$$

where μ is a measure of tastes and assumed constant over time, we obtain

$$S_t = ra + (rb - c)Y_{Nt} + cY_t + rd\mu - rA_{t-1}, \tag{1}$$

replacing Y_T by Y, as we may do since Y_N is already present in the regression. While it is far from clear that the tastes variable should enter additively, rather than influencing the coefficient of normal income, the regressions for saving actually fitted avoid nonadditive tastes effects. For components of saving we have

$$S_{it} = a_i + b_iY_{Nt} + c_iY_t + d_i\mu + r_0A_{t-1} - (r_0 + r_i)A_{i(t-1)}, \tag{1a}$$

[55] This implies the following formulation for the consumption function

$$C = Y_N - r(A^* - A_{t-1}) + (1 - c)Y_T,$$

which can also be derived by a somewhat different line of reasoning. Suppose that the fraction of normal income devoted to consumption is variable and depends on the gap between actual and desired assets. Then, for $Y_T = 0$, $c = fY_N$, where f is a function of $(A^* - A_{t-1})$. A simple function of $(A^* - A_{t-1})$, which has the desirable properties that it takes on the value one when $(A^* - A_{t-1})$ is zero and that it has a lower limit greater than zero, is

$$f = \frac{1}{g}\left(g - m\frac{A^* - A_{t-1}}{A^*}\right), g > m.$$

If $A^* = bY_N$, we obtain by substitution

$$C = \frac{1}{g}\left(g - m\frac{A^* - A_{t-1}}{bYn}\right)Y_N = Y_N - \frac{m}{gb}(A^* - A_{t-1}).$$

where $a_i = (r_0 + r_i)j_i - r_0a$; $b_i = (r_0 + r_i)k_i - r_0b - c_i$; and $d_i = (r_0 + r_i)m_i - r_0d$.

If we assume the household, or more plausibly socioeconomic groups of households, to be in asset equilibrium at the beginning of the period —i.e., $A_i^*{}_{(t-1)} = A_{i(t-1)}$—then $(A_t^* - A_{t-1})$ becomes simply $b\Delta Y_N$, while $A_{it}^* - A_{i(t-1)}$ becomes $k_i\Delta Y_N$, and we have

$$S_t = rb\Delta Y_N + cY_{Tt} \text{ or} \tag{2}$$

$$S_{it} = [(r_0 + r_i)k_i - r_0b] \Delta Y_N + c_iY_{Tt}. \tag{2a}$$

Alternatively, we may assume that A_t^* and A_{it}^* are quadratic functions of Y_N,

$$A_t^* = aY_{Nt} + bY_{Nt}^2 + f \text{ and } A_{it}^* = j_iY_{Nt} + k_iY_{Nt}^2 + f_i.$$

Assuming a zero constant term for mathematical convenience, this leads to

$$\frac{S_t}{Y_{Nt}} = ra + rbY_{Nt} + c\frac{Y_{Tt}}{Y_{Nt}} - r\frac{A_{t-1}}{Y_{Nt}}, \tag{3}$$

or adding $\dfrac{A_{t-1}}{Y_{Nt}}$ to both sides and ignoring capital gains

$$\frac{A_t}{Y_{Nt}} = ra + rbY_{Nt} + c\frac{Y_{Tt}}{Y_{Nt}} + (1 - r)\frac{A_{t-1}}{Y_{Nt}}.$$

For components of saving,

$$\frac{S_{it}}{Y_{Nt}} = a_i + b_iY_{Nt} + c_i\frac{Y_{Tt}}{Y_{Nt}} + r_0\frac{A_{t-1}}{Y_{Nt}} - (r_0 + r_i)\frac{A_{i(t-1)}}{Y_{Nt}}, \tag{3a}$$

where a_i and b_i are defined as above. Regressions of this type have been fitted both for savings and for asset items.

As normal income rises, we may divide the resulting changes in the desired stock of a particular type of asset into two components, one reflecting the increased size of the total portfolio and the other reflecting shifts in the preferred composition of the portfolio. For example, we expect corporate stock to be relatively more important in large portfolios than in small, so that desired holdings of stock will grow more rapidly than total net worth. To isolate the effects on asset acquisition of such shifts in portfolio composition as income rises, we plan in future work to fit a number of regressions of the general types discussed above, but with S_i/S or A_i/A as the dependent variable. Portfolio shifts may also occur, of course, as the result of changes in the relative rates of return on assets which are close substitutes in the services they perform, but cross-section data are not convenient for analyzing these shifts.

The logarithmic formulations

$$\log A_t = \rho \log \alpha + \rho\beta \log Y_{Nt} + \rho\theta \log \mu + (1 - \rho) \log A_{t-1}, \quad (4)$$

based on the assumptions

$$\frac{A_t}{A_{t-1}} = \left(\frac{A_t^*}{A_{t-1}}\right)^\rho \text{ and } A_t^* = \alpha Y^\beta_{Nt}\mu^\theta,$$

and

$$\log A_{it} = \rho_i \log \alpha_i + \rho_i\beta_i \log Y_{Nt} + \rho_i\theta_i \log \mu + (1 - \rho_i) \log A_{i(t-1)},^{56}$$

$$(4a)$$

based on the assumptions

$$\frac{A_{it}}{A_{i(t-1)}} = \left(\frac{A_{it}^*}{A_{i(t-1)}}\right)^{P_i} \text{and } A_{it}^* = \alpha_i Y_{Nt}^{\beta_i}\mu^{\theta_i},$$

have considerable appeal, but suffer from two disadvantages. First, it is not convenient to introduce a term in transitory income and, second, zero values are likely to occur in the cross section for specific types of assets.[57] For these reasons, regressions of the form (4) are shown for net worth only. In later work we plan to fit similar regressions for individual assets to grouped data, for which transitory income is expected to be close to zero and zero asset values are unlikely to occur.

IV. Empirical Results for Stock Regressions

1. FRB NET WORTH DATA

Data compiled by the Federal Reserve Board (FRB) from a stratified sample of 2,600 "families and unrelated individuals" for the year 1962, with an oversampling of upper income classes,[58] permit the derivation of the relations between the volume and composition of household net worth and household income. For this paper, we have had to work with grouped data for a single year published in the *Federal Reserve Bulletin* (March 1964), whereas our subsequent analysis of the Survey of Consumer Finances (SCF) panel data, collected by the University of Michigan Survey Research Center (SRC), permits the use of ungrouped data

---

[56] Note that this ignores the effect on the ith asset of disequilibrium in other asset holdings.

[57] A further disadvantage arises from the failure of the expressions for individual assets to aggregate to that for total assets.

[58] The over-all response rate was 86 per cent, but the rate was very much smaller in the upper income classes.

as well as data covering a much longer time span. However, the FRB survey focuses on net worth, covers a larger sample (particularly in the upper income brackets), gives some additional asset detail, and apparently has certain types of checks (notably against income tax data) not carried out in the SCF data. The FRB data have been appropriately weighted so as to be representative of all families (and unrelated individuals).

A comparison of the volume and composition of household net worth implied by the weighted FRB data with external time series aggregates can be made by multiplying the mean value of asset holdings by the number of families and unrelated individuals in the universe, both reported by the FRB for the end of 1962. The results can then be roughly compared with the time series estimates by Raymond W. Goldsmith, Robert E. Lipsey, and Morris Mendelson for nonfarm households, nonfarm unincorporated business, and agriculture as of the end of 1958;[59] we increase their figures for net worth and stock holdings by an estimated $50 billion to allow for the 15 per cent rise in the market value of equities from the end of 1958 to the end of 1962 and deduct an estimated $135 billion for consumer durables (other than automobiles) and currency not included in the FRB survey. With these crude adjustments, the FRB net worth of $1400 billion is modestly lower than the adjusted Goldsmith *et al.* figure of $1600 billion; part of this remaining difference is still conceptual since the coverage of FRB insurance is much narrower. For homes, the largest single item in net worth,[60] the estimates seem quite close. The most serious understatements in the FRB survey are for liquid assets, where the FRB figure is only about two-thirds of the external aggregate, and for insurance, where the proportion is even lower, but the latter difference appears to be more conceptual than statistical. There also appears to be a significant understatement in the FRB estimate for stock holdings, but it is not possible to tell precisely how much since stock in closely held corporations is grouped with other investments rather than with marketable stock in the FRB data. Though the time series aggregates are also subject to error, they are likely to be more reliable for financial assets. The deficiencies in the universe estimate of financial assets—especially liquid assets—from the FRB survey reflect in part underrepresentation of upper income groups (as discussed subsequently in another context), but also appear to reflect

[59] *Studies in the National Balance Sheet of the United States,* Vol. II, Princeton for NBER, 1963, pp. 68–69.

[60] Stock is a close second.

underreporting of holdings by respondents in the survey.[61] The understatement of liquid assets in consumer surveys has generally been assumed to be proportional to income, but there is no conclusive evidence that this is so. Indeed, there appears to be some reason to believe that proportionately more of the understatement is attributable to the upper than to the lower income groups.[62]

The relation of assets to income for families classified by income, which is essentially the only FRB data available for the purposes of our analysis, might be expected to give a fully satisfactory approximation of the relation of desired assets to normal income only under certain assumptions. First, the average time to adjust actual assets to desired assets for a given level of normal income should be not much over a year. In other words, actual assets should, on the average, be close to desired assets without any substantial disequilibrium component, an assumption which may be more valid for assets than saving but is questionable even for assets. As noted in Part II, if this assumption is incorrect, the relation of assets to normal income would be expected to give a somewhat lower income effect than the relation of desired assets to normal income in which we are interested. Second, it is assumed that available income is, on the average, close to normal income, a condition which is certainly not true at the low end of the income scale for a particular year and probably not at the upper end. The low end is likely to be particularly biased because of the inclusion of the retired group in the FRB sample. The only device available to us to get around these difficulties at least in part is to exclude the lowest and highest income classes in attempting to approximate the relation of desired assets to normal income and to examine the implications of omitting different income classes at the extremes. Third, it is assumed that the correlation of saving tastes with income is not very strong (e.g., the correlation between income for the ith group Y_i and tastes F_i in the relation for net worth $A_i = a + bY_i + F_i + u_i$). This seems to be a reasonable hypothesis.

Two additional technical problems involved in the use of the FRB data should also be mentioned. While data on the dollar value of assets by income class are provided, this is not true of the dollar value of income. This presents a major problem only for the open-end over-$100,000 income class where there is no satisfactory basis for estimating the average income. There is strong evidence that the external data pub-

---

[61] The FRB survey is less subject to the first type of deficiency than other available surveys, but it is not possible to tell without further analysis about the second type.

[62] See footnote 13.

lished by the Internal Revenue Service, which we used for estimating average income within an income class, would greatly overestimate the average income of the sample reporting to the FRB for incomes over $100,000. This, of course, is not surprising in view of the well-known difficulties of obtaining survey responses from the top income class, and simply provides another reason for omitting this group from our regression analysis. The other problem is that the income data are on a before-tax base so that it was necessary to convert them to a disposable income base, using the income and tax statistics for before-tax income groups published by the Internal Revenue Service for 1962. However, since these adjustments are fairly crude, a few key before-tax results will also be presented.

Plotting the average net worth (including the market value of automobiles) against average disposable income for households classified by 1962 before-tax income indicated that the relation was closer to logarithmic than to linear. Omitting the under-$3,000 and over-$100,000 income classes which are subject to special problems previously mentioned, the coefficient of determination adjusted for degrees of freedom ($\bar{R}^2$) is .91 for the logarithmic relation and .72 for the linear relation, both universe weighted results.[63] An examination of the logarithmic scatter still shows significant curvilinearity, with an apparent income elasticity of net worth in the neighborhood of one for disposable income between $3,000 and $7,500 and well above one thereafter, rising to 2.0 or so in the $10,000 to $100,000 range. In the latter range there is no consistent trend, but there is an indication of some decline in the $50,000–$100,000 bracket.

The distribution of net worth by income class indicates that 65 per cent of net worth is held by the households with an income elasticity of well over one. Actually the percentage falling into this category is likely to be higher than the raw figures suggest. Families with low current incomes will, on the average, have negative transitory incomes, which would be expected to affect income more than assets, so that the observed asset-to-income ratio will be well above normal. On the other hand, families with high current incomes and positive transitory income would be expected to have an observed asset-to-income ratio well below normal. As a result, the presence of extreme current income groups is likely to introduce a downward bias in the estimated income elasticities.

The income elasticities derived from the weighted log relations between the volume and composition of net worth and disposable income are presented in Table 1 for all households excluding the two extreme

[63] These results are somewhat lower than those obtained on a before-tax base.

income classes (under $3,000 and over $100,000), and in Table 2 for all households excluding four extreme income groups (under $5,000 and over $50,000). The income elasticity of net worth is estimated at 1.27 in the first table and at 1.51 in the second (with $\bar{R}^2$ of .91 and .93, respectively).[64] One qualification of these estimates—the tendency of transitory income to introduce a downward bias in these estimates, particularly in Table 1—has already been pointed out. Another limitation which should be mentioned is the possibility that, in the absence of precise information on income for the sample, we have overstated income significantly in the $50,000–$99,999 class, which would again lead to understatement of the elasticities in Table 1 and suggest that the correct values are closer to those in Table 2.[65]

An income elasticity of net worth significantly over one appears to be inconsistent with the "permanent income" hypothesis, which assumes proportionality between normal saving and normal income. In the absence of disequilibrium asset holdings, transitory income, and capital gains, the unitary income elasticity of saving in the permanent income hypothesis implies the same income elasticity for net worth, holding age constant. As suggested earlier, the existence of disequilibrium holdings and transitory income would not be expected to raise the estimated income elasticity of net worth. Nor is it clear why capital gains (which, of course, are largely unrealized) should have such an effect. If desired assets are determined only by normal income, the relation of normal income to assets should not be affected by whether assets are accumulated by saving or by capital gains. If desired assets are a function not only of normal income but also of average capital gains, then as a first approximation it might be assumed that capital gains are proportional to accumulated saving and hence to normal income. If this is true, then under the permanent income hypothesis the income elasticity of assets would be equivalent to the normal income elasticity of saving. Other assumptions would seem to be required—such as a higher propensity of upper income groups for variable price assets in conjunction with the treatment of capital gains as part of normal income—if these findings

[64] The corresponding elasticities are 1.19 and 1.38 on a before-tax base. It might also be noted that, when the four extreme groups are omitted, $\bar{R}^2$ in the linear relation of net worth to after-tax income is raised from .72 to .80.

[65] The average after-tax incomes used were $3,640 for the $3,000–$4,999 before-tax class, $5,480 for the $5,000–$7,499 class, $7,670 for the $7,500–$9,999 class, $10,120 for the $10,000–$14,999 class, $15,250 for the $15,000–$24,999 class, $25,350 for the $25,000–$49,999 class, and $43,800 for the $50,000–$99,999 class. The last figure was estimated to be $65,400 on a before-tax basis. We hope to check our estimates of average income as well as to improve on this analysis generally through access to the ungrouped data.

TABLE 1

*Weighted Log Regressions of Assets on Disposable Income as of December 31, 1962,
for Families and Unrelated Individuals with Before-Tax Incomes from $3,000 to $99,999,
FRB Survey of Financial Characteristics of Consumers*

Asset Items (equity in)	Income Slope (and standard error)	Constant Term (and standard error)	Coefficient of Determination (adjusted for degrees of freedom)
Total net worth	1.269 (.047)	.611 (.088)	.911
All tangible assets	1.037 (.010)	.0004 (.019)	.993
Own home	1.034 (.012)	− .110 (.022)	.991
Automobile	1.043 (.017)	−2.227 (.031)	.982
Business, profession	1.213 (.082)	−1.200 (.154)	.754
Life insurance, annuities, retirement plans	1.471 (.007)	−2.358 (.013)	.999
All liquid and investment assets	1.248 (.070)	− .308 (.132)	.815
Liquid assets	1.072 (.056)	−1.064 (.105)	.837
All investment assets	1.309 (.078)	− .844 (.147)	.796
Stocks	1.668 (.113)	−2.354 (.212)	.753
Marketable bonds	2.749 (.168)	−8.077 (.315)	.790
Other	− .967 (.107)	− .905 (.200)	.533
Miscellaneous assets	2.127 (.189)	−4.150 (.355)	.638
Less: personal debt (excludes autos)	.635 (.062)	−1.824 (.116)	.592

Note: See Table 3 for definitions of asset items.

TABLE 2

Weighted Log Regressions of Assets on Disposable Income as of December 31, 1962,
for Families and Unrelated Individuals with Before-Tax Incomes from $5,000 to $49,999,
FRB Survey of Financial Characteristics of Consumers

Asset Items	Income Slope (and standard error)	Constant Term (and standard error)	Coefficient of Determination (adjusted for degrees of freedom)
Total net worth	1.508 (.056)	.068 (.114)	.935
All tangible assets	1.118 (.010)	− .175 (.021)	.996
Own home	1.122 (.014)	− .303 (.028)	.993
Automobile	1.064 (.023)	−2.262 (.047)	.977
Business, profession	1.705 (.083)	−2.306 (.169)	.892
Life insurance, annuities, retirement plans	1.513 (.008)	−2.447 (.016)	.999
All liquid and investment assets	1.688 (.075)	−1.293 (.152)	.909
Liquid assets	1.565 (.016)	−2.151 (.033)	.995
All investment assets	1.713 (.100)	−1.753 (.205)	.851
Stocks	1.572 (.202)	−2.168 (.414)	.538
Marketable bonds	4.053 (.150)	−10.952 (.307)	.935
Other	1.786 (.093)	−2.714 (.190)	.878
Miscellaneous assets	.758 (.231)	−1.174 (.473)	.160
Less: personal debt (excludes autos)	.652 (.110)	−1.878 (.224)	.402

Note: See Table 3 for definitions of asset items.

are to be reconciled with the permanent income hypothesis.[66] It is possible to examine the income elasticities of the major categories of assets classified by their capital gains potential, i.e., by fixed and variable value asset groupings, to provide some information on the relative propensities of upper income groups to hold variable value assets and thus provide insights into the relation between the normal income elasticities of assets and savings. Such information is, of course, of great interest in its own right.

The data in Tables 1 and 2 suggest that income elasticities of assets are about one or significantly above for all major categories of net worth, with the single exception of personal indebtedness (exclusive of mortgage and automobile debt).[67] The latter constitutes only about 2 per cent of net worth (Table 3). The elasticities indicated in Table 2, with minor exceptions, are higher than those in Table 1 and are associated with significantly higher correlations. Perhaps the most interesting difference between the two sets of results are those for liquid assets (including U.S. savings bonds but excluding currency), where the second set points to an elasticity of 1.57 (with $\bar{R}^2$ over .99) vs. 1.07 for the first set (with an $\bar{R}^2$ of .84). There is also a substantial difference for equity in business, but in both cases the elasticity is significantly above one. The elasticities for other investment assets (including stock in closely held corporations) and miscellaneous assets (including those in trust) also differ greatly between the two sets.

Tangible assets seem to have an income elasticity not very different from one; life insurance, business investment, and stocks in the neigh-

---

[66] The possibility exists that, in the analysis of the FRB data, our inability to hold other factors constant, notably age, seriously affects the results. This possibility as well as the implications of explicitly adjusting for transitory income and asset disequilibrium will be investigated in the next section in the analysis of the SRC data. Empirical evidence on the comparative size of income elasticities for assets and for savings will be presented in a subsequent section.

[67] Our estimates of both the income elasticity of net worth and of individual components of assets may reflect in part interest rate or rate of return effects as a result of differential taxation in upper and lower income groups. The upper income groups receive less returns after taxes from an identical investment and have more tax incentive to invest in certain types of assets, notably tax-exempt bonds and variable price assets such as stock. Thus it could be argued that our income elasticities of net worth are biased downward and our income elasticities of tax-exempt bonds and stocks biased upward. Such biases do not arise from the cross-sectional nature of our data but might be expected in time series as well.

TABLE 3

Percentage Distribution of Assets as of December 31, 1962,
for All Families and Unrelated Individuals,
FRB Survey of Financial Characteristics of Consumers

Asset Items (equity in)	Per Cent of Total Net Worth
Total net worth	100.0
All tangible assets	29.3
Own home	26.5
Automobile	2.8
Business, profession	17.3
Life insurance, annuities, retirement plans	6.1
All liquid and investment assets	42.7
Liquid assets	11.4
All investment assets	31.3
Stocks	18.0
Marketable bonds	2.0
Other	11.2
Miscellaneous assets	6.8
Less: personal debt (excludes autos)	−2.1

Notes

Net worth in own home represents the respondent's estimate of market value of his principal residence as well as any vacation homes owned, less debt secured by such properties. Owner-occupied farm residences are included under business interests.

Net worth in automobiles represents the respondent's estimate of market value in the majority of cases. In the remaining cases, values from the Red Book of the National Market Reports, Inc., were used. Debts secured by automobiles were deducted.

Business interest consists of equity in farm and nonfarm sole proprietorships, partnerships, and closely held corporations in which the respondent considered himself to be active in management. Investment in business by self-employed professionals is also included here. Respondents were asked to value their businesses on two bases — book and market. The net worth concept used in this report incorporates businesses valued at book in most cases.

Equity in life insurance, annuities, and retirement plans consists of cash surrender value of life insurance (less loans secured by policies), the amounts that families could have withdrawn from retirement plans had they left their jobs on December 31, 1962, and amounts which had been paid for individual annuities as of December 31, 1962. The present value of annuities that were paying income in 1962 is not included in the estimate.

Notes to Table 3 (concluded)

Liquid assets consist of checking accounts at banks, savings accounts at banks, shares in savings and loan associations and credit unions, and U.S. savings bonds valued at face.

Stock consists of all publicly traded common and preferred stocks, shares in mutual funds and other investment companies, and shares in investment clubs, less net debit balances and loans secured by stocks. Shares were valued at market prices prevailing on December 31, 1962.

Marketable bonds consist of bonds, notes, bills, certificates, and debentures issued by the U.S. government, by state and local governments, by foreign and domestic corporations, and by foreign governments, less loans secured by such bonds. These securities were valued at par.

Other investment assets consist of mortgage assets (amount outstanding as of December 31, 1962), real estate valued at market less debt outstanding, and closely held or family businesses in which a family member was not active in management. Respondents were asked to value their interest in such businesses at market.

Miscellaneous assets consist of assets held in trust, amounts that family members could have withdrawn from profit-sharing and other deferred income plans had they left their jobs on December 31, 1962, and such assets as oil royalties, patents, and commodity contracts.

Personal debt consists of nonbusiness debt not secured by any of the asset types covered in the Survey. Examples are instalment debt on consumer durable goods other than automobiles, home repair and modernization loans, and debts to hospitals, doctors, and the like.

Total net worth consists of the various asset components of net worth described above less personal debt.

Income is defined as the total money income received in 1962 by all family members before any payroll deductions. The following components are included: salaries; commissions; net income from unincorporated businesses or professions, partnerships, and farms; dividends; interest; net income from rents; pension and social security payments; and any other periodic payments received by family members.

borhood of 1.5; and marketable bonds in the neighborhood of 3 to 4.[68] The most important assets by size of holdings were value of home, stocks, business, and liquid assets in that order (Table 3). The extremely high elasticity for marketable bonds presumably reflects the advantage

[68] The income elasticity for stocks estimated at 1.67 in Table 1 and 1.57 in Table 2 is less than the 1.98 figure for all income classes obtained from the relatively reliable distribution of stock ownership built up from dividend receipts reported to the U.S. Internal Revenue Service. See Jean Crockett and Irwin Friend, "Characteristics of Stock Ownership," *Proceedings of the Business and Economic Statistics Section,* American Statistical Association, 1963, p. 156. The income elasticity from the latter body of data excluding the retired is 1.95 (*ibid.,* p. 152).

to upper income groups of tax exemption on state and local government issues since, according to external data, tax-exempt bonds represent about 40 per cent of the marketable bonds held by individuals. In general, there is less relation between income elasticity and capital gains (or loss) potential or risk (anticipated variance in capital value or in return) than might have been expected on a priori grounds.

Because of differences in coverage, it is difficult at this time to make precise comparisons of these income elasticities with those derived in earlier studies.[69] However, the slightly larger than unitary elasticity for automobiles (less related debt) seems reasonably close to the results obtained in prior cross-section and in the Houthakker-Haldi panel studies but lower than the results in most time series studies, including the careful analysis carried out by Chow. The slightly larger than unitary elasticity for homes (less mortgage) appears close to the time series result derived by Muth, though higher than in a number of other analyses. On the other hand, the netting out of mortgage debt may significantly affect the estimated elasticities. The income elasticity for liquid assets (excluding currency) seems more consistent with the Friedman and Meltzer time series than with the Feige and Watts-Tobin cross-section results, though this cannot be stated with any certainty because of the inclusion of U.S. savings bonds in the FRB data as well as other noncomparable items.

In order to test, albeit crudely, the relative usefulness of total assets or net worth compared with income in explaining the composition of assets, the weighted logarithmic relations between component items of assets and net worth less that component are presented in Tables 4 and 5, which may be compared with the corresponding income relations in Tables 1 and 2.[70] The income relations provide better fits for tangible assets and insurance. The asset relations are better for business and investment assets. Pooling results from the regressions covering the $3,000–$99,999 and the $5,000–$49,999 income groups, there is not much basis for choosing between income and assets as an explanation of variation in holdings of liquid assets, stocks, and marketable bonds.

---

[69] We hope to be able to do this subsequently by making, at least in crude fashion, some of the necessary conceptual adjustments from the SCF data and by eventual access to the details of the FRB data.

[70] The absence of a total savings tastes variable might be expected to bias the results in favor of the asset relations; on the other hand, there may be fully offsetting negative correlations between tastes for different asset items.

TABLE 4

Weighted Log Regressions of Assets on Net Worth Less Indicated Asset Items as of December 31, 1962, for Families and Unrelated Individuals with Before-Tax Incomes from $3,000 to $99,999, FRB Survey of Financial Characteristics of Consumers

Asset Items (equity in)	Adjusted Net Worth Slope (and standard error)	Constant Term (and standard error)	Coefficient of Determination (adjusted for degrees of freedom)
All tangible assets	0.689 (.027)	0.186 (.069)	.900
Own home	0.699 (.025)	0.002 (.067)	.913
Automobile	0.728 (.036)	−2.424 (.106)	.851
Business, profession	1.003 (.040)	−1.755 (.113)	.897
Life insurance, annuities, retirement plans	1.052 (.044)	−2.669 (.128)	.888
All liquid and investment assets	1.011 (.037)	−0.491 (.093)	.913
Liquid assets	0.828 (.029)	−1.411 (.084)	.917
All investment assets	1.106 (.038)	−1.367 (.102)	.923
Stocks	1.333 (.087)	−3.043 (.249)	.765
Marketable bonds	2.188 (.101)	−9.454 (.301)	.868
Other	0.771 (.068)	−1.285 (.194)	.641
Miscellaneous assets	1.453 (.171)	−4.436 (.499)	.501
Less: personal debt (excludes autos)	0.489 (.044)	−2.083 (.129)	.635

Note: See notes to Table 3 for definitions of asset items.

TABLE 5

Weighted Log Regressions of Assets on Net Worth Less Indicated Asset Items as of December 31, 1962, for Families and Unrelated Individuals with Before-Tax Incomes from $5,000 to $49,999, FRB Survey of Financial Characteristics of Consumers

Asset Items (equity in)	Adjusted Net Worth Slope (and standard error)	Constant Term (and standard error)	Coefficient of Determination (adjusted for degrees of freedom)
All tangible assets	0.619 (.027)	0.435 (.072)	.914
Own home	0.634 (.026)	0.235 (.072)	.921
Automobile	0.642 (.033)	−2.086 (.104)	.879
Business, profession	1.152 (.042)	−2.275 (.127)	.935
Life insurance, annuities, retirement plans	0.923 (.042)	−2.185 (.128)	.906
All liquid and investment assets	1.217 (.039)	−1.105 (.106)	.949
Liquid assets	0.981 (.033)	−1.915 (.099)	.946
All investment assets	1.238 (.050)	−1.794 (.142)	.924
Stocks	1.119 (.121)	−2.319 (.366)	.622
Marketable bonds	2.536 (.136)	−10.652 (.429)	.871
Other	1.128 (.073)	−2.485 (.221)	.825
Miscellaneous assets	0.639 (.135)	−1.586 (.415)	.296
Less: personal debt (excludes autos)	0.434 (.067)	−1.899 (.210)	.443

Note: See notes to Table 3 for definitions of asset items.

Multivariate regressions of asset items on income and net worth and on income and net worth less that component pointed to similar results on the relative importance of income and assets as the simple regressions for all families in the $3,000–$99,999 income range included in Tables 1 and 4.[71] However, in view of the small number of observations, no attempt was made to compute similar multivariate regressions for the $5,000–$49,999 income range, which, as noted earlier, probably give better results. The data do not permit us to relate the composition of assets to the year's income and to initial or beginning-of-year net worth, which jointly represent the available resources for allocation over the year.

While these data are far from convincing, they suggest that income cannot be disregarded in analyzing the demand for liquid assets as well as for most other components of net worth. Of course, to the extent that net worth is determined by normal income, the use of either net worth or normal income as an explanatory variable in the demand functions for assets should give equivalent results. The difference in results may reflect various factors, notably, the fact that net worth is only imperfectly determined by normal income and that the income variable used includes transitory components which differ from normal income in their effect on desired and actual assets.

One further point should be considered in connection with the interpretation of the results presented in this section, viz., the implications of combining households with retired heads of households and other families. Most of such households, of course, are in the lower income brackets and are excluded when the extreme income classes are omitted. To the extent that such households are included, they could be regarded as having negative transitory income, which would introduce a downward bias in the estimated income elasticities as measures of the elasticities for other (i.e., nonretired) families.[72] The normal income elasticity of

---

[71] Both income and asset coefficients were generally (though not always) significant, but sometimes the statistically less important of the two had a negative sign, probably reflecting the differential effect of transitory elements on current income and assets.

[72] As noted earlier, however, it is probably preferable to consider our basic desired asset and asset-adjustment relations to apply to households in their working span, while the assets of retired persons are determined by their end-of-work-life assets (which, in turn, is a function of their normal income at that time), their retirement span, and the proportion of such assets that will be passed on as inheritances.

net worth for households with working heads in turn should be equivalent to or less than the elasticity relevant to time series analysis.[73]

2. SRC NET WORTH DATA

Data on assets, saving, and income were compiled by the Survey Research Center (SRC) from a panel of 1059 spending units for the years 1959, 1960, and 1961. Not all asset or saving items were collected for each year, but total savings were collected for the two-year period 1960-61, assets for the beginning and end of the two-year period, income and selected items of assets and saving for each of the three years covered by the panel, and income also for a preceding year (1958), expected income for a subsequent year (1962), and rough estimates of income for the years 1920, 1928, 1940, 1947, and 1955. Although the initial sample was randomly selected, the final panel sample of respondents for all three years is not a random sample of the population as a whole. "Younger consumer units were not introduced into the panel in succeeding years and respondents who moved were not followed. As a result, the members of our panel tend (1) to have higher

---

[73] If A_w represents assets during the work life, A_r assets of the retired, A total assets, A'_w assets of the retired at the end of their work life, i half the retirement span, Y_N normal income for the working population, and g the growth rate of income, and if we assume for simplicity that the relation of desired assets to normal income is linear in logs (i.e., $A_w^* = aY_N^b$), that the asset adjustment period is instantaneous, that a fraction f of A'_w is left as inheritances, and that no income is earned on assets, we can write as an approximation

$$A = \left[a + \frac{a(1+f)}{2(1+g)^{ib}} \right] Y_N^b$$

so that the income elasticity of A, which is of course b, would be the same as that of A_w. If we drop the most troublesome assumption for our purposes, that of immediate adjustment and write $A_w = raY_N^b + (1-r)(A_w) - 1$ where r is the speed of adjustment, the normal income elasticity for working households

$$E_w = \frac{braY_N^b}{raY_N^b + (1-r)(A_w)_{-1}}$$

is less than the corresponding elasticity for all households

$$E = \frac{b\left[ra + \dfrac{a(1+f)}{2(1+g)^{ib}} \right] Y_N^b}{\left[ra + \dfrac{a(1+f)}{2(1+g)^{ib}} \right] Y_N^b + (1-r)(A_w)_{-1}},$$

and both are less than b.

incomes, (2) to contain a higher proportion of home owners, and (3) to be older than the noninstitutional population of the United States as a whole."[74]

The saving data in this panel have been subjected to an interesting preliminary analysis by the Survey Research Center in *Consumer Behavior of Individual Families Over Two and Three Years,* largely by relating two-year total saving (in ratio form) to two-year per capita income (before taxes) and other selected family characteristics, along lines similar to earlier analysis of one-year saving by the Center. The analysis in this paper attempts, among other things, to make much greater use of the panel features of the data. However, in view of difficulties with the data, not all of which have yet been resolved, we are able to present at this time only part of the results we had hoped to have completed. Our analysis is confined to those families who reported information on all variables we were interested in, so that, instead of the 1059 panel members reporting some information for all three years, or the 921 panel members included in the SRC's more limited analysis of two-year total saving, our entire potential sample consisted of only 596 spending units. An examination suggested that data for a handful of households—largely those with extremely large saving-to-income ratios and, to a lesser extent, those with very large incomes—were highly questionable, so that it was decided to eliminate the twenty-five units with a ratio of annual savings (a two-year average) to normal disposable income (a five-year average) of over 75 per cent and the four other units with five-year disposable income of over $20,000 per annum. The fairly numerous cases of extremely high saving-to-income ratios generally seemed to be associated with the inclusion of capital gains in saving or with other distortions. The small number of high-income families in our potential sample is presumably largely a reflection of the original random sampling scheme, but may also reflect the difficulty of enlisting full cooperation from such households. The remaining 567 cases were divided into three groups which were analyzed separately: viz., 413 units headed by employees; 61 by self-employed persons including farmers; and 93 by retired persons.

In addition to the characteristics of each spending unit supplied by the Survey Research Center, we constructed a number of other variables on the basis of the data made available to us. Perhaps the most important of these include average disposable income for five years, which serves as a basic set of estimates of normal income; rough estimates of average disposable income for even longer periods based on data for 1928,

[74] *Consumer Behavior of Individual Families Over Two and Three Years,* p. 75.

1940, 1947, 1955, and 1958;[75] net worth at the end of 1961 and at the end of 1959; group averages of income, which serve as another set of estimates of normal income; and several different savings tastes variables. Since disposable income for each household was estimated by the Survey Research Center only for 1959, 1960, and 1961, it was necessary to convert the before-tax figure available for 1958 and 1962 to an after-tax base in order to obtain average disposable income for the five-year period 1958–62. This was done by multiplying the 1958 before-tax income for each household by the ratio of 1959 after-tax to 1959 before-tax income for the same unit, and multiplying the 1962 before-tax income by the ratio of 1961 after-tax to 1961 before-tax income.

Simply as a matter of convenience, net worth was not defined to include the stock of automobiles or other consumer durables (the latter not being available), but reflects all other items of assets and liabilities covered in the survey.[76] The net worth estimates for 1961 are probably much more reliable than those for 1959 since several components for 1959 were obtained in the later survey and presumably reflect a more significant memory bias. Moreover, both the value of stocks (i.e., equity securities) and the value of business for 1959 were available only in class interval form, introducing further errors of measurement.

The SRC data on net worth or stock of assets for 1961 are analyzed in this section. The more detailed analysis of saving or flow of assets appears in the following section. In both sections the data are unweighted, partly to save time at this stage of the analysis and partly to maintain comparability with the published SRC results.

Summary data on the end of 1961 net worth regressions derived from the SRC panel are presented in Table 6, both in logarithmic form to allow for the nonlinearities in the net worth relations noted earlier and for comparability with the FRB data, and in linear form for comparability with the later savings regressions. If we confine our attention

[75] In this long-run perspective, one estimate of normal income for the group with heads of households over 55 was obtained by taking the simple average of 1928, 1940, and 1947 incomes; for the 35–54 age groups as the average of 1940, 1947, and 1955 incomes; and for the under 35 age group as the average of 1947, 1955, and 1958 incomes. Still another estimate used an average of 1947 and 1955 incomes for all age groups. It was necessary to convert before-tax income to disposable income by applying average prevailing tax rates in an income class to all units in that class. All before-tax income data were available only by class intervals.

[76] An important omission in the SRC data on net worth consists of financial investment other than corporate stock and U.S. savings bonds. Such investment would tend to be concentrated more heavily among the upper income groups than other items of net worth, leading to a relative understatement of net worth for these groups.

TABLE 6

Regressions of 1961 Net Worth on Disposable Income and Other Variables, SCF Panel Data for Households with 1958-62 Disposable Income of Less Than $20,000

PART A: EMPLOYEES

Coefficient of	Logarithmic Regressions						
	1	2	3	4	5	6	7
Household income, 1958-62	1.64 (13.65)	1.07 (3.05)	.19 (.82)	.13 (.56)	1.51 (10.57)	.55 (5.17)	—
Group income, 1958-62	—	—	—	—	—	—	.11 (.59)
Historical household income[a]	—	—	—	—	.16 (1.66)	−.03 (−.43)	—
Household income, 1961	—	.56 (1.76)	.32 (1.50)	.35 (1.66)	—	—	.46 (5.40)
Household net worth, 1959	—	—	.70 (22.65)	.69 (21.84)	—	.70 (22.68)	.70 (22.52)
Normal capital gains[b]	—	—	—	.01 (1.26)	—	—	—
Age of head[c]	—	.64 (6.96)	.19 (2.99)	.19 (3.00)	—	.20 (2.90)	.19 (3.00)
Constant term	−5.49 (−5.28)	−7.26 (−7.04)	2.58 (3.16)	2.77 (3.35)	−5.67 (−5.43)	2.48 (3.05)	2.09 (1.39)
Normal income elasticity	1.64	1.63	1.72[d]	1.59[d]	1.68	1.75[d,e]	1.90
Speed of adjustment[h]	i	i	.16	.17	i	.16	.16
$\bar{R}^2$	.31	.38	.73	.73	.31	.72	.73

(continued)

TABLE 6 *(continued)*

PART A: EMPLOYEES (concluded)

		Linear Regressions			
8	9	10	11	12	13
3.25 (13.54)	–	2.24 (2.48)	.69 (1.07)	–	–
–	–	–	–	.92 (1.70)	–.12 (–.31)
–	–	–	–	–	–
–	2.87 (13.34)	1.02 (1.27)	.30 (.53)	2.68 (11.13)	.90 (4.80)
–	–	–	1.07 (20.18)	–	1.08 (20.22)
–	–	–	–	–	–
–	–	354.94 (5.78)	56.68 (1.23)	–	52.44 (1.14)
–8,226.65 (–4.99)	–6,535.04 (–4.20)	–16,373.79 (–7.55)	–6,149.89 (–3.80)	–11,146.66 (–3.56)	–5,001.01 (–1.98)
1.68	1.54[f]	1.68	g	1.89	g
i	i	i	g	i	g
.31	.30	.36	.68	.30	.68

(continued)

TABLE 6 *(continued)*

PART B: SELF-EMPLOYED INCLUDING FARMERS

	Logarithmic Regressions					
Coefficient of	1	2	3	4	5	6
Household income, 1958-1962	1.51 (6.43)	1.76 (3.34)	.55 (1.17)	.44 (.92)	1.39 (5.39)	.76 (3.06)
Historical household income[a]	—	—	—	—	.03 (.15)	-.11 (-.67)
Household income, 1961	—	-.18 (-.36)	.23 (.55)	.27 (.66)	—	—
Household net worth, 1959	—	—	.64 (5.72)	.64 (5.72)	—	.66 (6.03)
Normal capital gains[b]	—	—	—	.14 (1.63)	—	—
Age[c]	—	.41 (1.39)	.09 (.36)	.10 (.40)	—	.12 (.47)
Constant term	-3.07 (-1.52)	-4.95 (-1.99)	1.21 (.54)	1.70 (.74)	-2.27 (-1.07)	2.10 (.95)
Normal income elasticity	1.51	1.58	2.19[d]	1.99[d]	1.42	1.91
Speed of adjustment[h]	i	i	.20	.20	i	.19
$\bar{R}^2$	.41	.41	.62	.63	.36	.62

(continued)

TABLE 6 *(continued)*

PART B: SELF-EMPLOYED INCLUDING FARMERS (concluded)

	Linear Regressions		
7	8	9	10
8.47	—	7.55	3.18
(6.52)		(2.63)	(1.32)
—	—	—	—
—	7.55	1.42	1.95
	(5.73)	(.51)	(.89)
—	—	—	1.13
			(5.84)
—	—	—	—
—	—	601.02	1.59
		(1.36)	(.00)
−12,195.01	−5,589.77	−29,897.95	−20,839.98
(−1.26)	(−.57)	(−1.80)	(−1.56)
1.29	1.14[f]	1.36	g
i	i	i	g
.41	.35	.41	.63

(continued)

TABLE 6 *(continued)*

PART C: RETIRED

Coefficient of	Logarithmic Regressions					
	1	2	3	4	5	6
Household income, 1958–62	1.03 (5.04)	1.85 (4.31)	.24 (.98)	.18 (.74)	.88 (3.68)	-.04 (-.31)
Historical household income[a]	—	—	—	—	.25 (1.21)	.07 (.66)
Household income, 1961	—	-.58 (-1.93)	-.19 (-1.21)	-.17 (-1.13)		
Household net worth, 1959	—	—	.98 (15.89)	.96 (15.35)	—	.98 (16.23)
Normal capital gains[b]	—	—	—	.03 (1.23)	—	—
Age[c]	—	1.74 (2.46)	.01 (.03)	.04 (.10)	—	-.06 (-.17)
Constant term	.68 (.45)	-7.95 (-2.24)	6.40 (3.18)	6.61 (3.28)	.04 (.02)	6.92 (3.65)
Normal income elasticity	1.03	1.27	2.27[d]	.20[d]	1.13	1.26
Speed of adjustment[h]	i	i	.01	.02	i	.01
$\bar{R}^2$	.21	.26	.81	.81	.22	.81

(continued)

TABLE 6 *(continued)*

PART C: RETIRED (concluded)

Linear Regressions			
7	8	9	10
6.48	–	8.15	6.06
(6.31)		(2.68)	(3.04)
–	–	–	–
–	5.98	–1.22	–4.96
	(5.74)	(–.41)	(–2.53)
–	–	–	.98
			(11.76)
–	–	–	–
–	–	297.23	–23.51
		(1.53)	(–.19)
–2,349.31	–1,064.21	–17,819.96	–562.37
(–.81)	(–.36)	(–1.70)	(–.08)
1.19	1.08[f]	1.27	g
i	i	i	g
.30	.26	.31	.73

(continued)

TABLE 6 *(continued)*

PART D: EMPLOYEES BY AGE OF HEAD

| | Logarithmic Regressions | | | | | |
| | Under 35 | | | 35 to 44 | | |
Coefficient of	1	2	3	4	5	6
Household income, 1958-62	2.09	1.20	1.15	2.37	.11	.08
	(8.20)	(1.77)	(1.67)	(9.97)	(.23)	(.16)
Household income, 1961	—	-.41	-.38	—	.67	.68
		(-.71)	(-.65)		(1.60)	(1.62)
Household net worth, 1959	—	.76	.75	—	.64	.63
		(8.87)	(8.31)		(11.68)	(11.41)
Normal capital gains[b]	—	—	.01	—	—	.01
			(.45)			(.53)
Age[c]	—	-.06	-.05	—	.23	.22
		(-.30)	(-.28)		(.51)	(.49)
Constant term	-9.80	.78	.90	-12.03	.12	.28
	(-4.44)	(.38)	(.43)	(-5.79)	(.06)	(.13)
Normal income elasticity	2.09	3.22[d]	3.01[d]	2.37	2.15[d]	2.08[d]
Speed of adjustment[h]	i	.13	.14	i	.20	.20
$\bar{R}^2$	.37	.63	.63	.44	.74	.73

(continued)

TABLE 6 (concluded)

PART D: EMPLOYEES BY AGE OF HEAD (concluded)

Logarithmic Regressions					
45 to 54			55 and over		
7	8	9	10	11	12
1.20	−.12	−.39	1.55	.88	.87
(6.19)	(−.38)	(−1.16)	(5.35)	(1.57)	(1.54)
−	.37	.56	−	−.24	−.24
	(1.31)	(1.92)		(−.47)	(−.46)
−	.69	.65	−	.77	.76
	(14.06)	(12.99)		(10.67)	(10.48)
−	−	.04	−	−	.01
		(2.36)			(.24)
−	−1.02	−1.10	−	1.32	1.28
	(−1.69)	(−1.87)		(1.34)	(1.28)
−1.21	8.99	10.02	−4.22	−2.63	−2.43
(−.72)	(3.60)	(4.04)	(−1.75)	(−.63)	(−.56)
1.20	.81[d]	.48[d]	1.55	2.72[d]	2.67[d]
i	.17	.19	i	.12	.13
.25	.73	.75	.32	.77	.76

Note: Numbers in parentheses are T-tests for the coefficients immediately above.

[a]Average of 1947 and 1955 income before taxes.

[b]Ratio of household net worth (1959) plus estimated normal capital gains to 1959 net worth. Normal capital gains for the two years 1960-61 were estimated as 10 per cent of holdings of corporate stock in 1959, assuming a normal rate of capital gains of 5 per cent per year.

[c]Age of head minus 20 to approximate number of working years.

[d]Assuming same normal income in 1960 and 1961.

[e]Elasticity with respect to a weighted average of mean 1958-62 income and mean long-term income, the weights being determined by the regression coefficients.

[f]Elasticity with respect to current income.

[g]Meaningful estimates of the speed of adjustment and normal income elasticity cannot be computed from this regression.

[h]Fraction of the gap between desired and actual assets (or their logarithms) eliminated in a single year.

[i]Assumed to be one.

initially to those regressions which assume a short-term adjustment (within one year) to the level of desired assets, for the employee group (Part A of the table) the normal income elasticity of net worth indicated by the log regression—where normal income is defined as average disposable income for the five years 1958–62—is 1.64,[77] while for the self-employed (Part B) it is 1.51, and for the retired (Part C), where this concept of normal income is most questionable, it is 1.03. A weighted average of the first two elasticities which might be expected to approximate the corresponding FRB elasticities that eliminate the lowest and highest income groups would appear to be reasonably close to the FRB results. As might be expected from the fact that five-year average income is used, rather than single-year income as in the analysis of the FRB data, the SRC elasticities are slightly higher.[78] Some difference may also be expected, because of the more complete coverage of assets in the FRB data and because the FRB data are weighted to approximate the universe income distribution while the SRC data are not.[78a]

The logarithmic regressions based on ungrouped (SRC) data are quite sensitive to the treatment of the relatively few households for which net worth, as we have measured it, is zero or negative. For the most part these are cases in which instalment debt is reported but no assets other than automobiles and other durables, which have been omitted in our computation of net worth. This omission, of course, leads to a persistent understatement of net worth throughout the sample, but the omission becomes critical only when little or no other assets are reported, for then the percentage understatement is very large, introducing substantial distortion into the logarithmic, though not the linear, regressions. For employees, we experimented with several alternatives in handling these households, arbitrarily assigning to them net worths of $1, $100, and $1,000 and finally omitting them entirely, which is roughly equivalent to assigning them a net worth equal to the average value for other households in the sample with the same income (implying in most cases a net worth well above $1,000). The correlations were substantially higher for the last three alternatives than for the first. The estimated

[77] Under an alternative method of handling households with zero or negative computed values for net worth, this rises to 1.82, as discussed subsequently.

[78] Using single-year income, the elasticity for employees based on SRC data drops to 1.45.

[78a] The less than $18,000 average net worth implied by the S.R.C. data prior to elimination of any of the extreme cases (an average of $12,700 for employees, $52,300 for the self-employed, and $15,000 for the retired) is somewhat lower than the over-all F.R.B. total of $22,600. The elimination of the extreme cases reduces the S.R.C. estimates, but only for the self-employed is the reduction substantial.

income elasticity based on a simple logarithmic regression against five-year average income fell from 2.17 (setting net worth at one dollar) to 1.82 (setting net worth at $100) to 1.64 (setting net worth at $1,000) to 1.54 (omitting the cases of zero or negative net worth entirely).[79] Since with rare exceptions households may be expected to hold auto-moblies and durables with a value at least equivalent to their outstanding instalment debt and probably somewhat larger, and since all households may be expected to hold some liquid assets, in the form of currency if not bank deposits, the assumption of a minimum net worth of either $100 or $1,000 appears more reasonable than either of the other two alternatives; and the highest correlations are obtained under these assumptions, particularly when other relevant variables are included in the regressions. The logarithmic regressions in Table 6 are based on the assignment of net worths of $1,000 to the households with zero or nega-tive computed values. While this is not clearly preferable to the $100 figure, and some intermediate value might well be superior to either, we prefer to err in the direction of understating rather than overstating the income elasticity of net worth. Further, we obtain better agreement both with the income elasticity obtained from the FRB data and that obtained from the SRC data using linear regressions.

The linear regressions relating net worth to the five-year average of household income provide about as good a fit as the log regressions for those relations which assume a short-term adjustment (somewhat better in the case of the retired). The income slopes in the SRC linear regres-sions are substantially lower than the corresponding FRB results, but this may reflect at least in part the difference in the income groups covered. The mean income elasticities of assets implied by the linear relationships are very close to those in the log regressions for employees (and for the retired when age and transitory income are held constant), but are a little lower than in the log regressions for the self-employed.

While the SRC sample is very much smaller than the FRB sample, the additional information available for each household permits us to rectify three shortcomings of the FRB analysis. First, we can control the age of household head to investigate whether, given the correlation of age with income, the increase in the asset-to-income ratio as income rises may simply reflect the effect of age on net worth. In other words, the higher income families may have higher asset-to-income ratios only because they tend to be older families who have had more earning years

[79] For the linear regressions, the elimination of the households in question changed the estimated income elasticity only to 1.60 from 1.68 (obtained with no adjustment at all in the value of net worth).

over which to accumulate assets. Second, we can make some rough allowance for capital gains based on initial holdings of corporate stock. Since net worth grows through capital gains as well as through saving and since, further, some part of capital gains may in fact be anticipated and counted as part of normal income by the holders of variable value assets, the asset-to-income ratios of households experiencing capital gains may be pushed up relative to other households, either by the addition of unanticipated capital gains to the numerator (assuming savings is not curtailed to offset them) or through understatement of the denominator by the amount of anticipated capital gains. If upper income families are more inclined to hold variable value assets than lower income families, this may account to some extent for their higher asset-to-income ratios. Third, we can avoid or reduce biases in the income elasticity of assets due to temporary aberrations of the asset-to-income ratios, arising either from the presence of transitory income or from time lags in the adjustment of net worth to recent changes in normal income. As indicated in Part III we try to minimize the effect of transitory income by utilizing either a five-year average of household income or income for the occupational group to which the household head belongs, instead of single-year income. To allow for incomplete adjustment to the desired asset level at a given point of time, we introduce asset holdings at an earlier time.

The age effect is controlled for both by adding age as a continuous variable[80] to the regressions fitted and for employees by fitting separate regressions within four age groups—under 35 years, 35–44, 45–54, and 55 and over—to investigate nonlinear age effects as well as possible interactions between age and income effects. The introduction of age and current income into the instantaneous adjustment model has a negligible effect on the normal income elasticity (computed from the sum of the coefficients of current and normal income) for employees, even though the effect of age is highly significant. The elasticity is raised very slightly for the self-employed and somewhat more in the logarithmic model for the retired. The transitory income effect (measured by the coefficient of current income) is much smaller than the normal income effect for employees (though close to significant in the logarithmic regression), insignificant for the self-employed, and actually negative (though not significantly so) for the retired. When age is controlled by

[80] We have subtracted 20 from the age of head to approximate the number of working years, since, apart from inheritances, we expect wealth to be zero at the beginning of the working life. This is significant only for the logarithmic model which implies that the dependent variable approaches zero when any independent variable does so.

fitting separate regressions within each age group, the normal income elasticities for the instantaneous adjustment model are greater than unity in all cases and quite significantly so for the two younger age groups, for which elasticities greater than two are obtained.

If we turn from the assumption of an immediate or a short-term adjustment to the level of desired assets to allow for a delayed or prolonged adjustment, the correlations are increased, particularly for employees and the retired. The log regressions for employees and the self-employed imply that the adjustment time is neither very fast (say, close to one year) nor very slow (close to the entire earning span), with one-sixth of the gap between the logs of desired and actual net worth eliminated in a year for employees and one-fifth of the gap for the self-employed group.[81] Thus, according to these relationships, two-thirds of the gap would be eliminated within six years for employees and a higher fraction for the self-employed. The estimated normal income elasticity is slightly increased over the instantaneous adjustment model for employees and substantially increased for the self-employed.[82] The effect of age remains significant for employees, though not for the other two groups. The normal income effect is still somewhat larger than the transitory for employees and substantially so for the other two groups. For the four age groups of employees, income elasticities are above two for all except the 45–54 age group (where the elasticity falls below one). In two of the four cases, the elasticity rises compared with the immediate adjustment model. In all cases except the 45–54 group, the normal income effect remains greater than the transitory effect, and in two cases substantially so. Adjustment speeds are higher for the two age groups in the middle than for the youngest or oldest group.

When a proxy variable for normal two-year capital gains is introduced into the delayed adjustment logarithmic regressions, the normal income elasticity drops a little for employees (from 1.72 to 1.59) and for the self-employed (from 2.19 to 1.99). Some decline occurs for each of the age groups of employees, but it is large only for the 45–54 group, where the elasticity is already low. The coefficient of initial net worth, and therefore the estimated speed of adjustment, remains virtually

---

[81] The estimated speed of adjustment may be biased downward by reason of the crude handling of capital gains and the use of an imperfect approximation to savings tastes, but random errors in the measurement of lagged assets work in the opposite direction, so that no a priori statement can be made as to the probable direction of bias.

[82] For the retired, erratic results are obtained, which are quite sensitive to the inclusion of a capital gains proxy discussed below. It appears that for the retired, current net worth is almost entirely explained by initial net worth.

unchanged for all groups. The proxy variable which is used for normal capital gains in the logarithmic regressions is the ratio to initial net worth of initial net worth plus capital gains on 1959 holdings of corporate stock at a rate of 5 per cent annually, which of course falls far short of the actual, highly abnormal gains for the 1960–61 period.

The linear regressions, which do not provide as good a fit for employees, point to a speed of adjustment close to zero for all three employment status groups. The resulting estimates of income elasticities are unrealistically high, throwing considerable doubt on the validity of the linear model under the assumption of time lags in adjusting net worth to changes in normal income. The introduction of 1959 holdings of corporate stock as a proxy for capital gains in the 1960–61 period reduces the coefficient of net worth for the self-employed, retired, and three of the four age groups of employees. However, only in the case of the retired and one age group of employees do reasonable speeds of adjustment result. The effect of the lagged stock variable is positive and highly significant for the two older age groups of employees and for the retired. When linear regressions are fitted for net worth excluding corporate stock as a function of normal income and other variables, somewhat more reasonable speeds of adjustment are obtained for employees (.045) and for the retired (.11) but not for the self-employed. Estimated income elasticities of net worth excluding corporate stock run about 1.25 for both employees and the self-employed in the instantaneous adjustment linear model and rise to 5.11 in the lagged adjustment model for employees.

A quadratic relationship of net worth to normal income was also fitted for employees, yielding an income elasticity of 1.29, somewhat lower than the logarithmic and linear models, and a correlation which is also lower. In the lagged adjustment quadratic model, the correlation is a little higher than for the logarithmic or linear models. However, the implied speed of adjustment, while larger than in the linear model, is still very small, leading to an unreasonably high estimate of the income elasticity. In both cases the upward concavity of the asset-income function is attested by the positive and highly significant coefficients of the quadratic term.[83]

[83] The regressions actually fitted are:

$$NW61/Y_N = -.26 + .00011\ Y_N + .063\ W \qquad \bar{R}^2 = .12$$

$$NW61/Y_N = -.93 + .00006\ Y_N + .009\ W + .63\ Y/Y_N + .97\ NW59/Y_N \qquad \bar{R}^2 = .76,$$

where $NW61$ and $NW59$ are household net worth at the end of 1961 and 1959, respectively; Y_N is average household income, 1958–62; Y is 1961 income; and W is age of head minus 20. T-tests for the coefficient of Y_N are 3.30 and 3.41, respectively.

When normal income is defined as the mean of five-year income (1958–62) for the occupational group to which the spending unit belongs, a somewhat higher income elasticity (about 1.90) is obtained for employees in the instantaneous adjustment linear model and in the lagged adjustment logarithmic model and a still higher estimate (2.14) in the instantaneous adjustment logarithmic model. As noted earlier, such group income might be expected to give an unbiased estimate of the normal income effect, if transitory income averages close to zero for each group. For employees, mean income was available for seven subgroups with a range in income from $3,937 to $8,600.

A historical income variable which is an average of 1947 and 1955 disposable incomes does not add significantly to 1958–62 income in explaining variations in net worth for either employees or the self-employed, whether logarithmic or linear or short-run or long-run adjustment models are used. The adjusted normal income elasticities of net worth, where normal income is now defined as an average of the five-year (1958–62) and two-year (1947 and 1955) income averages weighted by the relative size of their coefficients, is not appreciably different from the elasticities based on the five-year income variable above. The historical income variable has a coefficient close to significant in the logarithmic instantaneous adjustment model, but loses all effect when 1959 net worth is added to the regression. This suggests that the relevant planning span for asset accumulation is relatively short-run or a period much shorter than the earning span, and seems to point to an even more rapid speed of adjustment to the desired asset level than is indicated in the delayed adjustment log regressions. It is possible, of course, that the virtually complete unimportance of the longer-term income variable reflects the households' difficulties in recalling such information.[84] The improvement in the correlations and the change (upward) in the income elasticities is quite small as the time span for incomes is lengthened successively from one year to two years to five years to sixteen years (1947–62),[85] with each year added making progressively less difference and with very little difference between the five year and longer-term results. Transitory income, as might be

---

[84] The fact that the longer-term income variable has not yet been converted from the old current (1947 and 1955) dollars to the more relevant recent (1958–62) prices tends to overstate the corresponding income slope in linear regressions (by a factor which is the average of income-weighted price increases from 1947 and 1955 to 1958–62), though not necessarily the associated income elasticity.

[85] The increase in income elasticity is from 1.45 to 1.68 for the instantaneous adjustment logarithmic model while the improvement in correlation is negligible.

expected, is much less important than normal income in the determination of net worth and, what may be more surprising, generally falls short of significance (except when normal income is measured by the average income for occupational groups).

Two different measures of historical income were used for the four age groups of employees. In addition to the mean of 1947 and 1955 incomes, another long-term income variable which varies with the age group was used. Neither alternative has much net effect on net worth, and even the direction of the effect is not consistent over the different age groups. There is some indication that for the youngest (under 35) age group there is a significant, if small, positive net effect on net worth over and above the 1958–62 average income in the instantaneous adjustment model, but this becomes insignificant when lagged net worth is introduced.

The major conclusion of this section is that the normal income elasticity of household net worth is significantly greater than one and in the neighborhood of 1.5 or above when the income extremes are excluded. This result is not altered when we hold constant both age of head and a crude approximation to recent capital gains. Close agreement as to the magnitude of the income elasticity is obtained between analyses based on the SRC and the FRB data and between immediate and delayed adjustment logarithmic and immediate adjustment linear models for employees, using the SRC data. A somewhat lower elasticity is obtained from an immediate adjustment quadratic model for employees, but this is still well above one. The linear and quadratic delayed adjustment models are less satisfactory than the logarithmic in that they imply extremely low speeds of adjustment to the desired asset level and extremely high income elasticities.

The income elasticity of net worth is much more erratic for the self-employed and retired, as might be expected in view of the much smaller samples. However, it appears not to differ much for the self-employed and employees, and is somewhat lower for the retired.

V. Empirical Results for Flow Regressions[86]

Part A of Table 7 presents, for employees, linear relationships for average annual total saving (excluding currency and consumer durables but including additions to houses), contractual saving (life insurance premiums plus payments on mortgage principal), changes in liquid assets (excluding currency but including U.S. savings bonds), net change in

---

[86] These are all based on the SCF data.

TABLE 7

Linear Regressions of Total Saving, Saving Components, and Consumer Investment Items (1960-61 Averages) on Disposable Household Income and Other Variables, SCF Panel Data for Households with 1958-62 Disposable Income of Less Than $20,000

Dependent Variable	Normal Household Income[a]	Current Household Income	Net Worth, 1959	Holdings of Individual Asset, 1959	Age[b]	Saving Tastes	Constant Term	Normal Income Elasticity	$\bar{R}^2$
Part A: Employees									
Total saving	.210 (8.72)						-560.90 (-3.41)	1.75	.154
	-.081 (-.64)	.278 (2.34)					-511.60 (-3.10)	1.64	.163
	-.077 (-.61)	.280 (2.35)	-.004 (-.49)			1.31[c] (.53)	-522.88 (-3.11)	1.69[d]	.160
Contractual saving	.060 (5.99)						-1.57 (-.02)	1.00	.078
	.103 (1.93)	-.041 (-.81)					-8.77 (-.13)	1.04	.077
	.107 (2.00)	-.046 (-.92)			-2.68 (-.94)	16.73[e] (.97)	31.26 (.33)	1.02	.076

(continued)

TABLE 7 *(continued)*

	Coefficient of								
Dependent Variable	Normal Household Income[a]	Current Household Income	Net Worth, 1959	Holdings of Individual Asset, 1959	Age[b]	Saving Tastes	Constant Term	Normal Income Elasticity	$\bar{R}^2$
Part A: Employees (continued)									
Changes in liquid assets	.112 (5.17)						−596.08 (−3.84)	5.41	.059
	−.053 (−.46)	.157 (1.47)					−541.20 (−3.63)	5.06	.061
	−.031 (−.27)	.149 (1.38)		−.050[f] (−3.23)	13.76 (2.31)	16.88[e] (.49)	−862.71 (−4.30)	5.70[d]	.090
Other investment	.034 (1.55)						−187.39 (−1.23)	g	.003
	−.158 (−1.35)	.184 (1.67)					−154.73 (−1.01)	g	.008
	−.150 (−1.28)	.184 (1.66)	−.004 (−.54)		−4.10 (−.66)		−69.37 (−.32)	g	.006

(continued)

TABLE 7 (continued)

Dependent Variable	Coefficient of						Constant Term	Normal Income Elasticity	$\bar{R}^2$
	Normal Household Income [a]	Current Household Income	Net Worth, 1959	Holdings of Individual Asset, 1959	Age [b]	Saving Tastes			
Part A: Employees (continued)									
Reduction in mortgage debt	.006 (.36)						87.65 (.76)	g	−.002
	.036 (.40)	−.028 (−.34)					82.59 (.71)	g	−.004
	−.047 (−.54)	.001 (.01)		−.072[h] (−6.47)	8.50 (1.92)		−46.18 (−.31)	−2.30[d]	.085
Reduction in instalment debt	.004 (.52)						−21.45 (−.40)	g	−.002
	.076 (1.82)	−.069 (−1.76)					−33.66 (−.62)	g	.003
	.039 (1.07)	−.045 (−1.32)		−.286[i] (−11.60)	2.43 (1.31)		−162.39 (−2.47)	−9.22[d]	.248

(continued)

TABLE 7 (continued)

Dependent Variable	Normal Household Income[a]	Current Household Income	Net Worth, 1959	Holdings of Individual Asset, 1959	Age[b]	Saving Tastes	Constant Term	Normal Income Elasticity	$\bar{R}^2$
				Coefficient of					
			Part A: Employees (continued)						
Net outlay on automobiles	.050 (6.31)						9.16 (.17)	.97	.086
	−.070 (−1.70)	.115 (2.95)					29.57 (.55)	.87	.103
	−.068 (−1.64)	.112 (2.87)			−1.15 (−.52)	8.94[e] (.66)	44.32 (.60)	.86	.100
Net outlay on other durables	.015 (5.09)						29.03 (1.46)	.76	.057
	.001 (.07)	.013 (.91)					31.36 (1.56)	.72	.057
	.002 (.11)	.010 (.70)	.001 (1.05)		−2.11 (−2.60)		84.12 (2.96)	.60	.068

(continued)

TABLE 7 (continued)

Dependent Variable	Normal Household Income[a]	Current Household Income	Net Worth, 1959	Coefficient of — Holdings of Individual Asset, 1959	Age[b]	Saving Tastes	Constant Term	Normal Income Elasticity	$\overline{R}^2$
Part A: Employees (concluded)									
Home additions and repairs	.047 (5.15)						−51.29 (−.82)	1.21	.058
	−.016 (−.33)	.060 (1.33)					−40.64 (−.65)	1.14	.060
	−.020 (−.43)	.053 (1.17)	.005 (1.83)		−1.99 (−.78)		22.18 (.25)	.84	.063
Part B: Self-Employed and Farmers									
Total saving	.357 (4.02)						−1083.79 (−1.64)	1.92	.205
	−.036 (−.15)	.412 (1.71)					−1189.38 (−1.83)	2.03	.230
	−.054 (−.20)	.424 (1.68)	.000 (.02)		−15.08 (−.47)	−7.16 (−.74)	−501.85 (−.41)	2.00[d]	.198

(continued)

TABLE 7 (concluded)

| | Coefficient of | | | | | | | | |
Dependent Variable	Normal Household Income[a]	Current Household Income	Net Worth, 1959	Holdings of Individual Asset, 1959	Age[b]	Saving Tastes	Constant Term	Normal Income Elasticity	$\bar{R}^2$
	Part C: Retired								
Total saving	.043 (.73)						-156.72 (-.94)	g	-.005
	.565 (3.18)	-.548 (-3.10)					-98.22 (-.61)	g	.084
	.557 (3.06)	-.535 (-2.95)	-.002 (-.27)		-4.52 (-.40)		134.16 (.22)	g	.066

Note: Numbers in parentheses are T-tests for the coefficient immediately above.

[a] Five-year average of household income, 1958–62.
[b] Age of head minus 20 to approximate number of working years to date.
[c] Ratio of household insurance premiums in 1959 to average household income 1958–60, multiplied by 1000.
[d] This is a short-run income elasticity of savings. Under the assumptions of the lagged adjustment model, the long-run elasticity for savings is zero.
[e] Ratio of household net worth in 1959 to average household income, 1958–60.
[f] Liquid assets, end of 1959.
[g] Meaningful estimates of the normal income elasticity cannot be computed from this regression.
[h] Mortgage debt, end of 1959, treated as a negative asset.
[i] Instalment debt, end of 1959, treated as a negative asset.

other investments, reduction in mortgage debt, reduction in instalment debt, and net outlays on automobiles (purchases less sales), on other durables, and on additions and repairs to owned homes for the two-year period 1960–61. Corresponding single-year relations for each of the three durable items in 1959, 1960, and 1961, for insurance premiums in 1959 and 1961, and for liquid saving in 1959 were also computed but are not shown. The choice of variables to be analyzed was dictated in part by availability of data. Each of the flow or saving variables for the two-year 1960–61 analysis was related to the five-year average disposable income, to a two-year average (the transitory income effect being obtained from the coefficient of this variable and the normal income effect being the sum of the five-year and two-year coefficients), to initial net worth, to the initial level of specific assets where available, to age, to family size dummy variables, and to two general savings tastes variables—the ratio of insurance premiums in 1959 to annual average disposable income for the three-year period 1958–60 and (for savings components) the ratio of net worth at the end of 1959 to the three-year average of disposable income.[87] Each of the saving variables for the single-year analysis was related to a three-year average of disposable income centered on that year, to disposable income for the same year, to initial net worth where available, to the initial level of specific assets where available, and to a general savings tastes variable which was the ratio of insurance premiums in 1959 to average 1958–60 disposable income for the 1960 and 1961 savings items and the more theoretically attractive ratio of two-year 1960–61 saving to five-year average income for the 1959 saving items. The table shows only selected regressions for the two-year savings items. The family size dummies were generally insignificant and are not shown. The savings tastes and age variables are for the most part shown only when they raise the correlation or show *T*-tests in the neighborhood of one or more.

For employees, the average annual marginal propensity to save out of normal disposable income during the 1960–61 period amounted to .20 or .21, representing a mean income elasticity of about 1.7, if neither initial assets nor saving tastes are introduced into the analysis. A comparison can be made between this estimate of about .20 and an estimate made by Kosobud based on a larger sample, including nonemployee

---

[87] Note that for individual savings components, with income given, initial net worth itself may serve as a savings tastes variable in addition to its role in reflecting the extent to which the household's desire for alternative types of assets is satisfied. However, when initial stock of the specific asset corresponding to the savings component is omitted from the regression, net worth plays still a third role, serving as a proxy for the missing asset item.

groups as well as employees (921 panel members), reporting all the required information for both 1960 and 1961, but using a somewhat different saving regression relating the two-year saving-to-income ratio to two-year per capita income, change in liquid assets in the preceding year, number of people in the spending unit, and age of head.[88] No asset or tastes variable appears in the Kosobud regression and only income is significant. Kosobud derives a marginal propensity to save of .09 but he appears to be relating an annual saving rate to two-year income, and our rough estimate of the more customary annual propensity to save based on his regression is over .14. Since this is a propensity to save out of before-tax income, the Kosobud result appears to be fairly close to ours, though in view of the inclusion of self-employed and retired groups in the former it is difficult to be precise.

In our model, the absence of an initial assets variable is highly questionable from a theoretical point of view unless the speed of adjustment to the desired level of assets is relatively slow, while the absence of some device for holding tastes constant also raises statistical difficulties. The elasticity discussed above may be interpreted as an approximation to a short-run elasticity of savings under our model, if the speed of adjustment is very slow, or as both a long- and a short-run elasticity under an alternative model which takes initial assets to be irrelevant to savings behavior.[89] We note that this elasticity of savings is quite similar in value to the income elasticity of net worth obtained in Table 6 when initial assets are omitted. It is also very close to the short-run elasticity of saving obtained when initial assets are introduced into the savings regression, since this does not change the normal income coefficient of employees appreciably. Nor does the introduction of age or of a saving tastes variable make any appreciable difference. The low initial assets coefficient implies a very slow—indeed close to zero—speed of adjustment, which is the same dubious result obtained from the linear regression in the preceding section relating assets to normal income and initial assets, and which implies an income elasticity for assets completely inconsistent with the instantaneous adjustment linear regressions and both the instantaneous and delayed adjustment logarithmic regressions for assets.

As noted earlier, the dubious result provided by the linear delayed adjustment model may reflect the basic nonlinearity of the relationship, with the result that the initial assets variable reflects much of the normal income effect so that the absolute value of the initial assets coefficient

---

[88] *Consumer Behavior of Individual Families Over Two and Three Years,* p. 87.
[89] The long-run (full-adjustment) elasticity of net saving under our model is, of course, zero.

is substantially biased downward. Alternatively if the true relationship is approximately linear, it could be argued that normal income, which is measured more accurately than assets, acts as a proxy for initial assets so that again the absolute value of the initial assets coefficient may be biased downward (and the income coefficient similarly biased downward). The use of an imperfect approximation to saving tastes should further tend to bias the estimated speed of adjustment downward, but random errors in the measurement of lagged assets work in the opposite direction. Thus errors in the estimate of certain initial assets would tend to be associated with an opposite error in the estimate of saving, which would introduce an upward bias in the estimated speed of adjustment in the saving regression. On the other hand, the general understatement of saving and assets characterizing survey data would not be expected to have any effect on the estimated speed of adjustment, though it would tend to understate the estimated income elasticity of saving. There is reason to believe, both on the basis of a priori considerations and a comparison of survey data with external aggregates, that both random and systematic errors are more serious for the savings than for the asset data.

Because of the unrealistically low estimate of the speed of adjustment obtained, any attempt to compute an income elasticity of net worth from the savings regression would lead to an unrealistically high figure. The results obtained appear to throw doubt on the adequacy of a linear savings function as well as to suggest that the biases introduced by measurement errors and other factors may be quite large. Savings functions which are quadratic in normal income will be discussed subsequently.

When the annual average of income during the two years is used as an explanatory variable in addition to the five-year average, the transitory income effect for employees (with transitory income, it will be recalled, measured here as the difference between the two-year and five-year average) is .28, compared with a normal income effect of .20 or .21, but the difference between the two effects is not significant.[90] As a result, the two-year average of saving is explained about as well by two-year average income alone as by a combination of the five-year and two-year averages. The two-year average income alone gives about the same income coefficient and correlation as the five-year or either of the relevant three-year averages.

The historical income variable, which is an average of 1947 and 1955 disposable incomes, does not add significantly to 1958–62 incomes in explaining variations in saving (Table 8). The adjusted normal income

[90] The significance of this difference is measured by the significance of the five-year income coefficient.

TABLE 8

Linear Regressions of Total Saving, Contractual Saving, and Liquid Saving (1960-61 Averages) on Historical Household Income and Other Variables, SCF Panel Data for Households with 1958-62 Disposable Income of Less Than $20,000

Coefficient of	Employees		Self-Employed and Farmers		Retired	
	1	2	3	4	5	6
	Total Saving					
Household income, 1958-62	.199	.199	.400	.392	.022	.032
	(7.05)	(6.06)	(3.67)	(3.01)	(.31)	(.36)
Historical household income	.029	.036	−.131	−.105	.073	.075
(mean of 1947 and 1955)	(.70)	(.82)	(−.78)	(−.59)	(1.13)	(1.15)
Household net worth, 1959	−	−.002	−	−.003	−	−.004
		(−.29)		(−.16)		(−.51)
Age of head[a]	−	−3.78	−	−13.25	−	−7.10
		(−.54)		(−.40)		(−.59)
Savings tastes[b]	−	1.16	−	−4.69	−	−
		(.46)		(−.48)		
Constant term	−593.27	−544.33	−844.06	−300.55	−192.48	173.71
	(−3.47)	(−2.20)	(−1.24)	(−.24)	(−1.09)	(.27)
Normal income elasticity	1.91	1.96	1.45	1.55[c]	d	d
$\bar{R}^2$	.153	.148	.196	.158	.004	−.010

(continued)

TABLE 8 (continued)

Coefficient of	Employees		Self-Employed and Farmers		Retired	
	1	2	3	4	5	6
	Contractual Saving					
Household income, 1958-62	.051 (4.32)	.044 (3.23)	.129 (2.61)	.191 (3.37)	.043 (3.13)	.048 (2.87)
Historical household income (mean of 1947 and 1955)	.026 (1.50)	.030 (1.66)	.027 (.35)	.019 (.25)	-.008 (-.65)	-.008 (-.61)
Household net worth, 1959	—	.002 (.64)	—	-.013 (-1.72)	—	-.001 (-.85)
Age of head[a]	—	-3.45 (-1.19)	—	23.05 (1.61)	—	-1.03 (-.44)
Constant term	-30.35 (-.42)	53.72 (.54)	-678.41 (-2.20)	-1283.45 (-2.54)	-16.57 (-.49)	35.92 (.29)
Normal income elasticity	1.28	1.24	4.30	5.80	1.21	1.40
$\bar{R}^2$	.081	.080	.148	.184	.089	.080

(continued)

TABLE 8 (concluded)

Coefficient of	Employees		Self-Employed and Farmers		Retired	
	1	2	3	4	5	6
	Change in Liquid Assets					
Household income, 1958-62	.109 (4.27)	.124 (4.85)	.049 (.83)	.063 (.98)	.006 (.08)	-.007 (-.09)
Historical household income (mean of 1947 and 1955)	.009 (.23)	.000 (.00)	-.050 (-.56)	-.057 (-.66)	-.006 (-.09)	-.006 (-.10)
Household net worth, 1959		—		.016 (1.80)		—
Liquid assets, 1959		-.047 (-3.52)		-.132 (-3.47)		.005 (.46)
Age of head[a]		14.01 (2.34)		1.86 (.11)		-3.53 (-.30)
Constant term	-578.71 (-3.76)	-872.41 (-4.36)	-357.94 (-.98)	-437.32 (-.76)	-38.01 (-.22)	141.75 (.23)
Normal income elasticity	5.68	6.03	d	d	d	d
$\bar{R}^2$	.056	.086	-.022	.126	-.022	-.042

Note: Numbers in parentheses are *T*-tests for the coefficients immediately above.

[a] Age of head minus 20 to approximate number of working years.

[b] Ratio of household insurance premiums in 1959 to average household income 1958-60, multiplied by 1000.

[c] This is a short-run elasticity of savings with respect to normal income, defined as a weighted average of five-year (1958-62) and two-year (1947 and 1955) income with weights determined by the regression coefficients.

elasticities of saving are a little higher for employees than the elasticities based on the five-year income variable alone.

For total saving, the family size dummies and the age variable all have negligible effects. The savings tastes variable (ratio of insurance premiums to normal income in the preceding year) is not at all significant, but its inclusion increases very slightly the income elasticity and the effect of lagged net worth. To allow for nonlinear age effects and to investigate possible interactions between income and age effects, the employee saving and related regressions were computed separately for each of four age groups—under 35, 35–44, 45–54, and 55 and over. The household saving regressions for individual age groups (Table 9) gave about the same marginal propensity to save out of normal income as the .20 figure for all age groups combined for the under 35 and the 45–54 groups, but a higher value for the 35–44 group and a lower value for the 55 and over group which is characterized by extremely low correlations. Correlations for the two youngest age groups, on the other hand, are substantially higher than for all ages combined. Only the 45–54 group showed a higher propensity to save out of transitory than out of normal income, but here the difference was close to significance. Thus both the age groups in the middle show relatively high propensities to save, the 35–44 group with respect to normal income and the 45–54 group with respect to transitory income. The family size effect was substantial (though still not significant) only for the youngest age group and the indication was that three or four person families saved more than either larger or smaller families. Age effects within age groups are still insignificant but larger than for employees as a whole, with a nonlinear pattern. Saving appears to fall with age for the youngest group, rise with age for the middle groups, and then fall again for the oldest group. The saving tastes variable has the expected positive effect only for the 45–54 age group, where it comes close to being significant. For the relatively small group aged 55 and over, the effect is negative and significant. This seems to be associated with the apparent large liquidation of other investment (corporate stock, etc.) by this group and the negative relationship between other investment and savings in the form of insurance (which dominates the saving tastes variable used).

Turning next to the components of saving and related items, we were able to utilize our lagged adjustment model only for changes in liquid

TABLE 9

Regressions of Total Savings, Saving Components, and Consumer Investment Items (1960-61 Averages) on Disposable Household Income and Other Variables, for Employees by Age of Household Head, SCF Panel Data for Households with 1958-62 Disposable Income of Less Than $20,000

PART A: TOTAL SAVING

| Age of Head | Coefficient of | | | | | Constant Term | Normal Income Elasticity | $\bar{R}^2$ |
	Household Income, 1958-62	Household Income, 1960-61	Net Worth, 1959	Age[a]	Saving Tastes[b]			
Under 35	.219 (6.36)					-500.44 (-2.29)	1.63	.255
	.220 (1.10)	-.000 (-.00)				-500.52 (-2.20)	1.63	.249
	.203 (.94)	-.011 (-.06)	.020 (1.23)	-10.37 (-.39)	-2.020 (-.57)	-285.77 (-.90)	1.43[c]	.240
35-44	.295 (6.17)					-1187.89 (-3.43)	2.46	.229
	.071 (.34)	.209 (1.10)				-1105.60 (-3.13)	2.34	.230
	.051 (.24)	.202 (1.05)	.011 (.66)	14.46 (.33)	-1.40 (-.28)	-1263.96 (-1.38)	2.11[c]	.215

(continued)

TABLE 9 (continued)

PART A: TOTAL SAVING (concluded)

Age of Head	Coefficient of					Constant Term	Normal Income Elasticity	$\bar{R}^2$
	Household Income, 1958-62	Household Income, 1960-61	Net Worth, 1959	Age[a]	Saving Tastes[b]			
45-54	.192 (3.83)					-562.41 (-1.46)	1.75	.111
	-.549 (-1.69)	.723 (2.31)				-517.01 (-1.37)	1.58	.145
	-.503 (-1.55)	.663 (2.10)	.005 (.31)	20.45 (.34)	9.15 (1.71)	-1371.23 (-.74)	1.45[c]	.149
55 and over	.118 (1.66)					-37.68 (-.10)	1.07	.029
	.242 (.88)	-.123 (-.47)				-40.82 (-.11)	1.09	.016
	.073 (.29)	.116 (.47)	-.035 (-2.84)	-42.64 (-1.21)	-12.53 (-2.33)	2000.71 (1.34)	1.72[c]	.206

(continued)

TABLE 9 *(continued)*

PART B: CONTRACTUAL SAVING

Age of Head	Coefficient of					Constant Term	Normal Income Elasticity	$\bar{R}^2$
	Household Income, 1958-62	Household Income, 1960-61	Net Worth, 1959	Age[a]	Saving Tastes[e]			
Under 35	.119 (6.69)					−274.92 (−2.44)	1.64	.276
	.328 (3.26)	−.192 (−2.11)				−338.96 (−2.95)	1.87	.297
	.299 (2.88)	−.175 (−1.89)		2.65 (.19)	67.92 (1.32)	−357.28 (−2.46)	1.71	.297
35-44	.054 (3.10)					35.73 (.28)	.91	.064
	.054 (.71)	−.000 (−.00)				35.63 (.27)	.91	.057
	.056 (.74)	−.009 (−.13)		−2.89 (−.18)	63.66 (1.78)	44.30 (.14)	.80	.066

(continued)

TABLE 9 *(continued)*

PART B: CONTRACTUAL SAVING *(concluded)*

Age of Head	Coefficient of					Constant Term	Normal Income Elasticity	$\bar{R}^2$
	Household Income, 1958-62	Household Income, 1960-61	Net Worth, 1959	Age[a]	Saving Tastes[e]			
45-54	.044 (1.95)					8.97 (.05)	.97	.025
	.145 (.98)	−.098 (−.70)				2.78 (.02)	1.03	.020
	.144 (.97)	−.094 (−.66)		21.15 (.77)	9.24 (.22)	−659.92 (−.79)	d	.008
55 and over	.087 (4.04)					−65.52 (−.59)	1.19	.206
	.100 (1.21)	−.013 (−.16)				−65.86 (−.58)	1.19	.193
	.099 (1.14)	−.014 (−.17)		−5.76 (−.48)	.26 (.01)	173.01 (.34)	1.16	.167

(continued)

TABLE 9 *(continued)*

PART C: CHANGE IN LIQUID ASSETS

Age of Head	Coefficient of				Constant Term	Normal Income Elasticity	$\bar{R}^2$
	Household Income, 1958-62	Household Income, 1960-61	Liquid Assets, 1959	Age[a]			
Under 35	-.003 (-.11)				92.38 (.58)	d	-.009
	-.201 (-1.41)	.183 (1.41)			153.25 (.94)	d	.000
	-.178 (-1.18)	.171 (1.28)	-.039 (-.67)	-1.13 (-.06)	123.88 (.58)	d	-.014
35-44	.157 (4.46)				-1039.51 (-4.06)	d	.131
	-.112 (-.73)	.251 (1.81)			-940.58 (-3.62)	d	.147
	-.090 (-.61)	.254 (1.88)	-.109 (-3.19)	27.95 (.90)	-1443.99 (-2.36)	d	.201

(continued)

TABLE 9 *(continued)*

PART C: CHANGE IN LIQUID ASSETS *(concluded)*

| | Coefficient of | | | | | Normal | |
Age of Head	Household Income, 1958-62	Household Income, 1960-61	Liquid Assets, 1959	Age^a	Constant Term	Income Elasticity	$\bar{R}^2$
45-54	.158 (3.11)				-847.28 (-2.18)	4.68	.073
	.177 (.53)	-.019 (-.06)			-848.49 (-2.17)	4.70	.064
	.257 (.74)	-.079 (-.24)	-.054 (-.94)	56.40 (.90)	-2490.43 (-1.29)	5.29^c	.060
55 and over	.135 (2.16)				-374.09 (-1.16)	2.46	.059
	-.198 (-.84)	.330 (1.46)			-365.70 (-1.14)	2.40	.077
	-.219 (-.99)	.369 (1.75)	-.041 (-3.26)	13.12 (.42)	-837.34 (-.62)	2.73^c	.198

(continued)

TABLE 9 (continued)

PART D: OTHER INVESTMENT

Age of Head	Coefficient of				Constant Term	Normal Income Elasticity	$\bar{R}^2$
	Household Income, 1958-62	Household Income, 1960-61	Net Worth, 1959	Age [a]			
Under 35	.037 (3.08)				-194.07 (-2.56)	9.24	.069
	-.108 (-1.60)	.133 (2.18)			-149.72 (-1.94)	6.32	.098
	-.124 (-1.74)	.137 (2.20)	.008 (1.39)	-5.69 (-.63)	-66.48 (-.63)	3.44	.099
35-44	.028 (1.03)				-116.89 (-.60)	d	.000
	-.123 (-1.05)	.140 (1.32)			-61.60 (-.31)	d	.006
	-.146 (-1.24)	.139 (1.30)	.013 (1.37)	-21.17 (-.87)	379.84 (.78)	-.69	.010

(continued)

TABLE 9 *(continued)*

PART D: OTHER INVESTMENT (concluded)

Age of Head	Coefficient of				Constant Term	Normal Income Elasticity	$\bar{R}^2$
	Household Income, 1958-62	Household Income, 1960-61	Net Worth, 1959	Age[a]			
45-54	.066 (1.37)				-328.90 (-.88)	d	.008
	-.833 (-2.69)	.877 (2.94)			-273.79 (-.76)	2.40	.073
	-.833 (-2.67)	.885 (2.91)	-.004 (-.25)	-3.95 (-.07)	-153.60 (-.09)	2.82	.056
55 and over	-.178 (-1.59)				595.18 (1.03)	d	.025
	.531 (1.26)	-.702 (-1.74)			577.34 (1.01)	d	.058
	.442 (1.05)	-.601 (-1.47)	-.026 (-1.26)	-67.57 (-1.13)	3437.94 (1.35)	d	.076

(continued)

TABLE 9 *(continued)*

PART E: REDUCTION IN MORTGAGE DEBT

| Age of Head | Coefficient of | | | | Constant Term | Normal Income Elasticity | $\bar{R}^2$ |
	Household Income, 1958-62	Household Income, 1960-61	Mortgage Debt, 1959	Age[a]			
Under 35	.033 (.76)				-115.70 (-.42)	d	-.004
	.104 (.41)	-.066 (-.29)			-137.59 (-.48)	d	-.012
	-.143 (-.51)	.079 (.33)	-.055 (-2.18)	9.29 (.28)	75.98 (.20)	-4.75[c]	.012
35-44	.023 (.84)				49.67 (.25)	d	-.002
	-.002 (-.02)	.023 (.21)			58.83 (.29)	d	-.010
	-.064 (-.56)	.046 (.45)	-.063 (-4.18)	-13.89 (-.59)	302.57 (.65)	-.59[c]	.107

(continued)

TABLE 9 *(continued)*

PART E: REDUCTION IN MORTGAGE DEBT *(concluded)*

| Age of Head | Coefficient of | | | | Constant Term | Normal Income Elasticity | $\bar{R}^2$ |
	Household Income, 1958-62	Household Income, 1960-61	Mortgage Debt, 1959	Age[a]			
45-54	-.018 (-.52)				162.13 (.63)	d	-.007
	.081 (.36)	-.096 (-.45)			156.10 (.60)	d	-.014
	.041 (.20)	-.113 (-.56)	-.119 (-3.98)	49.04 (1.27)	-1227.10 (-1.03)	-11.89[c]	.108
55 and over	.036 (1.61)				35.85 (.31)	.83	.026
	.081 (.93)	-.044 (-.54)			34.73 (.30)	.84	.014
	-.049 (-.72)	.034 (.54)	-.091 (-6.65)	-1.25 (-.13)	177.06 (.44)	-.34[c]	.440

(continued)

TABLE 9 *(continued)*

PART F: REDUCTION IN INSTALMENT DEBT

Age of Head	Coefficient of				Constant Term	Normal Income Elasticity	$\bar{R}^2$
	Household Income, 1958-62	Household Income, 1960-61	Instalment Debt, 1959	Age[a]			
Under 35	.031 (1.58)				-134.24 (-1.07)	3.61	.013
	.053 (.46)	-.020 (-.19)			-140.76 (-1.08)	d	.004
	.059 (.67)	-.037 (-.47)	-.358 (-9.00)	-18.45 (-1.63)	-144.14 (-1.15)	2.51[c]	.435
35-44	-.003 (-.15)				-8.81 (-.07)	d	-.008
	.170 (2.15)	-.162 (-2.25)			-72.35 (-.54)	d	.024
	.088 (1.22)	-.096 (-1.47)	-.269 (-5.58)	1.29 (.09)	-163.53 (-.56)	d	.212

(continued)

TABLE 9 *(continued)*

PART F: REDUCTION IN INSTALMENT DEBT *(concluded)*

Age of Head	Coefficient of				Constant Term	Normal Income Elasticity	$\bar{R}^2$
	Household Income, 1958-62	Household Income, 1960-61	Instalment Debt, 1959	Age[a]			
45-54	-.000 (-.04)				-13.08 (-.14)	d	-.009
	.072 (.92)	-.071 (-.94)			-17.53 (-.19)	d	-.010
	.055 (.74)	-.061 (-.86)	-.210 (-3.97)	-14.17 (-1.04)	354.79 (.84)	d	.106
55 and over	.015 (1.37)				-49.72 (-.89)	3.61	.015
	-.018 (-.43)	.032 (.82)			-48.90 (-.88)	d	.009
	-.002 (-.07)	.005 (.16)	-.258 (-4.97)	6.00 (1.20)	-283.29 (-1.34)	.71[c]	.297

(continued)

TABLE 9 (continued)

PART G: NET OUTLAY ON AUTOMOBILES

Age of Head	Coefficient of					Constant Term	Normal Income Elasticity	$\bar{R}^2$
	Household Income, 1958–62	Household Income, 1960–61	Net Worth, 1959	Age[a]	Saving Tastes[e]			
Under 35	.027 (1.61)					112.27 (1.06)	.59	.014
	−.233 (−2.51)	.239 (2.84)				191.94 (1.81)	.14	.071
	−.268 (−2.79)	.261 (3.05)		6.38 (.51)	65.24 (1.38)	149.30 (1.11)	−.13	.077
35–44	.056 (3.16)					−3.26 (−.03)	1.01	.067
	−.129 (−1.69)	.173 (2.50)				64.95 (.50)	.79	.105
	−.132 (−1.74)	−.181 (−2.61)		−26.50 (−1.67)	−4.65 (−.13)	541.06 (1.74)	.88	.111

(continued)

TABLE 9 *(continued)*

PART G: NET OUTLAY ON AUTOMOBILES (concluded)

Age of Head	Coefficient of					Constant Term	Normal Income Elasticity	$\bar{R}^2$
	Household Income, 1958-62	Household Income, 1960-61	Net Worth, 1959	Age[a]	Saving Tastes[e]			
45-54	.050 (3.74)					62.61 (.61)	.85	.106
	.058 (.65)	-.007 (-.08)				62.17 (.60)	.85	.098
	.056 (.63)	-.003 (-.03)		16.81 (1.01)	5.18 (.20)	-459.12 (-.91)	.90	.091
55 and over	.022 (1.21)					38.83 (.42)	d	.008
	-.067 (-.99)	.088 (1.36)				41.06 (.45)	.69	.022
	-.071 (-1.02)	.086 (1.30)		-11.84 (-1.21)	-.57 (-.04)	534.55 (1.29)	.52	.013

(continued)

TABLE 9 *(continued)*

PART H: NET OUTLAY ON OTHER DURABLES

Age of Head	Coefficient of				Constant Term	Normal Income Elasticity	$\bar{R}^2$
	Household Income, 1958-62	Household Income, 1960-61	Net Worth, 1959	Age[a]			
Under 35	.027 (4.08)				-13.45 (-.32)	1.09	.120
	.043 (1.14)	-.015 (-.44)			-18.44 (-.43)	1.15	.114
	.065 (1.65)	-.025 (-.73)	-.005 (-1.76)	-2.21 (-.44)	-36.29 (-.61)	1.63	.127
35-44	.011 (1.51)				69.83 (1.30)	.52	.010
	.005 (.15)	.006 (.20)			72.12 (1.31)	d	.002
	.001 (.03)	.002 (.08)	.003 (1.09)	6.58 (.97)	-31.24 (-.23)	d	.005

(continued)

TABLE 9 *(continued)*

PART H: NET OUTLAY ON OTHER DURABLES *(concluded)*

Age of Head	Coefficient of				Constant Term	Normal Income Elasticity	$\bar{R}^2$
	Household Income, 1958-62	Household Income, 1960-61	Net Worth, 1959	Age[a]			
45-54	.012 (3.30)				10.75 (.38)	.89	.082
	.017 (.68)	−.004 (−.18)			10.48 (.37)	.89	.074
	.017 (.69)	−.009 (−.38)	.002 (1.72)	−.19 (−.04)	15.77 (.11)	.56	.082
55 and over	.013 (2.29)				16.18 (.56)	.79	.067
	−.046 (−2.29)	.058 (3.04)			17.67 (.65)	.75	.183
	−.044 (−2.14)	.056 (2.81)	.001 (.67)	2.03 (.70)	−67.92 (−.55)	.74	.169

(continued)

TABLE 9 *(continued)*

PART I: HOME ADDITIONS AND REPAIRS

Age of Head	Coefficient of				Constant Term	Normal Income Elasticity	$\bar{R}^2$
	Household Income, 1958-62	Household Income, 1960-61	Net Worth, 1959	Age[a]			
Under 35	.021 (1.02)				100.95 (.76)	d	-.000
	.055 (.46)	-.031 (-.29)			90.51 (.66)	d	-.008
	-.015 (-.12)	.007 (.06)	.011 (1.18)	17.52 (1.10)	45.11 (.24)	d	.003
35-44	.042 (2.19)				20.11 (.15)	.93	.029
	.024 (.29)	.017 (.22)			26.64 (.19)	.91	.022
	.028 (.32)	.016 (.21)	-.002 (-.26)	6.04 (.34)	-89.83 (-.26)	d	.007

(continued)

TABLE 5 (concluded)

PART I: HOME ADDITIONS AND REPAIRS (concluded)

Age of Head	Coefficient of				Constant Term	Normal Income Elasticity	$\bar{R}^2$
	Household Income, 1958-62	Household Income, 1960-61	Net Worth, 1959	Age[a]			
45-54	.058 (3.74)				-167.03 (-1.40)	1.72	.105
	-.065 (-.64)	.120 (1.22)			-159.46 (-1.33)	1.63	.109
	-.064 (-.61)	.110 (1.09)	.004 (.70)	-8.41 (-.44)	94.22 (.16)	1.36	.098
55 and over	.056 (2.52)				-107.00 (-.92)	1.69	.083
	-.169 (-2.09)	.223 (2.89)			-101.33 (-.93)	1.62	.186
	-.138 (-1.80)	.183 (2.46)	.010 (2.62)	14.95 (1.37)	-742.73 (-1.60)	1.34	.280

Note: Numbers in parentheses are T-tests for the coefficients immediately above.

[a] Age of head minus 20 to approximate number of working years to date.

[b] The ratio of household insurance premiums in 1959 to average household income 1958-60 (multiplied by 1000).

[c] This is a short-run income elasticity of saving. Under the assumptions of the lagged adjustment model the long-run elasticity of net saving is zero.

[d] A meaningful estimate of the normal income elasticity cannot be computed from this regression.

[e] The ratio of household net worth at the end of 1959 to average household income, 1958-60.

assets and the two debt components.[91] For employees as a whole and for each age group, the marginal propensity to save in contractual form is substantial for normal income and is generally negligible for transitory income, which is reasonable.[92] The difference in the two income effects is significant for employees as a whole. The roles of normal and transitory income seem to be quite different for liquid saving where transitory income seems somewhat more important than normal income. This result is consistent over all age groups except for the 45–54 group, but the differences are not at all statistically significant. For other financial investment, which is something of a hodge-podge, the correlations are extremely low. The mean normal income elasticities are close to one for contractual saving but very much higher for liquid assets. Even for contractual saving, the normal income elasticity is considerably higher than one for the under 35 age group, and it is increased to somewhat above one for all age groups combined when the long-run average of 1949 and 1955 incomes is included as an additional explanatory variable. The data suggest that long-run income may be somewhat more important in explaining contractual saving than in explaining saving generally, at least for employees, but has little influence on saving in the form of liquid assets.

For reduction in debt, both income variables are almost irrelevant and only the initial levels of debt and age contribute to the explanation of these savings components. For each age group of employees and for all combined, the normal income elasticity of reduction in mortgage debt was found to be negative when the initial level of debt was held constant. This was due entirely to the greater propensity of the higher than the lower income groups to increase mortgage debt either to finance home additions and repairs or for other reasons. (No purchases of new homes were involved.) If cases of increasing mortgage debt are eliminated,[93] the income elasticity becomes positive. For reduction in

[91] In future work we plan to extend this model to net outlays on automobiles, when data on initial auto stocks have been developed, and possibly for homeowners to home additions, using value of house as the relevant asset stock. For insurance premiums on existing policies—a large component of contractual saving—the model is not particularly useful, while for other investment and outlays on other durables the relevant asset data are not available.

[92] The strongly negative effect of transitory income for the lowest age group suggests a time lag in adjusting contractual saving to rapidly rising income trends. Thus, for a given five-year average of income, the household with rapidly rising income has less contractual saving than the household with more gradual income growth.

[93] For employees, there were 37 such cases, of which two-thirds had incomes above average and one-third had incomes substantially above average.

instalment debt also, the income elasticities were negative for all employees and for the two age groups in the middle, holding the initial level of debt constant. This indicates a somewhat stronger tendency for the upper than the lower income brackets to increase instalment debt in this period.

For the three classes of consumer physical investment—including automobiles, other consumer durables, and additions and repairs to homes[94]—the marginal propensity with respect to transitory income seems substantially higher for automobile expenditures and somewhat higher for home additions and repairs than the normal income propensity, while for other consumer durables little difference exists between normal and transitory income effects. However, considerable variation appears among age groups. The transitory income effect on automobile expenditures is significantly higher than the normal income effect for the youngest age group and almost so for the 35–44 group, while the differences are much smaller for the two older groups. For additions and repairs, on the other hand, the normal income effect is slightly stronger than that of transitory income for the two younger groups (with correlations very low), while the transitory income effect is the stronger for the two older groups, with the difference significant for those 55 and over. For durables expenditures, the normal income effect is the stronger for all except the oldest group, where the transitory effect is significantly stronger. For the over 55 age group, which as noted earlier is based on a rather small sample, there is evidence that for all classes of consumer physical investment the propensity to invest out of transitory income is substantially higher than out of normal income, suggesting that, for these families, investment in durables does not have as urgent a claim on normal income as for the younger households. For employees as a whole, the normal income elasticities at the mean are about one for automobiles, somewhat lower for other durables, and somewhat higher for additions and repairs. In the last two cases, the inclusion of lagged net worth substantially reduces the estimated normal income elasticity.

The effect of family size is significant only for additions and repairs, with families of five persons or more spending more than smaller families. Liquid saving appears to decline steadily with family size, while the smallest households are most inclined to reduce mortgage debt and the largest are least inclined to reduce instalment debt. The effect of age is significant and positive for changes in liquid assets and reduction in

[94] Only additions are considered as part of investment and included in total saving, but we were not able to separate additions from repairs as a saving component at this stage of our analysis.

mortgage debt,[95] significant and negative for durables expenditures, and positive but not significant for reduction in instalment debt. Small negative effects occur for contractual saving,[96] other investment, automobile expenditures, and additions and repairs. The savings tastes variables shown for savings components (i.e., net worth at the end of 1959 either deflated by a three-year average of income centered on 1959 or not deflated) have positive, though not significant, effects for contractual saving, outlays on other durables, and home additions and repairs. The alternative savings tastes variable—the ratio of insurance premiums in 1959 to three-year average income—was significantly positive for contractual savings, reflecting the high correlation between insurance premiums in 1959 and in 1960–61, significantly negative for other investments,[97] and negative though not significant for reduction in mortgage debt.

When attention is directed to consumer investment in insurance premiums, changes in liquid assets, other consumer durables, and additions and repairs for individual years for the period 1959–61 (with insurance available for 1959 and 1961, liquid assets for 1959, and other variables for all three years), the marginal propensity to save out of normal income is significantly higher than that out of transitory income for insurance and additions and repairs in 1959, higher for other consumer durables (significantly so) and additions and repairs (not quite significant) in 1960, and somewhat higher for insurance in 1961. Transitory income seems more important for other consumer durables in 1959 and somewhat more important for additions and repairs in 1961. For automobiles, the transitory propensity is significantly higher than the normal propensity in 1960, but there is no significant or even consistent difference between the two in 1959 and 1961. Thus, the evidence is reasonably strong that the normal propensity is higher than the transitory for insurance, but the evidence is not consistent from year to year for auto-

[95] The positive effect of age on reduction in mortgage debt, holding initial level of debt constant, probably reflects not only the reluctance of older families to incur new debt, but also the mechanical fact that the same debt level is likely to be associated with a relatively expensive house, largely paid for, in the case of a middle-aged family, and a relatively inexpensive house, recently purchased, in the case of a young family. Monthly payments (debt reduction) are expected to be larger in the first case than in the second.

[96] The negative effect for contractual savings, in conjunction with a strong positive effect for reduction in mortgage debt, implies a substantial negative effect of age on savings in the form of insurance, the other major component of contractual saving.

[97] Possibly this suggests a pattern of savings tastes in which those households that are strongly insurance-minded are disinclined toward such investments as corporate stock, bonds other than U.S. savings bonds, and real estate.

mobiles, other consumer durables, and additions and repairs. Change in liquid assets in 1959 seems completely uncorrelated with either income component.

Of the three saving or related items for which corresponding initial asset holdings are already available—i.e., changes in liquid assets, reduction in mortgage debt, and reduction in instalment debt—the apparent speed of adjustment was relatively high for instalment debt (.35) and much lower for mortgage debt (.08) and liquid assets (.05). When regressions are derived for each age group separately, the speed of adjustment tends to rise with age for mortgage debt but to fall for instalment debt.[98] For these three items, long-run income elasticities for the associated asset stocks may be estimated from the saving regressions, if we ignore the effects of disequilibrium in holdings of other types of assets. Dividing the sum of the two income coefficients by an appropriate function of the speed of adjustment as estimated from the lagged asset coefficient, we obtain a normal income elasticity of 7.34 for liquid assets, 1.09 for mortgage debt, and .25 for instalment debt. The figure for liquid assets is considerably higher than that obtained from the FRB data, while no direct comparison is available for the debt items.

For entrepreneurs or the self-employed and farmers (Part B of Table 7), the marginal propensity to save seems higher than for employees, amounting to .40 or .41 for transitory income and from .36 to .38 for normal income. However, again the difference between the two coefficients is not significant. Once more also the coefficients of the net worth and saving tastes variables are insignificant. The mean normal income elasticities of saving for the self-employed are not very different from those for employees, running around 2.0. Historical income is even less important for the self-employed than for employees, but the inclusion of this variable lowers the estimated normal income elasticity, bringing it into closer agreement with that obtained for net worth.

Because of the smallness and the nonhomogeneity of the sample (combining farm and nonfarm entrepreneurs), rather erratic results were obtained for saving components and these are not shown. The major difference between entrepreneurs and employees lies, of course, in the much greater role played by business saving for the entrepreneurs. The marginal propensity of entrepreneurs to channel income into business saving was about half of their over-all normal saving propensity,

---

[98] The annual speed of adjustment (r) in the 1960–61 equations is measured as $r = 1 - \sqrt{1 + 2c}$, where c is the algebraic value of the coefficient of the initial specific assets variable. This computation ignores the effect on particular savings components of disequilibrium in holdings of other assets.

while it was entirely negligible for employees. Though the propensity to save in this form was higher for normal than for transitory income, the difference is not statistically significant. The marginal propensity of entrepreneurs to save in contractual form was also substantial and somewhat higher than for employees; again only normal income was of any importance in the determination of saving in this form.

The income elasticity obtained for business savings was surprisingly low, in the neighborhood of unity, while that for contractual saving (which may include some elements of business saving) was much higher than for employees. For liquid saving in 1960–61, the marginal propensity to save out of transitory income was very large and significantly greater than out of normal income, which is in the same direction as the result for employees. The speed of adjustment to the desired level of liquid assets is faster than for employees (.12). Mortgage debt was increased rather than decreased, on the average, by entrepreneurs but the marginal propensity to reduce debt is positive, unlike the result for employees. The income elasticity for reduction of instalment debt is again negative. The speed of adjustment is somewhat lower than in the case of employees for mortgage debt (.04) and somewhat higher for instalment debt (.82), and in the last case the difference between the two occupational groups is statistically significant. The implicit income elasticities for asset stocks are higher than for employees in the case of mortgage debt, much lower in the case of liquid assets, and negative in the case of instalment debt. As for employees, the relative size of the entrepreneurial marginal propensities to save out of normal and transitory income is not consistent from year to year for automobiles, other consumer durables and additions and repairs. Elasticities for these items are lower than for employees. The effect of age is negative and significant for durables outlays, and positive and close to significance for reduction in mortgage debt; these results are consistent with the findings for employees.

For the retired (Part C of Table 7), current income is completely unrelated to saving (or dissaving), while normal or five-year average income is not much better in this respect, with a positive but statistically insignificant coefficient. The comparative unimportance of current or short-run income for this group of consumer units is not surprising. However, when both five-year average and current income are included as explanatory variables, the current income coefficient is significantly negative while the five-year average income coefficient is positive, but not significantly so. This is a strange result and may reflect the fact that our measure of initial net worth is inadequate and that current income for the retired acts as a proxy for initial net worth (which may be the primary determinant of saving or dissaving for the retired) to a greater extent than does five-year average income. Thus the major components of saving which account for the negative current income coefficient and positive five-year coefficient are liquid assets and to a much lesser extent other investments, both of which might be expected to be liquidated by the retired. Initial assets, when included in the regression with normal and current income, has a negative but again insignificant coefficient. The unimportance of initial assets for the retired is difficult to explain and may again reflect the fact that income acts as a proxy for initial assets. Historical income seems somewhat more important than five-year average income for this group but neither is significant. The only major component of saving that is significantly related to either income variable is contractual saving, which is positively and significantly correlated with five-year average income. Contractual saving, which is positive (and averages $68 per household), helps to account for the surprisingly small dissaving of retired households (averaging $14), with liquid assets and other investments representing the major dissaving items. Net outlays on automobiles, other durables, and additions and repairs are positively and significantly correlated with five-year average income, while the effects of transitory income are negligible in all three cases. The income elasticities for automobiles and other durables are higher than for employees. The elasticity for reduction of instalment debt is negative as for the other two groups.

Table 10 presents selected saving-to-income ratios separately for employee homeowners and employee renters. Renters represented only about one-fourth of our sample and had lower mean incomes than homeowners ($4,842 vs. $6,811) and total saving amounting to only about one-fourth of homeowner saving, with liquid saving about the same for the two groups and contractual saving accounting for most of the difference. Outlays for automobiles and other durables were also lower for renters.

The independent variables we have used appear much more adequate to explain the saving behavior of renters than of homeowners, accounting for one-third of the variance of total and contractual saving and 40 per cent of the variance of liquid saving for renters. In the lagged adjustment model, the income elasticity of total saving is considerably higher for each group taken separately than for both groups combined and is quite similar for the two groups. In the immediate adjustment model, the elasticity for homeowners is lower and that for renters very much higher than for both combined, with the weighted average again higher. The elasticity for liquid saving, in particular, is much larger for renters than

TABLE 10

Linear Regressions of Total Saving, Saving Components, and Consumer Investment Items (1960-61 Averages) on Disposable Household Income and Other Variables, for Employees by Tenure of Dwelling Unit, SCF Panel Data for Households with 1958-62 Disposable Income of Less Than $20,000

Coefficient of	Renters			Homeowners		
	1	2	3	1	2	3
	Total Saving					
Household income, 1958-62	.225	-.200	-.345	.183	-.062	-.064
	(5.67)	(-1.32)	(-2.23)	(5.90)	(-.38)	(-.39)
Household income, 1960-61		.403	.473		.235	.252
		(2.91)	(3.43)		(1.52)	(1.62)
Net worth, 1959			.044			-.009
			(2.30)			(-.97)
Age of head[a]			8.60			-5.03
			(1.31)			(-.51)
Constant term	-870.24	-792.33	-722.47	-305.97	-263.41	-131.76
	(-4.14)	(-3.88)	(-2.66)	(-1.34)	(-1.14)	(-.40)
Normal income elasticity	4.99	4.52	2.83[b]	1.32	1.25	2.68[b]
$\bar{R}^2$	.241	.295	.337	.101	.105	.105

(continued)

TABLE 10 (continued)

Contractual Saving

Coefficient of	Renters			Homeowners		
	1	2	3	1	2	3
Household income, 1958-62	.025 (5.25)	.023 (1.20)	.002 (.13)	.050 (3.75)	.098 (1.38)	.088 (1.20)
Household income, 1960-61		.002 (.12)	.015 (.88)		-.046 (-.68)	-.037 (-.54)
Age of head[a]			-1.57 (-1.99)			-1.40 (-.33)
Saving tastes[c]			70.08 (4.54)			-10.47 (-.58)
Constant term	-1.72 (-.07)	-1.32 (-.05)	43.64 (1.50)	131.65 (1.33)	123.38 (1.23)	189.06 (1.36)
Normal income elasticity	1.01	1.01	.69	.72	.75	.72
$\bar{R}^2$	.213	.205	.340	.042	.040	.036

(continued)

TABLE 10 (concluded)

Coefficient of	Renters			Homeowners		
	1	2	3	1	2	3
	Change in Liquid Assets					
Household income, 1958-62	.232	-.201	-.183	.101	.050	.063
	(6.62)	(-1.53)	(-1.32)	(3.63)	(.34)	(.43)
Household income, 1960-61		.411	.416		.049	.047
		(3.41)	(3.37)		(.36)	(.34)
Liquid assets, 1959			-.053			-.048
			(-1.71)			(-3.18)
Age of head[a]			14.72			16.91
			(2.52)			(2.08)
Constant term	-1011.28	-931.83	-1295.28	-562.32	-533.37	-904.56
	(-5.44)	(-5.24)	(-5.93)	(-2.73)	(-2.67)	(-3.20)
Normal income elasticity	10.07	9.12	10.14[b]	5.40	5.28	5.88[b]
$\bar{R}^2$	.304	.372	.407	.039	.036	.068

Note: A small number of employees who were not either renters or homeowners are omitted from this table. Numbers in parentheses are T-tests for the coefficients immediately above.

[a] Age of head minus 20 to approximate number of working years.

[b] This is a short-run elasticity. The long-run income elasticity of savings is zero under the assumptions of the lagged adjustment model.

[c] Household net worth, 1959, divided by average income 1958-60.

for homeowners. The effect of transitory income on total saving is significantly greater than that of normal income for renters, while for homeowners there is rather little difference in the two effects. For renters, both contractual saving and other investment seem to be much more strongly related to initial net worth or the ratio of initial net worth to normal income than to either of the income variables. The effect of age on total saving is positive and quite large for renters, though not significant, while it is negative and relatively small for homeowners.

We have indicated earlier our reservations about the linearity of the saving function, in terms of both the apparent nonlinearity of the asset-to-income relationship and the insignificance of lagged net worth in the linear saving regressions and the unrealistically low speeds of adjustment implied. When the ratio of saving to normal income is related to normal income and other variables (Table 11)—a formulation consistent with a quadratic relationship between saving and income—lagged net worth becomes significant or nearly so for all three employment status groups. However, the speeds of adjustment, though somewhat increased, still seem unrealistically low. Correlations are lower for total saving (though as high or higher for some components).[99] However, correlation coefficients are not directly comparable between the two models since in the present case only the relatively small variance of the saving-to-income ratio is to be explained. In the neighborhood of mean income, the deviations of actual from computed saving appear to be somewhat smaller using the quadratic model, while an examination of the households with incomes over $10,000 suggests that there is little to choose between the two models in this range.

For employees, there is strong evidence of nonlinearity for total saving and for liquid saving in the highly significant coefficient of the quadratic term, and some indication of nonlinearity for reduction in instalment debt, reduction in mortgage debt, and outlays on other durables. In the last two cases, the relationship with income appears to be concave downward. For the self-employed also, there is an indication that the relationships are concave upward for total saving and change in liquid assets, and concave downward for outlays on other durables, though the coefficients are not significant. In addition, there is significant nonlinearity for contractual saving and for reduction in mortgage debt, with the relationships concave upward. For the retired, the effect of income on all three durables items is concave upward, significantly so for automobiles and other durables.

[99] Correlations are higher for liquid saving and about the same for the two debt items.

TABLE 11

Regressions of Saving-to-Income and Investment-to-Income Ratios on Disposable Household Income and Other Variables (1960-61 Averages) SCF Panel Data for Households with 1958-62 Disposable Income Less Than $20,000

	Coefficient of							
	Normal Income [a]	Current Income [b]	Net Worth, 1959 [c]	Holdings of Individual Asset, 1959 [c]	Age of Head [d]	Constant Term	Normal Income Elasticity	$\bar{R}^2$
Total Saving								
Employees	.013 (3.61)	.255 (2.76)			-.000 (-.37)	-.229 (-2.33)	1.50	.046
	.013 (3.75)	.274 (2.95)	-.012 (-1.95)		.000 (.31)	-.248 (-2.51)	1.67[e]	.053
Self-employed including farmers	.040 (1.78)	.892 (2.28)			-.004 (-.61)	-.944 (-1.93)	1.81	.102
	.038 (1.74)	.786 (1.99)	-.029 (-1.46)		-.001 (-.16)	-.780 (-1.57)	2.48	.120
Retired	.003 (.13)	-.321 (-2.56)			-.003 (-.86)	.432 (1.85)	f	.053
	.006 (.29)	-.213 (-1.60)	-.012 (-2.19)		-.002 (-.53)	.321 (1.37)	f	.092

(continued)

TABLE 11 (continued)

	Coefficient of							
	Normal Income[a]	Current Income[b]	Net Worth, 1959[c]	Holdings of Individual Asset, 1959[c]	Age of Head[d]	Constant Term	Normal Income Elasticity	$\bar{R}^2$
Saving Components for Employees								
Contractual saving	.002 (1.10)	-.000 (-.00)			-.000 (-.16)	.049 (1.18)	f	-.004
	.002 (.99)	-.006 (-.15)	.004 (1.47)		-.000 (-.65)	.055 (1.32)	f	-.001
Change in liquid assets	.010 (3.41)	.250 (3.37)			.001 (1.22)	-.328 (-4.15)	3.13	.052
	.010 (3.60)	.219 (3.13)		-.059[g] (-7.50)	.002 (2.79)	-.302 (-4.07)	4.01[e]	.165
Reduction in mortgage debt	-.001 (-.24)	.017 (.26)			.001 (1.17)	-.010 (-.14)	f	-.004
	-.004 (-1.68)	.042 (.67)		-.072[h] (-6.63)	.002 (2.76)	-.074 (-1.11)	-2.19[e]	.092

(continued)

TABLE 11 (continued)

	Coefficient of							
	Normal Income[a]	Current Income[b]	Net Worth, 1959[c]	Holdings of Individual Asset, 1959[c]	Age of Head[d]	Constant Term	Normal Income Elasticity	$\bar{R}^2$
Saving Components for Employees (continued)								
Reduction in instalment debt	.001 (.73)	−.030 (−.90)			−.000 (−.68)	.029 (.82)	f	−.003
	.002 (1.52)	−.023 (−.80)		−.285[i] (−11.63)	.001 (1.81)	−.026 (−.82)	−2.15[e]	.245
Net outlay on automobiles	.001 (.70)	.093 (2.77)			−.000 (−.90)	−.043 (−1.21)	.96	.016
	.001 (.62)	.089 (2.64)	.002 (1.03)		−.000 (−1.19)	−.040 (−1.10)	.89	.016
Net outlay on other durables	−.001 (−1.33)	.008 (.60)			−.000 (−2.27)	.023 (1.71)	.57	.009
	−.001 (−1.37)	.007 (.53)	.000 (.59)		−.000 (−2.33)	.024 (1.76)	.56	.008

(continued)

TABLE 11 (concluded)

			Coefficient of					
	Normal Income[a]	Current Income[b]	Net Worth, 1959[c]	Holdings of Individual Asset, 1959[c]	Age of Head[d]	Constant Term	Normal Income Elasticity	$\bar{R}^2$
			Saving Components for Employees (concluded)					
Home additions and repairs	.001 (.70)	.041 (1.10)			-.000 (-.85)	-.004 (-.09)	f	-.001
	.001 (.57)	.034 (.90)	.005 (1.87)		-.001 (-1.43)	.003 (.09)	f	.005

Note: Denominator for ratios is five-year average of household income, 1958-62. Numbers in parentheses are T-tests for the coefficients immediately above.

[a]Five-year average of household income, 1958-62, divided by 1000.
[b]Average income, 1960-61, divided by normal income.
[c]Divided by normal income.
[d]Age minus 20 to approximate number of working years.
[e]This is a short-run elasticity. The long-run elasticity of saving is zero under the assumptions of the lagged adjustment model.
[f]A meaningful estimate of the normal income elasticity cannot be computed from this regression.
[g]Liquid assets.
[h]Mortgage debt.
[i]Instalment debt.

For employees, the income elasticity of total saving is the same as in the linear model when lagged net worth is included in the regression, but otherwise a little lower (1.5). However, for change in liquid assets, the elasticity is considerably lower than in the linear form (3 or 4 compared with 5 or 6). For reduction in mortgage debt and outlays on automobiles and other durables, the elasticities are much the same as in the linear model. The effects of age and of net worth considered as a saving tastes variable are somewhat enhanced in the quadratic model.

For the self-employed, the elasticity for total saving is a little higher (2.5) than in the linear form when initial net worth is included in the regression. For the retired, the marginal propensity to save out of normal income is .04 at the mean, compared with .02 for the linear model when current income is also included in the regression. The effect of transitory income is still large and negative but no longer significant when lagged net worth appears in the regression. The transitory income effect is no longer negative for liquid assets, though it remains significantly so for other investment. Business saving for the self-employed again has an income elasticity around unity, while contractual saving again has a very high elasticity. The marginal propensity to reduce mortgage debt is again positive at mean income and that for liquid saving is the same as for the linear model when initial liquid assets are included in the regressions. The income elasticity for reduction of instalment debt is negative for all three employment status groups, as in the linear model.

Table 12 presents for employees the relationships between total saving and related items for each consumer unit in 1960–61 and both group income (the 1958–62 mean income of the occupational group to which the unit belongs) and the unit's income for the two-year period covered, as well as other variables. The measure of the normal income effect obtained from these regressions as the sum of the group income and household income coefficients conforms essentially to a long-run concept of normal income. However, the implicit measure of transitory income must be assumed to contain substantial components of permanent income as well. Therefore, it is not surprising that the estimates of the two income effects are generally quite similar. However, substantial (though not quite significant) differences still appear for contractual saving and liquid saving. For change in liquid assets the transitory income effect is higher than the normal income effect, with marginal propensities of .13 and .05, respectively. For contractual saving, the situation is reversed with marginal propensities of .08 for normal income and .05 for transitory income. Furthermore, the income elasticities differ somewhat from those obtained from the regressions using

TABLE 12

Linear Regressions of Total Saving, Saving Components, and Consumer Investment Items (1960-61 Averages) on Group Disposable Income and Other Variables for Employees, SCF Panel Data for Households with 1958-62 Disposable Income of Less Than $20,000

	Mean Income for Occupational Group, 1958-62	Household Income, 1960-61	Asset Stock, 1959	Age[a]	Constant Term	Normal Income Elasticity	$\bar{R}^2$
Total saving	.178 (3.46)				-383.27 (-1.14)	1.51	.026
	-.027 (-.51)	.209 (8.27)			-407.65 (-1.31)	1.54	.163
	-.025 (-.45)	.214 (7.52)	-.003[b] (-.39)		-428.36 (-1.36)	1.61[c]	.161
Contractual saving	.080 (3.87)				-131.01 (-.98)	1.35	.033
	.034 (1.48)	.047 (4.38)			-136.48 (-1.04)	1.36	.074
Change in liquid assets	.030 (.68)				-63.81 (-.22)	d	-.001
	-.097 (-2.00)	.130 (5.70)			-78.93 (-.28)	1.59	.070
	-.080 (-1.65)	.132 (5.86)	-.037[e] (-2.82)		-135.49 (-.49)	2.56[c]	.086

(continued)

TABLE 12 (continued)

	Mean Income for Occupational Group, 1958-62	Household Income, 1960-61	Asset Stock, 1959	Age[a]	Constant Term	Normal Income Elasticity	$\bar{R}^2$
Other investment	.048 (1.14)				-285.91 (-1.02)	d	.001
	.018 (.35)	.034 (1.47)			-302.60 (-1.05)	d	.004
Reduction in mortgage debt	.026 (.77)				-39.77 (-.18)	1.31	-.001
	.027 (.72)	-.001 (-.07)			-39.62 (-.18)	1.31	-.003
	-.001 (-.03)	-.042 (-2.29)	-.071[f] (-6.41)	8.31 (1.88)	-54.31 (-.23)	-2.16[c]	.084
Reduction in instalment debt	.018 (1.13)				-108.79 (-1.06)	d	.001
	.021 (1.18)	-.003 (-.39)			-108.42 (-1.05)	d	-.001
	.019 (1.21)	-.013 (-1.81)	-.289[g] (-11.74)	2.64 (1.42)	-245.83 (-2.41)	.83[c]	.249

(continued)

TABLE 12 *(concluded)*

	Mean Income for Occupational Group, 1958-62	Household Income, 1960-61	Asset Stock, 1959	Age[a]	Constant Term	Normal Income Elasticity	$\bar{R}^2$
Net outlays on automobiles	.044 (2.65)				45.26 (.42)	.86	.014
	−.007 (−.42)	.052 (6.22)			39.22 (.38)	.88	.097
Net outlays on other durables	.014 (2.38)				31.58 (.82)	.74	.011
	.000 (.06)	.014 (4.56)			29.95 (.79)	.75	.057
	−.001 (−.21)	.012 (3.36)	.001[b] (1.08)		92.01 (2.06)	.54	.068
Home additions and repairs	.048 (2.60)				−65.20 (−.54)	1.27	.014
	.005 (.23)	.044 (4.61)			−70.36 (−.60)	1.29	.060
	.000 (.02)	.036 (3.36)	.005[b] (1.62)		−37.97 (−.32)	.97	.064

Note: Numbers in parentheses are *T*-tests for the coefficients immediately above.
[a] Age of head minus 20 to approximate number of working years.
[b] Net worth.
[c] This is a short-run elasticity. The long-run elasticity of saving is zero under the assumptions of the lagged adjustment model.
[d] Meaningful estimates cannot be computed.
[e] Liquid assets.
[f] Mortgage debt.
[g] Instalment debt.

ungrouped variables only, being a little higher for contractual saving and considerably lower, though still well above one, for liquid saving. Theoretically, these elasticities are unbiased if transitory income within each group is approximately zero (while some bias due to transitory income may still remain in the elasticities of Table 7), and in any case they show considerably closer agreement with the asset elasticities of Table 2.

VI. Summary and Conclusions

In Part I we have presented a simple general model of consumer saving and investment behavior, in which desired total assets or net worth is primarily a function of normal income and tastes; actual net worth, which at any point of time represents a delayed adjustment to desired net worth, is a function of normal income, transitory income, capital gains (which may be treated partly as normal and partly as transitory income), beginning-of-period net worth, and tastes; and saving is, apart from capital gains, simply the difference between end and beginning of period net worth.[100] The optimum asset structure depends, of course, not only on the variables explaining total assets and saving but also on the relative rates of return and risks of individual items of assets and liabilities, while the composition of saving during any period will depend as well on the initial values of these items.

Part II summarizes the results obtained by others in prior analysis of the determinants of consumer demand for total assets and saving and for individual items of saving or investment. It points out the very wide range of results derived in estimating the role played by income and initial assets in the determination of the demand for assets, saving or investment and discusses the difficulties in resolving these differences.

Part III presents the plan of our analysis; we have undertaken to correct some important deficiencies in the earlier work, but have not been able to complete all of our analysis for this paper. The empirical work in this paper is based on cross-section data on total and individual items of both assets (or stocks) and saving (or flows). We attempt to integrate the asset and saving analysis, to experiment with different mathematical forms, and to use several approaches to the measurement of normal (and transitory) income and to holding tastes constant. Unfortunately, the results of some of the more promising approaches

[100] In this paper we have ignored problems of capital transfers since they do not seem to affect significantly any of our conclusions.

are not yet available, and some were not conspicuously successful, but several interesting findings do emerge from the analysis in this paper.

The most noteworthy of the substantive findings in Part IV (on asset stocks) and Part V (on saving or flows) is that the long-run normal income elasticity of total net worth and the short-run normal income elasticity of total saving are substantially higher than one, a result which is inconsistent with the usual version of the "permanent" income hypothesis. With minor exceptions, only for consumer investment in tangible assets such as housing and consumer durables and in associated debt do both the long-run normal income elasticity of assets and the short-run normal income elasticity of saving appear to be in the neighborhood of one, while for most major categories of business, liquid, or financial investment, at least one and generally both of these elasticities appear to be well over one. The influence of transitory income on total saving—particularly on changes in liquid assets—seems to be somewhat greater than that of normal income, but the reverse is true for contractual saving and for total assets. The difference is especially marked for contractual saving.

A puzzling result of our analysis is the conflicting evidence relating to the planning span for total asset accumulation. While we are disposed to believe that the relevant period is relatively short, i.e., a period effectively much shorter than the earning span, there is as much evidence to contradict as to support this supposition. On the other hand, the significance of the initial assets coefficient in the parabolic saving form and the fact that this coefficient is significantly different from one in the logarithmic asset form tend to support our lagged adjustment model as opposed to a model which considers initial assets irrelevant.

The Theory of Investment Behavior

DALE W. JORGENSON

UNIVERSITY OF CALIFORNIA AT BERKELEY

1. Introduction

Business investment behavior is one of the areas of modern economic research that is being studied most intensively; empirical studies are accumulating rapidly,[1] and at the same time important developments

[1] A very detailed review of the literature through 1960 has been provided by R. Eisner and R. Strotz, "The Determinants of Business Investment," in D. B. Suits, *et al.*, *Impacts of Monetary Policy*, Englewood Cliffs, 1963, pp. 60–338. A more concise review of developments through 1962 has been presented by E. Kuh, "Theory and Institutions in the Study of Investment Behavior," *American Economic Review*, May 1963, pp. 260–268. Empirical studies published since 1962 include: S. Almon, "The Distributed Lag between Capital Appropriations and Expenditures," *Econometrica*, January 1965, pp. 178–196; W. H. L. Anderson, *Corporate Finance and Fixed Investment*, Boston, 1964; A. Bourneuf, "Investment, Excess Capacity, and Growth," *American Economic Review*, September 1964, pp. 607–625; R. Eisner, "Investment: Fact and Fancy," *American Economic Review*, May 1963, pp. 237–246; Eisner, "Capital Expenditures, Profits, and the Acceleration Principle," *Models of Income Determination*, Studies in Income and Wealth 28, Princeton University Press for National Bureau of Economic Research, 1964, pp. 137–176; Eisner, "Realization of Investment Anticipations," in J. S. Duesenberry, E. Kuh, G. Fromm, and L. R. Klein, eds., *The Brookings Quarterly Econometric Model of the United States*, Chicago, 1965; E. Greenberg, "A Stock-Adjustment Investment Model," *Econometrica*, July 1964, pp. 339–357; B. Hickman, *Investment Demand and U.S. Economic Growth*, Washington, 1965; D. W. Jorgenson, "Capital Theory and Investment Behavior," *American Economic Review*, May 1963, pp. 247–259; Jorgenson, "Anticipations and Investment Behavior," in *Brookings Quarterly Econometric Model;* E. Kuh, *Capital Stock Growth: A Micro-Econometric Approach*, Amsterdam, 1963; J. R. Meyer and R. R. Glauber, *Investment Decisions, Economic Forecasting and Public Policy*, Boston, 1964; G. J. Stigler, *Capital and Rates of Return in Manufacturing Industries*, Princeton for NBER, 1963.

in the economic theory of investment behavior are taking place.[2] As yet, there is very little common ground between the empirical and theoretical approaches to this subject. From a certain point of view this is a desirable state of affairs.[3] Econometric studies of investment behavior date back no more than thirty years.[4] Only recently have data on investment expenditures suitable for analysis by econometric methods become available. If empirical studies are forced prematurely into a theoretical straitjacket, attention may be diverted from historical and institutional considerations that are essential to a complete understanding of investment behavior. On the other hand, if theoretical work is made to conform to "realistic" assumptions at too early a stage in the development of empirical work, the door may be closed to theoretical innovations that could lead to improvements in empirical work at a later stage.

While there is some surface plausibility in the view that empirical and theoretical research are best carried out in isolation from each other, this view is seriously incomplete. Econometric work is always based on highly simplified models. The number of possible explanations of investment behavior, which is limited only by the imagination of the investigator, is so large that, in any empirical investigation, all but a very few must be ruled out in advance. Insofar as the necessary simplifications restrict the possible explanations of investment behavior, these simplifications constitute, at least implicitly, a theory of investment behavior. Such theories can be compared with each other most expeditiously by reducing each to its basic underlying assumptions, after which empirical tests to discriminate among alternative theories can be

[2] See, for example, the following papers: K. J. Arrow, "Optimal Capital Policy, The Cost of Capital, and Myopic Decision Rules," *Annals of the Institute of Statistical Mathematics,* 1964, pp. 21–30; "Optimal Capital Adjustment," in K. J. Arrow, S. Karlin, and H. Scarf, eds., *Studies in Applied Probability and Management Science,* Stanford, 1962; K. J. Arrow, M. Beckmann, and S. Karlin, "Optimal Expansion of the Capacity of the Firm," in K. J. Arrow, S. Karlin, and H. Scarf, eds., *Studies in the Mathematical Theory of Inventory and Production,* Stanford, 1958; A. S. Manne, "Capacity Expansion and Probabilistic Growth," *Econometrica,* October 1961, pp. 632–649; E. Zabel, "Efficient Accumulation of Capital for the Firm," *Econometrica,* January-April 1963, pp. 131–150; and the following books: T. Haavelmo, *A Study in the Theory of Investment,* Chicago, 1960; F. A. Lutz and D. G. Hague, eds., *The Theory of Capital,* London, 1961; P. B. D. Massé, *Optimal Investment Decisions,* Englewood Cliffs, 1962; V. L. Smith, *Investment and Production,* Cambridge, 1961; B. Thalberg, "A Keynesian Model Extended by Explicit Demand and Supply Functions for Investment Goods," *Stockholm Economic Studies,* Pamphlet Series, No. 3, 1964.

[3] This point of view has been put forward by K. Borch, "Discussion," *American Economic Review,* May 1963, pp. 272–274.

[4] J. Tinbergen, *Statistical Testing of Business Cycle Theories,* Part I, "A Method and its Application to Investment Activity," Geneva, 1939.

designed. Far from forcing empirical studies into a theoretical strait-jacket, judicious use of a theoretical framework is essential to the proper direction of empirical work.

The view that theoretical and empirical research should be carried out in isolation is incomplete in a second respect. The use of economic theory as a source of possible explanations for investment behavior frees econometric work from reliance on empirical generalizations that have not been subjected to rigorous econometric tests. There is a very real danger that econometric models of investment behavior may be made to conform prematurely to assumptions that are "realistic" by the standards of empirical work not based on econometric methods. Just as premature reliance on "realistic" assumptions may be stultifying to the development of economic theory, so reliance on historical and institutional generalizations may restrict the development of econometric models unduly. The paramount test for "realism" of an econometric model is its performance in econometric work. If a model does not perform satisfactorily by the standards of econometrics, it must be rejected, however closely it parallels historical and institutional accounts of the same economic behavior.

The point of departure for this paper is that progress in the study of investment behavior can best be made by comparing econometric models of such behavior within a theoretical framework. Ideally, each model should be derived from a common set of assumptions about the objectives of the business firm. Differences among alternative models should be accounted for by alternative assumptions about the behavior of business firms in pursuing these objectives. It will undoubtedly be surprising to some that a theoretical framework is implicit in the econometric models of investment behavior currently under study. The objective of this paper is to make this framework explicit in order to provide a basis to evaluate evidence on the determinants of investment behavior. This objective can only be attained by a thoroughgoing reconstruction of the theory of investment. Once the theory of investment is placed in a proper setting, the arguments advanced for pessimism about combining theoretical and empirical work largely evaporate.

In providing a framework for the theory of investment behavior, the first problem is to choose an appropriate basis for the theory. Two alternative possibilities may be suggested. First, the theory of investment could be based on the neoclassical theory of optimal capital accumulation. There are three basic objections to this possibility, the first of which is that a substantial body of noneconometric work on the motivation of business firms, mainly surveys of businessmen, suggests that "marginalist" considerations are largely irrelevant to the making of business decisions. This evidence has been subjected to careful scrutiny by White,[5] who concludes that the data accumulated by the surveys are so defective, even by the standards of noneconometric empirical work, that no reliance can be placed on conclusions based on them. A second objection is that previous attempts to base the study of investment on neoclassical economic theory have been unsuccessful,[6] but this argument will not withstand critical scrutiny. First, none of the tests of the neoclassical theory reported in the early literature was based on a fully rigorous statement of the theory. Secondly, the assumptions made about the lag between changes in the demand for capital services and actual investment expenditures were highly restrictive. Frequently, the lag was assumed to be concentrated at a particular point or to be distributed over time in a very simple manner. Tests of the neoclassical theory were carried out prior to the important contribution of Koyck to the analysis of distributed lags and investment behavior.[7] Despite these deficiencies, the pioneering tests of the neoclassical theory reported by Tinbergen reveal substantial effects for the price of investment goods, the change in this price, and the rate of interest.[8] Similarly, tests reported by Roos reveal substantial effects for the price of investment goods and rate of interest.[9] Klein's studies of investment in the railroad and electric power industries reveal substantial effects for the rate of interest.[10]

A third and more fundamental objection has recently been restated by Haavelmo, who argues that a demand schedule for investment goods cannot be derived from neoclassical theory:[11]

What we should reject is the naive reasoning that there is a demand schedule for investment which could be derived from a classical scheme of producers'

[5] W. H. White, "Interest Inelasticity of Investment Demand," *American Economic Review,* September 1956, pp. 565–587.

[6] J. Meyer and E. Kuh, *The Investment Decision,* Cambridge, Mass., pp. 7–14.

[7] L. M. Koyck, *Distributed Lags and Investment Analysis,* Amsterdam, 1954.

[8] Tinbergen, *Statistical Testing,* see also the discussion of Tinbergen's results by T. Haavelmo, "The Effect of the Rate of Interest on Investment: A Note," *Review of Economic Statistics,* February 1941, pp. 49–52.

[9] C. F. Roos and V. S. Von Szeliski, "The Demand for Durable Goods," *Econometrica,* April 1943, pp. 97–122; Roos, "The Demand for Investment Goods," *American Economic Review,* May 1948, pp. 311–320; Roos, "Survey of Economic Forecasting Techniques," *Econometrica,* October 1955, pp. 363–395.

[10] L. R. Klein, "Studies in Investment Behavior," in *Conference on Business Cycles,* New York, National Bureau of Economic Research, 1951.

[11] Haavelmo, *Theory of Investment,* p. 216.

behavior in maximizing profit. The demand for investment cannot simply be derived from the demand for capital. Demand for a finite addition to the stock of capital can lead to any rate of investment, from almost zero to infinity, depending on the additional hypothesis we introduce regarding the speed of reaction of capital-users. I think that the sooner this naive, and unfounded, theory of the demand-for-investment schedule is abandoned, the sooner we shall have a chance of making some real progress in constructing more powerful theories to deal with the capricious short-run variations in the rate of private investment.

We will show that it is possible to derive a demand function for investment goods based on purely neoclassical considerations. While it is true that the conventional derivation of such a demand schedule, as in Keynes' construction of the marginal efficiency of investment schedule,[12] must be dismissed as naive, there is a sense in which the demand for investment goods can be taken to depend on the cost of capital; such a theory of investment behavior can be derived from the neoclassical theory of optimal capital accumulation.

A second possible basis for the theory of investment is the assumption that business firms maximize utility defined more broadly than in the characterization of objectives of the firm in the neoclassical theory of optimal capital accumulation. This basis has been suggested by Meyer and Kuh:[13]

Partial recognition of institutional changes has led in recent years to shift the theory of the firm, and consequently of plant and equipment investment, from a profit maximization orientation to that of utility maximization. Primarily, this move represents a growing belief that profit maximization is too narrow to encompass the full scope of modern entrepreneurial motives, particularly once the previously assumed objective conditions are released from *ceteris paribus,* and the theory seeks to explain a much wider range of behavioral responses.

This position has recently been supported with much force by Simon: ". . . I should like to emphasize strongly that neither the classical theory of the firm nor any of the amendments to it or substitutes for it that have been proposed have had any substantial amount of empirical testing. If the classical theory appeals to us, it must be largely because it

---

[12] J. M. Keynes, *The General Theory of Employment, Interest and Money,* New York, 1936, esp. Chapter 11, pp. 135–146.

[13] Meyer and Kuh, *Investment Decision,* p. 9.

has a certain face validity . . . rather than because profit maximizing behavior has been observed."[14]

In putting forward this view, Simon ignores the entire econometric literature on cost and production functions, all of which is based on the neoclassical theory of the firm. A recent survey of this literature by Walters[15] enumerates 345 references, almost all presenting results of econometric tests of the neoclassical theory of the firm which are overwhelmingly favorable to the theory. The evidence is largely so favorable that current empirical research emphasizes such technical questions as the appropriate form for the production function and the appropriate statistical specification for econometric models of production based on this theory. We conclude that Simon's statement that the alternatives to the neoclassical theory of the firm have had no substantial amount of empirical testing is correct. However, his characterization of the empirical evidence on the neoclassical theory is completely erroneous.

One possible reaction to a proper assessment of the support for the neoclassical theory of the firm from econometric studies of cost and production functions is to reject out of hand studies of investment behavior not based explicitly on the neoclassical theory, such as the study of Meyer and Kuh. In fact, the theoretical basis for the econometric model of investment behavior proposed by Meyer and Kuh is consistent with the neoclassical theory of optimal capital accumulation. Their appeal to a less narrow view of entrepreneurial objectives is not essential to the interpretation of the empirical results they present. We conclude that the objections to the neoclassical theory of the firm as a basis for the theory of investment behavior are ill-founded. Furthermore, the appeal to a broader view of entrepreneurial objectives than that which underlies this theory is not required by evidence either from econometric studies of cost and production functions or from studies of investment behavior. The neoclassical theory of optimal accumulation of capital is a far more powerful theory than the "broader view" suggested by Simon and others in the sense that a much narrower range of conceivable behavior is consistent with it than with the amorphous utility-maximizing theory. Accordingly, we will employ a theoretical framework based on the neoclassical theory of the firm for constructing a theory of investment behavior.

[14] H. A. Simon, "New Developments in the Theory of the Firm," *American Economic Review*, May 1962, p. 8.

[15] A. A. Walters, "Production and Cost Functions: An Econometric Survey," *Econometrica*, April 1963, pp. 1–66.

The objective of explaining investment behavior on the basis of the neoclassical theory of the firm cannot be described as novel. This objective is clearly in evidence in Tinbergen's pioneering monograph, *Statistical Testing of Business Cycle Theories*. Subsequently, a similar objective was adopted by Roos and by Klein.[16] In these early studies of investment behavior, the neoclassical theory was employed to provide a list of possible explanatory variables for investment expenditures. The rate of interest, the level of stock prices, the price of investment goods, and changes in the price of investment goods were used along with other variables such as profits, output, and changes in output. Little attention was paid to the manner in which the rate of interest and the price of investment goods enter the demand for capital services or the demand for investment goods. Both variables enter only through the *user cost* of capital services.[17] There is no effect of the price of investment goods except in combination with the rate of interest and vice versa. We conclude that, although the objective of explaining investment behavior on the basis of the neoclassical theory of the firm is not new, this objective remains to be fully realized.

2. The Neoclassical Framework

In formulating a theory of investment behavior based on the neoclassical theory of optimal capital accumulation, a great number of alternative versions of the theory could be considered. Reduced to its barest essentials, the theory requires only that capital accumulation be based on the objective of maximizing the utility of a stream of consumption. This basic assumption may be combined with any number of technological possibilities for production and economic possibilities for transformation of the results of production into a stream of consumption. In selecting among alternative formulations, a subsidiary objective must be borne in mind. The resulting theory of capital accumulation must include the principal econometric models of investment behavior as specializations,

---

[16] See footnotes 9 and 10. See also L. R. Klein, *The Keynesian Revolution,* New York, 1947, esp. pp. 62–68, pp. 196–199; Klein, "Notes on the Theory of Investment," *Kyklos,* vol. 2, Fasc. 2, 1948, pp. 97–117; Klein, *Economic Fluctuations in the United States, 1921–1941,* New York, 1950, esp. pp. 14–40.

[17] A complete discussion of the concept of user cost has been given by W. A. Lewis, "Depreciation and Obsolescence as Factors in Costing," in J. L. Meij, ed., *Depreciation and Replacement Policy,* Amsterdam, 1961, pp. 15–45. See also Keynes, *General Theory,* pp. 66–73; A. P. Lerner, "User Cost and Prime User Cost," *American Economic Review,* March 1943, pp. 131–132; F. A. Lutz and V. Lutz, *The Theory of Investment of the Firm,* Princeton, 1951; A. D. Scott, "Notes on User Cost," *Economic Journal,* June 1953, pp. 364–384.

but the theory need not encompass possibilities for the explanation of investment behavior not employed in econometric work.

The essentials of a theory of optimal capital accumulation that meets this basic objective are the following: The firm maximizes the utility of a consumption stream subject to a production function relating the flow of output to flows of labor and capital services. The firm supplies capital services to itself through the acquisition of investment goods; the rate of change in the flow of capital services is proportional to the rate of acquisition of investment goods less the rate of replacement of previously acquired investment goods. The results of the productive process are transformed into a stream of consumption under a fixed set of prices for output, labor services, investment goods, and consumption goods. These prices may be considered as current or "spot" prices together with forward prices for each commodity or, alternatively, as current and future prices together with a normalization factor, which may be identified with current and future values of the rate of time discount or interest rate. Both current and forward prices are taken as fixed by the firm. Alternatively, current and future prices together with current and future values of the rate of interest are taken as fixed. Under these conditions, the problem of maximizing utility may be solved in two stages. First, a production plan may be chosen so as to maximize the present value of the productive enterprise. Secondly, consumption is allocated over time so as to maximize utility subject to the present value of the firm. In view of our concern with the theory of business investment behavior, we will consider only the first of these problems. It should be noted that, under the assumption of fixed prices, the choice of a production plan is independent of the subsequent allocation of consumption over time. Two firms with different preferences among alternative consumption streams will choose the same plan for production.

This version of the neoclassical theory of the firm is not the only one available in the literature on capital theory. From a certain point of view, the objective of maximizing the present value of the firm is only one among many possible objectives for the firm. In a recent survey paper on the theory of capital, Lutz remarks that "It is one of the surprising things about capital theory that no agreement seems to have been reached as to what the entrepreneur should maximize."[18] Alternative criteria discussed in the literature include maximization of the average internal rate of return, maximization of the rate of return on capital owned by the firm, investment in any project with an internal

[18] F. A. Lutz, "The Essentials of Capital Theory," in Lutz and Hague, *Theory of Capital,* p. 6.

rate of return greater than the ruling market rate of interest, and so on. None of these criteria can be derived from maximization of the utility of a stream of consumption under the conditions we have outlined. Maximization of the present value of the firm is the only criterion consistent with utility maximization. This approach to the theory of optimal capital accumulation was originated by Fisher and has recently been revived and extended by Bailey and by Hirshleifer.[19] The essential justification for this approach is summarized by Hirshleifer, as follows:

> Since Fisher, economists working in the theory of investment decision have tended to adopt a mechanical approach—some plumping for the use of this formula, some for that. From a Fisherian point of view, we can see that none of the formulas so far propounded is universally valid. Furthermore, even where the present-value rule, for example, is correct, few realize that its validity is conditional upon making certain associated financing decisions as the Fisherian analysis demonstrates. In short, the Fisherian approach permits us to define the range of applicability and the short-comings of all the proposed formulas—thus standing over against them as the general theoretical solution to the problem of investment decision under conditions of certainty.[20]

A second controversial aspect of the version of the neoclassical theory outlined above is the assumption that the set of technological possibilities confronted by the firm can be described by a production function, where the flow of output is a function of flows of labor and capital services and the flow of capital services is proportional to the stock of capital goods obtained by summing the stream of past net investments.[21] The concept of capital service is not essential to the neoclassical theory. A production function relating output at each point of time to inputs of labor and capital services at that point of time may be replaced by a production function relating output at every point of time to inputs of investment goods at every point of time; this description of the set of

[19] I. Fisher, *The Theory of Interest,* New York, 1930. M. J. Bailey, "Formal Criteria for Investment Decisions," *Journal of Political Economy,* October 1959, pp. 476–488. J. Hirshleifer, "On the Theory of the Optimal Investment Decision," in E. Solomon, ed., *The Management of Corporate Capital,* Glencoe, 1959, pp. 205–228.

[20] *Ibid.,* p. 228.

[21] For a discussion of this assumption and some of its implications, see J. Robinson, "The Production Function and the Theory of Capital," *Review of Economic Studies,* Vol. 21, No. 54, 1953–54, pp. 81–106; R. M. Solow, "The Production Function and the Theory of Capital," *Review of Economic Studies,* Vol. 23, No. 61, 1955–56, pp. 101–108; J. Robinson, "Reply," *Review of Economic Studies,* Vol. 23, No. 62, 1955–56, p. 247; J. Robinson, "Some Problems of Definition and Measurement of Capital," *Oxford Economic Papers,* June 1959, pp. 157–166; K. J. Arrow *et al.,* "Symposium on Production Functions and Economic Growth," *Review of Economic Studies,* June 1962.

production possibilities is employed by Fisher; moreover, it may be characterized abstractly so that even the notion of a production function may be dispensed with, as is done by Malinvaud.[22] The description of the set of technological possibilities by means of a production function as presented by Fisher is a specialization of the description given by Malinvaud. The further assumption that the relationship between inputs of investment goods and levels of output may be reduced to a relationship between output at each point of time and a corresponding flow of capital services involves a specialization of the description of technological possibilities given by Fisher.

In the neoclassical literature, two basic models of the relationship between flows of investment goods and flows of capital services have been discussed, namely, a model of inventories and a model of durable goods. At the level of abstraction of Fisher's description of the set of production possibilities, no distinction between inventories and durable goods is required. For both inventories and durable goods, the acquisition of a stock of productive goods may be represented as an input to the productive process at the time of acquisition. For inventories, the individual items "used up" at different points of time may be represented as the output of a subprocess representing the holding of stocks; these outputs may be inputs into other subprocesses. For durable goods, the outputs of the corresponding stockholding process are the services of the goods rather than the individual items of the stock; the services of the durable goods may be inputs into other parts of the productive process.

The basis for the distinction between inventories and durable goods lies in the relationship among the initial input and the various outputs from the stockholding process. For inventories, the outputs provided by the stockholding process are customarily treated as perfect substitutes. For each item held in stock, the ultimate consumption of that item can occur at one and only one point in time. By contrast, the outputs provided by durable goods are treated as if they were perfectly complementary. The output of the service of a durable good at any point of time is assumed to bear a fixed relation to the output of the same service at any other point of time. The assumptions that outputs provided by a given input of investment goods are perfectly complementary or perfectly substitutable are highly restrictive. Nevertheless, the simplification of the neoclassical theory for these limiting cases and the practical importance of these cases are very great. A far more substantial proportion of the literature on capital theory is devoted to these two limiting

[22] E. Malinvaud, "Capital Accumulation and Efficient Allocation of Resources," *Econometrica*, April 1953, pp. 233–268.

cases than to the theory of production at the level of abstraction of the descriptions of technology given by Fisher or by Malinvaud. In the following we assume that the conventional neoclassical description of a durable good is appropriate for each investment good considered.

A second assumption required for a relationship between output at each point of time and the corresponding flow of capital services is that the services of investment goods acquired at different points of time are perfect substitutes in production. Accordingly, the flow of capital services from each investment good is proportional to the stock of capital that may be obtained by simply adding together all past acquisitions less replacements. This assumption is highly restrictive; the assumption can be justified primarily by the resulting simplification of the neoclassical theory. We discuss only a single investment good. Under the assumptions outlined above, there is only a single capital service. This simplification is also completely inessential to neoclassical theory.

Finally, we assume that the flow of replacement generated by a given flow of investment goods is distributed over time in accord with an exponential distribution. This assumption implies that the flow of replacement investment at any point of time is proportional to the accumulated stock of investment goods. Again, this assumption is only one among many possibilities. Alternative assumptions employed in practice include the following: First, replacement is equal to investment goods acquired at some earlier point in time; second, replacement is equal to a weighted average of past investment flows, with weights derived from studies of the "survival curves" of individual pieces of equipment.[23] For empirical work the exponential distribution of replacements is of special interest. While empirical studies of "survival curves" for individual pieces of equipment reveal a wide variety of possible distributions, there is a deeper justification for use of the exponential distribution. This justification arises from a fundamental result of renewal theory, namely, that replacement approaches an amount proportional to the accumulated stock of capital whatever the distribution of replacements for an individual piece of equipment, provided that the size of the capital stock is constant or that the stock is growing at a constant rate (in the probabilistic sense).[24] This asymptotic result may be used as the basis for an approximation to the distribution of replace-

[23] A summary of research on the lifetimes of capital equipment as given by A. Marston, R. Winfrey, and J. C. Hempstead, *Engineering Evaluation and Depreciation,* 2nd ed., New York, 1953.

[24] For a statement of the basic theorem, see E. Parzen, *Stochastic Processes,* San Francisco, 1962, pp. 180–181.

ments; for any investment good, the stream of replacements eventually approaches a stream that would be generated by an exponential distribution of replacements. Accordingly, the exponential distribution may be used as an approximation to the distribution of replacements for the purpose of estimating the stream of replacements. A simple indirect test of the validity of this approximation has been carried out by Meyer and Kuh.[25] For any distribution of replacements except the exponential distribution, one would expect to observe an "echo effect" or bunching of replacements at lags corresponding to points of relatively high density in the conditional distributions of replacements for individual types of equipment. Meyer and Kuh report no evidence for such an effect.

To summarize, we consider a version of the neoclassical theory in which the objective of the firm is maximization of its present value. This may be derived from the objective of maximizing the utility of a consumption stream subject to a fixed set of production possibilities and to fixed current and future prices and interest rates. Since the choice of a production plan is entirely independent of the corresponding choice of a consumption stream, two individuals with different preferences among consumption streams will choose the same production plan. Secondly, we consider a description of technological possibilities in which output at each point of time depends on the flow of labor and capital services at that point of time, the flow of capital services is proportional to the stock of capital goods, and replacements are also proportional to the stock of capital goods. This description of technology is a specialization of the descriptions given by Malinvaud and by Fisher. The essential justification for this specialization is that the resulting theory of optimal capital accumulation is sufficiently broad to include the principal econometric models of investment behavior as special cases.

3. Optimal Capital Accumulation

To develop the theory of investment behavior in more detail, we must first define the present value of the firm. For simplicity, we limit the analysis to a production process with a single output, a single variable input, and a single capital input. Where Q, L, and I represent levels of output, variable input, and investment in durable goods and p, w, and q represent the corresponding prices, the flow of net receipts at time t, say $R(t)$, is given by:

$$R(t) = p(t)Q(t) - w(t)L(t) - q(t)I(t). \tag{1}$$

[25] Meyer and Kuh, *Investment Decision*, pp. 91–94.

Present value is defined as the integral of discounted net receipts; where $r(s)$ is the rate of time discount at time s, net worth (W) is given by the expression:

$$W = \int_0^\infty e^{-\int_0^t r(s)\ ds} R(t)\ dt. \tag{2}$$

For purposes of the following discussion, we may assume that the time rate of discount is a constant without loss of generality. Accordingly, the present value of the firm may be represented in the simpler form:

$$W = \int_0^\infty e^{-rt} R(t)\ dt.$$

Present value is maximized subject to two constraints. First, the rate of change of the flow of capital services is proportional to the flow of net investment. The constant of proportionality may be interpreted as the time rate of utilization of capital stock, that is, the number of units of capital service per unit of capital stock. We will assume that capital stock is fully utilized so that this constant may be taken to be unity. Net investment is equal to total investment less replacement; where replacement is proportional to capital stock, this constraint takes the form:

$$\dot{K}(t) = I(t) - \delta K(t) \tag{3}$$

where $\dot{K}(t)$ is the time rate of change of the flow of capital services at time t. This constraint holds at each point of time so that $\dot{K}, K$, and I are functions of time; to simplify notation, we will use K in place of $K(t)$, I in place of $I(t)$, and so on. Secondly, levels of output and levels of labor and capital services are constrained by a production function:

$$F(Q, L, K) = 0. \tag{4}$$

We assume that the production function is twice differentiable with positive marginal rates of substitution between inputs and positive marginal productivities of both inputs. Furthermore, we assume that the production function is strictly convex.

To maximize present value (2) subject to the constraints (3) and (4), we consider the Lagrangian expression:

$$\mathcal{L} = \int_0^\infty [e^{-rt}R(t) + \lambda_0(t)F(Q, L, K) + \lambda_1(t)(\dot{K} - I + \delta K)]\ dt, \tag{5}$$

$$= \int_0^\infty f(t)\ dt,$$

where:

$$f(t) = e^{-rt}R(t) + \lambda_0(t)F(Q, L, K) + \lambda_1(t)(\dot{K} - I + \delta K).$$

The Euler necessary conditions for a maximum of present value subject to the constraints (3) and (4) are:

$$\frac{\partial f}{\partial Q} = e^{-rt}p + \lambda_0(t)\frac{\partial F}{\partial Q} = 0, \tag{6}$$

$$\frac{\partial f}{\partial L} = -e^{-rt}w + \lambda_0(t)\frac{\partial F}{\partial L} = 0,$$

$$\frac{\partial f}{\partial I} = -e^{-rt}q - \lambda_1(t) = 0,$$

$$\frac{\partial f}{\partial K} - \frac{d}{dt}\frac{\partial f}{\partial \dot{K}} = \lambda_0(t)\frac{\partial F}{\partial \dot{K}} + \delta\lambda_1(t) - \frac{d}{dt}\lambda_1(t) = 0,$$

and also:

$$\frac{\partial f}{\partial \lambda_0} = F(Q, L, K) = 0, \tag{7}$$

$$\frac{\partial f}{\partial \lambda_1} = \dot{K} - I + \delta K = 0.$$

Combining the necessary conditions for labor and output, we obtain the marginal productivity condition for labor services:

$$\frac{\partial Q}{\partial L} = \frac{w}{p}. \tag{8}$$

Of course, output, labor, wages, and prices are all functions of time. The difference between this marginal productivity condition and the corresponding condition of the "static" theory of the firm is that condition (8) holds at every point of time over the indefinite future whereas the marginal productivity condition of the "static" theory of the firm holds only at a single point in time. A similar marginal productivity condition for capital services may be derived. First, solving the necessary conditions (6) for $\lambda_1(t)$:

$$\lambda_1(t) = -e^{-rt}q,$$

the necessary condition for capital services may be written:

$$\lambda_0(t)\frac{\partial F}{\partial K} - \delta e^{-rt}q - re^{-rt}q + e^{-rt}\dot{q} = 0.$$

Combining this condition with the necessary condition for output, we obtain the marginal productivity condition for capital services:

$$\frac{\partial Q}{\partial K} = \frac{q(r + \delta) - \dot{q}}{p} = \frac{c}{p}, \tag{9}$$

where:

$$c = q(r + \delta) - \dot{q}. \tag{10}$$

Again, output, capital, prices, and the rate of time discount are functions of time so that these conditions hold at every point of time over the indefinite future.

Expression (10) defines the implicit rental value of capital services supplied by the firm to itself. This interpretation of the price $c(t)$ may be justified by considering the relationship between the price of capital goods and the price of capital services. First, the flow of capital services over an interval of length dt beginning at time t from a unit of investment goods acquired at time s is:

$$e^{-\delta(t-s)} \, dt.$$

If $c(t)$ is the price of capital services at time t, then the discounted price of capital services is $e^{-rt}c(t)$, so that the value of the stream of capital services on the interval dt is:

$$e^{-rt}c(t)e^{-\delta(t-s)} \, dt.$$

Similarly, if $q(s)$ is the price of capital goods at time s, then the discounted price of capital goods is $e^{-rs}q(s)$, so that the value of a unit of investment goods acquired at time s is:

$$e^{-rs}q(s).$$

But the value of investment goods acquired at time s is equal to the integral of the discounted value of all future capital services derived from these investment goods:

$$e^{-rs}q(s) = \int_{s}^{\infty} e^{-rt}c(t)e^{-\delta(t-s)} \, dt,$$

$$= e^{\delta s} \int_{s}^{\infty} e^{-(r+\delta)t}c(t) \, dt.$$

Solving for the price of capital goods, we obtain:

$$q(s) = e^{(r+\delta)s} \int_s^\infty e^{-(r+\delta)t} c(t)\, dt,$$

$$= \int_s^\infty e^{-(r+\delta)(t-s)} c(t)\, dt.$$

To obtain the price of capital services implicit in this expression, we differentiate with respect to time:

$$\dot{q}(s) = [r(s) + \delta]q(s) - c(s),$$

so that:

$$c = q(r + \delta) - \dot{q},$$

which is expression (10) given above for the implicit rental value of capital services.

The conditions describing the neoclassical model of optimal capital accumulation may also be derived by maximization of the integral of discounted profits, where profit at each point of time, say, $P(t)$, is given by:

$$P(t) = p(t)Q(t) - w(t)L(t) - c(t)K(t). \tag{11}$$

The integral of discounted profits, say, W^+, is given by the expression:

$$W^+ = \int_0^\infty e^{-rt} P(t)\, dt. \tag{12}$$

The side condition for investment may be disregarded, since investment does not enter into the definition of profit (11); substituting the side condition for the shadow price of capital services into the profit function, we obtain:

$$W^+ = \int_0^\infty e^{-rt}[p(t)Q(t) - w(t)L(t) - \{q(t)[r(t) + \delta] - \dot{q}(t)\}K(t)]\, dt.$$

To maximize this function subject to the production function, it suffices to maximize profit at each point of time subject to the production function. But this yields the marginal productivity conditions (8) and (9) and the production function (4) itself. Reintroducing the side conditions (3) and (10), we obtain the complete neoclassical model of optimal capital accumulation.

The integral of discounted profits is not the same as the integral defining present value of the firm. The difference between the two is given by:

$$W - W^+ = \int_0^\infty e^{-rt}[R(t) - P(t)] \, dt$$

$$= \int_0^\infty e^{-rt}[\{q(t)[r(t) + \delta] - \dot{q}(t)\}K(t) - q(t)I(t)] \, dt$$

$$= \int_0^\infty e^{-rt}[q(t)\delta K(t) + q(t)r(t)K(t) - \dot{q}(t)K(t) - q(t)\dot{K}(t)$$

$$- q(t)\delta K(t)] \, dt$$

$$= q(0)K(0),$$

which is the value of capital stock on hand at the initial point of time. The present value of the firm is the sum of the integral of discounted profits and the market value of the assets of the firm. Since the market value of the assets of the firm is fixed, maximization of the integral of discounted profits results in the same path for accumulation of capital as maximization of present value of the firm. To summarize, the neo-classical model of optimal capital accumulation may be derived by maximizing present value of the firm, by maximizing the integral of discounted profits of the firm, or simply by maximizing profit at each point of time.

In taking maximization of profit as the objective of the firm, profit is defined in a special sense, namely, net receipts on current account less the implicit rental value of capital services. This concept of profit would agree with the usual accounting definition of profit only in rather unusual circumstances, for example, where the firm actually rents all the capital services it employs. The price of capital services is then a market price and the rental value of the services is an actual outlay. Where the firm supplies capital services to itself, the implicit rental value of capital services $c(t)$ is a shadow price which may be used by the firm in the computation of an optimal path for capital accumulation. For optimal capital accumulation, the firm should charge itself a price for capital services equal to the implicit rental value and should then maximize profit at each point of time in the usual way. It is very important to note that the conditions determining the values of each of the variables to be chosen by the firm—output, labor input, and investment in capital goods—depend only on prices, the rate of interest, and the rate of change of the price of capital goods for the current period. Accordingly, in the neoclassical theory of optimal capital accumulation, the firm behaves at each point of time as in the "static" theory of the firm, provided that the price of capital services is taken to be equal to the corresponding implicit rental value. Of course, in the "static" theory the marginal productivity condition (9) holds only at a single point in time.

The complete neoclassical model of optimal capital accumulation consists of the production function (4) and the two marginal productivity conditions (8) and (9):

$$F(Q, K, L) = 0, \quad \frac{\partial Q}{\partial L} = \frac{w}{p}, \quad \frac{\partial Q}{\partial K} = \frac{c}{p},$$

and the two side conditions (3) and (10):

$$I = \dot{K} + \delta K,$$

$$c = q(r + \delta) - \dot{q}.$$

The production function and marginal productivity conditions hold at each point of time. The side conditions are differential equations also holding at each point of time. Combined, these conditions determine the levels of output, labor input, and capital input, together with the level of investment and the shadow price for capital services.

The interpretation of condition (3) determining the level of investment is the source of some difficulty in the literature. If the level of investment is bounded, the derivative of the level of capital services must be bounded. But this implies that the level of capital services itself must be continuous. Since we have assumed that the production function is twice differentiable, a sufficient condition for continuity of the level of capital services is continuity of the prices—*w, p, c.*

One interpretation of condition (3) is that the initial value of the level of capital services may be chosen arbitrarily. This interpretation has been suggested by Haavelmo and by Arrow.[26] If the initial level of capital services is derived from the production function and the marginal productivity conditions and if the initial value of capital is fixed arbitrarily, optimal capital accumulation may require an unbounded initial level of investment. In management science, this interpretation of the problem may be of some interest, though even there the interpretation seems somewhat forced, as Arrow points out.[27] For empirical work this interpretation is completely artificial since firms are viewed as making new decisions to invest continuously over time. To maximize present value at each point of time, a firm following an optimal path for capital accumulation must maximize present value subject to the initial condi-

[26] Haavelmo, *Theory of Investment,* pp. 162–165. Arrow, "Optimal Capital Adjustment," in *Studies in Applied Probability,* p. 2.

[27] *Ibid.,* p. 6, fn. 1.

tion given by the optimal path up to that point. But this results in a new optimal path which is precisely the same as the old from that point forward. Accordingly, if the optimal path for capital accumulation is continuous, the initial value of the level of capital services may not be chosen arbitrarily in the maximization of the present value of the firm. At each point it is precisely that for which the initial level of investment is bounded, namely, the level of capital services derived from the production function and the marginal productivity conditions. A possible objection to this view is that firms must begin to accumulate capital at some point in time. But at such a point the initial level of capital services is not given arbitrarily; the initial level must be zero with a positive derivative.

4. The Theory of Investment Behavior

Beginning with the neoclassical model of optimal capital accumulation, we may derive differentiable demand functions for labor and capital services and a differentiable supply function for output, say:

$$L = L(w, c, p), \tag{13}$$

$$K = K(w, c, p),$$

$$Q = Q(w, c, p).$$

The problem of deriving the demand for investment goods as a function of the rate of interest is a subtle one. Haavelmo expresses the view that the demand for investment goods cannot be derived from the profit-maximizing theory of the firm. This is a consequence of his interpretation of the demand function for capital services and condition (3) determining the level of investment from replacement and the rate of change of demand for capital services. According to this interpretation, finite variations in the rate of interest with all other prices held constant result in finite changes in the demand for capital services. As the rate of interest varies, demand for investment goods assumes only three possible values—negatively infinite, positively infinite, or the value obtained where the initial level of capital services is precisely equal to the demand for capital services. Investment demand has a finite value for only one rate of interest. In this interpretation, the demand function for capital services is analyzed by means of comparative statics, that is, by comparing alternative production plans at a given point of time. Any attempt to derive the demand for investment goods as a function of the rate of interest by such comparisons leads to nonsensical results, as Haavelmo correctly points out.

However, an alternative interpretation of the demand function for capital services and condition (3) determining the level of investment is possible. Under the hypothesis that the firm is following an optimal path for capital accumulation and that the optimal path is continuous, the initial level of capital is always equal to the demand for capital services. By imposing this condition at the outset, the demand for investment goods as a function of the rate of interest at any point of time may be analyzed by means of comparative dynamics, that is, by comparing alternative paths of capital accumulation, each identical up to that point of time and each continuous at that point. The demand for investment goods is given by condition (3):

$$I = \dot{K} + \delta K,$$

where the level of capital services, *K,* is fixed; but from the demand function for capital services (13), this condition implies that for fixed values of the price of output and the price of labor services, the implicit price of capital services must remain unchanged. Holding the price of investment goods constant, the rate of change of the price of investment goods must vary as the rate of interest varies so as to leave the implicit price of capital services unchanged. Formally, the condition that variations in the rate of interest leave the implicit price of capital services unchanged may be represented as:

$$\frac{\partial c}{\partial r} = 0;$$

holding the price of investment goods constant, this condition implies that the own-rate of interest on investment goods, $r - \dot{q}/q$, must be left unchanged by variations in the rate of interest.

We assume that all changes in the rate of interest are precisely compensated by changes in the rate of change of the price of current and future investment goods so as to leave the own-rate of interest on investment goods unchanged. Under this condition the discounted value of all future capital services, which is equal to the current price of investment goods, is left unchanged by variations in the time path of the rate of interest. The condition that the time path of the own-rate of interest on investment goods is left unchanged by a change in the time path of the rate of interest implies that forward prices or discounted future prices of both investment goods and capital services are left unchanged by variations in the rate of interest. For a constant rate of interest, this condition may be represented in the form:

$$\frac{\partial^2 e^{-rt} c(t)}{\partial r \partial t} = 0.$$

Like the previous condition, this condition holds at every point of time.

To derive the demand for investment goods as a function of the rate of interest, we first differentiate the demand for capital services with respect to time, obtaining:

$$\dot{K} = \frac{\partial K}{\partial w} \cdot \frac{\partial w}{\partial t} + \frac{\partial K}{\partial c} \cdot \frac{\partial c}{\partial t} + \frac{\partial K}{\partial p} \cdot \frac{\partial p}{\partial t}.$$

For simplicity, we consider only the case in which $\dfrac{\partial w}{\partial t} = \dfrac{\partial p}{\partial t} = 0$, that is, the price of output and the price of labor services are not changed. In this case, we obtain:

$$\dot{K} = \frac{\partial K}{\partial c} \cdot \frac{\partial c}{\partial t}.$$

Differentiating the implicit price of capital services with respect to time, we have:

$$\frac{\partial c}{\partial t} = \frac{\partial q}{\partial t}(\delta + r) + q\frac{\partial r}{\partial t} - \frac{\partial^2 q}{\partial t^2}. \tag{14}$$

To derive the demand for investment goods, we combine expression (14) for the rate of change of capital services with condition (3) for the rate of investment, obtaining:

$$I = \frac{\partial K}{\partial c}\left[\frac{\partial q}{\partial t}(\delta + r) + q\frac{\partial r}{\partial t} - \frac{\partial^2 q}{\partial t^2}\right] + \delta K,$$

which depends on the rate of interest and the price of investment goods through the rate of change of capital services. Differentiating this investment demand function with respect to the rate of interest, we obtain:

$$\frac{\partial I}{\partial r} = \frac{\partial^2 K}{\partial c^2} \cdot \frac{\partial c}{\partial r} \cdot \frac{\partial c}{\partial t} + \frac{\partial K}{\partial c}\frac{\partial^2 c}{\partial t \partial r} + \delta\frac{\partial K}{\partial c} \cdot \frac{\partial c}{\partial r}.$$

But $\dfrac{\partial c}{\partial r} = 0$, since changes in the rate of interest are compensated by changes in the rate of change of the price of investment goods so as to leave the implicit price of capital services unchanged. This condition implies that:

$$\frac{\partial^2 q}{\partial t \partial r} = q.$$

Secondly, $\dfrac{\partial^2 e^{-rt} c(t)}{\partial r \partial t} = 0$, since changes in the time path of the rate of interest leave the time path of forward or discounted prices of capital services unchanged. This condition implies that:

$$\frac{\partial^2 c}{\partial t \partial r} = c.$$

Combining these two conditions, we obtain:

$$\frac{\partial I}{\partial r} = \frac{\partial K}{\partial c} \cdot c < 0,$$

so that the demand for investment goods is a decreasing function of the rate of interest.

We conclude that it is possible to derive the demand for investment goods as a function of the rate of interest on the basis of purely neoclassical considerations. However, the demand for investment goods depends on the rate of interest through a comparison of alternative paths of capital accumulation, each continuous and each depending on a time path of the rate of interest. Although this conclusion appears to be the reverse of that reached by Haavelmo, his approach to the demand for investment goods is through comparative statics, that is, through comparison of alternative production plans at a given point of time. The demand function for investment goods cannot be derived by means of such comparisons. As a proposition in comparative statics, any relation between variations in the rate of investment and changes in the rate of interest is nonsensical.

To summarize, the complete neoclassical model of optimal capital accumulation consists of the production function (4), the two marginal productivity conditions (8) and (9), and the side condition (10). An alternative form of this model consists of the demand functions for capital and labor services, the supply function for output:

$$L = L(w, c, p),$$

$$K = K(w, c, p),$$

$$Q = Q(w, c, p);$$

and the demand function for investment goods:

$$I = \frac{\partial K}{\partial c}\frac{\partial c}{\partial t} + \delta K,$$

$$= I\left(w, c, p, \frac{\partial c}{\partial t}\right).$$

The demand for investment goods depends on the change in the demand for capital with respect to a change in the implicit price of capital services, the time rate of change in the price of capital services, and the level of replacement demand. Where the time rates of change of the price of labor services and the price of output are not zero, the demand function for investment goods may be rewritten:

$$I = \frac{\partial K}{\partial w}\frac{\partial w}{\partial t} + \frac{\partial K}{\partial c}\frac{\partial c}{\partial t} + \frac{\partial K}{\partial p}\cdot\frac{\partial p}{\partial t} + \delta K,$$

$$= I\left(w, c, p, \frac{\partial w}{\partial t}, \frac{\partial c}{\partial t}, \frac{\partial p}{\partial t}\right).$$

5. Alternative Theories of Investment Behavior

The neoclassical theory of demand for investment goods just outlined may be contrasted with the theory current in the literature. Most recent accounts of the theory of demand for investment are based on Keynes' *General Theory,* in which the criterion for optimal investment behavior is that any project with an internal rate of return greater than the ruling rate of interest is undertaken.[28] An investment demand schedule is constructed by varying the rate of interest and plotting the quantities of investment undertaken for each value of the rate of interest. The criterion for optimal investment behavior used by Keynes is inconsistent with maximization of the present value of the firm, as Alchian and Hirshleifer have pointed out.[29] Nevertheless, a substantial portion of the current literature on the investment demand function is based on a straightforward reproduction of Keynes' derivation. Alchian lists a number of examples from the literature prior to 1955; examples from the

---

[28] Chapter 11, "The Marginal Efficiency of Capital," especially p. 136.

[29] A. A. Alchian, "The Rate of Interest, Fisher's Rate of Return over Costs and Keynes' Internal Rate of Return," in *Management of Corporate Capital,* p. 70; and J. Hirshleifer, in *ibid.,* pp. 222–227. This conclusion of Alchian and Hirshleifer contradicts the position taken by Klein in *The Keynesian Revolution.*

current literature are provided by the recent work of Duesenberry and Tarshis.[30] Keynes' construction of the demand function for investment must be dismissed as inconsistent with the neoclassical theory of optimal capital accumulation.

An alternative construction of the demand function for investment goods has been suggested by Fisher.[31] In Fisher's theory any project with positive present value is undertaken. Keynes appears to have identified his construction of the marginal efficiency of capital schedule with that of Fisher, as Alchian points out.[32] There are two difficulties with Fisher's construction. First, the construction is carried out by means of comparative statics so that the resulting schedule may be interpreted as a theory of demand for capital services for which no demand function for investment goods exists. Second, the construction is not internally consistent in a second sense pointed out by Alchian, since ". . . we cannot in full logical consistency draw up a demand curve for investment by varying only the rate of interest (holding all other prices in the impound of *ceteris paribus*)."[33] The relevant prices are forward prices of all commodities; but altering the rate of interest amounts to altering certain forward prices. It is inconsistent to vary the rate of interest while holding such prices fixed. This inconsistency may be eliminated by stipulating that variations in the rate of interest must be precisely compensated by changes in the time rate of change of the price of investment goods. The price of investment goods at a given point of time is held fixed; the rate of change of the price of investment goods varies with the rate of interest. The construction of the demand function for investment goods involves a comparison among alternative paths of optimal capital accumulation; all paths are identical up to the point of time for which the investment function is constructed. Such a theory of investment behavior is internally consistent and may be derived by means of comparative dynamics.

Klein has attempted to derive a demand function for investment goods on the basis of profit maximization. His treatment, though suggestive, is

[30] J. S. Duesenberry, *Business Cycles and Economic Growth,* New York, 1958, pp. 49–85. Duesenberry asserts that Keynes' derivation is based on "profit maximization" (p. 85). L. Tarshis, "The Marginal Efficiency Function," *American Economic Review,* December 1961, pp. 958–985. Tarshis asserts that the Keynesian theory is based on that of the "profit-maximizing firm" (pp. 958–959).

[31] Fisher, *Theory of Interest,* pp. 159–176.

[32] Alchian, in *Management of Corporate Capital,* p. 67. Klein (*Keynesian Revolution,* p. 62) follows Keynes in identifying these two distinct approaches to the construction of the marginal efficiency schedule.

[33] Alchian, *Management of Corporate Capital,* p. 71.

marred by a number of inconsistencies. In his first attempt, the stock of investment goods is defined as the integral of past flows of investment, but the flow of investment is employed as a stock in the production function and in the definition of "discounted profit."[34] A second attempt involves the identification of the flow of capital services with the flow of depreciation.[35] In both attempts, quantities measured as rates of capital service per unit of time are added to quantities measured as rates of investment per unit of time, which is self-contradictory. This inconsistency carries over to the empirical implementation of the resulting investment function, where the price of investment goods is identified with the price of capital services.[36] An internally consistent treatment of the theory of investment along the lines suggested by Klein leads to a comparative statics theory of demand for capital services in which no demand function for investment goods exists.

Another branch of the current literature is based on the view that no demand function for investment goods exists. We have already cited Haavelmo's support of this position. A similar view may be found in Lerner's *Economics of Control*. Lerner argues that, under diminishing returns, the firm has a downward sloping demand curve for capital services but that, except where there is no net investment, the rate of investment is unbounded:[37]

. . . there is no limit to the rate per unit of time at which [the individual] can acquire assets by buying them, borrowing money for the purpose if he has not enough of his own. This indefinitely great rate of "investment" means that he can move at once to the position . . . which makes the (private) marginal productivity of capital equal to the rate of interest. Once he gets there, there is no tendency for further expansion. . . .

This view is the same as that expressed by Haavelmo. A recent restatement of this position has been given by Witte, who concludes, with Lerner and Haavelmo, that ". . . the continuous function relating the rate of investment to the rate of interest at the micro level has no foundation in the ordinary theory of the firm."[38] We have demon-

---

[34] Klein, *Keynesian Revolution,* esp. pp. 196–199.

[35] Klein, in *Kyklos,* Vol. 2, fasc. 2, 1948, pp. 97–117; and his *Economic Fluctuations.*

[36] *Ibid.* The price of investment goods (p. 21 and p. 85) is identified with the price of capital services (p. 15).

[37] A. P. Lerner, *The Economics of Control,* esp. pp. 330–338.

[38] James G. Witte, Jr., "The Microfoundations of the Social Investment Function," *Journal of Political Economy,* October 1963, pp. 441–456.

strated that it is possible to derive the demand for investment goods from the comparative dynamics applied to the ordinary neoclassical theory of the firm. The conclusion reached by Haavelmo, Lerner, and Witte concerning a demand function for investment goods derived on the basis of comparative statics is, of course, correct.

An attempt has been made by proponents of the view that the demand function for investment goods does not exist to rehabilitate the Keynesian marginal efficiency of investment schedule. Alternative versions of this rehabilitation are presented by Haavelmo, Lerner, and Witte.[39] The essentials of the argument are that, at a given rate of interest, a certain price for investment goods is required to equate the marginal productivity of capital with the implicit price of capital services; but the higher this price the lower the rate of interest, so that a rising supply curve for investment goods implies that the amount of investment goods produced will increase as the rate of interest falls. A fundamental difficulty with this view is that it fails to account for the purchase of new investment goods by the users of capital equipment.[40] Witte summarizes this consequence of the view as follows: ". . . the rate-of-investment decision is the rate-of-output decision of supplying enterprises and not the rate-of-input decision of capital-using firms."[41] In the same vein Haavelmo writes, ". . . it is, actually, not the users of capital who demand investment, it is the producers of capital goods who determine how much they want to produce at the current price of capital."[42] A further attempt along these lines of the rehabilitation of the Keynesian marginal efficiency of investment schedule has been presented by Clower.[43] His argument follows that of Haavelmo, Lerner, and Witte in assuming that demand for capital services is equal to supply. However, Clower intro-

[39] Haavelmo, *Theory of Investment*, pp. 194–197. See also: B. Thalberg, "An Analysis of a Market for Investment Goods," in Lutz and Hague, *Theory of Capital*, pp. 161–176, and "A Keynesian Model Extended by Explicit Demand and Supply Functions for Investment Goods," in *Stockholm Economic Studies*, Pamphlet Series, No. 3, 1964. Lerner, *Economics of Control*, pp. 333–334. Witte, in *Journal of Political Economy*, October 1963, pp. 445–447.

[40] A second difficulty with this view is that an increase in the price of investment goods may result in a rise or a fall in the supply of investment goods, depending on the relative capital intensity of the investment goods and consumption goods industries. Lerner, for example, assumes implicitly that investment goods are produced with no capital services. This difficulty was pointed out to me by James Tobin.

[41] *Ibid.*, p. 448.

[42] Haavelmo, *Theory of Investment*, p. 196.

[43] R. W. Clower, "An Investigation into the Dynamics of Investment," *American Economic Review*, March 1954, pp. 64–81.

duces a demand for investment goods which is not necessarily equal to the supply of investment goods. The excess or deficiency of demand over supply is net accumulation of capital. This view also fails to account for the purchases of new investment goods by the users of capital equipment.

For internal consistency, the rehabilitation of the Keynesian marginal efficiency of investment schedule requires either a changing rate of interest, as suggested by Haavelmo, or a changing price of capital goods, as suggested by Lerner.[44] For if the rate of interest and the price of investment goods are fixed over time and the marginal productivity of capital is equal to the implicit price of capital services, the firm's demand for investment is determinate; this demand is precisely equal to replacement demand so that net investment is zero. Under these circumstances, the rate of investment demand by users of capital equipment is independent of the rate of interest so that the price of investment goods must be that at which this rate of investment will be supplied by investment goods producers. But then if the marginal productivity of capital is to be equal to the implicit price for capital services, the rate of interest is uniquely determined, which is inconsistent with variations in the rate of interest from whatever source.

To complete the rehabilitation of the Keynesian marginal efficiency of investment schedule, interpreted as the level of investment resulting from a market equilibrium in investment goods corresponding to a given rate of interest, market equilibrium must be studied in a fully dynamic setting. The demand for investment goods must be derived from a comparison among alternative paths of optimal capital accumulation. It remains to be seen whether such a rehabilitation can be carried out in an internally consistent way.

[44] Haavelmo, *Theory of Investment,* p. 196. Lerner, *Economics of Control,* diagram, p. 336.

COMMENT

On Crockett-Friend and Jorgenson

BY JAMES TOBIN, YALE UNIVERSITY

I agree with Jorgenson's general defense of the neoclassical theory of the firm. As he says, its usefulness is by no means confined to static conditions. As long as expectations are assumed certain, maximization of the present value of the firm is as powerful a principle for dynamic theory as profit maximization has been for static theory. A dynamic theory based on this principle has much more to say, and can handle many more complexities, than is often appreciated.

Jorgenson's specific example, however, is only barely dynamic. His firm can maximize present value simply by maximizing profits at every point in time. The firm confronts no intertemporal trade-offs, in which profits now must be weighed against profits later. It purchases capital *services* at a market rental, just as it purchases labor at a market wage. There is a perfect market in capital goods; capital is homogeneous in quality regardless of its vintage; and capital evaporates exponentially, so that future depreciation is also independent of vintage. Thus, any surviving capital can always be sold at the prevailing price of new capital goods. Therefore if, as Jorgenson assumes, the rental of capital services correctly reflects interest, depreciation, and the change in price of capital goods, the firm will be indifferent in choosing between renting and owning. The present value of such future rentals just equals the current price of capital goods.

I would like to make a parenthetical semantic remark: Jorgenson calls the rental just discussed, specifically $q(r + \delta - \dot{q}/q)$, user cost. To anyone who learned about user cost from the appendix to Chapter 6 of Keynes' *General Theory*, this terminology seems surprising. Keynes assumed that the decline in the value of a stock of goods during a period depends on the intensity of use, not just on the passage of time, hence the term *user* cost. Keynes' assumption is notably absent from most modern capital theory, including Jorgenson's. I find it confusing to see a rental which is just a time or ownership cost called user cost.

By assuming diminishing returns to scale, Jorgenson makes the size of his firm determinate within the framework of pure competition and certain expectations. However, the sale of the services of owned capital is an activity with constant returns to scale, and in Jorgenson's world of perfect competition and perfect knowledge, the scale of ownership by any one individual is indeterminate.

Given the time path of the price of the product p, the wage rate w, and the rental on capital c, Jorgenson's firm decides upon the paths of output Q, employment L, and use of capital services K. Indeed, these paths will simply maximize profits $pQ - wL - cK$ at each point in time, subject to the production function. If the time paths of p, w, and c are continuous, then so are the paths of Q, L, and K.

However, as Jorgenson points out, there is no reason to assume that markets will never present an individual firm with jumps in p, w, and c. If they do so, the firm's profit-maximizing response involves jumps in Q, L, and K. In Jorgenson's firm there are no frictions or speed-of-adjustment costs to make profitable any delay at all in responding to new conditions.

Many economists—Jorgenson cites Haavelmo and Lerner—have concluded that such an individual firm has no demand schedule for *net investment* $\dot{K}$ but only a demand schedule for capital K. These theorists think that if conditions change the optimal rate of use of capital services, the firm will immediately shift to the new optimum—by renting more or less capital or by buying or selling capital goods. This is not a surprising conclusion. It is the use of capital services, proportional to the stock not to the flow, which is related to the determining prices. Similarly, the firm has a demand schedule for labor services, not for their rate of change. No one is dismayed that a frictionless firm is expected to shift in no time from one employment level to another.

The investment demand schedule which these economists have sought and not found is a relationship at a given point in time t_0 between investment $\dot{K}(t_0)$ (or $\dot{K}(t_0) + \delta K(t_0)$) at that time and the rate of interest $r(t_0)$, *holding constant all other current and expected prices*. This is the marginal efficiency schedule which Keynes purported to draw at the aggregate level, which Lerner and Haavelmo doubted existed for an individual firm, which Lerner tried to justify on macroeconomic grounds. Now varying $r(t_0)$ to the individual firm, holding all other relevant prices constant, is bound to cause the break-even rental $c(t_0)$ to vary also. Indeed all hypothetical values of $r(t_0)$ except one involve a jump at t_0 in the optimal $K(t)$. Moreover, one cannot escape the conclusion that, except for the one value of $r(t_0)$ which keeps $c(t_0)$ adjusted to the existing capital stock, $\dot{K}(t_0)$ must be either $+\infty$ or $-\infty$.

Jorgenson does not escape this conclusion either, but by asking a different question he arrives at what he identifies as an investment demand schedule. He does not hold all other prices, present and future, constant while he varies $r(t_0)$. Instead he compensates the variation of $r(t_0)$ by changes in present and future $q(t)$ so that $c(t_0)$ remains the same.[1] Thus $K(t_0)$ is independent of these compensated variations in r, but the subsequent path $K(t)$ is not. And in particular $\dot{K}(t_0)$ will depend on r!

Maybe there is some question to which this is the answer, but it is not the question to which Jorgenson finds previous answers so unsatisfactory. There is no reason to assume that expected prices of capital goods accommodate themselves so obligingly to interest rate variations. Unless they do so, Jorgenson's investment demand schedule cannot serve the analytical purposes for which such a schedule is desired, and one must look elsewhere for a determinate theory of investment. At the level of a single firm, this may be derived from frictional or adjustment costs; at the level of the whole economy, it may be derived from capacity limitations on production of investment goods (although here Lerner's famous solution is, as Jorgenson points out, far from foolproof).

It would be desirable to have a neoclassical theory of consumer investment to place alongside the theory of business investment. In such a theory it would be necessary to state payoffs in utility rather than in money, to recognize imperfections in rental and second-hand markets, and to allow for true Keynesian user cost. A model of this kind would, I think, suggest some differences between real and financial investments by households which do not appear in the Crockett-Friend paper.

Their model is considerably less theoretical. In their view, each household has a desired total and composition of net worth, depending on its normal income and its tastes, and on the yields and risks of various assets and debts. Crockett and Friend explain flows of household investment and saving as a process of stock adjustment, without worrying with Jorgenson why adjustments should not be instantaneous.

While I am sympathetic to this approach to empirical data, I think the authors' formulation is too static. Not all flows should be interpreted simply as efforts to eliminate discrepancies between actual and desired stocks. Desired stocks change, and there would be nonzero flows even if the household were continuously in adjustment. Even for the same normal income, for example, a household's desired wealth will change in total and in composition with time and age. I suspect that reformulation along these lines might improve the authors' empirical estimates of adjustment speeds, which are so far rather unsatisfactory.

The main purposes of the Crockett-Friend project, of which this con-

---

[1] For example, if $\dot{q}(t)/q(t)$ is increased for all $t \geq t_0$ by the same amount as a once-and-for-all rise in r at t_0, then $c(t_0)$ is unchanged. Future $c(t)$ are increased, but since they are discounted more heavily their present value is still $q(t_0)$.

ference paper is a progress report, are to estimate normal income elasticities of demand for wealth and its components, and to estimate speeds of stock adjustment. The data are cross sections, and the authors rely especially on cross sections containing observations in the same households for more than one year.

A principal finding is that the ratio of net worth to normal income increases with wealth and income. Crockett and Friend suggest that this finding is inconsistent with saving theories which contend that "permanent" saving is a constant fraction of permanent income. However, their finding is relevant to this suggestion only when age is controlled. When net worth and normal income are compared across age groups, wealth will appear to have an income elasticity above one, even if saving does not. Crockett and Friend do try to control for age, but their age brackets are so broad as to leave the issue in doubt.

A potential test of great interest concerns households just retired or about to retire. If those which had enjoyed larger earned incomes had by this age accumulated relatively larger net worth, simple permanent income models that assume all saving is for retirement would be called into question. The Crockett-Friend findings for retired households do appear to be inconsistent with those models and to suggest an estate motive for saving. But these findings must be interpreted with caution because of the vagaries of "income" reporting for persons already retired.

Other problems in interpreting the apparent high income elasticity of demand for wealth arise from the possibilities that the net worth of high-income households may be disproportionately swollen by inheritances and unrealized capital gains.

In line with much recent work, Crockett and Friend devote considerable attention to the measurement of normal income free from transient components. They use two devices—averaging of several annual incomes reported for the household and averaging of incomes of members of an occupational group. Neither device adds appreciably to the explanatory power of two-year disposable income. However, calculations based on groupings which allow for age are yet to be reported. When this is done, it may be possible to use the age profile of income for people with a given occupation and education in computing their permanent incomes. In principle, normal income should be forward looking not backward looking.

So far the authors' calculations of speeds of adjustment are not very encouraging. It is scarcely surprising that total wealth at the end of 1961 is related to wealth two years earlier. It is disconcerting that wealth at the end of 1959 is not much help in explaining 1960-61 flows. With respect to individual assets, few stocks were available for use in the flow regressions, and these were used only in their "own" regressions.

Crockett and Friend are properly concerned with eliminating spurious relationships due to persistent differences among households in "tastes" —both general thriftiness and preferences for the services of particular consumer assets. As is well known, these differences can obscure stock-flow relationships in cross sections. The authors' device of classifying households by saving behavior in a year not used in the regression does not, on the whole, produce significant results. It would be better, as far as possible, to exploit the panel nature of the data to examine changes in the behavior of identical households.

The paper is a progress report on a large-scale empirical research project, and the main thing a discussant can do is to cheer the authors on their promising line of inquiry. Perhaps it is not too irreverent for this discussant, who has in the past labored in the same field, to remind the authors of the challenge to all of us presented by the near constancy of the aggregate ratio of household saving to disposable income in the U.S. since the Korean War. Have our detailed researches yet provided the forecaster and policy-maker with a better guide than the rule of thumb that 5 per cent of disposable income is saved? Will they give advance warning if and when this rule of thumb is breached? We should gear our research to these questions and not be satisfied with statistical explanations of household differences for their own sake.

On Crockett-Friend and Jorgenson

by zvi griliches, university of chicago

In the conventional approach, "theory" gives one the demand for capital as a level and comparative statistics tells how much capital stock will be demanded at different relative prices, but from neither can one derive a unique optimal adjustment path from one equilibrium position to another. There are two aspects to this position:

First, defining equilibrium as the stationary solution ($dk/dt = 0$) concedes the possibility that markets are out of equilibrium during the investment process. Given full adjustment to the previous situation, there is no positive net investment unless something (e.g., prices) *changes* and disrupts the previous equilibrium. In this sense, net investment is viewed as a disequilibrium phenomenon.

Second, without adding additional constraints on the possible range of adjustment or a concept of "cost of change," the instantaneous *rate* of investment could be infinite in response to a once-and-for-all shift in the exogenous variables.

Jorgenson's contribution, and it is an important one, is to show that under certain conditions, when prices are and have been changing smoothly, both problems need not arise and it is possible to derive a unique relationship between the rate of investment and the variables influencing it.

If things are continuously and smoothly changing, one may assume that the firm is always in equilibrium—that all marginal conditions are satisfied everywhere along the accumulation path. This allows one to define different paths of accumulation and associate comparative dynamic statements saying, e.g., that accumulations paths differing only in the level of the ruling rate of interest can be characterized by larger or smaller investment rates.

It should be pointed out, though, that the solution to these problems is achieved through a very severe restriction on the scope of the original question. In the Jorgenson model, one cannot answer the question of what happens to the rate of investment if the rate of interest or other prices *shift* to a new permanent level in one move or if a change occurs in depreciation rules. A discontinuous jump to a new accumulation path is not admissible. Since these are the types of questions that Haavelmo and others wanted to answer, solving a more restricted problem, while very useful, does not necessarily imply that they were wrong or that *their* problem has been solved.

The conventional position, having got as far as theory would carry it —to the demand for capital but not for investment, proceeded to "solve" the problem by introducing ad-hoc "partial adjustment," "cost of change," or "liquidity constraint" theories, which explained why and how a particular desired change in capital levels is spread out over a substantial period of time. The theoretical underpinnings of these additions were very weak, but they did force one immediately into a consideration of lags and of a larger list of possible variables, making the theory empirically much more promising and effective.

By limiting himself only to continuous changes, Jorgenson shows that this type of ad-hockery is redundant as far as the original problem is concerned. It can be solved in a smooth world within the original theoretical model without invoking various dubious lag hypotheses. But this may be an illusory gain. To be effective econometrically, the Jorgenson theory will also have to be broadened to include some lag or "cost of change" hypotheses. As of now, it implies that dk/dt (net investment) $= 0$, whenever wages, prices, or interest rates are constant, irrespective of their previous paths. Adding some lag hypothesis did solve the infinite derivative problem in the original model. Since some lag hypothesis will also be necessary in this model, it is not all that clear what will be the final contribution of solving the infinite derivative problem separately. It is clear, though, that the comparative dynamics apparatus developed by Jorgenson will prove very useful in future elaborations of this and similar models. A very important problem still remains unsolved, however: the form and determinants of the optimal adjustment path from one equilibrium position to another. We hope to be able one day to derive it as an implication of our theoretical model, instead of just tacking on something "reasonable" at the end. Showing that these lag hypotheses are not necessary to solve one problem (the derivation of an internally consistent investment function) does not make them any less important.

I have only a brief comment on the Crockett-Friend paper. Their theory should allow for a replacement component of saving, since their saving is gross saving (at least in some of its components). Thus, the coefficient of assets is equal to the difference between the rate of depreciation (replacement) and the rate of adjustment. This may explain why they get, on the face of it, such unreasonably low estimated rates of adjustment. One should add to these the appropriate average maintenance and replacement coefficient associated with the given level of assets.

ON JORGENSON

BY ROGER F. MILLER, UNIVERSITY OF WISCONSIN

Jorgenson's paper does a great deal to expose the misunderstandings at the heart of the controversy on whether or not an investment demand function is derivable from the neoclassical theory of the firm. In brief, the neoclassical theory contains a demand-for-capital-services function; to get capital services, the firm acquires capital assets (or another firm acquires them and rents them to the producing firm); and acquisition of additional capital assets is *defined* to be gross investment. The demand for investment is derived from the demand for capital assets, which in turn is derived from the demand for capital services. There are, thus, three demand functions involved, all intimately related, and either all exist or none exists. The existence of any one is unaffected by the fact that it may be a simple transformation of another in a simple model. Nor is it affected by the fact that it is a derived demand. Most demands *are* "derived"! It may be that there is little point to introducing the *concept* of investment in such a model, but this is a distinct objection unrelated to the controversy.

More consequential is the problem of the continuity and continuous differentiability of the demand-for-capital-assets function. At any point where this function is not continuously differentiable, the investment function becomes discontinuous. If the demand-for-capital-assets function is also discontinuous, the fact that the neoclassical model allows instantaneous adjustments has been interpreted as implying that the amount of investment at such a point is unbounded when expressed as a rate per instant of time. Jorgenson's paper adds nothing to the solution of this problem because he merely finesses the problem completely.

Following the apparent intent of the neoclassicists, Jorgenson makes adjustments instantaneous, and he also *imposes* continuity on the variables he discusses. In particular, his introduction of $\dot{K}(t)$ in (3) and its treatment in the present value maximizing exercise which follows is tantamount to assuming that $\dot{K}(t)$ is continuous and differentiable from the beginning. His later interpretation of condition (3) is less than helpful because it seems to imply that the assumed continuity is a result of the analysis. In condition (3) Jorgenson defines investment as "$I(t) = \dot{K}(t) + \delta K(t)$, where $\dot{K}(t)$ is the time rate of change of the flow of capital services at time t." If $\dot{K}(t)$ is not differentiable or is discontinuous at t, this is inappropriate because $\dot{K}(t)$ is undefined. Jorgenson has simply assumed that such occasions do not arise, and thus sheds no light on this aspect of the controversy.

Jorgenson's contribution is interesting and valuable in spite of his having finessed the unboundedness issue, to which I will return below. It is, however, unfortunate that Jorgenson muddied the waters by discussing, however briefly, the arguments and evidence for aggregate investment functions, which might be very closely approximated by continuous functions even if firm or plant investment functions are not, but which are at best very tenuously related to the microfunctions mentioned in the first paragraph above. Apart from this, I believe the Jorgenson paper is a worthwhile opposite extreme to the case of once-and-for-all adjustment where the capital stock for a given "firm" is a fixed amount.[1] In the latter case, it is clear that in determining the initial (and permanent) capital stock of a given plant, the amount of capital (and thus the amount of investment in *that* enterprise) is nega-

[1] See Vernon L. Smith, "The Theory of Investment and Production," *Quarterly Journal of Economics,* February 1959, and Roger F. Miller, "A Note on the Theory of Investment and Production," *Quarterly Journal of Economics,* November 1959.

tively related to the rate of interest and to the cost of capital assets.[2] Because this conclusion carries through in Jorgenson's instantaneous adjustment model, there is a strong presumption in favor of this relation holding for intermediate lagged adjustment cases.

While I welcome Jorgenson's explication of the neoclassical framework, I feel that one of his contributions is exposing the rather severe restrictions one must impose upon the model in order to deal with some of the important questions of concern to economists. I strongly doubt that the prominent neoclassicists, were they alive and well read today, would find much interest in a model which assumes away uncertainty with regard to the future, lags in adjustment, difficulties of aggregation and composition, discontinuities, etc. Jorgenson's analysis should help to bury this Caesar, as well as praise him.

I believe the day has passed when our analyses have surpassed our observational and computational capabilities. Jorgenson's introductory remarks are to the point. It is just because of this that I think it is unfortunate that Jorgenson chose to sidestep the unboundedness problem. I wish to make it clear that I am not concerned with the "realism" of the model, but with the domain of its application. For most purposes, it may be perfectly satisfactory to regard a fully continuous model as a sufficient approximation to our essentially discrete activities. I strongly suspect that not all purposes are served equally by this approximation, and that for investment timing for a particular firm or individual discontinuities may be of the essence. If this is so, the relevant discontinuities should be recognized and the model constructed so as to allow for them.[3] In the conference discussion it was pointed out that adoption of "period analysis" using discrete time intervals, or of a lagged adjustment function, represent two ways of avoiding the discontinuity problem. Neither of them is fully consistent with the instantaneous-adjustment full-equilibrium framework of the neoclassicists, however, and both merely sidestep the controversy in another dimension. Because both Jorgenson and the discussants thus leave the controversy in an unsatisfactory state, I should like to put forward a few comments and suggestions on dealing with nondifferentiability and discontinuity problems which I hope may resolve the present controversy and have much wider applicability as well.

As a preface to my suggestions, I feel it is necessary to point out that the concept of a function is independent of the concepts of differen-

---

[2] The result comes from finding $(\partial X_2/\partial r)$ and $(\partial X_2/\partial W_2)$ from (68) in Miller (*ibid.*, p. 678).

[3] This is, of course, one of the principal motivations of the model presented in the Miller-Watts paper included in this volume.

tiability, continuity, or boundedness, although the latter properties make functions more tractable to traditional mathematical manipulations. Thus, to say that the investment function is unbounded at any time for which the demand-for-capital-assets function is discontinuous does not imply that the investment function does not exist. However, it does raise questions as to the economic sense of the function as it is defined. We do a disservice to the science of economics (and to the discipline of mathematics as well) if we bind ourselves too rigidly to conventional and convenient mathematical formulations and definitions. I believe this is precisely the heart of the problem in this controversy: it is much ado about nothing, where the nothing in question is the time between t and t (i.e., $dt = 0$). In particular, there is a confusion between the instantaneous time rate of change of capital assets and the quantity of investment which takes place at any instant. The latter is clearly what we are interested in; the former is useful only if it leads to the latter.

Without loss of generality, the ensuing discussion is simplified and clarified by assuming that we have the following function for the quantity of capital assets demanded as a function of the continuous variable t over the interval from $t = 0$ to $t = 4$:

$$
\left.
\begin{array}{lll}
\text{(a)} & K(t) = 2.0t & \text{for } 0 \le t < 1. \\[4pt]
\text{(b)} & K(t) = 2.0 - 0.5(t - 1) & \text{for } 1 \le t < 2. \\[4pt]
\text{(c)} & K(t) = 4.0 + 0.2(t - 2) + 0.1(t - 2)^2 & \text{for } 2 \le t \le 4.
\end{array}
\right\} \quad \text{(I)}
$$

The units in which $K(t)$ is measured are whatever is appropriate for the way K is defined, say, tons of machinery. This yields the following diagram:

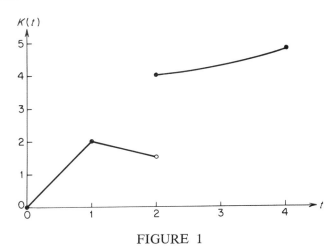

FIGURE 1

Clearly, the amount of net investment that has taken place over any finite interval of t between 0 and 4 is a finite and determinable quantity. This is true despite the fact that the instantaneous time rate of change of the stock of capital assets is unbounded at $t = 2$. For example, if $0 \leq \epsilon \leq 1$, then the cumulative amount of net investment that takes place over the interval from $(2 - \epsilon)$ to $(2 + \epsilon)$ is equal to $2.5 - 0.3\epsilon + 0.1\epsilon^2$ tons of machinery. This is simply derived by subtracting $K(2 - \epsilon)$ found in (b) from $K(2 + \epsilon)$ found in (c). As $\epsilon \to 0$, this converges on $I(2) = 2.5$, however, which understates the actual amount of investment taking place at $t = 2$.

To develop the correct formulation of the investment function which can be applied to demand-for-capital-assets functions of this type, it is convenient to start with Jorgenson's definition of gross investment at t:

$$I(t) = \delta K(t) + \dot{K}(t), \tag{3}$$

where δ is a positive fraction representing the quantity of capital assets which disappear through depreciation. This investment function serves perfectly well for any instant except $t = 1$ or $t = 2$ in our example above.

(a) $\dot{K}(t)$ is not defined at either of these critical values. The economic sense of this term, however, is the amount of additional K demanded to provide for immediate future production, so that we are only interested in the right-hand derivatives of $K(t)$ with respect to time. We may define such a right-hand derivative as $\lim_{\epsilon \to 0} [\dot{K}(t + \epsilon)]$ and substitute this for $\dot{K}(t)$ in the expression for $I(t)$, removing this difficulty.

(b) At $t = 2$ we face another difficulty with respect to depreciation. At any t, depreciation applies to the pre-existing stock of capital assets, not to the amount being newly acquired (otherwise $\delta K(t)$ would have to be included in (3) above as a third term). To capture this feature, consider $K(t - \epsilon)$ as a sequence and find $\lim_{\epsilon \to 0} [\delta K(t - \epsilon)]$ as a replacement for the first term in (3) above. At $t = 2$ this limit is 1.5δ, not 4.0δ.

(c) Finally, at $t = 2$ there is nothing in (3) to capture the instantaneous jump from $K = 1.5$ to $K = 4.0$. This can be remedied in the same manner as the depreciation technique by including in $I(t)$ the $\lim_{\epsilon \to 0} [K(t + \epsilon) - K(t - \epsilon)]$, which in our example is $4.0 - 1.5 = 2.5$.

The modifications of the preceding paragraph, plus the recognition that $K(t) \geq 0$, yield the following gross investment function:

(a) $I(t) = \lim_{\epsilon \to 0} \delta K(t - \epsilon) + \lim_{\epsilon \to 0} \dot{K}(t + \epsilon) + \lim_{\epsilon \to 0} [K(t + \epsilon) - K(t - \epsilon)]$

(b) $I(t) \geq \lim_{\epsilon \to 0} (\delta - 1)K(t - \epsilon),$

$$\left.\right\} \text{(II)}$$

where (IIb) overrides (IIa) in case of a conflict, and merely says that it is impossible to disinvest more capital than is available. Applied to our example, the gross investment function is, with arguments ordered as in (IIa) above:

(a) $I(t) = 2.0\delta t + 2.0 + 0.0$ for $0 \leq t < 1$

(b) $I(t) = \delta(2.5 - 0.5t) + (-0.5) + 0.0$ for $1 \leq t < 2$

(c) $I(t) = 1.5\delta + 0.2 + 2.5$ for $t = 2$

(d) $I(t) = \delta(4.0 - 0.2t + 0.1t^2) + (0.2t - 0.2) + 0.0$ for $2 < t \leq 4$

$$\text{(III)}$$

Notice that the third term is always zero except where $K(t)$ is discontinuous. The resulting diagram for *net* investment ($I(t)$ less depreciation) is:

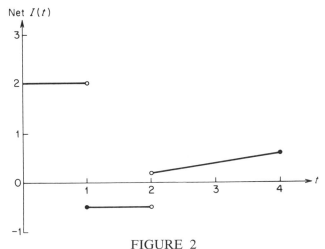

FIGURE 2

The "limiting" processes I have introduced above are simply rules for finding which numbers are the appropriate ones to enter into the function at a given t. As such, they are matters of definition and should not be confused with the distinct limiting process which is involved in defining a derivative.[4]

[4] Furthermore, the investment function defined in (II) is Stieltjes-integrable back to the demand-for-capital-assets function (given the appropriate constants of integration) if we assume that in the neighborhood of any point of nondifferentiability ($t = 1$) or discontinuity ($t = 2$) of the demand-for-capital-assets function there exists some interval including that point over which the function is continuous and differentiable. The relative unfamiliarity of Stieltjes-integration (as opposed to the more common Reimann-integral) is a mathematical, and not an economic, consideration.

The question remains in what units $I(t)$ is expressed. This is not a trivial question since it is not obvious that the third term has the same time dimensionality as the first two. The appearance of the terms in an equation can be deceptive, however, since any term can have a coefficient (necessarily equal to one and therefore not apparent) which is expressed in units appropriate to make the term have the desired units. In Jorgenson's formulation, since $\dot{K}(t)$ is a time derivative, it has (by itself) units of capital assets flowing per instant of time. If no other coefficient is added, $I(t)$ and all other terms must have the same units. This requires, for example, that δ be defined as the fraction of existing assets that disappear (flow away) per instant of time due to depreciation. Both terms, and the corresponding terms in my (IIa) and (IIb) above, represents an amount of capital assets per instant (e.g., tons of machinery per instant) such that, *if* continued at a constant level over the interval from t to $t + 1$, the total change in the stock of capital assets *would* exactly equal the sum of the terms in the equation. The third term in my formulation has exactly the same interpretation: it is the change in the stock of capital assets that takes the form of a discrete jump *at the instant t,* and is thus an instantaneous rate in the same sense as the other terms. In the example above, notice that the rate of net investment at $t = 2$ is 2.7. If that rate of net investment were to continue constant at that level over the interval from $t = 2$ to $t = 3$, the stock of capital assets would increase by precisely 2.7 tons of machinery (from 4.0 to 6.7), and the demand-for-capital-assets function (*if* that rate of net investment were maintained) would have to be modified accordingly to be:

$$K(t) = 4.0 + 2.7(t - 2) \text{ for } 2 \leq t \leq 3. \tag{Ic'}$$

In this case, of course, we would also have

$$\lim_{\epsilon \to 0} \dot{K}(t + \epsilon) = 2.7 \text{ for } 2 \leq t < 3.$$

I can see no mathematical or economic objections to the manner in which I have redefined the investment function. I would not have pursued it to this extent if I did not feel that the technique employed was sufficiently useful and unknown to make its exposition a useful contribution per se. In addition, it should lay to rest the unfortunate controversy over whether or not a sensible investment function is derivable from the neoclassical model of the firm. My investment function may not be so easy to manipulate as a continuous and differentiable one, but that is a small matter of mathematics and not a fundamental matter of economics. As redefined in this comment, the investment function frees us from the necessity of assuming continuity of prices or of capital services while allowing the retention of the assumption of instantaneous adjustment to new optimal levels of capital services input. This may be a small gain attained at a high price. If so, it is only because we are slavishly pursuing the letter rather than the spirit of neoclassical economics.

REPLY TO TOBIN AND GRILICHES

JEAN CROCKETT AND IRWIN FRIEND

To begin with Tobin's last question as to whether our detailed micro-economic studies provide better forecasting devices for aggregate personal saving than the "7 per cent rule," we have several rather obvious answers to make. We agree that sophisticated models now in existence probably could not have given more accurate predictions of saving over the last twelve years than that saving would be 7 per cent of disposable income. However, we hope that our models will eventually be able to improve on this rule, since the saving-income ratio has departed substantially from 7 per cent within the memory of man and is quite likely to do so again.

The interesting stability of the ratio in recent years may be the product of offsets among the effects of a number of changing variables. For example, the increasing proportion of retired with their relatively low savings ratios may offset the increasing proportion of homeowners with their relatively high savings ratios; or the increased economic confidence which has made households willing to assume continually increasing amounts of indebtedness relative to disposable income—a process which can hardly go on indefinitely—may offset a natural tendency for the savings ratio to rise with income. Even if such offsets are not the explanation of the recent stability, there are still many savings-income functions (including our own) which may give approximate constancy of the savings ratio over a particular income range but which would have quite different implications for higher incomes. If the normal income elasticity of assets and savings is significantly above one, as our analysis strongly implies, the constant savings ratio cannot be expected to persist except through other influences offsetting the income effects. Our analysis, if it is correct, gives insights into the implications of alternative economic policies which cannot be obtained from observation of the approximate constancy of the savings ratio.

It is our belief that the best path to an adequate understanding of aggregate saving behavior involves two steps: (1) the development and estimation of a satisfactory microeconomic model, toward which we believe that we have made some progress in this paper, and (2) the development of aggregate forecasting procedures based on the microeconomic parameters. The second is a far from trivial problem to which we have hardly addressed ourselves here, except insofar as we have tried to free our estimated income effects from biases due to the correlation of other cross-sectional variables with income. In addition to this, it is necessary to solve the aggregation problem and to allow for the influence of factors which are variable over time but whose effects cannot be determined in the cross section.

Quite apart from the question of forecasting aggregate savings, the present kind of investigation of the size and composition of household portfolios has implications for the capital markets, since consumers are very important elements in the supply of and demand for various types of funds. We find it rather amusing that Tobin is concerned with the implications of a "constant" ratio of aggregate personal saving to disposable income in recent years for our "detailed researches" in this area, without experiencing or at least expressing a similar concern about the corresponding implications of a "constant" investment-income ratio.

As to the more specific criticisms which Tobin makes of our paper, he first argues that our model is too static since we do not allow for changes in desired asset stocks over time. We have specifically allowed for changes in desired stocks when normal income varies, as it must if it is based on anything less than expected lifetime income, and even then if expectations are revised as additional information is accumulated. In addition, we entirely agree with Tobin that desired asset stocks also change with age. This is implicit in the balancing of the utility of an extra dollar of consumption against the utility of the present and discounted future services of an extra dollar of assets, particularly for assets whose major services occur in the future, since the discounted value of such services rises over time. While we did incorporate age as an explanatory variable for desired assets in the preliminary version of our paper to which Tobin's comments refer, we have made much greater use of age in the present version than we were able to do earlier. The various techniques we have used for holding age constant do not improve our empirical estimates of adjustment speeds in linear regressions, and these are in any case quite reasonable for the logarithmic regressions.

Second, Tobin suggests that we have not adequately controlled for age in arriving at the conclusion that the income elasticity of net worth is greater than one. In the present version of our paper, age is controlled by (a) including age as a continuous variable in net worth regressions, (b) fitting separate regressions within four age groups, and (c) including age as a continuous variable in the regressions within age groups to take care of the possibility of strong but nonlinear age effects. Our results have not been altered in any significant way by this extension of our earlier analysis.

Third, Tobin mentions the possible problems introduced by disproportionately high inheritances and unrealized capital gains for the upper-income groups in interpreting the high income elasticity of demand for wealth. Disregarding the effect of capital gains, we do not see how inheritances per se could result in an upward bias in the estimated income elasticity of wealth if there is a unitary income elasticity of demand for saving. However, capital gains do pose a problem which we considered in the original version of our paper. In addition to the evidence presented there that this problem does not seriously affect our conclusion on the income elasticities for wealth and saving, we have introduced a crude proxy for capital gains in the present version of our net worth regressions, and while this reduces income elasticities slightly, they remain well above unity. The capital gains proxy also improves somewhat the estimated adjustment speeds in the linear regressions.

Fourth, Tobin criticizes our saving tastes variables and suggests that it would be better to hold tastes constant by considering changes in the behavior of individual households over time. Here we agree entirely with the desirability of such an approach and had pointed this out in our paper. We were greatly disappointed that the body of data which we analyzed did not permit the use of this approach. Data for two distinct time periods were available only for three items, and even here the periods were too close together to produce much change in normal income and thus permit accurate estimation of a normal income elasticity. We hope to utilize the 1950-60 BLS consumer expenditures data to study changes in the saving behavior of socioeconomic or other groups over a ten-year period, somewhat in the manner of Duesenberry and Kistin. One of the authors has already used this approach in a forthcoming analysis of the aggregate postwar data for different countries, the other in an analysis of Greek household expenditure data.

Finally, Tobin notes that neither our separation of income into normal and transitory components nor our introduction of initial asset levels adds much to our correlations. This is not true for total assets, where the introduction of transitory income (as well as initial assets) improves the correlations and has a significantly different impact from normal income. Unfortunately, Tobin's caveat is true for total saving, although it should be emphasized that the primary reason for both of these devices was to produce (we hoped) a relatively unbiased estimate of the income elasticity rather than to raise correlations. Thus, turning to the major components of saving, we find that the effect of normal income on contractual saving is significantly higher than that of transitory income in the linear regressions for employees, even though the separation of the two effects does not raise the correlation, while in the quadratic regressions for liquid saving (which provide much the best fit) both transitory income and the second-degree term in normal income are highly significant for employees and the self-employed. Furthermore, for both groups, lagged assets are highly significant and raise the correlations for liquid saving in both the linear and quadratic models, though the implied adjustment speeds are rather low for employees.

For mortgage debt also, a very important savings component for homeowners, the introduction of initial debt levels raises the correlations; and since there was some tendency to increase mortgages, even though no purchases of new homes were involved, this is not quite so mechanical as it may seem. Incidentally, the comment that assets stocks were used only in their "own" savings regressions is not quite correct. Total net worth was frequently included, in addition to specific asset stocks, to represent all other assets, but did not prove significant or add to the correlation.

As to Griliches' comment that our estimated speed of adjustment for net worth may be understated because of our failure to allow for depreciation in housing, he is quite correct if we wish to consider our regressions as referring to total saving rather than merely to saving in the form of financial assets and if we consider only the saving but not the assets regression; but the adjustment is not quantitatively important even for the total saving regressions. With a depreciation rate of .035 per year for housing, which seems high but is used by Muth in the study discussed in our paper, and with a value of house estimated to account for about one-third of total net worth, depreciation should amount to perhaps 1 per cent of net worth. Thus .01 should be added to the estimated speed of adjustment in the total saving regressions. However, in the assets or net worth regressions, it is not necessary to make any adjustment of this type since assets are measured at a market value rather than on an undepreciated cost basis.

REPLY TO TOBIN, GRILICHES, AND MILLER

BY JORGENSON

The comments by Griliches, Miller, and Tobin should convince even the most blasé observer that the theory of investment behavior is a difficult and far from settled branch of economic theory. Even within the extremely simple framework I have used, elementary confusions arise, ambiguities persist, issues remain unresolved.

Tobin is correct in pointing out that there is no reason to assume that markets will never present an individual firm with jumps in prices. But it would be equally correct to say that there is no reason *not* to assume that firms will never be presented with jumps. The selection of an appropriate assumption is entirely a matter of analytical convenience. If jumps have interesting consequences, these consequences should be studied and tested against data. If continuity of prices has interesting consequences, these consequences are equally deserving of study.

In the theory of investment behavior, the assumption of jumps in price levels rules out any consequences at all. On the other hand, the assumption of continuous price levels has interesting and unsuspected consequences, namely, a rigorous theory of investment behavior based on the neoclassical theory of optimal capital accumulation. Keynesians receive the additional benefit of a "correct" sign for the change in investment with respect to variations in the rate of interest. In view of these consequences, it is difficult to interpret Tobin's remark to the effect that the resulting investment demand schedule "cannot serve the analytical purposes for which such a schedule is desired" as anything but a simple misunderstanding.

To sum up, the answer to the question whether demand for investment goods is a function of the rate of interest is that it all depends on what you hold constant. If Tobin insists on holding constant all present and *future* prices of investment goods (while varying the rate of interest), investment is unbounded except for a single value of the price of capital services. On the other hand, if present and *forward* prices of investment goods are held constant, there exists a perfectly well-defined investment demand function that depends on the rate of interest.[1] Tobin follows Haavelmo and Lerner in identifying two separate questions: (1) Is demand for investment goods a function of the rate of interest? (2) What happens to investment when the rate of interest varies with all present and *future* (not *forward*) prices held constant? Only when it is realized that there is no necessary connection between the two questions can a complete and unambiguous answer to the first question be given.

I intended the theory of investment behavior developed in my paper and econometric work on investment to be less directly related than Griliches supposes. Two different theoretical positions are commonly employed to rationalize empirical work. One is based on the Keynesian marginal efficiency of investment schedule, and the other on a theory of demand for capital services.

In view of the previous literature on the theory of investment, it may be surprising that both these positions can be developed within the same theoretical framework. Now that this fact has been demonstrated, tests to discriminate between the two approaches can be undertaken. As Griliches suggests, in empirical applications both positions are associated with substantial ad-hockery. Before the two positions can be tested against each other in any definitive way, it will be necessary to reduce the ad-hockery in each.

Miller's suggested modification of my theoretical framework is based on an unfortunate slip. The problem is one of appropriate dimensions. Using discrete time, we often write something like:

$$K_{t+1} = I_t + (1 - \delta)K_t.$$

A relationship like this can also be written using continuous time:

$$\frac{K(t + \epsilon) - K(t)}{\epsilon} = I(t) - \delta K(t),$$

where $\epsilon = 1$. When we employ such a relationship only at discrete points of time—t, $t + 1$, and so on—the time interval, $\epsilon = 1$, may be suppressed. However, where we pass to continuous time, letting $\epsilon \to 0$, it is important

---

[1] Tobin asserts that "there is no reason to assume that expected prices of capital goods accommodate themselves so obligingly to interest rate variations." In the conventional approach, one might argue similarly that there is no reason to assume that present and future prices obligingly hold themselves constant. Both of these arguments are beside the point. The investment demand schedule, like most economic relationships, is based on conjectural variation. Real income does not obligingly stay constant while we study changes in the demand for a commodity resulting from changes in its price. We hold it constant *by assumption*. Similarly, in studying investment demand, we hold whatever is held constant to be constant *by assumption*. Needless to say, changing the assumption usually changes the results.

to make the time interval explicit. The dimensions of the left-hand side variable are units of investment goods *per period of time;* these units correspond to those of $I(t)$ and $\delta K(t)$, both of which are measured as investment goods *per period of time.* Now taking the limit:

$$\lim_{\epsilon \to 0} \frac{K(t + \epsilon) - K(t)}{\epsilon} = \dot{K}(t) = I(t) - \delta K(t),$$

we obtain quantities which are still measured as investment goods *per period of time.*

The difficulty with Miller's expression II (a) is that the quantity $K(t + \epsilon) - K(t - \epsilon)$ is measured in investment goods, not investment goods per period of time. The appropriate expression is $[K(t + \epsilon) - K(t - \epsilon)]/2\epsilon$, since 2ϵ, the time interval, is measured in units of time and the ratio is measured as investment goods *per period of time.* Thus, Miller adds investment goods, a stock, to investment goods per period of time, a flow, which is self-contradictory. This is an elementary point, but it is essential to a correct formulation of the continuous time version of the basic relationship between gross and net investment. Miller's results are vitiated by this error.

PART II

Financial Aspects

Estimates of the Cost of Capital Relevant for Investment Decisions Under Uncertainty

MERTON H. MILLER

UNIVERSITY OF CHICAGO

AND

FRANCO MODIGLIANI

MASSACHUSETTS INSTITUTE OF TECHNOLOGY

For discussion at the Conference, we distributed a lengthy and detailed paper in which we attempted to develop methods for estimating the cost of capital relevant for investment decisions under uncertainty and to apply these methods to a cross-sectional sample of large electric utilities for 1954, 1956, and 1957. Much of this material had a direct and important bearing on the subject of the conference, particularly the latter sections of the paper which contrasted our estimates with several of the alternative measures of the cost of capital currently used in empirical studies of investment behavior.

Other parts of the paper, however—especially the review of the underlying theory of valuation under uncertainty, the discussion of the various theoretical and practical problems involved in the estimation, and the fairly extensive testing of the basic specification—were clearly of less direct concern to the Conference's central theme, except as supporting material for a critical evaluation by the discussants and those with a direct interest in the area of finance.

In revising our paper for inclusion in this volume, therefore, we decided to confine ourselves primarily to those portions of the original document most closely related to the central purpose of the Conference. Thus we have focused on our specific estimates of the cost of capital, on comparisons with alternative measures, and on the problems inherent in trying to develop continuous historical series. The remaining portions have been summarized and cut down to the bare minimum necessary for explaining and interpreting the results. Readers interested in a fuller development are referred to the *American Economic Review* for June 1966, which contains an unabridged, though slightly revised, version of the original paper (referred to hereafter as the "unabridged version").

I. Introduction

In its simplest form, the central normative proposition of the micro-theory of capital is that the firm should adjust its capital stock until the marginal rate of return on further investment (or disinvestment) is equal to the cost of capital. Under conditions of perfect certainty—which is the assumption on which most of classical theory has been developed—the concept of the cost of capital presents no particular difficulty; it is simply the market rate of interest. Since all securities must have the same yield in equilibrium under certainty, there is only one such rate per period and it is, in principle, a directly observable magnitude. Under real world conditions, however, we are confronted not with one, but with a bewildering variety of securities, with very different kinds and priorities of claims to portions of the (uncertain) future earnings of the firm. Since these securities will also, in general, have different anticipated yields, it is by no means clear which yield or combination of yields is the relevant cost of capital for rational investment planning. Nor, because it is based on anticipations, is the cost of capital any longer a directly observable magnitude. It must, rather, somehow be inferred from what *is* observable, namely, the market prices of the various kinds of claims represented by the different securities.

Although most (but not all) recent studies of investment behavior have shown some awareness of these difficulties, a common approach in empirical work has been simply to ignore the problem and to use, without comment or explicit justification, some standard index of current, nominal yields on high-grade corporate bonds (or even government bonds) as a measure of the cost of capital. Other writers use both a series on current bond yields to represent the cost of debt capital and a current profit series to measure the "availability" and hence, presumably, also the "cost" of equity capital. Still others have tried indexes of share prices, current dividend yields, or current earnings yields alone or in various averages with bond yields along the lines suggested in the standard texts on corporation finance. How much error is involved in the use of such measures is still unknown, though even a cursory survey of the underlying theory suggests many grounds for apprehension on this score; but we cannot be sure. Too little work has yet been done to permit even a rough calibration of these series as proxies for the cost of capital, let alone to provide acceptable alternative series.

The results that follow should be thought of as first steps toward closing this gap in our understanding and measurement of the cost of funds relevant to investment decisions. They are only first steps partly because of the very limited coverage of the estimates (three years for one industry)[1] and partly because the underlying model from which the estimates are derived is a special and still incompletely tested one. In particular, the interpretation of our estimates as the "cost of capital" rests on the assumptions of perfect capital markets and rational behavior by investors and by the corporate managers responsible for the actual investment decisions. Neither of these assumptions, needless to say, is likely to be enthusiastically accepted by those working in this field. In their defense, however, the following points are perhaps worth noting. (1) Our concern in this paper (and in the series of earlier papers on which it builds) is almost entirely with large, well-established firms. Though relatively few in number, these firms account for a disproportionately large share of total investment and in some major industries (such as our utilities or the steel industry) for virtually all of it. For such firms, we feel that the assumption of perfect capital markets— which implies, among other things, that, over the relevant range of funds requirements and except for very short intervals of time, there is no constraint on the total of funds from all sources that a firm can obtain at the going "cost of capital" to finance its investment outlays— cannot be ruled out as implausible, at least to a first approximation. For smaller firms, on the other hand, which are known to face severe limitations in their ability to expand their equity capital, the assumption may be largely inappropriate, and we would regard other kinds of models (stressing "availability" considerations) as more promising. (2) Insofar as rational behavior is concerned, the great virtue in that assumption is that it leads to a direct and simple connection between

[1] The sample consists of sixty-three separate firms representing all of the (consolidated) systems classified as of 1950 as Class A by the Federal Power Commission; plus those of the smaller Class B systems, whose assets devoted to electricity generation were at least $15 million in 1950. The sample years are 1954, 1956, and 1957.

the cost of capital and market valuation. To some, of course, such a defense will smack of looking for a missing wallet under the lamppost because the light is better there. But we do not yet know that the wallet is not there! There will be time enough to try working with more complicated behavioral assumptions when the evidence shows that the assumption of rationality fails (and precisely how it fails). As it turns out, some of the implications of the assumption of rational investor behavior stand up quite well when confronted with the data (see the unabridged version). The issue of the rationality of investment policy by corporate management is a more delicate one, and the final answer will have to wait until estimates of the cost of capital of the kind developed here have been tried out in studies of investment behavior.

With tests of this sort kept in mind as the ultimate goal, we turn now to the immediate task at hand. We shall begin in section II by providing an operational definition of the cost of capital and developing therefrom a link between the cost of capital and market valuation. The perfect market and rational behavior model of valuation will then be sketched out and the basic estimates of market-required rates of return and their relation to the cost of capital will be presented along with a very brief account of the estimating methods employed. Section III compares the estimates of the cost of capital with various popular alternative measures, with particular emphasis on average yield measures of the kind emphasized in the conventional literature on corporation finance. We conclude in section IV with some tentative suggestions on the problem of developing time series estimates of the cost of capital.

II. Valuation and the Cost of Capital

As used throughout, the term cost of capital (C) will be taken to mean the minimum prospective rate of yield that a proposed investment in real assets must offer to be worthwhile undertaking from the standpoint of the current owners of the firm. Under conditions of perfect capital markets, there is a one-for-one correspondence between "worthwhileness" in the above sense and the current market value of the owners' interest. If the management of the firm takes as its working criterion for investment (and other) decisions, "maximize the market value of the shares held by the current owners of the firm," then it can be shown (see, e.g., Hirshleifer [6])[2] that this policy is also equivalent to maximizing the economic welfare or utility of the owners. Thus, under the assumptions, valuation and the cost of capital are intimately related.

---

[2] Numbers in brackets refer to Bibliography at end of paper.

1. THE SIMPLE CERTAINTY MODEL

The precise relation between them is most easily seen in the context of a simple certainty model, in which all real assets are assumed to yield uniform, sure income streams in perpetuity and in which the market rate of interest (r) is given and constant over time. If, in addition, we assume perfect capital markets, rational investor behavior, and no tax differentials on different sources of income, then it can readily be shown that the equilibrium current market value (V) of any firm (i.e., the sum of the market values of all securities or other claims to its future earnings) is given by

$$V = \frac{1}{r} X \tag{1}$$

where X is the (uniform) income per period generated in perpetuity by the assets presently held. The term $1/r$ in (1)—the reciprocal of the interest rate—is commonly referred to as the market "capitalization rate" for sure streams since it represents the factor the market applies to a unit income flow to convert it to a capital stock.

For an expansion of real assets to be worth undertaking from the standpoint of the current owners of such a firm, the investment must lead to an increase in the market value of their holdings. If we let dA equal the purchase cost of the assets acquired, dS^o the change in value of the holdings of the original owners, and dS^n the market value of the additional securities issued to finance the investment, then differentiating (1) with respect to A yields:

$$\frac{dV}{dA} = \frac{dS^o}{dA} + \frac{dS^n}{dA} = \frac{dS^o}{dA} + 1 = \frac{dX}{dA}\frac{1}{r}. \tag{2}$$

It follows that the cost of capital (C) must be the reciprocal of the market capitalization rate for earnings since from (2), $dS^o/dA \geq 0$ if and only if $dX/dA \geq r$, i.e., if and only if the rate of return on the new investment is equal to or greater than the market rate of interest.[3]

2. EXTENSION TO THE CASE OF UNCERTAINTY

When we turn from a world of certainty to one of uncertainty, the problem of relating the cost of capital to market valuation becomes a

---

[3] We have here stated (and shall continue to state) the conditions for optimality of investment decisions in terms of the rate of return or internal yield on investment. Although it is well known that there may be cases in which such a rate of return cannot be adequately or unambiguously defined (see, e.g., Hirshleifer [6]), such cases are largely ruled out by our additional simplifying assumption.

much more formidable one for which no completely general solution is yet available. We have at least been able to show, however (see [10]), that if we retain the assumptions of perpetual streams, rational investor behavior, perfect markets, no taxes (and no "growth" in a sense to be more precisely defined later), then an analog of the certainty valuation formula (1) does carry through to the case of uncertainty. In particular, if we restrict attention to what we have called a "risk equivalent class" of firms, then the equilibrium market valuation of any firm in such a class can be expressed as

$$V = \frac{1}{\rho_k} \bar{X} \qquad (3)$$

for all firms in class k, where V is the sum of the market values of all the firm's securities, $\bar{X}$ is the *expected* level of average annual earnings generated by the assets it currently holds, and $1/\rho_k$ can be interpreted as the market's capitalization rate for the expected value of uncertain, pure equity earnings streams of the type characteristic of class k. Hence, by a straightforward extension of the reasoning in the previous section, the cost of capital for a proposed expansion in scale by any firm in the class is simply ρ_k. The precise value of ρ_k will, of course, be different from class to class, presumably increasing with the market's uncertainty about the level of future long-run earnings in the class (and reflecting also the nature and extent of the covariation with the returns in other classes). Though the various ρ's themselves are not directly observable, they can, in principle, be inferred from the market valuations, e.g., by regressing the observed V on estimates of $\bar{X}$ over a cross section of firms within a class.

An important implication of (3) is that the market value of a firm depends only on its real earning power and on the market capitalization rate for pure equity streams of its class and not at all upon the particular mix of security types that characterize its financial structure. This independence of value and financial structure is basically a reflection of the assumption of perfect capital markets—an assumption implying, among other things, that for comparable collateral, the supply curve of borrowed funds for individuals is the same as that for corporations. Hence, if corporations making heavy use of borrowed funds should sell, say, at a premium relative to unlevered corporations in the same class, rational investors could always obtain a more efficient portfolio by selling the "overvalued" levered shares, purchasing the "undervalued" unlevered shares, and restoring the previous degree of leverage by borrowing against the shares on personal account. And the converse is true if levered shares should sell at a discount, in which case the "arbitrage" operation involves selling the unlevered shares, buying the levered shares, and unlevering them by also buying a pro rata share of the firm's debts.[4]

With reference to the cost of capital, the independence of market value and financial policy implies, of course, that the cost of capital relevant for investment decisions is also independent of how the investment is to be financed, even though the particular securities considered may, and in general will, have very different expected yields. This seeming paradox disappears as soon as it is recognized that the independence property also requires that the common shares in levered corporations have higher expected yields than those of less levered corporations in the same class—a differential which can be thought of as compensation for the greater "riskiness" attaching to levered shares. Thus, the apparent gain in terms of the cost of capital coming from the ability of a firm to finance an investment with "cheap" debt capital is offset (and with rational behavior in a perfect market exactly offset) by the correspondingly higher cost of equity capital.

3. THE EFFECT OF CORPORATE INCOME TAXES

When we extend the analysis to allow for the existence of corporate income taxes and the deductibility of interest payments, the picture changes in a number of respects, the most important being that market value and financial structure are no longer completely independent. To see what is involved, let us again denote by $1/\rho_k$ the capitalization rate in a given class for pure equity streams available to investors (i.e., streams of expected net profits after taxes in unlevered firms), by $\overline{X}$ a firm's expected total earnings (now to be taken as earnings before taxes as well as interest), and by τ the (constant) marginal and average rate of corporate income taxation. Then the market value of an unlevered firm can be expressed as:

$$V_u = S_u = \frac{\overline{X}(1 - \tau)}{\rho_k}, \qquad (4)$$

where $\overline{X}(1 - \tau)$ is the unlevered firm's earnings after taxes. The value of a levered firm with D of debt or other securities whose payments are tax

---

[4] A fuller account of the arbitrage mechanism and proof of the independence proposition is given in our [10]. It is perhaps worth noting that the independence proposition can be proved under assumptions much weaker than those necessary to develop equation (3). In particular, neither the perpetuity assumption nor the concept of a risk equivalent class is essential (see, e.g., the discussion in our [9], pp. 429–430, and also Hirshleifer [5]).

deductible and P of preferred stock or other nondeductible senior securities can be shown to be (see our [12]):

$$V \equiv S + D + P = \frac{\bar{X}(1 - \tau)}{\rho_k} + \tau D. \tag{5}$$

Note that in (5), the expression $\bar{X}(1 - \tau)$ no longer represents the firm's earnings after taxes or any other standard accounting concept when D is not zero and hence when $\bar{X}$ includes some tax deductible interest. To avoid confusion, therefore, we shall hereafter refer to $\bar{X}(1 - \tau)$ as "tax adjusted" earnings using the symbol $\bar{X}^\tau$ for earnings after taxes in the ordinary accounting sense (i.e., for the sum of expected net profits after taxes, preferred dividends, and interest payments as they actually come on to the market for sale to the various security purchasers).[5]

As to the meaning of (5), it says, in effect, that the government pays a subsidy to firms using certain sources of capital which under current law would include bonds, notes, and other firm contractual obligations of indebtedness but not preferred stocks (with some minor exceptions) or common stocks. The addition to the present worth of the firm occasioned by these tax savings is the corporate tax rate times the market value of the debt—the latter being, of course, the present worth, as judged by the market, of the future stream of tax deductible payments.

Since the deductibility of interest payments thus makes the value of the firm a function of its financial policy, it must also make the required yield or cost of capital a function of financial policy. To see the precise nature of this dependence, let dS^o, as before, stand for the change in the market value of the shares held by the current owners of the firm, dS^n for the value of any new common shares issued, dP for the value of any new preferred stock issued, and dD for the value of any new tax-deductible debt issued, with $dS^n + dP + dD = dA$. Then from (5) we have:

$$\frac{dV}{dA} = \frac{dS^o}{dA} + \frac{dS^n}{dA} + \frac{dP}{dA} + \frac{dD}{dA} = \frac{dS^o}{dA} + 1 = \frac{d\bar{X}(1 - \tau)}{dA}\frac{1}{\rho_k} + \tau\frac{dD}{dA}, \tag{6}$$

from which it follows that the cost of capital or required yield on a tax-adjusted basis is

$$C = \rho_k\left(1 - \tau\frac{dD}{dA}\right) \tag{7}$$

---

[5] The relation between the various concepts can easily be established by observing that expected taxes paid will be $\tau(\bar{X} - \bar{R})$ so that $\bar{X} = \bar{X}^\tau + \tau(\bar{X} - \bar{R})$ and hence $\bar{X}(1 - \tau) = \bar{X}^\tau - \tau\bar{R}$. Further discussion of these concepts along with the basic proofs for the tax case will be found in our [12].

since $(dS^o/dA) \geq 0$ if and only if $(d\bar{X}(1 - \tau)/dA)$ is equal to or greater than the right-hand side of (7).

In connection with (7), the two extreme cases of financing methods are of particular interest. For an investment financed entirely by equity capital—and in this context equity capital includes nondeductible preferred stock—dD/dA will equal zero. Hence the required tax-adjusted yield or "marginal cost of equity capital" is ρ_k. For an investment financed entirely by debt or other sources of capital whose payments are tax deductible, dD/dA is unity, implying that the "marginal cost of debt capital" is $\rho_k(1 - \tau)$.

The term marginal cost has been put in quotation marks to emphasize that, while these extreme cases serve to illuminate the meaning of (7), neither is directly relevant for actual decision-making at the level of the firm. For companies with reasonable access to the capital markets, as would certainly be true of those in our sample, investment and financing decisions (including decisions to retire outstanding securities) are made continually and largely independently. Since particular investment projects thus are not, and in general cannot be, linked to particular sources of financing, the relevant cost of capital to the firm must be thought of as essentially an average of the above costs of debt and equity capital, with weights determined by the long-run average proportions of each in the firm's program of future financing. If we denote this "target" proportion of debt as L, then the weighted average cost of capital can be expressed as $C = C(L) = \rho_k(1 - \tau)L + (1 - L)\rho_k$, or, more compactly, as $C = C(L) = \rho_k(1 - \tau L)$, where the notation $C(L)$ will be used when we want to emphasize that the cost of capital is a *function* of the target debt ratio L.

Notice, finally, that while the definition of the cost of capital has become a good deal more complex as a result of the introduction of income taxes, the problem of estimation remains essentially the same. It still involves only the estimation of a single capitalization rate—in this case, $1/\rho_k$, the capitalization rate for unlevered, pure equity streams in the class. The difference between the cost of equity and debt capital introduces no new difficulties because the cost of debt capital does not depend on the market rate of interest on bonds, but only on the above capitalization rate and the tax rate. Hence $1/\rho_k$ remains a sufficient parameter both for economists seeking to explain rational investment behavior and for firms planning their investment programs on the basis of given financial policies.[6]

4. GROWTH AND VALUATION[7]

Up to this point, we have focused attention entirely on the role of current earning power and financial policy as determinants of the value of the firm. There are, of course, very many other factors that influence real world valuations and some that may well be large enough and systematic enough to warrant incorporating them directly into the model rather than impounding them in the general disturbance term. Of these, one of the most important is "growth potential," in the sense of opportunities the firm may have to invest in real assets in the future at rates of return greater than "normal" (i.e., greater than the cost of capital).

Clearly, translating such a concept into operational terms is a task of formidable proportions and one for which no universally applicable solution can be expected. For industries such as the electric utilities, however—where the growth in earnings has been (and will presumably continue to be) reasonably steady—rough, but tolerable, approximations to growth potential can probably be obtained by exploiting the so-called constant-growth model. In particular, suppose that a firm has the opportunity to invest annually an amount equal to $100 k$ per cent of its tax-adjusted earnings ($k \leqq 1$), on which investments it will earn a tax-adjusted rate of return of ρ^*, greater than $C = C(L)$, its average cost of capital. (These assumptions imply, among other things, that earnings will grow at the constant rate of $k\rho^*$ per year.) And suppose further that these especially profitable opportunities are expected to persist over the next T years, after which only normally profitable opportunities will be available. Then, by analogy to the solution we have derived for the

---

[6] The independence of the cost of equity capital (and hence also of debt capital) from the interest rate is, of course, an independence only within a partial equilibrium framework. In a general equilibrium setting, there is necessarily a very direct connection between the interest rate (which may be regarded, to a first approximation, as the yield on assets generating sure streams) and the various ρ_k (which are the expected yields on assets generating streams of various degrees of uncertainty). But while the connection is direct (since they are mutually determined in the process of market clearing and jointly reflect such underlying factors as the level of wealth, the composition of the stock of real assets, and attitudes toward risk), there is no reason to believe that they will always move closely together over time.

[7] Since all the main earnings and cost of capital concepts have now been introduced, we shall hereafter, in the interests of simplicity, drop all subscripts and superscripts on the variables where there is no danger of ambiguity.

certainty case (see [9], footnote 15) the current market value of the firm can be expressed as

$$V = \frac{1}{\rho}\overline{X}(1 - \tau) + \tau D + k\overline{X}(1 - \tau)\left[\frac{\rho^* - C}{C(1 + C)}\right]T, \qquad (8)$$

where the first two terms, as before, represent the capitalized value of the current tax-adjusted earning power plus the tax benefits on debt, and the last term is the contribution to value of the future growth potential.

Despite the heroic simplifications invoked in its derivation, the above expression for growth potential is still by no means a simple one. It is the *product* of three separate elements: the profitability of the future opportunities as measured by the difference between ρ^* and $C(L)$; the size of these opportunities $(k\overline{X}(1 - \tau))$; and how long they are expected to last (T). None of these component terms is directly observable, though some such as $k\overline{X}(1 - \tau)$ (and possibly ρ^*) might be approximated by extrapolating recent past experience. In this paper, we take the simplest way out by focusing on the most tractable component $k\overline{X}(1 - \tau)$, the level of investment opportunities, and impounding the others in its regression coefficient.

As an empirical estimate of investment opportunities, we have used in the subsequent estimating equations the quantity $(1/5(A_t - A_{t-5})/A_{t-5}) \cdot A_t$. That is, we have used a linear five-year average growth rate of total assets times current assets denoted for simplicity hereafter as $\triangle\overline{A}$. This particular form of average, for reasons still not entirely clear to us, yields consistently higher gross and net correlations with total value than other simple averages we have tried. But the differences are not large and the estimates of the other coefficients are not sensitive to the specific measure used.

5. DIVIDEND POLICY, VALUATION AND THE COST OF CAPITAL

Under ideal conditions of perfect capital markets, rational investor behavior, and no tax discrimination between sources of income, dividend policy would present no particular problem. In such a setting, we have shown [9] that, given a firm's investment policy, its dividend policy will have no effect whatever on the current market value of its shares or on its cost of capital; and that despite the impressions of some writers to the contrary (see, e.g., Lintner [7]), this conclusion is equally valid whether one is considering a world of certainty or uncertainty. Dividend policy serves to determine only the division of the stockholders' return between current cash receipts and capital appreciation, and the division of the firm's equity financing between retained earnings and external flotations.

The picture becomes considerably more complicated, however, as soon as we weaken the assumptions to allow for the present tax subsidy to capital gains and for the existence of brokerage fees and flotation costs. Under these conditions, a firm's dividend policy can, in general, be expected to have some effect on its market value though the precise amount of the effect is impossible to determine a priori.

Given this uncertainty as to the size and, to some extent, even the direction of the dividend effect, the indicated course might seem to be simply to add a dividend term with an unspecified coefficient to the structural equation (8) and let the sample determine its value. From such a valuation equation we could, of course, also go on to derive an extension of the cost of capital formula (7) running in terms of dividend policy as well as debt policy.[8]

The trouble with such an approach, however, is that if it is applied in a straightforward fashion, as in Gordon [3] or Durand [2], the resulting estimate of the dividend coefficient will inevitably be strongly biased upward (and the key earnings coefficient correspondingly biased downward). Since the precise mechanism generating this bias has been described at length in our [11] and will be further referred to below, we need not dwell on the matter further at this point beyond observing that the difficulty arises from the widespread practice of dividend stabilization. With current dividends based in large part on management's expectations of long-run future earnings, the dividend coefficient in the regression equation will reflect this substantial informational content about $\overline{X}(1 - \tau)$ along with the true effect, if any, of dividends per se on valuation.

Because of this confounding of the earnings and dividend coefficients, our approach here will be to omit the dividend variable entirely and to focus on the problem of estimating the earnings coefficient (which is, of course, to be interpreted as the capitalization rate for earnings for companies following the sample average dividend policy). As it turns out, tests of the dividend effect (presented in detail in the unabridged

---

[8] Although the procedure for deriving the marginal and average costs of capital in the dividend case is analogous to that for the leverage case, the derivation is considerably more complicated. Further difficulties arise from the fact that, in such a setting, maximizing market value is no longer always equivalent to maximizing the economic welfare of the owners. Since these and related problems are largely peripheral to the main concerns of this paper, further discussion of them will be deferred to a separate paper.

version) indicate that it is quite small in this industry for the years under study and can safely be neglected for our main purposes here.

6. SIZE AND VALUATION

All the valuation equations considered so far have been written as linear homogeneous functions of the independent variables, implying, among other things, that a given proportionate change in the values of all the independent variables leads to an equal proportionate change in the market value of the firm. The results of previous valuation studies (see, e.g., Gordon [4]) suggest, however, that the true market capitalization rate for the expected earnings of large firms may tend to be larger than that of small firms in the same industry.

As was true of the growth effect, there are a number of possible ways of incorporating this size or scale effect into the model. By far the simplest is merely to add a constant term to the valuation equation. The resulting nonhomogeneous equation must then be interpreted as the linear approximation over the sample range to the underlying nonlinear relation, and the coefficient of the earnings variable as the (constant) marginal capitalization rate in the industry. The magnitude and direction of the scale effect would be indicated by the size and sign of the constant term. A negative constant term would confirm that the average capitalization rate is less than the marginal rate and hence that the average capitalization rate tends to rise with increasing size of firm. A positive value for the constant term, on the other hand, would imply decreasing returns to scale in valuation.

7. THE ECONOMETRIC MODEL AND THE METHOD OF ESTIMATION

Our analysis of the theory of valuation thus leads to the following structural equation:

$$(V - \tau D) = a_0 + a_1 \overline{X}(1 - \tau) + a_2 \overline{\Delta A} + U, \qquad (9)$$

where a_1 is the marginal capitalization rate for pure equity streams in the class and hence the key parameter for deriving the cost of capital, a_0 is an intercept term whose size and sign will measure any effects of scale on valuation, a_2 is a measure of the effects of growth potential on value, and U is a random disturbance term. Note that since the theory implies that the coefficient of the leverage variable D is equal to the marginal corporate tax rate τ, we shall, to increase the efficiency of estimation, so constrain it by incorporating it with the dependent variable.

Least-squares estimates of the coefficients of (9) will be efficient and unbiased only if, among other things, the variance of the disturbance term U is a constant, independent of the size of the firm, and the disturbances are not correlated with the independent variables. Unfortunately, neither of these conditions can reasonably be expected to hold in our sample.

As for the variance of the disturbances, one would certainly suppose that the errors in a valuation equation, including errors in measuring $(V - \tau D)$, are of the multiplicative rather than the additive variety. And indeed, check of the simple scatter of value on measured earnings suggests that the error term is approximately proportional to the size of firm. Any attempt to fit (9) directly, therefore, would be highly inefficient and in our sample (where the largest firm is on the order of 100 times the smallest) the results would be completely dominated by a handful of giant companies.

In the present context, there are at least two approaches worth considering as possible solutions for this problem of heteroscedasticity: (i) dividing (9) through by $(V - \tau D)$ and re-expressing the structural relation in so-called "yield" form; or (ii) weighting each observation in inverse proportion to the size of the firm and hence to the size of the standard deviation of the error. The former leads to the estimating equation

$$\frac{\bar{X}(1 - \tau)}{V - \tau D} = a'_1 + a'_0 \frac{1}{V - \tau D} + a'_2 \frac{\overline{\Delta A}}{V - \tau D} + u', \qquad (10)$$

where $a'_1 = \rho =$ the reciprocal of the capitalization rate for pure equity streams (or, equivalently, the "marginal cost of equity capital"), $a'_0 = a_0\rho$, $a'_2 = -a_2\rho$, and $u' = -\rho(U/V - \tau D)$, with Var (u') approximately a constant for all firms.

While an approach of this kind has the virtue of simplicity, it suffers from the fact that the variable $(V - \tau D)$ enters into the denominator of the ratios on both sides of the equation. This is not only somewhat unesthetic—since we are, in effect, using V to explain V—but will lead to biased estimates to the extent that $(V - \tau D)$ contains stochastic elements independent of those in the numerator of the ratios. In the present case, this will mean that the coefficients of the growth and size variables will be too high (i.e., less negative) and that the estimate of the cost of capital (from the intercept term a_1) will be correspondingly too low. Since $(V - \tau D)$ certainly does have a stochastic component—impounded in the term U in (9)—and since we have, at this stage, no basis for judging how large the resulting bias really is, we obviously cannot afford to rely on estimating equations of this form. We shall therefore rely primarily on the weighted regression approach.

Assuming that the standard deviation of the error term in (9) is roughly proportional to size of firm, the required weighting can be effected by the relatively simple expedient of deflating each of the variables by the book value of total assets, denoted by A. Our reason for using total assets as a deflator rather than, say, total sales (as, e.g., in Neilsen [13]) is mainly that in the utility industry at least such deflated terms as V/A, D/A, or $\bar{X}(1 - \tau)/A$ have natural and useful economic interpretations in their own right. The equation to be fitted, then, will be of the form

$$\frac{V - \tau D}{A} = a_0 \frac{1}{A} + a_1 \frac{\bar{X}(1 - \tau)}{A} + a_2 \frac{\overline{\Delta A}}{A} + u, \tag{11}$$

with $u = U/A$ and Var $(u) = $ a constant.

One question that immediately arises in connection with (11) is the status of the constant term. Recall that we are interpreting the basic valuation equation (9) in the original, undeflated variables as a linear approximation over the sample range, with its constant term a_0 serving as a measure of the effect of scale on valuation. To preserve this interpretation, we must, therefore, regard the derived deflated regression (11) as homogeneous, that is, as being fitted with no constant term and with the coefficient of the variable $1/A$ now measuring the size effect.

A potentially much more serious problem than heteroscedasticity is that posed by the lack of independence between the disturbance term in (11) and the independent variables, particularly the key earnings variable $\bar{X}(1 - \tau)/A$. That variable is defined, it will be recalled, as the market's expectation of the long-run, future earning power of the assets currently held by the firm. Since it is an expectation, it is not directly observable or measurable and the best that can normally be done is somehow to approximate it from the firm's published accounting statements. This best, unfortunately, is likely to be none too good even in an industry, such as the electric utility industry, where there is substantial uniformity of accounting conventions among firms, where there are (at least in our sample period) no firms suffering net losses, and where large, year-to-year random fluctuations in reported earnings seem to be relatively rare.

The implications of these inevitable errors in the measurement of earnings for the problems at hand are perhaps most easily seen by expressing the underlying structure as the following *system* of equations (where, to simplify the notation, we let $V^* = (V - \tau D)/A$, $X^* =$

$\bar{X}(1 - \tau)/A$ = the "true" unobservable expected earnings, X = deflated earnings as measured from the accounting statements, and Z_i, $i = 1 \ldots m$ stand for all other relevant variables (including constants, where appropriate):

$$V^* = \alpha X^* + \sum_{i=1}^{m} \beta_i Z_i + u \qquad (12a)$$

$$X = X^* + v \qquad (12b)$$

$$X^* = \sum_{i=1}^{m} \gamma_i Z_i + w \qquad (12c)$$

where some γ_i and β_i may be zero, and with the error terms assumed to be independent of each other and to have mean zero and (constant) variances σ_u^2, σ_v^2, and σ_w^2 respectively. In other words, the value of the firm depends on expected earnings and certain additional explanatory variables; measured earnings are merely in approximation to true expected earnings, the error of measurement being v; and lastly, at least some of the explanatory variables are also correlated with (and hence convey information about) the true but unobservable X^*.

The equations above thus constitute a simultaneous system in which V^* and X are, in effect, the endogenous variables, and the Z_i are the exogenous variables. It follows, then, that if we attempt to fit by direct least squares the single equation.

$$V^* = aX + \sum_{i=1}^{m} b_i Z_i + u' \qquad (13)$$

in which V^* is regressed on the Z_i and the endogenous, measured earnings X, the error term u' will not be independent of X and the coefficients of (13) will be biased. More concretely, it can readily be shown (see, e.g., Chow [1], esp. pp. 94–98) that, in the limit for large samples, the coefficients of X will be given by

$$a = \alpha \frac{\sigma_w^2}{\sigma_w^2 + \sigma_v^2}$$

which is less than the true value α and the more so the larger the variance of the error of measurement σ_v^2 and the better proxies the included exogenous variables are for earnings (i.e., the smaller the value of $\sigma_w{}^2$).[9] As for the other variables, the coefficients will be given by

$$b_i = \beta_i + \gamma_i\alpha \frac{\sigma_v{}^2}{\sigma_w{}^2 + \sigma_v{}^2} = \beta_i + \gamma_i[\alpha - a]$$

and thus may be larger or smaller than their true values (β_i) depending on the direction of correlation with X^* (i.e., on the sign of γ_i).[10]

Recasting the original structure in the form of (12) not only serves to clarify the nature of the biases introduced by errors of measurement, but also suggests a remedy, namely, an instrumental variable approach. For reasons of computational simplicity as well as ease of interpretation in the present context, we shall implement this approach by means of a two-stage procedure formally equivalent to the two-stage least-squares method of Theil [14]. (See also Madansky [8].) Operationally, this means first regressing the endogenous variable X on all the instrumental variables Z_i, thereby obtaining estimates g_i of the coefficients γ_i in (12c). From these estimates, a new variable $\bar{X}$ is formed, defined as $\sum_{i=1}^{m} g_i Z_i$, and thus constituting an estimate of X^* from which, if our assumptions are correct, the error of measurement v will have been purged. If $\bar{X}$ is then used in the second stage as the earnings variable in (13) in place of X (and if the conditions for identification are met), the resulting estimates of a and the b_i can be shown to be consistent estimates of α and the β_i in the basic structural equation (12a).

As for the specific exogenous or instrumental variables to be used, we have already considered two, growth and size. In addition—for reasons discussed in detail in the unabridged version—we shall use total assets, two capital structure variables (D/A and P/A), and total dividends paid.

---

[9] The above expression for the bias in the earnings coefficient was derived on the assumption that (13) was fitted *with* a constant term. If the equation were fitted without a constant term (and if, as we have assumed, there is no constant term in the true specification), then the apparent bias will be considerably smaller. The reason is, of course, that the bias, by flattening the slope of the regression, tends to produce a positive intercept even where none really belongs. Hence forcing the regression through the origin and eliminating the artificial intercept offsets some of the distortion. The offset is only partial, however, and forcing the regression through the origin cannot be regarded as a satisfactory substitute for the more elaborate methods for eliminating the bias to be introduced below.

[10] Note that even if some $\beta_i = 0$ (implying that the corresponding Z_i really has no effect on market value) its estimate b_i might still be positive if $\gamma_i > 0$. And the b_i might be quite large if γ_i is large and if the measurement error in X is substantial (so that a is considerably smaller than α). This is, of course, precisely the "information effect" or proxy variable bias we were concerned about in connection with the dividend variable (see section II 5).

III. The Results

1. THE VALUATION EQUATION

The two-stage least-squares estimates of (11) for the three sample years are presented in Table 1. Since our concern here is primarily with

TABLE 1

Two-Stage Least-Squares Estimates of the Basic Valuation Model
(Dependent Variable: $(V - \tau D)/A$ *)*

| | Coefficients of | | | | Adjusted | Ratio of Adjusted |
Year	Earnings $(\bar{X}^\tau - \tau \bar{R})/A$	Size $1/A \cdot 10^7$	Growth $\overline{\Delta A/A}$	Mult. R	Standard Error	Standard Error to Mean, V/A
1957	16.1	−.280	1.36	.88	.057	.052
	(.46)	(.08)	(.23)			
1956	16.7	−.114	.896	.87	.057	.051
	(.40)	(.07)	(.21)			
1954	19.7	−.244	.299	.73	.063	.053
	(.45)	(.07)	(.18)			

the cost of capital rather than valuation per se, we shall not comment on these estimates in any detail. Suffice it to say that the results compare quite favorably in terms of explanatory power—as measured, for example, by the ratio of the standard error of the regression to the mean value of V/A—with those that have been obtained in other valuation studies using very different (and to us, at least, very unsatisfactory) specifications. Of particular interest, of course, is the behavior of the growth variable. Future growth potential (though small relative to current earning power and the tax subsidy to debt in terms of contribution to total market value) apparently increased steadily in absolute and relative importance over this period and by 1957 accounted for something over 10 per cent of total market value for the average firm in the sample.

For further reference and comparison, we present in Table 2 two alternative sets of estimates of the valuation equation. The first is the direct least-squares regression of $(V - \tau D)/A$ on measured earnings, with the constant term suppressed. As can be seen, the differences from the two-stage estimates are generally quite small, a result not really

TABLE 2

Direct Least-Squares Estimates with Measured Earnings

Part A: Value Form (Dependent Variable: $(V - \tau D)/A$)

Year	Coefficients of			Mult. R	Adjusted Standard Error	Ratio of Adjusted Standard Error to Mean, V/A
	Earnings $(\bar{X}^\tau - \tau \bar{R})/A$	Size $1/A \cdot 10^7$	Growth $\Delta A/A$			
1957	16.0 (.44)	-.277 (.08)	1.39 (.23)	.88	.057	.052
1956	16.6 (.39)	-.111 (.07)	.926 (.21)	.87	.057	.051
1954	19.2 (.43)	-.205 (.07)	.466 (.17)	.75	.063	.053

Part B: Yield Form (Dependent Variable: $(\bar{X}^\tau - \tau \bar{R})/V - \tau D)$)

Year	Coefficients of			Mult. R	Reciprocal of Constant Term and Its Implied Standard Error	Ratio of Standard Error of Regression to Mean of Dependent Variable
	Constant	Size $(1/V - \tau D) \cdot 10^6$	Growth $\Delta A/V - \tau D$			
1957	.0592 (.002)	.166 (.04)	-.0516 (.02)	.58	16.8 (.44)	.07
1956	.0582 (.001)	.066 (.04)	-.0325 (.01)	.39	17.4 (.38)	.07
1954	.0506 (.001)	.121 (.04)	-.0124 (.01)	.45	19.8 (.45)	.07

very surprising in the light of the suppression of the constant term.[11] The differences turn out to be considerably larger (particularly in 1954) when the constant term is not suppressed and, indeed, it is only in the case of the two-stage estimates that the constant term really does approach zero. The differences become larger still when other tests of the basic specification (notably those concerned with the leverage and dividend variables) are considered.

The second panel shows the estimates obtained by direct least-squares regressions in the "yield form" of equation (10) above. The main drawback of this approach, it will be recalled, comes from the presence of $V - \tau D$ in the denominators of variables on both sides of the equation, which imparts an upward bias to the coefficients of the independent variables and a consequent downward bias to the crucial constant term. Since the direction of the bias is known, however, we can use equations of this form to provide at least a rough check on the reasonableness of the estimates obtained by the more roundabout, two-stage approach.

To facilitate comparison with the estimates in Table 1, a column has been added showing the reciprocal of the constant term, which is the estimate of the capitalization factor for earnings implied by the observed constant terms in the yield equations. As predicted, the capitalization factors obtained via the yield equations are indeed all higher than those obtained via the two-stage approach. The gap between the two sets of estimates tends to widen somewhat over time, but the differences are never very large. This close agreement should remove any lingering fears that major distortions in the estimates may somehow have been introduced in the two-stage approach. At the same time, it suggests that the simpler yield equations may still have a useful role to play in valuation studies, particularly where the interest is mainly in determining the direction of changes in the cost of capital over time rather than developing precise estimates or testing the basic specification as developed here.

2. THE COST OF EQUITY CAPITAL

Turning now from valuation to the other side of the coin, the cost of capital, we show in Table 3 the estimates of the cost of equity capital implied by the earnings coefficients of Table 1. For comparison, the table also shows two other measures of the cost or "ease of acquisition" of equity capital frequently used by economists in investment studies, namely, the average earnings-to-price ratio and the reciprocal of the

[11] See footnote 9.

TABLE 3

Estimated Cost of Equity Capital and Some Alternative Measures of Equity Costs

Year	Estimated Cost of Equity Capital (ρ)		Average Earnings Yield on Shares ($\bar{\pi}^\tau/S$)		Reciprocal of Ratio of Price to Book Value (B/S)		Average Tax and Leverage Adjusted Total Earnings Yield, $(\bar{X}^\tau - \tau R)/(V - \tau D)$	
	Amt. (1)	As Per Cent of 1954 (2)	Amt. (3)	As Per Cent of 1954 (4)	Amt. (5)	As Per Cent of 1954 (6)	Amt. (7)	As Per Cent of 1954 (8)
1957	.062 (.002)	122	.070	106	.64	105	.056	110
1956	.060 (.001)	118	.070	106	.63	103	.056	110
1954	.051 (.001)	100	.066	100	.61	100	.050	100

ratio of the average price to the book value of the shares. Notice that all three measures indicate a rise in the cost of equity capital between 1954 and 1957, but our measure indicates a steeper and more substantial increase over the interval. The causes and implications of this apparently lesser responsiveness of the standard measures will become clear in subsequent discussion.

Insofar as levels are concerned, notice that the average earnings yield happens to be consistently higher than our estimate of the cost of equity capital. We say happens to be to emphasize that, under our model of valuation, there is no "normal" or even simple relation to be expected between the two concepts. The earnings yield for any company is not a given fixed number for each member of the class, but rather a function whose arguments include the cost of equity capital for the class, the firm's growth potential, its leverage policy, and its size. The sample mean earnings yield shows only the combined effect of these different and, to some extent, offsetting influences.

3. VALUATION, GROWTH, AND THE COST OF EQUITY CAPITAL

Because of the distortions resulting both from leverage effects and from the fact that the market value of shares incorporates the capitalized value of growth opportunities, we must conclude that the earnings-to-price ratio—which together with long-term interest rates is the most widely used measure of the cost of capital in investment studies—is unlikely to provide an adequate approximation.

The first of these distortions—that arising from leverage—could be handled by falling back on a measure of market yield somewhat different from the earnings-to-price ratio, though related to it. Let us suppose first that there were no corporate income taxes. Then we know that, in the absence of valuable growth opportunities, the fundamental valuation equation, expressed in yield form, would be simply $\bar{X}/V = \rho$. The ratio of expected total earnings to total market value—which may be thought of as a "leverage-corrected" yield—would thus provide a direct estimate of ρ. In principle, any firm could so approximate its cost of equity capital from its own company data, although, of course, as a practical matter, a better estimate would be obtained by averaging over a large group of similar firms so as to wash out any random noise in $\bar{X}$ or V. When we allow for taxes and the consequent tax subsidy on debt the picture becomes slightly more complicated, but a direct approximation of ρ still exists. The appropriate yield—see (5)—now becomes $(\bar{X}^\tau - \tau\bar{R})/(V - \tau D)$, the ratio of total tax-adjusted earnings to total market value minus the value of the tax subsidy.

This method of direct approximation breaks down, however, in the presence of growth. The leverage adjusted yield will be systematically too low as an estimate of ρ for any company with growth potential as will be the group average yield for any sample that contains significant numbers of growth companies. Nor will the movements of the yield over time conform well with changes in ρ to the extent that the market's evaluation of future growth potential changes over time (and, of course, much of the short-term variation visible in share prices stems precisely from this source). Some idea of how sizable the distortions of level and movement of the yield relative to ρ can be—even in such a low-growth industry as our electric utilities and even over such a short span of time —is provided by a comparison of our estimates of the cost of equity capital in the first column of Table 3 with those of the tax and leverage adjusted yield, $[(\bar{X}^\tau - \tau\bar{R})/(V - \tau D)]$, in the last column of that table.

One somewhat surprising aspect of this comparison, already noted above, is the relative stability of the leverage-adjusted yield series over this period. Because of the many uncertainties surrounding estimates of

Figure 1

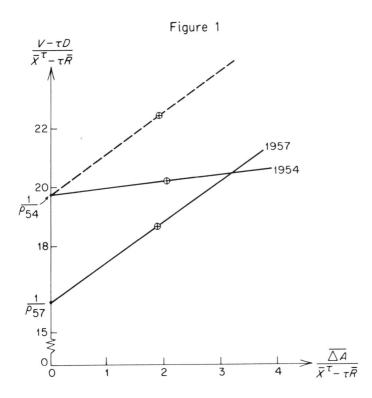

future growth potential and because of the sensitivity of current market values to even small changes in projected growth rates, one would expect the growth component in the denominator of the yield ratio to be quite volatile, and hence that the market yield would tend to swing quite substantially in response to these continuing re-evaluations. Some idea of why this "normal" pattern did not obtain during our sample period can be gained from Figure 1. The solid-line functions plotted there are the basic value regressions of Table 3 for the beginning and ending years, 1954 and 1957, expressed in ratio form as

$$\frac{V - \tau D}{\overline{X}^\tau - \tau \overline{R}} = a_1 + a_2 \frac{\overline{\Delta A}}{\overline{X}^\tau - \tau \overline{R}}$$

(and hence ignoring the minor size effect). The dependent variable is thus the reciprocal of the tax- and leverage-adjusted yield; the intercept a_1 is our estimate of $1/\rho$; and the slope a_2 is the coefficient of growth in the V equation.[12]

Notice that in 1954, at the beginning of the period, the market's estimate of the growth potential of the industry was quite low. Because the slope was so flat, the approximate sample mean value of $(V - \tau D)/(\overline{X}^\tau - \tau \overline{R})$—indicated by the circled cross—differed only very slightly from the estimate of $1/\rho$ implied by the intercept. By 1957, however, a striking increase had taken place in the market's valuation of the prospects for continuing profitable growth in the industry. As can be seen from the broken line—which has been plotted with 1954 intercept and 1957 slope—this large revaluation would have pushed the average value of $(V - \tau D)/(\overline{X}^\tau - \tau \overline{R})$ up by nearly 15 per cent to 22.4 (equivalent to a yield of about .044) if no other changes had occurred. But instead of this "pivoting" around a stable intercept of $1/\rho_{54}$, our estimates indicate that a simultaneous and quite substantial drop in the intercept took place (i.e., rise in the cost of equity capital). So substantial was this drop, in fact (when combined with the slight fall in the mean value of the growth variable itself), that the upward push of the revaluation of growth was more than offset; and the mean value of $(V - \tau D)/(\overline{X}^\tau - \tau \overline{R})$ actually fell by about 10 per cent.

Although these compensating movements in ρ and the market's evaluation of growth "explain" the relative stability of the tax- and leverage-adjusted yield during the sample period, the explanation may

---

[12] The use of the reciprocal of the yield rather than the yield itself is simply a matter of convenience since the presence of growth impounded in V would lead to a nonlinear relation between $(\overline{X}^\tau - \tau \overline{R})/(V - \tau D)$ and growth as measured by $\overline{\Delta A}/(V - \tau D)$.

strike the reader as somewhat paradoxical. Growth potential, after all, is the opportunity to invest in the future in projects whose rates of return exceed the cost of capital. One would expect, therefore, that a rise in the cost of capital would normally be associated with a *fall* in growth potential. There are a number of possible explanations for the opposite behavior in the present instance, but discussion of them is perhaps best postponed until we have first provided estimates of the average cost of capital relevant for investment decisions.

4. THE REQUIRED YIELD OR AVERAGE COST OF CAPITAL

As emphasized earlier, the relevant cost of capital for investment decisions at the level of the firm is the average cost of capital, $\rho(1 - \tau L)$, where L measures the "target" proportion of debt in future financing. The average cost is thus not a fixed number, but a schedule or function whose arguments are ρ (which is an "external" property of the class or industry determined by the market) and L (which is a matter of "internal" company policy). Although the average cost of capital, unlike the cost of equity capital, is thus in principle different for each firm in the industry, we can get some idea of its value and behavior for the typical electric utility by using a typical or average value for L. The obvious candidate, of course, is the actual sample average of D/A for each year, since D/A measures the average proportion of debt in past financing and this proportion is likely to be quite stable (particularly when averaged over the industry). Estimates with these values for L are shown in Table 4, columns 1 and 2. (For notational convenience, we shall hereafter refer to these estimates as $C(\overline{D}/\overline{A})$, using $C(L)$ to mean the function itself and $C(D/A)$, i.e., without the bar on D/A, to refer to the function evaluated not at the industry mean, but at a particular company's value of D/A.)

These estimates $C(\overline{D}/\overline{A})$ of the average cost of capital are, of course, always below the corresponding estimates of ρ (Table 3, column 1); but the movements over time of the two series are closely similar since, as expected, the sample mean value of $\overline{D}/\overline{A}$ is quite stable. Notice also that the estimates of ρ and hence of $C(\overline{D}/\overline{A})$ conform quite closely in their movements with the average yield on AAA bonds in the industry (Table 4, columns 3 and 4)—probably the most popular surrogate for the cost of capital in investment studies. This conformity is particularly interesting since the rate of interest on bonds enters only very indirectly into our calculations of ρ and $C(\overline{D}/\overline{A})$ and, as can be seen from columns 5 and 6, the implied average rate of interest in our sample does not even seem to conform well with the AAA series. From the

TABLE 4

Average Cost of Capital and Some Comparison Series

| Year | Average Cost of Capital, $C(\bar{D}/A)$ | | Yields on AAA Public Utility Bonds[a] | | Sample Mean Yield on Debt (R/D) | | Sample Mean Yield on Preferred Stock (Pdv/P) | | Weighted Average Yields | | | | Growth-Adjusted Average Yield[b] $(\bar{X}^\tau - \tau\bar{R})/V - G$ | |
| | | | | | | | | | With Book Value Weights $\bar{C}_B(\overline{D/A})$ | | With Market Value Weights $\bar{C}_M(\overline{D/V})$ | | | |
	Amt. (1)	As Per Cent of 1954 (2)	Amt. (3)	As Per Cent of 1954 (4)	Amt. (5)	As Per Cent of 1954 (6)	Amt. (7)	As Per Cent of 1954 (8)	Amt. (9)	As Per Cent of 1954 (10)	Amt. (11)	As Per Cent of 1954 (12)	Amt. (13)	As Per Cent of 1954 (14)
1957	.046	128	.043	137	.029	112	.047	115	.034	104	.042	108	.047	122
1956	.045	125	.039	126	.029	112	.046	112	.035	106	.043	110	.045	115
1954	.036	100	.031	100	.026	100	.041	100	.033	100	.039	100	.039	100

[a] Monthly average for December (from *Federal Reserve Bulletin*).

[b] With G equal to growth coefficient in Table 1 times sample mean value of $\overline{\Delta A/A}$.

economic point of view, this parallelism between movements in ρ and the AAA yields would seem to suggest that, over this short interval at least, the movements of both series were dominated by factors affecting the supply of and demand for capital generally. Changes, if any, in investors' tastes for risk-bearing or in their evaluation of the riskiness of this industry in relation to others were apparently not large enough (except possibly in 1957) to cause any significant divergence of movement in the period under study.

It is also instructive to contrast our estimates of the average cost of capital with those that would be obtained by following the prescriptions laid down in much of the traditional literature of corporation finance. Essentially, these call for computing the weighted sum of the market yields of each type of security, the weights being the "target" proportions of each security in the capital structure. That is, if we let i equal the earnings-to-price ratio (our $\bar{\pi}^\tau/S$), p the preferred yield (our $\overline{Pdv}/P$), r the average rate of interest on bonds (our $\bar{R}/D$), l the target debt ratio, and l' the target preferred ratio, then the weighted average cost of capital function under the traditional view can be expressed as $i(1-l-l') + p(l') + r(1-\tau)(l)$. Where the target weights l and l' are computed at book value as is usually recommended (i.e., with $l=D/A$ and $l'=P/A$ and $(1-l-l')=B/A$ in our notation), we shall refer to the resulting average as $\bar{C}_B(D/A)$; where they are taken at market value (i.e., with $l=D/V$ and $l'=P/V$ and $1-l-l'=S/V$), we shall refer to the average as $\bar{C}_M(D/V)$, with unbarred values of the argument standing as before for a single company value and barred values for industry means. Estimates of both $\bar{C}_B(\overline{D/A})$ and $\bar{C}_M(\overline{D/V})$ for the typical firm in the sample, using actual sample mean values of i, p, and r, as well as of the book and market value measures of l and l' in each case, are shown in Table 4, columns 9–12.

As can be seen from Table 4, both the levels and the time paths of $\bar{C}_B(\overline{D/A})$ and $\bar{C}_M(\overline{D/V})$ differ significantly from those of $C(\overline{D/A})$. The largest discrepancies arise in the case of the widely advocated $\bar{C}_B(\overline{D/A})$ measure, which is substantially below $C(\overline{D/A})$ in all three years and which shows only a very slight rise over the period. The market value estimates, $\bar{C}_M(\overline{D/V})$, are considerably closer to those of $C(\overline{D/A})$, but they too fail to indicate the sizable increase in the cost of capital which seems to have occurred during this period.

5. RECONCILIATION WITH CONVENTIONAL AVERAGES

To understand precisely why these three methods of estimating the average cost of capital gave such different answers for the years under study (and why they are likely to continue to diverge for other years and other industries), it is helpful to begin by showing how these estimates would relate to each other in a much simpler world in which no growth potential ever existed. In such a world, we have seen that the ratio $(\bar{X}^\tau - \tau\bar{R})/(V - \tau D)$—the tax- and leverage-adjusted yield of the previous section—would be a measure of our ρ, the cost of equity capital. Hence, from the standpoint of any individual firm, the $C(L)$ function can be expressed as

$$C(L) = \frac{\bar{X}^\tau - \tau\bar{R}}{V - \tau D}(1 - \tau L) = \frac{\bar{X}^\tau - \tau\bar{R}}{V} \cdot \frac{1 - \tau L}{1 - \tau D/V}. \qquad (14)$$

The weighted average cost of capital function with market value weights is

$$\bar{C}_M(D/V) = \frac{\bar{\pi}^\tau}{S} \cdot \frac{S}{V} + \frac{\overline{Pdv}}{P} \cdot \frac{P}{V} + \frac{\bar{R}(1 - \tau)}{D} \cdot \frac{D}{V} = \frac{\bar{X}^\tau - \tau\bar{R}}{V} \qquad (15)$$

and with the book value weights

$$\bar{C}_B(D/A) = \frac{\bar{\pi}^\tau}{S} \cdot \frac{B}{A} + \frac{\overline{Pdv}}{P} \cdot \frac{P}{A} + \frac{\bar{R}(1 - \tau)}{D} \cdot \frac{D}{A}. \qquad (16)$$

Notice first that for the special case of $L = D/V$—i.e., when the target leverage coincides with current leverage at market value, D/V, the function $C(L)$ takes the value $C(D/V) = (\bar{X}^\tau - \tau\bar{R})/V = \bar{C}_M(D/V)$. In other words, if a firm's current and future target leverage is D/V, it will get precisely the same estimate for its average cost of capital regardless of whether it chooses to multiply its current tax- and leverage-adjusted yield by $(1 - \tau D/V)$, to compute the weighted average of the current yields of its outstanding securities with market value weights for each, or to simply use the ratio of expected tax-adjusted earnings to total market value. A similar equivalence of estimates (at least to a very close degree of approximation) would also hold, of course, for economists concerned with "typical" values for the industry and using industry mean values of D/V and of the various yields, i.e., $C(\overline{D/V}) \cong \bar{C}_M(\overline{D/V})$.[13]

[13] Although the equivalence holds for individual company data and for industry averages, there is one important case in which the equivalence very definitely does *not* hold. This is the common case of the firm following the weighted average approach of (15) or (16) with current (or prospective future) company weights, but using industry-wide averages of the component yields so as to obtain more reliable estimates. The trouble here is that the market yield on shares (and to some extent the yields on preferred and bonds as well) are increasing functions of leverage. Hence, for a firm whose target leverage is greater (smaller) than the average for the industry mean yield will be an underestimate (overestimate) of its own yield and the resulting average cost of capital will be too low (high). This problem does not arise under our (14), of course, since $(\bar{X}^\tau - \tau R)/(V - \tau D)$ is not a function of firm policy (as is $\bar{\pi}/S$) but an estimate of the external, market-given parameter, ρ.

Note also that if V equals A—which would tend to be the case if there were no growth past or future—then $\overline{C}_B(\overline{D}/A)$ becomes the same function as $\overline{C}_M(D/V)$ and, by extension, as $C(L)$. In this special case of no growth, therefore, all three company and industry-wide estimates will coincide.

This simple picture changes quite drastically, however, as soon as growth potential is introduced. The function $C(L)$ must now be expressed as

$$C(L) = \frac{\overline{X}^\tau - \tau\overline{R}}{V - \tau D - G}(1 - \tau L) = \frac{\overline{X}^\tau - \tau\overline{R}}{V - G} \cdot \frac{1 - \tau L}{1 - \tau\left(\dfrac{D}{V - G}\right)}, \quad (17)$$

where G is the market's current valuation of future growth potential. Hence, as can be seen by referring back to (15), there no longer exists any concept of L for which the function $C(L)$ will be the same as $\overline{C}_M(D/V)$. Note also that in the special case in which future growth potential constitutes the only major source of divergence between V and A, $(\overline{D/A}) \cong (\overline{D/V - G})$ so that our estimates of the average cost of capital $C(D/A)$ would be closely approximated by the ratio $(\overline{\overline{X}^\tau - \tau\overline{R}}/V - G)$. The actual sample mean values of that ratio (with G taken as the product of the growth coefficient in Table 1 and the mean value of our growth variable $\overline{\triangle A/A}$) are shown in columns 13 and 14 of Table 4. As can be seen, the approximation to $C(\overline{D/A})$ is indeed quite close in 1956 and 1957; but it is less satisfactory in 1954 where the growth contribution is small, both in absolute terms and relative to the other sources of divergence between V and A.

Where the ratio $(\overline{\overline{X}^\tau - \overline{R}}/V - G)$ is a good approximation to $C(\overline{D/A})$, it will, of course, also follow that both measures will exceed $\overline{C}_M(\overline{D/V})$ which, as we saw above, is given approximately by $(\overline{\overline{X}^\tau - \tau\overline{R}}/V)$. As for the relation between the popular $\overline{C}_B(\overline{D/A})$ and $C(\overline{D/A})$, note that we can express the ratio $(\overline{\overline{X}^\tau - \tau\overline{R}}/V - G)$ approximately as

$$\left(\overline{\frac{\overline{X}^\tau - \tau\overline{R}}{V - G}}\right) = \left(\overline{\frac{\overline{\pi}^\tau}{S - G} \cdot \frac{S - G}{V - G}}\right) + \left(\overline{\frac{Pdv}{P} \cdot \frac{P}{V - G}}\right)$$

$$+ \left(\overline{\frac{\overline{R}(1 - \tau)}{D} \cdot \frac{D}{V - G}}\right) \quad (18)$$

$$\cong \left(\overline{\frac{\overline{\pi}^\tau}{S - G}}\right)\left(\frac{\overline{B}}{A}\right) + \left(\overline{\frac{Pdv}{P}}\right)\left(\frac{\overline{P}}{A}\right) + \left(\overline{\frac{\overline{R}(1 - \tau)}{D}}\right)\left(\frac{\overline{D}}{A}\right),$$

since the assumption $V - G \cong A$ implies $D/V - G \cong D/A$, $P/V - G \cong$

P/A and $S - G/V - G \cong B/A$. Comparison with (16) shows that the weights in the two expressions are essentially the same; but since $(\overline{\pi\tau}/S) < (\overline{\pi\tau}/S - G)$, $\overline{C}_B(\overline{D/A})$ too will necessarily fall short of $C(\overline{D/A})$ when growth is present, and the gap will be larger, the larger is the contribution of growth to the value of the shares.

Once again, then, we see that attempts to infer the cost of capital directly from market yields rather than by the more detailed, cross-sectional estimating procedures developed in this paper break down in the face of growth. Where growth is present, all the popular, short-cut approximations will underestimate the cost of capital; and where the market changes its evaluation of growth potential over time (as is inevitable in view of the nature of growth), the time path of the yield measures may give a quite misleading picture of the true changes in the cost of capital. In particular, in our sample it happens that the market's evaluation of growth increased substantially over the period, thereby causing the yield measures to understate seriously the rise in capital costs that appears to have been taking place at the same time. As noted earlier, it is somewhat paradoxical that these two changes should have occurred simultaneously, since an increase in the cost of capital should tend to reduce what the market is willing to pay for given investment opportunities. We can perhaps throw some light on this paradox by taking a closer look at our growth coefficients and their implicit components.

6. A FURTHER ANALYSIS OF THE VALUATION OF GROWTH

The growth term in our basic valuation equation (see section II 4) is of the form

$$k\overline{X}(1 - \tau)\left[\frac{\rho^* - C}{C(1 + C)}\right]T,$$

where k is the ratio of investment to tax-adjusted earnings, C is the average cost of capital, ρ^* is the tax-adjusted rate of return on new investment, and T is a measure of the length of time for which the opportunities to invest at the rate ρ^* are expected last. In the actual estimating equations, we have taken as our growth variable an estimate of $k\overline{X}(1 - \tau)$, the level of future investment opportunities. Hence, if one accepts the underlying model, the observed coefficients of the growth variable can be interpreted as an approximation to $[\rho^* - C/C(1 + C)]T$.

Now that we have estimates of C, the average cost of capital for a typical firm, we can attempt some further decomposition of these growth coefficients and, in the process, we hope, gain some additional insights into the market's appraisal of the growth potential in this industry. In particular, it should be possible, from what we know about past earnings and about the regulatory process governing earnings in the industry, to make at least a rough approximation of ρ^*.

An obvious first candidate as an approximation to ρ^* is, of course, the current, tax-adjusted rate of return on assets, $(\overline{X}^\tau - \tau \overline{R})/A$. Such a measure, however, is almost certainly an underestimate of ρ^* since we know that there are components of total assets—actually, of total liabilities—that regulatory commissions systematically exclude from the rate base.[14] Some idea of the extent of this underestimate is provided by our knowledge that during these years most of the state commissions were still setting the "reasonable return on the rate base" in the neighborhood of the classical 6 per cent. By contrast, the sample average values of $\overline{X}^\tau/A$—$\overline{X}^\tau$ rather than tax-adjusted earnings $\overline{X}(1 - \tau)$ being the relevant earnings concept in rate setting—were only .054, .056, and .055 per cent in 1954, 1956, and 1957, respectively. One simple adjustment, therefore, would be to blow up each sample mean value of tax-adjusted earnings by the ratio of 6 per cent to the sample mean value of $\overline{X}^\tau/A$. The rates of return thus adjusted, as well as the original unadjusted rates of return, are presented in Table 5, along with the estimates of T they imply.

These results would seem to suggest the following as the resolution of the paradox described in the previous section. The observed rise in the market's valuation of the industry's growth potential, in the face of the sharp rise in the cost of capital during the period, cannot reasonably be attributed to any compensating increase in the expected rate of return on future investment. No sharp upward trend in earnings rates, adjusted or unadjusted, is visible in the data; nor would such a trend be expected in view of the regulatory controls over the level of earnings. What seems to have been happening rather is that early in the period investors came to recognize that the regulatory authorities were setting rates at levels

---

[14] A further word of caution is necessary because the so-called accounting rate of return (earnings after depreciation divided by net assets) is not the same as the ordinary internal rate of return when a firm is growing. This discrepancy does not seem likely to create any very serious problems insofar as the valuation equations or estimates of the cost of capital are concerned since in those equations assets appear only as a deflator and since an explicit growth variable is included. It may, however, raise difficulties for comparisons of the kind being attempted here. We say may, because the ρ^* in our formula is not the usual internal rate of return, but the so-called "perpetual rate of return" (see [9], p. 416), and the relations between that rate and the accounting rate of return have, to our knowledge, nowhere yet been explored. We are indebted to Sidney Davidson and Robert Williamson for some helpful discussions on this general point.

that would probably permit firms in the industry to earn somewhat more than the cost of capital on any new capital invested. The subsequent rise in the cost of capital narrowed the margin of gain somewhat; but its effects on valuation were more than offset by an increase in the length of time that favorable terms for new investment were expected to persist. The actual numerical estimates of the expected duration of growth opportunities, as presented in Table 5, are not, of course, to be taken seriously in view of the many approximations, theoretical and empirical, involved in their computation. But upward revaluation of growth prospects (or at least in increasing awareness of growth potential on the part of investors) is very definitely indicated.

IV. Some Concluding Observations

As emphasized at the outset, this paper should be regarded by economists as a first step toward developing historical estimates of the cost of capital relevant for investment decision-making by business firms. It will have adequately fulfilled its objectives if it has succeeded in convincing economists working with investment functions that there *is* a cost of capital problem, that some of the major econometric problems that have prevented progress in the area to date can be overcome, and that the averages and yield measures of the kind recommended in much of the traditional literature on corporation finance as measures of the cost of capital are likely to be treacherous and unreliable.

As for the direction to be taken by future research, clearly one urgent need is further testing of the basic, rational, behavior-perfect, capital market specification. Some confirmatory evidence for the model is provided in our unabridged paper and further tests on the same sample will be provided in sequel papers. But it would obviously be desirable to have independent tests by others and on samples which are a little fresher, both in age and extent of handling.

Even after a basic specification is agreed upon, there remain numerous perplexing problems of estimation, notably those connected with the crucial growth effect. If the market's expectation of future growth opportunities changed seldom, slowly, or only in response to movements of other more readily measurable variables such as sales, profits, or even dividends, then the task would be the difficult but still essentially straightforward one of extrapolation. In practice, however, the market's valuation of growth potential often changes abruptly, substantially, and with little readily apparent relation to changes in observable economic series.

TABLE 5

Analysis of the Growth Effect

Year	Growth Coefficient[a] (G)	Average Cost of Capital[b] $C(\overline{D/A})$	Average Tax-Adjusted Return on Assets (ρ_1^*)	Average Return Assuming 6 Per Cent Return After Taxes (ρ_2^*)	Implied Value of T [c] (in years)	
					For ρ_1^*	For ρ_2^*
1957	1.36	.046	.047	.052	51	11
1956	.90	.045	.048	.052	12	6
1954	.30	.036	.046	.052	1	1

[a] From Table 1.

[b] From Table 4, column 1.

[c] Computed as $G\left[\dfrac{(C)(1+C)}{(\rho^* - C)}\right]$.

While we, and we hope others, will continue to experiment with the extrapolative approach, we suspect that a somewhat more indirect attack may in the long-run prove more fruitful. In particular, instead of attempting to correct for the elusive and changing growth component in the value of growth companies, effort might be directed to finding and identifying companies that the market seems to regard as essentially no-growth companies—and growth here does not mean expansion, but opportunities to invest large sums at rates of return above the cost of capital. The search for such no-growth firms might proceed either by further decomposing the growth term along the lines of the last part of the previous section, with a view to finding the firms for which $\rho^* \cong C$, or by constructing scatters similar to those in Figure 1 for a series of widely spaced years and observing which firms seem continually to cluster in the near neighborhood of the "pivots." Once a sample of no-growth firms has thus been obtained, estimates of ρ can be made relatively simply and quickly via the leverage-corrected yield route discussed in section III. This approach, or variants relying on a judicious interplay of time series and cross-sectional estimation, should enable us, within a reasonable span of time and with a reasonable amount of effort, to obtain a usable time series of the estimated cost of capital.

Needless to say, even these hoped-for time series estimates would have to be handled quite gingerly in investment studies. It is not to be expected, for example, that the desired capital stock will always adjust quickly to the current level of the cost of capital. Because of the substantial decision-making costs involved, the cut-off rate or required minimum yield on new investments is likely to be changed only infrequently by large firms (typically, but by no means exclusively, on the occasions when external financing is contemplated). By suitably smoothing or lagging the series, however, it should be possible to incorporate at least the major changes in the level of the cost of capital that have occurred as the economy has swung over the last forty years from boom to severe depression, to a postwar prosperity widely regarded as temporary, and finally to a long period of sustained prosperity interrupted by only minor recessions and with fears of major future depressions largely absent.

Finally, we should like to stress once more that the measure of the cost of capital described in this paper should prove primarily relevant for the investment behavior of large corporate enterprises. For smaller firms, other measures—including more conventional measures of interest rates and of those rather elusive factors that may be lumped under the heading of availability of funds—might be a good deal more to the point.

BIBLIOGRAPHY

1. Chow, G., *The Demand for Automobiles in the United States,* Amsterdam, 1957.
2. Durand, D., *Bank Stock Prices and the Bank Capital Problem,* Occasional Paper 54, New York, NBER, 1954.
3. Gordon, M., "Dividends, Earnings and Stock Prices," *Review of Economics and Statistics,* May 1959.
4. ———, *The Investment, Financing and Valuation of the Corporation,* Homewood, Ill., 1962.
5. Hirshleifer, J., "Investment Decision Under Uncertainty," *Quarterly Journal of Economics* (forthcoming).
6. ———, "On the Theory of Optimal Investment Decision," *Journal of Political Economy,* August 1958.
7. Lintner, J., "Dividends, Earnings, Leverage, Stock Prices and the Supply of Capital to Corporations," *Review of Economics and Statistics,* August 1962.
8. Madansky, A., "On the Efficiency of Three-Stage Least-Squares Estimation," *Econometrica,* January-April 1964.
9. Miller, M., and Modigliani, F., "Dividend Policy, Growth and the Valuation of Shares," *Journal of Business,* October 1961.
10. Modigliani, F., and Miller, M., "The Cost of Capital, Corporation Finance and the Theory of Investment," *American Economic Review,* June 1958.
11. ———, "Reply," *ibid.,* September 1959.
12. ———, "Corporate Income Taxes and the Cost of Capital: A Correction," *ibid.,* June 1963.
13. Neilsen, S., *Market Value and Financial Structure in the Railroad Industry,* Hartford, 1961.
14. Theil, H., *Economic Forecasts and Policy,* 2d rev. ed., Amsterdam, 1961.

Corporation Finance:
Risk and Investment

JOHN LINTNER

HARVARD UNIVERSITY

All modern studies of investment decisions and their financing must build essentially upon Irving Fisher's *The Theory of Interest* [11],[1] published more than a third of a century ago. As Kuh [22] has remarked, "the foundations of capital theory in its modern form have been best articulated [in this work]. . . . It is a theory at the level of microeconomic choice and at the level of total market price determination which has the major ingredients, correctly related to each other, that a capital theory should have." In this basic model of the capital markets, all the individual participants' perceptions of their "real" investment opportunities and their market opportunities to borrow or lend, on the one hand, and their "initial endowments" of income (or funds) and their personal time preferences (or utility functions), on the other, mutually interact to provide Pareto-optimal, stable equilibrium market prices (interest rates).

The theory assumed that "investment opportunities," along with utility functions and initial endowments, were given; its rigorous analysis was confined to comparative statics under certainty; and even in this context, it was at best ambiguous in multiple-period cases with non-constant interest rates (Hirshleifer [17]). Much work remained to be—and, happily, has since been—done on the rational derivation of relevant (real) "investment opportunity functions" from more basic considerations and data; on the dynamics of adjustment processes; and, quite

NOTE: The research reported in this paper was financed from the grant of the Ford Foundation to the Harvard Business School for financial research. This generous support is gratefully acknowledged.
[1] Numbers in brackets refer to Bibliography at end of paper.

recently, on the development of a rigorous analysis of the crucial role and effects of uncertainty on investment and financing decisions and on market equilibrium. But a granite cornerstone in the foundations of future work had been securely put in its place. Subsequent efforts ignore or disregard Fisher at their peril.

In this paper we undertake to identify the variables required in a structural equation to explain investment outlays. In section I we assume that Fisher's perfectly competitive model under certainty is an adequate theoretical model of investment behavior. We examine the various forms of accelerator-capacity relationship in the light of certain real-world complications consistent with certainty of expectations, and point up additional variables required by Fisher's framework even under the restrictions involved in the assumption of certainty.

In section II, we examine the modifications required when the Fisher framework is extended to incorporate the fact of uncertainty. We retain under uncertainty the assumption that firms are optimizing at all times by making the decisions that will maximize the market value of their equity (given the level of "the market" as measured, say, by the Standard & Poor or Dow-Jones index); and continue to assume that all securities markets are purely competitive with no frictions or imperfections whatsoever. Nevertheless, to determine optimal capital outlays in this rigorous neo-Fisherian model, the fact of uncertainty is shown to *require* the inclusion of several financial and risk variables (such as leverage and retained funds) that would have no place at all if the world were really characterized by prescience so that the traditional certainty models would be adequate. The latter part of this section summarizes the author's model of investment and financial policy under uncertainty. Using the assumption that bonds (as well as stocks) are risk assets to their owners, we show that investment is inversely related to leverage—in contrast to the implications of the *MM* model based on an assumption that corporate debt is a riskless asset to its owners.

Section III of the paper then specifies a statistical model of investment outlays based on the foregoing theoretical-economic model; briefly discusses certain important problems of estimation, and of identification, in working with data generated under conditions of uncertainty; and presents the empirical results of applying the model to explain the plant and equipment expenditures of manufacturing corporations over the period 1953-63. Not only are correlations unusually high, but *t*-ratios are uniformly good, and forecasts into 1964 are reassuring.

I. Analysis Under Certainty

THE ROLE OF ACCELERATOR-CAPACITY VARIABLES
IN THE FISHER MODEL UNDER CERTAINTY

The initial formulation of the accelerator relationship held that net investment (change in capital stock) would not only be proportional to the actual current change in output,

$$I_t = K\Delta O_t, \tag{1}$$

but also that its elasticity to capital stock would be unity. Even if we retain Fisher's classical assumption of certainty for the nonce and also defer our consideration of all factors impounded in *ceteris paribus,* it is clear that reliance on this rigid form of the accelerator involves accepting certain underlying assumptions about the factual situation. In particular, even with other things equal under certainty, this particular formulation assumes that (a) production functions are homogeneous of order one, (b) the existing capital stock of potential buyers of plant and equipment is at the desired level at the beginning of the period, (c) suppliers of capital goods (in contrast) have sufficient excess capacity to meet all demands promptly at existing prices, and (d) the elasticity of expectations of capital goods buyers is zero.

Some of these restrictive assumptions are more serious than others. The linear homogeneity of production functions is probably an adequate approximation for present purposes. Also, lack of excess capacity on the part of suppliers and long production periods for capital goods merely serve to introduce a distributed lag of actual investment expenditures trailing the initiating change in outputs. (See Eisner and Strotz [10].) While this reduces the short-run elasticities, the long-run elasticity of capital to output would still be unity if the other relevant conditions were satisfied. If the elasticity of expectations of capital goods buyers is greater than zero, the elasticity of capital stocks to output will generally be increased and a variable measuring growth in output may need to be added.

If the remaining critical assumption is not accepted, more substantial modifications are required. It has long been recognized (indeed, since 1917 by J. M. Clark himself) that equation (1) will not hold whenever the existing capital stocks of the potential buyers of plant and equipment were already in excess of desired levels. An alternative formulation of the basic "acceleration" approach, free of this defect, substitutes an assumption that investment will be determined by the *discrepancy* between the (known) current capital stock and a desired level which, in turn, is assumed proportional to (actual or expected) output. A still more flexible formulation of this "capacity" version of the "acceleration family" of models introduces a distributed lag of actual investment, after assuming realistically that only some fraction of an existing discrepancy between desired and actual capital can be (or will be) acquired in any particular time interval. This more flexible version of the general "capacity" variant of the acceleration family of models thus relies on an equation of the form:

$$I_t = \gamma(BO_t - K_{t-1}),\qquad(2)$$

where γ is an adjustment coefficient equal to the fraction of the "capacity gap" eliminated per period, and B is the fixed (desired) capital-output ratio.

Still more flexible versions of the accelerator can, of course, be obtained by dropping the a priori requirement that the capital-output elasticity coefficient K in equation (1) is unity, and by combining this more flexible version of the initial accelerator model with its capacity variant, to specify investment as a function of the level of output, change in output, and the capital stock at the beginning of the period:

$$I_t = f(O_t, \Delta O_t, K_t).\qquad(3)$$

The relation between current output and beginning capital stock may, of course, be subsumed in some measure of the utilization of capacity along the lines introduced by de Leeow [4] and others.

OTHER FACTORS REQUIRED EVEN UNDER CERTAINTY AND PERFECT CAPITAL MARKETS

It is clear that at least the more flexible forms of accelerator relationships form an *essential part* of any valid theory of investment. They represent essential determinants of the position—and of the shifts in the position—of Fisher's investment opportunity function. But quite apart from considerations introduced by the fact of uncertainty, it is clear that in the context of Fisher's basic framework, even the most sophisticated and flexible versions of a generalized "accelerator principle"—such as equation (3)—would a priori be expected to be an adequate representation of the true structure of empirical investment behavior *only* under severely restrictive *ceteris paribus* assumptions. If the *ceteris* of these accelerator-capacity formulations are not, in fact, *paribus* to an acceptable degree of approximation, reliance on these models as an adequate representation of the structure of investment decision-making behavior would involve a certain degree of myopia.

Many more elements in the economy were allowed—and expected—to vary in Fisher's model than in even the most flexible version of the accelerator genus. Fisher's model of the real investment and financial sectors was (implicitly to be sure) embedded in a general equilibrium model of the entire economy including factor and product markets. While the immediately relevant product prices and factor costs were taken to be exogenously given at any one time, they were determined by interactions with the rest of the economy and subject to change over time. Changes in wage rates relative to labor productivity, for instance, or changes in the efficiency of economic life or other factors affecting the real cost of physical capital will directly affect the position and shape of the investment opportunity function, even if all accelerator-capacity factors were unchanged. Similarly, changes in marginal labor costs *relative* to marginal real capital costs per unit of output, by inducing substitutions of capital for labor along a given production function, will shift the position of the investment opportunity function even under certainty. If data on these factors have in fact been changing in the real world over the time period of interest, adherence to Fisher's model would require that such variables be added to the list of accelerator-capacity variables in statistical analyses of investment behavior.

Correspondingly, in Fisher's framework—even under conditions of prescient certainty and blissfully perfect markets throughout—the position and shape of the investment opportunity function determine the amount of investment only in conjunction with the line of "financial market opportunities." As is well known, the amount of investment is determined by moving along the (real) investment opportunity function to the point at which net increments in present value are no longer positive—in the continuous case, the point of tangency between the real investment opportunity function and the financial market opportunity line. Fisher was as sure that a change in the market interest rate—the relevant "cost of funds" in his model under certainty—would change the amount of investment without changing the position or shape of the real investment opportunity function as he was that a change in the latter would alter the amount of real investment when market opportunity lines and the rate of interest were unchanged.

To rely on traditional accelerator-type models as complete explanations of real investment behavior would, in the strictest theoretical terms, be equivalent to relying on one blade of Marshall's famous scissors. To rely on unaugmented accelerator-type models as an empirically adequate representation of real investment behavior would be to act upon a presumption that changes in the financial markets, in *financial* (as opposed to *real*) investment opportunities, and in the explicit (or implicit "opportunity") cost of funds, are uniformly ignored by all business decision-makers, and thereby to deny the relevance of "the main body of the maximization principle in economic theory."[2] In the specification of the statistical models fitted in the latter part of this paper, I consequently include variables for the labor and (real) capital costs of output, for output growth, and for financial costs (interest rates), along with the levels and change in level of output, capital stock, and capacity utilization.

Our structural equations must include all these variables if they are to be consistent with the basic Fisher framework of investment decisions and capital markets. (Whether the effects of all these variables come through loud and clear in the face of uncertainty and noise in the data is, of course, an empirical question which we defer to the latter parts of this paper.) Although our list of variables is already substantially longer than called for by accelerator-capacity models, it should be emphasized that up to this point our analysis has been conducted entirely within Fisher's own assumptions of perfect certainty and perfectly competitive market structures. For this reason, it will be noted, we have as yet not introduced certain other variables often included in investment equations —notably, current (or lagged) dollar profits or retained funds, current (or lagged) profit *rates,* initial endowments of funds, or assets. Within Fisher's idealized world of perfect competition and certainty, *these* factors affect the amounts of borrowing and lending and thereby the level of interest rates; but, given the level of interest rates, they do not affect the amount of investment, and with certainty none of them would affect the expectations of *future* profitability on incremental real investments incorporated in the investment opportunity function.

Before turning to the effects of uncertainty, there is one further real-world factor which must be considered briefly. Fisher did not develop the effects of corporate taxes upon optimal investment criteria, but the existence of a modern corporate tax structure is perfectly consistent with standard assumptions of certainty. Jorgenson's[3] recent work has elegantly filled in this gap in the theory. By maximizing net worth subject to a general neoclassical production function and the constraint that the growth in capital stock is investment less replacement, he shows [19] that the marginal productivity of capital is equal to the ratio of the user cost of capital to the price of output, where the user cost in turn is proportional to the cost price of capital goods. The factor of proportionality is a weighted sum of the depreciation rate and the market

---

[2] The slightly ungrammatical phrase is taken from Eisner [9], p. 139.

interest rate. Both weights involve the corporate tax rate. The other factor in the depreciation term is the proportion of replacement chargeable against income for tax purposes, and the other factor affecting the impact of the interest rate is the proportion of interest charges in total financial costs. Because of the latter term, leverage would affect optimal investment decisions, even in a world of certainty whenever there was a modern corporate income tax and, because of the favored treatment of the interest expense in such a tax, both the optimal capital stock and the level of current investment would vary directly with leverage.[3] The Jorgenson marginal productivity of capital term, involving the appropriate combination of tax, interest and depreciation rates, and leverage, is included in our later statistical analysis.

II. Analysis Under Uncertainty

THE FORMATIONS OF EXPECTATIONS:
MODIFICATIONS AND ADDITIONAL FACTORS
SUGGESTED BY THE FACT OF UNCERTAINTY

All the *factors* which would affect investment decisions under idealized conditions of certainty obviously must be included in the structural specification of investment behavior under uncertainty. The *variables* representing these factors may or may not be different under uncertainty: such items as beginning-of-period capital stock or interest rates can be introduced as known data; the variables representing other such crucially important elements as outputs may need to be modified or supplemented because it is the uncertain expectations of the future output levels (and associated operating costs) that determine the expectations of future profitability which directly affect current investment decisions.

Unfortunately, we have relatively little firm knowledge of the way such expectations of uncertain future outcomes are formed. Presumably they reflect some amalgam of past experience adjusted by new information. As an empirical matter, it has become common to assume (following the lead of Friedman [13]) that these judgments of the relevant future magnitudes reflect current judgments of "permanent" or "true" output levels, which are free of the random or transient components in the unfiltered and unadjusted raw data on current outputs. In this

---

[3] As shown in [19], p. 249, the optimal capital stock, given output and sales prices, is inversely proportional to the user cost, which in turn varies inversely with leverage, *ceteris paribus*. Jorgenson's cost variable is described in more detail in footnote 33 below.

approach, it is generally considered reasonable to believe that, at least to a first-order approximation, these current estimates of "sustainable" outputs are formed in terms of a simple "learning" theory that reduces arithmetically to an exponential smoothing (or some similar weighted average) of past observed data on outputs. It may be noted, however, that this approach presumes that decisions are made on the basis of "point estimates" of future data, whereas all the modern neo-Bayesian economic-statistical theory of rational decision-making under uncertainty argues the relevance and importance of the entire probability distribution except in special cases. Since it is very unlikely that corporations (or their shareholders!) are "linear in money" with respect to their capital budgets and since relevant "loss functions" are surely not symmetrical, nor quadratic utilities adequate to reflect preferences [27, p. 18] and [35], it seems clear that some variable measuring risk or degree of uncertainty may well be required along with measures of expected values.

It might have been argued that, even in a world of certainty, the level of orders and of order-backlogs would be as useful a measure (particularly in durable goods industries) as current output levels in judging future sales. When uncertainty is admitted into the analysis, their a priori relevance is greatly strengthened, for these are current data which bear *directly* on the future. Moreover, changes and trends in the level of orders and order-backlogs can probably be expected to have as much or more *expectational* significance as changes and trends in outputs; and, as Hart [15] has recently proposed, the level of the ratio of orders to capacity may play an even more critical role in the formation of the expectations which determine investment decisions.

The presence of uncertainty also suggests the need for still other variables to measure the expectations that are relevant to investment decisions. In a maximizing world, investment decisions depend upon estimates of future profitability, which in turn depend upon operating costs and sales prices as well as output levels. In a world of certainty, future data on each would be known. Judgments of each are required in the real world of uncertainty. The current levels of (and recent changes and trends in) the ratio of product prices to unit labor costs, and in the ratio of product prices to the costs of real capital, thus properly belong in the specification of determinants of investment outlays. Alternatively, current levels, changes, and trends in profit margins may be used. As in the case of the judgment of future output levels, there are important empirical questions regarding the way in which these expectations are formed and how much effect they have in practice.

Nevertheless, the expectations of future profit margins are, in principle, relevant on a par with expectations of output levels.

Up to this point—except for the brief comment on the possible relevance of a risk or dispersion variable in output and margin expectations —our discussion of the effects of uncertainty has pointed up the probable need for different or additional variables to capture the future expectations relevant to investment decisions under uncertainty. These modifications or additions were all required to capture under uncertainty the expectations that managements hold with respect to the specific determining variables which we saw would determine investment decisions if the future were known exactly in advance. With the exceptions noted, the modifications and additions have related to the same list of determining factors that would be operative under certainty.

The changes and additions required in the finance sector of the model by the fact of uncertainty are much more fundamental. Under certainty, only the risk-free interest rate (adjusted for corporate taxes, if any) and the "tax shield" of depreciation allowances would be relevant to investment decisions. Current profits, dividends, retained funds, current assets or liabilities, funded debt, and net worth would—in strict theory—all be completely irrelevant. But once uncertainty—and certain other facts of life which would be of no consequence were it not for the fact of uncertainty—are admitted into the analysis, the situation is basically altered.

Suppose, for the moment, that there were no taxes and financial markets were really such that the Modigliani-Miller fundamental proposition [31], [32], and [33] was valid. The aggregate market value of all the securities (stocks and bonds combined) issued by any corporation would be independent of its debt-equity ratio or, more generally, of the mixture of claims upon its cash flows. This aggregate market value in turn would depend upon both the expected value and the risks associated with the corporations' cash flows (before interest charges), and upon expectations of their future growth as a result of further investment outlays. In this simplified world without taxes, the minimum marginal expected return required to justify new investment (the company's "cost of capital") would be independent of its existing capital structure and of the mix of fund sources utilized to finance its current (or future) capital budgets, but, even so, it would depend upon risk as well as upon the pure interest rate.

The introduction of corporate taxes in this model, of course, makes the relevant cost of capital depend upon tax rates and leverage as well. But in this framework, with corporate debt assumed to be riskless, corporate taxes make the market value of the corporate entity a necessarily increasing function of the degree of leverage. Rather remarkably, therefore, within the *MM* model addressed to an uncertain world, the relevant cost of capital is inferred to be a declining function of the degree of leverage,[4] just as it is implicitly in Jorgenson's model derived without introducing uncertainty. Within the *MM* framework, the more leverage a company has, the further down its marginal efficiency of capital schedule it can profitably and properly move—i.e., the larger the fraction of the projects submitted to its capital budgeting committee which should be approved.[5] This *MM* model thus predicts a positive association between leverage and investment outlays under uncertainty, just as under certainty. This prediction is, of course, contrary to what many of us have observed in the field interviewing and working with corporate financial officers; it also does not accord with some recent statistical evidence [36]. The proposition is further tested later in this paper.

This surprising prediction, of course, follows logically from the rather severe assumptions of the *MM* model. But if, instead, one accepts the assumption made in my own work that corporate bonds as well as corporate stocks are risky assets to their owners and if, in particular, it is recognized and consequently assumed that, for any given stochastic EBIT stream, an increase in fixed financial charges exponentially increases the probability of default and risks of loss on forced refinancing, thereby reducing expected returns by *more* than the mere interest charge on the added debt—then the troublesome inferences of the *MM* model no longer follow in strict theory under uncertainty, even within purely competitive markets with no imperfection whatsoever.

In my own theoretical work, I have assumed that all risk assets are traded in a single purely competitive capital market in which all investors are risk-averters with explicit joint (Gaussian or log-Gaussian) probability distributions over the end-of-period outcomes of the n risk-assets in the market. By introducing these additional assumptions into Fisher's model of capital market equilibrium under certainty, the equilibrium vector of market values of all risk-assets are simultaneously determined. (See Lintner [27] and [28].) Within this Fisherian model adopted to

---

[4] Note from equation (8) in [33], p. 442, that the required return net of tax declines linearly with leverage.

[5] Presumably institutional restrictions take over before leverage approaches 100 per cent, but the model is silent on how or where.

uncertainty, I then regard the ith company's bonds and its stock as different risk assets (each with its own vector of attributes) being traded in the perfectly fluid and purely competitive market of all stocks and bonds. I allow for the fact that the risks of holding corporate bonds and stocks (even of the same company) differ substantially because they have different variances and because their returns are subject (to at least a significant degree) to different influences, including different intercorrelations with other risk assets and with different exogenous variables.

In this Fisher framework adapted to uncertainty, the market values of the ith company's bonds and of its stock will each reflect its own vector of attributes (including its own row or column of the master variance-covariance matrix). In particular, the differential effect on the market value of a company's common stock of a given action by the company is *not* determined by first finding its differential effect upon the aggregated "entity" value of the company and then merely subtracting bond values (as for *MM*), but rather is determined directly as its effect on the common stock itself. (Any action by a company, of course, affects both the market value of its bonds and of its equity in the competitive equilibrium, but the effect of the action shareholder's welfare is measured directly by the latter.)

Within this model (even with the vector of all future investment outlays and "earnings" invariant), maximization of equity value occurs with positive leverage (except in limiting cases of a priori low relevance) and the degree of optimal leverage is a unique function of the set of parameter values pertaining to any given case. Apart from the effects of taxes, the minimum marginal expectation of return on new real investment which will justify the issuance of debt for (some or all of) its financing—the marginal "cost of debt capital"—is a continuously rising function of the amount of debt or the degree of leverage. (This is true even in the simpler versions of the model in which the interest is not assumed to be a rising function of leverage. The introduction of rising interest costs merely compounds the effect.) This result reflects both the marginal effect of leverage on the expectations of earnings before interest charges noted above, as well as its more commonly recognized impact on variances of rates of returns.[6] Both these considerations are directly attributable to the fact of uncertainty as such, and both are cumulative in their effect (i.e., both have positive second derivatives with leverage). In contrast, the favorable treatment accorded

---

[6] For a more precise statement, see also item (d) on p. 227 below.

interest expense in the tax laws—a factor common to the certainty case and our model under uncertainty—provides at most a linear offset. In the presence of a modern corporate tax structure, the marginal cost of debt capital under uncertainty must consequently be an orthodox U-shaped function, rising beyond some moderate amount of leverage. (This is true, incidentally, in both the short and long run.)

It follows immediately that, given any dividend or retention policy, there is an optimal degree of leverage. I have shown elsewhere [25] that, in the Fisher model of capital markets adapted to uncertainty, there is an optimal dividend payout policy,[7] given probabilistic investment opportunities (and any given level of leverage). A fortiori, there is an optimal mix of retentions and leverage for each company in the market.

In finding what this optimum is under any given set of expectations, the firm is assumed to act in accordance with standard maximizing principles: at any point along the "expansion path" of standard production theory (i.e., as the tentative size of the firm's capital budget is increased), it equates the *marginal* (not the average[8]) cost of each source, retentions and debt. If the firm is at a point on its "funds-for-investment-outlays" production function which is not on the "expansion path," these marginal costs in turn get equated by its using the cheaper source until it is no longer cheaper. Now for any given retention ratio, the marginal costs of debt are U-shaped when plotted against leverage (as noted above); but an optimizing firm will always be operating on the rising, right-hand side of this curve. The reason is simply that the marginal costs of retention are themselves a continuously rising function of the degree of leverage with which the retentions are associated. Since the maximizing firm uses debt instead of retentions as long as debt is cheaper, it will continue to use debt until marginal debt costs have become as large as marginal retention costs.

It must also be noted that these marginal debt costs are necessarily larger than the yield on the outstanding debt for four compounding

---

[7] In this paper for simplicity, I am confining the analysis to the joint optimization of dividends-retentions policy, debt, and real investment. (See also footnote 18.) It should be noted, however, that there will also be an optimal dividends-retention policy vis à vis common stock financing as a result of differentials in tax rates on ordinary income and capital gains (as pointed out in both Modigliani and Miller [32] and Lintner [24]) if investor's incomes differ, even if their probability distributions are identical and there are no issue or transfer costs. Relaxing the latter assumptions also introduces definite investor preferences for dividend policy even in the absence of taxes (see Lintner [24]).

[8] The average is acceptable if and only if it is equal to the marginal cost.

reasons.[9] The yield on outstanding debt is in the nature of an average return to the bond owner; the relevant costs to the company and its shareholders are higher[10] because: (a) issue costs are often relatively substantial compared with buyer yields at the time of issue; (b) increasing leverage, other things being equal, increases lender's risks, which results (even in purely competitive markets with no imperfections) in interest rates that are an increasing function of borrower's leverage and which makes the relevant marginal cash flow costs to the borrower higher than the stated interest charge on the immediate increment of debt (this difference between the relevant marginal and the average interest cost is itself a rapidly increasing function of leverage); (c) as noted earlier, for any given stochastic EBIT stream, an increase in fixed financial charges exponentially increases the risks of default and risks of loss to the company and its shareholders on forced refinancings, thereby reducing expected returns by more than even the relevant issue and marginal interest charges on the added debt; and, finally, (d) increasing leverage increases the variance of the distribution of the present values[11] of the relevant cash flows (associated with any given stochastic EBIT stream which reflects a given vector of investments) which crucially affect the *current* market values of equities in a purely

[9] See footnote 12.

[10] Because of the prevalence (among economists and elsewhere) of the belief that a "weighted average cost of capital" rule is appropriate under uncertainty, we should note that the "weighted average cost of capital" is usually a weighted average of the earnings yield on the stock and the market yield (or coupon rate) on debt (using equity and debt as weights). In terms of our model, this weighted average alternative is *too low* because (1) the relevant debt cost is *necessarily* (and usually very much) *greater* than the average debt yield used in the weighted average formula, and (2) the cost of retentions or new issues for equity is also higher than the earnings yield whenever we allow for the facts that the future is uncertain, that we know still less about the more distant future, and that most investors are "risk averters." (See Lintner [25].) In sum, the weighted average cost usually used is too low because, in the face of the uncertainties of life, it understates the required returns for the use of equity capital, and it doubly understates the marginal expected returns which must be required to justify the use of debt. Moreover, these understatements are mutually reinforcing in the sense that the greater the "spread" on the equity side (i.e., the difference between the marginal rates which are really required to justify the use of equity and the current earnings yield of the stock), the greater will be the corresponding spread (above marginal cash costs on a yield basis) on the debt, and vice versa.

[11] Alternatively, and in more traditional language, we find that increased leverage increases the variance of profit *rates,* and a fortiori the variances of prospective growth rates. (Stock prices were shown to be inversely related to the variance of growth rates in Lintner [25].) The marginal prospective return on new investment financed with debt must be enough higher than the combined costs of (a), (b) and (c) above to offset this further variance effect on stock values.

competitive capital market. (See Lintner [27].) The third and fourth factors together determine the relevant risk premium involved in debt financing in excess of issue costs and its relevant marginal cash costs.[12]

The maximizing firm will increase the size of its capital budget until the marginal *expected* return no longer exceeds the marginal cost of capital along its expansion path—i.e., the equalized marginal costs of debt and of retentions. Under uncertainty, this optimal intersection of "m.e.c." and "m.c.c." will occur where the marginal cost curve is rising with increased budget size. It follows that the marginal cost of added retentions and of added leverage are not only equal but rising at the equilibrium point.[13]

Finally, a distinction between long-run and short-run equilibrium is required. So far in my discussion of the derivations of the costs of capital and the optimal finance mix, I have implicitly been discussing the analogue under uncertainty of the "long-run equilibrium" analysis of the traditional "comparative statics (or dynamics)" under certainty. I firmly believe—and always have[14]—that (target) dividend payout ratios (or retention rates), target or ex ante maximal debt-equity ratios, and capital budgeting criteria in the long-run planning context are mutually determined. Other things being given, relatively greater volumes of more promising and profitable investment opportunities on the average (or expected over the long pull) lead to greater retentions (lower dividend payouts) and greater leverage; while *expected* values pertaining to investments being the same, greater "business risks" or ex ante variances in average and marginal EBIT streams lead to lower retentions (higher cash dividend payouts) *and* lower leverage. In this way, *ceteris paribus,* the target dividend payout ratio and the ex ante expected average (or ex ante maximal) debt ratios are mutually determined along with the "cost of capital" (used to determine the optimal ex ante size of capital budgets) in terms of long-run expectations (in the economist's sense).[15] These long-run expectations, in turn, involve judgments

---

[12] It should be noted that the sizes of (c) and (d) are increasing functions of factors (a) and (b); (c) and (d) themselves are additive; and (b) will also be an increasing function of the combined effect of (c) and (d).

[13] For the no leverage case, see Models II–VI in Lintner [25]. The same conclusion that the marginal cost of retentions is necessarily rising at the optimum, of course, holds as well for any given degree of leverage. The costs of leverage are also rising at the optimum, since they are rising throughout the relevant range, *ceteris paribus.*

[14] See my [23] and [26].

[15] Liquidity considerations may also be included in this simultaneous long-run ex ante optimization along the lines laid out in Anderson [2], Chap. III.

of the company's investment opportunity functions and the operating characteristics of the business, along with the characteristics of competitive reactions in the firm's product and factor markets and the other properties of the stochastic processes within which it lives.

In terms of *shorter-run equilibria,* however, the situation is basically different in one important respect. Although the *target* dividend payout ratios (as well as the debt-equity ratios and criteria for determining the size of the capital budget) are simultaneously determined in the theoretical context of a comparative dynamic, stochastic, long-run equilibrium analysis, along with somewhat more flexible "speed-of-adjustment" coefficients[16] (to control the response of cash dividends to cyclical and stochastic changes in earnings), cash dividend payments in line with these predetermined standards constitute a top priority claim on funds during short-run fluctuations. Given the fact of substantial uncertainty, the assumption that companies are seeking to maximize the value of their equity, the crucial dependence of market values on shareholders expectations, and the extraordinarily high "information content" of changes in dividend payments in the eyes of shareholders as they form their expectations—such action by companies is perfectly rational (i.e., maximizing behavior under uncertainty) in terms of strict theory. There is also substantial evidence that this theoretical formulation describes actual practice with respect to dividend payments very well.[17]

In our theoretical model, consequently, short-run optimization occurs subject to the constraint of dividend outflows at each point in time in accordance with the established dividend policy (except for infrequent

[16] These standards for speed-of-adjustment factors within each company are established in a similar manner on the basis of the mutual interrelationships expected between the volume of profitable investment opportunities and other parts of the sources and uses of funds flows over the cycle. For a fuller discussion of dividend determination, see Lintner [23] and [26]. It should be emphasized that the theoretical (and practical) conclusions drawn in the text here depend only on company's *adherence* to an established dividend policy; they do not depend upon the ultimate resolution of any differences there may be on whether the policy itself is denominated in terms of reported "earnings" or cash flows, for instance, as Brittain [3] has concluded.

[17] See, for instance, the three references in the preceding footnote. Important additional confirmation is provided by Glauber [14]. In a canonical correlation analysis of all sources and uses of funds of forty-four chemical companies in three postwar years of extreme expansions and three years of contraction, he found that the dividend earnings relationship was uniformly the first and dominant factor in the analysis; it was also the most stable. Subject to this orthogonal factor, the residuals revealed a complex interaction among working capital, real investment, and liquidity decisions.

crisis situations requiring immediate re-examination of the company's entire set of long-run expectations and policies). As in the traditional short-run theory of the firm (in which price and volume decisions are taken subject to the constraint of a fixed stock of real capital), our model of short-run adjustments assumes that firms simultaneously adjust and optimize over time the volume of their real investment, the amount (and forms) of their outside financing (if any), and their working capital and liquidity positions, all subject to predetermined requirements for dividend payments.

In this short-run context (quarter to quarter or year to year), the cost-of-funds factor in investment decisions works out as follows. The cost of the debt used will clearly be equal to its marginal costs, which in the relevant range, it will be recalled, rises with the degree of leverage in an essentially exponential manner, due not only to the rising marginal explicit cash costs of debt but even more to the rapidly increasing additional risk premiums required because of the greater "borrower's risk" being borne as leverage increases. Further, the *opportunity cost* of using some more retained funds to increase the current size of the capital budget is the foregone opportunity to repay debt, as Duesenberry [6] has emphasized. The cost of retained funds for investment is thus also given by the *marginal* cost-of-debt function. The cost of using either debt or retained funds to finance investments is thus *higher* than the quoted interest rate by amounts that increase rapidly with leverage.[18]

Note particularly that this *cost* of using either debt or retained funds to finance investment will, other things being the same, vary *inversely* with the amount of retained funds.[19] For any given level of investment outlay, the availability of more retained funds enables the firm to have less debt outstanding at the end of the period. Alternatively, we can say that more retained funds permit the financing of a given level of invest-

---

[18] Space does not permit any detailed discussion of the place of common stock financing in the model. Suffice it to say that such issues will be made only at such times as the (essentially long-term) standards of acceptable debt and liquidity positions are being strained by current (and prospective) profitable investment outlays *and* when market conditions are sufficiently favorable to bring the full costs of a new equity issue down to or below the costs of other funds (or of foregone investment). With the principal exceptions of utilities and small, rapidly growing, ambitious firms, such conditions apparently occur infrequently, and we will simply assume here that the costs of equity are equal to or greater than the cost of debt.

[19] Note also that, given dividend policy, the relevant cost of funds in the short run also varies inversely with the amount of dollar profits. See following comment in the text.

ment at lower marginal costs than would otherwise be possible.[20] It also follows that, for any given size (or schedule) of marginal costs of debt capital, the optimal scale of investment outlays will be an increasing function of the amount of retained funds currently available.[21]

Given uncertainty and risk aversion on the part of shareholders, this conclusion that, other things being equal, the availability of greater retained funds should increase the real investment outlays of optimizing decision-makers is rigorously implied by the theoretical model. This is true without introducing tax considerations or any imperfections whatsoever (not even transactions costs), and it is true under uncertainty *cum* risk aversion even though the result is foreign to classical doctrine based on the traditional assumption of prescience. Uncertainty and risk aversion do make a big difference, in theory as well as in practice![22] Not only are profits and flow variables (which would be irrelevant under certainty) required as legitimate and essential elements in the neo-Fisherian theory of the structural determinants of optimal investment outlays under uncertainty; but entirely new content and values are introduced into the relevant "interest rate" variables.

[20] The *value* to the firm of the availability of some finite increment of retained funds is thus *greater* than indicated by the marginal cost of currently outstanding debt. For it is equal to the (integral of the) marginal costs of the *larger* amount of debt that would have been outstanding had the marginal retained earnings not been available, and the relevant debt cost function is highly concave upward for reasons already given.

To avoid misunderstanding, the reader should keep in mind that we are here in a short-run context—the values involved are the *shadow prices* of existing supplies of retained earnings; except within the limits of flexibility in "speed-of-adjustment" factors in dividend policy (this flexibility in practice is largely confined to "rounding up" or "rounding down" to even nickels or dimes in per-share dividends) we are not referring to adjustments in the amounts of retained earnings available.

[21] This analysis has ignored issue costs, which make the marginal costs of increases in debt greater than those marginal savings of reductions in debt. The analysis has also assumed that managements' judgments and reactions are symmetrical with respect to the effects of increases or decreases in current debt levels on *future* borrowing costs and "safety margins" or "flexibility." The effect of all such considerations would be to make the favorable marginal effect of retained funds on investment outlays greater when they were short of capital requirements than when they were in excess of the volume of otherwise profitable investments.

[22] In the same connection, the reader will recall earlier conclusions regarding the effects of leverage. The presence of uncertainty involves cumulatively rising costs which convert the linearly declining marginal cost of debt function (found with taxes under certainty) into a U-shaped curve; and optimizing firms will necessarily operate on the *rising* portion of the curve.

III. Statistical Analysis

In this section we present the results of a statistical analysis of the determinants of the plant and equipment outlays of all U.S. manufacturing companies over the forty-four quarters in 1953–63. The analysis, incorporating accelerator, financial, and risk variables, is based directly on the theory developed in the previous section. All financial data used were drawn from the F.T.C.-S.E.C. *Quarterly Financial Reports,* except that interest rates were taken from the *Federal Reserve Bulletin* and Standard and Poor's data on stock prices and seasonally adjusted earnings were used. Hickman's careful estimates [16] of constant dollar capital stocks and quarterly interpolations of his annual estimates of declining-balance depreciation rates provided the data for these series. Output was measured by the Federal Reserve Board index of manufacturing production, and capacity utilization by de Leeuw's index. Hart kindly made his data on the orders-to-capacity ratio available and these were supplemented with O.B.E. data on backlogs. The series on labor cost per unit of output was taken from the Bureau of the Census *Business Cycle Developments.*

Several essentially statistical problems must be considered before we specify the particular models fitted and present the results. The first problem arises from the fact that investment decisions taken at any point in time—on the basis of the expectations as of that point in time and hence upon current and past data then available—result in expenditures over a succession of future periods. From the work of Koyck [21], Solow [36] and Jorgenson [19], we know that, in principle, the form of this distributed lag can be determined by including one or two lagged values of the dependent variable as explanatory variables in the equation being fitted. But given the character of the experiments which have been run for us in the real world and the available collinear data, these procedures run the serious risk that the autoregressive properties of the dependent variable itself will swamp the effects of other explanatory variables. In this event—even though very high R^2's, good Durbin-Watson (D.W.) ratios, and low standard errors of estimate are obtained as a matter of course—the estimates obtained are essentially those of a pure autoregressive model,[23] and the parameter values for the other variables of more theoretical interest can be quite unstable and misleading. In particular, if by chance the estimates obtained for the auto-

---

[23] As an illustration, see comments of Jorgenson in [20], commenting on his own model.

regressive terms differ from their true values, the estimates for the structural decision variables will almost inevitably be biased. Fortunately, other alternatives are available.[24] The one utilized in the work reported here was the use of the independent estimates of the lag structure of manufacturers' investment outlays behind their appropriations developed in Almon's recent study [1].[25] Use of these exogenous estimates of the relevant lag structure enables us to confine the list of explanatory variables in our equations to those representing the determinants of investment *decisions,* and thereby to avoid the ambiguities and risks involved in the use of lagged investment terms.

A somewhat similar problem is imposed by the common time trends in much of the data. Apart from the use of cross sections with which we are not now concerned, one quite effective device for handling this problem—much used in consumption studies following the pioneering work of Duesenberry [5] and Modigliani [30]—is, of course, to fit the model to the data in ratio form. This precedure was also followed in this paper. Specifically, investment outlays in real terms and all explanatory variables (not already in ratio form or having the dimensions of interest rates) were deflated by beginning-of-period capital stock.

The fact that the Almon weights represent the time pattern between *appropriations* and the subsequent expenditures on investment goods raises another troublesome issue.[26] Clearly, the first period in Almon's lags dated from appropriations may not be the quarter in which the *decision* was taken, nor is it necessarily even the immediately following

[24] See, for instance, Eisner [7] and de Leeuw [4]. The Eisner approach requires the use of large numbers of lags for each relevant explanatory variable; even when put in first difference form to reduce collinearities, the latter problem remains and the large number of lags in the explanatory variables rules out the approach as a practical matter in fitting the theory advanced in this paper. De Leeuw's approach of testing various previously defined weight patterns is directly used in this study, employing the Almon weights which were developed after de Leeuw's work.

[25] These have also been used by Resek in [36].

[26] There is clearly much to be said in favor of undertaking two separate studies, one to establish the set of factors which together determine investment *decisions* and their associated appropriations, the other to establish the structure and parameter values of the realization function relating the appropriated inputs (together with subsequent information and "surprises") to the later expenditures. Such research should surely be encouraged. It seemed, however, that the essential purposes of the present investigation could best be served by following the more usual practice of relating the theoretical model of decisions-to-invest directly to the resulting spending on investment goods. Within the restricted compass of the empirical work reported here, this was the primary tack taken. In the final stages of our work, however, some additional runs were made including measures of the current quarter's conditions, which we hoped would pick up cancellations and other effects of "surprises."

one. There are lags between decisions and appropriations, just as there are between the latter and actual spending. As in Anderson's earlier work [2], the appropriate time span between the conditions initiating decisions and the first period of spending was estimated empirically. Specifically, for the ith period of weighted-summed explanatory variables, the denominator of the dependent variable was beginning-of-year real capital stock, but differently dated numerators were tried. The dependent variable I_{t+i}/K_{t-1} with $i = 1$ proved to be consistently superior to no lead ($i = 0$) or to a two- or three-period lead.

Another problem is reflected in the fact that all the initial "fits" to the data left unacceptably low Durbin-Watson statistics, generally in the range .4–.6. Much of this autocorrelation doubtless arises from the fact that Almon's best lag distribution for all manufacturing showed a D.W. statistic of only about .9 when investment outlays were predicted from appropriations. Further autocorrelation is introduced by our own treatment of the data. Our use of data with a given quarter's time index[27] (as inputs into the Almon-weighted sums which are our explanatory variables) in effect assumes that these particular input data control the investment *decisions* made within the quarter. In point of fact, of course —as Hart [15] has aptly said—"deciding to invest is a process rather than an event." Consequently, it can be argued that the *inputs into* the Almon lags should themselves be moving averages rather than data for a single quarter. Our use of the latter inputs then involves using data with a form of autocorrelated "observational error."

Although autocorrelated residuals, as such, do not bias parameter estimates, they do reduce their efficiency. The use of lagged values of the dependent variable was ruled out for reasons given above.[28] But the device recommended by Johnston [18] and Theil [39] to reduce autocorrelations and improve estimating efficiency was employed—*all* variables, dependent and independent, were converted to the form $X'_t = X_t - rX_{t-1}$. The residuals on the first pass suggested an r of .8, which led to a substantial improvement. Successive recalculations using r values from .4 through 1.0 indicated, however, that the optimum value

---

[27] This does not, of course, mean that only *data* for the given quarter were used as inputs. For instance, the inputs into the Almon weights for, say, the second quarter of 1956 include the capacity utilization ratio, retained funds and leverage of that quarter, along with first differences as of that quarter, and lagged (i.e., beginning-of-quarter) interest rates, and so on. Also, exponentially smoothed values or trend values as of a given quarter were tested for some variables.

[28] We should perhaps also note that use of the new unbiased estimating technique developed by Taylor and Wilson [38] was ruled out by the fact that the lagged dependent variable does not enter our model as an explanatory variable in its own right.

for *r* was .9, and this value was used in preparing the final estimates since it minimized both the standard error of estimate and the remaining autocorrelation, and did so consistently for the various equations presented below.

Finally, we have to recognize the fact that in a world of uncertainty, as noted earlier, rational investment decisions depend upon the *expectations* (in the sense of economists) of future profitability, rather than upon known data on nonrandom outcomes. And there is as yet very little firm knowledge of how these expectations are generated.

Along with the current capital stock and real costs, the theoretical economic model tells us that expectations of such items as future outputs and profit margins are basic determinants of the position of the firm's real investment opportunity function; but economic theory does not tell us precisely what available numbers (reflecting current situations and past experience) are processed in precisely what ways to produce the inherently unobservable judgments regarding these theoretically relevant future magnitudes. Similarly, the theoretical economic model tells us that, in addition, financial and risk elements are required to determine the optimal point on the expected real investment opportunity function. It goes as far as to require the inclusion of interest rates, retained funds, and leverage (as a risk as well as a financial cost variable); but it does not tell us in advance, for instance, what particular form of the leverage variable will best measure the essentially subjective risk content of the variable. In the circumstances, one must experiment with real world series to see which ones (on standard statistical-econometric tests) perform best as empirical counterparts or representations of the theoretically required decision elements.[29]

Previous studies have established the great if not dominant role of capacity-accelerator considerations in empirical investment behavior,[30] although it is not entirely clear which *form* of the relationship is most significant and reliable. In view of the special focus of the present paper on the theoretical and empirical significance of long-term finance and risk considerations in investment decisions, we consequently structured our empirical work in the following way. Along with each of several

---

[29] In part, this is because the *economic* theory per se takes the primary probability judgments (like von Neumann-Morgenstein utility functions or the classical preference functions) as *givens,* and merely derives optimal decision rules from these; in part, it is because the formation of these basic expectations doubtless involves personal and social psychological factors along with strictly economic considerations.

[30] See Kuh's fine summary [22], especially pp. 264–267, and Meyer and Glauber [29].

standard (and some new) accelerator or capacity variables, interest rates and their smoothed first difference, as well as leverage (with and without allowance for retained funds), were added in different forms and combinations to the equations to be fitted. The resulting estimates of parameters and summary statistics were then examined to determine whether the finance and risk variables were *consistently* significant on standard statistical grounds *regardless* of the choice of variables to represent accelerator considerations. Given some uncertainty about the optimal choice of the latter variables, this research strategy clearly provides a stronger test of the sign and importance of the finance and risk variables of crucial interest to this paper than would results based on estimates of a single equation combining them with only one of the several plausible and theoretically motivated accelerator-capacity variables. Using two of the apparently better and more interesting accelerator-capacity variables, we also examined which representation of leverage seemed to produce the best over-all results. At a later stage, each of six variables representing real costs or profit margins in some form were then added to the best sets of variables from previous runs in order to determine the marginal effect of these further variables, but less systematic study was given to these variables in view of the focus of the present effort. Finally, since all the basic runs in the study were based on the use of data available at the decision-making stage to forecast subsequent investment outlays, some additional runs were made in the final stages of our work that also included measures of the current (i.e., outlay) quarter's conditions, which we hoped would pick up "surprises" and the falsifications of earlier expectations associated with cancellations. Apart from their own intrinsic interest, these runs provided a further test of the inherent stability and importance of the finance and risk considerations which are of primary concern to this study.

Although many of the input data were already in seasonally adjusted form, seasonal dummies were included in all runs. Although very small and uniformly insignificant (except for the second quarter), their continued inclusion represents an element of conservatism in the estimates of corrected R^2 and standard errors of estimate.[31] As a general point of reference, it may also be noted that the total contribution of the three seasonal dummies to R^2 ranged narrowly about .035. In addition, time trends were included in all equations fitted in order to guard against the possibility that some of the other variables included were merely serving as proxies for excluded variables which were also associated

---

[31] Since two needless degrees of freedom (for the third and fourth quarters) were allowed for in their calculation.

with "time." The contribution of the time trend variable to R^2 was generally less than the total for the seasonal dummies. This clearly reflected our earlier decision to estimate all equations in ratio form with I_{t+1}/K_{t-1} as the dependent variable.

Before proceeding to the presentation and discussion of our detailed results, we should explain the symbols used and the measurement of the variables included in the statistical work and tables.

SYMBOLS

I_t represents the seasonally adjusted plant and equipment outlays of manufacturing companies (S.E.C.-F.T.C. series), deflated by a price index constructed as a 2–1 weighted average of the Department of Commerce implicit GNP deflators for producers' durable equipment and nonresidential construction. I_{t+1} indicates the value for the quarter following the reference date.

K_t is a quarterly interpolation of Hickman's estimates of manufacturers' stocks of real capital in 1954 dollars. K_{t-1} indicates the value at the beginning of the reference quarter.

O_t is an unweighted average of the Federal Reserve Board's Index of Production for manufacturing over the three months in the indicated quarter.

U_t is de Leeuw's index of the utilization of manufacturing capacity for the current quarter.

(CR_t) represents capital requirements, $1.111 U_t - 1 + d_t$, where d is the quarterly rate of (real) declining balance depreciation interpolated from Hickman's annual estimates. The first two terms give the percentage change in capacity needed to bring capacity to its optimum relation to present output (expressed as a percentage of present capacity) when the optimum rate of operations is taken to be 90 per cent. This is the measure of capital requirements used by de Leeuw in [4] without the inclusion of an additional term to reflect the needs associated with projected future growth.[32]

J is Jorgenson's ratio of the current price of output (P_o) to the (current dollar) user cost of capital services (c), which was computed according to Jorgenson's formulas and procedures as given in [19] and

---

[32] Several experiments were run with "growth" included in a new CR variable; but, with any of these "growth-CR" variables in the equation, the coefficient on the growth component entered (in addition) as a separate variable was always strongly negative. With the CR variable defined as in the text, outlays reflecting steady expectations of growth will be reflected (with other things) in the constant term. I had no luck formulating a variable which would pick up varying expectations of growth.

[20].[33] It should particularly be noted that the user cost factor (c) is a function of the current quarter's effective income tax rate, and bookkeeping depreciation, as well as the price level of capital goods, the interest rate, and the debt-to-asset ratio. This J term was used as a multiplicative form with the above three accelerator or capacity variables.[34] If, for instance, other things being equal, investment increases with capacity utilization U, it is rational for the increment reflecting a favorable value of J to be larger as utilization is higher, and vice versa. Similarly with CR. Indeed, the product term $J(CR)$ is especially attractive inasmuch as it varies in the appropriate way the otherwise arbitrary assumption (used in computing CR) that the optimal capacity provides for a 90 per cent utilization ratio. In point of fact, the desired capital stock in relation to output will clearly be higher the more favorable the relation J between output prices and user costs of capital. Finally, we note that Jorgenson has shown [19] that desired capital stock K^* will be proportional (in my notation) to the product $J \cdot O$, say $K^* = \alpha J O$. If investment is equal to a fraction β of the discrepancy between K^* and the existing capital stock, we have $I_t = \beta(\alpha J O - K_{-1})$ or $I_t/K_{t-1} = \beta[\alpha J(O_t/K_{-1}) - 1]$. This is the equation fitted in our work after reinterpreting the right side as *inputs* into the investment expenditures stream (i.e., applying Almon weights to the terms on the right-hand side) and allowing for the lag between decisions and initial outlays.

It should particularly be noted that Jorgenson's analysis was carried through under the assumption of certainty. His demonstration that the optimal capital stock is proportional to the product of J and an accelerator term sugests that we may regard the effects that interest rates, taxes, and leverage *would* have under certainty as being incorporated in such a "compound accelerator" term in our equations. Any further effects of interest rates and leverage variables, found when they are entered as

[33] Ignoring capital gains (as he does), Jorgenson's formula for c is

$$c = q\left(\left[\frac{1 - uv}{1 - u}\right]d + \left[\frac{1 - uw}{1 - u}\right]r\right),$$

where u is the ratio of direct taxes paid to corporate profits before taxes, the current quarter's effective tax rate; d is the declining balance depreciation rate; r is the interest rate; v is the ratio of capital consumption allowances currently taken to the current replacement cost of capital assets; and w is net monetary interest to total capital cost. Since Jorgenson is working in a world of certainty, total capital cost is the product of the interest rate and total capital so that w reduces to the debt-to-asset ratio; and current replacement cost is computed as the product dKq, where q is the current price of capital goods.

[34] Entering J (or its reciprocal) linearly in the equation did not result in significant coefficients, though the signs were generally appropriate.

additional separate variables in the equation, can thus reasonably be regarded as their impact upon risk under real world conditions of uncertainty.

r is the interest rate variable, measured by the average of the monthly Baa rates (Moody's) during the quarter, as given in the *Federal Reserve Bulletin*. This rate was used instead of the Aaa or long-term government bond rate generally used by other investigators because it provides a much better measure of the cost of funds to the average corporation. The Baa rate, of course, reflects both the current level of the fully risk-free rate and allowances for leaders' risk, but it reflects the costs *to the borrowers* which *they* expect with assurance to discharge. The latter is clearly the relevant matter for borrower's investment decisions, not the fully risk-free rate itself.

$tr(\triangle r)_{t-1}$ is the trend in the Baa rate. This variable was measured by a weighted average of past quarterly changes in the Baa rate, using linearly declining weights for four quarters.[35] With the Baa rate entered separately in the equation, this variable reflects expectations of costs of new funds and, in particular, it is an index of the *difference* between the average costs and the incremental costs of new debt.

LTD is long-term debt, measured by all debt due in more than one year to banks and other lenders, as shown in the F.T.C.-S.E.C. *Quarterly Financial Reports* for manufacturing corporations.

RF represents retained funds, measured by net profits after taxes, *less* cash dividends charged to surplus, *plus* depreciation and depletion.

NW is net worth, measured by total assets less total liabilities (current liabilities, plus *LTD* plus other noncurrent liabilities). The F.T.C.-S.E.C. reports do not segregate preferred stock, but this item is known to have been sufficiently small and stable as to introduce little bias.

$K is capital stock expressed in current dollars, computed by reflating Hickman's estimates of constant dollar capital stock by the price index of the prices of capital goods (indicated under I_t above).

SP is the market value of equity indexed by twice the Standard and Poor index of the market prices of 425 industrial securities (which is, of course, adjusted for all stock splits and dividends). Ideally, it would have been desirable to have made a further adjustment for net new issues, but this did not prove feasible on a careful basis within the time available for the present study.

---

[35] I.e., $tr(\Delta r)_{-1} = .4(\Delta r)_{t-1} + .3(\Delta r_{t-2}) + .2(\Delta r_{t-3}) + .1(\Delta r_{t-4}) = .4r_{t-1} - .1\sum_{i=2}^{5} r_{t-i}.$

TABLE 1

Regression Coefficients, t-Ratios, and Partial Correlation Coefficients for Interest Rates and Leverage, with Alternative Accelerator-Capacity Requirement Variables

Accelerator-Capacity Variable Denoted by X_i	Constant	X_i	LTD-RF	r	$tr(\Delta v)_{t-1}$	Time	R_c^2	σ_{est}	D.W.
O_t/K_{t-1}	.011	.1396	− .3188	−1.7169	−10.9730	.00001	.7282	.0032	1.71
		3.39	− 5.24	−1.45	− 3.21	0.14			
		.497	− .663	− .238	− .477	−.024			
U_t	.018	.0636	− .3853	−3.049	− 5.777	.0002	.7202	.0032	1.64
		3.19	− 5.66	−3.00	− 1.85	3.76			
		.474	− .691	.452	.298	.537			
$(CR)_t$	.023	.1614	− .3019	−2.046	−10.698	.0001	.7261	.0032	1.70
		3.34	− 4.98	−1.80	− 3.14	2.01			
		.491	− .644	− .291	.469	.322			
$J(O_t/K_{t-1})$	.013	.0093	− .3196	−1.614	− 6.321	.00013	.6562	.0036	1.41
		1.32	− 4.47	−0.73	− 1.81	1.37			
		.219	− .603	− .123	− .294	.225			
$J(U)_t$	.013	.0099	− .3079	−2.138	− 5.923	.0002	.6508	.0036	1.38
		1.09	− 4.37	−1.00	− 1.70	2.77			
		.181	− .595	− .166	− .276	.424			
$J(CR)_t$	.023	.0195	− .2975	−2.269	−10.1674	.0001	.7265	.0032	1.70
		3.35	− 4.92	−2.06	− 3.05	2.18			
		.492	− .639	− .329	− .458	.346			

The leverage variables used in the study were computed by forming ratios with LTD and $(LTD - RF)$, respectively, in the numerator and using each of the variables NW, $\$K$ and SP in the denominator.

THE RESULTS[36]

Table 1 presents the regression coefficients, t-ratios, and partial correlation indexes obtained when the following equation was fitted to the data:

$$\frac{I_{t+1}}{K_{t-1}} = (SD) + b_1 + b_2 X_i + b_3 \frac{LTD - RF}{SP} + b_4 r + b_5 [tr(\Delta r)_{t-1}] + b_6 T,$$

$$(1)$$

where (SD) indicates three seasonal dummies, and X_i represents the particular "accelerator-capacity" variable (see list Table 1) which was used. As previously indicated, in this and all other equations reported, all explanatory variables (except, of course, the SD's and time) were the weighted sums of past data cumulated to the period in question using the Almon weights; also, all equations were fitted with all variables in differenced form. Incidentally, it should be kept in mind that the R_c^2's, adjusted for degrees of freedom, which are given in the tables indicate the fraction of the variance of the quarterly differences of I_{t+1}/K_{t-1} which are accounted for by the explanatory variables. If, instead, these results are transformed into the corresponding fraction of the variance of I_{t+1}/K_{t-1} itself (without differencing) which is explained, the R_c^2's, would be given much higher values. For instance, a standard error of estimate of .36 per cent implies an adjusted R_c^2 of .935 on this alternative basis. Similarly, a σ(est) of .32 per cent corresponds to an R_c^2 of .955, and a σ(est) of .30 per cent to an R_c^2 of .959.

In terms of the theoretical model developed in section II, the rationale for the structure of equation (1) should be clear. Given any particular accelerator-capacity variable to measure the volume of new investment (as a percentage of existing capital stock) which *would* be undertaken *ceteris paribus if* financing and risk considerations were neutral, the other terms are included to measure the effects of the latter factors. Specifically, the Baa rate (r) reflects the average cost of outstanding debt at current bond prices, which serves as the base for judging the (before-tax) cost of new debt and thus is one factor directly influencing the risk of debt and the costs of funds. In addition to reflecting expectations of

---

[36] The author is very grateful to George Schussel for his effective handling of all the computer work involved in this study.

rates, the trend in the Baa rate $(tr(\triangle r)_{t-1})$ indexes the difference between the marginal costs of debt and the average cost since it is a rising linear function of the latter difference. (A negative value of $tr(\triangle r)_{t-1}$, of course, does not necessarily imply that the marginal cash cost of new borrowing is below the average cost of outstandings, but rather that this differential is smaller than at other times when the interest-trend term has positive values.)

The theoretical analysis further showed that the difference between the marginal cash costs of debt and its average cost is also an increasing function of leverage. Our leverage variable is included in the equation to reflect both these important effects.

The tests of the significance of these fund-cost and risk factors, in conjunction with different choices of accelerator-capacity variables, which are reported in Table 1, utilizes leverage measured by $(LTD - RF)/SP$ because on a priori grounds this form of the leverage variable was expected to best reflect and incorporate the different elements involved in the theoretical content of the leverage variable. Specifically, the basic theoretical analysis showed that the marginal (opportunity) costs of the use of debt and retained funds for investment outlays should be the same. The underlying model of behavior thus points directly to the use of $LTD - RF$ rather than long-term debt alone in the numerator of the leverage variable. Similarly, the whole analysis is based on the fact that the relevant risks (and hence the economic costs in the form of the minimum required *expected* returns) depend fundamentally upon ex ante judgments of vectors looking into the future of *expected* values of earnings and cash flows, together with their stochastic properties, variances, and risks. Equity values reflect both these critical matters, and do so with a directness and degree of precision which is lacking in either book net worth or even the current dollar value of the net fixed capital stock. A further reason for believing that equity value is the superior and more relevant denominator in the leverage variable is that the impediment to new investment posed by any given stock of debt varies inversely with equity prices because of the alternative of issuing new shares on more favorable terms as market prices rise, and conversely.

Table 1 shows that, over these forty-four quarters of recent experience in manufacturing, leverage is very strongly and *negatively* related to investment, regardless of whether the output-capital stock ratio, de Leeuw's capacity utilization index, or his "capital requirements" measure—or any of the three multiplied by Jorgenson's measure of the marginal productivity of capital—was used to represent accelerator-

TABLE 2

Regression Coefficients, t-Ratios, and Partial Correlation Coefficients for Alternative Leverage Variables in Equations with Interest Rates and O_t/K_{t-1}

Leverage Variable Denoted by X_i	Constant	O_t/K_{t-1}	r	X_i	$tr(\Delta r)$	Time	R_c^2	σ_{est}	D.W.
$\dfrac{LTD}{NW}$	.027	.1158	-2.7835	-1.3046	-12.3870	.00014	.5815	.0039	1.12
		2.29	-1.88	-2.36	- 2.78	1.42			
		.360	- .303	.370	- .426	.233			
$\dfrac{LTD-RF}{NW}$	.025	.0846	-2.1459	-1.3888	-12.2684	.00016	.6048	.0038	1.25
		1.70	-1.43	-2.82	- 2.88	1.57			
		.276	- .235	- .430	- .438	.257			
$\dfrac{LTD}{\$K}$	.021	.2438	-3.2590	-1.4597	-15.3326	.00035	.7084	.0033	1.61
		4.81	-2.85	-4.82	- 4.08	3.79			
		.631	- .434	- .631	- .568	.540			
$\dfrac{LTD-RF}{\$K}$	.017	.1708	-2.2414	-1.224	-16.1186	.003	.6736	.0035	1.51
		3.62	-1.75	-4.12	- 3.93	3.17			
		.522	- .283	- .572	- .533	.472			
$\dfrac{LTD}{SP}$	.017	.1031	-2.5410	-0.2707	-12.4810	0.00006	.7166	.0032	1.62
		2.476	-2.192	-4.988	- 3.525	0.666			
		.386	- .348	- .645	- .512	.112			
$\dfrac{LTD-RF}{SP}$	.011	.1396	-1.7169	- .3188	-10.9730	.00001	.7282	.0032	1.71
		3.39	-1.45	-5.24	- 3.21	0.141			
		.497	- .238	- .663	- .477	.024			

TABLE 3

Regression Coefficients, t-Ratios, and Partial Correlation Coefficients for
Alternative Leverage Variables in Equations with Interest Rates and $J(CR)$

Leverage Variable Denoted by X_i	Constant	$J(CR)$	r	X_i	$tr(\Delta r)_{t-1}$	Time	R^2_c	σest	D.W.
$\dfrac{LTD}{NW}$	.036	.0185	−2.962	−1.249	−12.148	.0002	.5985	.0039	1.17
		2.63	−2.18	−2.31	− 2.86	3.18			
		.406	− .345	− .363	− .436	.473			
$\dfrac{LTD\text{-}RF}{NW}$	.032	.0149	−2.168	−1.352	−12.384	.0002	.6223	.0038	1.31
		2.15	−1.54	−2.81	− 3.03	2.97			
		.342	− .251	− .428	− .456	.449			
$\dfrac{LTD}{\$K}$	.039	.0311	−4.069	−1.226	−13.150	.0005	.6962	.0034	1.56
		4.56	−3.76	−4.28	− 3.62	5.79			
		.610	− .537	− .586	− .522	.700			
$\dfrac{LTD\text{-}RF}{\$K}$	.030	.0246	−2.744	−1.145	−15.050	.0004	.6827	.0034	1.56
		3.81	−2.35	−4.00	− 3.88	5.43			
		.541	− .370	.561	.548	.676			
$\dfrac{LTD}{SP}$	.026	.0138	−3.011	− .2538	−11.584	−.0001	.7101	.0033	1.59
		2.28	−2.76	−4.57	− 3.34	−2.37			
		.360	− .423	− .611	− .491	.372			
$\dfrac{LTD\text{-}RF}{SP}$	.023	.0195	−2.269	−0.297	−10.167	.0001	.7265	.0032	1.70
		3.35	−2.06	−4.92	− 3.05	2.18			
		.492	− .329	− .639	− .458	.345			

capacity considerations in the equation. In all six equations, the negative leverage coefficient had a t-ratio of over 4.3, and the partial correlation coefficients on the leverage variable ranged upward from .60. In both respects, incidentally, the leverage variable was actually "more significant" than the accelerator-capacity variable in any of the equations.

The coefficients on the Baa rate and its trend-change were both negative in all six equations (in spite of the inclusion of "time" as a separate variable). In the first three equations with "simple" accelerator-capacity variables, the negative coefficients on the two interest rate variables all had t-ratios of 1.45 or better, and one or the other showed a t of 3.0 or more in each equation. It will be recalled that the interest rate is an important component of Jorgenson's marginal productivity of the capital term J used multiplicatively with the accelerators in the last three equations. Perhaps this partially explains the generally less satisfactory performance of the separate interest rate variables in these runs. It should be noted, however, that the separate interest rate variables have t-ratios of 2.1 and 3.0, respectively, when the product of J and (CR) is used to measure investment needs and profitability.

Perhaps the most surprising result in the table is that the combination of the marginal capital productivity term J with either O_t/K_{t-1} or U_t reduced the over-all R_c^2's and D.W. statistics, as well as the t-ratios for the individual variables in the equation. But the over-all results when the product $J(CR)_t$ is used are quite good and compare favorably with those obtained when either capital requirements (CR) or a simple accelerator (O_t/K_{t-1}) is used in the equation. Each of these three accelerator variables leads to equations with standard errors of estimate of .32 per cent and D.W. statistics of 1.7+ over the forty-four quarters of data.

Table 2 shows that in these data, when the equations are fitted using the simple accelerator (O_t/K_{t-1}) and both interest variables (and "time"), the impact of leverage on investment is consistently negative and "significant" according to the usual standards, regardless of which of the six leverage variables is chosen. The same conclusion holds (Table 3) when the compound marginal productivity of capital *cum* capital requirements term $J(CR)_t$ is substituted for the simple accelerator. And in both bases, both interest rate terms are consistently negative and generally "significant" regardless of the leverage variable.

The use of the excess of long-term debt over retained funds in the numerator of the leverage variable (rather than long-term debt itself) generally led to higher t-ratios on the leverage term, and higher D.W. statistics and lower estimating errors for the equation, as expected from theoretical considerations. With both "accelerators," this was consistently the case when either book net worth or the market value of the equity were used in the denominator of the leverage variable, although the comparison is reversed when the current value of the stock of real capital (K) is used in the denominator.

As expected on theoretical grounds, the use of the market value of the equity as the denominator of the leverage ratio led to uniformly superior results to those obtained when either book net worth or the current value of net real capital stock was used as the "base" of the leverage measure. With both accelerators, and with $LTD - RF$ as with LTD alone in the numerator, the D.W. ratio and the t-ratio on the leverage term was higher, and the estimating error of the equation was lower, with SP than with NW or $K. While none of the differences between individual pairs of regression coefficients using different numerators or different denominators in the leverage variable was "statistically significant," the over-all pattern and general consistency of the results, together with theoretical considerations, justify continued use of $(LTD - RF)/SP$ as the preferred measure of the leverage variable.

Theoretical considerations also indicate that, under rational optimizing behavior, there will be significant interaction between the interest rate and leverage variables. Higher interest rates mean that the risks associated with any given degree of leverage are higher and also that the *incremental* risk associated with any increment in leverage will be greater. Similarly, higher leverage would in theory add to the deterrent effects of any given level (or increase) in interest rates. Unfortunately, it was not possible to get any meaningful measures of these incremental interaction effects by simply adding the new product term $r[(LTD - RF)/SP]$ to the earlier equations because of the collinearities involved. As an alternative, the latter multiplicative form of compound interest-rate and leverage variable was introduced in place of the interest rate and leverage separately. As illustrated in Table 4, this procedure did raise the precision of the estimate of the regression coefficient as shown by the higher t-ratios, and this was true whether or not time was included as a separate variable in the equation. Not only did the t-ratios of the compound interest-leverage variable show unusually high values of 6.6 and 7.0, but the smoothed rate of change of the interest rate and the accelerator terms both had t values of 3.7 or better. These latter (clearly very satisfactory) values were, however, somewhat lower than those obtained when the interest rate and leverage were entered separately in the equation; and the standard errors of estimate over the observation period for the equations as a whole, and the values of the D.W. statistics, were about the same with both forms of the equation.

TABLE 4

Regression Results for Interest and Leverage as Separate Variables and as a Product Term, with and Without Time Trend

Constant	O_t/K_{t-1}	r	$\frac{LTD-RF}{SP}$	$r[\frac{LTD-RF}{SP}]$	$tr(\Delta r)_{t-1}$	Time	R_c^2	σ_{est}	D.W.
.0110	.1438	−1.572	−.3218	—	−11.257	—	.7356	.0031	1.71
	5.11	−2.67	5.72	—	−4.13	—			
	.648	−.406	−.690	—	−.567	—			
.0053	.1396	—	—	−8.039	−10.904	—	.7406	.0031	1.69
	5.01	—	—	−7.00	−4.07	—			
	.636	—	—	−.755	−.556	—			
.0115	.1396	−1.7169	−.3188	—	−10.9730	.00001	.7282	.0032	1.71
	3.39	−1.45	−5.23	—	−3.20	0.14			
	.497	−.238	−.663	—	−.477	0.02			
.0055	.1274	—	—	−8.3607	−10.406	.00003	.7364	.0031	1.70
	3.75	—	—	−6.62	−3.70	0.63			
	.530	—	—	−.741	−.525	0.105			

Altogether, this evidence provides little basis for the choice between entering interest and leverage separately or as a single compound term. In either case, the D.W. statistic is a very satisfactory 1.7; the standard error of the equation is only about .31 per cent of the capital stock—or less than $250,000 of investment outlay at annual rates on the average in 1954 dollars—and the error of forecasts of investment for the second and third quarters of 1964 were consistent with this (percentage) figure.

Although these investigations were focused primarily upon the effects of financial and risk considerations (*with* accelerator effects) on investment outlays, we should also briefly note the results of including other terms in the equations presented to pick up the independent effect of certain factors reflecting relative real costs and profit margins, both as current data and (by changes or trends of changes) as elements of expectations. The comments can properly be brief because, whatever significance for future research our results may have, the findings were negative. Specifically, none of the separate variables for profit margins (either on sales or net worth) or their first differences or trends, the ratio of product price to labor cost or its first difference or trend, or the ratio of labor to real capital cost proved to be significant when added as an additional variable to our basic equations.[37] In each case, the addition of the term produced a t-ratio of less than 1.2 on the variable and failed to improve the over-all equation. The same negative results were also obtained when stock price, equity earnings yields, or retained funds were added as separate variables (except that retained funds always had a positive sign and were often "significant" as a separate variable *if LTD* rather than the theoretically preferred form $(LTD - RF)$ was used in the leverage variable). In the same way (perhaps because of our use of the Almon weights on past values of all explanatory variables), the addition of either the first differences or the smoothed rate of change of any of the accelerator variables shown in Table 1 frequently produced "wrong" signs on these terms and no "significant" and "right" signs on these added variables in any of the equations tested. Neither did the orders-capacity variable, which has been suggested by Hart [15], prove to be a significant additional variable in our equations—a finding that may be due to our use of data for *all* manufacturing (rather than the durable sector separately) or to the period since 1953 when supply bottlenecks were of less importance than they had been in earlier years.

---

[37] This did not merely reflect the order in which the variables were introduced. In several tests, these variables were put in early and "fell out" as financial-risk variables were added.

Finally, it should be recalled that all of our basic runs and tests were undertaken with a view to explaining investment outlays in terms of the fundamental determinants of the *decisions* to make real investments. To this end, in view of the spreading of the actual resulting expenditures over time, *all* explanatory variables consisted of data which had been cumulated to the given index quarter using Almon's weights (and the explanatory data cumulated to the tth period were used to determine investment in the $(t + 1)^{th}$ quarter to allow for the so-called "decision lag"). But not all decisions or initial commitments result in final expenditures on a fixed time schedule without speed-up, deferral, or cancellation. This is clearly established by studies of the "realization function" relating appropriations to actual subsequent outlays and also by studies of the differences between the expenditures planned for future quarters, as reported in S.E.C. surveys, and the actual amounts later expended (see, e.g., [34] and [12]).

In the final stages of our work, consequently, some additional runs were made that also included a measure of *current* conditions in the tth quarter, which we hoped would pick up cancellations and other positive and negative effects of "surprises" on the actual investment outlays in the $(t + 1)^{th}$ quarter. Since previous studies have found that the discrepancy between actual and "expected" sales is the factor most closely related to differences between actual and expected investment outlays, the variable used was the percentage difference between actual output and "expected" output in the tth quarter. ("Expected" output was estimated by the exponentially smoothed value of the stream of past quarterly outputs with a smoothing constant of .1). For the results see Table 5.

This "surprise" or "sales discrepancy" variable proved to be positive and significant with a *t*-ratio of 2.37 or better. The statistical results over the observation period were improved. The D.W. statistic was raised to over 1.9, and the standard error of estimate of I_{t+1}/K_{t-1} was reduced to .30 per cent or less. The forecasting errors for $I_{64:2}$ and $I_{64:3}$ were also somewhat improved by the addition of this "surprise" term. Most relevant to the basic concerns of the present paper, however, is that the addition of the current sales "surprise" variable produced little change in the regression coefficients of the leverage variables $(LTD - RF)/SP$ or $r[(LTD - RF)/SP]$ and that their *t*-ratios remained high (4.6 or more for the former, and 5.6 or more for the latter). The addition of the surprise term raised the *t*-ratio on the Baa rate as a separate variable to more than 3.0 when a time trend term was not included in the equation; with "time" included separately, the coefficient on the Baa rate was still negative and "significant" at about the .1 level. The addition of the sales surprise term reduced the t-ratios on the smoothed rate of change of the Baa rate, but its t-ratios still remained above 2.15. It will also be noted that the addition of the tth periods sales surprise raised the precision of the estimate of the coefficient on the basic accelerator variable O_t/K_{t-1} which is cumulated with the Almon weights.

In view of Hickman's [16] earlier finding of negative time trends in investment equations, which appeared to imply a gradual weakening of investment demand due to technical progress, attention should also be called to the fact that all the time trends in our equations are essentially zero or positive. The models fitted here include financial and risk variables, while no such terms were included in his equations. Our results consequently suggest that the negative time trends he obtained probably reflect the powerful effects of these other factors upon which we have focused rather than any persistent marginal depressing effect of technological change. In particular, they suggest that the ratio of new investment to capital stock will be maintained if output is kept strong in relation to real capital stock and finance-risk factors are held neutral.

IV. General Conclusions

As developed in section II, the neo-Fisherian model of purely competitive security markets of risky bonds and stocks traded by risk-averse investors leads directly to a unified theory of rational corporate financial and investment policy, under the traditional assumption that management's objective is to maximize the market value of the equity of its shareholders. In this theory, as in Fisher's earlier model under certainty, *both* financial and accelerator or capital-requirements variables are *required* by the optimizing economic theory itself in the specification of the statistical model intended to represent the structure of investment decisions and behavior. In keeping with this theory, the present paper has sought to throw light on the simultaneous influence of both sets of considerations upon investment behavior. Rather than undertaking a race (or alternative choice test) between allegedly competing subtheories of investment, the statistical work has sought to test and implement the unified structure suggested by the theory.

Since the empirical work was confined to data for all manufacturing for the eleven years 1953–63, with limited forecasts beyond that period, the econometric results are not conclusive at this stage. Further work with individual industries, longer forecast periods, different time spans, and other data will be required for that. But the results suggest the

TABLE 5

Regression Results with a "Surprise" Variable,
with and Without Time Trend

Constant	O_t/K_{t-1}	r	$\frac{LTD\text{-}RF}{SP}$	$r[\frac{LTD\text{-}RF}{SP}]$	$tr(\Delta r)_{t-1}$	S	Time	R_c^2	σ_{est}	D.W.
.0086	.1571	−1.714	−.2707	—	−7.214	.0488	—	.7665	.0029	1.92
	5.81	−3.08	−4.75	—	−2.35	2.40	—			
	.701	−.461	−.626	—	−.369	.375	—			
.0028	.1514	—	—	−7.265	−7.144	.0484	—	.7729	.0029	1.91
	5.72	—	—	−6.50	−2.44	2.50	—			
	.690	—	—	−.735	−.377	.384	—			
.0077	.1648	−1.459	−.2750	—	−7.642	.0498	−.00002	.7601	.0030	1.93
	4.11	−1.30	−4.59	—	−2.18	2.38	−0.26			
	.576	−.218	.618	—	−.350	.378	−0.045			
.0027	.1537	—	—	−7.197	−7.174	.0492	−.000005	.7665	.0029	1.92
	4.55	—	—	−5.60	−2.41	2.37	−0.112			
	.609	—	—	−.687	−.377	.373	−0.019			

Note: S, the "surprise" variable, is measured by the percentage difference between actual output and *expected* output, the latter being computed as the exponentially smoothed value of the stream of past quarterly outputs with a smoothing constant of .1.

desirability of further work along these lines, since the quarterly data for all manufacturing over this decade do quite consistently bear out the expectations of the theory.

In terms of these data, the most important finding is the fact that leverage (and one or more interest variables) were highly significant and *negatively* related to investment outlays. This was consistently true with different accelerator-capacity variables in the equation; with long-term debt alone, or its excess over retained funds, used in the numerator of the leverage variable; and with either numerator used with any of three denominators in the leverage variable. As suggested by the theory, the ratio $(LTD - RF)/SP$ seemed to be clearly superior to the other leverage variables regardless of the accelerator-capacity component of the equation. No strong basis was found for choosing between entering the interest rate and leverage-retained earning variable separately in the equation or using one variable which is a multiplicative combination of them, although the *t*-ratios on the latter leverage variable were higher (5.6+). The smoothed rate of change of the Baa rate remained highly significant and negative regardless of the form of the leverage variable and regardless of whether the level of the Baa rate was entered separately or as part of a compound interest-leverage term.

All explanatory variables were cumulated to the index quarter, using Almon's weights to allow for the distributed lag of investment outlays after decisions and appropriations. We also found that all explanatory variables in these basic equations retained their significance and were in general little changed by the addition of a current (i.e., noncumulated) actual-to-expected sales-discrepancy term to measure cancellations and other positive and negative effects of "surprises" (see Table 5). With this additional term, the Durbin-Watson statistics were 1.9+, and standard errors of estimate were under .30 per cent of I_{t+1}/K_{t-1}, which is the equivalent of an adjusted R_c^2 on investment itself of .96+. Time trend terms were nonnegative in all equations incorporating finance and leverage terms and were virtually zero in the final equations presented.

In one important respect, the results did not conform to those expected on the basis of theory: like other investigators, we failed to find significant effects and coefficients for any of several relative real cost variables tested as separate variables added to the equation.

BIBLIOGRAPHY

1. Almon, Shirley, "The Distributed Lag Between Capital Appropriations and Expenditures," *Econometrica,* January 1965, pp. 178–196.

Corporation Finance: Risk and Investment   253

2. Anderson, W. H. L., *Corporate Finance and Fixed Investment,* Boston, 1964.
3. Brittain, John A., "The Tax Structure and Corporate Dividend Policy," *American Economic Review,* May 1963, pp. 272–287.
4. de Leeuw, Frank, "The Demand for Capital Goods by Manufacturers: A Study of Quarterly Time Series," *Econometrica,* July 1962, pp. 407–423.
5. Duesenberry, James, *Income, Saving, and the Theory of Consumer Behavior,* Cambridge, Mass., 1949.
6. ———, *Business Cycles and Economic Growth,* New York, 1958, Chap. V.
7. Eisner, Robert, "A Distributed Lag Investment Function," *Econometrica,* January 1960, pp. 1–29.
8. ———, "Investment: Fact and Fancy," *American Economic Review,* May 1963, pp. 237–246.
9. ———, "Capital Expenditures, Profits and the Acceleration Principle," in *Models of Income Determination,* Studies in Income and Wealth 28, Princeton for NBER, 1964.
10. ———, and Strotz, Robert H., "Determinants of Business Investment," in *Impacts of Monetary Policy,* Englewood Cliffs, 1963, pp. 60–333.
11. Fisher, Irving, *The Theory of Interest,* New York, 1930.
12. Friend, Irwin, and Bronfenbrenner, Jean, "Plant and Equipment Programs and Their Realization," in *Short-Term Economic Forecasting,* Studies in Income and Wealth 17, Princeton for NBER, 1955, pp. 53–98.
13. Friedman, Milton, *A Theory of the Consumption Function,* Princeton for NBER, 1957.
14. Glauber, Robert R., "Cyclical Dynamics of Financial Liquidity in Manufacturing Corporations: An Econometric Analysis," unpublished Ph.D. dissertation, Harvard Business School, 1965.
15. Hart, Albert G., "Capital Appropriations and the Accelerator," *Review of Economics and Statistics,* May 1965, pp. 123–136.
16. Hickman, Bert G., *Investment Demand and U.S. Economic Growth,* Washington, 1965.
17. Hirshleifer, Jack, "On The Theory of Optimal Investment Decision," *Journal of Political Economy,* August 1958, pp. 329–352.
18. Johnston, Jack, *Econometric Methods,* New York, 1963.
19. Jorgenson, Dale, "Capital Theory and Investment Behavior," *American Economic Review,* May 1963, pp. 247–259.
20. ———, "Anticipations and Investment Behavior" Working Paper No. 40, Committee on Econometrics and Mathematical Economics, Institute of Business and Economic Research, University of California at Berkeley.
21. Koyck, L. M., *Distributed Lags and Investment Analysis,* Amsterdam, 1954.
22. Kuh, Edwin, "Theory and Institutions in the Study of Investment Behavior," *American Economic Review,* May 1963, pp. 260–268.

23. Lintner, John, "Distribution of Incomes of Corporations Among Dividends, Retained Earnings and Taxes," *American Economic Review,* May 1956, pp. 97–113.

24. ———, "Dividends, Earnings, Leverage, Stock Prices and the Supply of Capital to Corporations," *Review of Economics and Statistics,* August 1962, pp. 243–269.

25. ———, "Optimal Dividends and Corporate Growth Under Uncertainty," *The Quarterly Journal of Economics,* February 1964, pp. 49–95.

26. ———, "Discussion of Corporate Dividend Policy," *American Economic Review,* May 1964, pp. 302–306.

27. ———, "The Valuation of Risk Assets and the Selection of Risky Investments in Stock Portfolios and Capital Budgets," *Review of Economics and Statistics,* February 1965, pp. 13–37.

28. ———, "Security Prices, Risk and Maximal Gains From Diversification," *Journal of Finance,* December 1965.

29. Meyer, John R., and Glauber, Robert R., *Investment Decisions, Economic Forecasting and Public Policy,* Cambridge, Mass., 1964.

30. Modigliani, Franco, "Fluctuations in the Savings-Income Ratio: A Problem in Economic Forecasting," *Studies in Income and Wealth 11,* New York, NBER, 1949, pp. 371–440.

31. ———, and Miller, Merton, "The Cost of Capital, Corporation Finance and the Theory of Investment," *American Economic Review,* June 1958, pp. 261–297.

32. ———, "Dividend Policy, Growth and the Valuation of Shares," *Journal of Business,* October 1961, pp. 411–433.

33. ———, "Taxes and the Cost of Capital: A Correction," *American Economic Review,* June 1963, pp. 433–442.

34. ———, and Weingartner, Martin, "Forecasting Uses of Anticipatory Data on Investment and Sales," *The Quarterly Journal of Economics,* February 1958, pp. 23–52.

35. Pratt, John, "Risk Aversion in the Small and in the Large," *Econometrica,* January-April 1964, pp. 122–136.

36. Resek, Robert W., "Investment by Manufacturing Firms: A Quarterly Time Series Analysis of Industry Data," *Review of Economics and Statistics* (forthcoming).

37. Solow, Robert M., "On A Family of Lag Distributions," *Econometrica,* April 1960, pp. 393–406.

38. Taylor, Lester D., and Wilson, Thomas A., "Three-Pass Least Squares: A Method for Estimating Models With a Lagged Dependent Variable," *Review of Economics and Statistics,* November 1964, pp. 329–346.

39. Theil, Henri, and Nagar, A. L., "Testing the Independence of Regression Disturbances," *Journal of the American Statistical Association,* December 1961, pp. 793–806.

COMMENT

On Miller-Modigliani and Lintner

by j. fred weston

university of california, los angeles

The Miller and Modigliani paper is a curious combination of impressive formal analysis resting on inconsistent and mutually contradictory premises. Drawing on their earlier work, they make assumptions and define terms so that they may conclude that financial policy does not affect the firm's cost of capital under certainty and with no income taxes.

With income taxes, a subsidy is provided to debt. The consequence would be that firms would use the maximum amount of debt. But the observed facts indicate that this is obviously not true.

Miller and Modigliani resort to the concept of a "target debt ratio," denoted as *L,* to explain why observed debt ratios are not as high as their model implies. A target debt ratio implies some policy on financing mix by a firm. But this is precisely what traditional business finance has argued and what Miller and Modigliani have denied. Their reference to "the maximum permitted by lenders" is an imprecise way of saying that the cost of debt at some point rises sharply with increased leverage —implying an optimal debt-to-equity ratio.

The theoretical underpinnings of their empirical materials are therefore confused. Their development of the theoretical model is marred by loose statements and unsupported assertions such as the following: "For companies with reasonable access to the capital markets, as would certainly be true of those in our sample, investment and financing decisions (including decisions to retire outstanding securities) are made continuously and largely independently over time."

What does "reasonable access to the capital markets" signify in analytical terms? What is their evidence that investment and financing decisions are made "continuously and largely independently over time"? Surely such critical assertions should not be made without evidence or reference to other studies which provide evidence.

After an extended discussion of theoretical models, the equation which they use in their statistical tests turns out to be a rough empirical approach. The value of the firm is related to the factors generally considered important in the business finance literature. These factors include earnings, dividend policy, growth rate, leverage, and size of firms. Their results, then, critically depend on how the variables are measured and the nature of their sample.

The Miller-Modigliani study is focused on the electric utility industry. A number of characteristics of the regulated industry can influence the generality of their results and even interpretation of their significance for the electric utility industry. First, if the earnings of a utility company exceed or fall below some range, a rate adjustment may take place. Second, a review of the opinions of utility commissions indicates a preference for investment financed from outside equity compared with retained earnings. This attitude certainly influences dividend policy. Third, the effect of regulation is to create a tendency toward uniformity in both leverage and dividend policies. For example, if higher debt ratios lead to higher earnings, the higher profits may be reduced by rate adjustments. On the other hand, if earnings are low because leverage ratios are low, commissions are unlikely to make compensatory rate adjustments. The influence of regulation is to make for conformity in financial policies—a consequence which should greatly influence the interpretation of the empirical results.

In this connection, the empirical measurements of Lintner present another set of problems. Lintner studies the plant and equipment outlays of all U.S. manufacturing corporations over the forty-four quarters of 1953–63. The Miller-Modigliani studies focus on cross-section analysis of an industry for which product homogeneity is emphasized. Lintner employs a time series analysis covering a wide variety of industries. This substantially departs from the Miller-Modigliani concept of industries representing homogeneous risk classes.

It is interesting to note that the underlying theoretical models differ as well. Miller and Modigliani seek to explain the value of the firm, while Lintner seeks to explain investment outlays. He emphasizes that financing decisions and investment decisions are mutually determined. This strong belief is in direct contrast with the counter assertion of Miller and Modigliani.

Lintner argues that the marginal cost of financing is represented by the marginal cost of debt. He suggests that the marginal cost of debt is likely to rise exponentially for a number of reasons. But since the equity holders are in a junior position to the creditors of a company, the factors that cause the cost of debt function to rise sharply are likely to cause the cost of equity function to rise even more.

Lintner objects to the use of the weighted average method of calculating the cost of capital. In theory the marginal cost of capital should be measured as we measure the marginal cost of any inputs. We formulate a function and take the partial derivatives with respect to the inputs being varied. Lintner argues that the weighted average cost method of calculating the cost of capital is wrong because the average cost is used rather than the marginal cost of debt and equity financing. But this objection can be met conceptually by using the marginal costs rather than the average costs.

Lintner's objection to the use of weighting appears to confuse (1) increasing the size of the capital budget by the use of debt or equity and (2) changing the debt-equity mix. This goes to the heart of the difficulty in calculating the cost of financial inputs. For calculating the marginal cost of physical (real) labor and capital inputs, the points of tangency of the isoproduct and isocost lines for different levels of output are connected. The isoquants representing different levels of value of the firm for different combinations of debt and equity unfortunately involve interdependence. To change the debt-to-equity mix not only influences the cost of debt, but influences the cost of equity as well. Altering the financing mix changes both the earnings of the company *and* the appropriate capitalization rates to be employed. The theoretical problem is formidable and the measurement problem appears to require some approximation methods for working purposes.

Lintner asserts that the opportunity cost of using more retained funds to increase the current size of the capital budget is the foregone opportunity to repay debt, "as Duesenberry has emphasized." Neither Duesenberry nor Lintner provides evidence that the opportunity cost of increasing the size of the capital budget is the foregone opportunity to repay debt. Why is not retirement of equity another alternative use of retained funds? Would not the decision to retire debt or to retire equity be a function of the marginal decreases in the cost of funds resulting from applying retained earnings in the one direction or the other?

Particularly in the latter section of the paper where Lintner is formulating statements about the behavior of the cost of capital function, it would be useful to have the arguments presented in a more precise analytical framework. Without a clear statement of the complete model that is being used, it is not certain what the linkage is between the data and model, between measurement procedures and the meaning of the results.

ON MILLER-MODIGLIANI

BY IRWIN FRIEND, UNIVERSITY OF PENNSYLVANIA

The most interesting part of the paper by Miller and Modigliani consists of an econometric implementation of their basic model of firm

valuation and cost of capital, which is applied to cross-section data for
electric utilities in 1954, 1956, and 1957. This model assumes that the
cost of capital for a firm in a given risk class is, apart from the very
important tax complication (for which they adjust explicitly), invariant
to capital structure.

Their theory leads to a basic structural equation in which the value of
the firm, apart from tax (and size of firm) effects, is determined by two
terms.[1] The first is the capitalization of current earnings before interest,
represented as the product of such earnings (which can be measured
directly) and the reciprocal of the cost of equity capital,[2] which cannot
be measured directly but is assumed to be a constant for all firms of
given size in the industry. The second term is the value placed on the
growth potential, expressed empirically as the product of expected
growth in the book value of assets (based on the most recent five-year
growth rate) and another "constant," which in theory is an inverse
function of the cost of capital and a direct function of the rate of return
on new investment and of the duration of the period for which profitable
new investment opportunities are expected to persist. The cost of financing for an all-equity structure, which is different from the total cost of
financing in the Miller-Modigliani model only as a result of the tax
savings associated with debt, is estimated as the reciprocal of the regression coefficient of the current earnings variable in this structural equation.

My reaction to such an approach to estimation of the cost of financing
is that, while it is intriguing, it is also questionable. If the measure of
expected growth is a poor one, the current earnings variable (expressed
as a ratio of the book value of assets) may act as a proxy for such
growth so that its coefficient is biased upward and hence the estimated
cost of capital would be biased downward. More important, there is a
much more direct approach to the estimation of the cost of capital which
avoids both this statistical difficulty and the theoretical necessity of
assuming the irrelevance of capital structure, apart from tax savings, to
the over-all valuation and cost of financing of the firm.[3] This alternative
approach, which appears preferable both on statistical and theoretical
grounds, consists of estimating the cost of equity (which is no longer
the cost for a pure equity stream) as the sum of a dividend yield plus an
estimated growth rate in earnings and dividends, and obtaining the

---

[1] For statistical reasons, all variables are divided by the book value of assets in
the equations actually fitted.

[2] This is the cost of capital for an all-equity structure in that risk class.

[3] The Miller-Modigliani approach permits the incorporation of leverage variables
into their basic structural equation, but this may aggravate the statistical difficulties, particularly if the irrelevance assumption is justified.

over-all cost of capital as the market-value weighted sum of the costs of equity and senior capital (adjusted for tax effects). There are, of course, major problems involved in estimating the expected growth rate—including decisions on the use of the past objective record, forecasts used by financial analysts, the duration of the period for which growth is to be projected, etc.—but these same problems exist in the implementation of the Miller-Modigliani econometric model. I (as well as others) have used this approach in the past, and it is my impression that it would yield significantly higher estimates of the cost of capital for the electric utilities than the Miller-Modigliani figures ranging from 3.6 per cent in 1954 to 4.6 per cent in 1957, which seem to me to be implausibly low (and indeed are not much higher than the yield on AAA public utility bonds).

In estimating the regressions coefficients in their basic structural equation, Miller and Modigliani substitute normalized earnings for reported earnings in order to eliminate measurement errors from the key earnings variable in the equation. Their method of normalizing earnings is to regress reported earnings on five different variables including dividends, with normalized earnings measured as the expected value of the dependent variable in this regression. Of the variables tested, the unabridged version of their paper seems to indicate that only dividends exert a major influence on normalized earnings, though one other variable—strangely enough, the ratio of preferred stock to assets—was also significant. It is not clear in their analysis that dividends alone would not have sufficed as a proxy for normalized earnings. The authors do not discuss other alternatives which have been used for normalizing earnings, some of which seem preferable to me.[4] Actually, the change in the coefficients of the earnings variable in their basic structural equation, as a result of the substitution of normalized for reported earnings, does not appear to be very large. The only noteworthy difference between the normalized and reported earnings coefficients is that the former imply an increase in the cost of capital from 1954 to 1956 and 1957 in both regressions fitted, i.e., with and without a constant term, while the latter yield almost the identical results in the regression without a constant term but point to a decrease in the cost of capital in the regression with a constant term (which is the regression the authors like least). Intuitively, in spite of an increase in interest rates, stability or even some decrease in the cost of capital over this period does not seem

---

[4] For example, see Irwin Friend and Marshall Packett, "Dividends and Stock Prices," *The American Economic Review,* September 1964.

implausible to me in view of the reasons for believing there was a reduction in the required risk differential on equity.[5]

Though they devote considerable attention to the rise in their estimates of the cost of capital from 1954 to 1957, I do not really understand the explanation of this phenomenon offered by Miller and Modigliani. The average cost of capital according to them rises from 3.6 to 4.6 per cent, while the yields on AAA public utility bonds rise from 3.1 to 4.3 per cent. Disregarding what I consider to be an unreasonably low figure for the cost of capital at the beginning of this period, the Miller-Modigliani estimates appear to imply that there was no lowering of the risk differential on equity over this period—a result which, to me at least, seems dubious.

In view of these and other reservations (including a feeling that the authors have been less than charitable in their references to the state of the arts), my over-all reaction to the paper is that it is a stimulating but unsuccessful attempt to measure an elusive but highly important economic parameter, the cost of capital. As the authors point out, the goal is extremely important and difficult of attainment. It is no reflection on the ingenuity displayed in this paper to suggest that the goal has yet to be attained.

REPLY TO FRIEND AND WESTON

BY MILLER AND MODIGLIANI

We are grateful to Friend for pointing out so specifically, succinctly, and frankly those aspects of our approach to measuring the cost of capital about which he has serious misgivings. It is apparent that his objections spring largely from his qualms about our actual numerical estimates of the cost of capital, which strike him as implausibly low and as moving over time in the wrong direction. These qualms, quite understandably, have led him to search for possible shortcomings in our procedures that might be responsible for estimates seemingly so wide of the mark. In

[5] Similarly, in the authors' unabridged version of their paper, which incorporates dividend policy as an additional explanatory variable in their basic structural equation, I do not understand the authors' preference for two-stage or normalized results vs. direct least-squares results. In the latter, dividend policy is significant in 1954, with higher payout associated with higher market value, but not at all in 1956 and 1957, while in the former the payout ratio is not significantly related to market value in any year, but there is an upward drift in its impact on market value over this period. Intuitively again, the direct least-squares results (including the other regression coefficients in the equation) seem fully as plausible as the two-stage results.

what follows we shall try to indicate why we do not share his doubts and why we persist in believing that our estimates, properly interpreted, are plausible and sensible. Before doing so, however, it may be useful first to consider his methodological objections.

As one possible reason for the low estimates he points out that "the current earnings variable . . . may act as a proxy for [expected] growth . . . and hence the estimated cost of capital would be biased downward." We have acknowledged in our paper that our measure of expected growth opportunities is only an approximation and that, to the extent that it is measured subject to error, biases in the other coefficients may well creep in. But we have some grounds at least for believing that any likely bias from the correlation between earnings and growth in the present case could hardly be large enough to change the picture dramatically. Not only is there no particular reason to expect a priori any systematic correlation between the level of current earnings (relative to assets) and future growth potential in a regulated industry such as this one, but the data themselves give no hint of such correlation. The simple correlations between earnings and our growth variable (see Appendix B, Table 2, of the unabridged version) are virtually zero or negligibly negative in all three years. Granted that our measure of growth is far from perfect, and hence that we cannot be absolutely sure that there is no correlation between earnings and the *true* measure, our measure of growth cannot really be so bad (judging by how well it does perform in the valuation regressions) that it would fail to pick up any correlation between growth and earnings strong enough to have a noticeable effect on the results.

Friend's second possible explanation of the peculiar results is that we have used a "questionable" and certainly too roundabout method of estimation in preference to a "much more direct" method of estimating the cost of capital. By direct, he means first estimating the cost of equity capital as the sum of an estimate of the expected dividend yield and some estimate of the expected growth rate of dividends or earnings, and then obtaining the over-all cost of capital as a weighted average of this cost of equity, current debt, and preferred stock yields (adjusted for tax effects). In his view, this approach is superior to ours "both on statistical and theoretical grounds." It is also his impression (based on his own work and that of others) that his method "would yield significantly higher estimates of the cost of capital for the electric utilities."

This is, indeed, a major point of contention, since we would have regarded as one of the major methodological contributions of our paper precisely that it provided an effective alternative to the traditional piecemeal approach to the cost of capital that Friend describes and recommends.

By "preferable on theoretical grounds," he means, apparently, that his approach "avoids the theoretical necessity of assuming the irrelevance of capital structure, apart from tax savings, to the over-all valuation of the firm." It is true, of course, that our *estimates* were computed on that assumption and that such an assumption is also implied in our model of rational valuation. But this has nothing to do with our *method* of estimation. Before discussing results based on the assumption, we first tested that assumption and found that it was indeed consistent with the data in our sample (see Table 4 of the unabridged version). If these tests had turned out differently, so would the final results we presented.

It is also true, of course, that his "direct" method avoids the necessity of considering explicitly the relation between capital structure and valuation. But it does so only at the cost of having a less useful and less informative result. At best, his approach will provide an estimate of a single point on the cost of capital *function,* namely, the point corresponding to the actual current sample value of the capital structure (and the current levels of any other variables that affect valuation). Hence, in contrast to our approach, the results of the piecemeal approach cannot be used for policy-making or policy evaluation purposes by individual firms or regulatory bodies.

Even more puzzling is Friend's claim that his method is "statistically superior." He certainly cannot mean by this that his concept of growth is a simpler one than ours or that it presents fewer problems to the estimator. Indeed, the opposite is closer to the truth. His growth component, after all, is nothing more or less than the expected capital gain on a share of common stock, and this expectation must reflect not only growth in our sense (i.e., of advantageous future investment opportunities) but also expected financial policy (i.e., the extent to which future asset expansion will be financed from retained earnings). If, nevertheless, Friend still feels more comfortable with his approach to growth rather than with ours, that is, of course, his privilege; but other investigators should at least not be misled into thinking that his approach offers any clear-cut advantage over ours.

As to whether the Friend method, properly implemented, will indeed turn out to yield substantially higher estimates than ours, that is anybody's guess. We have our doubts since we do not really think our estimates are unreasonably low for reasons to be indicated later. In any event, we too, in another connection, happen to have made some computations of expected equity yields along the lines he describes for a number of companies, including some also in our utility sample. It was not our experience that such yields, after correction for leverage, were substantially and systematically higher than the pure equity yields implied by the results in the present paper. We wonder whether Friend may not have derived his impression that equity yields in this period were quite high from the reported figures on *realized* yields or rates of return. These *ex post* yields were indeed rather high on the whole; but since they contain a very substantial amount of what must surely be regarded as unanticipated capital appreciation, they are hardly likely to be good measures of the kind of *ex ante* or required yields that he and we are concerned with.[1]

Friend's third methodological objection is that we have based our main conclusions on one particular set of test results involving a very special "method of normalizing earnings," i.e., our two-stage, instrumental variable approach to estimation. On this point, a casual reader of his comments is likely to come away with the impression that our use of the two-stage estimates is simply a peculiar matter of taste on our part. We seem to prefer two-stage estimates with constant suppressed to direct least-squares estimates with or without constant. He, on the other hand, would prefer our direct least-squares estimates and would presumably be even happier with estimates derived from another "normalizing" approach developed by him and Marshall Puckett.

Actually, of course, we base our discussion of the cost of capital on the estimates without a constant term not because we enjoy suppressing constants or feel that those estimates are more in line with our prejudices but because the basic theoretical specification requires the constant to be so treated and because the tests of that specification presented in our paper give no evidence that the constant term is other than zero. We used a two-stage instrumental variable approach because, under our assumptions, such estimates would at least have the property of consistency whereas the direct least-squares estimates are open to bias from measurement errors in the key earnings variable (and particularly so if a constant term were to be included). It is for the same reason, of course, that we "preferred" our approach to the alternative method of Friend and Puckett. Ingenious as their method may be, it cannot be expected to yield consistent estimates, as they themselves have acknowledged.[2]

[1] Our suspicions about the unanticipated nature of much of the realized capital gains over this period are strongly reinforced by the findings of F. Ardetti in his as yet unpublished dissertation, *"Risk and The Required Return on Equity,"* Massachusetts Institute of Technology, 1965, esp. Chapter IV.

[2] I. Friend and M. Puckett, "Dividends and Stock Prices," *American Economic Review,* September 1964, p. 669.

In any event, anticipating that our instrumental variable procedure might be unfamiliar to some and might cause just such uneasiness as Friend has shown, we took the precaution of providing some alternative "calibrating" estimates derived from a more conventional method. This approach, which represents what we called the "yield formulation," does rely on familiar direct least-squares estimation. It can be expected to be free at least from bias stemming from the measurement error in earnings, though subject to certain other sources of bias that should tend on balance to underestimate the cost of capital. Comparison of the estimates derived from these very different procedures (see Table 6 and surrounding text in the unabridged version) shows that they are quite close and stand in the predicted relation to each other. If, therefore, our two-stage estimates are "implausibly low," this cannot be attributed to any serious distortions introduced through our "normalization" procedure.[3]

Having failed to find anything in Friend's methodological objections that could account for the "implausibility" of the estimates, a few words may now be in order in defense of their reasonableness. We suspect that some of Friend's misgivings stem from his concentration on our estimates of the so-called weighted average cost of capital or tax-adjusted required rates of return given in Table 4. The tax-adjusted rate is a measure about which it is difficult to make intuitive judgments because the concept of income on which it is based does not correspond to any of the more commonly used accounting concepts. Furthermore, because of the way we controlled for size of firm, the estimates presented apply directly only to the largest firms (strictly speaking, to firms of infinite size). Adjusting to average size our estimates of the tax-adjusted required rates of return for 1956 and 1957 come to 4.6 and 4.8 per cent, respectively. If we next convert from a tax-adjusted to the more familiar *before-tax* basis, these estimates imply *before-tax* required rates of return for companies of average size in this industry of 9.5 and 10 per cent, respectively. Such values certainly do not strike *us* as being preposterously low.

Nor is it meaningful to compare, as Friend does, our tax-adjusted average rate with the before-tax bond yield since our required rate is so substantially affected by the sizable tax subsidy on the very high degree of leverage that is found in this industry. The more sensible comparison,

---

[3] There is equally little ground for Friend's concern over the fact that, in the first-stage regressions on the instrumental variables, the dividend variable alone seems to account for most of the correlation. As we pointed out in the unabridged version, virtually identical estimates (though, of course, with somewhat higher standard errors) are obtained when dividends are not included among the instrumental variables in the first stage.

if one is to be made, would be between the bond yield and our estimated cost of equity capital or tax-adjusted required return for an unlevered firm. The latter figure, again adjusting for size, we find to be 5.3 per cent in 1954, compared with a bond yield of 3.1 per cent, implying a "risk premium" of some 70 per cent. By 1957, the required equity yield had risen to 6.4 per cent, compared with a bond yield of 4.3 per cent, implying a risk premium of just below 50 per cent. Premiums of this size do not strike us as unreasonably low for an industry like the electric utilities consisting of regulated but protected monopolies, none of which suffered any losses (or even sizable declines in earnings) either during the sample period or for several prior years, despite the fact that some of these were years of recession. Note also that our estimates, properly interpreted, do seem to indicate a falling trend in the risk premium of the kind that Friend's intuition led him to suspect. If anything, this fall in the "risk differential on equity" strikes us as rather remarkably large for the period 1954-57. For, though we share his feeling that a substantial downward adjustment in risk premiums probably took place between the late 1940's and the middle 1950's (reflecting the growing confidence in the economy's resistance to severe depression), our guess would have been that more of the adjustment had occurred before the end of 1954.

There are still other ways to put our estimates in a more meaningful perspective from which to bring intuition to bear. For example, starting from our 1957 estimate of the average tax-adjusted cost of capital, one finds that after adjusting for average size of firm and average leverage the required rate of return or yield on levered common stock implied by our results is on the order of 8.5 per cent, which, again, hardly seems preposterously low.[4] As a further and particularly telling consideration suggesting that our estimates of the tax-adjusted cost of capital are not substantially too low, we may point out that the convenional 6 per cent return after taxes on the rate base is equivalent to about 5.2 per cent when converted to our tax-adjusted basis (see section III of our paper). Since there seems to be clear and undisputed evidence that investors during this period were willing to pay significant premiums for growth potential, they must presumably have been projecting a tax-adjusted cost of capital or required yield that was less than 5.2 per cent. With an implied ceiling of this order of magnitude, our estimates of 4.6 and 4.8 per cent as the required yields in 1956 and 1957 can hardly be con-

---

[4] Curiously enough, our implied yields on levered equity shares of utilities in this period are actually somewhat higher than those reported by Professor Friend in his paper with Puckett.

sidered as implausibly low. On the contrary, we suggest that it will be the Friend estimates, if they turn out to be very substantially above ours, that will have to be regarded as implausibly high!

Summing up, then, we can find no basis for Friend's repeated assertions that our estimates of the tax-adjusted cost of capital for the utility industry are far too low. And since we certainly respect his judgment in matters pertaining to the capital markets, we are led to suspect that he did not dig deeply enough into our perhaps overlong paper to appreciate what our estimates really mean or how they relate to other, more familiar concepts of yield.

Turning now briefly to Weston's critical remarks it should be noted that, with one exception to be discussed below, his comments really have little bearing on the problem of main concern in this paper, namely, how to estimate the cost of capital. His quarrel is rather with the presumed "theoretical underpinning" of our model of valuation. Since these underpinnings have been discussed at length in several of our previous papers and will be further explored in sequels to the present paper, there is no point in rehashing the matter here. Suffice it to say, for the sake of the record, that we do not agree that our target leverage ratio is the same as the optimum financing mix of traditional discussions of finance—an optimum such that deviations in either direction would adversely affect the value of the shares. As for his strictures on our failure to present any direct evidence for our working assumptions of rational behavior and perfect capital markets, we were frankly astonished to see this sort of ploy in what purports to be a serious critique. We would have thought it had long been accepted among economists that standard working assumptions of this kind can only be effectively tested by testing their consequences. And that, of course, is precisely what most of our paper is about! We also feel that his comments on this matter come with particular ill grace since he has interlarded his own remarks with a number of dubious, unsupported assertions about electric utilities—assertions much more susceptible to direct check than our working assumptions.

Weston's one substantive point is that external regulation of earnings and financial policies in the electric utility industry may reduce the "generality" and "significance" of our results, particularly those bearing on the relation between financial policy and the cost of capital. There are really two distinct kinds of questions involved here. First, does the mere fact that the financial policies may have been *imposed* on the managements of some firms create problems of estimation or interpretation? Here the answer is clearly no. Our concern is solely with what investors are willing to pay for the different packages of earnings and financial policy that actually do come onto the market for sale. For establishing the empirical relations between the prices of various packages, the questions of why they differ or who really makes them up are wholly irrelevant. On the other hand, a serious estimation problem might arise if regulation of financial policy was so pervasive and so uniform that all the packages on the market were virtually alike. When we first began the study, this was indeed our greatest fear about the sample. As it turns out, however, there does happen to be considerable variation within the industry—less so certainly than we would like, but enough to rule out the possibility that our zeroish results for debt and dividend policy reflect merely a fit to a single point with some random variation in its immediate neighborhood. Weston could have discovered this himself either by looking at the table of means and standard deviations of the variables presented in the appendix of the unabridged version, or by looking at the results of the direct least-squares regressions where there was apparently enough variability, in some years at least, for the financial policy variables to show up as highly significant and in the classical direction. All this is not to say, of course, that we regard our assumptions, procedures, or results as unexceptionable; but we do think such severe critics should present us at least with a bill of particulars.

PART III

Consumer Assets

The Distribution of Population

Within Urban Areas

RICHARD F. MUTH

INSTITUTE FOR DEFENSE ANALYSES

I

Most papers on the subject of investment are concerned with how much of it takes place. This one, however, is primarily interested in where investment in housing occurs. More precisely, it is concerned with the distribution of population within urban areas, especially the distribution of population between the central city (the largest political city) and its suburbs, and the total amount of land used by the urban area. One of the most striking phenomena of recent years has been the relatively large growth in population of the suburban parts of urban areas and the accompanying rapid increase in land area used for residential and other urban purposes. It is not generally realized, however, that the outer parts of central cities have tended to grow at greater relative rates than those parts closest to the city center.

In many popular and some scholarly discussions of urban growth and related problems, the rapid growth of the outer parts of urban areas of recent years is viewed as haphazard or capricious and unplanned, implying that it is necessarily bad. In other, more sophisticated discussions, urban decentralization is viewed primarily as a "flight from blight"—that is, as an attempt by people to escape the poor housing, the age, excessive population densities, or other undesirable features of central cities. Both kinds of discussion often suggest that urban decentralization has gone too far and urge various kinds of governmental action to reverse it. As economists, most of us would be tempted to seek an explanation for urban decentralization in factors such as changes in the relative costs of living in different parts of urban areas. One obvious factor that might affect these relative costs is the growth of automobile transportation and the building of express highways. In addition, governmental programs, such as the federal income tax advantage to owner-occupied housing and the FHA and VA mortgage programs, have probably encouraged decentralization.

This paper presents some of the results of my study of the spatial aspects of urban housing markets that are relevant to the analysis of urban decentralization. Section II contains a very brief summary of the theoretical framework which underlies the empirical work described later. Section III discusses some of the factors that would be expected to be related to the relative rate of decline in population densities with distance from the city center, describes the measures of these factors used here, and presents a preliminary regression analysis made in an attempt to appraise their empirical importance. This analysis is continued in section IV, which also examines the effects of these and other factors on the distribution of population between the central city and its suburbs and the total land used by urban areas. In this last I am especially interested in the extent to which suburbanization is simply an extension beyond its borders of the distribution of population within the central city and to what extent it is something different. My conclusions and some of their implications are summarized in the final section.

Admittedly, my analysis has few implications for the determinants of the total volume of investment in nonfarm residential real estate. Apart from providing some explanation for where such investment takes place, it may also be suggestive of the form in which housing investment takes place. If, for example, my analysis were to imply a continuation of past rates of urban decentralization, it would also suggest that investment in housing in the future would continue to be disproportionately in the form of new units rather than additions and alterations to existing units and in houses rather than apartments. Continued decentralization might also imply greater investment in new public facilities in newly built communities and greater expenditures under governmental programs such as urban renewal, which are designed in part to halt decentralization.

II

Because accessibility to employment and purchasing opportunities has value, the price consumers pay for housing of any given quality would be expected to decline with distance from the central business district (CBD) of an urban area. It can easily be shown that, for any given residential location to be an equilibrium one for the household occupying it, the following must hold:[1]

$$-(p_k/p) = (T_k/pq), \tag{1}$$

where p is the price per unit of housing, p_k is the change in housing price per unit change in distance from the CBD (k), q is the quantity of housing consumed, and T_k is the change in transport costs incurred by the household per unit change in distance. The last is assumed to include both direct money outlay and the money equivalent of time spent in travel. Since T_k is positive, equation (1) implies that housing prices are smaller at greater distances from the CBD. The truth of the proposition stated in the previous sentence can also be seen from the following consideration. If housing prices were invariant with distance but households located at greater distances incurred greater transport costs, it would be in the interest of the latter to offer more for the services of housing closer to the CBD than its occupants currently pay. In the process, housing prices would rise close to the CBD and decline at greater distances from it.

The fall in housing prices with distance from the CBD implies that the rent per unit of residential land must also decline with distance. For, if this were not the case, firms producing housing close to the CBD would earn larger incomes than the more distantly located firms. Rents would then be bid up in locations close to the CBD and bid down in distant locations. Along with the decline in land rents with distance from the CBD, land will be substituted for other productive factors in producing housing, provided that, as seems likely, the variation of construction costs is small relative to that of land rents throughout the urban area. As a consequence of this substitution, the output of housing per unit of land in both physical and value terms declines with distance from the CBD.

The variation of housing prices also affects the per capita consumption of housing in different parts of the urban area. Given real incomes and tastes for housing versus other commodities, equilibrium of the consumer in the presence of declining housing prices requires that housing be substituted for other commodities or that the per capita consumption of housing be greater at locations more distant from the CBD. Secondly, since higher-income CBD-worker households consume more housing per capita than lower income ones, they have an incentive on

---

[1] This relationship was presented in my earlier paper "The Spatial Structure of the Housing Market," *Papers and Proceedings of the Regional Science Association,* Volume 7, 1961, pp. 207–220. The present paper is a continuation of the earlier one.

this account to locate at greater distances from the CBD where housing prices are lower. However, to the extent that differences in income of CBD-worker households result from wage income differences, higher-income households would value travel time more highly, T_k would be greater for them, and they would tend to locate closer to the CBD on this account alone.[2] On balance, though, the effect operating on location through greater consumption would be expected to predominate. It would seem likely that the income elasticity of marginal transport costs would be less than or equal to unity, while the income elasticity of housing demand is probably at least equal to unity and perhaps as high as two. Finally, like higher-income households, households with stronger tastes for housing consume more of it and have an incentive to locate in locations where housing prices are lower. Thus, in addition to the pure substitution effects of housing prices on quantity consumed, the consumption of housing per capita tends to be greater at greater distances from the CBD because higher-income CBD-worker households and households with stronger tastes for housing tend to locate there.

Population density is identical to the output of housing per unit of land divided by the per capita consumption of housing. The forces summarized in the preceding three paragraphs imply that population densities decline with distance from the CBD, both because the numerator declines and because the denominator increases. In my earlier paper I presented and evaluated estimates of the negative-exponential approximation to the pattern of population densities in large U.S. cities:[3]

$$D(k) = D_0 e^{-D_1 k}, \qquad (2)$$

where $D(k)$ is gross population per unit of land at a distance k from the CBD, D_0 is the central density or level of population density when extrapolated to the CBD, and D_1 is the density gradient. The negative-exponential function in distance alone was found to explain about one-half of the variation in gross population density by census tract in forty-six large U.S. cities in 1950 and the fit was about the same in cities of different sizes and in different parts of the country. While too many departures from the negative-exponential pattern of decline were found to be consistent with sampling variability, there was no significant tendency for the log density-distance regressions to exhibit predominantly positive or negative curvature.

[2] I failed to spell this out in my earlier paper.

[3] *Ibid.* I also gave one rationale for this particular functional form. The reader is referred to my earlier paper for a fuller explanation of the estimates I made.

If, in addition to (2), it is assumed that the incremental supply of land to the housing industry is

$$L'(k) = \xi k, \tag{3}$$

where $(\xi/2\pi)$ is the fraction of space surrounding the CBD that is used for residential purposes, certain other relationships can be readily derived. The total population living not more than k miles from the CBD is (assuming the CBD is of negligible width)

$$P(k) = \int_0^k D(v)L'(v)\, dv \tag{4}$$

$$= \frac{\xi D_0}{D_1^2} f(D_1, k),$$

where $f(D_1, k) = 1 - (1 + D_1 k)\, e^{-D_1 k}$.

If one supposes that the central city of the urban area occupies a circular area of radius k_1 surrounding the CBD, its population, P_1, is given by

$$P_1 = \frac{\xi D_0}{D_1^2} f(D_1, k_1). \tag{5}$$

Likewise, on the supposition that the urbanized area is circular with a radius k_2 surrounding the CBD and assuming that (2) holds outside the central city as well, a similar expression for urbanized area population, P, can be derived. Taking P as given by other forces, the latter defines central density, D_0, in terms of P, D_1, ξ, and k_2:

$$D_0 = \frac{P D_1^2}{\xi f(D_1, k_2)}. \tag{6}$$

Hence, using (6), equation (5) can be rewritten as

$$P_1 = \frac{P f(D_1, k_1)}{f(D_1, k_2)}. \tag{7}$$

The radius of the urbanized area is determined by the strengths and elasticities of urban and agricultural demands for land.[4] For practical purposes, however, an urbanized area is defined by the Bureau of the Census as essentially all the land area surrounding a city for which population densities exceed a certain minimum amount. Substituting this minimum density into equation (2) defines k_2.

---

[4] This point is discussed in more detail in my "Economic Change and Rural-Urban Land Conversions," *Econometrica,* January 1961, pp. 1–23.

In considering differences among cities and/or over time, provided that the definition of urbanized area remains the same, differentiation of (2) yields (asterisk means natural log of)

$$dk_2^* = \frac{dD_0^*}{D_1k_2} - dD_1^*, \tag{8}$$

while from (6)

$$dD_0^* = dP^* + \left(2 - \frac{\partial f_2^*}{\partial D_1^*}\right) dD_1^* \tag{9}$$

$$-d\xi^* - \frac{\partial f_2^*}{\partial k_2^*} dk_2^*,$$

where

$$\frac{\partial f_2^*}{\partial D_1^*} = \frac{\partial f_2^*}{\partial k_2^*} = \frac{(D_1k_2)^2 e^{-D_1k_2}}{f(D_1, k_2)}$$

Substituting for dD_0^* in (9) and solving for dk_2^*,

$$dk_2^* = \alpha dP^* - (1 - 2\alpha)dD_1^* - \alpha d\xi^*, \tag{10}$$

where

$$\alpha = \frac{f(D_1, k_2)}{D_1k_2(1 - e^{-D_1k_2})}.$$

Since from the integrated form of (3),

$$dL^* = d\xi^* + 2dk_2^*, \tag{11}$$

where L is the total land area occupied by the urbanized area,

$$dL^* = \beta dP^* - 2(1 - \beta)dD_1^* + (1 - \beta)d\xi^*, \tag{12}$$

where $\beta = 2\alpha$. Similarly, from (7),

$$dP_1^* = dP^* + \left\{\frac{\partial f_1^*}{\partial D_1^*} - \frac{\partial f_2^*}{\partial D_1^*}\right\} dD_1^* + \frac{\partial f_1^*}{\partial k_1^*} dk_1^* - \frac{\partial f_2^*}{\partial k_2^*} dk_2^*, \tag{13}$$

$\partial f_1^*/\partial D_1^*$ being defined analogously with $\partial f_2^*/\partial D_1^*$ in (9). Substituting (10) for dk_2^* in (13),

$$dP_1^* = (1 - \gamma) dP^* + 2(\delta - \gamma) dD_1^* + 2\delta dk_1^* + \gamma d\xi^*, \tag{14}$$

where

$$\gamma = \frac{D_1k_2}{(e^{D_1k_2}-1)} \quad \text{and} \quad \delta = \frac{1}{2} \frac{\partial f_1^*}{\partial D_1^*}.$$

Thus, on the assumptions made earlier, equations (14) and (12) express central city population and land used by the urbanized area in terms of the urbanized area population, the relative rate of decline of population densities with distance from the CBD, and the fraction of space surrounding the CBD which is used for residential purposes. (The central city population depends also on the radius of central city, which, in turn, depends mainly upon the vagaries of the political process and, apart from matters relating to municipal finance, has little economic significance.) The density gradient, in turn, may be influenced by many factors. Some of these influences, together with the variables used to describe them, are enumerated in the following section.

III

This section presents some preliminary regression estimates of the quantitative influence of various forces upon the density gradient. First, however, brief mention should be made of some of the reasons for including the variables used in my empirical analysis.

As equation (1) of the last section suggests, the relative rate of decline in housing prices with distance from the CBD varies directly with the marginal cost of transport and inversely with per capita expenditures on housing. It was argued in the last section that, because of the decline in prices with distance, the output of housing per unit of land declines, the per capita consumption of housing increases, and therefore their ratio—population density—declines with distance from the CBD. Furthermore, the more rapid the relative decline in housing prices with distance, the more rapid the decline in land rents and hence the output of housing per unit of land. In addition, the substitution of housing for other commodities because of relative price differences is stronger the more rapid the relative decline in housing prices. The incentive for higher-income CBD-worker households and households with above-average tastes for housing to locate at greater distances from the CBD is also stronger, so an increase in the rate of price decline would produce a more rapid increase in the per capita consumption of housing with distance on both counts. It follows, then, that the density gradient varies directly with the marginal cost of transport and inversely with per capita expenditures on housing. Measured density gradients might also depend on the spatial configuration of nonresidential uses of land and on factors affecting people's tastes for housing in different parts of the urban area.

In my earlier paper I described and gave the reasons for including the following variables in the analysis of differences in density gradients among cities:[5]

Present Designation	*Earlier Designation*	*Name*
MILINE	X_1	Miles of line of local transit systems per square mile of urbanized area, 1950
VEHMIL	X_2	Vehicle miles operated per mile of line, local transit systems, 1950
AGESMA	X_3	Age of the Standard Metropolitan Area (SMA), 1950
GROPOP	X_4	Proportion of SMA population growth in 1920–50
CAREGS	X_5	Car registrations per capita in principal SMA counties, 1950
URBINC	X_6	Median income, families and unrelated individuals, urbanized area, 1949
MANCIT	X_7	Proportion of manufacturing employment in the central city, 1947
RETCBD	X_8	Proportion of SMA retail sales in the central business district, 1954
SUBSTD	X_9	Proportion of central city dwelling units substandard (in need of major repair and/or lacking running water), 1950
MFGEMP	X_{10}	Proportion of urbanized area manufacturing employment (male) in manufacturing, 1950
DENCIT	X_{11}	Average density of the central city
URBPOP	X_{12}	Log_e of urbanized area population, 1950
DENGRA	—	Log_e of the density gradient, 1950.

---

[5] "The Spatial Structure of the Housing Market," pp. 214–217, especially Table VII.

Throughout the empirical part of this study I shall designate variables by six-letter code names rather than by more conventional symbols.

In addition to the above, I have included several other variables in the subsequent analysis, which are the following:

Designation	Name
180CIT	1 if "waterfront" city (see below), 0 otherwise
PEROOM	Proportion of central city dwelling units with more than one person per room, 1950
CITINC	Median income of families and unrelated individuals, central city of the urbanized area, 1949
POPNEG	Proportion of the central city population which was Negro, 1950
AGEDUS	Proportion of the central city's dwelling units which were built prior to 1920, 1950
SMAMFG	Log_e of manufacturing production worker employment in the standard metropolitan area, 1947
REGION	1 for urbanized areas in the South (of Washington, D.C.) and West (St. Louis, Mo.), 0 otherwise
RADCEN	Average distance from the CBD to the boundary of the central city (k_1 of Section II)
CNTPOP	Log_e of the population of the central city of the urbanized area, 1950
LNAREA	Log_e of the land area occupied by the urbanized area, 1950

The reasons for including this latter set as well as some modifications and extensions of my original list of reasons for including the variables used in my previous paper are described immediately below.

The most important variable affecting the average per capita expenditure on housing in a city is income. As noted in the discussion of the effect of income on the optimal location for a household in the preceding section, while an increase in income tends to increase both the marginal costs of transport and expenditures for housing, the latter effect would be expected to be the stronger. An increase in the average level of income in the urban area would thus be expected to reduce the density gradient. There are several other reasons for the demand for housing to grow more rapidly in the outer parts of cities as income increases and, hence, for density gradients to vary inversely with income. If higher-income households have stronger preferences for newer housing, an increase in the average income level of the city would increase the relative demand for new housing, and the latter is typically located in the outer part of the city. Or, if preferences for good- as opposed to poor-quality housing increase with the income level of a household, the concentration of poor-quality housing in the central parts of the city would mean a relative decline in the demand for housing there with an increase in income. Finally, for various reasons higher-income households may have stronger preferences for space than for other characteristics of housing or for single-family housing. Since space is relatively cheaper in the outlying parts of the city, population and housing output might increase more rapidly near the edges of the city with a growth in income for this last reason.

Another important determinant of housing consumption, and thus the price gradient, is the price of housing services. But the impact of differences in housing prices on the price gradient depends critically upon the price elasticity of housing demand. If the latter is −1, as some previous research would suggest,[6] then expenditure for housing, which is price times quantity purchased, would be the same irrespective of the level of housing prices. The most likely alternative to a unit elasticity of housing demand is an elastic one, in which case expenditures on housing would vary inversely and the price gradient would vary directly with the level of housing prices. The greater the price gradient, the greater the incentive for higher-income CBD-worker households or households with stronger preferences for housing to locate at greater distances from the city center, and so the greater the increase in the per household consumption of housing with distance.

The size of the price gradient also affects the rate of decline in the value of housing produced per square mile of land with distance. If housing prices were to increase, for example, because of an increase in property tax rates, the effect on variations in the intensity of residential land use with distance would depend upon the effect on the price gradient only. But if housing prices vary because of an increase in nonland costs or in the supply of land to the housing industry, the effect on the rate of decline in residential land use intensity depends upon the effects of factor cost changes on the optimal way to produce housing in the different parts of the city. Because it would appear that the relative importance of land declines as land rents do with distance from the CBD and, if anything, the elasticity of land supply to the housing industry is likely to increase, it can be shown that an increase in either nonland costs or in the supply of land to the housing industry would reduce the rate of decline in the value of housing output per square mile with distance from the CBD.

[6] See my "The Demand for Non-Farm Housing," Arnold C. Harberger, ed., *The Demand for Durable Goods,* Chicago, 1960, pp. 72–73; and Margaret G. Reid, *Housing and Income,* Chicago, 1962.

Housing prices depend upon construction costs and the level of land rents as well as upon interest and property tax rates. There is virtually no data available on intercity variation in the latter three factors. However, in cities which are built on the edge of a lake or ocean, such as Chicago or Miami, the total supply of land up to any given distance from the CBD is only about half of that in other cities, so that one might expect land rents would be greater in waterfront cities than in others of comparable size. To take account of such conditions, I have used a dummy variable 180CIT which takes the value 1 for waterfront cities and 0 for others.[7] One might also expect that land rents and thus housing prices would be greater in larger cities, and the city size variable discussed below might be expected to reflect this possibility. I have also tried a measure of residential construction costs for 1949 (CONCST) to account for some of the possible variation in housing prices among cities.[8] But since the latter was available for only twenty-eight of the thirty-six cities studied here and did not show up very strongly when included in regressions for these, it was omitted from the comparisons made here.

I initially included city size as a test for the omission of some important variable, for I could not think of any very convincing reasons why the density gradients should be negatively related to size itself. Indeed, to the extent that traffic congestion increases with city size when other measures of transport cost are held constant, marginal transport costs and hence the density gradient might be expected to increase with size. The negative association between size and the estimated density gradient is to be explained, I believe, by the less-than-unit elasticity of substitu-

[7] This is admittedly a very crude procedure. For example, Seattle, which is mostly built on a narrow corridor of land between Puget Sound and Lake Washington, obviously has less land surrounding the CBD than other waterfront cities. On the other hand, Boston is built on a sector of approximately 270 degrees surrounding Massachusetts Bay. More land surrounds Boston's CBD than Chicago's, but still more surrounds the CBD of cities such as Indianapolis. There is also the problem of how to treat cities such as St. Louis whose CBD's are separated from much of the surrounding land area by major rivers. But, because land costs are but a small fraction of the price of housing, it did not seem worthwhile to attempt to construct a more sophisticated land availability variable unless preliminary investigation suggested that this factor might be of decided importance. Cities treated as waterfront cities and assigned the value 1 for the 180CIT variable are: Buffalo, Chicago, Cleveland, Detroit (because of the national boundary), Miami, Milwaukee, San Diego, and Seattle.

[8] This is the Boeckh index for brick structures (1926–29 U. S. average = 100), and I wish to thank its compiler, E. H. Boeckh of Washington, D.C., for making these unpublished data available to me. I found the Boeckh index to be significantly associated with housing consumption both over time and among different cities in 1950 in my "The Demand for Non-Farm Housing."

tion of land for other factors in producing housing. As I have argued in another paper,[9] the elasticity of housing supply is inversely related to the relative importance of land. With a less-than-unit elasticity of substitution in production, the relative importance of land declines with distance from the CBD as land rents do, and, consequently, the elasticity of housing supply per unit of land increases. With an increase in total population and the resulting rise in housing prices in all parts of the city, the output of housing and residential population increase relatively more rapidly in the outer parts of the city.

As is discussed more fully below, my earlier results showed a significant negative relation between SUBSTD and the estimated density gradients. To test the possibility that it is not dwelling-unit condition itself but rather some variable or variables closely related to it that accounts for this association, several other taste variables were introduced into the comparisons later. These relate to characteristics of the inhabitants of poor-quality dwellings rather than to dwelling-unit condition as such. They are: the proportion of central city dwelling units with more than one person per room in 1950 (PEROOM), which is another measure of crowding; the median income of families and unrelated individuals in 1949 for the central city (CITINC); and the proportion of the central city population which was Negro in 1950 (POPNEG).[10] About the last of these, it is frequently argued that the expansion of Negro and other minority groups in the older parts of cities has led the former residents of these areas to seek new neighborhoods and has thus promoted a rise in property values in the outer parts of the city.[11] In these later experiments I also included the proportion of the central city's dwelling units which were built prior to 1920 (AGEDUS) to test the hypothesis that households have an aversion to living in the central city because of the age of its dwelling units.[12]

Equation (15) in Table 1, which was estimated by conventional least squares, was presented in my earlier paper.[13] Of the indicators of

[9] "The Derived Demand Curve for a Productive Factor and the Industry Supply Curve," *Oxford Economic Papers,* New Series 16, July 1964, pp. 221–234.

[10] Data on persons per room was obtained from *Census of Housing: 1950,* Vol. I, Part 1, Washington, 1953, Table 29. The other variables were obtained from *Census of Population: 1950,* Vol. II, Part 1, Washington, 1952, Table 92, and Vol. II, Table 34.

[11] See, in particular, Homer Hoyt, *One Hundred Years of Land Values in Chicago,* Chicago, 1933, p. 317.

[12] Data on age of dwelling units were obtained from *Census of Housing: 1950,* Vol. I, Part 1, Table 30.

[13] "The Spatial Structure of the Housing Market," Table VII, p. 216.

transport cost, the coefficients of VEHMIL and CAREGS each have the expected signs, and the latter is numerically more than twice its standard error. The coefficient of URBINC is negative as would be anticipated, though a little smaller than its standard error. The coefficient

TABLE 1

Initial Regression Analyses of the Determinants of DENGRA[a]

Explanatory Variable	Equation (15)	Equation (16)	Equation (17)
MILINE	.037	.038	—
	(.044)	(.046)	
VEHMIL × 10⁻⁶	−4.8	1.8	2.2
	(4.7)	(5.9)	(4.8)
AGESMA	.081	.075	—
	(.070)	(.082)	
GROPOP	.024	−.050	—
	(.89)	(1.9)	
CAREGS	−7.0[b]	−9.2[b]	−9.3[b]
	(3.0)	(3.8)	(2.5)
URBINC × 10⁻³	−.40	1.5	−.19
	(.55)	(1.5)	(.32)
MANCIT	1.5[b]	1.5[b]	1.0[b]
	(.69)	(.74)	(.57)
RETCBD	−2.3	−1.3	—
	(1.8)	(1.9)	
SUBSTD	−2.8[b]	−.87	−2.4[b]
	(1.5)	(2.1)	(1.3)
MFGEMP	1.4	1.4	—
	(.99)	(1.0)	
DENCIT × 10⁻³	−.020	−.034	—
	(.046)	(.055)	
URBPOP	−.62[c]	−.63[c]	−.47[c]
	(.22)	(.23)	(.13)
PEROOM	—	−2.1	—
		(2.8)	
CITINC × 10⁻³	—	−1.9	—
		(1.4)	
POPNEG	—	−2.9[b]	−2.8[b]
		(1.8)	(1.1)
AGEDUS	—	−1.2	—
		(2.3)	
180CIT	—	—	−.39
			(.29)

Notes to Table 1

[a] Data for the following cities were used in the regressions summarized in this and all subsequent tables:

Akron, Ohio	Detroit, Mich.	Philadelphia, Pa.
Baltimore, Md.	Flint, Mich.	Pittsburgh, Pa.
Birmingham, Ala.	Fort Worth, Texas	Portland, Oregon
Boston, Mass.	Houston, Texas	Providence, R.I.
Buffalo, N.Y.	Indianapolis, Ind.	Richmond, Va.
Chicago, Ill.	Los Angeles, Cal.	Rochester, N.Y.
Cincinnati, Ohio	Louisville, Ky.	St. Louis, Mo.
Cleveland, Ohio	Memphis, Tenn.	San Diego, Cal.
Columbus, Ohio	Milwaukee, Wisc.	Syracuse, N.Y.
Dallas, Texas	New Haven, Conn.	Toledo, Ohio
Dayton, Ohio	New Orleans, La.	Utica, N.Y.
Denver, Colo.	Omaha, Nebr.	Washington, D.C.

The selection of cities is described in my "The Spatial Structure of the Housing Market," p. 210; p. 215, n. 17; and p. 217, n. 20.

[b] Significant at the one-tail 0.10 level.

[c] Significant at the two-tail 0.20 level.

of MANCIT is rather strongly positive; but the retail sales variable, while having a strongly positive simple correlation with DENGRA, has the wrong sign in (15). Of the taste variables, only SUBSTD has a coefficient that is large relative to its standard error and is of the right sign. As mentioned earlier, equation (15) indicates a strong tendency for the relative rate of decline in population density to decrease with increasing city size.

The coefficient of SUBSTD in equation (15) appears to be consistent with the "flight from blight" hypothesis—that is, that people have an aversion to living in the central cities of urbanized areas because of the poor quality of its dwelling units. However, many factors are associated with poor housing quality, and I included four of these in equation (16) to try to determine whether it is poor housing quality itself rather than some related factor which people seek to avoid. Indeed, from (16) it would appear that SUBSTD's coefficient in (15) really reflected the racial composition of the central city population. Since Negroes have lower incomes than whites, they tend to inhabit poorer-quality housing. In (16), the coefficient of POPNEG is much larger than that of SUBSTD, both numerically and relative to its standard error. In equation (17), however, from which the variables whose coefficients in (16) are negligible or have the wrong sign have been deleted, the coefficient of SUBSTD is again rather strongly negative.

The coefficients of PEROOM and AGEDUS in (16), while both negative as might be expected, are both smaller than their standard errors. CITINC has the wrong sign for a taste variable, but from (16) it would appear that it is a better income variable than URBINC. On practical grounds, there is little distinction between the two since the simple correlation between them is + .94, and I prefer URBINC on a priori grounds. As will be demonstrated in the following section, however, the effects of these two variables on the distribution of population between the central city and its suburbs and on the total land area occupied by the urbanized area appear to be quite different. Finally, the coefficient of 180CIT, the dummy variable for waterfront cities included in (17), has the sign opposite to that which would be anticipated but is moderately large in relation to its standard error. Since I wanted to include this variable in the further analysis of central city population and urbanized area land area discussed in section IV, I decided to retain it in the density-gradient equation.

IV

One of the most important possible shortcomings of the analysis summarized in the preceding section is the bias that might result from treating certain of DENGRA's explanatory variables as independent in conventional least-squares regressions when, in fact, they are jointly determined. This section will examine this question by re-estimating equation (17) using the method of two-stage least squares. In addition, I will present two-stage least-squares estimates of equations (14) and (12), using first the determinants of DENGRA and then DENGRA itself as explanatory variables. The distribution of population between the central city and its suburbs and the land area used for urban purposes both provide additional tests of my analysis of factors influencing the spread of population within urbanized areas and are of interest for their own sakes.

Of the explanatory variables included in the regression equations summarized in Table 1, one might argue that CAREGS, MANCIT, and SUBSTD should be treated as jointly dependent with DENGRA. Where cities tend to be more spread out or have smaller density gradients for reasons other than lower marginal transport costs, one would expect the demand for automobile transport and thus car ownership to be greater, other things being the same. The negative regression coefficient observed earlier might be due partly, or even wholly, to the effect of DENGRA on CAREGS rather than the reverse. Similarly, it might be argued that the distribution of population exerts a strong influence on the distribution of employment places because employers seek to reduce labor costs by locating close to the residences of their workers. It is hard to analyze the validity of such a contention because little is known empirically about the relative importance of the determinants of location of employment places in cities. I am rather inclined to dismiss it, however, because I suspect that factors such as transport costs on material inputs and final products and land costs for assembly-line type plants are likely to be much more important empirically than intracity differences in wage costs, but there is no good evidence to back up these suspicions. Finally, it is frequently argued that slums result from the decline in demand for land near the city center which has accompanied improvements in transport costs. If so, and if the other measures of transport costs included fail to remove all the variation in DENGRA on this score, then the coefficient of SUBSTD may partly reflect the effects of lower transport costs.

To test possibilities such as these, the regression coefficients of the more important variables discussed thus far were estimated, using the method of two-stage least squares. In applying this method, one must specify and use data on the predetermined variables which appear in other equations of the model. From other work I have done, it would appear that SUBSTD depends upon the following variables discussed earlier: AGESMA, GROPOP, URBPOP, and CITINC. In addition, it would appear that SUBSTD is related to the proportion of the population one year old and over in 1950 who resided in the same dwelling unit in 1949 and 1950, designated as SAMHOU.[14] Conventional least-squares regressions using CAREGS as the dependent variable indicated that, in addition to DENGRA and SUBSTD, coefficients of VEHMIL, URBINC, RETCBD, and DENCIT had meaningful signs and were large relative to their standard errors. These results, not shown here, suggested using these last four variables as predetermined variables in the two-stage least-squares analysis. While it would have been desirable to treat MANCIT as endogenously determined as well, I did not do so

[14] Data were obtained from *Census of Population: 1950,* Vol. II, Part 1, Table 86. This variable, which is negatively associated with SUBSTD, probably reflects the effects of rent control. Its effect was negligible in 1960.

because so little is known about the locational determinants of manu-facturing plants within cities.[15]

In addition to the variables already noted, three other predetermined variables were used in the analysis. These are: the natural log of manu-facturing production worker employment in the Standard Metropolitan Area (SMAMFG);[16] a dummy variable which takes the value 1 for

TABLE 2

*Two-Stage Least-Squares Estimates
of Determinants of DENGRA*

Explanatory Variable	Equation (18)
VEHMIL $\times 10^{-6}$	4.2 (5.5)
CAREGS[a]	-6.3^{b} (3.9)
URBINC $\times 10^{-3}$	$-.21$ (.34)
MANCIT	.78 (.66)
SUBSTD[a]	-1.5 (1.8)
URBPOP	$-.47^{c}$ (.13)
POPNEG	-2.6^{b} (1.3)
180 CIT	$-.43$ (.31)

[a] Treated as simultaneously determined.

[b] Significant at the one-tail 0.10 level.

[c] Significant at the two-tail 0.10 level.

[15] Evelyn M. Kitagawa and Donald J. Bogue (*Suburbanization of Manufacturing Activity within Standard Metropolitan Areas,* Oxford, Ohio, 1955, pp. 49–60), using a set of economic and demographic variables similar to those used here, were able to explain only about one-fifth of the variation among SMA's in the proportion of manufacturing employment outside the central city in 1947, and none of the explanatory variables taken separately showed a very strong associa-tion with the dependent variable.

[16] The data are taken from *ibid.*

urbanized areas in the South (below Washington, D.C.) and West (beyond St. Louis, Mo.) and 0 for others (REGION); and the average distance from the CBD to the boundary of the central city (k_1 of sec-

TABLE 3

*Two-Stage Least-Squares Estimates
of the Determinants of CNTPOP,
Using Determinants of DENGRA,
Equation (19)*

Explanatory Variable	Actual Coefficients	Predicted Coefficients[a]
VEHMIL $\times 10^{-6}$	.45 (1.6)	2.2
CAREGS[b]	-1.5 (1.5)	-3.3
URBINC $\times 10^{-3}$	-1.1[c] (.43)	$-.11$
MANCIT	.39[c] (.18)	.41
SUBSTD[b]	$-.88$ (.78)	$-.78$
URBPOP	.92[c] (.063)	.46
POPNEG	.50 (.50)	-1.4
180 CIT	$-.023$ (.083)	$-.43$
RADCEN	$-.024$ (.16)	1.1
CITINC $\times 10^{-3}$	1.2[c] (.37)	$-$
REGION	$-.0081$ (.11)	$-$

[a] Assuming $\gamma = 0.30$, $\delta = 0.56$.

[b] Treated as simultaneously determined.

[c] Significant at the one-tail 0.10 level.

tion II here designated as RADCEN).[17] The reasons for including these last three variables will be described below.

The resulting two-stage least-squares estimates of DENGRA's determinants are shown in Table 2. While the coefficients of CAREGS and MANCIT are both a little smaller numerically than the corresponding conventional least-squares estimates shown in Table 1, the greatest difference is in SUBSTD's coefficient. In equation (18) this coefficient is only about six-tenths as large numerically as in (17), and it is now decidedly smaller than its standard error. Thus, there is considerable doubt whether locational preferences and, hence, the relative decline in population densities in cities is affected at all by the condition of the central city's housing stock. SUBSTD's coefficient in (18) is still large enough numerically to be of some practical importance, however, as explained more fully in the final section. When the actual values of DENGRA were plotted against the ones calculated from equation (18) there was little indication of nonlinearity or heteroscedasticity.

In Table 3 two-stage least-squares estimates of equation (14), using the determinants of DENGRA rather than this variable itself, are presented in the first column. The variable to be explained is CNTPOP, the natural log of the central city population.[18] The coefficients of URBINC, MANCIT, and URBPOP are all significant by the usual standards of evaluation. The last, however, is not significantly different from unity, which is a more appropriate null hypothesis. Of even greater interest to me is the consistency of the estimated coefficients with my equation (14), which in effect assumes that suburban population is determined by extrapolating the behavior of population densities within the central city out to the suburbs, and the coefficients shown in Table 2. The predicted values shown in the second column were derived from the coefficients in Table 2, together with evaluations of γ and δ shown in equation (14). The latter were made using my estimated density gradients, the k_1 or RADCEN measurements described earlier, and similar measurements made of k_2, the urbanized area radius.[19] The

[17] As measured from the Census tract maps in *Census of Population: 1950,* Vol. III, Washington, 1952. For each city, at most eight measurements separated by 45 degrees were made and averaged. The direction of the first measurement was selected at random from among 0 to 40 degrees by five-degree intervals. Measurements were made only in those directions from the CBD in which the urbanized area extended.

[18] The data are from *Census of Population: 1950,* Vol. I, Part 1, Washington, 1952, Table 17.

[19] The measurements were made from the urbanized area maps in *Census of Population: 1950,* Vol. II.

average values of these parameters for the forty-six cities for which I have estimated density gradients are $\gamma = 0.30$ and $\delta = 0.56$.

Comparing the columns in Table 2 giving the actual and predicted coefficient, the coefficients of MANCIT and SUBSTD agree quite closely, while those of CAREGS disagree by about one standard error of the actual coefficient. The actual coefficients of URBINC and URBPOP, however, are much larger numerically than the predicted values. That of URBPOP indicates that the central city population increases more rapidly as the urbanized area population grows than would be expected from the variation of population density within the central city. The coefficient of URBINC suggests that, as income grows, the suburban population grows more rapidly than would be expected from extrapolating the greater relative growth of the outer parts of the central city. One possible explanation for this discrepancy is the inducements to home ownership provided by the federal income tax advantage and federal mortgage programs. Such inducements would tend to increase the relative demand for housing in the outer parts of urban areas because single-family housing is relatively cheaper there. Their impact would be strongest in the suburban areas in the short run because vacant and agricultural land is more readily converted to new residential uses. Many other explanations could be offered, of course. Finally, the coefficient of POPNEG is positive, though not much larger than its standard error, whereas a negative one would be expected. This last suggests that, while an increase in the proportion of the central city population which is Negro may stimulate the demand for housing in the outer parts of the central city, it has no effect per se on the distribution of population between the central city and its suburbs.

One other coefficient in equation (19), that of CITINC, is statistically significant by anyone's standards and, as explained more fully later on, of substantial practical importance. In some initial regressions, using CNTPOP as the dependent variable, a weak but positive coefficient for URBINC was found. Since the latter is contrary to what would be anticipated, CITINC was included in the regression as well as to see if its omission was responsible for the positive coefficient of URBINC. One explanation for the positive coefficient of CITINC is that higher-income households have an aversion to living among lower-income ones within the central city. There are two difficulties with this interpretation, however. An aversion to certain kinds of neighbors would be expected to be related to more visible phenomena such as housing quality or race. But, more important, in equation (16) CITINC's coefficient was rather strongly negative; if the presence of low-income households in the central city increases the demand for housing in the suburban parts of the urbanized area, it would be expected to do so in the outer parts of the central city as well.

A better explanation can be found, I believe, in considering the effect of low-income households on taxes paid by higher-income central city residents. If the incomes of, say, the lower third of central city households were to fall, taxes collected from them directly or indirectly through property taxes would fall. At the same time, central city expenditures for health and welfare purposes, which are financed in substantial part by taxes collected within the central city, would probably rise. The net effect would be an increase in taxes for higher-income central

TABLE 4

*Two-Stage Least-Squares Estimates
of the Determinants of CNTPOP,
Using DENGRA, Equation (20)*

Explanatory Variable	Actual Coefficients	Predicted Coefficients[a]
URBPOP	.96[b]	.70
	(.061)	
DENGRA[c]	.22[b]	.52
	(.099)	
RADCEN	.17[b]	1.1
	(.11)	
180 CIT	.080	−.21
	(.078)	
URBINC × 10^{-3}	−1.1[b]	−
	(.38)	
POPNEG	.78[b]	−
	(.30)	
CITINC	1.3[b]	−
	(.33)	
REGION	.0092	−
	(.10)	

[a] Assuming $\gamma = 0.30$, $\delta = 0.56$.

[b] Significant at the one-tail 0.10 level.

[c] Treated as simultaneously determined.

city households and business firms. Such a tax increase would have no differential effect on housing demand within the central city but would reduce the attractiveness of central city relative to suburban locations.

In Table 4 an alternative form of equation (19), in which DENGRA itself rather than its determinants is included among CNTPOP's explanatory variables, is shown. Like equation (19), (20) indicates that with an increase in URBINC the demand for suburban housing increases relatively more than would be anticipated from the increased housing demand in the outer parts of the central city. In addition, with DENGRA and URBPOP held constant, an increase in the fraction of the central city population which is Negro leads to an increase in the central city population, again suggesting that the racial composition of the central city affects the relative demand for housing within the central city but less so between the central city and its suburbs. The coefficient of CITINC is again strongly significant in (20) and virtually the same magnitude as in (19). Finally, the coefficient of URBPOP is much larger than would be anticipated on the basis of equation (14), while that of DENGRA is much smaller. Together, these comparisons suggest that the factors making for an outward movement of population away from the CBD operate in the same direction but with less force between the central city and its suburbs than within the central city. This finding is directly contradictory to most popular and scholarly explanations of so-called "suburban-sprawl."

The actual values of CNTPOP were plotted against those calculated from equation (19); the scatter of points exhibited as much linearity and homoscedasticity as one could hope for. The fit was also extremely tight, but this is misleading for two reasons. First, the relevant goodness-of-fit measure for explaining CNTPOP is to be derived from the reduced-form equation for CNTPOP. And, second, the size of the urbanized area population would affect the size of the central city population on virtually any hypothesis, naive or otherwise. In CNTPOP's reduced form, R^2 is 0.99, compared with 0.94 when URBPOP alone is included; thus, the other variables employed by the model account for about four-fifths of the variance of (the log of) CNTPOP which is unaccounted for by urbanized area size alone. Furthermore, R^2 in the reduced form for DENGRA is 0.65, while the reduced form for land area explains about five-sixths of the variance not accounted for by population size. It should also be noted that conventional least-squares estimates for the central city population and land area structural equations (not shown) are substantially different from the two-stage least-squares estimates in several important instances and, where different, accord less closely with my a priori expectation.

I would now like to consider the determinants of the land occupied

TABLE 5

Two-Stage Least-Squares Estimates
of the Determinants of LNAREA,
Using Determinants of DENGRA,
Equation (21)

Explanatory Variable	Actual Coefficients	Predicted Coefficients[a]
VEHMIL × 10⁻⁶	−.44 (3.3)	−2.9
CAREGS[b]	5.2[c] (3.1)	4.4
URBINC × 10⁻³	.38 (.88)	.15
MANCIT	.20 (.43)	−.55
SUBSTD[b]	−.089 (1.2)	1.0
URBPOP	.81[c] (.13)	.98
POPNEG	1.4[c] (.97)	1.8
180 CIT	.036 (.18)	.05
CITINC × 10⁻³	−.74 (.72)	−
REGION	.37[c] (.24)	−
SMAMFG	.11 (.11)	−

[a] Assuming $\beta = 0.65$.

[b] Treated as simultaneously determined.

[c] Significant at the one-tail 0.10 level.

TABLE 6

*Two-Stage Least-Squares Estimates
of the Determinants of LNAREA,
Using DENGRA, Equation (22)*

Explanatory Variable	Actual Coefficients	Predicted Coefficients[a]
URBPOP	.49[b] (.25)	.65
DENGRA[c]	−.61[b] (.37)	−.70
180 CIT	−.18 (.20)	−.24
MANCIT	1.1[b] (.69)	−
SUBSTD[c]	−2.0[b] (1.5)	−
CITINC × 10^{-3}	−.78[b] (.51)	−
REGION	.22 (.24)	−
SMAMFG	.21[b] (.15)	−

[a] Assuming $\beta = 0.65$.

[b] Significant at the one-tail 0.10 level.

[c] Treated as simultaneously determined.

by the urbanized area, LNAREA,[20] summarized in Tables 5 and 6. In the former the determinants of DENGRA are included, while DENGRA itself is used in the latter. Each of the tables shows both the actual two-stage least-squares estimates and the values of the coefficients predicted by equation (12), the coefficients of Table 2, and an average value for β of 0.65.[21] As was the case in the CNTPOP regressions, the actual coefficient of CAREGS would seem to be quite consistent with the predicted value, but in (21) the coefficients of both URBINC and POPNEG agree fairly well with their predicted values. The coefficient of

[20] The data are from *Census of Population: 1950*, Vol. I, Part 1, Table 17.

[21] β was evaluated in a way analogous to that described earlier for γ and δ.

URBPOP is a bit low but differs less drastically from its predicted value than in the CNTPOP regressions. The major disagreements now seem to be the coefficients of MANCIT, which is too large, and SUBSTD, which is too small. The latter indicates that, while the condition of the central city housing stock may influence the relative demand for housing in the outer relative to the inner parts of the central city, it has no effect upon the demand for suburban vs. central city housing. The coefficient of MANCIT might be explained by a smaller degree of substitutability of land for other productive factors in manufacturing than in the production of housing or a smaller variation in land rentals for industrial than for residential land. In either case, a shift of manufacturing plants from the suburbs to the central city coupled with a reverse shift of residences would tend to increase the urbanized area demand for land since the reduction in manufacturing demand would be numerically smaller than the increased residential demand.

Also included among the explanatory variables in Tables 5 and 6 are three which would not be expected to reflect differences in the relative rate of population density decline within the central city. CITINC was included for essentially the same reason here as in the CNTPOP regressions; initial results indicated that increasing values of URBINC are associated with decreasing amounts of urbanized land area. The LNAREA coefficients of CITINC seem to be consistent both in magnitude and sign with those in the CNTPOP regressions. REGION was included because an earlier regression exhibited predominantly positive residuals for urban areas in the South and West. The positive coefficient might result from a lower agricultural demand for land and hence lower land rentals for urban users in areas outside of the Northeast. SMAMFG was included because the positive coefficient for MANCIT observed in earlier regressions was thought to result from its intercorrelation with the former. Adding SMAMFG did indeed make MANCIT's coefficient smaller, though in (21) it remains larger than predicted by equation (12). The positive coefficient of SMAMFG may reflect the fact that manufacturing is more land intensive than other nonresidential uses of land, so that the greater the employment in manufacturing given population size, the greater the demand for urban land.

In Table 6 the coefficients of URBPOP and DENGRA both indicate a smaller response of total land used by the urbanized area than would be anticipated on the basis of the spread of population within the central city. The result here is similar to that observed in equation (20), though in (22) the differences between actual and predicted coefficients are less than one standard error of the former. The other variables included in equation (22) would seem to be consistent with the interpretation I gave for their coefficients in (21). Finally, plotting the actual values of LNAREA against the values calculated from (21) revealed little departure from linearity and homoscedasticity.

V

The principal conclusion I would draw from the material presented above is that urban decentralization is far from haphazard and only in small part a "flight from blight." Rather, the distribution of population in urban areas would appear to be consistent with a set of variables which can be given plausible interpretations in terms of the relative demand and supply of housing in different locations. The distribution of population between the central city and its suburbs and the total land occupied by an urban area are to an important extent, though not solely, explainable by the same forces that affect the spread of population within the central city.

Car registrations per capita, which I have interpreted as a proxy for the costs of automobile transport, is probably the quantitatively most significant variable affecting the intraurban distribution of population. The coefficient of CAREGS was a little over one and a half times its standard error in the DENGRA equation and almost two-thirds larger than its standard error in the LNAREA equation. Though only as large as its standard error in the CNTPOP equation, it was also only a standard error less than the value predicted by the hypothesis that the suburban population distribution is simply an extrapolation of the central city's. More important, however, CAREGS increased from about 0.26 to 0.35 during the 1950's in the cities studied here. Such an increase would be sufficient according to equation (18) to reduce the relative rate of decline of population densities within the central city by about 57 per cent. According to the actual values of coefficients of equations (19) and (21), it would reduce the central city population by about 14 per cent, holding the urbanized area population and other factors constant, and increase the total land used by the urbanized area by about 60 per cent. The observed increase in automobile ownership, then, could indeed have important effects upon urban population distribution.

The size variable (URBPOP) is the most significant of all statistically, and it too is of great practical significance. During the 1950's the increase in urbanized area population averaged about 30 per cent for the cities studied. Such an increase would reduce density gradients by about 15 per cent according to equation (18) and increase the land area occupied by the urbanized area by almost 30 per cent. The central city population would tend to grow only slightly less rapidly or about half as rapidly depending upon whether one believes the actual or predicted coefficient in equation (19). During the 1950's the fraction of SMA manufacturing employment in the central city fell by about 9 percentage points, from 0.71 to 0.62. Such a decline would reduce the density gradient by about 7 per cent and the central city population by a little less than 4 per cent. A growth in income of about 3 per cent per year would, in a decade, raise the 1950 average both for URBINC and CITINC of $3,000 by about $1,000. Such an increase would reduce the relative rate of population density decline by almost 20 per cent; thus, even though URBINC's coefficient is hardly statistically significant in the DENGRA equation, it could still be of some practical importance. In the CNTPOP equation the effects of increases in URBINC and CITINC tend to cancel, while in the LNAREA equation growth in both by the same amount would tend to reduce area by approximately one-third.

On the whole, it is hard to make a strong case statistically for the condition of the central city housing stock having any effect on urban population distribution at all. The coefficient of SUBSTD is less than its standard error in the DENGRA equation, only slightly larger in the CNTPOP equation and negligible in the LNAREA equation. In the first two, however, the coefficient is still large enough to be of some practical importance. During the 1950's the proportion of substandard central city dwellings fell from 0.20 to 0.11 in the cities studied here, mostly, I believe, because of the growth in income during the decade. Such a decline would tend to increase the density gradient by about 14 per cent and the central city population by about 8 per cent. Because of the dramatic increase in dwelling unit condition during the 1950's, one would have to argue that urban decentralization during the decade was a delayed response to previously existing poor-quality housing to try to salvage the "flight from blight" hypothesis.

A much better case can be made on purely statistical grounds for the hypothesis that decentralization has occurred because of the relative growth in central city's Negro population. POPNEG's coefficient was about twice its standard error in the DENGRA and LNAREA equations. I have not yet calculated the 1960 proportion of the central city's population which was Negro, but I doubt that the proportion could have increased more than 50 per cent or by 7 percentage points over the 1950 average of a little under 14 per cent. An increase of 7 percentage points would reduce the density gradient by approximately 20 per cent and increase land area by around 10 per cent. Thus, the effects of a changing racial composition of the central city population would certainly be small relative to those of increased automobile transportation. And, according to equation (19), relative increases in the Negro population of the central city cannot account at all for the suburbanization of population.

It would appear that the distribution of population between the central city and its suburbs and the land used by the urbanized area are largely governed by the same forces influencing population distribution within the central city. But two qualifications must be made to this statement. From my CNTPOP and LNAREA regressions, an influx of lower-income persons into the central city would tend to increase the proportion of the urbanized area's population which is suburban and also its total land area. The best explanation for this effect, I believe, is the increase in the tax burden on higher-income central city households and upon business firms which the inmigration of low-income persons would imply. Secondly, my results imply that the central city population and, to a lesser extent, the land area occupied by the central city and its suburbs tend to respond less than would be anticipated to factors that reduce the relative rate of population density decline within the central city. Such a result might follow from a long-run disequilibrium in 1950 in urbanized area population distribution, which could have resulted from the depression of the 1930's and the war and postwar adjustments of the 1940's. I hope to test this last hypothesis by repeating the analyses of CNTPOP and LNAREA for 1960. Some preliminary results seem to suggest that the regression coefficients of the more important variables were quite similar for 1950 and 1960. Another possible explanation for the discrepancy between the actual and predicted coefficients of equations (19) and (20) is that a greater fraction of total land area is held vacant in the suburbs in anticipation of more intensive future development. But, if anything, the apparent attenuation in the suburbs of forces making for decentralization is inconsistent with the statements one frequently hears that urban decentralization has been carried too far.

Finally, I would like to consider the total effects of all the changes during the 1950's on urban decentralization and examine their consistency with observed changes in central city populations and total land area used for urban purposes. Altogether the changes discussed above would imply a decline in density gradients of about 60 per cent, or from a 1950 average for the cities studied here of around 0.30 to 0.12. These same changes would imply an increase in central city populations of around 20 per cent according to the actual coefficients of equation (19), compared with an actual increase of about 9 per cent. However, a value for the coefficient of CAREGS only one standard error larger numerically than the actual coefficient in (19) would convert the expected increase to 4 per cent. Likewise, the coefficients of equation (21), together with the changes in the explanatory variables that took place during the 1950's, would imply an increase in land area of about 62 per cent, against about 82 per cent which was actually observed. Again, if CAREGS's coefficient were one standard error larger, the expected increase would be over 95 per cent. It would certainly appear, then, that my analysis of population distribution based upon differences among urbanized areas in 1950 is broadly consistent quantitatively with the urban decentralization observed during the past decade.

An Econometric Analysis of the Role
of Financial Intermediaries in
Postwar Residential Building Cycles

GORDON R. SPARKS

UNIVERSITY OF MICHIGAN

The purpose of this paper is to develop a model of the residential construction sector of the U.S. economy, with particular emphasis on the financial factors that provide a link between construction activity and the monetary sector. The study was undertaken as part of a larger project to incorporate monetary policy variables into the econometric model constructed by the Research Seminar in Quantitative Economics at the University of Michigan.[1] As this is an annual model designed for short-run forecasting and policy analysis, the equations for the residential construction sector have been estimated from postwar annual data.

Our model consists of a set of equations which determine the flow of funds through financial intermediaries and their influence on construction activity. The rate of accumulation of savings deposits is assumed to depend on interest rates and personal financial saving. The inflow of deposits together with interest rates and other variables then determine the volume of commitments made by financial institutions

NOTE: This paper is based on a Ph.D. dissertation undertaken at the University of Michigan with financial support provided by a Ford Foundation fellowship. However, the conclusions, opinions, and other statements presented here are those of the author and not necessarily those of the Ford Foundation. I am indebted to Daniel B. Suits, James C. T. Mao, Harold T. Shapiro, Warren L. Smith, and Ronald L. Teigen for their valuable comments.

[1] For a description of this model, see [14] and [16]. Numbers in brackets refer to Bibliography at end of paper.

to supply residential mortgage funds. The supply of mortgage commitments then affects housing starts and residential construction expenditures. Equations for housing starts and the supply of mortgage funds are formulated in section I of the paper and the empirical results are presented in section II. Equations for savings deposits are given in section III and the implications of the model for monetary policy are discussed in section IV.

I. Housing Starts and the Mortgage Market

The most striking feature of housing starts in the postwar period has been the countercyclical behavior of this series. Building has typically risen sharply during periods when the general level of economic activity was approaching a cyclical trough. During the early stages of an upswing, housing starts have continued to increase but have reached a peak well in advance of the peaks indicated by the National Bureau reference cycles.[2] Most students of the housing market have considered the supply of mortgage credit to be the major cause of this behavior. For example, Grebler[3] gives the following characterization of postwar residential building cycles: "Given long-run demand and supply forces favorable to residential building, short-run cycles in housing construction were associated for the most part with changes in the supply of mortgage funds and credit terms, which in turn were greatly influenced by the level of total economic activity. When that level was rising and high, the expanded demand for funds by business, which is relatively insensitive to increased cost of borrowing, tended to reduce the availability of funds for housing, which is highly sensitive to changes in the cost of borrowing."

Among the proponents of this view, there has been some disagreement over the importance of the legal maximum interest rates on mortgages insured by the Federal Housing Administration or guaranteed by the Veterans Administration. Guttentag [6] argues that the effect of the rate maxima has been greatly exaggerated. He emphasizes the demand side of the market for mortgage funds and argues that housing demand is more highly sensitive to changes in mortgage credit terms than to changes in the flow of current income. A similar view is expressed by Alberts [1].

A graphical exposition of this theory is given in Figure 1. For pur-

[2] See [17], Chart 1A.

[3] [5], p. 104.

FIGURE 1

Allocation of Funds Between Mortgages and Bonds

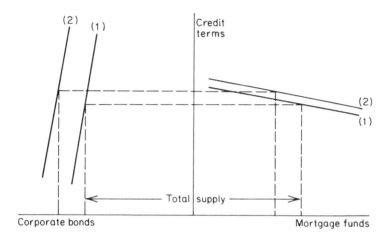

FIGURE 2

Fixed-Rate Theory

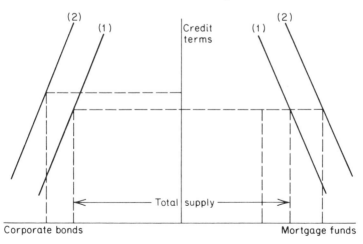

poses of illustration, we assume a fixed supply of funds to be allocated between corporate bonds and mortgages. The demand for mortgage funds is assumed to be highly responsive to changes in credit terms while the demand by corporations is assumed to be inelastic. A rise in income causes both schedules to shift upward but has a greater effect on corporate demand, resulting in a shift of funds away from mortgages.[4] The fixed-rate theory, advanced by Warren Smith [15] and others, is illustrated in Figure 2. According to this view, the spread between the ceiling rates on insured and guaranteed mortgages and yields on other securities has an important influence on the supply of mortgage funds. Assuming that the interest rate is at the statutory maximum at the initial equilibrium, an upward shift in the schedules results in a reallocation of funds from mortgages to corporate bonds, leaving an excess demand in the mortgage market.

A rather different approach to the explanation of fluctuations in housing starts is taken in a recent study by Maisel [12], who emphasizes the importance of changes in vacancies and the inventory of houses under construction. According to his theory, the lag in the response of builders to changes in demand and the lag between starts and completions lead to an inventory cycle. He includes among the determinants of housing starts, vacancies at the beginning of the period, net household formations, removals (from the housing stock), and the ratio of rents to construction costs as a measure of the income from building or owning houses. As a measure of the cost and availability of credit, he uses a lagged moving average of the Treasury bill rate. Maisel emphasizes that the impact of credit conditions is on the supply side of the housing market rather than on the demand side. He argues that there is little relationship between credit conditions and final demand as measured by net household formations, but that changes in credit conditions influence the willingness of builders to increase their inventories under construction.

We have attempted to combine Maisel's approach with a more detailed treatment of the supply of mortgage funds. Housing starts (HS) are assumed to depend on the following variables.

1. Inventory of houses under construction plus vacancies at the beginning of the period. In terms of first differences, the sum of these two variables was represented by housing starts less net household formations (HF), using the following identities and disregarding removals:

---

[4] Denoting the credit elasticities of demand for corporate funds and mortgages by e_{bc} and e_{mc}, respectively, and the income elasticities by e_{by} and e_{my}, respectively, the condition for a shift of funds away from mortgages is $e_{bc}/e_{mc} < e_{by}/e_{my}$.

$\triangle$(vacancies) equals completions minus net household formations minus removals.

$\triangle$(inventories under construction) equals starts minus completions.

2. Ratio of rents (R) to construction costs (C) at the beginning of the period.

3. Mortgage credit terms (Cr).

4. Net household formations (HF). This variable was used with the reservation that the available data supplied by the Bureau of the Census is subject to considerable sampling variability [18]. As noted by Maisel [11], even the direction of change in net household formations may be in error.

5. Disposable income (Y). We have included an income variable as a determinant of the demand for owner-occupied as opposed to rental units. High income may stimulate the demand for home ownership and lead to an increase in single-unit starts. Total starts will be affected if, as is likely to be the case, there is a lag in the reaction to increased vacancies of rental units. Assuming a linear relationship, our equation for housing starts becomes

$$\Delta HS = \alpha_0 - \alpha_1(HS - HF)_{-1} + \alpha_2\left(\Delta \frac{R}{C}\right)_{-1} - \alpha_3\Delta Cr + \alpha_4\Delta HF + \alpha_5\Delta Y.$$

Since mortgage credit terms cannot be assumed to be exogenous to the housing market, a model of the mortgage market is also required. The demand for residential mortgage funds comes from three sources: builders, investors in rental units, and individuals purchasing existing or custom-built homes. The major sources of supply are the four main types of financial intermediaries: savings and loan associations, mutual savings banks, life insurance companies, and commercial banks—plus the Federal National Mortgage Association. An important institutional feature of this market is the use of forward commitments under which an investor agrees to lend a specific amount of money at a given interest rate within a specified period of time. A residential builder generally seeks a commitment for permanent mortgage financing from a financial institution before construction is begun. According to Klaman,[5] commercial banks will usually make short-term loans to finance construction only after a builder has obtained such a commitment. Thus, the willingness of financial institutions to enter into forward commitments is likely to have an important impact on housing starts. Accordingly, we have formulated the demand for mortgage funds in terms of the demand for

[5] [9], p. 168.

loans disbursed without prior commitment plus forward commitments. This variable, denoted by *MC,* is assumed to depend on the same factors as housing starts. Thus, we have

$$\Delta MC = \beta_0 - \beta_1(HS - HF)_{-1} + \beta_2\left(\Delta\frac{R}{C}\right)_{-1} - \beta_3\Delta Cr + \beta_4\Delta HF + \beta_5\Delta Y.$$

On the supply side of the mortgage market, our basic approach to the explanation of the mortgage lending of financial intermediaries is expressed by the following equation:

$$\Delta MC_i = \gamma_{i0} + \gamma_{i1}\Delta^2 SD_i + \gamma_{i2}\Delta REP_i - \gamma_{i3}\left(\Delta\frac{M_i}{SD_i}\right)_{-1} - \gamma_{i4}\Delta r$$
$$+ \gamma_{i5}\Delta Cr.$$

The volume of mortgage loans and commitments (MC_i) made by the ith lender is assumed to depend on the inflow of savings deposits (ΔSD_i) and repayments on outstanding mortgages (REP_i), the ratio of mortgage holdings (M_i) to deposits at the beginning of the period, mortgage credit terms (Cr), and a market rate of interest (r) which represents the yield on alternative investments.

In order to avoid the problem of simultaneous-equation estimation bias, we solved the above model to obtain a reduced form equation for housing starts, which did not contain the mortgage credit term variable explicitly. This procedure has the additional advantage of eliminating the need for a quantitative measure of credit terms. The interest return on mortgages is an inadequate indicator to the extent that changes in credit conditions are reflected in changes in loan-to-value ratios and maturities.

Equating supply and demand in the mortgage market, we obtain

$$\sum_i \Delta MC_i + \Delta FNMA = \Delta MC,$$

where the term FNMA represents net purchases of mortgages by the Federal National Mortgage Association. Substituting the supply and demand functions, we obtain an equation from which an expression for the variable ΔCr can be derived as follows:

$$\sum_i [\gamma_{i0} + \gamma_{i1}\Delta^2 SD_i + \gamma_{i2}\Delta REP_i - \gamma_{i3}\left(\Delta\frac{M_i}{SD_i}\right)_{-1} - \gamma_{i4}\Delta r + \gamma_{i5}\Delta Cr]$$
$$+ \Delta FNMA$$

$$= \beta_0 - \beta_1(HS - HF)_{-1} + \beta_2\left(\Delta\frac{R}{C}\right)_{-1} - \beta_3\Delta Cr + \beta_4\Delta HF + \beta_5\Delta Y$$

$$\Delta Cr = \frac{1}{\gamma_5 + \beta_3} \left\{ \beta_0 - \beta_1(HS - HF)_{-1} + \beta_2\left(\Delta\frac{R}{C}\right)_{-1} + \beta_4\Delta HF + \beta_5\Delta Y \right.$$

$$\left. - \sum_i [\gamma_{i0} + \gamma_{i1}\Delta^2 SD_i + \gamma_{i2}\Delta REP_i - \gamma_{i3}\left(\Delta\frac{M_i}{SD_i}\right)_{-1} - \gamma_{i4}\Delta r] - \Delta FNMA \right\},$$

where $\gamma_5 = \sum_i \gamma_{i5}$. Substituting this expression in the housing starts equation we obtain

$$\Delta HS = \alpha'_0 - \alpha'_1(HS - HF)_{-1} + \alpha'_2\left(\Delta\frac{R}{C}\right)_{-1} + \alpha'_4\Delta HF + \alpha'_5\Delta Y$$

$$+ \alpha'_3 \left\{ \sum_i [\gamma_{i0} + \gamma_{i1}\Delta^2 SD_i + \gamma_{i2}\Delta REP_i - \gamma_{i3}\left(\Delta\frac{M_i}{SD_i}\right)_{-1} - \gamma_{i4}\Delta r] \right.$$

$$\left. + \Delta FNMA \right\},$$

where $\alpha'_j = \alpha_j - \dfrac{\alpha_3\beta_j}{\gamma_5 + \beta_3}$; $j = 0, 1, 2, 4, 5$; and $\alpha'_3 = \dfrac{\alpha_3}{\gamma_5 + \beta_3}$.

Because of the limited number of degrees of freedom provided by postwar annual data, the coefficients in the above equation were estimated in two stages. First the γ_{ij} were estimated from regressions using the ΔMC_i as the dependent variables.[6] The α_j were then estimated from a regression of housing starts on the estimated changes in the total supply of mortgage funds $\Delta(MC + FNMA)$ along with the other independent variables appearing in the reduced form equation.[7] The results of these regressions are reported in the next section.

[6] These regressions do not represent the true reduced forms which would be obtained by substituting the expression derived above for ΔCr in the equations for the supply of mortgage funds. Since the expressions resulting from this substitution would contain all the exogenous variables in the model, a source of bias is introduced to the extent that the omitted exogenous variables are correlated with those included.

[7] A reviewer of this paper has objected to the use of sixteen observations to estimate the more than sixteen parameters appearing in the above equation. We have simply followed the usual method of estimating the reduced form coefficients in a simultaneous system and gained degrees of freedom by first obtaining direct estimates of the structural coefficients γ_{ij}. Our procedure differs from a straightforward application of two-stage least squares in that we have used the supply of funds in the first stage regressions rather than the credit term variable that appears in the structural equations. Because of this modification we have not attempted to adjust the standard errors in the second-stage regression to take account of errors in the estimates of the first-stage coefficients so that the former are likely to be biased downward.

II. Empirical Results

SAVINGS AND LOAN ASSOCIATIONS

The regression results for mortgage lending of savings and loan associations are shown in Table 1. The values of the dependent variable MC_1 were computed as the sum of mortgage loans made (ML_1) plus the change in outstanding commitments during the year. Since no data on outstanding commitments were available for the earlier years, the equations were fitted to the period 1957–64.

As a measure of the rate of return on alternative investments, the long-term U.S. rate was used since the nonmortgage security holdings of savings and loan associations consist mainly of U.S. government securities.[8] This variable did not obtain a significant coefficient as might be expected from the institutional considerations. According to Klaman,[9] "Compared with other major financial institutions in the mortgage market, savings and loan associations are singularly limited by law and tradition to the specialized role of home mortgage lenders. In home mortgage markets they specialize, also, in providing conventional loans directly to individual borrowers in local markets and thus are less flexible than other financial institutions in adjusting investment programs to changes in capital market conditions."

Between 1949 and 1963 the ratio of mortgage holdings to savings and loan shares varied within a fairly narrow range of 93 to 99 per cent while the average annual increase in shares has been about 15 per cent, indicating that the inflow of savings capital has been the major influence on mortgage lending. In addition, at the end of 1963, conventional as opposed to government-insured or guaranteed mortgages made up 87 per cent of total mortgage holdings. Thus, the ceiling rates have been of little importance.

The third equation in Table 1 was fitted with the coefficient on repayments constrained to be unity. The unconstrained coefficient obtained seems unreasonable and is likely to be biased upward. During periods when the level of mortgage lending and construction is high, advance payoffs of loans rise due to the sale of existing properties. Thus repayments are not exogenously determined but are influenced to some extent by the volume of mortgage loans made.

---

[8] Federal associations are restricted by law from holding state and local government or private securities, and state-chartered institutions are subject to similar limitations [4].

[9] [9], p. 18.

TABLE 1

Mortgage Lending of Savings and Loan Associations

Period	Dependent Variable (bill. $)	$\Delta^2 SD_1$ (bill. $)	ΔREP_1 (bill. $)	$\left(\Delta \dfrac{M_1}{SD_1}\right)_{-1}$	Δr_{us} (per cent)	Constant Term	$\bar{R}^2$	df
1957–64	ΔMC_1	1.106 (.116)	1.482 (.141)	−44.601 (11.067)	−.2197 (.5789)	−.1551	.969	3
1957–64	ΔMC_1	1.124 (.094)	1.487 (.124)	−42.840 (8.908)		−.2028	.976	4
1957–64	ΔMC_1	1.090 (.185)	1.000	−37.760 (17.342)		.3117	.905	5
1949–64	ΔML_1	.9159 (.1836)	1.000	−27.914 (9.191)		.2633	.848	13

TABLE 2

Mortgage Loans and Commitments of Mutual Savings Banks, 1952–64

$\Delta^2 SD_2$ (bill. $)	ΔREP_2 (bill. $)	$\left(\Delta \dfrac{M_2}{SD_2}\right)_{-1}$	Δr_{cb} (per cent)	$\Delta (r_m - r_{cb})$ (per cent)	Constant Term	$\bar{R}^2$	df
1.226 (.273)	−.1086 (.7686)	−21.215 (11.641)	−1.338 (.762)		.9880	.822	8
1.230 (.256)		−20.787 (10.609)	−1.331 (.718)		.9533	.842	9
1.331 (.205)	.6203 (.7350)	−15.076 (11.169)		1.636 (.674)	.5374	.858	8
1.345 (.201)		−19.038 (9.971)		1.430 (.618)	.7593	.863	9

Using a one-sided t-test with five degrees of freedom, both coefficients in the constrained regression are significant at the 5 per cent level and the coefficient on $\triangle^2SD_1$ is significant at the 1 per cent level. Because of the limited amount of data available on outstanding commitments, the equation was fitted to the period 1949–64, using $\triangle ML_1$ as the dependent variable. In this case, both coefficients are significant at the 1 per cent level.

MUTUAL SAVINGS BANKS

In contrast to savings and loan associations, the portfolio regulations and policies of mutual savings banks permit them to take advantage of changing yield differentials. The laws of the seventeeen states in which mutual savings banks operate generally permit investment in bonds of state and local governments and corporations. Their portfolio choices are likely to be responsive to the level of the ceiling rates on government-insured and guaranteed mortgages since a relatively high percentage of their mortgage holdings are FHA and VA loans and they have generally been reluctant to resort to discounting.[10]

The equations were fitted to the period 1952–64 for which commitments data were available and the results are shown in Table 2. The corporate bond rate (r_{cb}) was used to represent the rate on competing assets. Slightly better results were obtained using the differential between the average of the FHA and VA ceiling rates (r_m) and the corporate bond rate. In both cases, the repayments variable was not significant.

LIFE INSURANCE COMPANIES

Like mutual savings banks, life insurance companies have a wide degree of flexibility in their choice of assets, but their responsiveness to short-run changes in available funds and yield differentials is limited by the practice of planning ahead a year or more.[11] They make extensive use of forward commitments which typically cover a time period from about three months on existing homes to six to twelve months for new construction and up to two and a half years for apartment houses.[12]

The regression results obtained for the period 1954–64 are shown in Table 3. The equations were fitted using the corporate bond rate and the differential between the average of the FHA and VA ceiling rates and the corporate bond rate. In contrast to the mutual savings bank

[10] [4], p. 175.
[11] [9], Chapter 6.
[12] [10], p. 186.

TABLE 3

Mortgage Loans and Commitments of Life Insurance Companies, 1954-64

$\Delta^2 SD_3$ (bill. \$)	ΔREP_3 (bill. \$)	$\left(\Delta \dfrac{M_3}{SD_3}\right)_{-1}$	Δr_{cb} (per cent)	$\Delta(r_m - r_{cb})$ (per cent)	Constant Term	$\bar{R}^2$	df
.6606 (.8900)	−.1708 (1.348)	−25.178 (24.008)	−2.689 (.986)		1.0313	.640	6
.5966 (.3565)			−2.839 (.619)		.7687	.681	8
.1050 (.8848)	1.428 (1.155)	−9.801 (28.496)		2.233 (1.018)	.2101	.553	6
1.102 (.445)				2.973 (.818)	.4834	.562	8

results, somewhat better equations were obtained using the former variable. In both cases, neither repayments nor the ratio of mortgages to deposits[13] was significant.

COMMERCIAL BANKS

Although commercial banks hold a considerable volume of mortgage loans, we decided to exclude them from our model because of the lack of available data comparable to those used for the other financial institutions. No data are published on outstanding commitments or mortgage loans made, except for the mortgage recordings series which covers only loans of $20,000 or less. In addition, the available figures on mortgage holdings include short-term credits in the form of construction loans or interim financing provided to builders and other real estate mortgage lenders, as well as long-term permanent loans.[14]

Regression equations relating changes in mortgage holdings to inflows of time deposits and market rates of interest yielded unsatisfactory results. For example, using the state and local bond yield (r_{s1}) as the rate on competing assets, the following was obtained for the period 1949–63:

$$\Delta^2 M_4 = -.0908 \ \Delta^2 SD_4 - 28.870 \left(\Delta \frac{M_4}{SD_4} \right)_{-1} - .8733 \ \Delta r_{s1} + .3340.$$
$$\quad\quad (.0711) \quad\quad\quad (7.825) \quad\quad\quad\quad\quad\quad (.5518)$$

$$\bar{R}^2 = .522.$$

The coefficient on the state and local bond yield is significant at the 10 per cent level, but time deposits enter insignificantly and with a negative sign. We also tried the long-term U.S. rate and the Treasury bill rate but obtained insignificant coefficients in both cases.

Since most of the explanatory power in the above equation comes from the lagged ratio of mortgage holdings to time deposits, we reran the regression using lagged time deposits and the state and local bond yield. The following equation was obtained:

$$\Delta^2 M_4 = .2856 \ \Delta^2 (SD_4)_{-1} - .9283 \ \Delta r_{s1} - .0883.$$
$$\quad\quad (.0600) \quad\quad\quad\quad (.4498)$$

$$\bar{R}^2 = .648.$$

This result suggests that there is a lag of one year before a change in the rate of inflow of time deposits induces a change in the rate of

---

[13] Deposits in the case of life insurance companies were defined as reserves plus dividend accumulations less policy loans. See section III below.

[14] [8], p. 205.

accumulation of mortgages. However, to the extent that the significant coefficient on the lagged inflow of time deposits reflects the lag between commitments and the acquisition of mortgage loans, the equation is unsatisfactory for our purposes. Some estimate of the volume of commitments made by commercial banks would be required to incorporate their mortgage lending into our model.

HOUSING STARTS

On the basis of goodness of fit and significance of individual regression coefficients, the following equations were chosen to estimate mortgage lending of savings and loan associations, mutual savings banks, and life insurance companies, respectively:

$$\Delta MC_1 = 1.090 \ \Delta^2 SD_1 + 1.000 \ \Delta REP_1 - 37.760 \left(\Delta \frac{M_1}{SD_1}\right)_{-1} + .3117,$$
$$ (.185) (17.342)$$

$$\Delta MC_2 = 1.345 \ \Delta^2 SD_2 - 19.038 \left(\Delta \frac{M_2}{SD_2}\right)_{-1} + 1.430 \ \Delta(r_m - r_{cb}) + .7593,$$
$$ (.201) (9.971) \phantom{\left(\Delta \frac{M_2}{SD_2}\right)} (.618)$$

$$\Delta MC_3 = .5966 \ \Delta^2 SD_3 - 2.839 \ \Delta r_{cb} + .7687.$$
$$ (.3565) (.619)$$

The estimated values from these equations plus net purchases of mortgages by the Federal National Mortgage Association were added together to obtain estimated changes in the total supply of mortgage funds, which were then used to estimate the housing starts equation.[15] Using the variables introduced in section I, the following regression was obtained from data for the period 1949–64:

$$\Delta HS = -.2372 \ (HS - HF)_{-1} + 2.519 \left(\Delta \frac{R}{C}\right)_{-1} + .3256 \ \Delta HF$$
$$ (.0624) \phantom{\ (HS - HF)_{-1} +} (.578) \phantom{\left(\Delta \frac{R}{C}\right)} (.0868)$$

$$+ .6961 \ \Delta Y + 3.159 \ \Delta(MC + FNMA) - 3.3902.$$
$$ (.2672) (.859)$$
$$\bar{R}^2 = .904.$$

[15] It should be noted that no adjustment was made to take account of changes in the average amount loaned per dwelling unit. This will depend on such factors as the average price per dwelling unit, the loan-to-value ratios, and the mix between single- and multiple-unit starts.

FIGURE 3

Housing Starts, 1949-64

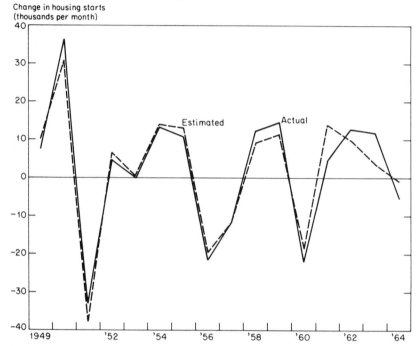

The variables are defined as follows: *HS* is housing starts (thousands per month); *HF* is net household formations (thousands per month); *R/C* is the ratio of the rent component of the Consumer Price Index to the Boeckh Index of residential construction costs for the month of December (1957–59 = 100); *Y* is personal disposable income (billions of 1954 dollars); and *MC + FNMA* is the supply of mortgage funds (billions of dollars). All the coefficients are more than three times their standard errors with the exception of the coefficient on disposable income, which is 2.6 times its standard error. The actual and estimated values of the annual changes in housing starts are plotted in Figure 3. The estimated values are generally very close to the actual, but the relatively large errors in 1961 and 1963 are somewhat disturbing.

III. Savings Deposits

In order to measure the indirect effects of changes in interest rates on the supply of mortgage funds via changes in the flows of deposits into financial intermediaries, equations for these inflows were also estimated. Our basic approach was to relate the net increase in deposits ($\triangle SD_i$)

in the ith institution to the following variables: (1) personal financial saving (FS); (2) stock of financial assets except corporate stock[16] held by households at the beginning of the year (FA_{-1}); (3) rate of interest paid on the deposits (r_i); (4) rate of interest paid on commercial bank time deposits (r_{td}); and (5) yield on short-term government securities (r_{sg}). Consumer credit outstanding at the beginning of the period (CC_{-1}) was also tried, but was significant only in the case of life insurance reserves. The regressions were fitted to first differences of the above variables and the results are shown in Table 4.

SAVINGS AND LOAN SHARES

The results obtained for savings and loan shares indicate a high degree of responsiveness to changes in yields on alternative financial assets. The significant coefficient on the commercial bank time-deposit rate reflects the shifts that occurred in 1957 and 1962 in response to the increases in the time-deposit rate, which resulted from raising the maximum allowable rate under Regulation Q. Similarly, the coefficient on the yield on short-term government securities reflects shifting into marketable securities during periods of high interest rates as a result of the short-run stickiness of the rate paid on savings and loan shares. The unwillingness of these institutions to raise their rates in periods of tight credit conditions arises from the nature of their role as intermediaries. A rise in market rates of interest increases the yield obtainable on newly acquired securities but does not affect the outstanding portfolio, while an increase in the rate paid on deposits must be extended to all accounts.[17]

This sensitivity of savings and loan shares to interest rate differentials may be questioned on the ground that savings and loan associations cater to small unsophisticated investors. However, survey data published by the United States Savings and Loan League indicates that this may not be the case.[18] For each of the three associations surveyed, over 50 per cent of the accounts contained less than $1,000, but over 60 per cent of the deposits were in accounts of $5,000 or more.

Because of the insignificant and implausible coefficient obtained on the savings and loan rate, the equation was rerun with this coefficient constrained to be equal in magnitude but opposite in sign to the coefficient on the time-deposit rate. This regression is shown in the second row of Table 4.

---

[16] Corporate stock was excluded because of the large year-to-year changes in market value which tend to dominate the changes in total financial assets.

[17] [7], pp. 112–113.

[18] [19], pp. 18–19.

TABLE 4

Savings Deposits, 1949-63

Dependent Variable	ΔFS (bill. \$)	ΔFA_{-1} (bill. \$)	ΔCC_{-1} (bill. \$)	Δr_i (per cent)	Δr_{sg} (per cent)	Δr_{td} (per cent)	Δr_{sd} (per cent)	Constant Term	$\bar{R}^2$	df
$\Delta^2 SD_1$ (savings and loan shares)	.0362 (.0340)	.0351 (.0102)		-.5271 (1.607)	-.3412 (.1117)	-1.619 (.716)		.1255	.609	9
$\Delta^2 SD_1$ (savings and loan shares)	.0614 (.0308)	.0259 (.0084)		1.569	-.3862 (.1133)	-1.569 (.754)		.0513	.565	10
$\Delta^2 SD_2$ (mutual savings bank deposits)	.0466 (.0303)	-.0071 (.0093)		2.355 (.935)	-.5126 (.1149)	.4610 (.6824)		-.1460	.683	9
$\Delta^2 SD_2$ (mutual savings bank deposits)	.0440 (.0280)			2.360 (.829)	-.5043 (.1052)			-.2363	.721	11
$\Delta^2 SD_3$ (life insurance reserves)	.0685 (.0276)	.0073 .0077	-.0912 (.0446)		-.0426 (.0875)		-1.620 (.938)	.4299	.630	9
$\Delta^2 SD_3$ (life insurance reserves)	.0710 (.0237)		-.0728 (.0391)				-1.190 (.747)	.4592	.659	11

MUTUAL SAVINGS BANK DEPOSITS

Mutual savings bank deposits also appear to be quite sensitive to interest rates. Significant coefficients were obtained on the rate paid on the deposits and the short-term government security rate. Since the rate on commercial bank time deposits and the stock of financial assets did not enter significantly, the regression was rerun omitting these variables.

LIFE INSURANCE RESERVES

As a measure of the savings of policyholders held by life insurance companies, we used reserves plus the accumulated value of dividends left on deposit less policy loans outstanding. Policy reserves are amounts set aside according to legal requirements to meet future obligations, net of future premium payments and interest earnings, prescribed under currently outstanding insurance contracts. Unlike deposits in other financial institutions, they are accumulated according to an agreed schedule of premium payments, only part of which represent additions to reserves, the remainder being the cost of insurance provided. However, a policyholder may at any time terminate his contract and withdraw his reserve, or he may use his reserve as collateral for a loan from the company.[19] Thus, life insurance reserves should be included among the financial assets of households, but they are undoubtedly viewed differently from other savings deposits.

In contrast to savings and loan shares and mutual savings bank deposits, the regression results obtained for life insurance reserves did not indicate a significant relationship to market rates of interest. However, significant coefficients were obtained on financial saving and consumer credit outstanding at the beginning of the period. A weighted average of the interest rates paid on savings and loan shares, mutual savings bank deposits, and commercial bank time deposits (r_{sd}) was also included in the regressions. The coefficient obtained was significant at the 10 per cent level and may reflect a shift toward low-reserve insurance plans in response to increases in the rates of interest paid by other financial institutions.

---

[19] In practice, the cash value of a policy is not exactly equal to the reserve because the calculation of the reserve makes no allowance for administrative expenses incurred by the company.

IV. Conclusions and Policy Implications

ANALYSIS OF THE SAMPLE PERIOD

The effects of changes in interest rates and other exogenous variables can now be analyzed by substituting the equations for mortgage lending and savings deposits into the housing starts equation. Lumping together the exogenous factors affecting the supply of funds other than market rates of interest into a single term denoted by E, we obtain the following relationship:

$$\Delta HS = -.2372\,(HS - HF)_{-1} + 2.519\left(\Delta\frac{R}{C}\right)_{-1} + .3256\,\Delta HF + .6961\Delta Y$$

$$+ 3.159\,\Delta FNMA - 3.473\,\Delta r_{sg} - 13.486\,\Delta r_{cb} + E - 3.3902 + u,$$

where u represents the unexplained residual variation. The contributions of each of these variables to the explanation of housing starts are given in Table 5. The figures shown were computed by multiplying the regression coefficients by the observations for each year expressed as deviations from their means. The β-coefficient for each column was computed as the ratio of the standard deviation of the numbers in the column to the standard deviation of the dependent variable, the sign being determined by the sign of the regression coefficient.[20] This statistic provides a summary measure of the relative importance of each factor.

As can be seen from the table, the supply-of-funds hypothesis is confirmed by the behavior of housing starts in the recession years of 1954 and 1958. In both of these cases, the low rate of increase of final demand, as measured by the household formations and disposable income terms, was offset by the effect of a sharp decline in interest rates. However, it should be noted that this process was reversed in the recovery years of 1955 and 1959 when the rise in interest rates was offset by the upturn in final demand. Furthermore, during the mild downturn of 1960, the decline in interest rates did not compensate for the sharp fall in demand which occurred, resulting in a considerable decline in housing starts from the 1959 level.

---

[20] This formula yields the usual β-coefficient for those columns which involve a single independent variable. If y_i and x_i denote the observed values of the dependent variable and a particular independent variable, expressed as deviations from means, and b is the regression coefficient, we have

$$\beta = \frac{\sqrt{\Sigma(bx_i)^2}}{\sqrt{\Sigma y_i^2}} = b\,\frac{\sqrt{\Sigma x_i^2}}{\sqrt{\Sigma y_i^2}}.$$

TABLE 5

Contributions of Exogenous Variables to Explanation of Changes in Housing Starts

(thousand units per month; deviations from means)

Variable	ΔHS	$(HS-HF)_{-1}$	$\left(\dfrac{\Delta R}{C}\right)_{-1}$	Final Demand, ΔHF & ΔY	ΔFNMA	Interest Rates	E	u
β-coefficient		− .410	.479	.419	.135	− .339	.297	
Contribution								
1949	5.3	17.7	− 2.5	− 5.8	1.4	4.1	−7.0	−2.6
1950	34.1	14.8	19.7	− 5.7	− .2	2.0	−1.9	5.4
1951	−35.4	− 2.5	−19.6	− 7.2	0	− 3.0	−7.8	4.7
1952	2.7	1.3	2.3	− 2.7	− .3	.3	3.5	−1.7
1953	− 2.3	− 1.0	4.1	− 3.5	− .5	− 2.2	1.4	− .6
1954	11.2	− 5.1	10.6	.6	− .7	9.9	−3.5	− .6
1955	8.6	− 4.6	3.8	11.9	.8	− 3.6	3.2	−2.9
1956	−23.8	− 2.6	− 7.0	− 2.5	.8	− 5.4	−5.2	−1.8
1957	−13.9	− 2.0	− 3.0	− .2	1.5	− 7.7	−2.6	0
1958	10.1	1.4	.8	− 2.7	−3.0	8.2	2.3	3.0
1959	12.4	− .5	− 1.0	13.6	5.6	−13.1	4.7	3.1
1960	−24.3	2.8	− 4.5	−13.2	−3.2	3.4	−6.3	−3.5
1961	2.4	− .9	2.8	1.9	−1.9	4.9	4.7	−9.2
1962	10.6	− 1.6	0	− 1.1	− .1	1.8	8.7	3.0
1963	9.7	− 9.0	− 2.2	7.0	−3.4	1.9	6.9	8.4
1964	− 7.6	− 8.3	− 4.5	9.5	3.2	−1.7	−1.3	−4.6

As indicated by the β-coefficient, the level of inventories of units under construction and vacancies, and the relationship between rents and construction costs also make an important contribution to the explanation of housing starts. Increases in construction costs during periods of rapid increase in building and decreases during periods of declining activity have had a considerable impact on the subsequent volume of starts. The contribution of the inventory variable indicates the presence of a backlog of demand relative to available housing in the years 1949 and 1950 and an accumulation of inventories resulting in a downward pressure on new starts during the periods 1953–57 and 1961–64.

The column in the table headed by the symbol E includes all the variables in the equations for mortgage lending and savings deposits except rates of interest on marketable securities. The significant positive influence indicated in the expansionary years of 1955, 1959, 1961, and 1962 reflects the effect on personal financial saving of the sharp increases in disposable income that occurred. The figures also suggest that the substantial increase in the rate of accumulation of savings deposits by households during the recent period of 1961–63 has played a key role in maintaining the high volume of housing starts that took place. This increase in the flow of funds through financial intermediaries occurred as a result of the rapid increase in household holdings of financial assets in general, rather than as a result of shifting out of marketable securities in response to a decline in interest rates, as was the case in earlier periods of increasing building activity such as 1954 and 1958.

COMPARISON WITH MAISEL'S MODEL

In a recent study of the residential construction sector [12], Maisel obtained the following regression equation using quarterly data for the period 1950–62:

$$St_0 = -172.9 - 20.25 \left(\frac{1}{3} \sum_{j=2}^{4} i_{-j} \right) - .1441 \ V_{-1} + .3177 \ St_{-1}$$
$$\qquad\qquad\qquad (6.73) \qquad\qquad\qquad\qquad (.0367) \qquad\quad (.1420)$$

$$- \ .2357 \ St_{-3} + 2.673 \left(\frac{R}{C} \right)_{-1} + 2.456 \ Rem_0 + .5908 \ \Delta HH_0.$$
$$\quad (.0780) \qquad\quad (.905) \qquad\qquad (1.500) \qquad\quad (.3330)$$

$$R^2 = .85.$$

The variables were defined as follows: St is housing starts; i is the Treasury bill rate on new issues; V is the deviation of vacancies from a straight trend at the start of the quarter; R is the rent component of the Consumer Price Index; C is the residential cost component of the GNP implicit price index; Rem is an estimate of net removals; and $\triangle HH$ is net household formation in the quarter.

This model differs from our own in several important respects. First, the large role played by demand in our equation conflicts with the statistical results obtained by Maisel, who argues that final demand is relatively stable in the short run and thus is not an important factor in cyclical fluctuations. He uses net household formations and net removals from the stock of houses to represent final demand, while we have included an income variable as a determinant of the demand for owner-occupied as opposed to rental housing. In addition, we have used the series on household formations published by the Bureau of the Census, which indicates much greater year-to-year variation than the series used by Maisel.

The inventory variable is also treated somewhat differently in our model. We assume that housing starts depend on the inventory of units under construction and vacancies at the beginning of the period, while in Maisel's model housing starts are assumed to be a function of vacancies and the change in inventories under construction during the previous quarter, the latter being represented by starts lagged one and three quarters. Furthermore, in the regression equations presented, starts lagged one quarter enter with a positive sign implying that a buildup of inventories has a stimulating rather than depressing influence on new starts. This result is not surprising because of the presence of serial correlation in the quarterly data but constitutes a serious weakness in Maisel's statistical model.

The effect of credit conditions is represented in Maisel's model by a lagged moving average of the Treasury bill rate. He experimented with mortgage yields and the spread between mortgage yields and bond yields but obtained better results using a short-term rate. He argues that the latter variable provides a better measure of the cost and availability of credit. In our model, the short-term rate affects the availability of credit through its influence on the flow of deposits into financial intermediaries. Our results also indicate that long-term rates have an important influence in a model which takes account of other factors affecting the supply of funds.

INTEREST RATE MULTIPLIERS

In order to calculate the effect of changes in interest rates on expenditures, we estimated residential construction expenditures (H), measured in billion 1954 dollars, as a linear function of housing starts during the current year (HS), and housing starts during the last six months of the previous year (HS^*_{-1}). Using annual first differences for the period 1949–64, the following regression equation was obtained:

$$\Delta H = \underset{(.0079)}{.0930} \ \Delta HS + \underset{(.0077)}{.0343} \ \Delta HS_{-1}^* + .3368. \qquad \bar{R}^2 = .925.$$

Using this equation and an estimate of 1.629 billion 1954 dollars for the additional expenditures induced by an exogenous change of \$1 billion in construction expenditures, we obtained the multipliers shown in Table 6. This figure was obtained from the inverse of the most recent version of the University of Michigan econometric model of the U.S. economy. It indicates the magnitude of the income effects of the increase in construction expenditures but does not take account of the feedback to the housing sector through interest rates, disposable income, or financial saving.

In the last column of Table 6, we have shown the effect on GNP of a decrease of one percentage point in the short-term rate accompanied by

TABLE 6

Interest Rate Multipliers

	Short-Term Government Security Rate $(\Delta r_{sg} = -1.00)$	Corporate Bond Rate $(\Delta r_{cb} = -1.00)$	$\Delta r_{sg} = -1.00$ $\Delta r_{cb} = -.23$
Housing starts (thousands per month)	3.473	13.486	6.574
Residential construction expenditures (billion 1954 dollars)	.3230	1.254	.6114
GNP (billion 1954 dollars)	.5262	2.043	.9960
GNP (billion 1964 dollars)[a]	.6351	2.466	1.202

[a] Calculated from the constant dollar figures by multiplying by 1.207, the GNP deflator for 1964 obtained from the *Survey of Current Business*, February 1965.

a decrease of .23 in the corporate bond rate. This relationship between the two interest rates represents the historical average which was derived from a regression of changes in the corporate bond rate on changes in the short-term rate. As can be seen from the table, a decrease in the short-term interest rate of 1 percentage point (e.g., from 4 to 3 per cent) will lead to an increase in GNP of about a half billion 1954 dollars, assuming no change in the corporate bond rate, and an increase of about one billion 1954 dollars, assuming an induced change of .23 in the corporate bond rate. Similarly, the multiplier for a 1 percentage point decrease in the corporate bond rate is about two billion 1954 dollars. These figures indicate that monetary policy has a substantial impact on the residential construction sector, but that the resulting changes in GNP will be small relative to the cyclical fluctuations experienced in the postwar period. For example, the largest year-to-year change in interest rates occurred in 1959 when the short-term rate rose by 2.02 per cent and the corporate bond rate by .59. According to the above multipliers, this rise in interest rates reduced the growth of GNP by 2.3 billion 1954 dollars from $29.6 billion to the observed increase of $27.3 billion. Thus the residential construction sector exerts some stabilizing influence but does not provide a mechanism by which monetary policy alone can be expected to achieve short-run stabilization.

Statistical Appendix

Financial flows are in billion dollars and interest rates are in per cent per annum. The source of the data is the *Federal Reserve Bulletin,* unless otherwise noted.

RESIDENTIAL CONSTRUCTION DATA

1. Nonfarm residential construction expenditures, billions of 1954 dollars (*H*). Source: *Survey of Current Business.*

2. Nonfarm private housing starts (*HS*) and housing starts during the last six months of the year (*HS**), thousands per month. Source: Housing and Home Finance Agency, *Housing Statistics,* January 1965, and *Historical Supplement,* October 1961. Data for 1947–58 multiplied by the following factors, derived from those given in [12]: 1947–56—1.200; 1957–I—1.188; 1957–II—1.175; 1958–I—1.163; 1958–II—1.150.

3. Net household formations, thousands per month (*HF*). Source: U.S. Bureau of the Census, *Current Population Reports,* Series P-20, No. 130. Calendar year changes in the number of households were

obtained by interpolation. The figure for March 1961 was adjusted upward by 1 per cent to make it comparable with succeeding years.

4. Ratio of the rent component of the Consumer Price Index to the Boeckh Index of residential construction costs for the month of December, 1957–59 = 100 (R/C). Source: *Housing Statistics*.

5. Personal disposable income, billions of 1954 dollars (Y). Source: *Survey of Current Business*.

6. Estimated mortgage funds supplied by financial intermediaries (MC). Source: regression equations for mortgage lending of savings and loan associations, mutual savings banks and life insurance companies.

7. Net purchases of mortgages by the Federal National Mortgage Association (FNMA).

SAVINGS AND LOAN ASSOCIATIONS

1. Mortgage loans made (ML_1).

2. Mortgage loan commitments outstanding at the end of the year (COS_1).

3. Mortgage holdings at the end of the year (M_1).

4. Mortgage repayments (REP_1). Source: computed as the difference between mortgage loans made and the change in mortgage holdings during the year.

5. Savings and loan shares (SD_1).

MUTUAL SAVINGS BANKS

1. Mortgage loans made (ML_2). Source: 1948–60: [13], p. 169; 1961–64: estimated from changes in mortgage holdings by assuming repayments to be 10 per cent of total mortgage holdings at the beginning of the year.

2. Mortgage loan commitments outstanding at the end of the year (COS_2). Source: 1951–58: interpolated from data given in [13], p. 229; 1959–64: *Federal Reserve Bulletin*. Total commitments were estimated from data for New York state by multiplying by 1.7.

3. Residential mortgage holdings at the end of the year (M_2).

4. Mortgage repayments (REP_2). Source: 1951–60: computed as the difference between mortgage loans made and the change in mortgage holdings during the year; 1961–64: assumed to be 10 per cent of total mortgage holdings at the beginning of the year.

5. Mutual savings bank deposits (SD_2). Source: *Federal Reserve Bulletin; Supplement to Banking and Monetary Statistics,* Section 1, Banks and the Monetary System, 1962.

LIFE INSURANCE COMPANIES

1. Nonfarm mortgage loans made (ML_3).

2. Mortgage loan commitments outstanding at the end of the year (COS_3). Source: Life Insurance Association of America. Total commitments were estimated from the available data by multiplying by 1.5.

3. Nonfarm mortgage holdings at the end of the year (M_3). Source: *Federal Reserve Bulletin;* Institute of Life Insurance, *Life Insurance Fact Book,* 1964.

4. Mortgage repayments (REP_3). Source: computed as the difference between mortgage loans made and the change in mortgage holdings during the year.

5. Life insurance reserves plus dividend accumulations less policy loans (SD_3). Source: *Federal Reserve Bulletin; Life Insurance Fact Book.* Dividend accumulations for 1948–52 were estimated from dividends paid.

COMMERCIAL BANKS

1. Residential mortgage holdings at the end of the year (M_4).

2. Time deposits adjusted at commercial banks at the end of the year (SD_4). Source: *Federal Reserve Bulletin; Supplement to Banking and Monetary Statistics.*

INTEREST RATES

1. Long-term U.S. government bond rate (r_{us}).

2. Aaa corporate bond rate (r_{cb}).

3. Average of FHA and VA ceiling rates (r_m). Source: *Federal Register.*

4. Standard and Poor's state and local bond yield (r_{s1}). Source: *Survey of Current Business; Business Statistics.*

5. Rate on nine- to twelve-month U.S. government notes and bonds (r_{sg}).

6. Rate paid on savings and loan shares (r_1). Source: [19]. Rates paid 1948–1957 were estimated from dividends paid.

7. Rate paid on mutual savings bank deposits (r_2). Source: 1948–60: [13], p. 87; 1961–63: [19].

8. Rate paid on commercial bank time deposits (r_{td}). Source: [19].

9. Weighted average rate on savings and loan shares, mutual savings bank deposits and commercial bank time deposits (r_{sd}).

TABLE 7

Residential Construction Data

Year	ΔH	HS	ΔHS	ΔHS*	HF	ΔHF	Δ(R/C)	ΔY	ΔMC	ΔFNMA
1948		91.4		- 9.9	132.8		- .9			
1949	- .2	98.9	7.5	24.0	127.9	- 4.9	7.9	2.3	1.436	.454
1950	4.3	135.2	36.3	18.7	91.4	-36.5	-7.7	17.2	2.422	- .077
1951	-2.6	102.0	-33.2	-32.9	74.2	-17.2	1.0	6.0	-1.050	- .009
1952	- .1	106.9	4.9	11.2	69.5	- 4.7	1.7	6.6	3.571	- .084
1953	.8	106.8	- .1	- 6.4	52.2	-17.3	4.3	11.4	2.111	- .161
1954	1.8	120.2	13.4	25.6	67.6	15.4	1.6	1.9	4.410	- .232
1955	2.8	131.0	10.8	- 3.7	86.6	19.0	-2.7	16.5	2.244	.260
1956	-2.0	109.4	-21.6	-20.1	67.7	-18.9	-1.1	13.5	- .975	.255
1957	- .9	97.7	-11.7	- 5.4	70.2	2.5	.4	6.9	- .894	.489
1958	.9	110.0	12.3	23.9	74.4	4.2	- .3	2.5	5.721	- .952
1959	3.3	124.6	14.6	- 1.9	103.3	28.9	-1.7	14.4	- .281	1.761
1960	-1.3	102.5	-22.1	-21.6	65.5	-37.8	1.2	7.1	1.479	-1.011
1961	0.0	107.1	4.6	12.8	67.0	1.5	.1	10.4	5.428	- .617
1962	1.9	119.9	12.8	9.9	48.8	-18.2	- .8	15.2	5.680	- .032
1963	1.1	131.8	11.9	12.4	63.5	14.7	-1.7	11.5	5.185	-1.066
1964	.1		- 5.4			2.3		20.9	1.451	1.003

TABLE 8

Financial Intermediaries

Part A: Savings and Loan Associations

Year	ΔML_1	$\Delta^2 COS_1$	$\Delta^2 SD_1$	ΔREP_1	$\Delta(M_1/SD_1)$
1948					.032
1949	.029		.297	.167	−.009
1950	1.601		.012	.871	.045
1951	.013		.595	.147	−.010
1952	1.367		.973	.442	−.008
1953	1.150		.563	.416	.003
1954	1.202		.837	.536	−.003
1955	2.286		.370	1.251	.019
1956	− .930		.098	.069	−.015
1957	− .165	.009	− .192	− .175	−.007
1958	2.022	.594	1.300	.680	−.004
1959	2.969	−.803	.543	1.075	.023
1960	− .847	.264	.952	− .262	−.007
1961	3.060	.475	1.184	1.225	.004
1962	3.390	−.227	.608	2.218	.011
1963	3.980	.061	1.618	1.837	.014
1964	− .151	−.296	−2.174	1.777	

Part B: Mutual Savings Banks

Year	ΔML_2	$\Delta^2 COS_2$	$\Delta^2 SD_2$	ΔREP_2	$\Delta(M_2/SD_2)$
1951					.059
1952	− .052	.942	.822	.140	.026
1953	.217	.207	.071	.116	.028
1954	.711	.587	.184	.211	.036
1955	.825	− .675	− .133	.439	.051
1956	− .128	− .665	.017	.034	.037
1957	− .977	.194	− .182	−.113	.011
1958	.899	1.304	.682	.229	.015
1959	.081	−1.823	−1.402	.446	.028
1960	.002	.891	.427	− .212	.026
1961	.467	.721	.764	.200	.015
1962	1.186	.748	.910	.221	.019
1963	1.046	−1.518	− .059	.317	.032
1964	.743	.765	1.409	.390	

(continued)

TABLE 8 *(concluded)*

Part C: Life Insurance Companies

Year	ΔML_3	$\Delta^2 COS_3$	$\Delta^2 SD_3$	ΔREP_3	$\Delta(M_3/SD_3)$
1953					.009
1954	1.006	1.118	.115	.404	.016
1955	1.177	−1.680	.309	.425	.023
1956	.093	− .003	− .122	.001	.022
1957	−1.378	.160	− .176	−.186	.006
1958	.016	.875	.238	.417	.000
1959	.633	− .588	.731	.401	−.001
1960	.150	− .035	−1.047	−.294	.008
1961	.611	.162	.464	.786	.004
1962	.626	.639	.315	.401	.005
1963	1.447	− .045	.507	.666	.009
1964	1.044	− .139	.075	.590	

Part D: Commercial Banks

Year	$\Delta^2 M_4$	$\Delta^2 SD_4$	$\Delta(M_4/SD_4)$
1948		− .886	.028
1949	− .523	− .213	.015
1950	1.145	− .174	.047
1951	− .916	1.377	.011
1952	.079	1.262	.002
1953	− .181	.186	−.004
1954	.490	.192	.006
1955	.509	−1.670	.027
1956	− .620	.703	.007
1957	− .973	3.344	−.031
1958	1.301	1.465	−.011
1959	.285	−4.309	.014
1960	−1.687	2.778	−.023
1961	.821	5.269	−.027
1962	1.394	4.530	−.017
1963	.737	−1.941	

TABLE 9

Interest Rates

Year	Δr_{us}	Δr_{cb}	$\Delta(r_m - r_{cb})$	Δr_{sl}	Δr_{sg}	Δr_1	Δr_2	Δr_{td}	Δr_{sd}
1949	.13	-.16	.16	-.19	.00	.08	.16	.00	.09
1950	.01	-.04	-.04	-.23	.12	.00	.08	.00	.04
1951	.25	.24	-.28	.02	.47	.06	.06	.20	.16
1952	.11	.10	-.10	.19	.08	.12	.35	.00	.15
1953	.26	.24	.01	.53	.26	.12	.09	.00	.08
1954	.39	-.30	.42	-.35	-1.15	.08	.10	.20	.17
1955	.29	.16	-.16	.16	.97	.05	.14	.10	.12
1956	.24	.30	-.28	.40	.94	.11	.13	.20	.18
1957	.39	.53	-.25	.67	.70	.22	.17	.50	.33
1958	.04	-.10	.27	-.04	-1.44	.10	.13	.11	.12
1959	.64	.59	-.37	.39	2.02	.16	.12	.15	.15
1960	.06	.03	.28	-.22	-.56	.31	.33	.20	.27
1961	.11	-.06	-.12	-.27	-.64	.06	.22	.15	.13
1962	.05	-.02	-.05	-.28	.11	.23	.33	.47	.34
1963	.05	-.07	.07	.05	.26	.06	.05	.13	.08
1964	.15	.14	-.14	-.01					

TABLE 10

Household Financial Variables

Year	ΔFS	ΔFA	ΔCC
1948		7.2	2.828
1949	− 1.852	7.4	2.907
1950	4.644	11.0	4.090
1951	2.121	14.1	1.222
1952	5.176	20.0	4.784
1953	.344	20.3	3.992
1954	− 2.918	21.6	1.071
1955	3.759	27.7	6.343
1956	2.187	26.4	3.527
1957	− .895	25.6	2.636
1958	.172	29.8	.159
1959	4.921	38.0	6.413
1960	− 4.596	24.7	4.486
1961	4.996	38.6	1.650
1962	5.174	42.7	5.486
1963	3.157		

HOUSEHOLD FINANCIAL ASSETS AND LIABILITIES

1. Personal financial saving (*FS*). Computed from the formula *FS* equals (personal saving plus imputed depreciation) minus (purchases of houses for owner-occupancy plus alterations and repairs minus net increase in mortgage debt) plus (increase in consumer credit). Source: personal saving and imputations: *Survey of Current Business;* other variables: *Federal Reserve Bulletin* and *Flow of Funds Supplement,* 1963.

2. Stock of financial assets except corporate stock at the end of the year (*FA*).

3. Consumer credit outstanding at the end of the year (*CC*).

BIBLIOGRAPHY

1. Alberts, William W., "Business Cycles, Residential Construction Cycles, and the Mortgage Market," *Journal of Political Economy,* June 1962, pp. 263–281.

2. Benavie, Arthur, "The Impact on the Strength of Monetary Controls of Asset Shifts Involving Intermediary Claims," unpublished Ph.D. dissertation, University of Michigan, 1962.

3. Feige, Edgar L., *The Demand for Liquid Assets: A Temporal Cross-Section Analysis,* Englewood Cliffs, 1964.

4. Gies, Thomas G., Mayer, Thomas, and Ettin, Edward C., "Portfolio Regulations and Policies of Financial Intermediaries," in *Private Financial Institutions,* Englewood Cliffs, 1963, pp. 157–263.

5. Grebler, Leo, *Housing Issues in Economic Stabilization Policy,* New York, National Bureau of Economic Research, Occasional Paper 72, 1960.

6. Guttentag, J. M., "The Short Cycle in Residential Construction," *American Economic Review,* June 1961, pp. 275–298.

7. Kendall, Leon T., *The Savings and Loan Business: Its Purposes, Functions and Economic Justification,* Englewood Cliffs, 1962.

8. Klaman, Saul B., "The Availability of Residential Mortgage Credit," *Study of Mortgage Credit,* U.S. Senate Committee on Banking and Currency, Subcommittee on Housing, 85th Congress, 2nd Session, Washington, 1958.

9. ———, *The Postwar Residential Mortgage Market,* Princeton for NBER, 1959.

10. Life Insurance Association of America, *Life Insurance Companies as Financial Institutions,* Englewood Cliffs, 1962.

11. Maisel, S. J., "Changes in the Rate and Components of Household Formation," *Journal of the American Statistical Association,* June 1960, pp. 268–283.

12. ———, "A Theory of Fluctuations in Residential Construction Starts," *American Economic Review,* June 1963, pp. 359–383.

13. National Association of Mutual Savings Banks, *Mutual Savings Banking: Basic Characteristics and Role in the National Economy,* Englewood Cliffs, 1962.

14. Research Seminar in Quantitative Economics, *Econometric Model of the U.S. Economy,* University of Michigan, 1964 (mimeographed).

15. Smith, W. L., "The Impact of Monetary Policy on Residential Construction, 1948–1958," *Study of Mortgage Credit,* U.S. Senate Committee on Banking and Currency, Subcommittee on Housing, 85th Congress, 2nd Session, Washington, 1958.

16. Suits, Daniel B., "Forecasting and Analysis with an Econometric Model," *American Economic Review,* March 1962, pp. 104–132.

17. U.S. Bureau of the Census, *Business Cycle Developments.*

18. ———, *Current Population Reports,* Series P-20, No. 125.

19. U.S. Savings and Loan League, *Savings and Loan Fact Book,* 1964.

Consumer Expenditures
for Durable Goods

MARVIN SNOWBARGER AND DANIEL B. SUITS

UNIVERSITY OF MICHIGAN

This paper presents the findings of research on the demand for consumer durables, using cross-sectional data from the Survey of Consumer Finances. The annual surveys, conducted by the Survey Research Center at the University of Michigan, of 1960, 1961, and 1962 contained a reinterview (panel) sample of 1059 households.[1] The data are analyzed by the Sonquist-Morgan Automatic Interaction Detector (AID) program,[2] developed for the IBM 7090 computer. Essentially, this is a method for searching a large body of data for important relationships. It differs from most research procedures in that it seeks out the most important variables without having them prespecified. The program is discussed in section I.

Section II presents an application of the AID program to consumer investment decisions. The program is used to examine the characteristics that distinguished households who subsequently buy a specific durable from those that do not. The individual durables studied are television sets, refrigerators, washers, furniture, and automobiles.

Since automobiles are the major component of consumer durable expenditure, the phenomenon of the two-car family has special implications for the industry and the national economy. In section III, the program is used to study multiple-car ownership.

---

[1] The 1960–62 panel and its characteristics are discussed in R. Kosobud and J. Morgan, *Consumer Behavior of Individual Families over Two and Three Years,* Survey Research Center, 1964.

[2] John Sonquist and James Morgan, *The Detection of Interaction Effects,* Monograph No. 35, Survey Research Center, 1964.

I. The Method of Analysis

Regression and related techniques are often used to analyze cross-section data, but the diversity of individual consumer behavior and the complex intercorrelations and interactions preclude a straightforward linear regression. Cross tabulations often provide a better profile of consumer behavior, but still require the analyst to select the "control" variables in advance. As a practical matter, however, he rarely knows all the important variables, especially where complex interactions are involved. The Automatic Interaction Detector (AID) program provides an alternative by which the data can be scanned to identify the most important variables and their interactions.

The program is essentially a way of partitioning the total sample of observations by a sequence of dichotomies. At each stage the computer attempts to use the variables to divide the existing subsets. Each subset is partitioned by the variable yielding the maximum R^2. The procedure terminates when individual subsets are either sufficiently homogeneous or contain a minimum number of observations. Upon completion, the computer output specifies a "tree" of two-way splits, providing a picture of the relationship by defining a series of increasingly complex interactions.

At each step the program scans several variables, but selects only one of them. An important feature of the program is its ability to allow every variable the chance to become a predictor at each stage. In any split, some variables may be highly correlated with the partitioning variable, but not sufficiently powerful to make the split. A highly correlated variable at one stage may return to partition a group later in the tree. Information about the status of all variables is contained in the printed output of the program. In particular, the relative discriminating power of each variable is shown at every stage of the program, making it possible to compare the one ultimately chosen with all alternatives. This contributes to an understanding of why one variable appears rather than another, and how great the difference between them was. Any interpretation of the tree must be supported by an analysis of the splits that "almost" occurred.

If the program is allowed to run without constraint, it may split off a very small group. These splits must be recognized for their extreme variation, but disregarded in the final analysis.

Each variable appearing in the tree makes a contribution to the explanation of the dependent variable. Its relative strength is indicated by a "partial R^2." The total of all these "partial R^2's" is equal to the proportion of the total variation "explained" by the splits in the tree.

TABLE 1

List of Variables Used in Panel Analysis

Variables	Code Categories
pendent[a]:	
ether purchased TV	Purchased; did not purchase
ether purchased refrigerator	Purchased; did not purchase
ether purchased washer	Purchased; did not purchase
ether purchased furniture	Purchased; did not purchase
ether purchased automobile	Purchased; did not purchase
dependent:	
tter or worse off than year ago	Better; same; worse; uncertain
pect to be better off year from now	Better; same; worse; uncertain
:e of place	Central cities; urban places; rural places
e of head	18-24; 25-34; 35-44; 45-54; 55-64; 65-
mber of adults	0; 1; 2; 3; 4; 5; 6; 7; 8 or more
mber of children under 18	0; 1; 2; 3; 4; 5; 6; 7; 8 or more
e of youngest child under 18	2-3; 3-4; 4-5; 5-6; 6-9; 9-14; 14-18
e of oldest child under 18	2-3; 3-4; 4-5; 5-6; 6-9; 9-14; 14-18
rital status	Married; single; widow; divorced; separated
ngth of marriage	0-1; 2; 3; 4; 5-9; 10-20; over 20 years
:e residence established	Pre-1939; 1940-49; 1950-54; 1955-56; 1957; 1958; 1959; 1960
ising status	Owner; renter
ither head employed now	Employed; unemployed; retired
mber of weeks head worked	13 or less; 14-26; 27-39; 40-47; 48-49; 50-52
mber of weeks wife worked	13 or less; 14-26; 27-39; 40-47; 48-49; 50-52
e's employment status	Worked 2 years ago; worked last year
)PR/disposable income	Percentage scale
posable income	Dollar scale
centage of income received by wife	Percentage scale
naining instalment debt on A/R	Dollar scale
naining instalment debt on cars	Dollar scale
naining instalment debt on durables	Dollar scale
naining instalment debt on other	Dollar scale
ther expect to buy TV	Definitely; probably; undecided
ther expect to buy refrigerator	Definitely; probably; undecided
ther expect to buy washer	Definitely; probably; undecided
ther expect to buy furniture	Definitely; probably; undecided
ther expect to buy automobile	Definitely; probably; undecided

These variables are part of the independent variables unless they are the dependent able in a particular run.

FIGURE 1

Factors Related to Purchase of a Television Set

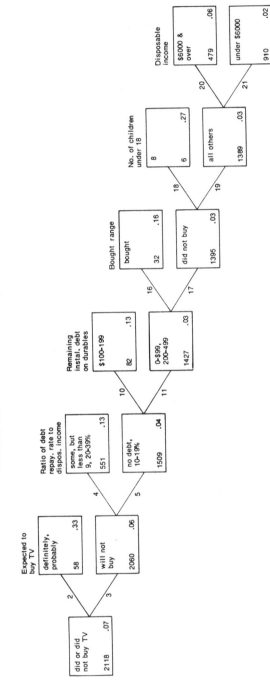

Variation explained: 15 per cent.
Source: 1960-62 Survey of Consumer Finances. N-1059.

II. Purchase of Durables

The AID program is used in this section to study the purchase of consumer durables. The Survey of Consumer Finances, conducted by the Survey Research Center, contains information on the purchase of television sets, refrigerators, washers, furniture, and automobiles, together with extensive attitudinal, demographic, and economic data. The 1960–62 Surveys contained a panel of 1059 households, each of which was interviewed three times. Information is available describing the position of the family at each interview, and its purchase behavior during the past year. For each durable, the attempt was made to relate the characteristics of the family at one interview to its subsequent purchasing behavior as determined from the following interview. Since three interviews were conducted, two observations were available for each household. The complete data set used in this analysis consists of 2118 observations.

Specifically, the data were arranged in the following way. A particular durable was selected and the value 1 assigned to a household if it purchased the durable between 1960 and 1961. Otherwise, the household was assigned the value 0. Corresponding data for the independent variables were compiled as of January 1960. This yields 1059 households, each of which is known either to have purchased or not to have purchased the durable between January 1960 and January 1961. All data for these households were obtained at most one year prior to the actual purchase.

The procedure was repeated for the same households, but using purchase behavior of the period 1961–62. The data for the independent variables were compiled as of January 1961, yielding an additional 1059 observations. All data for these households are, likewise, no later than one year prior to the actual purchase behavior.

Combining the two groups of data produces the data set of 2118 observations. The several variables used in the study are listed in Table 1.

The relationship of the independent variables to the purchase of a television set is shown in Figure 1. The first box shows that, of the 2118 interviews, 7 per cent were followed by the purchase of a television set. The first branch of the tree shows that "plans to buy a TV" is the most important information distinguishing purchasers from nonpurchasers. Among households with expressed intentions to buy, 33 per cent bought, compared with only 6 per cent of those who did not plan to buy. Although two-thirds of families "planning to buy" actually failed to do so, the group was too small to be split again.

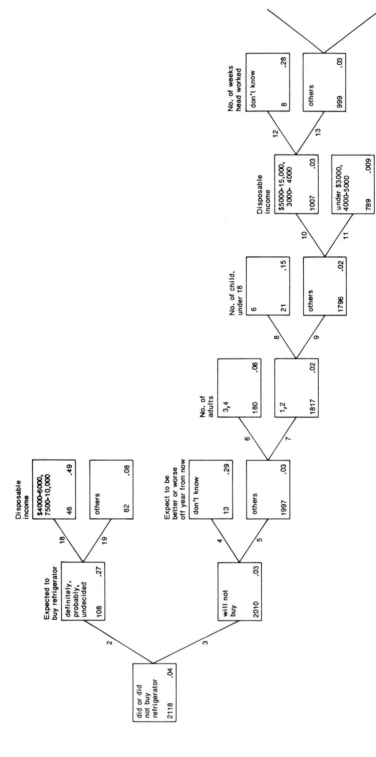

FIGURE 2

Factors Related to Purchase of Refrigerator

Variation explained: 23 per cent.
Source: 1960-62 Survey of Consumer Finances. N-1059.

FIGURE 2 (concluded)

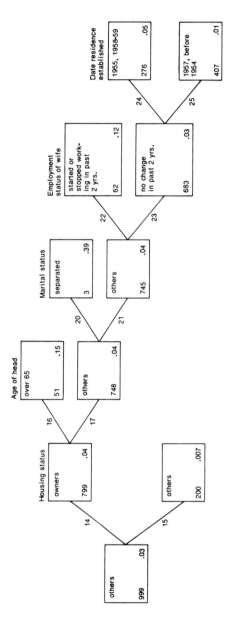

The next branch of the tree shows the importance of the annual repayment rate of consumer debt in distinguishing purchasers from non-purchasers.[3] Among households expressing no intention to buy, a large number of purchases (13 per cent) was made by households whose debt repayment rate as a percentage of income was either very low or very high. Fewer purchases are found among households with a moderate debt repayment to income ratio. Among the latter, families with moderate amounts of instalment debt bought television sets.

The final branches of the tree show the influence of "buying a range," the "number of children under 18," and "disposable income." Neither the purchase of a range nor the number of children under 18 provide useful information. The number of observations in these two splits is thirty-two for the former, and six for the latter. After taking account of all the other influences, however, disposable income still produces a difference in behavior.

Figure 2 displays the AID tree purchases of a refrigerator. Forty-nine per cent of the households planning to buy, and having income in the $4,000–$6,000 and $7,500–$10,000 range, actually bought a refrigerator. The lengthy series of splits on the bottom of the tree shows that extreme variability, arising for a number of reasons, will produce many small partitions. An interpretation must be selective. Splits 7, 10, 14, and 24 highlight the characteristics of households with no prior intentions of buying a refrigerator. Households of one or two adults (split 7), with middle to high income (split 10), who are homeowners (split 14), and recently established (split 24), are more likely to buy refrigerators than households without these attributes. Results for washers, furniture, and automobiles are similar and are shown in Figures 3, 4, and 5.

The purchasing behavior shown by the five trees exhibits a number of important common elements. In every case, expressed purchase intentions are the first criterion for identifying eventual buyers. Nevertheless, less than half of those households planning to buy will carry out their intentions. Other characteristics separate buyers from nonbuyers.[4] These usually include debt position and disposable income. In no case did the two general attitudinal variables ("better off than a year ago," "expect

[3] George Katona, *The Powerful Consumer,* New York, 1960, pp. 186 ff.

[4] Buying intentions and their fulfillment are discussed in *1962 Survey of Consumer Finances,* Survey Research Center, 1963, Ch. 8.

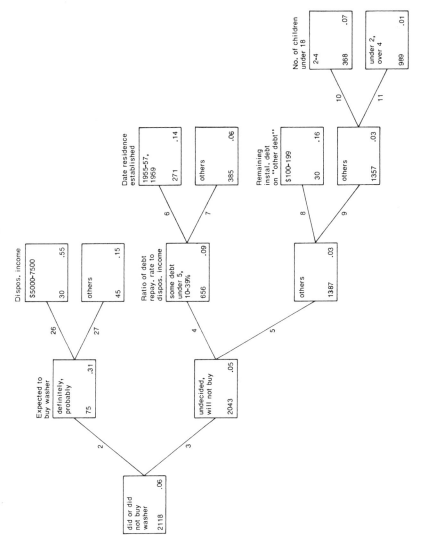

Variation explained: 15 per cent.
Source: 1960-62 Survey of Consumer Finances. N-1059.

FIGURE 4

Factors Related to Purchase of Furniture

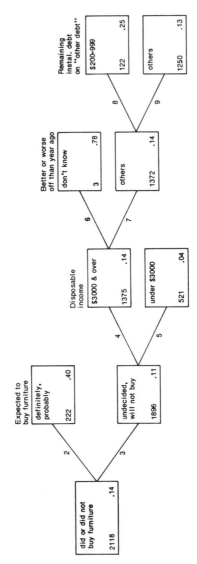

Variation explained: 16 per cent.
Source: 1960-62 Survey of Consumer Finances. N-1059.

FIGURE 5

Factors Related to Purchase of Car

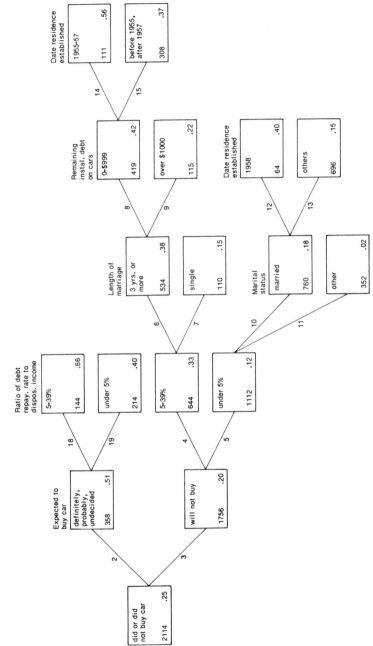

Variation explained: 28 per cent.
Source: 1960-62 Survey of Consumer Finances. N-1059.

TABLE 2

Multiple-Car Ownership Among All Spending Units [a]

Year	Percentage of Spending Units Owning More Than One Car
1963	18.5
1962	18.5
1961	14.3
1960	14.4
1959	12.3
1958	11.8
1957	10.4
1956	9.6
1955	8.8
1954	7.6
1953	7.7

Source: *Survey of Consumer Finances.*

[a] A spending unit is defined as all related persons living together who pool their incomes. Husband, wife, and children under 18 living at home are members of the same spending unit.

to be better off a year from now") contribute to an understanding of the specific purchase behavior.[5]

The possible complementarity or substitutability of durable purchases was studied by including among the independent variables explaining the purchase behavior with regard to any one good the observed purchase behavior with regard to each of the others. For example, in attempting to distinguish buyers of television sets from nonbuyers, the AID program considered whether the household bought, say, an automobile during the same period. If purchases of automobiles and tele-

[5] There is a considerable literature on the role of "buying intentions," "attitudes," and consumer demand. Substantive issues are represented, in part, by the following publications: J. Tobin, "On the Predictive Value of Consumer Intentions and Attitudes," *Review of Economics and Statistics,* February 1959, pp. 1–11; Eva Mueller, "Consumer Attitudes: Their Influence and Forecasting Value," in *The Quality and Economic Significance of Anticipations Data,* Princeton for National Bureau of Economic Research, 1960, pp. 149–174; Eva Mueller, "Ten Years of Attitude Surveys: Their Forecasting Record," *Journal of the American Statistical Association,* December 1963, pp. 899–917.

FIGURE 6

Percentage of Spending Units Owning More Than One Car
and New U.S. Passenger Car Registrations, 1953-63

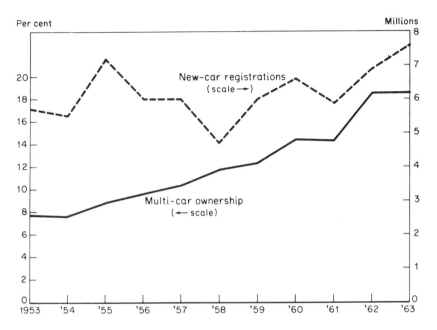

Source: *Ward's Automotive Yearbook;* Survey of Consumer Finances.
Note: A spending unit consists of all related persons living together who pool their incomes.

vision sets are complementary, we should expect known purchases of one to be frequently accompanied by purchase of the other. If the two purchases are substitutes, known purchase of one should be frequently accompanied by failure to purchase the other. In either case, known purchase of the one good should show up as a discriminator. The general failure to do so suggests that the purchases are not generally related in either fashion.

The foregoing analysis highlights the vast complexity of consumer behavior. If we imagine the trees to be employed to predict the behavior of families, it is clear that, regardless of our information, the best bet is that any given family will *not* purchase the durable in question. The rare exceptions are those like the subsample of families who both expect to purchase a washer and whose income is in the $5,000–$7,500 bracket. Since 55 per cent of such families went on to buy a washer, the odds

TABLE 3

Variable List Used in 1957 and 1962-63
Multiple-Ownership Study

Variables	Code Categories
Dependent:	
Whether family owns more than one car	Multiple owner; not multiple owner
Independent:	
Age of head	18-24; 25-34; 35-44; 45-54; 55-64; 65-
Number of children under 18	1; 2; 3; 4; 5; 6; 7; 8 or more
Number of adults	1; 2; 3; 4; 5; 6; 7; 8 or more
Age of the youngest child	Under 2; 2-3; 3-4; 4-5; 5-6; 6-9; 9-14; 14
Age of the oldest child	Under 2; 2-3; 3-4; 4-5; 5-6; 6-9; 9-14; 14
Number of dependents not living in	0; 1; 2; 3 or more
Marital status	Married; not married
Home owner status	Owner; renter
Head self-employed or not	Self-employed; works for someone else
Disposable income	Dollar scale
Percentage income received by wife	Percentage scale
Place of residence	Central cities; urban; rural

of identifying a buyer among them are slightly better than even. The real power of the method lies in its ability to help identify the complex of factors associated with consumer behavior, even though their combined influence is small compared with the total of other things.

III. Multiple-Car Ownership

This section of the paper is an investigation of the phenomenon of the multiple-car-owning family.[6] As shown in Table 2, the percentage of families owning more than one car has more than doubled in the last decade, rising from 7.7 per cent in 1953 to 18.5 per cent in 1963.

[6] There has been survey work done on multiple-car ownership. See Mordechai Kreinin, "Analysis of Used Car Purchases," *Review of Economics and Statistics,* November 1959, pp. 419–425; Mordechai Kreinin and Charles Lininger, "Ownership and Purchases of New Cars in the United States," *International Economic Review,* September 1963, pp. 310–324; John Lansing and Nancy Barth, *Residential Location and Urban Mobility: A Multivariate Analysis,* Survey Research Center, December 1964. Also, see the annual issues of the *Survey of Consumer Finances,* Survey Research Center.

FIGURE 7
Cross-Sectional Characteristics of Multiple-Car Ownership, 1957
(nonowners excluded)

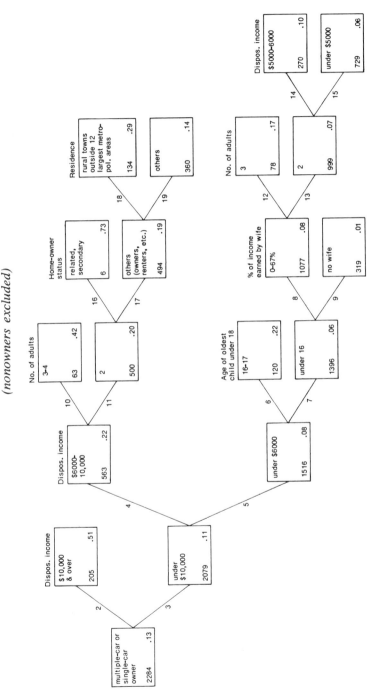

Variation explained: 27 per cent.
Source: 1957 Survey of Consumer Finances. N-3041.

FIGURE 8

Cross-Sectional Characteristics of Multiple-Car Ownership, 1962–63
(nonowners excluded)

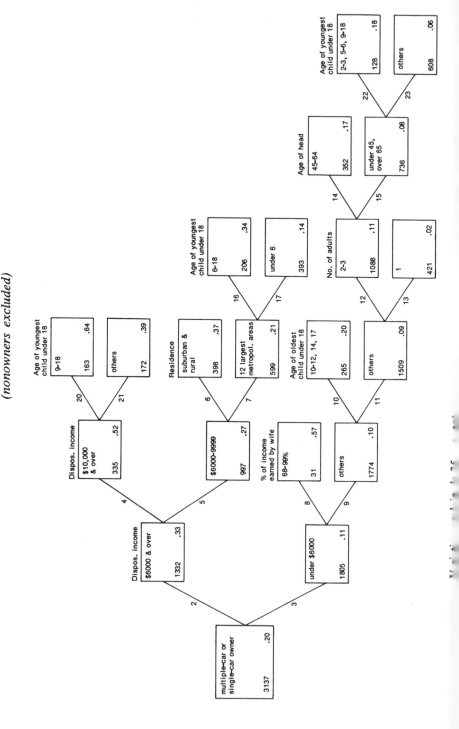

Figure 6 shows the growth in multiple-car-owning families in relation to total new automobile demand.

AID runs were designed to study the cross-sectional characteristics of multiple-car-owning families. The data are from the 1957 Survey of Consumer Finances and the 1962 and 1963 Surveys of Consumer Finances. One AID run was made on the 1957 data. Another, with identical variables, was made on the 1962–63 data. The list of variables is given in Table 3. The runs were designed to study multiple owner-ship among car owners. Therefore, all households that did not own cars (i.e., nonowners) have been excluded from these two runs. The 1957 multiple ownership AID run is in Figure 7. The 1962–63 AID run is in Figure 8.

Both the 1957 and the 1962–63 trees separate households into three income groups: under $6,000, $6,000–$10,000, and $10,000 and over.

TABLE 4

Proportion of Variation Explained by Each Variable in 1957 and 1962-63 Multiple-Ownership Study

(per cent)

	1957	1962 - 63
Age of head	2.1	1.1
Number of children under 18	1.1	4.0
Number of adults	1.5	2.4
Age of youngest child	2.3	5.1
Age of oldest child	2.2	3.4
Number of dependents not living in	.3	.7
Marital status	.3	—
Home-ownership status	.9	1.2
Head self-employed or not	.2	.3
Disposable income	13.0	10.6
Percentage of income received by wife	1.1	3.4
Place of residence	2.5	2.5
Total explained variation	27.3	34.6

Note: Detail may not add to total because of rounding.

[a] $TSS(I)/TSS(T)$ = Percentage of "explained variation" attributable to each predictor (I).

FIGURE 9

Cross-Sectional Characteristics of Multiple-Car Ownership, 1957
(single-car owners excluded)

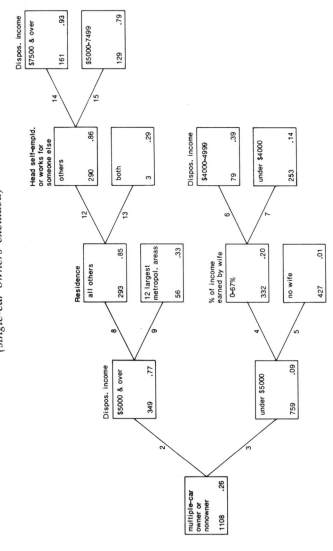

Variation explained: 71 per cent.
Source: 1957 Survey of Consumer Finances. N-3041.

FIGURE 10

Cross-Sectional Characteristics of Multiple-Car Ownership, 1962-63
(single-car owners excluded)

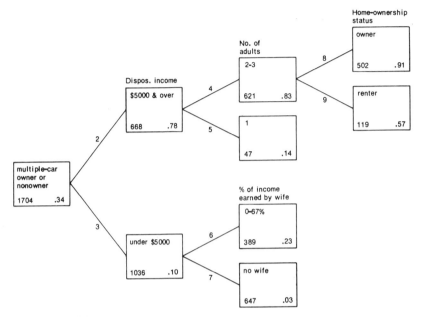

Variation explained: 74 per cent.
Source: 1962-63 Survey of Consumer Finances. N (1962)-2117. N (1963)-2036.

Multiple ownership among low-income families in 1957 is strongly influenced by older children and working wives. The impact of older children is the only major influence on low-income families in 1962–63.

Multiple-car ownership among middle-income families is explained by place of residence in both periods. Disregarding the minor splits in 1957, urban cities outside the twelve largest metropolitan areas and rural towns are the best discriminators. Middle-income households in the central cities are unlikely to be multiple owners. The pattern appears to be stable between 1957 and 1962–63.

Among upper-income groups, the age of older children is important in the 1962–63 tree. The upper-income group is not split in 1957.

The broad characteristics of the AID trees in these two periods are primarily captured by the division of multiple owners into three distinct income classes. In addition, the discriminating features of the three groups are somewhat different. Residence seems to influence middle-income families more than either of the two other income groups, but the impact of children, especially in the teen-age groups, appears in various guises in all income groups. In the 1957 tree, only low-income multiple owners were characterized by children in certain age groups. By 1962–63, the influence of older children was diffused throughout the separate income groups. One way or another, the variables explaining multiple ownership in terms of family composition were more important in 1962–63.

Table 4 shows the partial R^2's, calculated from the two AID trees. These statistics show the relative strength of the variables. A comparison of the variables over time indicates their changing importance. While disposable income is seen to be the single most important factor, it declined in importance between 1957 and 1962–63. The combined set of variables measuring the number and ages of children under 18 rank second to income, and have risen in importance. The wife's contribution to household income has also become more important in distinguishing two-car owners.

As a supplement to the analysis of the distinction between single- and multiple-car owners, it is useful to explore the distinction between multiple-car owners and those households with no car at all. Again, AID trees were created for the two periods, 1957 and 1962–63, with the dependent variable being ownership of more than one car or of no cars. The variables and data were identical to those used in the runs described above. The resulting trees are in Figures 9 and 10.

The remarkable feature of these two trees is the amount of variation explained by the selected predictors: 71 per cent of the variation is explained in 1957, and 74 per cent in 1962–63, percentages that are extremely high for survey data.

Both trees show that approximately 20 per cent of low-income families with working wives are multiple-car owners. There is virtually no multiple-car ownership among low-income families when the wife does not work. Among middle- and upper-income groups, multiple ownership appears to be associated with residence outside the largest metropolitan areas in 1957, but with home ownership in 1962, 1963. Actually, the statistics from the print-out show that the 1957 sample "almost" split on home ownership, which was nearly as powerful as residence with which it is, in any case, highly correlated. Thus, the residence variable masked the influence of home ownership. In the 1962–63 sample, home ownership was sufficiently powerful to cause the split, with place of residence not even "close"; 91 per cent of homeowners in the middle- and upper-income group were multiple-car owners.

FIGURE 11

Factors Related to Becoming a Multiple-Car Owner

(nonowners excluded)

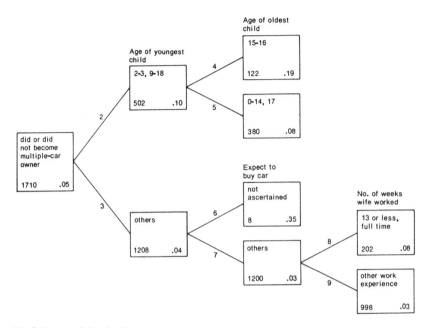

Variation explained: 18 per cent.

Source: 1960-62 Survey of Consumer Finances. N-1059.

The two preceding analyses represent attempts to distinguish the automobile ownership *status* of households. The reinterview character of the 1962–63 survey, however, further permits us to observe eighty-six households in the act of becoming multiple-car owners. Although this is a very small sample of occurrences, it reinforces some of the earlier findings. The analysis is carried out by treating the acquisition of a second car exactly as we did the purchase of a durable in section II above, using the same independent variables. The resulting tree, shown in Figure 11, differs from the other trees in this section in the failure of income, place of residence, and home-ownership status to appear. The only two important factors that seem to distinguish families about to become multiple-car owners from others are the ages of the children and the wife's work status.

This has important consequences for the future of the automobile market. The sharp rise in the teen-age percentage of total population experienced in recent years has been an important factor in the growing proportion of families who are multiple-car owners. This percentage has now almost reached its peak and is no longer making a strong contribution to the growth in multiple-car ownership. On the other hand, the proportion of married women who are employed will doubtless continue to rise for some time and will continue to exert an upward influence on the multiple-car component of total automobile demand. (See Figures 12 and 13.)

FIGURE 12

Percentage of U.S. Population in 10-19 Age Bracket, 1950-75

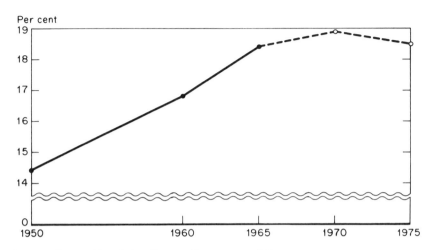

Source: *Current Population Report*, Department of Commerce.

FIGURE 13

Percentage of Married Women in Labor Force, 1950-64

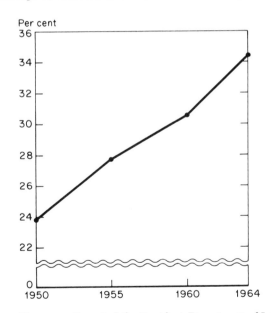

Source: *Manpower Report of the President*, Department of Labor.

A Model of Household Investment
in Financial Assets

ROGER F. MILLER AND HAROLD W. WATTS

UNIVERSITY OF WISCONSIN

I. Introduction

The theory of consumer behavior, generally considered to include household behavior, is elaborately presented in a static, strictly consuming framework in most economic texts. Various more sophisticated aspects of household behavior have been given specialized attention in some texts and journal articles, but for the most part these have been concerned with elucidating some fine theoretical points and providing a research framework for a very limited range of empirical applications.[1]

To a considerable extent, the lack of more ambitious attempts to examine household behavior can be explained by the limitations of available data. More fundamentally, attempts to create richer models run afoul of mathematical intractability or of gross distortion of the richness of alternatives available to humans in their economic activities.[2]

NOTE: The authors acknowledge substantial assistance from the following organizations: the Social Systems Research Institute, Wisconsin Alumni Research Foundation, and State of Wisconsin, all through the University of Wisconsin; the National Bureau of Economic Research; the Brookings Institution; the Ford Foundation; and the National Science Foundation. They have not only supported the authors in their endeavors, they have also helped to finance the data acquisition program which makes implementation of a model of the scope encompassed in this paper possible. (See footnote 3 below.) In addition, we are indebted to many of our colleagues for their support and aid, in particular to Guy Orcutt and Martin David.

[1] See the references cited in the Bibliography at the end of the paper.

[2] Especially compare the articles by Bear [1] and Miller [6] cited in the Bibliography.

The Social Systems Research Institute at the University of Wisconsin is developing a library with extremely rich data, especially on a very large shifting panel of households over a period of thirteen or more years, with emphasis on assets and incomes data matched from various sources.[3] To take full advantage of these data when they become completely available for analysis, we consider it important to have a fairly detailed model of household behavior with respect to the available variables.

In particular, we wish to focus on explaining the choices individuals make with respect to ownership of financial assets, and with respect to use of their time. We need a model that simultaneously determines the size, composition, changes, and management of portfolios, as well as other productive expenditures of effort, all at a given time (or short period) and also over time. We wish to explore the cumulative effect of time spent in various activities such as portfolio management, the effects of aging, and cross-sectional as well as longitudinal differences in behavior associated with different demographic positions at one time and over time.

For example, increased effort on portfolio management may result in the investor choosing more rationally among alternative investments in the capital market. It is also true that the effort and attention required to manage a portfolio in an optimal fashion are substitutes for other income-producing activities of the individual, such as overtime or secondary employment. Indeed, to the extent that tax considerations increase the relative rewards of portfolio management and induce persons to devote more attention to it, the increased rationality of their decisions *may* increase real productivity enough to compensate for the loss of product entailed in their foregone alternative work plus any ill effects of tax-induced misallocation of financial resources.

We consider our "model investor" to be an expected utility maximizer with a horizon extending to his death. More shortsighted individuals can be subsumed in the model by giving them a high rate of discounting future satisfactions. A person's utility depends upon his consumption, upon the use he makes of his time, and upon his estate value at time of death. To maximize his expected utility, he makes a plan for his entire

[3] The Wisconsin Assets and Income Studies within the Institute are bringing together detailed income tax records with sample survey data, social security data, and other sources, matched up by name, address, and social security number. Tax data for 1947–59 have been collected and are in the final stages of processing. A large, stratified subsample of Wisconsin taxpayers has been interviewed and the data are nearly ready for integration with tax data.

future, but this plan is subject to constant revision as his circumstances and information vary.

In formulating this model, it became clear that the more or less discrete behavior of individuals existing in continuous time raised problems that neither continuous-action models nor discrete-period models could handle adequately. For those activities in which timing is of the essence, such as trading in assets, both the discreteness and timing of actions are variables that must be determined within a model which also recognizes the continuity of time and the near continuity of many personal actions or external events (such as price quoting on a stock exchange). To capture these features, we have dichotomized the model. Section II below is concerned with the long-range planning of broadly conceived over-all decision problems, while section III presents a model of short-run suboptimizing behavior with regard to portfolio composition changes. In so doing, we have been more concerned to explicate than to manipulate the model and its two complementary parts. In section IV we make some comments on features of the model and tentatively advance some potential hypotheses that the model may produce.

We have tried to embrace in our model many of the features of some of the more limited models in the recent literature, the most important of which are listed in the Bibliography at the end of the paper. To avoid drawing attention to the violence we may have done to the work of other scholars in the process of our synthetic translation, we make no specific references or parallels with these works. Our indebtedness to others in this present endeavor is nonetheless warmly acknowledged.

II. The Household's Over-All Decision Problems

In general, we will not distinguish single-person from multiple-person households. For the latter, we disregard the problem of combining the preferences of the individual household members into a single, well-behaved preference function for the household as a unit. For the major economic decisions we wish to discuss, this appears to be an acceptable simplification. The principal income earner is likely to be the principal investment decision-maker and is likely to be the most heavily insured family member. It is this "head of the family," born at $t = 0$, to whom we refer principally in what follows when we speak of a "person's" decisions.

This does not mean that we disregard the fact that the family head's decision will be affected by the structure of the household. For any one household at any one time, we take as given the age, sex, and relationship composition of that household. Similarly we take the head's principal occupation and job as given, as well as his age and education cohort, and his history of the use of his time and of his past investments. These things are very important in explaining cross-sectional variations and will also vary over time for a given household. Such uncertainty as the planner may have with respect to these changes over time will not be considered to affect his current plans.

Further, we ignore problems of the composition of consumption, at any one time and over all time, by assuming that the allocation of consumption expenditures among commodities can be treated as an independent suboptimizing problem. We will, however, define a price index of consumption commodities for any time τ, $P_c(t, \tau)$, which is assumed to be computed with weights corresponding to the amounts of commodities the particular household actually consumes or plans to consume at time τ, relative to the base prices for this same bundle of goods at time t. If we then define $C(t, \tau)$ as the total amount of the household's planned consumption expenditures at τ, the plan being made at t, the "real" consumption expected for τ is

$$\gamma(t, \tau) = \frac{C(t, \tau)}{\bar{P}_c(t, \tau)}, \tag{1}$$

where $\bar{P}_c(t, \tau)$ is the household's expected value of the future price index. The latter results from integrating the household's price index over all possible future consumption good price configurations (each computed with different weights as the consumption pattern changes appropriately), each such index multiplied by the subjective probability density that the household assigns to that particular price configuration.

Finally, we will assume that problems of evaluating, investing in, and subsequently consuming the services of durable consumers goods are completely subsumed in the above suboptimization process. This means, among other things, that the decision to live in and enjoy the services of a particular home is being considered as independent of the decision to invest in the title to the home: 200 year leases which lapse at the death of the head (or of his surviving spouse) are available as alternative ways of acquiring the services of the home. The investment in the title to the home is thus a separate financial investment.

In addition to deciding on consumption expenditure, the household chooses an allocation of time amongst a variety of activities. The principal occupation of the head being given, the household decides on other employment (including both overtime or a second job for the head, as well as employment of the other household members), on home management (including maintenance), on portfolio management, on time spent on education, and on pure leisure time, including time spent in pure consumption. In addition, the household may hire labor services from nonhousehold members, to aid in either home or portfolio management. If we let $L(t, \tau)$ be the vector of planned (at t) allocation of time (at τ) amongst all possible uses, and $\bar{y}(t, \tau)$ the vector of expected direct financial remunerations for the corresponding elements of $L(t, \tau)$, then the expected budget restraint for τ will include $L(t, \tau)' \bar{y}(t, \tau)$. Elements of $\bar{y}$ for employment outside the home will be positive, those for purchasing of outside labor will be negative, and those for pure consumption will be zero. Those for education may have any real number as a value, depending upon whether the receipts of scholarship or fellowship awards exceed tuition and other educational costs or not. Elements of $\bar{y}$ for portfolio management will be zero, although there exists a shadow price or wage rate based on the effect such activity has on the income from the portfolio itself.

In addition to its role in the budget constraint, $L(t, \tau)$ enters into another set of constraints which recognize that total time is limited, that some opportunities are not available, and that some activities overlap or otherwise interact. Formally, we define $R(t, \tau)$ as a matrix of constraint coefficients and require that

$$R(t, \tau) \, L(t, \tau) \leq \underline{0}, \tag{2}$$

where $\underline{0}$ is the null vector. In order for this formulation to be satisfactory, we require that the first element of the L be the constant "one" (so that the first element of $\bar{y}$ is "zero"), to allow for a vector of restraint constants as the first column of R. If L is an $n \times 1$ vector, R is $m \times n$, and $m > n$.

We regard the restraints in (2) as of considerable importance for our model and wish to provide some additional analysis with respect to the matrix R. For any given arbitrary interval $d\tau$, the integral of $\iota' L(t, \tau)$ is restricted to the total amount of time available to all household members over the interval, where ι is the $n \times 1$ vector of ones for household members' times and zeros for purchased times and for the initial element. One row of R will, therefore, be ι' with the initial element being replaced by a number whose integral is the negative of that total amount of available time. Naturally, that initial element will itself vary with the composition of the household and so is variable over time. If a subset of elements of L relates to a given member of the household, a similar restraint in R could be formulated for that person alone. If there is one such special restraint for each household member (as there should be), then the row of R described in the second and third sentences of this paragraph would simply be the summation of the individuals' restraints, redundant (not independent), and could be dispensed with.

In addition, there may be effective upper and lower limits to the quantity of time that can be spent by one household in any activity. This is probably the case with home management, so that there will be one row of R with a negative first element and positive coefficients for each person's home management function, including those of hired servants, plumbers, etc., and also a row of R with a positive first element (smaller than the absolute value of the negative first element in the row just discussed) and with negative coefficients for each person's home management activity. The first of these rows recognizes the upper limit, the second recognizes the lower limit on the amount of home management needed. The sizes of the upper and lower limits are determined by the size of the household, its aggregate consumption, etc., all of which vary over time. Similarly, the coefficients will be different from one another to the extent that persons in the household are not equally efficient in carrying out home management tasks. Because these relative efficiencies will not be constant for all household tasks, separate restraints of this nature are required for each task for which the coefficients are recognized to be different. Furthermore, the distribution of capability for performing these tasks varies over time as children mature and are trained, etc., so that the coefficients themselves are variable over time.

If a person is completely unqualified for a particular type of activity, he has no opportunity to use his time in that activity. For such a person, there is a row of R with all zeros except for a positive coefficient in the column corresponding to the location of the element of L for that activity by that person. If more than one person in the household is similarly limited with respect to a particular occupation, a similar single restraint will handle all of them at once since a subset of the restraints are non-negativity restraints (requiring all elements of L to be nonnegative). If a person becomes qualified by education and experience for a job he could not have held before, his separate restraint changes (acquires a negative first element) as a function of this past use of his time in education and work.

Even the restraints recognizing a limited amount of total time available need not have unitary coefficients. Activities can be performed simultaneously (e.g., a routine home management task such as paying the bills may take place concurrently with such pure consumption activities as listening to a Bartok composition and consuming gin and bitter lemon). An added complication is the interaction of these activities (excessive consumption of gin might prevent the person from seeing the bills for which he is trying to write checks). Such nonlinear terms are not directly incorporated into the restraint in (2) above. Since we have already noted that R is a function of past activities, however, such interactions can be incorporated into an explicit expression for this effect:

$$R(t, \tau) = \Gamma[L(\nu, \tau); t; \tau], \qquad (3)$$

which incorporates within it a lag operator or other integral of elements of L over the interval $0 < \nu < \tau$.

We have been using a notation which indicates that consumption and time use are continuous in time. In fact, of course, persons carry out more or less discrete activities in a continuous time space. Consumption and time use are not highly variable activities, for a given household over time, however, and we think it does little violence to reality to treat these activities as average flow rates over time. When it comes to trading in assets, however, discreteness of activity is an important feature of the decision processes we wish to describe. Between transactions, the holding of assets is a truly continuous activity. Asset prices vary over time in a very nearly continuous fashion. Buying and selling assets, however, are highly discrete activities in which timing is of the essence. Indeed, the interval between transactions is a variable which itself needs explanation. The major problems of portfolio management per se are postponed to the next section, where they are dealt with in a suboptimizing model. For the moment we are concerned only with the flow of cash income in τ in the form of interest and dividends, as anticipated in t— $D(t, \tau)$; the "flows" of net long- and short-term realized capital gains— $G(t, \tau)$ and $H(t, \tau)$ respectively; the flow of total appreciation due to price changes—$A(t, \tau)$; the total value of the portfolio in τ—$V(t, \tau)$; the flow of current (at τ) saving into the portfolio—$S(t, \tau)$; and the effort expended in portfolio management (an element, say $L_n(t, \tau)$, in the L vector).

All these scalars are intimately related. Furthermore, to the extent that they are future values, they are not known with certainty, but the decision-maker for the household has a subjective probability distribution over future prices and dividends that, evaluated in terms of his past portfolio management experience and current information, allows him to make subjective probability statements about certain rates of change or flow. The detailed portfolio management model of the next section elucidates the shorter-run, day-to-day activity of the household's "investment manager," but in the model of this section we are more concerned with the complete consumption and long-run investment plans of the household. Clearly these are interdependent models and must be consistent in any statements about the household's behavior.

For the purposes of this section, we regard the portfolio as a wholly owned mutual investment fund corporation, for which the investment manager of the household is the chairman of the board. The corporation will experience and realize capital gains and losses at unknown dates but at reasonably predictable long-term rates. The corporation's rate of dividend receipt is more predictable in both amount and time. In this section, we consider these rates to be net of all portfolio transactions costs except the capital gains tax.

Let $x_d(t, \tau)$ be the rate of cash income yield from the portfolio in τ as anticipated in t. The household's planner has a cumulative subjective probability distribution function over all possible values of $x_d(t, \tau)$ which is implicitly dependent upon his experience and information and explicitly dependent upon his cumulative lifetime amount of effort at portfolio management to τ, the rate of flow of new savings into the portfolio to τ, the total value of the portfolio in τ, and the time interval $(\tau - t)$:

$$\text{Prob } [x_d(t, \tau) \leq x_d^*] = X_d\left[x_d^*; \int_0^\tau L_n(t, v)\, dv; \int_t^\tau S(t, v)\, dv; \right.$$
$$\left. V(t, \tau); (\tau - t) \right] \quad (4)$$

The mean value of $x_d(t, \tau)$ is then

$$\bar{x}_d(t, \tau) = \int_{\text{(all } x_d^*)} x_d(t, \tau)\, dX_d[\ \ ]. \quad (5)$$

Let X_{di} represent the partial derivative of $X_d[\ \ ]$ with respect to the ith argument as they are arranged in (4). We hypothesize that

$$X_{di}\begin{Bmatrix}\geq 0\\ < 0\end{Bmatrix} \text{ as } i = \begin{Bmatrix}1\\ 2, 3, 4\end{Bmatrix} \text{ and as, for } i = 5,\ x_d^*\begin{Bmatrix}< \bar{x}_d(t, \tau)\\ > \bar{x}_d(t, \tau)\end{Bmatrix} \quad (6)$$

in such a manner that, for $\bar{x}_{di}(t, \tau)$ being the partial derivative of $\bar{x}_d(t, \tau)$ with respect to the ith argument of $X_d[\ \ ]$,

$$\bar{x}_{di}(t, \tau)\begin{Bmatrix}\geq 0\\ = 0\end{Bmatrix} \text{ as } i = \begin{Bmatrix}2, 3, 4\\ 5\end{Bmatrix} \quad (7)$$

and so that the variance of $x_d(t, \tau)$, defined in the usual way as

$$\text{Var}\,[x_d(t, \tau)] = \int\limits_{(\text{all } x_d{}^*)} [x_d(t, \tau) - \bar{x}_d(t,\tau)]^2\, dX_d[\quad], \tag{8}$$

has partial derivatives with respect to the $i = 2, \ldots 5$ arguments of $X_d[\quad]$ of

$$\text{Var}_i\,[x_d(t, \tau)] \begin{Bmatrix} > 0 \\ \leq 0 \end{Bmatrix} \text{ as } i = \begin{Bmatrix} 5 \\ 2, 3, 4 \end{Bmatrix}. \tag{9}$$

Finally, we also assume that all changes in the person's information state not subsumed under the second argument of $X_d[\quad]$ are anticipated to be purely random future shocks whose effects are already taken into account in the fact that the variance defined in (8) is positive for all $\tau > t$. The person is aware of his past and present experience, however, so that the variance in (8) is zero for $\tau \leq t$, and indeed,

$$\mathop{\text{Lim}}_{(t \to \tau;\ t < \tau)} \text{Var}\,[x_d(t, \tau)] = 0. \tag{10}$$

At the present time we leave open the question as to whether or not, for larger $\tau - t > 0$, the effects of arguments 2–4 of $X_d[\quad]$ can offset the effects of argument 5 in (9) above: as $t \to \tau$, the approach of Var $[x_d(t, \tau)]$ to zero may not be monotonic for all initial values of $\tau - t$. In part this reflects the fact that arguments 2–4 in $X_d[\quad]$ are controllable by the portfolio manager, within the limits of his constraints.

For a given value of $V(t, \tau) = V^*$ then, the flow of $D(t, \tau)$ is itself a variable with a subjective probability distribution, for

$$D(t, \tau) = x_d(t, \tau)V^*. \tag{11}$$

However, $V(t, \tau)$ is not a fixed value in general; its variability is expounded below. Before proceeding, however, we can define $x_a(t, \tau)$, $x_g(t, \tau)$, and $x_h(t, \tau)$ as rates of total appreciation and rates of net long- and short-term gain realization, respectively, similarly to $x_d(t, \tau)$ so that

$$A(t,\tau) = x_a(t, \tau)V^*,$$
$$G(t,\tau) = x_g(t, \tau)V^*, \text{ and} \tag{12}$$
$$H(t,\tau) = x_h(t, \tau)V^*.$$

With suitable change in subscripts from d to a, g, and h, all statements (4)–(10) can be repeated as statements (4)′–(10)′, (4)″–(10)″, and (4)‴–(10)‴ respectively, with precisely the same form and content (but not identical $X[\quad]$ functions) with the following exceptions:

$$X_{g3} \geq 0 \text{ so that} \tag{6a''}$$
$$\bar{x}_{g3}(t, \tau) \leq 0. \tag{7a''}$$

The statements in the preceding paragraphs are the result of much of the thinking that went into the formulation of the suboptimizing portfolio management model of section III below, and detailed justification is not called for in this section. They seem plausible enough to use without the suboptimizing model to justify their use in any event.

From a short-run point of view we do not regard the face or cash values of the household's insurance as part of its portfolio that needs management in the sense of our suboptimizing model. These values are thus not included in $V(t, \tau)$. Generally they represent long-run contractual arrangements. However, we do include any borrowings against the cash value in the debt portion of $V(t, \tau)$: any lender is interested in the net worth of the borrower, dead or alive, and the pledge of specific assets against particular borrowings is primarily a means of obtaining preferred interest rates, whether the asset be cash value of insurance, market value of a home, or marketable securities.

Denote by $N(t, \tau)$ the face value of the head's insurance contracts that he plans at t to have at τ, let

$$\eta(t, \tau) = \eta[N, t, \tau] \tag{13}$$

be the percentage of $N(t, \tau)$ that will be accumulated cash value rather than pure insurance at τ, and let

$$M(t, \tau) = m[\eta, t, \tau] \tag{14}$$

be the per dollar premium on N payable in τ. Naturally, if anyone could predict with certainty the day upon which they would become uninsurable (with the actual date of death as the extreme case for a person otherwise healthy), they would wait until the "last moment" before taking out insurance. Uncertainty with respect to insurability is of the essence of insuring. Finally, let $\theta(t, \tau)$ be the "pure (instant term) insurance" premium per dollar of face value minus cash value at τ. Thus the individual at t plans to pay a premium of $[M(t, \tau)N(t, \tau)]$ at τ, of which $\left\{\theta(t, \tau)[1 - \eta(t, \tau)]N(t, \tau)\right\}$ is the cost of the pure insurance he purchases at τ, the difference being an amount of saving by investing in cash value, in order to purchase a contract paying $N(t, \tau)$ in the event of death at τ, with $[\eta(t, \tau)N(t, \tau)]$ being the amount of $N(t, \tau)$ representing an accumulation of savings in the insurance contracts. In addition, the person receives nontaxable current (at τ) income, denoted $Y_N(t, \tau)$:

$$Y_N(t, \tau) = \left\{\frac{d\eta}{d\tau} - M(t, \tau) + \theta(t, \tau)[1 - \eta(t, \tau)]\right\}N(t, \tau). \tag{15}$$

This is simply the excess of the current increase of cash value above the current premium net of current pure insurance costs. (It is important to recall that t, τ, and v are "age dates" rather than calendar dates, where $t = 0$ at the time of the birth of the head of household.)

If we let $Z_w[W(t, \tau)]$ represent the estate tax on a net-of-tax estate value of $W(t, \tau)$ which would be left by the head of household were he to die at τ, then this net estate bequeathed is

$$W(t, \tau) = V(t, \tau) + N(t, \tau) - Z_w[W(t, \tau)]. \tag{16}$$

Let

$$U_w(t, \tau) = U_w[W(t, \tau)] \tag{17}$$

represent the utility which the head of household foresees (at t) himself as receiving (at τ) by being able to leave a net estate worth $W(t, \tau)$ should he die at τ. Let $\beta(t, \tau)$ be a subjective discounting function for future bequesting utility to bring it to a current present value, and let $\pi(t, \tau)$ be the conditional probability density of dying at τ given that the person is alive at t. Then the conditional probability that the person will live to τ, given that he is alive at t, is

$$\Omega(t, \tau) = \int_{v=\tau}^{\infty} \pi(t, v)\, dv = 1 - \int_{v=t}^{\tau} \pi(t, v)\, dv. \tag{18}$$

This is the probability that the individual will be able to enjoy the household consumption and activity at τ, at which time he presently looks forward to receiving $U_c(t, \tau)$ utility, where

$$U_c(t, \tau) = U_c[\gamma(t, \tau); L(t, \tau)]. \tag{19}$$

Let $\alpha(t, \tau)$ be a subjective discounting function for future consumption and time use utility to bring it to a current present value. If T is an age beyond which the person cannot expect to live, then the present value at t of his expected utility for his remaining lifetime is

$$U_T(t) = \int_t^T \left\{ \Omega(t, \tau)\alpha(t, \tau)U_c(t, \tau) + \pi(t, \tau)\beta(t, \tau)U_w(t, \tau) \right\} d\tau. \tag{20}$$

The person seeks to maximize $U_T(t)$ by his choices of all decision variables subject to his constraints, and in the light of his anticipations of future changes in those variables over which he has no control. We now turn to the task of completing the formulation of those constraints.

A person alive at t and expecting to be alive at τ anticipates paying taxes (at τ) on his consumption purchases, property, ordinary income, and long-term capital gains income, in the aggregate amount of

$$Z(t, \tau) = Z_c[C(t, \tau)] + Z_p[q(t, \tau); p(t, \tau)]$$
$$+ Z_y[Y_L(t, \tau) + Y_h(t, \tau) + D(t, \tau)] \tag{21}$$
$$+ Z_g[Z'_y(t, \tau); G(t, \tau); H(t, \tau)],$$

respectively, where $q(t, \tau)$ is a vector of asset quantities and $p(t, \tau)$ is the corresponding vector of asset market values; where $Y_L(t, \tau)$ is household income from employment net of the deductible portion of outside labor wages paid; where $Y_h(t, \tau)$ is the amount of short-term capital gains income that is legally includable in net taxable income:

$$Y_h(t, \tau) = Y_h[H(t, \tau); G(t, \tau)]; \tag{22}$$

and where $Z'_y(t, \tau)$ is the derivative of the $Z_y[\ ]$ function (the marginal tax rate on ordinary income).

Recognizing total rather than just taxable income (except for imputed incomes which are instantly identically consumed), an "instantaneous" budget identity for a household at τ is

$$S(t, \tau) \equiv L(t, \tau)'y(t, \tau) + A(t, \tau) + D(t, \tau) + Y_N(t, \tau) \tag{23}$$
$$- Z(t, \tau) - C(t, \tau) - M(t, \tau)N(t, \tau)$$

which also defines the anticipated time rate of savings net of insurance premiums as a function of other, previously defined flows. Since

$$\frac{d}{d\tau} V(t, \tau) = S(t, \tau) \quad \text{and} \tag{24}$$

$$\int_{v=t}^{\tau} \frac{d}{d\tau} V(t, v)\, dv = V(t, \tau) - V(t, t),$$

we have, for a person living through any given interval from t to τ,

$$V(t, \tau) = V(t, t) + \int_t^\tau L(t, v)'y(t, v)\, dv + \int_t^\tau A(t, v)\, dv + \int_t^\tau D(t, v)\, dv$$

$$+ \int_t^\tau Y_N(t, v)\, dv - \int_t^\tau Z(t, v)\, dv - \int_t^\tau C(t, v)\, dv \tag{25}$$

$$- \int_t^\tau M(t, v)N(t, v)\, dv.$$

This expression is deceptively simple since the third, fourth, and sixth terms on the right-hand side of (25) all involve the intermediate values of $V(t, v)$. An expression such as (25) exists for each sequence of intermediate values, of course, and by substitution we may obtain a differential equation involving simply the household's initial asset position, its choice variables through time, and the unknown and exogenously determined price vectors. There is a joint probability density function over the values of the unknown price vectors; the conditional densities may be multiplied into the appropriate terms in (25) and the resulting expression integrated over all possible values of the price vectors for any given $V(t, t)$ and given set of time paths of the decision variables; this yields an expected value of the portfolio, $\bar{V}(t, \tau)$, as a function of $V(t, t)$, the time paths of the decision variables, and the moments of the future price density function. Given $V(t, t)$, therefore we can associate a distribution function on $V(t, \tau)$ with each time path of the decision variables. The household then chooses that time path to T of the decision variables that maximizes its total expected utility in (20) subject to the expected budget restraint derived from (25), the expectation of the bequest restraint in (16), the expected time use restraints in (2), and the additional set of nonnegativity restraints:

$$\left\{ \begin{array}{l} q(t, \tau) \geq \underline{0} \\ c(t, \tau) \geq \underline{0} \\ V(t, \tau) \geq 0 \\ N(t, \tau) \geq 0 \end{array} \right\} \text{ and } \left\} \text{ for all } t \leq \tau \leq T, \right. \tag{26}$$

where $c(t, \tau)$ is a vector of consumption quantities.

Among other things, the above model determines the flow of funds from current employment income into the portfolio's total value as

$$Q(t, \tau) = S(t, \tau) - A(t, \tau) - D(t, \tau), \tag{27}$$

the flow of portfolio management labor through time, $L_n(t, \tau)$, and the marginal tax rates applicable to short- and long-term capital gains. All of these quantities are taken as given in the short-run portfolio management model presented in the next section. The utility function used there is also considered to have been derived from that in (20), recognizing that accumulated assets may be used both for financing future consumption and for providing a larger bequest.

III. A Submodel of Dynamic Portfolio Adjustment

PRELIMINARY REMARKS

This section develops a model for exploring a particular subgroup of the household's economic decisions, namely, its selection of an investment portfolio. The investor *qua* household decision-maker has the problem of allocating a given stock of accumulated resources among alternative forms of wealth. At any point in time, the current allocation will depend on past decisions. The question the investor must continually answer is whether there is a transaction at the present moment which would improve upon the current allocation in terms of the long-run objectives of the household. The model that follows provides a particular structure for analyzing this set of decisions.

THE ELEMENTARY TRANSACTION DECISION IN THE PURE APPRECIATION CASE

The model will be developed from a relatively simple decision problem. An investor has a particular inventory of assets at time t, the present. These assets are continuously divisible, have market-determined prices which vary continuously through time. No asset provides a current flow of income, and no asset has a fixed price.[4] All alternative assets have these same characteristics. The investor has a set of probability beliefs about the prices in the future and he must decide to retain his current portfolio or make a specific transaction.

The current portfolio may be described by a vector $q(t)$ with non-negative elements $q_i(t)$ denoting the number of units of asset i held at t. This vector remains constant over time except for discrete changes, $\triangle q(t)$, called transactions. The following identity holds for a sufficiently small ϵ:

$$q(t + \epsilon) = q(t) + \Delta q(t). \tag{28}$$

The prices of the assets at time t are described by the vector $p(t) = \{p_i(t)\}$. The current "value" of the portfolio, $V(t)$, may now be defined as:

$$V(t) = q'(t)p(t). \tag{29}$$

Except for the existence of transactions costs, any portfolio which has the same current value as $q(t)$ could be obtained by a suitable transaction. That is, any transaction, Δq, which satisfies $\Delta q'p(t) = 0$ and $\Delta q + q(t) \geq \underline{0}$ (all elements nonnegative) would be "feasible." If transaction costs are covered by the proceeds of the sale(s) involved in a transaction, the alternative transactions feasible at time t will satisfy

$$\Delta q'p(t) + K(\Delta q) = 0, \text{ and} \tag{30a}$$

$$\Delta q + q(t) \geq \underline{0}, \tag{30b}$$

---

[4] The market prices are expressed in terms of a bundle of consumption goods— they are "real" prices.

where $K(\Delta q)$ is the cost of transactions function. The function $K(\Delta q)$ is discontinuous at $\Delta q = \underline{0}$, i.e.:

$$K(\underline{0}) = 0 \tag{31a}$$

$$\lim_{k \to 0} K(k\Delta q) > 0, \tag{31b}$$

for all $\Delta q \neq \underline{0}$.

The cost function increases for larger transactions but not in proportion to the size. More precisely:

$$K(\Delta q) < K(k\Delta q) < kK(\Delta q) \tag{31c}$$

for all $\Delta q \neq \underline{0}$ and $k > 1$.

The investor's probability beliefs at time t about future prices are summarized in a sequence of subjective probability distributions:

$$F(p; t, \tau) = Pr[p(\tau) \leq p], \tau \geq t. \tag{32}$$

These probability distributions are conditioned by the investor's experience and the information available to him including, among many other things, the history of prices up to time t. At time $t + \triangle t$ new information will have been generated and the probability beliefs will be altered. The means of these distributions are specified to have the same property of continuity in time as the actual prices. This can be formalized as follows:

let

$$\bar{p}(t, \tau) = \int_{\text{all } p} p \, dF(p; t, \tau) \tag{32a}$$

and require that

$$\lim_{\tau \to t} \bar{p}(t, \tau) = p(t) \text{ and}$$

$$\lim_{t \to t'} \bar{p}(t, \tau) = p_t(t', \tau).$$

Any linear combination of future prices and, in particular, the future value of an arbitrary portfolio, q, will have mean

$$\bar{V}(t, \tau) = q'\bar{p}(t, \tau) \tag{32b}$$

and this will have similar continuity properties. The variance of the value of a portfolio in the subjective probability distribution is given by:

$$\text{Var}\,[V(t, \tau)] = \int_p [q'(p - \bar{p}(t, \tau))]^2 dF(p; t, \tau). \tag{32c}$$

The notion of increasing uncertainty about increasingly more remote events can be expressed through the further requirement that:

$$\frac{d \operatorname{Var} [V(t, \tau)]}{d\tau} > 0. \tag{32d}$$

An additional property, which is suggested by the notion of continuous price variation, is:

$$\lim_{\tau \to t} \operatorname{Var} [V(t, \tau)] = 0. \tag{32e}$$

The utility of the portfolio is a function of its value at each point in time and does not, given the value, depend on the composition. This utility function is derived from the over-all decision problem of the household in which the portfolio value is among the constraining resources for consumption and bequest plans. The utility of a given portfolio value V at time τ in the future will be denoted:

$$U(V; t, \tau). \tag{33}$$

This function is assumed to be monotonic, increasing in V for any given set of values for the other variables in the over-all optimization.

The expected utility at time τ from a constant portfolio q is simply:

$$\bar{U}(q; t, \tau) = \int U(q'p; t, \tau) \, dF(p; t, \tau). \tag{34}$$

The investor is assumed to focus on a particular average of these expected utilities:

$$\bar{\bar{U}}(q; a(h), t) = \int_0^\infty a(h) \bar{U}(q; t) \, t + h, \, dh, \tag{35}$$

where

$$a(h) \geq 0 \text{ for all } h \text{ and } \int_0^\infty a(h) \, dh = 1. \tag{36}$$

This is the criterion he uses for evaluating alternatives available to him. At time t the investor has the portfolio $q(t)$. He will choose the transaction $\triangle q$ which maximizes $\bar{\bar{U}}(q(t) + \triangle q; a(h), t)$ subject to the constraints (30a)–(30b). The discontinuity of the cost function, $K(\triangle q)$, prevents a simple use of calculus to describe the maximizing conditions. Most of the maximizing transactions will be at "corners," with all or most of the elements of $\triangle q$ equal to zero. As usual in such cases, there will be a certain range of price expectations, and utility functions for that matter, within which the maximizing value of $\triangle q$ will be unchanged.

The weighting function $a(h)$ may now be given a more complete rationalization. The investor operating in a world of uncertainty can be fairly confident of one thing—namely, that any portfolio he chooses at present will not continue to be the best available one as time passes and further information on prices and other matters accumulates. He may anticipate with confidence that sooner or later a further transaction, not now apparent, will be in order. One may interpret the $a(h)$ function as a subjective density function on the random interval from any point in time to the next time a transaction (other than the trivial no-change transaction) will become advantageous. He then chooses as a proximate goal to have as much value as possible to allocate at that time. Given this interpretation an average "horizon" may be defined as:

$$\bar{h} = \int_0^\infty ha(h)\,dh. \tag{37}$$

The distribution $a(h)$ is regarded as a characteristic of a particular investor. Further discussion of the relation between $a(h)$, or descriptive summaries of it, and other characteristics of the investor will be presented below.

Briefly, the investor is continuously revising his subjective probability distribution of future prices as more and more of the future passes into history. Other aspects of his economic situation may alter and hence change his utility of portfolio value functions. When these variations make it advantageous to carry out a transaction, he does so. Clearly this will happen only when the average expected utility is greater for some altered portfolio than for the current one in spite of the fact that the immediate result of carrying out the transaction will be a reduction of the real value of the portfolio by the amount of the transaction cost.

INCOME-PRODUCING ASSETS

So far the assets considered have been of a very simple sort. The prices of the assets and their relative variation provided the only basis for gain (or loss). It will be argued below that the addition of dividends does not alter the essential features of the model.

One of the assets, say, the first, can be considered to be cash. If the other assets yield dividends, they are assumed to be paid on periodic dates, say, each quarter. The dividend consists of a payment of cash to the holders of each asset in proportion to their holdings. It is clear that the value of each unit of each asset will fall by the amount of its respective dividend at the time the sales are made ex-dividend. This discontinuous break in the market prices does not, however, immediately affect the value of the investor's portfolio. His cash holding is larger and the total value of his dividend paying assets is smaller.

This suggests an alternative way of describing a dividend payment, i.e., as a cost-free and involuntary transaction in which a part of each asset is sold for cash. The investor who receives d_i dollars for each unit of his holding of asset i can regard the quantity of the ith asset as having been reduced by a factor $[1 - (p_0 d_i / p_i)]$ where p_0 is the real value of a dollar. This viewpoint requires some adjustment in the interpretation of units and prices. In the previous section the prices were market prices per unit of the asset and the units corresponded to usual notions of corporate "shares." Now the unit of the asset is more elastic—it can be taken to correspond to the share between any adjacent dividend dates, but it must be redefined as a larger number of corporate shares when a dividend is paid. The price per unit becomes continuous through dividend dates by this process. For purposes of relating to actual market prices of corporate shares, the reinterpreted price corresponds roughly to the share price at time t plus all dividends paid since the unit was equal to the corporate share.

The investor at time t, while reviewing his holdings and considering alternatives, may be regarded now as holding probability beliefs about both prices and dividends at future dates. These probability beliefs can be viewed as the product of a conditional distribution of dividend payments given prices and the marginal distribution of prices (the continuous ones). The objective function can now be expressed in parts, each representing the interval between dividend dates, and the portfolio in each interval reflecting the effect of the involuntary transactions implied by the dividend payments.

An approximation can be obtained by replacing the uncertain dividends by their conditional expectations, given prices, and then integrating over the future prices, as before, to find the expected utility. It is argued that the residual uncertainty about the exact size of the fractional adjustments in portfolio composition occasioned by dividend payments is of minor importance and that the primary source of uncertainty is the unknown future prices, including any distribution of cash. Following this argument, one can reinterpret the price vector in such a way as to include income-producing assets in the basic model without any further modification.

TRANSFERS BETWEEN PORTFOLIO AND CURRENT ACCOUNTS

A primary function of the portfolio is to receive the resources currently earned by nonportfolio activities of the household in excess of current consumption (or to disburse for covering a deficiency). The amounts of such transfers are determined by the household in allocating its expected total resources over its lifetime, including its opportunity to earn a return on invested resources. The portfolio allocation model will regard the schedule of transfers as exogenously determined at the time the household is considering possible transactions. The same average expected utility can be maximized, with the additional feature that there are discrete additions to or subtractions from the cash component at particular points in future time. There is no essential change in the constraint function, except that the total value to be allocated will change discontinuously at transfer dates.

It does not follow, of course, that the portfolio composition will not depend upon the presence of such transfers. A flow of cash into the portfolio allows for a limited amount of adjustment of the composition of the portfolio at very low transaction cost because of the very low cost of transactions in cash. Transactions will tend to be more frequent or larger, or both, when there are positive transfers into the portfolio. Similarly negative transfers may affect the pattern of transactions.

FIXED-DOLLAR OBLIGATIONS AND BORROWING

Bonds, loans, and other assets that specify payments of specific dollar amounts at specific dates form a group which does not fit comfortably among the assets considered above. One reason is that an important source of uncertainty about the future prices of such assets is uncertainty about future interest rates. But, as one considers future prices at times approaching a bond's maturity date, this source of uncertainty becomes insignificant. This phenomenon raises the possibility that the subjective probability distribution will not have the property postulated in (32d).

Another reason for regarding the debt instruments as special is that there are a limited number of factors which determine a large fraction of the variation of their (real) prices, the value of money, the interest rate(s), etc. About the only element of uniqueness associated with a particular debt issue is the risk of default, and for many issues that can be negligible. Consequently, the structure of bond prices, to the extent that we understand it, should be used to place restrictions on the investor's subjective probability distribution of bond prices.

The portfolio adjustment model would seem, otherwise, to be able to accommodate this type of asset. While there may be differences, and differences worth exploring, in the properties of an investor's subjective probability beliefs about the two classes of assets, at a higher level of abstraction they are quite comparable.

Borrowing of the household is another portfolio item that should be included in the model. Household debt can be treated as a negative fixed-price asset. The evaluation of the average expected utility will not be affected nor will the total value restraint. The nonnegativity restraints will be reversed for the debt variables and there may be upper bounds on debt, either absolute or related to other components of the portfolio (collateral).

OTHER ASSETS

A further category of portfolio assets should be mentioned. A substantial part of most portfolios is represented by assets that are not divisible, do not have currently observed market prices, and are not fixed in (dollar) price. Such items as real estate, both residential and nonresidential, equity in unincorporated enterprise, shares of closely held corporations, professional practice, etc., do not fit into the framework as it stands. The nondivisibility is a minor problem since most transactions in this model are of a discrete nature anyway. Other properties of these assets are more troublesome.

For assets of this sort that are currently owned by the investor, it is reasonable to assert that he has subjective beliefs about their present and future prices. Here, in the absence of organized and informed markets, explicit assumptions about the process of selling such assets have to be made. But the investor's beliefs about alternatives to his current holdings are not so easy to specify—the alternatives are so numerous and varied. The extent of the investor's information becomes quite crucial here and that, in turn, depends upon a prior choice of the investor to spend time and effort on acquiring information.

For many of these assets, the utility of ownership is not satisfactorily captured in terms of the realizable value—they are directly involved in nonportfolio activities of the household. For this part of the portfolio, it becomes necessary to augment the argument of the partial utility function that appears in the objective function. If the utility function (33) is replaced by:

$$U(V, q; t, \tau),\tag{33a}$$

the model can make a formal allowance for these effects. In the broader model, this phenomenon appears as a restraint on alternative uses of time, which depend upon ownership of specific assets. For example, one cannot be the manager of one's own grocery store without owning it.

TAXATION OF PORTFOLIO RETURNS

The model developed above has purposely obscured the distinction between portfolio gains that are realized in cash by an involuntary transaction, such as an interest or dividend payment, and those that accrue, whether realized or not, via price appreciation. The income tax laws on the other hand draw sharp distinctions between these forms. Roughly speaking, the interest and dividends are taxed as regular income, at the marginal rate determined by the household's nonportfolio income, realized gains at half that rate (if they are long-term) up to a maximum of 25 per cent, and unrealized gains not at all. Since an understanding of household investment behavior must not ignore the presence of taxation, we must see how the tax structure fits into the model.

The taxation of interest and dividend income can be introduced by a minor change in the rule for defining the involuntary transaction implied by a dividend or interest payment. In addition to the other changes in asset quantities, a change in a liability—taxes owed—must be introduced equal to the product of the income receipt and the marginal tax rate in the bracket the investor expects his total income to attain.

The taxation of realized gains enters the model at a quite different point. Here the act of realization is a voluntary transaction. The immediate effect of the gains tax on the portfolio is similar to a transaction cost, and it seems appropriate to introduce it in the same way. The constraint function is augmented by an additional term showing the amount of capital gains tax payable as a function of the transaction. The calculation of this tax liability requires added information on the basis (purchase price) and holding period for each separately acquired lot of a divisible asset. This, in practice, requires a simple inventory, in sharp contrast to the clumsy notation that is needed to give it formal expression. It is sufficient to note that, by distinguishing among lots acquired at different times, the analysis remains essentially the same. The tax liabilities do occasion a reduction in the current value of the portfolio, in the same fashion as transactions costs, and similarly constrain the set of feasible transactions.

The appropriate treatment of the contingent tax liability on unrealized gains is much less obvious. It seems inappropriate to charge the portfolio for taxes on gains as the gains accrue because the amount of tax is, in part, a variable the investor can control. The alternative of evaluating future portfolios on the basis of their net after-tax liquidation value also proceeds on an unrealistic hypothesis. However, it is also wrong to ignore the contingent liability completely. When an asset is sold and the gains taxes paid, there is no longer any uncertainty about that particular component of the portfolio gain. There has been a reduction in contingent tax liabilities and the decision model should reflect this. As a tentative compromise, the objective function could be modified to include an estimate of the contingent liability eliminated by a transaction. Let $\phi(\triangle q)$ denote the investor's expectation of the amount of gains tax he would eventually pay on the sales included in $\triangle q$ if he did not sell them now. Among the other alternatives he considers are sales in years with lower rates either because of changes of statutory rates or lower nonportfolio income, holding the asset until death, donating it to a university, etc. The expected utility of the portfolio at time τ can now be written:

$$\overline{U}((q + \Delta q); t, \tau) = \int U[(q + \Delta q)'p + \phi(\Delta q)] \, dF(p; t, \tau). \quad (38)$$

The added term partly offsets the immediate reduction in the portfolio produced by taxes on realized gains.

CONCLUDING REMARKS

The portfolio adjustment model developed above has several basic features that might be emphasized at this point. It is concerned with the essentially dynamic process of a household's adjustment to imperfectly foreseen changes in its environment. It makes use of a form of the expected utility hypothesis in an objective function that is only a proximate goal, one that we hope is reasonably consistent with the ultimate objectives. Finally, the model gives a large role to the subjective probability belief of the investor household. This last feature provides a vehicle for considering a wide range of supplementary hypotheses about how the investor acquires these beliefs.

IV. Conclusion

The introduction noted the need for a relatively ambitious and comprehensive model of household economic behavior to provide a coherent unifying framework for analyzing increasingly detailed and extensive household data. The model presented in section II represents our attempt to fill this need. The submodel in section III elaborates, and to some degree isolates, the decisions of the household that are concerned with portfolio management, which involve most prominently the choices among financial investments. This submodel illustrates, in our opinion, the usefulness of having an explicit over-all model standing behind the necessarily partial models we devise for particular problems. The nature and the cost of the simplifications required to achieve the partial isolation are much more apparent and are of interest in themselves.

Both the model and the submodel are, at present, rather long on notation and short on results. Further analytical and empirical work must be done and is, indeed, proceeding. At this point, however, it is possible only to indicate a few specific features of the model which seem to us particularly interesting and worth further study.

The formation and continuous revision of the subjective probability distributions have already been mentioned as worthy of further analysis. Acquiring and absorbing current information undoubtedly requires time and effort that have alternative uses. Both the value of current information and the capacity for assimilating it efficiently probably depend on the accumulated experience of the investor [2]. The model outlined above provides a link between the precision of the investor's expectation, as determined by inputs of effort, and the frequency of transactions, both of which are observable. Implications concerning investor specialization in particular classes of investments could also be sought. Recent work on adaptive forecasting [8, 9] has provided a mechanism that could be incorporated in the model to generate the expectations of future prices on the basis of past price movements.

The proximity of the proximate goal used as the objective function in the submodel is another feature that is of interest. The $a(h)$ function which determines this was explained earlier as a distribution of the interval between portfolio transactions and implicitly regarded as a relatively stable characteristic of the investor. Why, then, do some investors carry out transactions frequently and others only occasionally? It is tentatively proposed that the frequency will depend on the joint effects of portfolio size (total value), the amount and variety of "risky" securities in the portfolio, and the precision of the investor's price expectations. Work of a more theoretical nature could be carried out to determine the conditions under which such a proximate goal provides a satisfactory substitute for a more complicated ultimate objective.

While not intended as a substitute for the hard work that remains to be done, the foregoing remarks are offered as an indication of the directions such work might take. It is hoped that these remarks, together with the models outlined in the body of the paper, provide, even at this stage, a basis for critical comment and suggestions.

BIBLIOGRAPHY

1. Bear, Donald V. T., "The Relationship of Saving to the Rate of Interest, Real Income, and Expected Future Prices," *The Review of Economics and Statistics,* February 1961, pp. 27–36.
2. Clarkson, Geoffrey P. E., *Portfolio Selection: A Simulation of Trust Investment,* Englewood Cliffs, 1962.
3. Farrar, Donald E., *The Investment Decision Under Uncertainty,* Englewood Cliffs, 1962.
4. Hadar, Joseph, "A Note on Stock-Flow Models of Consumer Behavior," *Quarterly Journal of Economics,* May 1965, pp. 304–309.
5. Markowitz, Harry, *Portfolio Selection: Efficient Diversification of Investments,* New York, 1959.
6. Miller, Roger, F., "The Theory of Household Saving," *The Review of Economics and Statistics,* February 1963, pp. 1–15.
7. Modigliani, Franco, and Brumberg, Richard, "Utility Analysis and the Consumption Function—An Interpretation of Cross Section Data," in *Post Keynesian Economics* edited by Kurihara, K. K., New Brunswick, 1954, pp. 388–436.
8. Nerlove, M., and Wage, S., "On the Optimality of Adaptive Forecasting," *Management Science,* January 1964, pp. 207–224.
9. Theil, H., and Wage, S., "Some Observations on Adaptive Forecasting," *Management Science,* January 1964, pp. 198–206.
10. Tobin, James, "Liquidity Preference as Behavior Toward Risk," *The Review of Economic Studies,* February 1958, pp. 65–86.
11. Watts, Harold W., and Tobin, James, "Consumer Expenditures and the Capital Account," *Consumption and Saving,* edited by Irwin Friend and Robert C. Jones, Vol. II, Philadelphia, 1960, pp. 1–48.
12. Yaari, Menahem E., "On the Existence of an Optimal Plan in a Continuous Time Allocation Process," *Econometrica,* October 1964, pp. 576–590.
13. ———, "Uncertain Lifetime, Life Insurance, and the Theory of Consumption" (unpublished).

COMMENT

On Muth

BY LOUIS WINNICK, FORD FOUNDATION

As I see it, Muth's paper makes two contributions to urban economics. First, his regression analyses reaffirm the role of the automobile as a determinant of the development patterns of metropolitan areas. For a half century or more the technology of transportation has been recognized as the most powerful influence on the size and configuration of cities and their hinterlands. And since the 1920's Robert Murray Haig and others have singled out private automotive transport as the "exploder" of urban conglomerations. Given the growing ownership of automobiles and trucks, the speed of movement, and the economics of highway construction which permits lattice-type networks of movement impossible of attainment by any rail system, it was possible to foresee not merely the decentralization of population but its diffusion as well; that is, not only would there be a reduction in the density gradient moving outward from the center but there would also be an increase in the average distance between household and household, between establishment and establishment, and between households and establishments. Muth's work shows that higher car registrations are in fact accompanied by lower gradients—the higher the incidence of car use, the more our cities tend to look like Los Angeles rather than New York.

The second contribution that Muth makes is to show that gradient reductions take place inside as well as outside the city, that not only the suburbs but also the outer rings within municipal corporate lines have tended to become the destination of urban migrants. He rightly points out there has been too much loose talk about the "flight from blight" and about the dichotomy of city and suburb.

Where Muth falls short is in excusing himself from the task of relating population movements to investment behavior; the latter is, after all, the subject of our conference. I should like to make a few general remarks on this subject, mainly to point out a few reasons why investment gradients need not correspond to population gradients.

Plainly, a substantial portion of metropolitan investment has no discernible relation either to resident population or to population growth. A notable example of such investment is the very substantial office building booms of New York, Chicago, Washington, San Francisco, and Boston. The location of national or regional headquarters is based on factors other than population trends in the immediate rings of the new establishment.

This much is obvious, but what of residential construction? Surely, housing investment is sensitive to resident population. It ought to be and it is but, as described at an earlier National Bureau conference, the relation between population levels and the dollar volume of new housing is only a very general one and holds only over very long periods of time. A much better dependent variable is change in number of households. But would not change in households correlate closely with change in population? Here again, the answer is a qualified yes if one is looking at national or regional aggregates. But the relationship falls apart when one is looking at the intrametropolitan aspects of population, settlements, and residential investment.

Inherent in the nature of an urban population is that there are systematic differences in the locational choices made by different types and sizes of households. What this means is that changes in number of households need not be the same as changes in the number of people. We can illustrate this by beginning with the well-known fact that, at the same time as our largest cities were losing population, they were gaining households. Thus, as Table 1 shows, between 1950 and 1960 seven out of the ten largest cities decreased in population but increased in households. In New York City, for example, population declined by 110,000 but the number of households expanded by nearly 300,000. More to

TABLE 1

Change in Population and Households in Ten Largest Cities
Between 1950 and 1960

(per cent)

City	Population	Households
New York City	− 1.4	+12.6
Chicago	− 1.9	+ 8.2
Los Angeles	+25.8	+33.0
Philadelphia	− 3.3	+ 7.4
Detroit	− 9.7	+ 2.7
Baltimore	− 1.1	+ 5.2
Houston	+57.4	+59.3
Cleveland	− 4.2	+ 4.4
Washington, D.C.	− 4.8	+13.3
St. Louis, Mo.	−12.5	− 1.2

TABLE 2

Average Household Size, by Area
Inside the N.Y.–N.J. SMSA, 1960

1. All SMSA	3.1
2. New York City	2.9
3. Manhattan	2.4
4. Census tract 130 (Manhattan)	2.2

Note: SMSA = Standard Metropolitan Statistical Area.

the point, this increase in households was accompanied by the largest residential investment boom since the 1920's, new construction totaling some 314,000 dwelling units.

This phenomenon already noted in the 1920's (when Manhattan lost population but experienced a record apartment boom) reflects deep-seated life-cycle preferences. The suburbs attract relatively more of the large families in the child-rearing stage, the central city relatively more of the smaller households—the young and old adults without children. Further, similar locational patterns are evident within the central city. As one moves from the outer rings to the inner core, the proportion of one- and two-person households sharply increases. Thus, in 1960, average household size was 3.1 for the entire New York metropolitan area, but only 2.9 for New York City, 2.4 for Manhattan, and 2.2 for a typical census tract in which substantial new apartment construction occurred (see Table 2).

In the typical new center-city apartment house in New York, Chicago, or Philadelphia, 90 to 95 per cent of the apartments are occupied by single individuals or married couples without children. New York's Third Avenue, for example, where a mile of four- and five-story tenements were replaced with 20- to 30-story apartments actually experienced a population decline: working class families with children departed for the outer rings and were replaced by both well-to-do executives and not-so-well-to-do secretaries who paired up and accepted rent-to-income ratios of 30 per cent or more in order to live in a convenient location or at a fashionable address. It goes without saying that any meaningful analysis of intrametropolitan population movements or investment trends must place these life-cycle differentials in choice of housing type and location at the very forefront.

A second "institutional" fact that Muth tends to neglect in his research on population distribution is the legal constraint, such as zoning and building codes, that significantly affects the costs of particular housing types and locations. According to Muth, the locational decisions of households are influenced by the gradient in residential land values as one moves outward from the center of the city. The housing consumer is confronted with a price system for land which, in conjunction with his income and tastes, determines his ultimate choice. On this I have three comments. The first and least important is that gradients and slope lines are no longer adequate descriptors of the pattern of land values. Simple geographical configurations, such as pyramids, cones, and concentric circles, may have been at one time useful visual aids to an understanding of the distribution of rents and value. But, alas, the automobile which has so drastically changed the map of population has also apparently changed the map of land values. Instead of a single-peaked cone, there seem to be multipeaked irregular configurations full of unexpected bumps and valleys. Land values at many points in the business district are lower than in the secondary rings and high-rent neighborhoods and blocks are side by side with slums.

My more important comments are, first, that land values or land rents expressed on per acre or per square foot are not very revealing measures of final housing costs; and, second, that building costs cannot be assumed to be equal throughout a metropolitan area. The influence of land costs on housing costs is more pertinently measured as a relative, namely, the amount of land cost per room or per square foot of building space. The unit price of land must be multiplied by the quantity wanted or required by the zoning code for a given type of housing. A large apartment house in Manhattan built on land costing $40 per square foot may have a lower relative land price than a single family house in the suburbs built on land costing 50 cents a square foot. The former may require only 125 square feet per dwelling unit, the latter would typically require 6,000 square feet. In other words, the housing consumer can adjust to high land costs by sharply decreasing the quantity purchased. Just how high the coefficient of price elasticity may be would be difficult to calculate, one reason being that consumer responses are heavily constrained by zoning regulations, another reason being that apartment house sites and single-family house sites are far from being perfect substitutes, i.e., to a large extent, they are traded in different markets.

But at the same time as the housing consumer seeks to escape both transportation and land costs by choosing a central city apartment house, he is confronted by another cost—the relatively high cost of constructing high-rise fireproof structures that are customarily mandated in core areas by the building codes. The incremental costs for elevators and fire-proofing are quite substantial. The latter type of structure may cost fully twice as much to build per room as a low nonfireproof frame house or garden apartment. Other things being equal and excluding the cost of the land, a garden apartment in New York City may have a construction cost of as low as $12 per square foot of building space, a high-rise fire-proof building a minimum cost of $20 per square foot. This differential in building costs can be a much more significant determinant of final housing costs than are differential land prices.

In sum, my remarks therefore constitute a series of suggestions to Muth that he might find useful as he proceeds with his analysis of 1960 data. Even if he continues to confine himself to the population rather than the investment aspects of intrametropolitan change, he ought to build up both the demographic and the economic dimensions of his model, adding to the first by bringing in life-cycle subsets, adding to the latter by taking account of the effects on housing costs of building density—that is, the size of structures relative to the size of sites.

On Muth

BY VERNON G. LIPPITT, UNIVERSITY OF ROCHESTER

This study is an intriguing attempt to obtain empirical equations relating the distribution of population in urban areas of U.S. cities to factors determining that distribution. In the main, it is a cross-section study based on data for some forty-six cities in 1950, though the cross-section findings are applied to some time series data near the end of the report.

Perhaps because of my unfamiliarity with investigations in this field, I had to reread sections of the paper several times before they came clear. The organization and presentation of the material is not suitable for a beginner. The author's use of well-chosen abbreviations to desig-nate his variables was a helpful practice which, it seems to me, could well be more widely adopted. In some instances it would have clarified the variables if units of measure (or dimensions) had been specified. Is k measured in miles? Is income per capita in dollars or thousand dollars? Such information is needed to assess the relative importance of some terms in equations. What are the units for q, the quantity of housing consumed? Is it a *flow,* perhaps dollars per year at 1950 prices? How are quality differences in housing units allowed for? What about density gradient D_1? Change in persons per square mile per mile of increase in distance from the center of the city suggests itself, but dimensional analysis of some of the equations indicates that it is percentage change in density per mile of distance.

Since I am not qualified to discuss the findings from familiarity with the problems analyzed and since Louis Winnick has commented so ably on the practical considerations involved, I shall limit my remarks to a couple of questions about the logic underlying the research.

In the first section of the report, Muth summarizes findings of an earlier study of his which indicated that population density declines roughly exponentially from the city center.

$$D = D_0 e^{-D_1 k}.$$

In developing the logic underlying this finding, the author relates density to factors involving housing.

$$D = \frac{\text{persons}}{\text{land area}} = \frac{\text{housing services per land area}}{\text{housing services per person}}.$$

Housing services per land area declines with k, because land is cheaper relative to costs of the building at larger k; so more land is used per house as k increases.

Housing services per person increases with k. It is the logic underlying this second conclusion about which I have some doubts.

For an individual household choosing a house in a metropolitan area, the condition for indifference among sites of various distances from the central business district (CBD) is apparently: housing expenditures + transportation expenditures to CBD = constant, or

$$pq + T = \text{constant for various } k, \tag{1}$$

where q = quantity of housing service consumed by an individual household, say, dollars per year at 1950 prices (including land rental value); p = prices per unit of housing, dollars per unit of q; T = transportation expenditure to CBD for all purposes, say, dollars per year; k = distance from the CBD, say, miles.

The distance gradient becomes

$$\frac{d(pq)}{dk} + \frac{dT}{dk} = 0, \tag{2}$$

or, in terms of percentage changes,

$$\frac{1}{pq}\frac{d(pq)}{dk} = -\frac{1}{pq}\frac{dT}{dk}. \tag{3}$$

Case 1: If q is constant for the household at various k, we have

$$-\frac{1}{p}\frac{dp}{dk} = -\frac{1}{pq}\frac{dT}{dk} \tag{4}$$

which is Muth's equation (1).

Case 2: If the household considers letting q vary with k to help offset the change in T with k, then (3) becomes

$$-\frac{1}{p}\frac{dp}{dk} + \frac{1}{q}\frac{dq}{dk} = -\frac{1}{pq}\frac{dT}{dk}. \tag{5}$$

The rise in T may be offset by a decrease in q or in p, or in some combination of the two which makes the left side of equation (5) negative and equal to the right side.

Perhaps we can say that q changes with k because of a price effect and an income effect, the latter arising from the increase in T as k increases. In terms of percentage changes

$$-\frac{1}{q}\frac{dq}{dk} = E_p\frac{dp}{pdk} + E_Y\frac{dY}{Ydk}, \text{ where } dY = -dT. \tag{6}$$

Substitution of (6) into (5) yields

$$(1 + E_p)\frac{dp}{pdk} - E_Y\frac{dT}{Ydk} = -\frac{1}{pq}\frac{dT}{dk}. \tag{7}$$

Collecting like terms, we find

$$(1 + E_p)\frac{1}{p}\frac{dp}{dk} = \left(E_Y - \frac{Y}{pq}\right)\frac{dT}{Ydk}. \tag{8}$$

The right side is quite surely negative, since $E_Y < 1 < Y/pq$ normally. Hence, on the left, dp/dk must be opposite in sign to $(1 + E_p)$; i.e., dp/dk is negative if $0 > E_p > -1$ and positive if $E_p < -1$.

Substitution of this solution for $(1/p)(dp/dk)$ into (6) and noting $dY = -dT$, we find

$$(1 + E_p)\frac{1}{p}\frac{dq}{dk} = -\left(\frac{E_pY}{pq} + E_Y\right)\frac{dT}{Ydk}. \tag{9}$$

The quantity in brackets on the right will normally be negative, since usually E_Y will be smaller in magnitude than E_p multiplied by Y/pq. Thus the right side is positive, and $(1/q)(dq/dk)$ will be of the same sign as

Figure 1

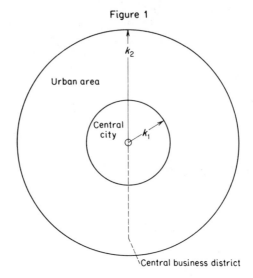

Figure 2

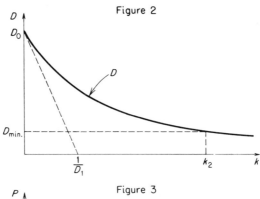

Figure 3

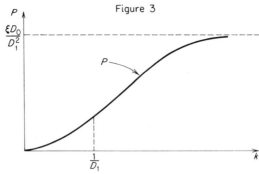

$(1 + E_p)$; i.e., dq/dk will be positive if $0 > E_p > -1$ and negative if $E_p < -1$.

In summary, it seems to me that Muth assumed in deriving his equation (1)—my equation (4)—that households would keep q constant as they decided where to locate. This leads to a negative price gradient because of the positive gradient in transportation costs. Then he concludes that the negative price gradient will lead to a positive gradient in q per capita because of price elasticity. It would seem better to permit both p and q to vary with k from the start of the analysis, with results indicated by my equations (8) and (9) above.

In the second section of his paper Muth analyzes "the distribution of population between the central city and its suburbs, and the total land used by urban areas."

The model used is that of a circular city with a small central business district, a central city of radius k_1 and population P_1, and an entire urban area of radius k_2 and population P_2 (Muth used P). (See Figure 1.)

Population density D is assumed to decline exponentially from the center of the city with constant gradient D_1 out to k_2.

$$D = D_0 e^{-D_1 k} \tag{10}$$

where D_1 is the percentage decrease in D per mile of increase in k (see Figure 2).

Total population within a circle of radius k is given by

$$P = \frac{\xi D_0}{D_1^2} f\{D_1, k\}, \tag{11}$$

where $f\{D_1, k\} = 1 - (1 + D_1 k)e^{-D_1 k}$ and $\xi = 2\pi$ times fraction of urban land area used for housing, assumed constant for all k (see Figure 3).

Urban land area used for housing is

$$L_2 = \tfrac{1}{2}\xi k_2^2 \quad \text{(Muth uses L instead of L_2.)} \tag{12}$$

From these three equations and the Census Bureau specification of a constant population density at the boundary of an urban area (with serves to eliminate D_0 from the equations), Muth derives equations to explain differences in the values of P_1 and L_2 among U.S. cities in terms of differences in their values of P_2, D_1, k_1, and ξ. All variables are expressed as percentage changes (or logarithmic differentials) between cities.

$$dP_1^* = (1 - \gamma) dP_2^* + 2(\delta - \gamma) dD_1^* + 2\delta dk_1^* + \gamma d\xi^* \tag{13}$$

$$dL_2^* = \beta dP_2^* - 2(1 - \beta) dD_1^* + (1 - \beta) d\xi^* \tag{14}$$

where β and γ are functions of (D_1k_2) and δ is a function of (D_1k_1).

Four comments suggested themselves to me regarding this formulation.

1. The fraction (ξ) of urban land area used for housing is apparently assumed constant for all k. It would seem more logical to assume that ξ would increase with k, as the proportion of land area devoted to commercial and industrial purposes tapers off with distance from the center of the city.

2. In my equations (13) and (14) the Greek-letter coefficients are functions of (D_1k_2) and (D_1k_1). Yet in the fitting of equations in the cross-section analysis it would appear that they have been treated as constants. Since D_1k_2 and D_1k_1 are known for various cities, it would seem desirable to calculate the Greek-letter coefficients directly to check on the assumed constancy or to enter their values in the equations as additional explanatory variables.

3. In my equation (13) the term involving dP_2^* (logarithmic differential of urban area population) apparently accounts for 94 per cent of the variance in dP_1^* (the logarithmic differential of central city population). Probably the urban area population term dP_2^* in equation (5) accounts for a large part of the variance in dL_2^* also. One wonders if it might not be good strategy to deflate by this dominant variable and use the ratios P_1/P_2 and L_2/P_2 as the dependent variables for analysis. It might then be possible to determine the contributions of the other explanatory variables independently of the total population effect.

4. Finally, I wondered about the use of the findings from cross-section analysis in the discussion of changes over time. In view of the developments of suburban business districts and of urban renewal projects in recent years, it would seem that dynamic changes may reflect considerably different causal forces from those that operated to determine the patterns of urban population distribution in a cross section as of 1950.

ON SPARKS

BY VERNON G. LIPPITT, UNIVERSITY OF ROCHESTER

I feel this is a competent paper; it is clearly and logically presented. Variables are clearly defined in a statistical appendix, with units of measure and sources given, and data recorded.

I applaud the use of year-to-year changes for dependent and independent variables. This reduces serial correlation and forces the coefficients in regression equations to reflect short-term relations between the variables rather than relations between their trends. Of course, using years for the time units and postwar years only restricts the number of degrees of freedom available, so that in several instances R^2 for a regression equation (adjusted for degrees of freedom) increases when one or two variables are omitted. It also prevents any investigation of time lags or leads of a few months' duration, such as one might expect in comparing housing starts and demand for mortgage funds.

As data for more postwar years become available, it may well prove desirable to investigate whether the form of relation between the annual change variables is linear, as assumed in the regression equation. It might also be interesting to split the data into earlier and later years to test the stability of the coefficients. I suspect that this might be a revealing, though humbling, test of many of our time series models. As the author notes, the large error terms in recent years suggest that the calculated equation for change in housing starts may be drifting off calibration. Included variables may be shifting in relative importance, or new variables may be coming into play.

There is little effort in this paper to develop a theoretical model, aside from the discussion of the income shifts and the fixed-rate theory as explanations of the shift of funds from the mortgage market to the corporate bond market in times of good business. And these alternative hypotheses were not tested because of the lack of good empirical data for credit terms. The variables included in the regression model are a combination of variables from consumer demand theory (income, relative prices, need based on demographic factors, available inventory of unoccupied dwelling units, and credit terms) plus variables from financial investment theory (inflows of saving deposits, repayments of loans, financial ratios, and relative rates of interest). A few comments may be in order on the choice and specification of these variables.

1. The equation for housing starts and the one for demand for mortgage funds are the same in form and in the explanatory variables. I wonder if there might not be an appreciable difference in timing between the housing starts variable and the demand for mortgage funds (including advance commitments). Probably use of annual data rules out detection of lags here. More important, one of these variables is a physical flow and the other is a money flow. The mortgage funds demanded differ from housing starts by a price, or unit value, variable which probably has changed over the years covered by the analysis, but which has not been included in the analysis. Mortgage credit demanded per housing start may have changed because construction costs have risen, the mix of dwelling units has shifted to higher average values,

or the average amount borrowed from financial intermediaries per start may have changed. In recent years mortgage borrowing seems to have been used as a cheap source of credit for purposes other than housing expenditures. A plotting of the series for change in supply of mortgage funds ($\triangle MC + \triangle FNMA$) does indicate an upward drift from 1949 to 1964 compared with the series for $\triangle HS$.

2. I have some reservations about the way in which the variable for credit terms was eliminated from the housing starts equation. Equations for demand and supply of mortgage funds were set equal, and solved for the credit terms variable $\triangle Cr$. This solution for $\triangle Cr$ was then substituted back in the housing starts equation, at least conceptually. The solution for $\triangle Cr$, while logically correct, might involve rather large errors, it seems to me. It depends essentially on the difference between the contributions to demand and supply of mortgage funds from all factors other than credit terms. So $\triangle Cr$ would pick up the time pattern of any omitted variables or nonlinearities of the demand and supply equations. I wonder if it might not have been better to use some direct measure of credit terms, even if it were not precise.

Of course, in the final equation for change in housing starts, the above solution for credit terms was not used. Instead, the series for supply of mortgage funds as derived from data for financial intermediaries (excluding commercial banks) was entered in place of the series for $\triangle Cr$. Some theoretical justification or discussion of this substitution would seem desirable. It is not the replacement for the credit term which is indicated by the reduced form calculations.

3. In the equations for net increase in saving deposits ($\triangle SD$) by type of financial intermediary, personal financial saving was used as an explanatory variable. Personal disposable income would have seemed a preferable behavioral variable to use, since it is more likely to be included in the over-all model of which these equations are a part.

Finally, note that "the purpose of this paper is to develop a model of the residential construction sector of the U.S. economy with particular emphasis on the financial factors that provide a link between construction activity and the monetary sector." The final equation for $\triangle HS$ and year-by-year values of the explanatory terms in Table 4 suggest that interest rates made an appreciable contribution to explaining $\triangle HS$ in several postwar years. Beyond the question of statistical significance lies the question of forecasting significance.

Can the year-to-year changes in the relevant interest rates be forecast reliably enough to make a useful contribution to forecasting housing starts? If the Research Seminar in Quantitative Economics is developing a model in which these interest rates are endogenous variables, I can see that we have a competitor to the SSRC model springing up.

How stable will the coefficients of the predictor equation remain through time? As noted above, the demand for mortgage loans in recent years seems to have been based increasingly on uses of funds other than for residential purchases. And as housing supply has caught up with demand in the postwar period, I wonder if the availability of mortgage funds and mortgage credit terms have become less effective in making residential housing activity a countercyclical force in the economy.

In any event this paper represents a good start, it seems to me, in an area where monetary factors may be expected to affect real demand and supply. If this model is to be incorporated into the ongoing forecasting effort under Daniel Suits at the University of Michigan, there is hope that it will be subject to continuous review, revision, and evaluation. That is the ultimate test of a model from the forecasting point of view.

ON SNOWBARGER AND SUITS

BY VERNON G. LIPPITT, UNIVERSITY OF ROCHESTER

The technique for successive dichotomous partitioning of a sample used in this paper to analyze what characteristics of buying units are related to purchase and ownership of consumer durables seems an ingenious one. The authors present this technique as an alternative to regression and related techniques used to analyze cross-section data— "an alternative by which the data can be scanned to identify the most important variables and their interactions." The claimed advantages of this technique are: (1) it provides "a better profile of consumer activity" in cross-section analysis where "the complex intercorrelations and interactions preclude a straightforward linear regression"; and (2) it does not "require the analyst to select the 'control' variables in advance"; it searches out the explanatory variables by uncovering significant differences in the dependent variable between dichotomous partitions on all recorded characteristics of the observation units.

A few comments on these claims would seem to be warranted.

First, it is not clear that this technique gets around the intercorrelation problem. The authors point out that: "In any split, some variables may be highly correlated with the partitioning variable, but not be sufficiently powerful to make the split." They suggest that "the relative discriminatory power of each variable is shown at every stage of the program" so that the investigator can analyze the splits that "almost" occurred. This deals with the problem qualitatively, but not quantitatively.

Second, regression techniques *can* handle some nonlinearities and interactions by use of dummy variables for each class on each characteristic and for subclasses determined by two-way classification.

Third, the fact that the AID program does not require advance specification of the explanatory variables indicates that the method does not involve the testing of a formal hypothesis of consumer behavior, except the hypothesis that the characteristics entered in the analysis do discriminate among buying units' probability of purchase. The technique is essentially a preliminary search technique, and should not be considered an alternative to regression analysis or analysis of variance techniques. As was indicated in the oral presentation, after using the AID program you "think up hypotheses for what the data show."

A review of the findings in this investigation reveals several interesting features.

1. In several cases a "successful" split involves breaking out a group of buying units characterized by two nonadjacent classes on some characteristic. See split 4 on television sets and washers (AIDPR levels of <9 per cent and 20–39 per cent), or split 18 on refrigerators (disposable income classes $4000–$6000 and $7500–$10,000), or split 6 on washers (residence established in 1955–1957 or in 1959). This may indicate significant nonlinearity in the influence of the classifying variable, but it does point up the incompleteness of this technique in not giving a picture of the way buying influences change when classes of that characteristics are placed in some rational order.

2. For split 4 on refrigerators we find that, among buying units who indicated they would not buy, purchases were most frequent among a group who answered "don't know" to the question "Do you expect to be better or worse off a year from now?" This is an odd explanatory variable. Perhaps it points to the need to find some characteristic distinguishing agnostic types or families beset by uncertainty whose buying behavior is most susceptible to outside influences.

3. It is noteworthy that relatively few further splits occur in the "high" group of the first split for household durables, i.e., among the group exhibiting high frequency of purchase. This group is characterized by their having expressed an intention to buy the appliance. Apparently this characteristic swamps the effects of all other characteristics. Given the intention to buy, few other characteristics discriminate strongly between the buying units *in this group* who do and do not carry out their intentions. Alternative explanations might be that in this

group with high probability of purchase a higher level of differentiating power (or *absolute* reduction of variance) is required for causing a split, or the small numbers of families may make it harder for a characteristic to be recognized as having a significant effect. If either of these explanations is true, I wonder about modifying the technique so that all of the buying units are searched together on successive splits after removing the influence of the characteristic found important on the prior split. The removal might be accomplished by subtracting from probability of purchase in the high group the difference between the proportion buying in the high and the low group.

Of course, it would be of interest to run the AID program on these buying units without including expectations or intentions variables also, to see how the demographic variables alone turn out.

4. It was interesting that time interval since marriage or since move to a new residence did not show up as very significant. Presumably this is either because newly married or recently moved buying units are too small in number to make their influence show up or because such units intend to buy and possession of that characteristic obscures the influence of the underlying factors motivating the buying intentions. Again the importance of analyzing the data with intentions data omitted is indicated, if the purpose is to derive demand determinants applicable to situations when intentions data are not available.

5. A significant omission from the variables used in analyzing the purchase data is a measure of the age of the given consumer durable at the time of the initial survey. It is sometimes stated that, among the group who do not express an intention to buy, breakdown or other enforced replacement is a frequent cause of purchase. Many market demand analyses give replacement demand an important place. It would have been interesting to see whether age of an appliance would have shown up as an important variable explaining unplanned purchases. It would be interesting to know, also, how omission of this variable may have affected the ability of other variables to cause splits.

6. The findings on second-car ownership are illuminating. With the intentions data omitted, we get more splits on the income and demographic variables among the high as well as low groups. The indication that the most relevant demographic factors are different for different income groups is, I think, an illustration of the most valuable type of insight with regard to interaction which the AID program is best suited to bring out. Such information would have marketing significance and some unlimited forecasting value. I say "limited" because the individual subclasses obtained after a few splits would be hard to forecast.

The forecasting of population by demographic characteristics becomes difficult if numbers in cells determined by several characteristics are required.

In summary, the AID technique of analysis used in this study can, it seems to me, provide useful information in a search for explanatory variables and in detecting some interactions. It should not be regarded as an alternative to regression or analysis of variance approaches in testing hypotheses or in evaluating quantitatively the over-all importance and systematic pattern of influence for an explanatory variable.

On Sparks, Snowbarger-Suits, Muth, and Miller-Watts

BY JAMES MORGAN, UNIVERSITY OF MICHIGAN

Gordon Sparks' paper is part of a program to introduce monetary factors in a meaningful way into the Klein-Suits-Goldberger-Suits-Locke Anderson-Suits Michigan model. He has selected a promising area where the supply of funds and interest rates should matter, namely, housing. He uses a two-stage analysis to explain first the flow of funds, and then uses that to help explain housing starts and residential construction expenditures. And he seems to have avoided using anything to explain itself: increase in dwelling units is not made a function of new family formation.

The paper by Marvin Snowbarger and Daniel Suits faces up directly to the problem that all our theorizing is accompanied by increasingly systematic and exhaustive exploration of the data, testing, and revision of models. Hence we are really not testing one hypothesis but selecting among many. The search procedure he uses loosens up the restrictions (additivity) with which we view data, and looks for what matters. It does it in a defined and reproducible way. His results should be looked upon as a first step toward the development of a better model or set of models. What is important about his findings is the evidence that both expenditures and income elasticities vary a great deal among different subgroups. The search for a single income elasticity may, therefore, be illusory. Economic policies which affect the incomes of different groups in different ways may well require knowing the separate income elasticities, not just the weighted average. The differences in level among subgroups matter. Even though some of the differences between subgroups may not lead to changes over time, others may. There may be substantial changes for instance in the number and proportion of families with working wives, teen-age children, or a dwelling in the suburbs.

Richard Muth's basic model implies that people have a general desire to be as close to the center of the city as possible, and are deterred by an increasing rent gradient. My disagreement is with these basic assumptions of the model rather than with the statistics. Bernard J. Frieden's new book *The Future of Old Neighborhoods*[1] shows a wide variety of rent gradients from one city to the next. Recent studies at the Survey Research Center have shown that more people would like to be farther out than the reverse. They want to have more space, to own their own homes, to have good schools, and to have access to outdoor recreation. The younger they are and the more outdoor activities they like, the greater their preference for living farther out. Even among those already fifteen miles or more from the center, 20 per cent would like to be farther out and only 10 closer in.[2]

Actual moving plans are in the same direction. In large cities of a million and a half or more, fewer than 40 per cent go downtown for purposes other than work even as often as once a month.[3] It seems likely that there are two groups, one of which is mostly made up of people without children who like being close to downtown, and the other made up of people who are only kept from real country-estate living by the costs of land and of the journey to work. There are certainly differences between cities as to the amount of employment available without even going downtown.

The frequency of passenger car ownership seems likely to be a result of past decisions about streets and public transport rather than a cause of urban spread. The Lansing-Mueller monograph shows that the age of a city, reflected by its population in 1900, is a major determinant of the proportion who use a car to get to work. Ranking the twelve largest metropolitan areas according to their population in 1900, one finds that the percentages using a car to get to work vary from 36 in New York and 63 in Chicago and 67 in Philadelphia to 79 in San Francisco, 86 in Detroit, 73 in Washington, D.C., and 91 in Los Angeles.[4] The use of two-stage least squares may avoid bias but it does not remove the doubt about whether cars are a cause or a result of urban spread.

Finally, the explanations of the two significant (but opposite in sign) coefficients for the median income in the central city and the median

[1] Cambridge, Mass., 1964.

[2] See John B. Lansing and Eva Mueller, *Residential Location and Urban Mobility*, Survey Research Center, University of Michigan, Ann Arbor, 1964, p. 24.

[3] *Ibid.*, p. 40.

[4] *Ibid.*, p. 92.

income in the urban area are ingenious, but since the two are correlated
.94 I have the uneasy feeling that this may be one more case where
multiple regression provides an excellent predictive mapping but does
not provide good explanations. Close examination may even show that
the result depends on one or two cases of "outliers."

FIGURE 1

A Theory of Time Use

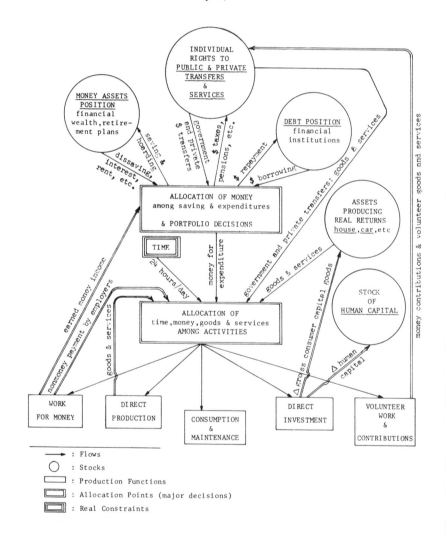

The paper by Roger Miller and Harold Watts is an excellent, tersely written attempt to formulate a stochastic and dynamic theory of the household and to attach a subtheory about its portfolio investment decisions. It repays close reading since it at least touches upon most of the main problems in such a theoretical model. It sees the household as making decisions about the allocation of its time, the spending or saving of its income, and the investing of the accumulated saving. I have only two suggestions and, unfortunately, they are for still more complexity before we can start simplifying and making it operational:

First, rather than one stock, the financial portfolio, there are really several: investments in financial assets; direct investments in real estate and business, which require more management time; debt (not connected with earning assets), which has motives and constraints of its own; consumer assets (houses, cars, etc.), which provide services directly and involve a commitment to a future stream of consumption (real behavioral problems are buried by treating all this like renting the service from oneself); human capital, whose value increases with investment in education or health; equity rights to public services and to public and private transfers, including social security and private pensions.

It is not important just how these are regrouped, but they cannot be forgotten. Many of them are mentioned in the paper, but not all, and the paper does not pretend to develop models of behavior with respect to the others. We are engaged at the Survey Research Center in a study of people's economic time allocations and have developed a graphic model (Figure 1) which is reproduced here both for its contribution and to make it easier to see what the Miller-Watts paper is about. The rich Wisconsin panel data will enable the development and testing of models of behavior with respect to the money assets (upper left circle). Our study deals with the allocation of time between the five activities at the bottom of the figure. It is useful to think of a household first allocating its time, money, and goods to activities, then making money allocations partly determined by the previous decisions, and finally making portfolio decisions about the way in which stocks of assets are held.

Secondly, we need a model that allows for learning, growth, and changes in taste. We know that people only think about an estate for their heirs if and when they get old and rich. We know their motivation to save feeds on past success in accumulating. George Katona has a forthcoming monograph with some new data indicating that the addition of a private pension plan to social security encourages people to save still more.[5]

I was certainly gratified by the amount of attention devoted to my paper by the discussants. It would be nice to be able to believe that it reflects an increased interest in urban problems on the part of economists generally, for I have become increasingly convinced that economists, and not merely a small group of dedicated specialists, have a great deal to contribute to understanding and solving urban problems. In this regard I was especially impressed by the comments of Vernon Lippitt, since it is my understanding that he has not previously done any work in this field.

Louis Winnick is certainly correct that there is more to the matter of where, within a metropolitan area, investment or even investment in housing takes place than mere population movements. I would like to have been able to present some empirical results on other aspects of the problem but time, both for my research and for presenting my results here at the conference, is, like housing, an economic good. Population movements since World War II have almost certainly contributed greatly to the location of postwar residential construction, however. The other major factor affecting the aggregate expenditures for housing in different parts of cities and thus residential construction, of course, is expenditures per capita. I have examined the variation of housing expenditures within the central city and believe that they are highly predictable; the occupant's income level would appear to be by far the major factor affecting these expenditures. The variation of median income by census tract within the central city, in turn, seems to be closely associated with age of dwellings and previous income level of the tract. Thus I would anticipate but cannot yet demonstrate that the variation of housing expenditure per capita between the central city and its suburbs could be largely explained in terms of the factors noted above.

Winnick's comparison of the difference between the relative change in population and in households in the ten largest U.S. cities over the

---

[5] George Katona, *Private Pensions and Individual Saving,* Survey Research Center Monograph 40, Ann Arbor, 1965. The model must be simple, but it does need to allow for some change in people's goals.

past decade, while interesting, is practically irrelevant for my purposes. The fact that in every case the percentage increase in households exceeded that of population probably reflects the great increase in incomes that occurred during the period. Earlier establishment of separate households by the young, longer maintenance of them by the aged, and less frequent sharing of quarters by single adults are among the ways by which the per capita consumption of housing is increased. For this phenomenon to make a difference for my purposes, however, there would have to have been differences among urbanized areas in the differential (change) in households relative to population between the central city and its suburbs. And even this would make no difference if one were able to explain the differential (change) in *per capita* expenditures for housing between the central city and its suburbs in terms of factors such as I noted in the preceding paragraph.

I quite agree with Winnick, and with the similar observation of Morgan, that there is a tendency for the average size of household to increase with distance from the CBD. But I feel this phenomenon is not very important quantitatively.

In part of my work, as yet unpublished, I have examined the relative change in average household size with distance as well as the change in housing expenditures per household and production per square mile of land in U.S. central cities for 1950. If anything, the association between average household size and distance is closer than that between the other two components of population density and distance. Housing expenditures per family and production per square mile each vary on the order of 20 per cent per mile, but average household size tends to increase on the order of only 1 per cent per mile within a given city. I once thought of including various demographic characteristics, such as number of children per family and fraction of adults of age 65 or more, in my analysis of variations in density gradients among the various cities for reasons similar to those set forth by Winnick and Morgan. When I had gathered the data, however, there was so little variation among cities in these measures that it hardly seemed worthwhile to use up my already limited residual degrees of freedom by including them. Thus, I do not feel that my neglect of the demographic considerations of which my critics make so much is a very important omission.

I also agree with the substance of Winnick's remarks on the importance of the substitution of construction outlay for land or space in the production of housing in response to differences in the price per unit of land and construction. I certainly did not mean to assume, however, that construction "costs" interpreted as total construction outlay or as a fraction of the total value of land plus structure are constant throughout the city; rather I assume that the variation in the price per unit of construction is small relative to that of land rents per square foot. Toward the beginning of section II of my paper I expressly noted the substitution of land for other productive factors in producing housing as land rents (per square foot) decline with distance from the CBD. Winnick is mistaken, I believe, when he argues in the last sentence of his penultimate paragraph that the differential in building expenditure is in any relevant sense a "determinant" of the way residential land is used. I would argue that the variation in building expenditure results from the variation of land rents relative to construction costs, both on a per unit basis. Only if construction costs *per unit* vary with distance can one say that "building costs" are in any meaningful sense a determinant of residential land use.

I must apoligize to Lippitt, as well as to any other reader with similar questions, for not being sufficiently clear as to the units of measurement I used. Distance, *k,* is indeed measured in miles, and it should be obvious from my equation (1) that the density gradient, D_1, is the relative change in population density per unit change in distance. Since the log of D_1 was used in my regression analysis, however, the coefficients shown would have been the same if distance had been measured in kilometers or rods. Income was measured in dollars, but the exponent shown in the stub of the various tables converts the units in which the income coefficients are expressed to thousand dollars. This should also have been clear from my discussion of the quantitative impact of various changes in section V.

Since *q* is housing consumption, it unambiguously relates to a flow of services per unit time. Actual measurement of this flow might be a very complicated problem when one is concerned with differences among different parts of a given city, and partly for this reason I did not attempt it. In principle, measurement of housing consumption would be similar to the measurement of, say, food consumption. When one attempts to combine quantities of diverse physical things into a single magnitude, as it is so frequently convenient to do for analytic simplicity, one does so by using an index number with prices as weights, though with well-known index number problems. The resulting measure is, of course, expressed in constant dollars of expenditure (per unit of time). To test the theory I have developed or to estimate certain parameters, however, it is not necessary to have such an index of housing consumption. Magnitudes such as population density and actual dollars of expenditure, both per household and per square mile of land, are much easier to measure, and I have concentrated my attention on them in my empirical work.

Contrary to Lippitt's assertion, I have not assumed that households keep housing consumption, q, constant in choosing their location. Rather, I have assumed, though not spelled out in my paper, that households maximize a conventional ordinal utility function $U = U(x, q)$, where x is dollars of expenditure (per unit of time) on all other commodities. The consumer is subject to the budget constraint $x + p(k)q + T(k, y) = y$, where T is expenditure for transportation and is a function of location as well as money income, y, the latter to allow for the opportunity cost of time spent in travel. There is nothing in this formulation which requires that q remain constant in any part of the household's decision process.

The first-order or necessary conditions for the constrained utility maximization are, first, the usual requirement that housing be consumed in such an amount in relation to other commodities that the marginal utility per dollar of expenditure be the same for housing and all other commodities and, second, my equation (1). The latter requires that no small change in location can increase the real income or consumption of the household. One set of sufficient conditions consists of the usual curvature properties of indifference curves plus the restriction that the rate of decline of housing price with distance not be so great that the saving in expenditure on that quantity of housing purchased at the optimal location for the household exceed the increased transportation expenditure which results from a small increase in distance.

Thus, in my formulation the appropriate value of q for the household to examine in deciding whether or not to move from a given location varies with distance because of the variation of housing prices with distance. When comparing different households, all of whom are assumed to be in their equilibrium locations, the sufficient conditions outlined above imply that those households in locations more distant from the CBD consume more housing relative to other commodities because housing prices are lower relative to other commodity prices at greater distances from the CBD. Lippitt's contention that my equation (1) holds only if q is invariant with distance follows directly from his assumption that the sum of housing expenditures and transportation expenditure is constant, an assumption for which there is certainly no economic rationale. Indeed, in my formulation constancy of this sum holds if and only if housing demand is perfectly inelastic. I submit, therefore, that Lippitt's contention is simply not correct.

With respect to Lippitt's other comments, there are certainly no logical grounds, though there could be empirical ones, which require one to assume that the fraction of land devoted to residential uses increase with k. I say "could be empirical ones" because other investigations I have not discussed here fail to reveal any evidence of increasing ξ. In particular I would expect a generally increasing ξ to impart a negative curvature to the relation between the log of gross population density and distance. In results reported in my earlier paper, such a curvature was not generally observed. And the direct inspection I have made for the south side of Chicago also fails to reveal any appreciable variation of ξ with distance or other measures of accessibility.[1] Lippitt is, of course, correct that the Greek-letter coefficients in my equations (10) through (14) may vary from city to city, and indeed I did calculate their values to obtain the average values used for interpreting my regression coefficients. I did not use the estimated city coefficients to weight the values of the various explanatory variables for the different cities as my equations (12) and (14) would suggest doing, however, because my D_1 values are sample estimates which are subject to appreciable sampling error. Had I used these in weighting the explanatory variables, I would have introduced appreciable measurement errors, and correlated ones at that, into all of the explanatory variables. It seemed to me that the specification error of not weighting is almost certainly likely to be less serious than the problem of correlated measurement errors in all the explanatory variables.

Since in my regressions I used logs for P_1, L, and P_2, it would seem to make little difference whether or not I deflate by P_2 as Lippitt suggests, especially since my computed regression equations give little indication of homoscedasticity. In comparing the increase in explained variance when all explanatory variables are included relative to that which is unexplained when size alone is included as I have done, a perfectly valid measure of the contribution of the other variables is obtained. Finally, as regards the propriety of the use of cross-section findings to explain changes over time, I would argue that consistency of regression estimates of the type I have presented with additional data, especially of a different type, is the best defense against the many objections to which an analysis such as mine might be subject. In fact, the so-called "dynamic changes" which Lippitt mentions are probably incorporated in my set of explanatory variables. The development of

[1] "The Variation of Population Density and Its Components in South Chicago," paper presented at the Regional Science Association Meetings, Ann Arbor, Mich., November 15, 1964.

suburban shopping centers is certainly not an exogenous force but is probably explainable in large part by the development of automobile transportation and increasing city sizes. To the extent that urban renewal has had any effects at all it would change the relative income level as between the central city and its suburbs, the racial composition of the central city population, the age and quality of the central city's housing stock, etc. Indeed, equations such as I have developed may well be useful in appraising the effects of urban renewal.

In first writing out my reaction to Morgan's comments, I was struck by how little disagreement there is between us. I will certainly agree that a wide variety of rent (presumably per unit of housing service) gradients, which I have argued are closely related to density gradients, exists in different cities. Indeed, I pointed this out in my earlier paper, delivered three years before the work Morgan cites; that paper and the present one are partly attempts to explain these differences. Although people may "want" to live further from the city center, in seeking to explain why they do not, Morgan mentions precisely the factors included in my equation (1)—transport costs and housing prices. Still another example is Morgan's expression of doubt as to the causal effect of car ownership on urban spread. I explicitly stated in my earlier paper that I used CAREGS as a surrogate variable for the many possible factors, some of which Morgan mentions explicitly, which may lead both to greater car ownership and urban spread.

There are a few differences between us, however. Morgan's remark about job opportunities not in the CBD seemingly implies that the effects of travel costs downtown on housing prices must certainly be weak. I tried to control for differences in the location of job opportunities by including the MANCIT variable, admittedly imperfect but the only such variable available for as many cities as I wished to study. More importantly, however, it appears to me that, in every city with which I am familiar, CBD and locally employed workers live throughout the city in significant numbers. Under such conditions, the two types of households must pay the same price (per unit) for housing at any given location. The fact that housing prices decline with distance from the CBD for locally employed workers implies that the money wages received by locally employed workers must likewise decline with distance. The fact of non-CBD employment by no means need weaken the effect of transport costs on housing prices.

Morgan's comments on the high intercorrelation between URBINC and CITINC might seem to imply that the coefficients of these variables are somehow tainted. I will readily admit that my explanation for the opposite signs of these two income variables in my equations (19) and (21) is a tentative one and not borne out by any additional evidence. From my Table 1 it appears quite certain that for these data the two income variables measure pretty much the same thing so far as the central city density gradient is concerned. But including CITINC in equations (19) and (21) actually corrected what appeared to me to be the wrong signs of the URBINC coefficients. This seems to me to be a step in the right direction, at least, and if due to "outliers" I am grateful for them.

In closing I would like to make one comment upon what I perceive to be a common objection of my three critics. This is the belief that if something conceivably important is omitted from the analysis the latter is necessarily suspect. I would argue just the reverse. A necessary, though certainly not sufficient, condition of a usable analysis is that it explain the phenomena it attempts to explain in terms of a limited set of data. The more limited the set of explanatory variables and, of course, the more consistent the model with observed data on the phenomena to be explained, the more useful is the analysis. If I were to attempt the risky business of criticizing my own work, I would be inclined to argue that, if anything, my explanation of urban population distribution requires too many variables rather than too few. To the comment that I have omitted other things from my explanation, I can only shout "hooray"!

Reply to Lippitt

by Snowbarger

I would like to thank Vernon Lippitt for his penetrating and insightful analysis of our paper. His comments will allow me to discuss, in more detail, some features of the AID program and its use in statistical anaylsis.

1. The AID program adds to the collection of statistical techniques that can be used to study the characteristics of empirical data. It is logically prior to the use of regression analysis and can be used to search data for interactions. An interaction variable can then be constructed and entered into a regression model. The AID program is not designed to supplant regression analysis.

The AID program can be used as an independent study device, or as a preliminary exploratory device within the framework of a complex statistical study. We have stressed the former feature in our study of multiple-car ownership (MCO). Without introducing regression techniques, a reasonably complete picture of MCO, and the dynamics of entry into the MCO market, is obtained. The MCO study could be placed into a regression framework and tested on other data.

Consumer expenditure on selected durables are explained by some interesting variables and their interactions. A consumer durable regression model can be constructed. The model might be used to predict individual household purchases. Or it might be aggregated to produce macropredictions.

The ideal use of the AID program allows the analyst to blend these two features into a complete statistical analysis. The AID program provides a profile of the data and uncovers the interactions. The complementary use of regression analysis provides significance tests, individual predicton models, macroprediction models, or both. The prediction may be attempted on a single cross section or on another panel. As an example of panel prediction, a model may be designed from one panel and then tried on another panel. In this manner, hypotheses may be tested. But before they can be tested they must be formulated. And this is precisely the advantage of the AID program when it is used prior to a regression analysis. It allows the researcher to design a hypothesis to fit or explain what he observes in the AID tree. The resulting hypothesis, within the framework of a complete regression model, may be tested on other data.

In summary, the AID program increases the efficiency of the research process. The application of the program to a set of data will reveal its structure. As the program is applied to data over time, stable relations may become apparent. The trees assist the researcher in formulating the hypothesis. The advantages are that better hypotheses may be designed, and premature testing (i.e., in regression) of hypotheses can be reduced. After the hypothesis is formulated, it should be tested on new data. The strength of the model will be revealed in its predictive ability.

2. There are several technical features of the AID program that increase its usefulness and flexibility. It can scan many more variables than it actually uses. Hence, a minimum of hunches and conditions needs to be imposed on the analysis. In addition, all variables may be entered unconstrained. When the variables enter the analysis unconstrained, nonadjacent groups may be selected or a split may occur containing a small number of cases. Neither problem should cause any concern. The computer output gives detailed information on the size of all groups. If nonadjacent categories are grouped together, and

there are a small number of cases, the regrouping can be disregarded. It might have occurred as a result of sampling error, etc. But if the regrouping contains a large number of cases, it might indicate an important result that should be considered by the analyst.

Splits that occur on a small number of cases (e.g., split 4 on refrigerators) are no problem. The order of splits is not important and these may be overlooked. The computer output should be studied carefully, however. When groups with a small number of cases are produced by the program, this is simply an indication that the program is working correctly. Individual behavior is not homogeneous and extreme variations are common. The program is looking for variation and does not stop to analyze the implications of the split. The research analyst must do this. (Small splits are actually an advantage because they warn the researcher of extreme skewness in the data.) This is why the problems of nonadjacent groups and small splits should cause no worry. The analyst must read and interpret all the output and not expect the tree itself to provide the answers.

There are several ways to get around the problems of nonadjacent groups and small splits. One solution is to not publish these "messy" things and carefully edit the tree to produce esthetically pleasing economic results. But if another person seeks to build on the analysis, he should be able to get the same results with the same data. The implication of these remarks is that there is a virtue in being able to reproduce another's work. Our trees are entirely reproducible by simply putting the data and the program on the computer.

Another way to avoid the problems of nonadjacent groups and small splits is to constrain and aggregate the variables that are to be used by the program. When a variable is constrained, the program is unable to split it on nonadjacent groups. A variable may be aggregated by reducing the number of code categories. (E.g., disposable income might be a ten-category variable with a range from $1000 to $50,000. It can be aggregated to five categories with the same range.) The effect of aggregation is to create a smaller number of code categories with a larger number of households in each category. Of course, to the extent that the researcher manipulates the variables in either of these two ways, he is dictating the "optimal" combinations to the program. (Carried to the limit, it means the AID analysis is superfluous. The researcher can use his personal feelings to design his own interactions and regroupings. The interactions thus designed are unlikely to be found in the data, however.) The result of doing either, or both, of these things is to reduce the flexibility of the program, reduce the variation explained by the tree, alter the structure of all interactions subsequent to the use of the constrained or aggregated variable, and, perhaps, even prevent the variable from being used.

The third way to handle the problems of nonadjacent groups or small splits is to enlarge the data set. This tends to reduce the impact of extreme variation and allows the program to isolate the dominant and pervasive characteristics of the data. This method will not entirely remove these problems, but it helps. We have used this technique in our paper in sections II, III. In section II we took the panel spanning two years and, rather than analyzing each year separately, we grouped the two years. The grouping had the effect of doubling our sample size. We, nevertheless, encountered these problems as the trees materialized. There are three reasons for this. First, the total two-year panel sample size of 2118 is not large, and the proportion of households purchasing a durable in a given year is small. Second, the purchase behavior of consumers for any of the five separate durables studied was not undergoing any large-scale change. Therefore, it was difficult to distinguish purchasers from nonpurchasers. Third, we did not have information on the age distribution of the current stock of durables. It seems certain that the stock characteristics of households are very important to purchase decisions of new durables.

In section III we grouped 1962 and 1963 data to increase our sample to over 4000 cases. The large number of sample points and the intensive growth of MCO allowed the program to isolate the dominant interactions with a minimum of extraneous splitting.

3. The output of the AID program can be carried to extremes. It is theoretically possible to continue splitting until every single data point is isolated. The point is that the concept of a final group, prior to this actual limit, is arbitrary. The researcher can call a group "final" at his discretion. One criterion that should be followed in defining a final group is that it be reasonably large in relation to the over-all sample. Hence, many seemingly final groups in the trees in our paper are not final at all. We have the computer output specifying many more splits on every final group in the trees. But we show no further splits because the group itself is small, or the mean of the group is small, or our analysis of the subsequent splits indicated that the program was unable to produce a dominant partition (i.e., a partition that contained a reasonably large number of cases).

4. Purchase intentions cause problems when they are used with other "objective" variables or predictors. Intentions may be part of a different stage in the causal process. They are unquestionably the

most efficient interaction term since they embody the objective economic determinants.

The purchase intentions variable was in the predictor list on every run on the panel data. It was the dominant variable in the purchase of the five durables. Purchase intentions were not part of the predictor list for the trees explaining the structure of MCO for 1957 and 1962–63. It would be meaningless to use current attitudes or intentions to explain ex-post MCO status.

We intend to re-examine the panel data and omit the purchase intentions variable. The sequential procedure of the AID program will then provide an even better picture of the influence of the objective economic variables. We also plan to use the panel data to examine purchase intentions as a dependent variable. The AID program will reveal the structure of interactions explaining these intentions.

PART IV

Producer Durables

Business Fixed Investment:
A Marriage of Fact and Fancy

W. H. LOCKE ANDERSON

UNIVERSITY OF MICHIGAN

Introduction

Several years ago Robert Eisner wrote a paper entitled, "Investment: Fact and Fancy."[1] Despite the author's explicit denial of such intent, there seemed little doubt that in his mind fact was to be equated with the acceleration principle and fancy with what is often called the "residual funds" theory of investment.[2] Eisner's provocative title is characteristic of the long-standing controversy between the accelerationists and the profiteers, which has so often been a source of enjoyable acrimony and occasionally even a source of enlightenment.

The basic position of the accelerationists is that capital goods must be loved to be worth purchasing. The basic position of the profiteers is that capital goods cannot be bought for love, alas, but only for money. Given the utter reasonableness of both of these propositions, it is not surprising that in recent years we have been treated to a number of

NOTE: This project was started when the author was on the staff of the Council of Economic Advisers and completed as a project of the Research Seminar in Quantitative Economics at Michigan, with support of the National Science Foundation.

[1] Robert Eisner, "Investment: Fact and Fancy," *American Economic Review,* May 1963, pp. 237–246.

[2] This theory is first clearly spelled out in John Meyer and Edwin Kuh, *The Investment Decision,* Cambridge, Mass., 1957, and further developed in James Duesenberry, *Business Cycles and Economic Growth,* New York, 1958.

econometric studies in which both capacity utilization and cost of funds variables have been shown to influence investment.[3]

In this study I have developed additional evidence in support of compromise. In brief, the equations which I shall present show investment expenditures to be functionally related to capacity utilization, retained earnings, net balance sheet positions, interest rates, and equity yields. The data, which are drawn from a variety of sources, have a much broader industrial coverage than that of most studies, embracing nearly all of producer durables and "other construction" in the national accounts.[4] Thus the results may be fairly directly incorporated into aggregative models for policy and prediction.

Before proceeding, I feel that I ought to say a few words on behalf of the much-maligned construction of highly aggregative models. I grant that because of collinearity, simultaneity, aggregation bias, and shortage of data points, variables as aggregative as those in the national accounts are not a very rich testing ground for economic hypotheses. Nonetheless, there are two good reasons for continuing to use them.

The first is that the less aggregative the approach to hypothesis testing is, the greater are the dangers that model building will degenerate into particular explanations for particular cases and that description will masquerade as theory. Broadly aggregative data provide a useful check on the generality of propositions established from less aggregative data.

The second reason is that policy formulation and forecasting often require quick and dirty estimates of economic parameters. If a policy maker needs to know the size of the accelerator, it is little help to him to be told that it is one value for manufacturing, another for public utilities, and some wholly unknown value for the remainder of industry which no one has yet bothered to investigate. Without a complete dis-

---

[3] See, for example: Frank de Leeuw, "The Demand for Capital Goods by Manufacturers," *Econometrica,* July 1962, pp. 407–423; Gary Fromm, "Inventories, Business Cycles, and Economic Stabilization," in *Inventory Fluctuations and Economic Stabilization,* U.S. Congress, Joint Economic Committee, 87th Congress, 2nd Session, Washington, 1962; John Meyer and Robert Glauber, *Economic Decisions, Economic Forecasting, and Public Policy,* Cambridge, Mass., 1964; W. H. Locke Anderson, *Corporate Finance and Fixed Investment,* Cambridge, Mass., 1964; Shirley Almon, "Investment Decisions: A Quarterly Time Series Analysis of Capital Appropriations in Manufacturing," unpublished; Robert Resek, "Investment by Manufacturing Firms: A Quarterly Time Series Analysis of Industry Data," unpublished.

[4] The coverage is approximately the same as that of Bert Hickman's study, *Investment Demand and U.S. Economic Growth* (Washington, 1965), to which the present study owes a considerable debt.

aggregative model which is set up to yield quick answers, aggregate models will continue to be very useful.

Theoretical Rationale

The starting premise of this investment model is the familiar profit-maximization assumption, whereby business carries its fixed investment to the point which equates the marginal rate of return to the marginal cost of funds. The operational problem in evaluating this premise is that neither the marginal rate of return (*mrr*) nor the marginal cost of funds (*mcf*) is directly observable. Hence it is necessary to evaluate the premise indirectly by conceptually specifying a model of the form:

$$mrr = f_1(I, Z_1), \tag{1}$$

$$mcf = f_2(I, Z_2), \tag{2}$$

$$mcf = mrr, \tag{3}$$

where Z_1 and Z_2 are the (vector) determinants of the positions of the *mrr* and *mcf* schedules as functions of investment (I). The two unobservables are eliminated from the system, which is solved for I, yielding:

$$I = g(Z_1, Z_2). \tag{4}$$

Measurements are made directly on (4), from which inferences about (1) and (2) are drawn.

As determinants of the position of the *mrr* schedule, I have used the level of output and the existing capital stock.

As Duesenberry has shown, one need not be a strict accelerationist to recognize the close link between utilization and investment.[5] If marginal costs rise with output along a schedule whose position is determined by the capital stock in existence, then the higher is output relative to the capital stock, the greater is the saving on variable cost to be obtained by shifting the marginal cost curve to the right through accumulating capital, and the higher is the rate of return on new capital.

As determinants of the position of the marginal cost of funds schedule, I have used the flow of retained earnings, the level of output, total outstanding liabilities, the value of assets other than fixed capital, the bond yield, and the dividend/price yield on equity.

The reason for including retained earnings is obvious. As for the balance sheet items, their inclusion is dictated by opportunity-cost

---

[5] Duesenberry, *Business Cycles,* Chap. 4.

considerations derived from the risks of illiquidity and indebtedness.[6] Other things equal, the higher noncapital assets are, the lower is the imputed cost of using funds for the accumulation of capital rather than noncapital assets, or the lower is the cost of decumulating noncapital assets to buy capital. The higher liabilities are, the higher is the cost of using funds for capital accumulation rather than debt retirement, or the higher is the cost of incurring further liabilities to finance capital expansion.

Along with the levels of liabilities and noncapital assets, some measure of businesses' ability to bear liabilities and its need to carry noncapital assets is required to determine the position of the imputed cost schedules. In both cases the level of output is probably a suitable variable, or in any case an adequate proxy which can be justified on grounds of simplicity.

The rate of interest is included to measure the market cost of raising funds through debt issue, and the dividend/share price ratio to measure the cost to existing stockholders of raising funds through equity issue.[7]

Taking these considerations together, we get relationships of the following sort (neglecting lags for the moment):

$$mrr = f_1(I, Q, K); \tag{5}$$

$$mcf = f_2(I, R, A, L, Q, s, r); \tag{6}$$

where I is investment, Q is output, K is capital stock, R is retained earnings, A is noncapital assets, L is liabilities, s is dividend/price ratio, and r is interest rate. If we normalize the dollar magnitudes for scale by taking them all as ratio to the capital stock and then make linear approximations, we get:

$$mrr = a_1 + a_2 \frac{I}{K} + a_3 \frac{Q}{K}; \tag{7}$$

$$mcf = b_1 + b_2 \frac{I}{K} + b_3 \frac{R}{K} + b_4 \frac{A}{K} + b_5 \frac{L}{K} + b_6 \frac{Q}{K} + b_7 s + b_8 r. \tag{8}$$

[6] For a further development of the rationale for including the state of the balance sheet, see Anderson, *Corporate Finance*, Chaps. 3 and 5.

[7] The cost to existing stockholders is actually some discounted earnings stream per share divided by the current price per share. Dividends are usually a better measure (except for scale) of normal earnings than current earnings are. Hence I use the dividend/price ratio rather than the earnings/price ratio.

Equating these and collecting terms with I/K on the left, we get:

$$\frac{I}{K} = c_1 + c_2 \frac{Q}{K} + c_3 \frac{R}{K} + c_4 \frac{A}{K} + c_5 \frac{L}{K} + c_6 s + c_7 r. \tag{9}$$

This is the model whose measurement has been the principal task of this study.

The Data

The data used to fit regressions corresponding to equation (9) come from a variety of sources to be described below. All dollar magnitudes are in billion 1954 dollars. All flows are annual. All stocks are measured at the end of the year. Bond and stock yields are measured in percentage points.

First, K (capital stock) and I (investment): The data on stocks, depreciation, and net and gross investment are derived from those prepared by the Department of Commerce.[8] They cover all stocks of producer durable equipment and "other construction" corresponding to the national accounts investment data, except those of agriculture and nonprofit institutions. The series have been extended through 1963, taking account of the July 1964 revisions in the national accounts.[9]

The Commerce Department provides four stock series corresponding to four different depreciation methods: straight-line, *Bulletin F* lives; straight-line, *Bulletin F* lives shortened by 20 per cent; double declining-balance, *Bulletin F* lives; double declining-balance, *Bulletin F* lives shortened by 20 per cent. Since there is little a priori basis for choice among these,[10] I have used each in turn to see which one seems to give the best results.

If the rate of growth of the capital stock is poorly measured, it will have a serious distorting effect on the measured coefficients of equation (9). There are two likely sources of such measurement error. First, the depreciation rate may be either higher or lower than the rate at which capital wastage really occurs. Second, the investment deflator may not accurately reflect changes in the productivity of capital goods.[11]

---

[8] These series were originally published in the *Survey of Current Business,* November 1962.

[9] The author would like to thank Robert Wasson of the Commerce Department for assistance in updating the series and removing the investment of nonprofit institutions. The tedious calculations involved in this process were ably performed by Charles Bischoff, a summer intern at the Council of Economic Advisers.

[10] If there were, the Commerce Department presumably would not have hedged.

[11] This possibility is raised by Hickman in *Investment Demand,* which gives an interesting account of the interrelationships among depreciation, capital productivity, and embodiment on pages 39–41.

Since either of these is quite likely to be the case with the data at hand, I have added an explicit time trend to the variables already included in equation (9). Its coefficient can compensate for any systematic trend in the error of measurement of the capital stock.

Second, Q (output): These figures from the national accounts include GNP originating in nonfarm business less that originating in finance, insurance, and real estate.[12] Thus the coverage is quite close to that of the capital series.

Third, R (retained earnings), A (noncapital assets), L (liabilities): With the exception of inventory stocks (which are unpublished stock series corresponding to the national accounts nonfarm inventory investment), all these figures come from the flow-of-funds accounts for nonfarm, nonfinancial business.[13] The retained earnings include noncorporate depreciation and proprietors' net investment plus gross corporate saving. The assets include inventories plus noncorporate and corporate financial assets. The liabilities include all corporate and noncorporate liabilities except one- to four-family mortgages. All financial variables are deflated by the investment deflator.

Fourth, s (equity yield) and r (bond yield): These are annual averages of Moody's industrial dividend/price ratio and Moody's industrial bond yield.[14]

Specification

The specification of equation (9) is incomplete, for it fails to indicate the lag structure. Moreover, a constraint had to be placed on some of the coefficients because of collinearity and a shortage of degrees of freedom.

Two specifications were ultimately adopted for measurement:

$$i_t{}^n = d_1 + d_2 \bar{u}_t + d_3 f_t + d_4 s_{t-1} + d_5 r_{t-1}; \tag{10}$$

and

$$i_t{}^g = d'_1 + d'_2 \bar{u}_t + d'_3 f_t + d'_4 s_{t-1} + d'_5 r_{t-1}. \tag{10'}$$

[12] The GNP originating in nonfarm business comes from Table 10 of the July 1964 *Survey of Current Business* and earlier issues. That originating in finance, insurance, and real estate comes from the series prepared by Martin Marimont and published in the *Survey of Current Business,* October 1962 and September 1964.

[13] Board of Governors of the Federal Reserve System, *Flow of Funds Accounts, 1945–62, 1963 Supplement,* updated with more recent estimates from the *Federal Reserve Bulletin.*

[14] These are available in *Business Statistics.*

The following is an explanation of the new notation employed:

$$i_i^n = \frac{I_t^N}{K_{t-1}} \text{ is the net investment rate;}$$

$$i_t^g = \frac{I_t^G}{K_{t-1}} \text{ is the gross investment rate;}$$

$$\bar{u}_t = 0.5 \frac{Q_t + Q_{t-1}}{K_{t-1}} \text{ is the output-capital ratio;}$$

$$f_t = \frac{A_{t-1}}{K_{t-1}} - \frac{L_{t-1}}{K_{t-1}} + 0.5 \frac{R_t + R_{t-1}}{K_{t-1}} \text{ is the financial position.}$$

The following are the justifications for the particular specifications adopted.

First, if the average effective depreciation rate on existing capital were a constant, the choice of i^n or i^g as the dependent variable would affect only the intercept of the equation. Since it is not constant (even for the declining-balance stock versions) because of variations in the useful-life mix of the stock, I initially tried using the depreciation rate as an independent variable. Its measured coefficients were implausible and insignificant. Yet when no account is taken of depreciation, neither (10) nor (10') is wholly satisfactory. Other things equal, higher depreciation ought to increase gross investment since it shifts the rate of return schedule, but it should lower net investment, since the supply of funds schedule is not infinitely elastic. Omitting the depreciation rate seemed the lesser of two evils, since its inclusion raised substantially the standard errors of the coefficients of other variables without contributing much to compensate for this.

Second, by averaging the output figures to approximate $Q_{t-1/2}$, the locus of final investment decision making is implicitly placed at the end of the year preceding the investment. Given that annual capital spending intentions surveys which are made before the preceding year's end are typically much poorer than those made soon after the beginning of the year, this seems like a good rough approximation.

Third, although the collapsing of the three internal cost of funds variables into a single variable was in part dictated by a shortage of data points and by the considerable collinearity which would otherwise occur, there are certainly analytical bases of justification. There is no reason to suppose that equal increments to noncapital assets (which are liquid) and liabilities should raise the imputed cost of funds for investment; if it did, firms could lower the cost by selling assets and buying back their liabilities. Hence the net position is what matters. Averaging R_t and R_{t-1} gives an approximation to the retained earnings flow at the end of $t-1$. This is used as a proxy for the expected flow during t. When this is added to $A_{t-1} - L_{t-1}$, it gives a variable which can be interpreted as the potential net position at the end of t if no investment is undertaken during t and no shares are issued. Apart from any equity issue, then, the further that investment is carried, the worse will be the end-of-year net position, and the higher will be the cost of funds.

Fourth, the bond and stock yields are lagged by a full year rather than the half year by which the other variables were lagged. This was done in the belief that decisions and arrangements to issue shares or long-term debt to finance capital spending are usually worked out quite far in advance of the spending undertaken.

It would be quite possible, of course, to quibble with the details of this specification. One might, for instance, prefer to have a nonadditive equation. I experimented with a log-linear form and got results which were not appreciably different from those of the linear form. Since a linear model lends itself to such ready economic interpretation and application, I preferred to stick with it. I also experimented with minor variations in the lag pattern, but these had little effect on the general characteristics of the results.

Results

The investment models given by equations (10) and (10′) were first fitted to data for which the dependent variable ranged from 1948 through 1963.[15] The fits were not especially impressive; and the standard errors of most of the coefficient were quite large. However, about half of the unexplained sum of squares was attributable to a very large residual for 1957. Since I firmly believe that the continuation of the mid-1950's investment boom into 1957 was collective madness *ex ante,* not to mention *ex post,* I had little compunction about pulling the 1957 observation and refitting the equations without it. The object of this was to increase the accuracy of the parameter estimates and not, of course, to raise the R^2. Anyone who feels that it is reprehensible to throw out maverick data points may feel free to double $1 - R^2$ in his own copy of Tables 1 and 2. All of the numbers in the tables as printed are based on calculations omitting 1957.

---

[15] These computations were ably and quickly performed by Wayne Vroman, a research assistant in the Research Seminar in Quantitative Economics, University of Michigan.

TABLE 1

Regression Results: Net Investment Rate

Capital Stock Series	Intercept	Coefficient of					$\bar{R}^2$
		$\bar{u}_t$	f_t	s_{t-1}	r_{t-1}	t	
A	-.1001	.1392	.1395	-.0068	-.0168		.9716
		(.0332)	(.0298)	(.0013)	(.0024)		
	-.1076	.1493	.1257	-.0070	-.0155	-.0003	.9692
		(.0394)	(.0420)	(.0014)	(.0037)	(.0007)	
B	-.1835	.1335	.1680	-.0078	-.0097		.9810
		(.0258)	(.0217)	(.0012)	(.0023)		
	-.1864	.1368	.1629	-.0079	-.0091	-.0002	.9790
		(.0301)	(.0303)	(.0013)	(.0034)	(.0006)	
C	-.0369	.0925	.1148	-.0091	-.0273		.9678
		(.0301)	(.0314)	(.0017)	(.0030)		
	-.0553	.1240	.0716	-.0096	-.0226	-.0013	.9714
		(.0352)	(.0412)	(.0016)	(.0042)	(.0009)	
D	-.0712	.0835	.1307	-.0115	-.0243		.9696
		(.0263)	(.0257)	(.0017)	(.0032)		
	-.1078	.1157	.0856	-.0122	-.0179	-.0017	.9781
		(.0266)	(.0299)	(.0015)	(.0040)	(.0008)	

TABLE 2

Regression Results: Gross Investment Rate

| Capital Stock Series | Intercept | $\bar{u}_t$ | Coefficient of | | | | $\bar{R}^2$ |
			f_t	s_{t-1}	r_{t-1}	t	
A	.0103	.1234 (.0287)	.1391 (.0265)	−.0077 (.0013)	−.0162 (.0022)		.9730
	.0036	.1323 (.0350)	.1268 (.0374)	−.0078 (.0012)	−.0151 (.0033)	−.0003 (.0006)	.9708
B	−.0072	.1379 (.0323)	.1261 (.0273)	−.0088 (.0015)	−.0184 (.0029)		.9748
	−.0126	.1439 (.0376)	.1169 (.0379)	−.0089 (.0016)	−.0174 (.0042)	−.0003 (.0008)	.9725
C	.0338	.1135 (.0272)	.1340 (.0284)	−.0093 (.0015)	−.0214 (.0027)		.9685
	.0230	.1255 (.0350)	.1176 (.0409)	−.0095 (.0016)	−.0197 (.0042)	−.0005 (.0008)	.9663
D	.0241	.1191 (.0288)	.1365 (.0281)	−.0114 (.0019)	−.0250 (.0035)		.9716
	.0092	.1322 (.0353)	.1181 (.0397)	−.0117 (.0020)	−.0224 (.0052)	−.0007 (.0010)	.9692

The results presented in Table 1 are those for equation (10), in which i^n is the dependent variable. Those in Table 2 are for equation (10'), in which i^g is the dependent variable. Each equation is estimated for each of the capital stock variants, and for each variant it is estimated with and without the trend variable.

There are very few noticeable differences between the coefficients in the two tables, except of course for the intercepts. The differences between the two columns of intercepts are not far from what one should expect from the average depreciation rates, which range from .085 for series A to .144 for series D. The pairs of corresponding slope coefficients rarely differ from each other by any amount which looks remarkable, given the standard errors. Neither set of equations seems to give fits that are systematically better than those of the other.

Likewise, there is little basis for choice among the various capital stock series to be found in comparisons of either over-all goodness of fit or significance of the output-capital ratio. The only place where one can detect any important differences is in the net investment rate equations. For the two declining-balance stock equations the coefficients of the output-capital ratios are noticeably increased by inclusion of the trend terms. This suggests that the declining-balance depreciation leads to an understatement of the growth in the capital stock, and hence to an understatement of the secular down-drift in u_t. When the time trend is explicitly included, the coefficients on u_t get larger and the trends have negative coefficients. The trend has the least effect on the coefficients of the equations using stock series B; this is the series with the highest growth rate of the four.

The output-capital ratio coefficients are all quite significant; in every case they are at least three times their standard errors. They give more explanatory contribution to the straight-line stock equations than to the declining-balance equations, which is what one should expect if these are in fact somewhat better stock series.

In almost all equations the financial position variable is also highly significant. Its significance level is reduced when the trend variable is included in the regression, however. Since both the profit rate and the net position have downward trends over the data period, the financial position is quite collinear with the trend.

The dividend yield variable is highly significant in every equation. Indeed, this consistent predictive contribution is something of a puzzle if the stock dividend yield measures only the cost of equity funds. Its effects are probably nonlinear (threshold) for individual firms and hence it ought not to be easily approximated in an aggregate linear equation. It seems likely therefore that it also measures expectational elements which influence both investment and stock prices, but are not adequately reflected in u_t.

The rate of interest is also highly significant in every equation. Since it has a marked upward trend over the data period, it is quite collinear with the trend variable. Nonetheless, its significance levels hold up well even when the trend is explicitly included.

The time trend itself is a positive explanatory nuisance in almost all cases. Except in capital stock variants C and D in the net investment equations, the inclusion of the time trend always reduces the adjusted R^2. In the two exceptions the adjusted R^2 is increased only slightly by the trend. These results give very little indication, therefore, that the Commerce Department's estimating procedures systematically and significantly distort the growth rate of the effective capital stock.

Incidentally, these results suggest that the recent findings of Hickman[16] may result in part from incomplete specification. He observes a significant negative trend in his flexible accelerator equations. This he attributes to a downtrend in the amount of capital desired per unit of output, as capital is conventionally measured. However, his specification does not include adequate accounting for the factors which have led to a secular uptrend in the position of the marginal cost of funds schedule. Lacking this accounting, he is forced to infer from an actual downtrend in the net investment rate at a constant output-capital ratio that there has been a decline in the desired amount of capital per unit of output. The data used in this study also show a significant negative trend if the variables standing for the marginal cost of funds are omitted. However, as soon as they are included, the trend ceases to be significant.

Conclusions

On the strength of the results given in Tables 1 and 2, it seems fairly clear that both capacity utilization and financial variables belong together in an adequate explanation of investment. If these were the only results to support this contention, one could justifiably be skeptical because of the formidable problems of drawing reliable inferences from time series aggregates. However, given the weight of evidence derived from less aggregative studies (see footnote 3) and the confirmation found in these aggregates, it is hard to see how one can remain a celibate accelerationist.

[16] Hickman, *Investment Demand*.

On the strength of the parameters of these equations, it is tempting to advance some conclusions about the effects of monetary and tax policies. At this writing I shall resist these temptations because of the dynamic complexities of the relationships among the variables involved. Quite apart from the macroeconomic feedbacks from investment to output and profits, one cannot change any of the variables in the equations without affecting most of the others. Not only are they linked together through accounting identities, but they are also interrelated through decision-making processes which determine borrowing and equity issue and through a technical relationship between the utilization rate and the retained earnings rate. Until these are adequately spelled out, it will not be possible to make even a partial equilibrium analysis of the effects of policy changes. Hence it seems best to close this tale with the wedding and leave the story of its progeny to a sequel volume.

Investment, Dividend, and External Finance Behavior of Firms

PHOEBUS J. DHRYMES

UNIVERSITY OF PENNSYLVANIA

AND

MORDECAI KURZ

STANFORD UNIVERSITY AND HEBREW UNIVERSITY, ISRAEL

Preliminaries and Summary

The relations among the investment, dividend, and external finance behavior of firms are often alluded to but seldom studied systematically. Quite clearly, given the institutional milieu of the modern corporation, there exists at least a presumption that these three aspects of the firm's decision-making process exhibit some interaction. Yet, in the current literature the view is frequently advanced that investment decisions are taken on solely "real" (nonfinancial) considerations, that dividend policies are characterized by a considerable degree of inertia, and that the financing of investment by internal or external funds is a mere detail.

To our knowledge, an explicit link among these three decisions has not been proposed and econometrically implemented. It is the purpose of this paper to study the question of establishing such a link and to elucidate the extent of the interdependence of these decisions. The

NOTE: We wish to acknowledge our gratitude to L. R. Klein and Edwin Kuh for several helpful suggestions and comments on an earlier version of this paper. We should also like to acknowledge the able research assistance of George Schink, Pietro Balestra, and Hajime Oniki. Financial support was in part provided through NSF grant GS 571 at the University of Pennsylvania, Office of Naval Research Grant 225 (50) at Stanford University, and through computer time made available to us by the Computer Center of the University of Pennsylvania.

approach employed makes use of a series of cross sections. Specifically, our sample consists of 181 industrial and commercial firms for which a continuous record exists over the period 1947–60. The "structural" form of this interrelated system will be estimated successively over the period 1951–60 in order to test the stability of structure, especially as it is related to business fluctuations.

Our main findings are the following: (1) A strong interdependence is evident between the investment and dividend decisions; the external finance activities of firms seem to be affected by the other two aspects of the firm's operation but do not seem much to affect them, except possibly during upswings or peaks. (2) There is compelling evidence to suggest that in estimating the structure one ought to use full information methods. (3) Elements of both the accelerator as well as the rate of profit theories of investment seem necessary in order to explain the empirical behavior of investment.

A Brief Review of the Literature

The three aspects of the firm's behavior on which this study is focused have been studied in the literature with varying degrees of intensity. Thus investment behavior has perhaps been studied most intensively.

The integration of investment theory with the neoclassical theory of the firms can be traced to Roos [20], Tinbergen [22, 23], and Klein [21].[1] An extensive survey of the work of the last two authors can be found in Meyer and Kuh [17]. Subsequent contributions have been numerous but are best omitted here since rather recently Eisner and Strotz [7] have provided a very complete review of such works.

It is perhaps accurate to say that the main results of such studies lie in providing tests concerning the empirical relevance of the accelerator, capacity-accelerator, or profits (or rate of profit) theories of investment. The issue is not yet satisfactorily resolved, but it appears that neither the capacity accelerator nor the profits theory is alone sufficient, but rather a combination of elements of both is probably necessary to provide a satisfactory account of the empirical behavior of investment.

In this connection it seems appropriate to cite, in some detail, a very important recent study by Kuh [13], which is, in some respects, similar to the one we propose to pursue here. Kuh investigates the investment, dividend, and external finance aspects of the firm's behavior in the following context. His basic sample consists of sixty industrial firms for which a continuous satisfactory record exists over the years 1935–55.

[1] Numbers in brackets refer to Bibliography at end of paper.

This sample was arrived at from a larger one by a process of selection which eliminated firms that were merged into others over the sample period, as well as those that were "too large"—owning gross assets over $120 million in 1953.

The work is divided in two distinct parts, a theoretical and an empirical one. In the theoretical part the interdependence of the three decisions is quite clearly recognized and an integrated model is presented combining the capacity-accelerator model of investment with the Lintner [16] model of dividend behavior. The empirical part, unfortunately, does not carry out this integration. There, investment is given by the usual capacity-accelerator model, so that it depends on the capital stock and sales, as well as on the observed sales-capital ratio, the latter being an approximation to the desired output-capital ratio of the accelerator theory. In this connection models are also tried in which the sales variable is replaced by a profit variable. It is found, however, that the former models are more in accord with the data than the profit ones. Dividends are explained by the well-known Lintner hypothesis, on which we have commented at length elsewhere [3]. They are thus made to depend on profits and past dividends, the model being essentially an adaptation of the usual flexible accelerator model of investment; here the role of the capital coefficient is played by the desired dividend-payout ratio.

Finally, external finance behavior is derived residually through the budgetary requirement that investment expenditures must equal retained earnings plus depreciation allowances plus external finance.

Thus, in this context there is a certain direction of causality; investment is independent of dividends and external finance; dividends depend only on profits (and lagged dividends) which may depend on investment, although the dependence is not explicit. Finally, external finance is more or less residually derived, and hence would depend on investment and dividends. Although Kuh does not state his model in these terms, the above is, we think, a very plausible interpretation of the spirit in which his econometric investigation is carried out.

His is a penetrating examination of the problems relating to testing homogeneity and stability of structures by an ingenious combination of cross-section and time-series data; the problem of simultaneity and interdependence to which our paper is addressed is, however, entirely overlooked in his econometric investigation. Kuh's estimation is carried out by single-equation methods and his results seem to bear out the capacity accelerator theory of investment and the homogeneous Lintner hypothesis on dividends.

A more recent study of investment behavior is that of Jorgenson [9]. His formal model considers the firm as determining its investment policy through maximization of net worth, defined as the present discounted value of current receipts minus outlays, where the latter includes, in addition to remuneration of the variable factors, expenditures on capital goods. However, his operational model through the convenient assumption of the Cobb-Douglas production function essentially reduces to the accelerator model. His major innovation is the introduction of general lag structures between the demand for additional capital stock, as arising because of a discrepancy between desired and actual capital stock, and the augmentation of the latter through deliveries of capital equipment. Another innovation consists of the systematic treatment of the replacement demand for capital. His sample consists of quarterly observations on certain classes of industrial aggregates.

Concerning the dividend behavior of firms, in addition to the work of Kuh [13] referred to above, one should mention the pioneering work of Lintner [15, 16]. The same approach is more or less followed by Darling [2], whose innovation consists in making the dividend function depend on the change in sales; the apparent success of this is probably a reflection of the type of dependence we wish to investigate here. In this connection it should be pointed out that we [3] have determined a substantial impact of investment on the dividend decision. Another recent study of dividend behavior is that of Brittain [1]. He follows the Lintner model quite closely, but reports that profits gross of depreciation is a better explanatory factor of dividend behavior than is profits net of depreciation.

The question of internal finance has not been systematically treated in the econometric literature, save for the work of Kuh which has a slightly different orientation from the one pursued in this paper. Thus, although frequent allusions are made in the literature to the interdependent character of these three aspects of the firm's behavior, rather little has been done in carrying out the implications of this view to the form of the econometric model to be estimated. One way of rationalizing this is to consider the current view in the literature as holding that the problem is being resolved in a sequential manner. Thus, investment decisions are implicitly viewed as being taken solely (or chiefly) on the basis of "real" considerations, and then once this decision is resolved the question of how to finance this undertaking is considered.

In the case of dividend behavior, the main work on the subject, viz., Lintner's [15, 16], views dividend disbursals as totally divorced from investment considerations. Yet, as noted above, we have determined a significant dependence of the dividend policy of electric utility firms on actual and anticipated investment. As an empirical matter Kuh and Meyer [14] report that 75 per cent of investment in manufacturing is internally "financed." The same authors in a previous work [17] list an impressive catalogue of reasons why such a preference might exist. While this phenomenon may, in some part, be due to the peculiarities of the tax structure of the United States it may also reflect imperfection in the capital market.

The view taken in this paper is rather simply put as follows. Quite generally a firm faces an outflow of funds represented by its variable and fixed costs, tax and dividend payments, as well as by its investment activities. On the other hand, it can rely on an inflow of funds represented chiefly by its sales and the proceeds through various forms of external finance, viz., by bond or stock flotation. To the extent that a plausible objective for a firm is to grow, provided its operations are profitable, and that the capital market is less than perfect, it would follow that investment and dividend outlays are quite clearly competitive.

On the other hand, the rather marked reliance on internal funds signifies a strong aversion to the use of the capital market. Thus, it would seem quite reasonable to suppose that the three decisions—to invest, to pay dividends, and to resort to external funds—are mutually determined. Hence, it is desirable to investigate this problem in the context of a simultaneous-equation model. If our conjecture about the *modus operandi* of the system is correct, then we should expect that the coefficients of the jointly determined variables—investment, dividends paid, and external finance—would be significant, at least in several instances, where they serve as explanatory variables.

The Model

THE STRUCTURE OF THE MODEL

In the discussion of the previous section it was pointed out that in our view a deficiency in the econometric investigations of the investment aspect of the firm's behavior is that the interaction of investment with certain financial variables was substantially overlooked.

Our objective here is to present a somewhat general equilibrium model of the firm's activities which attempts to remedy this deficiency and at the same time is sufficiently simple so as not to obscure the essential elements of the problem. Thus, at this stage, we shall not explicitly consider the technological constraint on the firm's activities in the form of a production function, nor the institutional characteristics of the factor and product market in which it operates, in the form of firm or industry factor supply and product demand functions.

We shall rather assume that production and marketing decisions predate the decision process we wish to study. The view we implicitly take is that investment affects output (and profits) only with a lag so that current investment affects only future output, and hence profits, and that current output and hence current profits are not affected by current investment.

While this may not be a perfectly valid view, it is, we believe, sufficiently accurate to serve at least as a rather useful simplification. We would think that the gains in simplicity obtained thereby more than offset any increased incidence of simultaneous-equation bias. Beyond that, it has of course been traditional to treat sales and profits, both current and lagged, as valid predetermined variables in cross-section studies on investment.

The general (schematic) structure of the model is as follows:

$$I_1 = f_1(I_2, D, EF1, EF2; X_1, X_2, \ldots X_n)$$

$$I_2 = f_2(I_1, D, EF1, EF2; X_1, X_2, \ldots X_n)$$

$$D = f_3(I_1, I_2, EF1, EF2; X_1, X_2, \ldots X_n) \tag{1}$$

$$EF1 = f_4(I_1, I_2, D, EF2; X_1, X_2, \ldots X_n)$$

$$EF2 = f_5(I_1, I_2, D, EF1; X_1, X_2, \ldots X_n)$$

Where I_1 is investment in fixed assets; I_2 is inventory and other short term investments; D is common stock dividends paid; $EF1$ is (net) external finance obtained by borrowing; $EF2$ is (net) external finance obtained by stock flotation; the X_i are predetermined variables, $i = 1, 2, \ldots$ n. The predetermined variables may include profits, depreciation, sales, long-term debt outstanding, etc., and will be introduced explicitly as the occasion arises.

In addition, the firm faces the "budget constraint"

$$I_1 + I_2 = EF1 + EF2 + P - D + Dep, \tag{2}$$

where P and Dep denote, respectively, profits and depreciation allowances.

If we use the constraint in (2), we can eliminate one of the (endogenous) variables of the system in (1). We have chosen to eliminate $EF2$; this was done chiefly because data on this variable were very difficult to obtain with any reasonable degree of reliability. At any rate stock flotation as a source of external finance, while not negligible, is

TABLE 1

Sources of Gross External Finance in Manufacturing, Mining,
Commercial, and Other Firms, 1954 - 56

Type of Firm	Bonds		Preferred Stock		Common Stock		Total (million dollars)
	Million Dollars	Per Cent	Million Dollars	Per Cent	Million Dollars	Per Cent	
1956							
Manufacturing	3,000	80.5	164	4.4	562	15.1	3,726
Mining	300	63.3	17	3.6	157	33.1	474
Commercial & other	259	79.4	8	2.5	59	18.1	326
Total	3,559	78.6	189	4.2	778	17.2	4,526
1955							
Manufacturing	2,043	68.2	165	5.5	786	26.3	2,994
Mining	198	47.8	10	2.4	206	49.8	414
Commercial & other	340	76.7	21	4.8	82	18.5	443
Total	2,581	67.0	196	5.1	1,074	27.9	3,851
1954							
Manufacturing	1,877	82.8	228	10.0	163	7.2	2,268
Mining	347	64.4	14	2.6	178	33.0	539
Commercial & other	317	75.3	62	14.7	42	10.0	421
Total	2,541	78.7	304	9.4	383	11.9	3,228

Source: *Statistical Bulletin*, Securities and Exchange Commission, February 1957.

of minor significance compared with bond flotation for most years and industries in our analysis. Table 1 will bear this out. Since our sample will consist largely of manufacturing and retail trade firms with a rather small representation of mining firms, it follows that our selection of bond finance as the principal source of external funds to be studied is not likely to lead to serious deficiencies.

Finally, we have chosen to regard short-term investment as a predetermined variable, so that our final system of equations to be estimated is reduced to three, viz., the dividend, the (fixed) investment, and the external finance equations. This last decision carries with it, in principle, serious deficiencies.

There are, however, several ameliorating circumstances: first, to the extent that a component of short-term investment is unintended inventory accumulation, we are clearly not committing a specification error; secondly, to the extent that the data for this series includes credit advanced to clients in the normal conduct of business (accounts receivable) this does not constitute a misspecification either; similarly for accounts payable; but to the extent that the series contains a component of intended inventory accumulation and short-term securities holdings for other than liquidity-transaction purposes, we are clearly committing a specification error. Unfortunately no detailed breakdown of the short-term investment series was available, so we have chosen to treat it as a predetermined variable. Thus, the model finally estimated is of the form

$$D = g_1(I, EF1; X_1, X_2, \ldots, X_n)$$
$$I = g_2(D, EF1; X_1, X_2, \ldots, X_n) \qquad (2)$$
$$EF1 = g_3(D, I; X_1, X_2, \ldots, X_n)$$

GENERAL COMMENTS ON THE FORM OF THE EQUATIONS

The Dividend Equation. One can look upon dividend disbursals as conveying information to the market on the inherent profitability of the disbursing firm as Modigliani and Miller [19] *inter alios* have argued. In fact they would contend that the dividend series contains "more information" than the profit series. Hence, it would appear that it is the policy of firms to maintain a steady dividend per share and to adjust it upward and downward only when a "permanent" change in their economic environment has taken place. As a matter of fact, it is more or less common for firms to maintain a constant dividend *per share.* But this in no way implies constancy in the dividend-profit ratio.

It is reasonable to suppose that dividend disbursals will depend on the rate of profit of the firm, its investment plans, and the external finance obtained through the bond market; the rationale for this last variable would be that external finance will enable the firm to carry out its planned dividend disbursals even when the rate of profit is low and investment programs are extensive.

The Investment Equation. The foundations of investment theory in the theory of the firm are too well-known to require repetition here. Clearly from this point of view investment would depend either on changes in the volume of output or on its rate of profit, which may be taken to lead to changes in the expected profitability of new investment. These two considerations are not totally unrelated, especially if the firm is assumed to operate with a neoclassical production function allowing substitution; if no substitution is allowed, then it is not clear that the rate of profit has any place in the investment function.

Our innovation here consists in introducing the other two jointly dependent variables, viz., dividends and external finance. We have already given some indication as to why we consider these variables relevant.

Clearly dividend disbursals and investment outlays represent competing demands on the resources available to the firm; thus it would be quite plausible to suppose that the investment activities of the firm will be affected by its dividend activities; postponement or curtailment of investment could conceivably result because of inability of the firm to carry out a given investment program, "optimally" determined by some "rational" criteria, and at the same time continue to make "satisfactory" dividend payments. To call such action "irrational" may be giving a correct label to the phenomenon but will not alter the facts—if, indeed, such is the factual state of affairs.

It would also be of interest to inquire whether such variables as depreciation (on this, see Meyer and Kuh [17]) are significant determinants of investment; if depreciation is an accurate index of deterioration of the capital stock due to its employment in the productive process, then depreciation would describe accurately that part of investment undertaken for replacement purposes. There are good reasons to believe, however, that depreciation does not accurately measure the using up of capital, and hence its introduction in the investment equation would only serve to portray more accurately the resources available to the firm for investment and dividend outlays. In addition, there is the question of the proper lags operating in the investment process; thus, it would be of interest to ascertain whether lagged rates of change of sales or past rates of profit significantly affect the decision to invest.

The introduction of the bond finance variable here has a motivation best understood in terms of imperfect capital markets. Thus, if in a given universe all firms belong to more or less the same uncertainty class, then market discrimination might be expected to take the form of restricting the amount a firm can borrow without raising the cost of obtaining long-term funds. Hence, we may conjecture, *ceteris paribus,* that the easier the access to this market—either in the amounts or in the terms on which the loans are granted—the larger the investment program a firm may undertake. Thus, in the investment equation dividends may be expected to have a negative impact, while external finance will have a positive one.

The External Finance Equation. Enough has been said in connection with the other two equations to make the hypothesized form of the external finance equation clear. One would expect to have this variable depend positively on investment, negatively on the market interest rate, and negatively on depreciation and profits. The relationship of external finance to dividends, however, is not very clear-cut. Thus, it is possible to argue that essentially because of a budgetary constraint, more dividends, other things being equal, mean more borrowing. But it is equally plausible to argue that for firms that are no longer growing rapidly more dividends need not induce further borrowing simply because their investment activities are somewhat restricted. Thus, there should not be any feedback from dividends to external finance.

Finally, it would be interesting to inquire whether there is any empirical merit to Kalecki's principle of increasing risk [11], i.e., whether the rate of borrowing depends on the magnitude of long-term debt already outstanding relative to the size of equity claims.

SOME ARGUMENTS FOR SIMULTANEOUS ESTIMATION OF THE MODEL

The question may perhaps arise as to why one might wish to apply simultaneous estimation techniques in estimating the model presented above. It might be argued that, since the firm represents a single unit of decision, the proper manner of looking at its decision-making process is one that views the firm as reacting to its economic environment, i.e., as making decisions in terms of the exogenous variables confronting it. Hence the appropriate econometric model should be a reduced form. After all we do not construct simultaneous-equation models of a household's consumption decisions.

This view, however, overlooks the simple institutional fact that the modern firm is a complex organization with a considerable degree of decentralization. The decisions made by one department have an impact on those made by another. Hence each department may be viewed as operating with certain decision rules which depend not only on exogenous variables but also on decisions arrived at by other departments, i.e., on variables which are endogenous to the firm. But in addition a firm has also a certain cohesiveness and such decisions must in some sense be made consistent, or the organism may not survive.

In this view of the firm's operations, the role of the highest executive echelons, say, the president and the board of directors, is rather unique. Their function is not to be the actual decision makers in the first instance, but rather to receive proposals, examine priorities, attempt to coordinate proposals, and make departmental decisions consistent with each other. In other words, it is their function to set the decision rule for each department and insure the proper and consistent execution of such rules. If one views the firm in this context, then it is quite clear that one should wish to employ simultaneous-equation techniques in estimating the parameters of the model given above. Thus, given that we hypothesize the existence of a meaningful structure of intrafirm decision-making, it is apparent that we should wish to estimate it by the most efficient econometric techniques. Furthermore, in so doing we may gain greater insight into the operations we wish to study, an insight that would be foregone if we simply confined ourselves to what in the context of our model would be reduced-form estimation.

Empirical Implementation

SAMPLE CHARACTERISTICS AND DEFINITION OF VARIABLES

The sample on which our study is based consists of 181 firms for which a continuous satisfactory record exists between 1947 and 1960. These firms are largely manufacturing and retail trade ones, although several are chiefly engaged in mining activities.

The sources of our data are the balance sheets and income statements of individual firms appearing in various issues of Moody's Manuals, although in some cases (about twenty) where data ambiguities or inconsistencies arose, the matter was rectified by direct correspondence with the firms involved.

It seems desirable at this stage to give a brief description of the characteristics of the firms in our sample, in terms of the type of activity pursued and of their size. Because the firms we used belong to numerous industrial subclassifications, we have stratified our sample through reclassification of firms into nine industrial classifications. This was done on the basis of the type of activity pursued by the individual firms.

TABLE 2

Classification Scheme

Variable	Description of Industrial Classification	Number of Firms	Per Cent of Total
C_1	Transportation equipment	17	9.32
C_2	Retail trade stores	21	11.61
C_3	Alcohol, tobacco, and food	21	11.61
C_4	Rubber, petroleum, and chemical products	30	16.58
C_5	Machine tools, agricultural equipment, and accessories	20	11.08
C_6	Electrical equipment and appliances	13	7.19
C_7	Building materials and equipment	18	9.95
C_8	Textiles, glass, pulp, and paper products	25	13.82
C_9	Mining, steel, steel products, and nonferrous metals	16	8.85
	Total	181	100.00

TABLE 3

Size Distribution of Sample Firms, Ranked by Book Value of Capital Stock, 1956

Size of Firm (million dollars)	Number of Firms	Per Cent of Total
0-49.9	18	9.95
50-99.9	41	22.65
100-149.9	26	14.36
150-199.9	15	8.29
200-299.9	18	9.95
300-499.9	17	9.39
500-999.9	20	11.05
1,000 and over	26	14.36
Total	181	100.00

A complete enumeration of the firms in our sample, grouped by industrial classification, as just explained, appears in the Appendix at the end of this paper. To reflect the sample stratification, we resorted to the standard analysis of covariance device of introducing (dummy) variables assuming the value 1 if a firm belongs to, say, the ith classification and zero otherwise. The variables corresponding to these classifications appear in Table 2.

It would appear from Table 2 that we have a very good cross section of mining and manufacturing firms, and quite a number of large retail stores. Our sample does not weigh very heavily any particular classification, although our firms tend to be mostly medium-sized and large ones. This is quite evident from Tables 3 and 4.

Table 3 classifies the sample firms by size of the (book value of the) capital stock. The median firm has capital stock of $160.2 million, the smallest and largest firms having, respectively, $16.5 million and $10,265.2 million. The smallest firms have a rather weak representation (9.95 per cent of the sample), while the largest firms have a somewhat stronger one (14.36 per cent of the sample). Essentially the same situation emerges if we classify the sample firms by size of sales. This classification appears in Table 4.

In this ranking, the median firm has sales of $438.7 million, the smallest and largest firms having, respectively, $38.2 million and $12,736.0 million. Again, the smallest firms are somewhat more weakly

TABLE 4

Size Distribution of Sample Firms, Ranked by Sales, 1956

Size of Firm (million dollars)	Number of Firms	Per Cent of Total
0-99.9	17	9.39
100-199.9	24	13.26
200-299.9	29	16.02
300-499.9	28	15.47
500-749.9	24	13.26
750-999.9	16	8.84
1,000-1,499.9	20	11.05
1,500-	23	12.71
Total	181	100.00

represented (9.39 per cent of the sample) than the largest firms
(12.71 per cent). Thus, our sample appears to be well stratified, in
terms of size as well as the type of activity pursued.

At this stage it is desirable to catalog and explain briefly the nature
of the variables entering into our investigation. We have already given,
in Table 2 above, the dummy variables associated with the industrial
classifications. In addition, the following basic variables are employed
(this list will also serve to define the symbolism employed in the subsequent development of our discussion):

S_t—sales at time t, undeflated.

$(EF1)_t$—long-term borrowing-external finance-at time t; this is simply the first difference of the book value of long-term debt outstanding
and thus represents net current long-term borrowing; it should be
remembered that this measure is somewhat biased by the transfer of
maturing long-term debt to the short-term category.

D_t—dividends (common) paid at time t.

I_t—gross fixed investment at time t.

K_t—book value of the capital stock at beginning of time t.

P_t—net profits (after taxes) at time t, undeflated.

$(LTD)_t$—net long-term debt outstanding at time t, in nominal terms.

$(Dep)_t$—depreciation allowances at time t.

N_t—net current position of the firm at time t, defined as the excess
of inventories, cash, short-term securities, and accounts receivable over
accounts payable and other short term liabilities.

R_t—interest payments at time t, on long-term debt outstanding. This
is admittedly a very poor measure of the relevant interest rate but it is
the only one available.

In actually carrying out the empirical implementation of the model,
we have chosen to normalize the jointly dependent variables by S_t. This
was done for two reasons: first, it tends to reduce heteroscedasticity
and hence make the stochastic characteristics of our sample correspond
more closely to the standard specification of the simultaneous-equation
models; second, since our objective is to isolate the determinants of the
investment-dividend-external finance decision process, this procedure
prevents our results from being unduly influenced by large firms simply
because of sheer size. Another related reason is the fact that one would
not expect the relation between investment and the appropriate accelerator variable to be identical in the case of a retail store and an aircraft
manufacturer. By relying on "intensive" variables, one tends to overcome such problems.

A list of the predetermined variables actually employed is given below:

N/K enters the model as a consequence of the use of the budget constraint to eliminate one of the equations of the system; the normalization employed here is to some extent motivated by portfolio theory considerations.

Dep/K represents the portion of the book value of the capital stock

TABLE 5

Simple Correlation Matrices, [a] *Endogenous Variables, 1951 - 60*

Variable	D/S	I/S	EF 1/S	D/S	I/S	EF 1/S
		1951			*1956*	
D/S	1.0000	.3018	−0.0854	1.0000	.3238	.0661
I/S		1.0000	.3735		1.0000	.4932
EF 1/S			1.0000			1.0000
		1952			*1957*	
D/S	1.0000	.2906	.0610	1.0000	.3871	.1522
I/S		1.0000	.6649		1.0000	.7414
EF 1/S			1.0000			1.0000
		1953			*1958*	
D/S	1.0000	.2793	.1630	1.0000	.4537	−0.0279
I/S		1.0000	.3346		1.0000	.3085
EF 1/S			1.0000			1.0000
		1954			*1959*	
D/S	1.0000	.1410	−0.0460	1.0000	.3049	−0.0316
I/S		1.0000	.3361		1.0000	.1012
EF 1/S			1.0000			1.0000
		1955			*1960*	
D/S	1.0000	.2816	−0.0499	1.0000	.3752	.0116
I/S		1.0000	−0.0200		1.0000	.0274
EF 1/S			1.0000			1.0000

[a] Critical values of $|r|$ for rejecting the hypothesis of zero correlation at the 5 and 1 per cent levels, respectively, are approximately .149 and .218.

written off as depreciation charges; its form is related to the following basic variable.

P/K is the rate of profit; it would have been better perhaps to have defined the numerator of this fraction as profits plus depreciation plus interest charges on the ground that, since it measures the (average) rate of return on the firm's capital resources, this ought to be measured gross of irrelevant bookkeeping items such as depreciation and interest charges.

$S_{-2}{}^* = (S_t - S_{t-3})/(S_{t-3})$ is the usual accelerator variable except that it is normalized by a lagged value of sales. It was felt, however, that it is the pressure of sustained relative increases in sales that affects investment.

$LTD/(K - LTD)$ is the leverage variable employed to test the principle of increasing risk. It is probably not a very accurate one, the rationale behind it being that businessmen are influenced by book rather than market value considerations.

EMPIRICAL RESULTS

It is instructive before we proceed to have a brief look at the matrix of simple correlation among the jointly dependent variables. This is given in Table 5.

Two features of these results are of particular interest; first, whenever significant, such correlations between dividends and investment are uni-

TABLE 6

Cyclical Peaks and Troughs, Identified by
Quarter, 1948 - 62

Year	Quarter	Peak or Trough
1948	4th	Peak
1949	2nd	Trough
1953	2nd	Peak
1954	2nd	Trough
1957	3rd	Peak
1958	1st	Trough
1960	2nd	Peak
1961	1st	Trough
1962	2nd	Peak

formly positive, a result that is somewhat surprising and difficult to accept at face value. Intrinsically these two quantities would not be expected to vary in the same direction. It will indeed be found that, in the proper structure to be estimated below, the impact of dividends on investment and vice versa is (contemporaneously) a negative one.

Secondly, it turns out that the simple correlation between dividends and investment is insignificant only for 1954 (a trough year as indicated by Table 6), that between investment and external finance is insignificant for 1955, 1959, and 1960 (in Table 6, all upswing or peak years), while the correlation between dividends and external finance is *significant* only for 1953 and 1957 (both peak years).

To the extent that one might wish to generalize on the basis of these results, it would appear that they simply demonstrate the substantial reliance of firms on internal financing. Apparently when profits increase rapidly in an upswing they are quickly absorbed into investment, obviating the need to resort to the capital market. On the other hand, when at the peak profits begin to get squeezed, we get a significant correlation of dividends with external financing, indicating that another sort of pressure is brought to bear on the firm's resources that forces increased reliance on the capital market.

THE SCOPE OF THE INVESTIGATION AND SOME TYPICAL SINGLE-EQUATION ESTIMATES

As stated earlier, it is our purpose to investigate the dividend, investment, and external finance decision-making process of the firm. Our contention is that these decisions are jointly determined and hence that the proper method of estimation is a simultaneous-estimation approach. Moreover, it is desirable to test the stability of structure as estimated. For one may argue that such simultaneity established by means of only one cross-sectional investigation is at best only a weak demonstration (in this connection, see Meyer and Kuh [12]). If, however, the structure so estimated can be shown to persist through time, then this would constitute additional support for our contention. Thus our procedure was to construct a model of this triad of decisions for the year 1956 and, after some experimentation, to decide on the variables that can significantly serve as explanatory variables. Then the model was estimated successively for the years 1951–60.

We first give (Tables 7, 8, and 9) what the statistical results would be if single-equation techniques were employed. Notice that the relationships thus estimated are significant if judged by the conventional *F*-test, although the correlation coefficients indicate that economically

TABLE 7

Single-Equation Estimates, Dividend Equation, 1951 - 60

Variable	1951	1952	1953	1954	1955	1956	1957	1958	1959	1960
C_0	0.157	0.0042	.0030	.0013	−0.0023	.0067	.0023	.0018	.0059	.0081
	(3.254)	(.892)	(.618)	(0.223)	(−0.418)	(1.266)	(.463)	(.352)	(1.003)	(1.576)
C_2	−0.0027	.9969	.9988	.0100	.0109	.0024	.0050	.0043	.0021	−0.0014
	(−0.447)	(1.160)	(1.477)	(1.408)	(1.590)	(.366)	(.803)	(.668)	(.305)	(−0.244)
C_3	.0001	.0121	.0096	.0125	.0145	.0058	.0081	.0039	.0056	.0013
	(.015)	(1.855)	(1.473)	(1.633)	(2.022)	(.833)	(1.232)	(.581)	(.759)	(.210)
C_4	.0156	.0306	.0325	.0355	.0320	.0252	.0250	.0214	.0259	.0192
	(2.594)	(5.397)	(5.679)	(5.486)	(5.030)	(3.865)	(4.056)	(3.353)	(3.688)	(3.127)
C_5	.0028	.0109	.0133	.0178	.0146	.0050	.0081	.0141	.0126	.0131
	(.447)	(1.813)	(2.236)	(2.545)	(2.167)	(.738)	(1.279)	(2.153)	(1.742)	(2.124)
C_6	−0.0028	.0048	.0075	.0123	.0131	.0072	.0061	.0061	.0036	.0004
	(−0.394)	(.723)	(1.134)	(1.578)	(1.741)	(.962)	(.857)	(.833)	(.454)	(.067)
C_7	.0128	.0256	.0302	.0335	.0261	.0220	.0250	.0268	.0277	.0222
	(1.915)	(4.089)	(4.844)	(4.649)	(3.574)	(2.893)	(3.484)	(3.807)	(3.638)	(3.350)
C_8	.0101	.0195	.0213	.0252	.0236	.0180	.0218	.0195	.0163	.0108
	(1.672)	(3.402)	(3.678)	(3.749)	(3.568)	(2.747)	(3.472)	(3.059)	(2.329)	(1.795)
C_9	.0254	.0390	.0367	.0420	.0379	.0342	.0343	.0327	.0338	.0268
	(3.680)	(5.690)	(5.588)	(5.655)	(5.243)	(4.662)	(4.821)	(4.363)	(4.197)	(3.831)
P/K	.0397	0,650	.0473	.0500	.0824	.0567	.0778	.0912	.0716	.0894
	(3.420)	(4.054)	(3.431)	(3.993)	(6.325)	(5.669)	(6.880)	(6.313)	(5.335)	(6.899)
N/K	−0.0023	−0.0043	−0.0022	−0.0017	−.004	−0.0028	−0.0048	−0.0051	−0.0041	−0.0044
	(−1.217)	(−2.066)	(−1.183)	(−0.886)	(−2.347)	(−1.384)	(−2.188)	(−2.110)	(−1.639)	(−1.771)
I/S	.0737	.0571	.0030	.0265	.0749	.0634	.0871	.1567	.0634	.1027
	(2.648)	(2.212)	(.115)	(.973)	(2.259)	(2.064)	(3.088)	(4.231)	(1.919)	(2.672)
$EF1/S$	−0.0688	−0.0589	.0863	−0.0014	−0.0127	−0.0171	−0.0646	−0.0749	−0.0330	.0235
	(−2.673)	(−2.611)	(2.611)	(−0.036)	(−0.311)	(−0.390)	(1.532)	(−2.099)	(−0.552)	(.914)
R^2	.2747	.3328	.2972	.2710	.3536	.3720	.4376	.4336	.3083	.4166
F-statistic	6.6823	8.4808	7.3440	6.5767	9.2046	9.8373	12.6705	12.4819	7.6490	11.7029

Note: $F_{.05} \approx 1.28$ $t_{.10} \approx 1.65$
     $F_{.01} \approx 1.45$ $t_{.05} \approx 1.97$

Number in parentheses is t-ratio.

Single-Equation Estimates, Investment Equation, 1951 - 60

Variable	1951	1952	1953	1954	1955	1956	1957	1958	1959	1960
C_0	.0194	.0286	.0254	.0655	.0255	.0407	.0197	.0320	.0370	.0416
	(1.307)	(1.561)	(1.286)	(3.849)	(2.123)	(3.004)	(1.361)	(3.088)	(2.716)	(4.359)
C_2	.0038	−0.0085	−0.0019	−0.0292	−0.0000	−0.0079	.0102	−0.0067	−0.0031	−0.0127
	(.219)	(−0.418)	(−0.087)	(−1.430)	(−0.005)	(−0.458)	(.607)	(−0.521)	(−0.185)	(−1.060)
C_3	−0.0023	−0.0009	.0017	−0.0193	.0049	−0.0018	.0179	−0.0014	.0057	.0003
	(−0.128)	(−0.043)	(.076)	(−0.875)	(.314)	(−0.100)	(1.000)	(−0.109)	(.328)	(.028)
C_4	.0390	.0313	.0603	.0334	.0275	.0338	.0490	.0310	.0449	.0318
	(2.431)	(1.618)	(2.945)	(1.661)	(1.866)	(1.906)	(2.921)	(2.370)	(2.665)	(2.613)
C_5	−0.0099	−0.0176	.0115	−0.0094	.0213	−0.0011	.0035	−0.0071	−0.0023	−0.0013
	(−0.591)	(−0.932)	(.568)	(−0.449)	(1.413)	(−0.070)	(.206)	(−0.545)	(−0.137)	(−0.110)
C_6	−0.0021	−0.0019	.0079	−0.0188	−0.0016	−0.0145	.0191	.0029	−0.0037	.0100
	(−0.110)	(−0.094)	(.353)	(−0.846)	(−0.100)	(−0.764)	(1.013)	(.202)	(−0.198)	(.739)
C_7	.0525	.0388	.0424	.0231	.0556	.0666	.0780	.0281	.0304	.0311
	(2.961)	(1.923)	(1.978)	(1.054)	(3.475)	(3.429)	(4.186)	(1.921)	(1.619)	(2.312)
C_8	.0021	.0191	.0275	−0.0082	.0118	−0.0017	.0390	.0048	.0125	.0131
	(.132)	(1.001)	(1.314)	(−0.407)	(.788)	(−0.092)	(2.326)	(.368)	(.748)	(1.075)
C_9	.0354	.0296	.0743	.0032	.0054	.0195	.0486	.0388	.0358	.0319
	(1.854)	(1.295)	(3.419)	(0.141)	(0.313)	(.956)	(2.490)	(2.502)	(1.808)	(2.241)
$(P/K)_{-1}$	−0.0296	.0148	.0155	−0.0592	−0.0429	−0.0336	−0.0179	−0.0234	−0.0168	−0.0347
	(−1.097)	(.488)	(.309)	(−1.179)	(−1.482)	(−0.918)	(−0.680)	(−0.867)	(−0.377)	(−1.210)
S^*_{-2}	.0329	.0016	.0058	.0264	.0795	.0404	.0216	.0101	.0135	.0305
	(2.157)	(.145)	(.518)	(1.778)	(5.049)	(2.527)	(1.148)	(.926)	(.748)	(2.199)
N/K	−0.0051	−0.0123	−0.0104	−0.0079	−0.0058	−0.0084	−0.0135	−0.0114	−0.0137	−0.0119
	(−1.045)	(−2.407)	(−1.707)	(−1.276)	(−1.303)	(−1.561)	(−2.452)	(−2.508)	(−2.145)	(−2.311)
D/S	.5755	.4598	.0157	.1554	.3460	.4164	.6386	.6599	.3760	.4197
	(2.879)	(2.075)	(.067)	(0.703)	(2.196)	(2.226)	(3.135)	(4.128)	(1.833)	(2.831)
$EF1/S$	.3302	.5540	.4695	.4824	−0.0251	.6579	1.0908	.3197	.2164	.0477
	(5.048)	(10.503)	(5.194)	(4.504)	(−0.283)	(6.942)	(14.556)	(4.582)	(1.569)	(.947)
R^2	.3887	.5616	.3179	.2762	.3738	.5012	.7089	.4639	.2470	.3844
F-statistic	9.8054	18.7331	7.4546	6.2848	9.2636	14.8345	34.7193	12.9828	5.5159	9.6451

Note: Number in parentheses is *t*-ratio.

TABLE 9

Single-Equation Estimates, External Finance Equation, 1951 - 60

Variable	1951	1952	1953	1954	1955	1956	1957	1958	1959	1960
C_0	.0186	.0084	.0336	.0223	.0206	.0132	.0070	.0275	.0114	.0382
	(1.509)	(.702)	(1.509)	(1.177)	(2.367)	(.914)	(.779)	(2.621)	(1.564)	(2.544)
$LTD/(K-LTD)$	-0.0118	-0.0008	.0360	.0165	.0012	.0105	-0.0008	-0.0000	-0.0022	.0007
	(-2.829)	(-4.551)	(1.704)	(0.924)	(.602)	(.810)	(-.687)	(-.056)	(-2.595)	(.544)
R/LTD	-0.1229	-0.0010	-0.0099	-0.1512	-0.1966	-0.1577	-0.0639	-0.1375	-0.0609	-0.9807
	(-0.551)	(-0.006)	(-0.091)	(-1.845)	(-1.435)	(-1.305)	(-0.721)	(-1.245)	(-0.863)	(-7.446)
DEP/K	.2151	-0.2218	-0.0706	-0.1205	-0.1241	.0152	-0.2690	-0.2871	-0.0797	-0.0112
	(1.946)	(-2.105)	(-0.924)	(-1.340)	(-1.310)	(.151)	(-2.737)	(-2.360)	(-0.977)	(-0.069)
P/K	-0.0528	.0438	-0.0091	.0138	-0.0035	-0.0098	.0403	.0229	-0.0045	-0.0049
	(-2.121)	(1.239)	(-0.384)	(0.715)	(-0.182)	(-0.665)	(2.276)	(.937)	(-0.321)	(-0.165)
D/S	-0.5243	-0.6441	.1382	-0.1986	-0.1258	-0.1672	-0.5218	-0.5361	-0.1126	-0.2749
	(-2.532)	(-2.897)	(.859)	(-1.552)	(-0.945)	(-1.286)	(-4.128)	(-3.510)	(-1.265)	(-1.416)
I/S	.3925	.7300	.2193	.2246	.0164	.3048	.4886	.3973	.0672	.0769
	(5.690)	(11.722)	(3.994)	(4.802)	(.277)	(6.997)	(15.175)	(5.487)	(1.736)	(.829)
R^2	.2239	.5138	.1095	.1222	-0.0059	.2392	.5862	.1435	.0340	.2198
F-statistic	9.6527	32.7078	4.6875	5.1756	.8249	10.3788	43.5010	6.0269	2.0490	9.4526

Note: Number in parentheses is t-ratio.

the explanatory power of such equations is not very great. The latter, however, is quite common in cross-section investment studies.

Consider the dividend equation first. In this connection, it should be noted that C_0 indicates the constant term, while the C_i, $i = 2, \ldots 9$, indicate the usual analysis of covariance contrasts; thus they may be interpreted as measures of the difference in the constant term among the various industrial classifications. In addition, it should be remarked that at the end of Table 7 we give the critical values of the F and t statistics at various levels of significance; the degrees of freedom of the F-statistic vary from equation to equation ranging from 165 to 180; the critical value for the t-statistic pertains to the conventional two-tailed test and the relevant degrees of freedom are approximately 165, though again this varies moderately from equation to equation. We shall not repeat this information for subsequent tables.

Returning now to the substantive results obtained, it is interesting to note that there is apparently quite a consistent difference in the dividend policies of firms in various industrial classifications as evidenced by the fact that the contrasts C_i, for $i = 9, 8, 7, 4$, turn out to be uniformly significant, while for $i = 6, 5, 3$, and 2 they are nearly uniformly insignificant. Thus the result seems to imply that, *ceteris paribus*, firms in mining, steel, etc. (9), textiles, glass, etc. (8), building materials and equipment (7), rubber, petroleum, etc. (4), tend to pay higher dividends (per dollar sales) than is the case for the remaining firms in our sample. The rate of profit variable, as was to be expected, turns out to be the most consistent factor in explaining dividends over the sample period. Another result of interest is that the investment variable turns out to be significant quite frequently (in eight cross sections) and appears to exert a positive influence on dividends. Now one might argue that investment, with a lag, affects the profitability of the firm's operations and hence would be expected to lead to greater dividend payments. On the other hand, it is difficult to rationalize this result in the context of our present investigation. The sign of the external finance coefficient, whenever significant, turns out to be negative. In both the case of investment and external finance, their coefficients appear to be in conformity with the signs of their respective simple correlations with the dividend variable.

Turning now to the investment equation, four features are worth noting. The rate of change in sales variables turns out to be significant in only five cross sections (1951, 1954, 1955, 1956, and 1960; with the exception of 1954 all are upswing or peak years); the rate of profit variable turns out to be uniformly insignificant. Of the contrasts, only

C_i for $i = 7$ and 4 turn out to be more or less consistently significant; notice, however, that the general constant, C_0, turns out to be more frequently significant in comparison with the general constant of the dividend equation. The external finance variable is nearly uniformly significant and its impact on investment is uniformly positive.

The astonishing result in the investment equation is the sign and nearly consistent significance of the coefficient of the dividend variable. While in discussing the dividend equation one could provide some rationalization for the positive sign of the coefficient of the investment variable, it is difficult to rationalize the positive sign of the dividend coefficient which points to the potential pitfalls of the single-equation approach and the ordinary tests of significance.

The external finance equation displays two interesting characteristics; there is no evidence that the firm's behavior in this aspect is affected by the type of activity it is engaged in, since the contrasts turned out to be uniformly insignificant and thus were omitted from the reported results. There is little evidence for the validity of the principle of increasing risk, although whenever the leverage variable is significant its coefficient turns out to be negative in conformity to the principle's implications. Finally it would appear that the most consistent determinant of external finance is investment, as one might expect.

The single-equation results in this section are quite instructive in a negative way. First, they demonstrate how dangerous it is to use single-equation techniques indiscriminately, when quite clearly the problems under consideration are fundamentally interdependent. Secondly, they show that the criterion of inclusion or exclusion of a variable from a regression based on the magnitude of the resulting multiple correlation coefficient as advocated by Hotelling [5] or Theil [14][2] is a very delicate criterion and should be used very cautiously indeed. In this context, if one is determined to use single-equation techniques, it is best to use as explanatory variables those which are truly exogenous, even though some explanatory power is lost thereby.

Estimation of the Dividend-Investment-External Finance Structure by Simultaneous-Equation Techniques

THE NEED FOR FULL INFORMATION METHODS

We have seen in the previous section that single-equation methods are beset by serious deficiencies in meaningfully tracing the interde-

---

[2] Pp. 206 ff.

TABLE 10

Correlation Matrix of Two-Stage Least-Squares Residuals, 1951 - 60

	Eq. (1)	Eq. (2)	Eq. (3)	Eq. (1)	Eq. (2)	Eq. (3)
		1951			*1956*	
Eq. (1)	1.0000	.6756	.1366	1.0000	.7517	−0.2722
Eq. (2)		1.0000	−0.1478		1.0000	−0.9492
Eq. (3)			1.0000			1.0000
		1952			*1957*	
Eq. (1)	1.0000	.8470	−0.3927	1.0000	.9099	−0.0384
Eq. (2)		1.0000	−0.7309		1.0000	.2152
Eq. (3)			1.0000			1.0000
		1953			*1958*	
Eq. (1)	1.0000	.8964	−0.5025	1.0000	.8603	.1955
Eq. (2)		1.0000	−0.1663		1.0000	.1191
Eq. (3)			1.0000			1.0000
		1954			*1959*	
Eq. (1)	1.0000	.9030	−0.0715	1.0000	.7608	−0.5608
Eq. (2)		1.0000	−0.4463		1.0000	−0.1303
Eq. (3)			1.0000			1.0000
		1955			*1960*	
Eq. (1)	1.0000	.6996	−0.2867	1.0000	.8682	.0169
Eq. (2)		1.0000	−0.0441		1.0000	−0.2147
Eq. (3)			1.0000			1.0000

pendence of the decision making processes we wish to investigate. Thus, simultaneous-equation techniques are clearly indicated. The question then naturally arises as to whether limited information methods, such as two-stage least squares, are appropriate or whether full information techniques are indicated.

It is, of course, the case that full information methods are more sensitive to errors of specification than limited information methods are. Nonetheless, one may suspect that the information content of the non-estimated equations is sufficiently high so that the gain in efficiency would outweigh the effects of propagating specification errors. This is so since we are dealing with a cross-sectional sample and the three decisions studied here are made more or less concurrently by the same group of people possessing substantially overlapping or similar information.

But, of course, the ultimate test as to whether full information methods are indicated is related to the correlation matrix of the, say, two-stage least-squares residuals of the three equations. In Table 10, we present the relevant correlation matrixes for the years 1951–60.

In Table 10, the dividend equation is termed equation (1), the investment equation is equation (2), and the external finance equation is equation (3). The model on which these correlations are based is that presented in Tables 7, 8, and 9. The impression is unmistakable, from Table 10, that full information methods are indicated in the present case.

The proper significance tests for this type of correlation coefficient are not adequately dealt with in the econometric literature. However, in view of the consistency of the two-stage least-squares estimates, it is not amiss to treat the residuals, at least asymptotically, as observations on the (unobservable) disturbances. This, of course, assumes no specification errors. If we take this view, then the proper test would be based on the distribution of the usual sample correlation coefficient. The appropriate number of degrees of freedom would be the number of observations less the number of estimated parameters in the two equations of interest. In our case, the degrees of freedom are not less than 150. On the basis of these considerations, it would appear that the critical values for rejecting the hypothesis of no correlation are $|r| = .159$ and $|r| = .208$, employing a two-tail test at the 5 and 1 per cent levels of significance, respectively.

Table 10 shows that the hypothesis is to be accepted only in the following instances; between dividend and external finance residuals for 1951, 1954, 1957, and 1960. In addition, the hypothesis is to be accepted also for the years 1955, 1959, and 1960 between the investment and external finance residuals. Interestingly enough, these are years of upswings or peaks. Thus, with the possible exception of upswing years, where apparently profits outrun investment and dividend requirements so that there is no effective (resource) constraint on the firms' operation, it would appear that the correlation coefficients are sufficiently high to warrant the conclusion that the efficiency of the parameter estimators would be appreciably increased by the use of full information methods. It might be instructive, however, before we present the main empirical results of our study, to examine briefly the limited information (two-stage least-squares) estimates of our model. These are presented in Tables 11, 12, and 13.

TABLE 11

Limited Information (2SLS) Estimates, Dividend Equation, 1951-60

Variable	1951	1952	1953	1954	1955	1956	1957	1958	1959	1960
C_0	.0277	.0172	.0157	.0132	.0100	.0196	.0222	.0093	.0094	.0259
	(2.7999)	(1.3136)	(1.0747)	(1.5090)	(1.2304)	(1.8840)	(1.5188)	(1.1085)	(.8668)	(2.1333)
C_2	−0.0047	.0044	.0028	.0042	.0047	.0056	.0095	.0035	.0030	−0.0046
	(−0.6301)	(.4832)	(.2584)	(.5017)	(.5252)	(.4844)	(.7920)	(.5138)	(.3892)	(−0.5898)
C_3	−0.0024	.0135	.0028	.0094	.0085	.0105	.0173	.0045	.0066	.0044
	(−0.3083)	(1.3755)	(.2380)	(.9864)	(.9249)	(.7792)	(1.3271)	(.6377)	(.8160)	(.5461)
C_4	.0289	.0478	.0470	.0417	.0429	.0474	.0641	.0317	.0322	.0378
	(2.4175)	(2.5982)	(2.1911)	(4.7282)	(4.9359)	(3.0207)	(2.8057)	(2.9074)	(2.3465)	(2.8913)
C_5	.0013	.0053	.0160	.0151	.0149	.0082	.0131	.0143	.0149	.0155
	(.1778)	(.5500)	(.9713)	(1.8857)	(1.8003)	(.8785)	(1.1106)	(2.0966)	(1.8820)	(1.9992)
C_6	−0.0018	.0050	.0040	.0104	.0086	.0052	.0179	.0078	.0021	.0069
	(−0.2070)	(.4920)	(.3480)	(1.0810)	(.9121)	(.5018)	(1.2377)	(1.0087)	(.2409)	(.7486)
C_7	.0307	.0456	.0445	.0384	.0434	.0543	.0866	.0370	.0307	.0419
	(2.1275)	(2.3471)	(2.6646)	(4.0349)	(3.9680)	(2.7453)	(2.3678)	(3.2034)	(2.5173)	(3.0755)
C_8	.0150	.0306	.0259	.0234	.0245	.0248	.0522	.0233	.0170	.0212
	(1.8553)	(2.3904)	(2.1047)	(3.0610)	(2.6935)	(2.0607)	(2.7126)	(3.0333)	(1.9699)	(2.2348)
C_9	.0428	.0549	.0650	.0446	.0449	.0524	.0802	.0451	.0352	.0485
	(3.0808)	(2.4140)	(2.4184)	(4.7073)	(4.8429)	(3.6863)	(2.7637)	(3.2743)	(2.5541)	(3.4583)
P/K	.0343	.0787	.0782	.0407	.0769	.0666	.0881	.0988	.0778	.0936
	(2.2171)	(3.0211)	(2.6281)	(2.7568)	(4.834)	(3.1867)	(3.9256)	(5.9616)	(5.1765)	(5.7570)
N/K	−0.0038	−0.0096	−0.0085	−0.0029	−0.0064	−0.0078	−0.0142	−0.0083	−0.0066	−0.0111
	(−1.3856)	(−1.9510)	(−1.7214)	(−1.2093)	(−2.4054)	(−1.8377)	(−2.2689)	(−2.2896)	(−1.6282)	(−2.3144)
I/S	−0.1812	−0.3393	−0.4008	−0.1481	−0.1773	−0.3071	−0.4798	−0.0417	−0.0307	−0.2931
	(−0.9624)	(−1.0504)	(−1.1298)	(−1.5108)	(−1.7433)	(−1.3858)	(−1.6344)	(−0.2445)	(−0.1476)	(−1.2723)
$EF1/S$	−0.0656	.1815	.6296	.1814	.2483	.3505	.4206	−0.0020	.3039	.1151
	(−0.6753)	(1.0781)	(2.1539)	(.8808)	(1.2511)	(.6248)	(1.0836)	(−0.0213)	(1.0728)	(1.7823)

Note: Number in parentheses is *t*-ratio.

TABLE 12

Limited Information (2SLS) Estimates, Investment Equation, 1951-60

Variable	1951	1952	1953	1954	1955	1956	1957	1958	1959	1960
C_0	.0362	.0427	.0462	.0636	.0293	.0494	.0574	.0452	.0617	.0466
	(1.7394)	(2.0186)	(1.7199)	(2.0680)	(.0309)	(2.1478)	(2.3086)	(3.1723)	(2.6136)	(4.4204)
C_2	.0025	−0.0073	−0.0097	−0.0019	.0124	−0.0033	.0061	.0013	.0079	−0.0078
	(.1422)	(−0.3503)	(−0.4062)	(−0.0584)	(.6352)	(−0.1396)	(.2726)	(.0797)	(.3275)	(−0.5940)
C_3	−0.0018	.0021	−0.0028	.0329	.0203	.0061	.0197	.0163	.0170	.0089
	(−0.0991)	(.0978)	(−0.1162)	(.8598)	(.9804)	(.2411)	(.8335)	(.8705)	(.6839)	(.6167)
C_4	.0578	.0627	.0803	.1457	.0729	.0777	.1050	.0858	.1196	.0596
	(2.4587)	(2.3626)	(2.7334)	(2.6593)	(3.2030)	(2.3379)	(3.1317)	(3.1028)	(2.3611)	(2.7069)
C_5	−0.0055	−0.0084	.0075	.0311	.0415	.0134	.0144	.0095	.0322	.0114
	(−0.3063)	(−0.4115)	(.3364)	(.8718)	(2.1673)	(.6302)	(.6211)	(.5370)	(.9827)	(.7408)
C_6	−0.0021	.0003	−0.0052	.0279	.0139	.0018	.0267	.0189	.0187	.0156
	(−0.1048)	(.0176)	(−0.2011)	(.7336)	(.6891)	(.0767)	(1.0394)	(.9613)	(.6470)	(1.0566)
C_7	.0745	.0636	.0650	.1367	.0966	.1173	.1585	.0944	.1112	.0615
	(2.9103)	(2.5649)	(2.1877)	(2.4950)	(4.2284)	(2.8252)	(3.5381)	(3.0214)	(2.0827)	(2.5238)
C_8	.0209	.0351	.0357	.0671	.0475	.0416	.0788	.0482	.0598	.0334
	(.9268)	(1.6274)	(1.4860)	(1.5482)	(2.0668)	(1.0849)	(2.7615)	(2.0881)	(1.6871)	(1.8133)
C_9	.0717	.739	.1082	.1491	.0607	.0748	.1348	.113	.1078	.0665
	(2.0278)	(2.0586)	(2.9748)	(2.2742)	(2.2236)	(1.8251)	(2.9326)	(3.3494)	(2.2296)	(2.3781)
$(P/K)_{-1}$	−0.0119	.0473	.1242	.2040	.0366	.0498	.0973	.1439	.2938	.0458
	(−0.3680)	(1.2614)	(1.2107)	(1.6125)	(.8487)	(.7674)	(1.5277)	(1.9012)	(1.4880)	(.7561)
S^*_{-2}	.0337	.0000	−0.0054	−0.0153	.0725	.0409	−0.0135	−0.0103	−0.0753	.0100
	(2.0252)	(.0071)	(−0.3603)	(−0.5759)	(3.7398)	(2.0248)	(−0.4020)	(−0.4477)	(−1.2534)	(.5051)
N/K	−0.0064	−0.0142	−0.0177	−0.0216	−0.0102	−0.0141	−0.0243	−0.0244	−0.0398	−0.0191
	(−1.2329)	(−2.6378)	(−2.0275)	(−1.9865)	(−1.8737)	(−2.0068)	(2.8265)	(−3.0674)	(−2.1392)	(−2.6342)
D/S	−0.2553	−0.5561	−1.2583	−2.9185	−0.8833	−0.8174	−1.2744	−1.0997	−2.0007	−0.4323
	(−0.3405)	(−0.8720)	(−1.1688)	(−1.9967)	(−1.9263)	(−1.0164)	(−1.4365)	(−1.5189)	(−1.4055)	(−0.7581)
$EF1/S$	.0851	.4695	.8029	1.4809	−0.1375	.2039	.5695	.1650	1.0848	.1295
	(.3719)	(3.4898)	(2.1078)	(2.7006)	(−0.3116)	(.2317)	(.9213)	(.5679)	(.9289)	(1.0516)

Note: Number in parentheses is t-ratio.

TABLE 13

Limited Information (2SLS) Estimates, External Finance Equation, 1951-60

Variable	1951	1952	1953	1954	1955	1956	1957	1958	1959	1960
C_0	.0186	.0051	.0438	.0259	.0241	.0195	.0213	.0324	.0118	.0728
	(1.0536)	(.2688)	(1.7777)	(1.2361)	(2.2899)	(1.2936)	(1.9536)	(2.6940)	(1.4741)	(3.3261)
$LTD/(K-LTD)$	-0.0118	-0.0005	.0337	.0111	.0011	.0091	-0.0008	-0.0000	-0.0021	-0.0004
	(-2.8772)	(-1.9915)	(1.5071)	(.5996)	(.5416)	(.6755)	(-0.5946)	(-0.0806)	(-2.5168)	(-0.2556)
R/LTD	-0.1489	-0.1611	.0016	-0.1701	-0.2641	-0.1871	-0.1081	-0.1857	-0.0613	-1.1784
	(-0.5681)	(-9.6545)	(.0128)	(-2.0045)	(-1.7469)	(-1.3453)	(-1.1051)	(-1.5837)	(-0.8754)	(-6.8722)
DEP/K	.2030	-0.3540	-0.0327	-0.2035	-0.1772	.0029	-0.3236	-0.3740	-0.0636	-0.3391
	(1.7329)	(-2.2743)	(-0.3177)	(-2.0577)	(-1.6725)	(.0238)	(-2.9077)	(-2.6794)	(-0.7321)	(-1.4703)
P/K	-0.0436	.1607	-0.0434	.0424	.0161	-0.0096	.0445	.0559	-0.0109	.1106
	(-1.3047)	(2.0572)	(-1.0145)	(1.7643)	(.6112)	(-0.4048)	(1.5571)	(1.5578)	(-0.5912)	(1.7708)
D/S	-0.6930	-1.9653	.2750	-0.6788	-0.3843	-0.2618	-0.7463	-0.9394	-0.0437	-1.8134
	(-1.1098)	(-1.9920)	(.4919)	(-2.8479)	(-1.3299)	(-0.7325)	(-2.3016)	(-2.7185)	(-0.2520)	(-2.6671)
I/S	.4710	1.3034	-0.0497	.3455	.1287	.2593	.4516	.5980	.0153	.6065
	(2.4308)	(4.1220)	(-0.1972)	(3.8562)	(1.0669)	(2.2752)	(4.8456)	(3.1997)	(.1486)	(1.9469)

Note: Number in parentheses is t-ratio.

At least two aspects of these results are worthy of comment. First, notice the reversal of sign of the coefficients of the investment variable in the dividend equation and that of the dividend variable in the investment equation. This does indeed demonstrate the type of erroneous conclusions one might be led to by using inappropriate econometric techniques.

The second interesting feature is that the single-equation results seriously understate the role of the rate of profit as a determinant of investment. The two-stage least-squares results show that variable to be occasionally significant in the investment equation, while the single-equation results never show it to be significant (often with an unacceptable sign).

No further comments seem to be warranted at this juncture, since we shall comment at length below on the structure of this triad of decision-making processes, when its parameters have been estimated by the appropriate econometric procedure, which our results so far suggest should be a full information one. The parameter estimates, however, do not differ markedly in two- and three-stage least squares, though the latter results are more efficient.

MAIN EMPIRICAL RESULTS

In dealing with the full information results of our estimation, it is well to bear in mind that while there are cogent a priori reasons why one might expect that such decisions as we are studying here are resolved simultaneously, nonetheless one cannot assert with any confidence that the feedbacks are equally strong in all directions. Hence one of the issues to be resolved by the empirical results is whether a fully simultaneous model, such as the one presented in the previous section, is the most appropriate or whether some other form such as a recursive one would be a more suitable version for the model. Admittedly, there is no clear-cut criterion by which to choose. We have tended to make this determination in terms of the interpretability of the results yielded in the context of the appropriate theoretical considerations. On this basis, it would appear that the fully simultaneous model gives more meaningful results and we shall, therefore, proceed to analyze its empirical implementation in some detail. The empirical results are contained in Tables 14, 15, and 16.

Consider the dividend equation first. One noteworthy aspect is the rather remarkable stability of both the significance pattern and magnitudes of the contrasts. While it might be difficult to argue definitively against the observation that this may be due entirely to the normaliza-

TABLE 14

Full Information (3SLS) Estimates, Dividend Equation, 1951-60

Variable	1951	1952	1953	1954	1955	1956	1957	1958	1959	1960
C_0	.0289	.0268	.0053	.0138	.0087	.0186	.0308	.0147	.0091	.0328
	(3.0240)	(2.6695)	(.4723)	(1.6619)	(1.1179)	(1.8804)	(2.4289)	(1.8858)	(.9025)	(3.3014)
C_2	-.0049	.0041	.0035	.0041	.0068	.0026	.0075	.0029	.0023	-.0059
	(-.6628)	(.4939)	(.3738)	(.4937)	(.7778)	(.2457)	(.6369)	(.4396)	(.3266)	(-.7700)
C_3	-.0022	.0129	.0034	.0092	.0106	.0069	.0156	.0055	.0062	.0059
	(-.2840)	(1.4304)	(.3299)	(.9858)	(1.1872)	(.5564)	(1.2383)	(.7859)	(.8201)	(.7472)
C_4	.0301	.0615	.0309	.0424	.0456	.0435	.0722	.0389	.0301	.0470
	(2.5859)	(4.1939)	(2.1453)	(5.5010)	(5.4389)	(3.1959)	(3.8542)	(3.8722)	(2.3217)	(4.2905)
C_5	.0014	.0110	.0084	.0154	.0171	.0073	.0148	.0134	.0122	.0164
	(.1914)	(1.2358)	(.8782)	(1.9273)	(2.1397)	(.8226)	(1.2704)	(1.9949)	(1.6402)	(2.1344)
C_6	-.0024	.0065	.0037	.0102	.0104	.0061	.0182	.0089	.0044	.0101
	(-.2808)	(.6968)	(.3627)	(1.0832)	(1.1384)	(.6222)	(1.3120)	(1.1710)	(.5364)	(1.1361)
C_7	.0315	.0553	.0294	.0388	.0446	.0498	.1039	.0442	.0294	.0503
	(2.2464)	(3.5559)	(2.4216)	(4.5331)	(4.3007)	(2.8570)	(3.5005)	(4.1319)	(2.5438)	(4.3522)
C_8	.0137	.0364	.0173	.0237	.0274	.0267	.0566	.0258	.0168	.0264
	(1.7094)	(3.3604)	(1.7457)	(3.1252)	(3.1130)	(2.2927)	(3.4431)	(3.4683)	(2.0608)	(3.0564)
C_9	.0423	.0767	.0411	.0453	.0479	.0499	.0945	.0542	.0361	.0575
	(3.1025)	(4.2083)	(2.3495)	(5.120)	(5.2868)	(3.8895)	(3.9039)	(4.2770)	(2.7521)	(4.7537)
P/K	.0332	.0491	.0721	.0409	.0819	.0634	.0660	.1012	.0702	.0751
	(2.4752)	(2.3130)	(2.7414)	(2.8356)	(5.2616)	(3.4194)	(3.3412)	(6.3468)	(5.0082)	(5.2006)
N/K	-.0040	-.0092	-.0043	-.0030	-.0073	-.0065	-.0138	-.0103	-.0053	-.0114
	(-1.6576)	(-2.1927)	(-1.2474)	(-1.4419)	(-2.8687)	(-1.8040)	(-2.5332)	(-3.0666)	(-1.3948)	(-2.8324)
I/S	-.1900	-.5752	-.1106	-.1625	-.1996	-.2727	-.6100	-.1663	-.0124	-.4518
	(-1.0667)	(-2.3977)	(-.5001)	(-2.5432)	(-2.1176)	(-1.5124)	(-2.7209)	(-1.1017)	(-.0633)	(-2.5995)
$EF1/S$	-.0770	.2646	.6890	.2087	.3604	.3289	.4272	-.0223	.3128	.1231
	(-.8388)	(1.9407)	(2.9665)	(1.3556)	(1.8633)	(.6715)	(1.1990)	(-.2395)	(1.1293)	(1.9467)

Note: Number in parentheses is t-ratio.

TABLE 15

Full Information (3SLS) Estimates, Investment Equation, 1951-60

Variable	1951	1952	1953	1954	1955	1956	1957	1958	1959	1960
C_0	.0562 (2.9868)	.0360 (2.3605)	.0352 (1.7951)	.0779 (2.9383)	.0313 (2.1768)	.0727 (3.4825)	.0463 (2.0629)	.0483 (3.4706)	.0657 (2.9005)	.0493 (4.8220)
C_2	.0009 (.0507)	.0129 (.9951)	.0076 (.3759)	.0062 (.2096)	.0172 (.8885)	-0.0080 (-0.3568)	.0072 (.3238)	.0023 (.1461)	.0045 (.1980)	-0.0097 (-0.7771)
C_3	-.0024 (-.1306)	.0219 (1.5934)	.0133 (.5967)	.0201 (.5855)	.0261 (1.2888)	.0032 (.1358)	.0233 (1.0010)	.0148 (.8151)	.0220 (.9458)	.0060 (.4448)
C_4	.0822 (3.9719)	.0958 (5.1432)	.1135 (4.7983)	.1857 (4.6702)	.0918 (4.6759)	.1300 (5.0582)	.0942 (3.2104)	.0989 (3.9044)	.1344 (2.8148)	.0618 (3.5059)
C_5	.0014 (.0849)	.0314 (2.2174)	.0262 (1.3235)	.0604 (1.9267)	.0481 (2.5908)	.0281 (1.3977)	.0146 (.6391)	.0202 (1.1669)	.0328 (1.0667)	.0119 (.8567)
C_6	.0002 (.0149)	.0120 (.8320)	.0098 (.4483)	.0199 (.5746)	.0198 (.9866)	.0217 (.9607)	.0212 (.8324)	.0190 (.9917)	.0261 (.9556)	.0155 (1.0980)
C_7	.1011 (4.4527)	.0781 (4.7017)	.0940 (3.9009)	.1639 (3.9948)	.1147 (5.6713)	.1868 (5.7198)	.1689 (4.1568)	.1196 (4.1999)	.1275 (2.5401)	.0610 (3.1452)
C_8	.0462 (2.2504)	.0544 (3.9923)	.0606 (2.9593)	.1014 (2.9762)	.0623 (2.9613)	.1022 (3.3186)	.0709 (2.7200)	.0721 (3.3576)	.0721 (2.1713)	.0298 (1.9612)
C_9	.1186 (3.9668)	.1314 (4.6803)	.1413 (5.0492)	.1918 (4.1124)	.0844 (3.6545)	.1422 (4.5389)	.1428 (3.4699)	.1628 (5.4355)	.1528 (3.3663)	.0624 (2.8230)
$(P/K)_{-1}$	.0234 (.4335)	.0042 (.2297)	.1340 (1.9058)	.1842 (2.1315)	.0806 (2.4284)	.1238 (2.4919)	.0090 (.2099)	.1402 (2.1097)	.2418 (1.3015)	-0.0108 (-0.2809)
S^*_{-2}	.0315 (1.9453)	.0071 (1.2251)	.0074 (.9380)	.0143 (1.4220)	.0627 (3.6952)	.0447 (2.6648)	.0357 (2.2093)	.0403 (2.0490)	-0.0076 (-0.1372)	.0241 (1.8978)
N/K	-0.0070 (-1.5260)	-0.0095 (-2.5345)	-0.0166 (-2.3955)	-0.0150 (-1.7010)	-0.0133 (-2.6445)	-0.0193 (-3.0976)	-0.0166 (-2.1921)	-0.0217 (-2.9701)	-0.0327 (-1.8591)	-0.0119 (-2.1800)
D/S	-1.3758 (-2.3716)	-1.1043 (-2.3017)	-1.9639 (-2.8860)	-4.2004 (-4.9679)	-1.3751 (-3.8710)	-2.3647 (-4.1750)	-0.8637 (-1.2435)	-1.6944 (-2.6593)	-2.6940 (-2.0022)	-0.4251 (-1.0417)
$EF1/S$	-.0943 (-.4472)	.3976 (3.1588)	1.0322 (3.0578)	1.0480 (2.1296)	-0.1781 (-0.4063)	-0.8921 (-1.1444)	.0912 (.1626)	-0.3760 (-1.4426)	.4722 (.4246)	.1064 (.9507)

Note: Number in parentheses is t-ratio.

TABLE 16

Full Information (3SLS) Estimates, External Finance Equation, 1951 -60

Variable	1951	1952	1953	1954	1955	1956	1957	1958	1959	1960
C_0	.0148	-0.0121	.0250	.0251	.0258	.0174	.0217	.0330	.0091	.0605
	(.8566)	(-0.7917)	(1.0803)	(1.7404)	(2.4713)	(1.2117)	(1.9916)	(2.7485)	(1.1639)	(2.8154)
$LTD/(K-LTD)$	-0.0115	-0.0008	.0149	.0106	.0007	.0032	-0.0004	-0.0003	-0.0017	.0001
	(-2.8806)	(-3.0161)	(.7424)	(1.1168)	(.3778)	(.2462)	(-0.3631)	(-0.2922)	(-2.1438)	(.0889)
R/LTD	-0.0660	-0.0145	-0.0321	-0.1591	-0.3001	-0.2066	-0.1374	-0.2086	-0.0889	-1.1594
	(-0.2556)	(-0.0857)	(-0.3369)	(-2.1438)	(-2.0968)	(-1.5273)	(-1.4366)	(-1.8885)	(-1.3550)	(-6.7665)
DEP/K	.2191	-0.2285	.0035	-0.2169	-0.1976	-0.0514	-0.3157	-0.3829	-0.0073	-0.2107
	(1.9411)	(-1.9049)	(.0396)	(-2.2400)	(-1.9292)	(-0.4376)	(-2.8443)	(-2.7616)	(-0.0859)	(-0.9338)
P/K	-0.0406	.1246	-0.0701	.0436	.0167	-0.0093	.0430	.0766	-0.0347	.1252
	(-1.2166)	(1.6509)	(-1.7543)	(1.8287)	(.6370)	(-0.3925)	(1.5073)	(2.1475)	(-1.9325)	(2.0083)
D/S	-0.6802	-1.0531	.6903	-0.6702	-0.3956	-0.2575	-0.7333	-1.2043	.3255	-1.8697
	(-1.0940)	(-1.1633)	(1.3617)	(-2.8198)	(-1.3703)	(-0.7254)	(-2.2664)	(-3.5257)	(1.9936)	(-2.7528)
I/S	.4785	1.0682	-0.2174	.3502	.1322	.2596	.4482	.7184	-0.1449	.6608
	(2.4752)	(3.5622)	(-0.9311)	(4.0191)	(1.0985)	(2.2882)	(4.8168)	(3.8733)	(-1.4538)	(2.1242)

Note: Number in parentheses is t-ratio.

tion we have chosen to impose on our endogenous variables, nonetheless such inference does not seem valid to us. It might be observed that the stability in the contrasts just noted seems entirely in accord with the single-equation conclusions based on Table 7. A rather important consequence of this finding relates to the well-known studies of Lintner [15, 16], as well as to those of others. We seem to find that the dividend decision function varies from one industrial classification to another, at least with respect to the constant term. Hence, it would not appear proper to deal with this relationship in simple aggregative terms. At least this aspect of nonhomogeneity must be taken account of.

The coefficients of the exogenous variables exhibit a substantial degree of stability over time. The coefficient of the net current position (N/K) is uniformly small and negative; it turns out to be insignificant for 1953, 1954, and 1959. It may be remarked that these were years of relatively low (corporate) inventory investment, and thus the insignificance of the net current position is best understood in terms of dominance of this variable by its inventory component. The result is then perfectly intelligible in view of the uniformly negative impact of investment on the dividend policy of firms.

The coefficient of the rate of profit variable is consistently positive and significant. There is some slight evidence of an upward trend in its magnitude, and while one might tend to attribute it to the rather prolonged expansionary behavior of the economy in the postwar years, the evidence is too slight to permit this interpretation to be pressed too vigorously.

The behavior of the investment and external finance coefficients is of considerable interest. First, comparing them with the single-equation results, we find a complete reversal of their sign. Beyond that, the full information results appear to indicate an interesting pattern of relationships. Thus, the external finance variable appears to be significant only in periods of upswings (1952, 1955) or peaks (1953, 1960). On the other hand, the coefficient of the investment variable appears to be significant (and negative) chiefly during the upturn and peak years, although this is not a strictly consistent phenomenon. These results clearly demonstrate the significant dependence of the dividend policy of firms on their investment decision, a result obtained also in connection with our study of the dividend policy of electric utility firms [3] in a slightly different context. In the light of these results, one ought to have serious reservations concerning the specification of Lintner's dividend relation. Our findings would lead us to believe that one could best interpret his relation as simply the reduced form of the appropriate dividend function. Thus it would appear that several useful variables have been omitted from consideration and the consequent incidence of specification bias would tend to vitiate his otherwise excellent and pioneering work. Incidentally a similar interpretation of Darling's [2] work would tend to explain why changes in sales tend to serve as a useful explanatory variable for the dividend behavior of firms.

Finally, one might remark generally that the behavior of the estimates of the coefficients of the dividend equation over the entire sample period is rather stable and relatively free of cyclical characteristics.

Turning now to the investment equation, we first note that certain contrasts turn out to be consistently significant, viz., C_i for $i = 9, 8, 7,$ and 4. The remaining contrasts tend, on the whole, to be insignificant. This is a result that departs from the single-equation findings. It might also be pointed out in passing that these are the same industrial classifications for which significant contrasts were also found in the dividend equation. The significance of these contrasts indicates some degree of nonhomogeneity in the investment behavior of firms and hence several cross-section studies, such as those of Eisner [6], commit a specification error when they neglect this aspect. It might also be remarked that the magnitude of these estimates remains relatively stable over the period.

The pattern of influence of the predetermined variables on the investment decision is of considerable interest. First, note that the net current position (N/K) variable is nearly uniformly significant and negative in impact. This is best understood in terms of the cash flow constraint referred to above (equation 2) and the remarks made in connection with this variable when discussing the dividend equation.

Beyond this, the results provide some basis for appraising the "profits" and "accelerator" versions of investment theory. At first glance, the results seem to favor slightly the accelerator version. The (two-year average) change of sales variable (S^*_{-2}) appears to exert a significant influence on investment during the long period of postwar investment boom (following 1955). During that period it is insignificant only for 1959. Its coefficient is also significant in 1951, during the Korean war boom. The (lagged) rate of profit variable (our view of the profits version is somewhat different from the conventional one) appears to be insignificant in upswing (1951, 1952, 1959) and peak years (1957 and 1960). Moreover, the coefficient of this variable, when significant, does not appear to exhibit as much stability as the coefficient of the change of sales variable.

One might be tempted to argue that the "profits" version of investment theory is less pertinent than the accelerator version. This is, e.g., the conclusion of Eisner [6] and Kuh [13], but it is a misleading one. First, their results are based on single-equation techniques and thus do not adequately reveal the structure of the decision-making process they wish to study. (In this respect our own single-equation results tend to corroborate theirs.) Secondly, in choosing between the two alternative versions, it is incorrect to rely only on the direct role each of the relevant variables is empirically determined to play in the investment equation. On the contrary, our results seem to imply that the "profits" version is a very consistent and useful way of looking at the empirical behavior of investment. For the rate of profit variable is a very consistent and very significant determinant of the dividend behavior of firms, while the dividend variable appears also as a very useful and consistent determinant of investment. Thus, profits seem to operate on investment in a rather complex way, both directly and indirectly through the impact they exert on the dividend and external finance behavior of firms. Thus, if we interpret the cross-section studies of investment by recent authors, such as Kuh [13] and Eisner [6], as relating to the reduced form of the investment function, then we can plausibly argue that their generally negative findings with respect to the profits version is simply a reflection of the fact that the reduced form confounds the various links through which the rate of profit affects the investment process, given the structure as set forth in our investigation.

The dividend impact on investment is quite pronounced and consistently negative and significant (except for 1957 and 1960, both peak years). This is again a sharp departure from the results obtained by single-equation methods and supports the interdependent view of this triad of decision processes. In conjunction with the similar situation found for the dividend equation, it demonstrates the competitive character of the investment and dividend demands on the firm's resources.

The external finance variable appears to have been significant only in the pre-1955 period. Its coefficient, however, is not very stable, although it is positive, as one might expect. This might indicate that equity financing has become relatively more significant since 1955. Beyond that, one is hard put to find any other interpretation.

Finally, turning to the external finance equation, we should note that contrasts were determined to be insignificant and hence were omitted from the final form of this equation. Beyond that, the results here provide considerable information on a number of rather minor but still interesting issues. One of these is the empirical relevance of the so-called principle of increasing risk [11]. This has received scant attention in the literature. A recent study that seems to have examined this issue is that of Meyer and Glauber [18]. Unfortunately, however, the manner in which they approach the problem is unsatisfactory; for they merely limit themselves to examining the significance of the simple correlation between investment and an appropriate leverage variable. But, admittedly, the connection between investment and leverage is not a simple and direct one, and conclusions based on so crude a measure as simple correlations are bound to be quite tenuous. When the problem is examined in its proper perspective, viz., as influencing the external finance activity of the firm and only through that its investment decision, then one sees that there is some validity to the notion of increasing risk, especially in periods (the pre-Accord years[3]) when market rationing could not adequately take place through interest rate variation. We see that the leverage variable does turn out to be significant in 1951 and 1952 as well as in 1959, and it is negative in sign. Its numerical coefficient, however, is quite small. In conjunction with this, our interest variable, although quite imperfect in construction, tends to be insignificant in 1951, 1952, and 1953 (a period adjacent to the Accord), while it is consistently significant and negative in impact thereafter. Again this result throws some light on a related question, viz., the impact of the interest rate on investment, to which the traditional single-equation approach has normally answered that the impact of the interest rate on investment is insignificant. In this structural context, however, we do see such an impact in the positive and significant impact of the external finance variable in the investment equation in certain years.

The depreciation variable behaves in the expected fashion in conformity with the implication of the flow-of-funds view. One might ask why depreciation and profits should not be aggregated into one variable when dealing with the external finance equation, again in the context of the flow-of-funds view. As the results indicate, this would have been statistically an unsound procedure since the coefficients of the depreciation and (rate of) profit variables are generally of different sign. Moreover, the sign of the rate of profit variable is not stable and displays a distinctly cyclical character. It tends to be positive during periods when economic activity slows down (1954, 1958), while it tends to be negative during upswing or peak years (1953, 1959). This is quite interesting and seems to be symptomatic of the following type of behavior. It is a well-known and documented fact that firms display marked reliance on internal funds. During the upswing, when profits are rapidly rising, the more profitable a firm is, the less likely it may be

---

[3] Treasury-Federal Reserve Accord, March 4, 1951.

to rely on external finance. On the other hand, during periods of tight money or during the downswing, when profits are generally squeezed, then firms lacking in internal funds may be more inclined to resort to the capital market. At such periods, however, it is also a well-established fact that noninterest related forms of credit rationing are relatively more prevalent. Hence it is the more profitable firms that tend to have access to the capital market. If we recall that we deal with a cross-sectional sample, the change in sign of the coefficient of the profitability variable is easily understood.

As might have been expected, the investment variable turns out to be a rather consistent determinant of external finance, although its coefficient does not display much stability, even when significant. The dividend variable seems to be a less consistent determinant of the external finance behavior of firms. Its coefficient in 1954, 1957, 1958, and 1960 is significant and negative, while in 1959 it is significant but positive. Although it is difficult to give a useful interpretation to this result, other than the fact that stock flotation is in general an alternative to bond finance, it at least serves to dispel one possible implication of the Lintner view of dividend behavior. Lintner seems to imply that firms manifest a strong desire to maintain a rigid dividend policy. Thus, it would appear that in years when profits are unusually low this alleged rigidity should lead to added borrowing. But in the two recession years of our sample (1954 and 1958) the coefficient of the dividend variable is significantly negative, and hence the rigidity view does not appear to be supported empirically.

Before concluding this section, it might be desirable to give a few negative results. As an alternative to the fully simultaneous model presented above, one might consider a recursive model. Thus, one might postulate that investment is independent of the dividend and external finance decisions, dividend decisions depend only on investment, while external finance depends on both the dividend and investment decisions. The results of this estimation, not presented here in the interest of conserving space, are generally similar to those obtained in the fully simultaneous model, except that in the investment equation the rate of profit variable is frequently insignificant, but whenever it is significant—in three years—it has a negative sign. If we note that the dividend variable in the investment equation has a significantly negative coefficient and that the rate of profit variable in the dividend equation is consistently very significant with a positive coefficient, then the phenomenon described seems to indicate that the simultaneous model is the more relevant of the two.

Another failure worth noting was connected with the introduction of lagged dividends $(D/S)_{-1}$ as an explanatory variable in the dividend equation. Aside from any other problems that might arise when lagged endogenous variables serve as predetermined variables, multicollinearity was so severe as to preclude any meaningful results. Hence this was abandoned. On the other hand, we performed some single-equation computations of the dividend equation using lagged dividends as an explanatory variable. It turns out that its coefficient is highly significant and positive although the remaining explanatory variables still retain their significance. We should point out in this connection that we do not consider very meaningful the introduction of lagged endogenous variables as explanatory variables in cross-section studies of the sort pursued here. Hence we are not particularly concerned with the severe incidence of multicollinearity in these equations.

Conclusion

The objective of this study was to determine the structure underlying the dividend-investment-external finance triad of decision-making processes. The aim was not so much to attain predictive sharpness but rather to aid our understanding of the complex of relations that bind these policies together and, in conjunction with information exogenous to the firm, determine its actions. Moreover, we were concerned with demonstrating the simultaneous character of these decision-making processes.

The sample employed was a cross-sectional one involving 181 manufacturing, mining, and retail trade firms for which we had a continuous record over the period 1947–60. The method of investigation consisted of estimating the structure of our model successively for the years 1951–60. The main findings are in brief the following:

1. The single equation approach obscures the character of these decision-making processes.

2. Full information (three-stage least-squares) estimation methods are indicated since the correlation coefficients of the limited information (two-stage least-squares) residuals turn out to be quite significantly different from zero.

3. There is a significant degree of interdependence between the investment and dividend decision-making processes, with the implication that if dividend policies are very rigid as some allege, then this rigidity may tend to hamper the investment activity of firms. On the other hand, our results tend to show that the investment requirements of firms tend to have a significant effect on their dividend behavior.

This result is in accord with the findings of Dhrymes and Kurz [3], in the case of electric utilities.

4. The external finance activity of firms seems to be strongly affected by their investment policies, but less so by their dividend policies.

5. There is considerable evidence that elements of the accelerator version of investment theory are empirically quite relevant. On the other hand, our results seem to indicate that this should not be interpreted as a denial of the usefulness of the profits (rate of profit in our view) version. The manner in which profits affect investment is quite complex. They may tend to register an impact in several directions through the manner in which they affect directly the investment, the dividend, and the external finance decision-making processes.

6. Although our results differ markedly from the results of several cited studies, nonetheless if we interpret their findings as pertaining to the reduced form of the structure we have estimated here, then their results become compatible with ours. Thus, our results are best understood as generalizing and putting into proper perspective several previous findings pertaining to the investment and dividend behavior of firms.

In conclusion, we should point out that we offer this study by way of a preliminary exploration of our topic. Quite clearly much may be done further to elucidate more clearly the cyclical variation of the structure of these decision-making processes. The rather crude method of successive cross sections used here, while it does very definitely point to the presence of some cyclical pattern, nonetheless does not adequately pinpoint it.

Beyond that there are some data problems relating to the measure of the capital stock, the market value of the firm, and the interest rate variables that might have been handled more adequately. But, despite these reservations, we think that several useful conclusions may be derived from this study.

Appendix

(The list of firms comprising our sample is given below by industrial classification.)

INDUSTRIAL CLASSIFICATION 1

Boeing Airplane Company
Curtiss-Wright Corporation
Douglas Aircraft Company, Inc.
Lockheed Aircraft Corporation
North American Aviation, Inc.
United Aircraft Corporation
American Car and Foundry Co.
Martin Company

INDUSTRIAL CLASSIFICATION 1 (CONT.)

Alco Products Incorporated
Pullman Incorporated
Baldwin-Lima-Hamilton Corp.
Chrysler Corporation
General Motors Corporation
Studebaker-Packard Corp.
American Motors Corp.
The White Motor Co.
Mack Trucks, Inc.

INDUSTRIAL CLASSIFICATION 2

Bond Stores, Inc.
J. C. Penney Company
Allied Stores Corporation
Associated Dry Goods Corp.
City Stores Company
Federated Department Stores, Inc.
Gimbel Brothers, Inc.
R. H. Macy & Co., Inc.
Marshall Field & Company
The May Department Stores Co.
American Stores Company
First National Stores Inc.
The Kroger Company
Safeway Stores, Inc.
W. T. Grant Company
S. S. Kresge Company
S. H. Kress & Company
G. C. Murphy Company
F. W. Woolworth Company
Montgomery Ward & Co., Inc.
Sears, Roebuck and Company

INDUSTRIAL CLASSIFICATION 3

The American Tobacco Company
Liggett & Myers Tobacco Company
R. J. Reynolds Tobacco Company
P. Lorillard Company
U.S. Tobacco Company
Philip Morris, Inc.
The Borden Company
National Dairy Products Corp.
National Distillers Products Corp.
Schenley Industries, Inc.
Hiram Walker–Gooderham & Worts Ltd.
Distillers Corp.–Seagrams Limited
General Mills, Inc.
Pillsbury Mills, Inc.
Penick & Ford, Ltd., Inc.
Armour and Company
The Cudahy Packing Company
Swift & Company
Wilson & Company, Inc.
General Foods Corporation
Standard Brands Inc.

INDUSTRIAL CLASSIFICATION 4

Abbott Laboratories
Merck & Company, Inc.
Parke, Davis & Company
Colgate-Palmolive Company
The Procter & Gamble Company
Gulf Oil Corporation
Phillips Petroleum Company
Shell Oil Company

INDUSTRIAL CLASSIFICATION 4 (CONT.)

Sinclair Oil Corporation
Socony Mobil Oil Company, Inc.
Standard Oil Company of California
Standard Oil Company—Indiana
Standard Oil Company—New Jersey
The Texas Company
The Firestone Tire & Rubber Company
The B. F. Goodrich Company
The Goodyear Tire & Rubber Company
United States Rubber Company
General Tire and Rubber Company
Eagle-Picher Company
American Home Products Corporation
Sterling Drug Inc.
Vick Chemical Company
Allied Chemical & Dye Corporation
American Cyanamid Company
The Dow Chemical Company
DuPont
Hercules Powder Company
Monsanto Chemical
Union Carbide

INDUSTRIAL CLASSIFICATION 5

Allis-Chalmers Manufacturing Co.
Deere & Company
International Harvester Company
J. I. Case Company
American Chain & Cable Company, Inc.
Blaw-Knox Company
Combustion Engineering, Inc.
Fairbanks, Morse & Company
Ingersoll-Rand Company
Link-Belt Company
Worthington Corporation
The Budd Company
Bendix Aviation Corporation
Dana Corporation
Eaton Manufacturing Company
The Electric Auto-Lite Company
Stewart-Warner Corporation
Thompson Products, Inc.
The Black and Decker Mfg. Co.
Ex-Cell-O Corporation

INDUSTRIAL CLASSIFICATION 6

General Electric Company
Westinghouse Electric Corp.
Cutler-Hammer, Inc.
The Electric Storage Battery Co.
McGraw-Edison Company
Minneapolis-Honeywell Regulator Co.
General Cable Corporation

INDUSTRIAL CLASSIFICATION 6 (CONT.)

Admiral Corporation
Motorola, Inc.
Philco Corporation
Radio Corporation of America
Zenith Radio Corporation
Avco Manufacturing Corp.

INDUSTRIAL CLASSIFICATION 7

Johns-Manville Corporation
National Gypsum Company
The Ruberoid Company
United States Gypsum Company
General Refractories Company
Alpha Portland Cement Company
Armstrong Cork Company
Smith-Corona Marchant, Inc.
International Business Machine Corp.
Lehigh Portland Cement Company
American Radiator & Standard Sanitary
  Corporation
Crane Company
Otis Elevator Company
Lone Star Cement Corporation
Harbison-Walker Refractories Company
Penn-Dixie Cement Corporation
Yale and Towne Manufacturing Co.
United States Pipe and Foundry Co.

INDUSTRIAL CLASSIFICATION 8

American Can Company
Continental Can Company, Inc.
Anchor Hocking Glass Corporation
Owens-Illinois Glass Company
Masonite Corporation
Libbey-Owens-Ford Glass Company
The Champion Paper and Fibre Co.

INDUSTRIAL CLASSIFICATION 8 (CONT.)

Container Corporation of America
Crown Zellerbach Corporation
International Paper Company
Kimberly-Clark Corporation
The Mead Corporation
Rayonier Inc.
St. Regis Paper Company
Scott Paper Company
Union Bag-Camp Paper Corp.
West Virginia Pulp and Paper Co.
Burlington Industries, Inc.
Cannon Mills Company
J. P. Stevens & Company, Inc.
United Merchants & Manufacturers, Inc.
Beaunit Mills, Inc.
American Viscose Corporation
Bigelow-Sanford Carpet Company, Inc.
Simmons Company

INDUSTRIAL CLASSIFICATION 9

The International Nickel Company of
  Canada, Ltd.
Bethlehem Steel Corporation
Inland Steel Company
Jones & Laughlin Steel Corporation
National Steel Corporation
Republic Steel Corporation
United States Steel Corporation
Armco Steel Corporation
Revere Copper and Brass, Inc.
Aluminum Company of America
Kaiser Aluminum and Chemical Corp.
Olin Mathieson Chemical Corp.
Reynolds Metals Company
The Anaconda Company
Kennecott Copper Corporation
Phelps Dodge Corporation

BIBLIOGRAPHY

1. Brittain, J. A., "The Tax Structure and Corporate Dividend Policy," *American Economic Review,* May 1964.
2. Darling, P. G., "The Influence of Expectations and Liquidity on Dividend Policy," *Journal of Political Economy,* June 1957.
3. Dhrymes, P. J., and Kurz, M., "On the Dividend Policy of Electric Utilities," *Review of Economics and Statistics,* February 1964.
4. Dobrovolsky, S. P., "Economics of Corporate Internal and External Financing," *The Journal of Finance,* March 1958, p. 35.
5. Eisner, R., "A Distributed Lag Investment Function," *Econometrica,* January 1960.

6. ———, "Investment: Fact and Fancy," *American Economic Review,* Papers and Proceedings, May 1963.

7. Eisner, R., and Strotz, R., "Determinants of Business Investment," in *Impacts of Monetary Policy,* Commission on Money and Credit, Englewood Cliffs, N.J., 1963.

8. Hotelling, H., "The Selection of Variates for Use in Prediction with Some Comments on the General Problem of Nuisance Parameters," *Annals of Mathematical Statistics,* September 1940, p. 271.

9. Jorgenson, D. W., "Anticipations and Investment Behavior," in J. Duesenberry *et al.* (eds.), *S.S.R.C. Econometric Model of the U.S.,* Chicago, 1965.

10. Kaldor, N., "Economic Growth and Cyclical Fluctuations," *Economic Journal,* March 1954.

11. Kalecki, M., "The Principle of Increasing Risk," *Economica,* November 1937.

12. Klein, L. R., *Economic Fluctuations in the United States, 1921–1941,* New York, 1950.

13. Kuh, E., *Capital Stock Growth: A Micro-Econometric Approach,* Amsterdam, 1963.

14. Kuh, E., and Meyer, J. R., "Investment Liquidity and Monetary Policy," in *Impacts of Monetary Policy,* Commission on Money and Credit, Englewood Cliffs, N.J., 1963.

15. Lintner, J., "The Determinants of Corporate Savings," in *Savings in the Modern Economy,* W. Heller (ed.), Minneapolis, 1953.

16. ———, "Distribution of Incomes of Corporations Among Dividends, Retained Earnings and Taxes," *American Economic Review,* Papers and Proceedings, May 1956.

17. Mayer, J. R., and Kuh, E., *The Investment Decision,* Cambridge, Mass., 1957.

18. Meyer, J. R., and Glauber, R. R., *Investment Decisions Economic Forecasting and Public Policy,* Graduate School of Business Administration, Boston, 1964.

19. Modigliani, F., and Miller, M. H., "The Cost of Capital, Corporation Finance and the Theory of Investment," *American Economic Review,* June 1958.

20. Roos, C. F., "A Dynamical Theory of Economics," *Journal of Political Economy,* October 1927.

21. Theil, H., *Economic Forecasts and Policy,* 2nd ed., Amsterdam, 1961.

22. Tinbergen, J., "Statistical Evidence on the Acceleration Principle," *Economica,* May 1938.

23. ———, *Statistical Testing of Business Cycle Theories,* Geneva, 1938.

24. U.S. Congress, Joint Economic Committee, *Variability of Private Investment in Plant and Equipment, Part I: Investment and Its Financing,* Washington, 1962.

COMMENT

On Dhrymes-Kurz and Anderson

BY HENRY A. LATANÉ, UNIVERSITY OF NORTH CAROLINA

There are two types of analysis used in dealing with the investment and financing decisions of the firm. The first is the standard marginal analysis based on certainty or point estimating models with modifications to reflect uncertainty. The second is to approach the problem from the point of view of the actual decision maker. Dhrymes and Kurz state that the objective of their study was to determine the dividend-investment-external finance triad of decision-making processes, thus apparently attempting to take the second approach. In any event I am going to use this approach in talking about the two papers.

Before making direct comments, I would like to take a few moments to develop a frame of reference. The problem we are dealing with—business fixed investment and the financing and dividend policies of the firm—are directly analogous to the types of decisions faced by the rational portfolio manager in handling financial assets and liabilities. The rational portfolio manager decides how much to withdraw for living and other expenses each year and how much to reinvest. This corresponds to the dividend decision. He also has two different types of problems. In the first place, he must form probability beliefs as to returns from individual assets under various states of nature. In some gambling and insurance situations risk can be virtually eliminated by diversification, but this is not true with most economic assets because of the covariance of yields. If one venture is profitable so will be others and vice versa. Probability beliefs about distributions of returns from various combinations of assets also are needed. In the second place, the portfolio manager must allocate his portfolio in the light of his beliefs about returns from available portfolios. The portfolio manager has the option to borrow and lend within restrictions, and in order to make rational choices he must have some trade-off function between returns and risk.

The rational entrepreneur has virtually the same problems. He must form probability beliefs not only about individual investment opportunities but also about returns to the firm as a whole if various alternative investment policies are adopted and various states of nature occur. He must decide upon proper financing or financial reserves. He too must have some trade-off functions between risk and return in order to make rational decisions.

I will talk first about the variables used by Dhrymes and Kurz, secondly about variables omitted in both papers, and finally about the trend in the cost of funds.

In the Dhrymes-Kurz model sales are used as a deflator for dividends and investment. Dividends divided by sales turn out to be positively correlated with investment divided by sales, and the coefficient of the dividend variable is significantly positive when used as one of the explanatory variables to explain the investment variable. They say "the astonishing result in the investment equation is the sign and nearly consistent significance of the coefficient of the dividend variable . . . it is difficult to rationalize the positive sign of the dividend coefficient which points to the potential pitfalls of the single-equation approach and the ordinary tests of significance." However, there is a plausible rationalization for this positive correlation. It is in the choice of sales as a deflator. Even if there is some small negative correlation between dividends per dollar of book and investment per dollar of book, as indeed would be expected if dividends and investment are accepted as alternative uses of funds, there would be a positive correlation between dividends per dollar of sales and investment per dollar of sales if there are significant differences in sales per dollar of book value. Consider, for example, a meat packer and a public utility. The meat packer pays a dividend equivalent to 5 per cent of book and invests 12 per cent of book, the public utility pays 6 per cent of book and invests 10 per cent of book. The dividend ratio is negatively correlated with the investment ratio. But the meat packer has $10 of sales for each $1 of book, while the public utility has only 25 cents of sales for each $1 of book, so the dividend-sales ratio for the meat packer is .5 per cent and the invest-ment-sales ratio is 1.2 per cent, while the corresponding ratios for the public utility are 24 and 40 per cent. The dividend-sales ratios are positively correlated with the investment-sales ratios. There may well be other reasons for preferring the full information approach to the single equation—indeed I am sure of it—but the positive correlation between the dividends and investment ratios used by Dhrymes and Kurz does not seem to me to be one of them.

Let us now consider the variables omitted from consideration. Pos-sibly the most striking example of this is Anderson's omission of the 1957 data. He says "Since I firmly believe that the continuation of the mid-1950's investment boom into 1957 was collective madness *ex ante,* not to mention *ex post,* I had little compunction about pulling the 1957 observation and refitting the equations without it. The object of this was to increase the accuracy of the parameter estimates and not, of course, to raise the R^2." I too would accept "collective madness" as a useful variable. The airline order curve for new equipment is a classic example of this sort. One airline ordered a new model and the race was on. I might agree with him that, in the absence of a good measure of collective madness, we should omit contaminated data. However, I would hesitate to claim that this procedure increased the accuracy of the parameter estimates unless the limited population about which I was talking were very clearly specified.

Probably a more serious omission in both papers is the omission of lagged variables in the explanatory equations. There are sound econometric reasons for this, but no one can claim that a model without lagged variables adequately reflects the structure underlying the dividend-investment-external finance triad of decision-making processes. This is particularly true as it affects the dividend decision. What the company has been paying in the past is a matter of prime concern to the directors who are deciding what to pay in the future. Not only does the omission of lagged dividends break with the actual decision process, but also it upsets the weights to be used with other estimating variables. For example, I have run simple cross-section regressions to explain the prices of the thirty stocks in the Dow Jones Industrial Average, using dividends and retained earnings only as the explanatory variables—all variables being deflated by book value. The regression coefficients vary widely from year to year, but the median values for the eight years 1956–1963 were as follows:

$$\hat{p} = 4 + 28D_t - 2RE_t.$$

If now we add the price last year to the explanation we get

$$\hat{p} = -2 + 5.6D + 3.0\,RE + .84P_{t-1}.$$

In three out of the eight years retained earnings carry more weight than dividends. Since the lagged price is available to anyone who is interested, it is clear that, in the actual decision-making context, retained earnings carry about as much weight as dividends. In the first equation the dividend variable acts as a proxy to take up the weight which should have been placed on past price.[1]

Finally, Anderson states that there is a secular uptrend in the position of the marginal cost of funds schedule. If he means only the interest rate when he says marginal cost of funds, I would agree. Not only are interest rates relatively high, but firms are economizing on their cash

[1] See Irwin Friend and Marshall Puckett, "Dividends and Stocks Prices" *American Economic Review,* September 1964, pp. 676–677.

balances, thus indicating that the cost of safe capital is relatively high. However, there is another type of capital—risk capital, whether derived from retained earnings or stock issuance—and there is no convincing evidence that the cost of this type of capital has increased. Industrial stock prices now average over twice book value compared with 1.2 times in 1950 and 1.4 times in 1957. Dividend yields have been cut in half. Part of this higher price-to-book ratio and lower dividend yields may have resulted from smaller uncertainty surrounding expected yields, but the reduction in uncertainty hardly has been enough to justify the assumption that the marginal cost of equity capital has risen.

On Dhrymes-Kurz and Anderson

by R. W. Resek, University of Illinois

In past years economists discussed the problems of business investment which were emphasized in these papers, but when the time came to make empirical estimates they frequently returned to either acceleration or capacity-output theories. This emphasis was not due to a lack of trying to bring in other factors but was largely forced upon them by the lack of data as well as by variables that failed to vary. The authors consistently tried to incorporate more information into the explanations, but the endeavors were generally not too successful.

More recently, empirical studies have been made which significantly extend the evidence supporting alternative theories that improve our explanation of investment. They accomplish this by complementing an already accepted theory—not competing with it.

The papers presented here both emphasize the cost and availability of funds and its effect on investment. A number of possible positions can be taken concerning the cost of funds.

One can say that the cost of funds is fixed for all firms in the economy by the appropriate rate of interest. Jorgenson takes this position in his empirical work[1] and places emphasis on it in his theoretical work as, for example, that presented in this conference. He does find, of course, that investment is a decreasing function of the rate of interest but the rate is not dependent on the internal financial structure of the firm.

Miller and Modigliani have made an important contribution in this area. Earlier in this Conference they attempted to achieve a real mea-

[1] Dale W. Jorgenson, "Capital Theory and Investment Behavior," *American Economic Review*, May 1963, pp. 247–259.

sure of the cost of funds. In their view, this cost may differ from firm to firm. It does however remain constant for any given firm, regardless of financial structure (apart from tax complications).

In contrast to these views, Lintner in his paper indicates the belief that cost of funds is related directly to the internal financial structure of a firm and may change according to the volume of investment being made by the firm.

The two papers presented here are consistent with this latter view. Anderson explicitly introduces an expression for the marginal cost of funds to the firm. His expression relates this cost to the cost of equity and bond financing and to the internal financial position of the firms in the industry. His model is estimated at a very high level of aggregation so the results may be obscured by aggregate relations. However, his lag structure is likely to minimize this problem.

Dhrymes and Kurz construct a model which emphasizes the total volume of funds available and allocation of these funds by the firm. This model does not put specific emphasis on other phases of the cost element but the approach is closely related to Anderson's.

Dhrymes and Kurz build a three-equation model based on the alternative sources and uses of funds for a firm. They depend on the accounting identity:

$$I_1 + I_2 = EF1 + EF2 + P - D + Dep. \tag{2}$$

This equation states that fixed investment (I_1) plus inventory and other short-term investment (I_2) are the uses of funds. These must equal the sources of funds. These are external finance from bonds $(EF1)$, external stock finance $(EF2)$, and the internally generated funds-profits (P) minus dividends (D) plus depreciation (Dep). They assume short-term investment to be predetermined for the model, as were profits and depreciation. Stock financing is assumed to be residually determined. Thus only three equations must be estimated. These are for fixed investment, dividends, and bond external financing.

Their particular specification of the model was:[2]

$$\frac{D}{S} = g_1 \left\{ \frac{I}{S} \frac{EF}{S} \frac{P}{K} \frac{N}{K} \right\}$$

$$\frac{I}{S} = g_2 \left\{ \frac{D}{S} \frac{EF}{S} \left(\frac{P}{K} \right)_{t-1} \frac{N}{K} \frac{S - S(t-3)}{S(t-3)} \right\}$$

$$\frac{EF}{S} = g_3 \left\{ \frac{D}{S} \frac{I}{S} \frac{P}{K} \frac{Dep}{K} \frac{R}{LTD} \frac{LTD}{K - LTD} \right\}$$

[2] Time subscripts are added only when they are not t.

The variables are defined in Dhrymes and Kurz (hereafter referred to as D-K). Several peculiarities in this specification seem immediately apparent. First, the normalization of variables is half related to sales and half to capital stock. One cannot help but wonder what the outcome would have been if capital stock had been used throughout. Since sales are likely to fluctuate more than capital stock, the results may be sizably affected by the sales. For example, if the investment equation is solved to the left,

$$I = h_2 \left\{ D, EF, S \cdot \left(\frac{P}{K} \right)_{t-1}, S \cdot \frac{N}{K}, [S - S(t - 3)] \frac{S(t)}{S(t - 3)} \right\}$$

Both profits and the net current position of the firm are multiplied by sales. D-K find that both of these variables are frequently significant. Because of their specification, they may be finding the effect of sales rather than profits. The same type of situation exists in each equation of the model. Moreover, the constant term may have a coefficient that is attributable to sales and that explains the variation which otherwise would be explained by the accelerator variable, $[S - S(t - 3)]$.

Secondly, one can question the lag structure used in the model. Considerable evidence has been accumulated indicating that there is a sizable lag between decisions to invest and the specific expenditure. The interest and belief in this lag is evidenced by this Conference's specific papers on anticipations and appropriations. Well-known papers by Almon[3] and de Leeuw[4] have made specific estimates of the size of the lag. One conclusion that might be reached from this point of view is that the investment decision is reached first and that the method of financing the investment is subsequently and separately determined. The decision concerning financing would take place when the money was actually spent. This might tend to indicate that a recursive model is called for. D-K indicate they attempted such a model unsuccessfully but since the lags employed in that attempt are unknown, the question remains unsettled.

An alternative approach (which I prefer) would be that, at the time investment decisions are made, tentative plans for financing are also considered. Certainly the variable cost of funds theory requires this view since the type of financing affects the cost of funds. This view says the D-K model is inappropriate because nearly all of the variables are used with no lag whatsoever while they should be lagged.

[3] Shirley Almon, "The Distributed Lag Between Capital Appropriations and Expenditures," *Econometrica,* January 1965, pp. 178–196.

[4] Frank de Leeuw, "The Demand for Capital Goods by Manufacturers: A Study of Quarterly Time Series," *Econometrica,* January 1962, pp. 407–423.

This question about the lags leads to a related problem concerning the identification of the model. P/K appears unlagged in the dividend model but lagged one year in the investment equation. This difference is not explained. Thus profits affect future investment but do not, at that same instant in time, affect the other future uses of funds, e.g., dividends. If the lag structure in the model is inappropriate, in particular if profits appropriately should appear with the same lag in both of the first two equations, then the investment equation is not identified and one will estimate only a linear combination of the first two equations. This problem is particularly troubling because this part of the specification is clearly uncertain, and as a result the investment equation estimates are unreliable.

Finally, the specific choice of variables can be questioned. In justifying the dividend equation, mention is made of the work of Lintner. His principal finding is that present dividends are largely dependent on past dividends. Dhrymes and Kurz did estimate this equation with this variable but they report that, ". . . multicollinearity was so severe as to preclude any meaningful results. Hence this was abandoned." This type of problem is acute whenever it arises, but it does not seem to be appropriate to exclude the single most important explanatory variable when the multicollinearity arises. The resulting misspecification is so severe as to preclude any meaningful results.

This particular problem arises since the lagged endogenous variable is the explanatory variable. Frequently this type of variable is employed to represent the lag structure, as suggested by Koyck and Jorgenson. In this type of usage the lagged endogenous variable serves as a proxy for most of the lagged dependent variables. Instead of such a proxy, it may be argued that it is preferable to avoid using the endogenous variable and to represent the lag in some other fashion. This argument does not apply to the present situation as the lagged dividends are, according to the theory, in and of themselves an important determinant of dividends.

Investment in the D-K model depends on the change in sales, profits, and variables indicating the financial position of the firm. Recent models have, in general, found that capacity adjustment mechanisms were at least as effective as those representing the acceleration principle through change in sales. A model employing sales and capital stock as variables is therefore a strong alternative to the use of change in sales.

The rate of profit is used in this equation as a variable, "which may be taken to lead to changes in the expected profitability of new investment." Generally profit theories depend on the cash flow arising from profits which lead to a lower cost of funds as well as future profits. This is indirectly taken into consideration in this model through the effects of profits on dividends and external finance and the resulting effect on investment. It is generally felt that profits and sales are highly correlated variables. Since sales enters as a first difference $[S - S(t - 3)]$ and profits directly, one cannot help but wonder whether the coefficients measure the relative importance of original variable versus first differences rather than the profits versus sales.

One should also question the information on internal funds of the firm contained in the investment equation. The financial position of the firm is indicated through dividends, external finance, and the net current position of the firm. The quantity of money available for investment is presumably contained in these. The cost of funds seems only to operate in affecting the external funds which in turn affect investment. The implication seems to be that the cost of funds schedule is perfectly elastic at a very low rate up to some critical value where it becomes perfectly inelastic. It seems much more realistic to say that the interest rate affects investment directly through the cost of funds as well as indirectly through the external financing. Even a firm with no external funds would be affected by the interest rate although the model does not allow for it.

Finally, the use of N/K by the authors should be considered. They indicate that this variable, ". . . enters the model as a consequence of the use of the budget constraint to eliminate one of the variables in the system." The nature of this relation and the sign this would imply for the coefficient are somewhat unclear. Anderson employs a similar variable lagged one period and gets a positive relation with investment, indicating that since current funds are available, investment will be higher. Dhrymes and Kurz find a negative value for the unlagged variable. This is somewhat harder to explain, but apparently means that funds have been used for current purposes and therefore investment could not take place during this period.

Up to this point we have commented on four major features of the specification of the D-K model. The normalization provides some question concerning what is being measured; the lag structure was not carefully formulated; the second equation is nearly underidentified; and finally the variables used in the equations certainly are not the only possible candidates for inclusion. These comments are nothing new for econometric work as every author must choose among mutually exclusive alternatives, but in this model specification problems seem particularly severe.

Three alternative sets of results are computed by D-K. These are one-stage, two-stage, and three-stage least squares. They reject ordinary least squares as inappropriate early in the paper. There can be no question but that they are correct in doing this and are providing a step forward, given their particular model. Their use of three-stage least squares is much more to be questioned. They justify it on the grounds that the correlation coefficients between the two-stage residuals are high. This is correct and it is true that this is the type of information that three-stage least squares use effectively.

On the other hand, the model employed may be greatly in error due to specification errors as discussed above. No estimating technique under consideration will provide consistent estimates of parameters under this type of situation. Two-stage estimates may be less affected by the specification errors than three-stage estimates, although true sampling properties are simply not known under this type of error. If this is true, their two-stage estimates may be more reliable than the three-stage values emphasized by the authors.

Let us turn now to the paper by Anderson. He sets up a two equation model explaining the marginal rate of return and the marginal cost of funds for firms. Since these must be equated by a rational investor, he then solves for investment and estimates the reduced form equation.

The marginal rate of return here is dependent on output and capital stock as well as the level of investment. This is reasonable and may be obtained from a capacity adjustment model. Marginal cost of funds depends on the internal financial position and the external cost of funds. The former here is noncapital assets minus liabilities plus retained earnings. This variable then represents approximately what the financial situation would be at the end of the period if all internally generated funds were used to improve this position. This formulation seems to be an excellent way to handle the generally difficult funds problem. In particular, Anderson seems to avoid the problem of collinearity that plagues alternative formulations of this variable.

The external cost of funds is measured by the equity yield and bond yield. However, it is clear that the yield on equities reflects more than the cost of equity funds. It is also greatly affected by the growth expectations of the firm. A firm with great prospects for growth would have a much lower yield than one with low growth prospects. Thus this stock variable reflects both expectations for output and cost of funds. The former, which I consider to be more important, would appropriately be considered as a determinant of the marginal rate of return of the firm. This in no way affects the reduced form model to be estimated but does significantly affect the interpretation to be put on the results obtained.

Anderson's results strongly support the hypothesis being tested and strongly support the cost of funds theories of investment behavior. Clearly, as he points out, the implications for governmental policy may be sizable but are likely to be complex.

Anderson uses very aggregate data, which may lead to problems related to the contrast between macrodata and use of what is essentially a microtheory. Anderson justified his model by saying that, ". . . policy formulation and forecasting often require quick and dirty estimates of economic parameters." Clearly the proof of this model will be in the forecasting ability of the equation obtained.

Together, these two papers provide a great deal of light on the internal financial behavior of firms and the effect of this on investment.

On Dhrymes-Kurz and Anderson

BY WILLIAM VICKREY, COLUMBIA UNIVERSITY

Dhrymes and Kurz examined the concept that in a large firm decisions on investment policy, dividend policy, and external finance are not the components of a single-decision vector arrived at by a unitary management on the basis of exogenous influencing factors; rather they are somewhat independent, though mutually interrelated, decisions arrived at and modified at different times and by different groups. This concept has considerable appeal as an attempt to improve understanding of the large organism. And it is reasonably plausible that this interrelated but nonmonolithic decision process can, to some extent, be represented by a structural model in which these interactions among the dependent variables can be exhibited. However, the results of this experiment do not seem to me to be as conclusive as the authors appear to believe.

The statistical results of their model are summarized in Table 1, in which the entries represent the range of the t-coefficients for the ten single-year cross sections, with some comments on their behavior. It is clear that the equations of the model are formally overidentified, which would provide an opportunity for the use of some test, such as the likelihood ratio, as an indication of whether the model fits the data sufficiently well compared with a less constrained one to maintain the hypothesis that the excluded coefficients are in fact zero. As it is, we are asked to take the stipulated constraints of the model more or less on faith and to suppress any suspicion we may have that knowledge of the leverage position of the firm or the interest rates that it pays might directly influence the decisions of those concerned with dividend policy, or of those concerned with investment.

If the derivation of a specific structure has any usefulness, over and above what can be done with direct least-squares estimation of the endogenous variables in terms of the exogenous ones, it lies in the coefficients in the first three lines, which express the internal structure of the decision mechanism concerning which we are seeking information. Unfortunately the results seem meager. The only coefficient to show a reasonable amount of consistency is the inhibiting influence of commitments as to dividends on investment decisions. Even this is somewhat suspect, inasmuch as current sales used to deflate investment and dividends also occurs as a component of the change in sales variable, which appears as an exogenous explanatory variable. As for taking the coefficients for the individual year structures at face value, it is really hard to believe that the composite internal decision structure of firms changes that much from one year to another. I cannot escape the impression that the model at hand is much too procrustean to provide us with any reliable insights into the internal structure of the firm.

As for the possible uses of the model for forecasting, it is my understanding that, as long as one does not anticipate any exogenously determinable change in the effective structure of the organism whose behavior is being predicted, straightforward least-squares regression of the single endogenous variables on the exogenous variables provides as good predictions as more elaborate methods. It is only when one expects to be able to predict independently some change in the structure that differs in character from changes occurring in the period of observation that knowledge of the specific structure becomes important, as when it is desired to predict the effect of a change in a tax rate that has been stable during the observation period. In the case at hand, I see little likelihood of there being available any such independent information of a general change in the internal organization of large businesses. Accordingly, the usefulness of the results for forecasting purposes would seem to me to reside in the single-equation least-squares results. Unfortunately, even these are not quite of the nature required, since the other endogenous variables are included in each of the single equations as explanatory variables, which makes a consistent forecast difficult.

Summary of Statistical Results of Dhrymes and Kurz

Variable	Variable Explained by the Equation		
	Dividends Per Unit of Sales	Investment Per Unit of Sales	Long-Term External Finance Per Unit of Sales
Endogenous Variables			
Dividends per unit of sales	−1	−1.0 : −4.9 small at peaks	−3.5 : +2.0 erratic
Investment per unit of sales	−0.6 : −2.7 erratic	−1	−0.9 : +4.8 erratic; mostly +
Long-term external finance per unit of sales	−0.8 : +2.9 erratic	−1.1 : +3.1 erratic	−1
Exogenous Variables			
Industry dummy variables	4, 5, 7, 8, 9 generally significant	4, 5, 7, 8, 9	excluded
Profits per unit of capital	+2.3 : +6.3 fairly stable	excluded	−1.8 : +2.15 erratic; + at peaks
Net short-term assets per unit of capital	−1.2 : −3.0 fairly stable	−1.5 : −3.1 fairly stable	excluded
Profits this year per unit of capital last year	excluded	−0.28 : +2.5 erratic	excluded
Relative change in sales over the past 3 years	excluded	−.13 : +3.6 mostly +	excluded
Debt-to-equity ratio	excluded	excluded	−3.0 : +1.1 mostly −
Interest rate on debt	excluded	excluded	−.08 : −6.7
Rate of depreciation allowances	excluded	excluded	−2.8 : +1.9 mostly −

By way of contrast, the statistical techniques employed in the Anderson paper are relatively simple-minded, and the results straightforward and convincing. My only comment is that it seems to me that, in attempting to reconcile the timing of variables relating to a whole year and those relating to a point in time, it would be preferable to relate the flow over a given year to an average of the stocks at the beginning and end of the year, rather than, as Anderson does, relate the stock at a point in time to an average of the flows for the preceding and subsequent periods. Not only do the data in the former case span only one year in time rather than two, but the former treatment seems to conform more closely to the data that would be uppermost in the mind of a decision maker at a given time. Even if he does not at a given time have before him the stock figures for the end of the current year, but only the flow data for, say, the first eleven months of the year, it seems plausible to say that he will be more strongly influenced by his rough knowledge of what the probable stock situation will be at the close of the year than he will by what the flow was for the preceding full year. Thus for an output-capital ratio it would seem preferable to use $2Q_t/(K_t + K_{t-1})$ rather than $(Q_t + Q_{t-1})/2K_{t-1}$, and similarly $2R_t/(K_t + K_{t-1})$ rather than $(R_t + R_{t-1})/2K_{t-1}$ as the retained earnings element in the financial position. Otherwise the results seem to speak for themselves.

Reply to Latané, Resek, and Vickrey

by Dhrymes and Kurz

We are indeed very grateful to the discussants of our paper for their detailed comments. We are, however, dismayed that a number of points raised are either adequately covered in our paper or involve an incomplete understanding of our arguments. We hope that the following paragraphs will aid in dispelling much of the misunderstanding and elucidate the issues. We shall examine the points raised by each discussant individually and conclude with some general comments.

It is our understanding that Henry Latané raises two points. First, he questions the omission of lagged dividends in the specification of the dividend equation of our model; this was also raised by other discussants and we shall deal with it below. Second, he maintains that our result relating to the reversal of sign in the coefficient of the dividend variable in the investment equation when one uses single- and simultaneous-equation techniques is the product of our normalization scheme. He goes on to say "The meat packer pays a dividend equivalent to 5 per cent of book and invests 12 per cent of book, the public utility pays 6 per cent of book and invests 10 per cent of book. The dividend ratio is negatively correlated with the investment ratio. But the meat packer has $10 of sales for each $1 of book, while the public utility has only 25 cents of sales for each $1 of book, so the dividend-sales ratio for the meat packer is .5 per cent and the investment-sales ratio is 1.2 per cent, while the corresponding ratios for the public utility are 24 and 40 per cent. The dividend-sales ratios are positively correlated with the investment-sales ratios." While no one will take exception to the arithmetic of the example, Latané appears to have entirely misunderstood the issue. First, it is well known that the fact that the (simple) correlation coefficient between the dependent and one of the explanatory variables in a multivariate regression is of a given sign *does not* imply that the corresponding multivariate regression coefficient *must be of the same* sign. Second, this example is completely irrelevant to the results we cite. What we find is the following. Noting that there is a body of thought which views the dividend policy of a firm as independent, at least in the short run, of its investment policy (and presumably independent of the error term in the relevant equation), we introduced dividends as an explanatory variable in our investment equation. The corresponding regression coefficient turns out to be significant and positive; when the same relation is estimated as part of the larger structure by simultaneous-equation techniques, then this same coefficient turns out to be significant and negative. This is a very important empirical result, which must not be confused with the problems, if any, induced by our normalization.

William Vickrey's two comments are that we have conducted no test for identifiability of the structure we have estimated, and that the results are too unstable to permit us an insight into the complex of the interdependence we seek to estimate. In regard to the first point, Vickrey suggests that we should have employed a likelihood ratio test. While there is no objection to performing such a test, it simply involves the extraction of characteristics roots of a certain matrix, we do not think that this is a particularly useful exercise. There is not much evidence to convince us that the error terms of the equations of our model have a joint normal distribution; if this is not so, then the execution of the likelihood ratio test is an empty exercise, the outcome of which is difficult to interpret.

Concerning the second point, Vickrey apparently bases his conclusion on the first three lines of his Table 1. This criticism, however, seems largely without foundation. A look at our Table 14 will indicate that, in the dividend equation, the investment variable appears uniformly with a negative sign, while the external finance variable, when significant, appears uniformly with a positive sign. Moreover, the contracting influence of investment on dividends is most apparent in peaks and upswings (1952, 1955, 1957, and 1960); the same is generally true of the external finance variable, whose positive influence on dividends is significant in 1952, 1953, 1955, and 1960.

Important conclusions can also be derived from the investment equation, in which the dividend variable is nearly invariably significant with a negative sign. Our results also indicate a sharp dichotomy in the role of the external finance variable; thus in the pre-Accord period this variable is quite significant and positive in its effect, while in the great investment boom of the mid-1950's it appears to have had no influence since its coefficient is uniformly insignificant from 1955 through 1960.

Thus, while not claiming that our paper constitutes the definitive work on this topic, we sharply disagree with Vickrey on his second point.

Our results give us a great deal of insight into the complex of the decision-making process we wish to study and, furthermore, hint at some very interesting cyclical patterns that bear more careful and systematic investigation—obviously the next step in this type of research.

Finally, to the best of our understanding, Resek makes the following points: (1) the "lag structure" in our model is not "properly specified"; (2) the second equation is "nearly underidentified"—whatever that may mean; (3) there is some ambiguity in the interpretation of coefficients in the investment equation; (4) several questions of misspecification are raised, in particular the exclusion of lagged dividends as an explanatory variable in the dividend equation.

In view of the fact that, as they are presented, the first two points are closely related we shall discuss them concurrently. In the first point we are taken to task for ignoring the work of Almon and de Leeuw relating to the lag between appropriations and expenditures in capital investment. On the other hand, in the second point we are taken to task for "underidentification" in that we enter the profit rate in the dividend equation and the lagged (one period) profit rate in the investment equation as explanatory variables without adequate justification.

Now if it is true, and surely one might wish to test it, that both elements of a rate of profit and elements of an accelerator theory govern investment behavior, and if Almon and de Leeuw are correct in pinpointing the specific lag structure between appropriations for investment and expenditures for investment, then it follows that our specification of the lagged rate of profit in the investment equation is a perfectly sensible specification. In particular, Almon's work shows that within a year after appropriation the bulk of it has actually been spent, while within six to eight quarters nearly all appropriations have been expended. Since her sample comprises two-digit manufacturing industries and certain manufacturing aggregates and since our sample consists mostly of firms which can be classed as manufacturing, it would appear that we acted properly in specifying the lagged rate of profit as an explanatory variable in the investment equation. Indeed, this "near underidentifiability" of which our model is accused is the logical consequence of taking into account the very works he urges us to take into account in an earlier passage. In this connection, we should mention that more complicated lag structures were attempted in specifying the role of the profit rate in the investment as well as the dividend equations, but these generally did not perform as well as the ones finally reported. Given the choice between the simple and the complex, other things being equal, we would of course choose the simplest specification possible. One possible explanation for Resek's views is that he may have overlooked the fact that investment in this context means investment expenditures, not appropriations.

We take it that there is no dispute in using the current profit rate as an appropriate explanatory variable in the dividend equation.

In his third point Resek raises a question of interpretation of the coefficients of the investment equation in particular. There appears to be some confusion in his mind about the meaning of the constant term and the coefficient of the rate of profit variable; he claims that "Because of their specification, they may be finding the effect of sales rather than profits." We do not think there is any ambiguity and should be glad to elucidate the matter. If we "solve" the investment equation by multiplying through by sales (S), then the coefficient of the linear term containing sales is, in fact, the decomposition of the constant term in our equation, a decomposition incidentally that reveals highly significant industrial classification contrasts.

The accelerator variable in our version is $S_t - S_{t-3}$. There cannot be any confusion in the manner Resek alleges "Moreover the constant term may have a coefficient that is attributable to sales and that explains the variation which otherwise would be explained by the accelerator variable, $[S - S(t - 3)]$." Now, in its usual empirical formulation the accelerator version of investment theory does not attribute investment to "sales" but rather to changes in sales, so it is difficult for us to understand Resek's criticism. The meaning of these two estimates is quite simple. The constant term relays the following information: consider any two firms, which are identical in every other respect except for their volume of sales. Then to the extent that there is a significant constant term, or a significant industrial classification contrast, the two firms would behave differently with respect to investment. Thus, the constant term of the equation captures a purely "size" effect; while the contrasts capture both a size *and* an effect that is to be attributed to the type of activity in which the firm in question engages.

On the other hand, consider any two firms which are identical in every other respect except that they differ in the variable $S_t - S_{t-3}$, i.e., one has grown more rapidly than the other. Then, to the extent that the coefficient of this variable is significant, our model would tell us that investment would differ between the two firms. This is what one customarily takes as the accelerator effect. Thus, far from confounding the issue, our formulation serves to differentiate clearly between effects that are to be attributed to size or industrial classification, and those that are to be attributed to the rapidity with which pressures are registered on the firm's productive capacity-accelerator effects.

There is only one valid criticism that can be made against our formulation, viz., that our accelerator variable is in effect $(S_t - S_{t-3})(S_t/S_{t-3})$. This induces a "bias" on the accelerator coefficient because of the presence of the second term in parentheses, a point not made by Resek. This is, however, innocuous in the present context since we are not particularly interested in the magnitude of that coefficient, nor are we interested in testing any hypothesis concerning its magnitude—other than whether the coefficient is significantly different from zero or not. A similar interpretation is to be placed on the rate of profit coefficient.

Finally, the question of specification raised by Resek concerns chiefly our omission of lagged D/S from the explanatory variables in the dividend equation. In our work with the dividend behavior of electric utilities, cited in our current paper, we showed that in our sample (which was a cross-sectional one) the simple Lintner hypothesis yields an optimal dividend pay-out ratio of 1.22. Since we refused to entertain seriously the notion that firms optimally desire to pay out as dividends $1.22 for every dollar of profits, we proceeded to show that an alternative specification of the dividend behavior of (electric utility) firms relying on essentially the same structure we use in the current study has as much explanatory power as the Lintner formulation. Moreover, in our specification we gain some additional insight into the structure of the dividend decision-making process. It is for this reason that we were not particularly perturbed when multicollinearity forced us to abandon the version Resek refers to, i.e., a specification in which $(D/S)_{t-1}$ appears as an explanatory variable in the dividend equation.

Perhaps it should be noted that the problem of multicollinearity is generally unrelated to the explanatory power of the omitted variable with respect to the explained variable. Here multicollinearity arises, and severely so, because $(D/S)_{t-1}$ is very highly correlated with $(P/K)_{t-1}$ and not because $(D/S)_t$ is highly correlated with $(D/S)_{t-1}$, which is what one might infer that Resek had in mind.

It seems fitting to conclude with a summary of the conceptual framework of this study. We view the firm as making the three decisions under consideration interdependently. The dividend behavior of the firm depends on the profitability of its operation, the type of activity it engages in, and the decisions it takes or reviews concurrently with respect to investment and external finance.

Investment depends on elements of the accelerator and rate of profit theories, perhaps with a lag between the appropriation and expenditure of funds on capital projects. Investment also depends on the decisions taken with respect to dividends and external finance.

Finally, external finance may depend on the interest rate, the leverage position of the firm, and the decisions with respect to dividends and investment.

Our results tend to substantiate this view of interdependence and incidentally show that investment and dividends are relatively little affected by external finance, while the latter is chiefly affected by the decisions of the firm regarding its dividend and investment policies.

PART V

Anticipations

Anticipations and Investment Behavior: An Econometric Study of Quarterly Time Series for Large Firms in Durable Goods Manufacturing

REYNOLD SACHS AND ALBERT G. HART

COLUMBIA UNIVERSITY

Investment behavior, in theoretical terms, seems very directly a matter of anticipations: present investment decisions can bear fruit in the form of new facilities only after a gestation lag of several calendar quarters, and in the form of added output and cost savings only over a period of several years after facilities are completed; hence rational decisions must relate to results to be expected in the fairly distant future. Empirically also, it may be taken as established that, when we organize the relevant data with time units of one year, an anticipations approach

NOTE: This paper is to be taken as an interim report on the Columbia University project in Expectational Economics supported by the National Science Foundation. Earlier reports (with more stress on capital appropriations and less on expenditures as objects of explanation) appear in A. G. Hart's article "Capital Appropriations and the Accelerator" (*Review of Economics and Statistics,* May 1965) and in R. Sachs' dissertation presented in May 1965 under the title "Manufacturers' Capital Appropriations as a Measure of Investment Decisions: An Econometric Study of Quarterly Time Series."

The authors wish to express appreciation for the financial support of NSF, for the cooperation of the Computer Center at Columbia University, and above all for the aid and counsel of Jon Cunnyngham (whose regression program has been used throughout). We have had invaluable guidance also from Franco Modigliani at the Massachusetts Institute of Technology, from James Duesenberry at Harvard University, from Shirley Almon at Wellesley, and from a number of associates at Columbia University.

has been validated by the proved usefulness of the various investment-intentions surveys. Data from such surveys are fairly useful as direct forecasts and highly useful as ingredients in predictive models. But for good reasons, econometric studies of investment behavior are shifting more and more to the analysis of quarterly data. Here studies which work only with *ex post* data have done at least fairly well. It must be considered questionable whether *ex ante* data can be made fruitful in a study which uses a quarterly time unit.

The discouragement of many investigators with *ex ante* investment data on a quarterly basis reflects a serious defect of the quarterly investment-intentions figures available from the Commerce-SEC survey. The time horizon of these figures is so short that they must measure primarily the *forecasts* of firms acquiring facilities for deliveries and the progress of work by their suppliers, rather than the *decisions* of the firms acquiring facilities. Only recently has the horizon of these inquiries been extended from one to two quarters in advance of the quarter when the data are collected. The present study, however, seeks to extend the horizon by using data for *capital appropriations,* exploiting systematically the quarterly survey by the National Industrial Conference Board.[1]

Appropriations Data in Relation to Investment Behavior

It is at first sight intuitively appealing to assert that to explain investment we must view it in terms of *investment decisions* and that the capital appropriations reported in the NICB survey constitute direct observation of such decisions. But the application of this assertion is not entirely straightforward and the simplifications involved in the second part of the assertion may be dangerous. In the first place, a decision on an investment project is not an event but a process; appropriation is clearly an interesting stage in that process, but cannot be certified in advance as an all-sufficient expression of the process as a whole. Both earlier and later stages may be important as objects of study as well as for policy formulation. In the second place, the investment decision as registered in an appropriation has dimensions which are not fully covered by a report only of the amount appropriated. Besides setting this amount, the investment decision must also embody a provisional distribution through time of expenditures to be made out

---

[1] Survey results, with some interpretation, are published regularly in *Newsweek* and the *Conference Board Business Record.* The data used in the present paper, however, incorporate unpublished revisions by the Department of Investment Economics at the NICB under the direction of Fred Stevenson, for which we wish to express our appreciation.

of the given capital appropriation. To actually apply the insight that appropriations may be taken to represent investment decisions, we need somehow to get past the difficulty that the appropriations survey tells us quarter by quarter about amounts appropriated,[2] but does not explicitly include any information about the distribution of resulting expenditures over time.

Other survey evidence suggests that respondent firms can furnish useful information about this time distribution of investment expenditures. The McGraw-Hill survey annually obtains an array of information about the prospective distribution over the oncoming three budget years of capital outlays under projects already budgeted for. If this information could somehow be crossed with that offered by the appropriations survey, we would be much closer to being able to measure both the size and timing dimensions of the investment decision. But for the present we are confronted with a situation where the appropriations survey is silent about future time distribution, while the investment-intentions surveys are silent about the dates at which decisions about investment projects crystallized.

Lacking actual survey data which cross appropriation dates and prospective expenditure dates, we can exploit the *ex ante* information offered by the appropriations survey only by trying to find in the record of appropriations an *implicit* pattern for inferring later expenditures. Having done so, we can compare this resulting *ex ante* model and a model that tries to explain investment expenditures from *ex post* data, and then match both against an eclectic model using elements of both.

Procedure of the Paper

The present study deals exclusively with the capital appropriations and expenditures of the durable goods producers among the 1,000 largest manufacturing corporations in the United States.[3] We prefer durable

---

[2] In fact, the survey yields information about these "amounts" both in flow and stock dimensions. The full array of NICB survey data for manufacturing industries (also, for a shorter period of observation, for public utilities) includes the *flow* of new appropriations by respondent firms during each quarter-year; the *backlog* (at the opening and close of the quarter) of funds appropriated and unspent; and *cancellations* during the quarter of funds appropriated but unspent. In addition, the survey collects data on actual capital expenditures by the firms which report appropriations.

[3] The Hart article cited in the beginning of the paper works entirely with aggregates for total manufacturing; the Sachs dissertation works separately with durables, nondurables (excluding petroleum because of its unique degree of concentration of appropriations in a single quarter), and their total. In addition, the Sachs dissertation complements the study of *levels* of appropriations, expenditures, and other variables with a study of their *changes*—measured by increments of logarithms.

goods to nondurable goods producers or to a combination of both because the former presumably do more advance planning and because the new orders variable, which in our preliminary studies has shown up as of crucial importance, has a more clear-cut meaning for durables than for nondurables manufacturers. We prefer working with the durable goods subaggregate data to working with available two-digit industry data, partly for lack of time to handle the problems of disaggregation and partly because the unavoidable complications of our report are already great enough without introducing additional dimensions through disaggregation. In view of the extent to which we have worked over the present data in the course of this study, the results are perhaps best viewed as hypotheses which should stand confrontation with the corresponding data for the two-digit durable goods manufacturing industries. Time lags and relative weights of variables should vary from industry to industry. But if our results are meaningful, the two-digit industries stage of the analysis should yield functions with a strong family resemblance to those presented in this study.

Our analysis passes through the following stages:

A. We first undertake to derive an explanation of capital expenditures in quarter (t) from appropriations data in antecedent quarters; the best model turns out to be one where the explanatory variables represent flows of appropriations in a series of successive quarters from $(t - 6)$ through $(t - 2)$.

B. We next compare the results of stage A with those of naive models based on autoregressions of expenditures. Here it is evident that the *ex ante* model incorporating appropriations is enormously superior to the autoregressive naive model, though there is an interesting partial correlation of expenditures with previous-quarter expenditures (after appropriations are taken into account) which suggests that random influences on expenditures probably tend to persist through two or three quarters rather than to exhaust themselves within one quarter.

C. We then take appropriations of quarter (t) as the object of explanation, considering an autoregressive naive model, a "pure-finance" model based upon cash flow and interest rates, an "accelerator" model based on the ratio of new orders to capacity, and an eclectic model. (The selection of these particular explanatory variables reflects extensive experimentation in the Sachs dissertation.) It turns out that the eclectic model is an enormous improvement over the naive model, a substantial improvement over the pure-finance model, and a moderate improvement over the accelerator model. The interest-rate variable appears highly significant in the pure-finance model, but very doubtful in the eclectic model where the ratio of orders to capacity as well as cash flow are also taken into account.

D. We then consider the possibilities of a "direct explanation" of capital expenditures from the accelerator and financial variables which in stage C were used to explain appropriations. The results are somewhat disconcerting; while the direct explanations of expenditures do not outperform the best appropriations model from stage A, they are considerably more powerful than one would expect from the results from stages B and C. We must infer that not all of the information relevant to expenditures which is carried by the financial and accelerator variables is incorporated in appropriations, but that some of the influences these variables represent somehow bypass the appropriations.

E. Next, we consider still more eclectic models which make use jointly of appropriations and of the financial and accelerator variables. These models considerably outperform either the pure appropriations models of stage A or the direct-explanation models of stage D. We must infer that capital appropriations embody a good deal of information relevant to expenditures which is not embodied in the several explanatory variables introduced at stage C. It should be noted, however, that to incorporate more such explanatory variables should reduce the apparent net contribution of appropriations data. It is conceivable that an optimum list of explanatory variables might pull this net contribution down until it became nonsignificant.

F. In stage F, we take up some indications on the behavior of Modigliani's *realization function*—working with *plan-image functions* and *indicators of surprise*. While an exhaustive exploration of this side of the problem would call for an enormously complex analysis, the results suggest that plans formulated as of the end of the third quarter before the expenditure may be taken as fairly firm, but that reactions to surprises of later dates are appropriate and significant.

G. A concluding section considers some basic limitations of this study and an agenda for further research.

A. Explanation of Capital Expenditures from Antecedent Appropriations

A series of regression equations for the explanation of capital expenditures from antecedent appropriations appears in Table 1. It will be immediately apparent that fairly handsome coefficients of determination result from extremely simple formulations, with an adjusted R^2 of 0.809, when we take account of appropriations in quarter $(t - 4)$ or of

TABLE 1

Regression Coefficients of Equations to Explain Capital Expenditures from Flow and Backlog of Appropriations

(million 1954 dollars per calendar quarter per unit of explanatory variable)

| | Noncausal Explanation, Pure Seasonal,[a] Eq. A-1 | Single Explanatory Term | | Multiple Explanatory Terms | | Plan Image, Consecutive Series of Flow of Dates (t-3) and Earlier, Eq. A-6 |
		Single Flow, Eq. A-2	Single Backlog, Eq. A-3	Single Flow with Preceding Backlog, Eq. A-4	Consecutive Series of Flows, Eq. A-5	
Adjusted R^2	0.1208	0.8085	0.8753	0.9028	0.9344	0.9040
Intercept[b]	1037 ± 87	482 ± 69	214 ± 64	170 ± 63	284 ± 54	363 ± 62
Backlog of appropriations unspent:						
B_{t-1}			0.186 ± 0.013			
B_{t-2}				0.124 ± 0.013		
Flow of (gross) new appropriations:						
A_{t-2}				0.291 ± 0.037	0.193 ± 0.052	
A_{t-3}					0.150 ± 0.064	0.310 ± 0.058
A_{t-4}		0.498 ± 0.046			0.136 ± 0.066	0.125 ± 0.080
A_{t-5}					0.042 ± 0.075	0.102 ± 0.088
A_{t-6}					0.154 ± 0.057	0.069 ± 0.063
Adjusted R^2 with C_{t-3} in eq.	0.1372	0.8212	0.9039	0.9244		

[a]Regression coefficients of seasonal dummy variables (which are included in all regression equations) are reported separately in Table A-2.

[b]Intercepts in all tables represent the *mean* level for all four quarters of the year (as opposed to direct results of the regression program, which used three seasonal dummies leaving the fourth seasonal regression implicit).

0.875 when we take account only of the backlog appropriated unspent at the opening of quarter $(t-1)$. These relations account, respectively, for 78 and 86 per cent of the variance left unexplained by a set of seasonal dummy variables.[4] The force of the explanation increases considerably if we extend these simple relations very slightly and use the most powerful combination of an appropriations-flow term with the backlog appropriated unspent just before the quarter of the appropriations (quarter $t-2$).[5] The most powerful explanatory equation of reasonably simple structure based on appropriations (equation A–5) yields an adjusted R^2 of 0.934 when we take account of appropriations in each quarter from $(t-6)$ up to $(t-2)$.[6]

An oddity of the data, for which we have no satisfactory explanation, is the consistency with which cancellations of unspent appropriations, taking place several quarters in advance of the expenditures to be explained, show a significant negative relation to the expenditures even after appropriations are taken into account. As may be seen from the last line in Table 1 (and from the repetition of the same phenomenon in the more complex situation reported in Table 2), adjusted multiple R^2's rise appreciably if this cancellations variable is included. The fact that the relationship is negative is scarcely surprising, since cancellations must above all register the unfavorable aspects of the news affecting investment decisions. But one might reasonably expect that this adverse news would register itself equally through holding down new

[4] These dummy variables are incorporated without exception in all our regression equations. We have avoided cluttering up the text tables with regression coefficients for the seasonal dummies; the variation of these coefficients from equation to equation can be traced in Table A-2 in the Appendix.

Note that the intercept values shown in each column are not those yielded directly by regression equations with three seasonal dummies, but implicit values which are obtained by adjusting the sum of these coefficients for the three dummies and the implicit fourth-quarter seasonal coefficient to equal zero.

[5] It would be inappropriate to combine appropriations-flow data for quarter $(t-2)$ with the backlog at the opening of quarter $(t-1)$ because the backlog at this date must be taken to include all funds appropriated in quarter $(t-2)$ with a very modest deduction for expenditures in the very quarter of the appropriation. But the backlog at the opening of quarter $(t-2)$ and the appropriations made during that quarter must be seen as clearly distinct pieces of information.

[6] The parameter of A_{t-5} is obviously nonsignificant; but it seems clearer at this stage to include it. The adjusted R^2 would rise to 0.936 if we economized one degree of freedom by omitting it.

The fact that the two highest parameters (0.193 and 0.154) appear for the most recent and most remote quarters suggests that appropriations of these quarters may be functioning to some extent as proxies for very recent and very remote quarters not included. However, in a similar equation both A_t and A_{t-1} were included but turned out to have regression coefficients far smaller than their standard errors and these terms were therefore rejected on the basis of statistical significance.

TABLE 2

Regression Coefficients of Equations to Explain Capital Expenditures (Using Autoregression) from Antecedent Expenditures and from Synthetic Combinations of Antecedent Expenditures with Appropriations Data

(million 1954 dollars per calendar quarter per unit of explanatory variable)

	Noncausal Explanation: Autoregression			Synthetic Explanation: One Autoregressive Term with Appropriations Terms Specified		
	Latest Expenditure, Eq. B-1	Three-Term Practical,[a] Eq. B-2	Four-Term Optimal,[a] Eq. B-3	Single Backlog, Eq. B-4	Single Flow Term,[b] Eq. B-5	Consecutive Series of Five Flow Terms,[a] Eq. B-6
Adjusted R^2	0.8408	0.7932	0.8990	0.9265	0.9390	0.9441
Intercept	105 ± 85	462 ± 111	253 ± 82		64 ± 53	140 ± 68
Autoregressive terms:						
X_{t-1}	0.903 ± 0.075		1.055 ± 0.069		0.698 ± 0.055	0.494 ± 0.125
X_{t-2}		1.264 ± 0.127				
X_{t-4}		−0.706 ± 0.127	−0.298 ± 0.069			
Flow of new appropriations:						
A_{t-2}					0.224 ± 0.031	0.163 ± 0.044
A_{t-3}						0.119 ± 0.048
A_{t-4}						0.064 ± 0.058
Adjusted R^2 with C_{t-3} in eq.	0.8675	(0.7875)	0.8984		0.9504	0.9561

[a]To avoid understating the contribution of autoregressive terms, we started the derivation of each equation with a continuous series of three, four, or five terms, but eliminated those terms whose inclusion *reduces* the adjusted R^2. Hence the absence from eq. B-2 of X_{t-3}, from eq. B-3 of X_{t-2} and X_{t-3}, and from eq. B-6 of A_{t-4} and A_{t-6}.

[b]Eq. B-5 may be taken to represent also the combination of a single flow term with the appropriate backlog, since term B_{t-2} has no adjusted partial correlation when added to eq. B-5. Note that the single-appropriations term which is most useful is A_{t-2}. The inclusion of X_{t-1} has a strong effect on the relative explanatory value of the appropriations flow terms. To use A_{t-2} in place of A_{t-4} in eq. A-2 lowers the adjusted R^2 from 0.8085 to 0.6179; to use A_{t-4} instead of A_{t-2} in eq. B-5 lowers the adjusted R^2 from 0.9390 to 0.8638.

CHART 1

Capital Expenditures, Appropriation, and
Explanatory Variables, Quarterly, Seasonally Adjusted, 1953-63
(monetary figures in billion 1954 dollars)

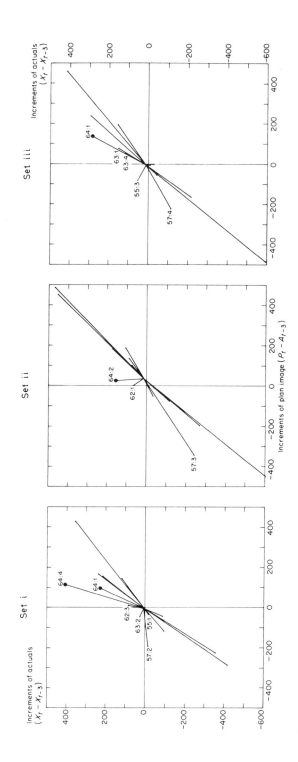

appropriations. This oddity would suggest that some pieces of information which register real influences on expenditures somehow bypass the stage of new appropriation and yet are registered in cancellations.

B. Explanation of Expenditures from Autoregressive Terms

A second set of regression equations, using autoregressive terms, appears in Table 2. Since capital expenditures are a very smooth series (as may be seen from the graph of seasonally adjusted data in Chart 1), it is not surprising that the coefficient of determination is as high as 0.841 using the directly antecedent level of expenditures (X_{t-1}) alone (equation B–1), or is 0.899 using the two autoregressive terms (X_{t-1}) and (X_{t-4}).[7] But it is clear from the outset that such noncausal "explanations" cannot dominate the explanation from appropriations data, since equation B–3 leaves 10.1 per cent of the variance unexplained compared with 6.6 per cent left unexplained by equation A–5 with its series of appropriations-flow terms. We should note further that the contrast would be still sharper if we were searching for "practical" relations which could be used to forecast expenditures (X_t) from data actually available before the opening of quarter (t). In this case, with data of quarter $(t-1)$ not being available, the best we could do with an autoregression would be to use (X_{t-2}) and (X_{t-4}) with an adjusted R^2 of 0.793 (equation B–2). But since the unavailable data in the appropriations-expenditure relation (A_{t-1}) made no net contribution, equation A–5 is already a practical forecasting relation. On this footing, the unexplained variance after the autoregression has been used to its limit is 20.7 per cent compared with 6.1 per cent from the appropriations-expenditure relation.

In any clear-cut choice between an explanation of expenditures from antecedent capital appropriations and a pseudo-explanation from autoregression, therefore, we can cheerfully choose the appropriations. But there is still an interesting question to consider: taking account of appropriations, do autoregressive expenditure terms make any *partial* explanatory contribution? This may be answered by comparing the synthetic equations in Table 2 with their corresponding numbers in Table 1: B–4 with A–3; B–5 with A–2 and A–4; B–6 with A–5. It

[7] Since we want to be sure not to set too low a baseline with our autoregressive "explanation," we present in Table 2 the combination of autoregressive terms ranging all the way to (X_{t-6}), which gives the highest adjusted R^2. To include the strongest of the omitted autoregressive terms (namely X_{t-3}) would raise the *unadjusted* R^2 only from 0.914 to 0.915 and would lower the adjusted R^2 from 0.899 to 0.897.

turns out that the autoregressive term (X_{t-1}) enables us to scale down the residual variance by 61.6 per cent when we take account only of a single appropriations-backlog term; by 50.7 per cent when we take account only of a single appropriation-flow term; by 37.2 per cent when we take account of a single appropriation-flow term and the antecedent backlog; and by 14.8 per cent when we take account of a series of successive appropriations-flow terms.[8]

While the apparent net explanatory contribution of the autoregressive term (X_{t-1}) diminishes sharply as we use more sophisticated appropriations patterns, it does not appear to converge upon zero: the regression coefficient for (X_{t-1}) in equation B–6 is significantly different from zero, with a t-value of 3.95. Our interpretation of this result is that there is probably considerable persistence from quarter to quarter in the economically "random" elements of capital expenditure. Since a large proportion of capital expenditures must be for projects in which spending goes on over two or more successive quarters, any random forces which affect the list of *active projects* in a given quarter should affect *expenditures* in two or more successive quarters. This rationalization obviously calls for testing in later work.

C. *Explanation of Capital Appropriations from Financial and Accelerator Variables*

The next stage of analysis brings us to a set of equations (Table 3) which for the first time in the paper offer analytical content of the sort that is ordinarily presented in analyses of investment behavior. The analysis may be characterized as a competition between financial and accelerator-type explanations, resulting in a merger. The variables selected for this paper represent the outcome of an extended screening process in the Sachs dissertation. While the resulting correlations are highly respectable (and are supported by substantial confirmation in the results obtained in the dissertation from a study of increments of logarithms of the variables), it should be remembered that the data have been all too thoroughly searched for handsome statistical relations. Hence, as was mentioned above, the empirical results should

[8] These terms cannot quite be reduced to conventional partial correlations since the presence of term X_{t-1} slightly shifts the choice of appropriations terms that yield the most efficient representatives of each approach.

Note that in the right-hand half of Table 2, we have simplified by using only (X_{t-1}) to represent autoregression. Using (X_{t-4}) as well would have raised the adjusted R^2 from 0.939 to 0.944 in equation B–6 and from 0.944 to 0.946 in equation B–6.

TABLE 3

*Regression Coefficients from Equations to Explain Capital Appropriations
from Financial and Accelerator Variables and Combinations Thereof*
(million 1954 dollars per calendar quarter per unit of explanatory variable)

| | Noncausal Explanation | | Financial Explanation | |
| | | | Cash Flow Only, | Bond Yield Only, |
	Pure Seasonal, Eq. C-1	Auto-regression, Eq. C-2	Eq. C-3	Eq. C-4
Adjusted R^2	0.0321	0.6724	0.2908	0.4788
Intercept	1169 ± 153	404 ± 158	-228 ± 398	3187 ± 403
Autoregressive terms:				
A_{t-1}		0.897 ± 0.113		
A_{t-4}		-0.234 ± 0.111		
Bond-yield terms:				
R_t				
R_{t-1}				
R_{t-4}				-543 ± 102
Cash-flow terms:				
F_t			0.738 ± 0.207	
F_{t-1}				
F_{t-4}				
Stock-price increment terms:				
ΔS_t				
ΔS_{t-4}				
Orders-capacity terms:				
O_t				
O_{t-1}				
O_{t-2}				
O_{t-7}				
O_{t-9}				
Adjusted R^2 with C_t in eq.	0.0811	0.6859	0.	0.6232

(continued)

TABLE 3 *(concluded)*

| Financial Explanation, Bond Yield with: | | Accelerator Explanation, Ratio of | Eclectic Explanation, Orders − Capacity Ratio with Financial Variables | |
Cash Flow Only, Eq. C-5	Cash Flow & Stock-Price Increment, Eq. C-6	Orders to Capacity, Eq. C-7	Bond Yield Only, Eq. C-8	Cash Flow with Bond Yield, Eq. C-9
0.6882	0.7939	0.8233	0.8563	0.8678
2103 ± 455	1460 ± 384	−2286 ± 327	−2357 ± 421	1967 ± 735
−340 ± 175	−532 ± 79			
				−494 ± 82
−248 ± 147				
0.689 ± 0.145	0.640 ± 0.149			0.411 ± 0.098
	0.261 ± 0.149			
			0.332 ± 0.116	
11.2 ± 5.7				
22.9 ± 6.0				
		453 ± 173	506 ± 161	
		267 ± 265	437 ± 154	
		238 ± 170		387 ± 85
			−290 ± 125	300 ± 72
			187 ± 113	
0.7043	0.8209	0.8300	(0.8563)	0.8828

probably be viewed not as reports on tests of hypotheses but rather as formulations of hypotheses to be tested on two-digit industries and on data more recent than the period of observation.

To set a baseline, we begin with a purely seasonal explanation (equation C–1) and a naive autoregressive one (equation C–2). It is evident that capital appropriations show even less pronounced seasonal fluctuations than expenditures do, and that the autoregressive relation is also much weaker. The rationalization offered above for the autoregressive tendency of expenditures—that a given project is likely to enter the figures in two or more successive quarters—is probably inapplicable to appropriations, since from our knowledge of the capital-budgeting process, it seems likely that each project will generate only one main appropriation. But we should mention that, if we *had* found a strong autocorrelation, it might have been explained by a possible "bandwagon effect," by which one company's go-ahead decision on a major project may set off a cluster of parallel appropriations by competing or complementary companies, spread over two or three quarters.

We begin the substantive analysis of appropriations (equation C–3) by considering cash flow alone. The resulting coefficient of determination (0.291) is significant, yet so low as to indicate that the model is grossly incomplete and hence uninteresting since other reasonably simple models can do so much better. In fact, as will be seen from equation C–4, using the yield on high grade long-term industrial bonds results in an adjusted R^2 substantially higher than with cash flow alone.

Combining the bond yield with cash flow results in a coefficient of determination of 0.688 (equation C–5); taking the current state of bond yield and cash flow along with the increment of stock prices four quarters previous (equation C–6) yields a coefficient of 0.794. This seems to be the best the data will yield with a purely financial equation.[9]

On the accelerator side, experimentation in the Sachs dissertation indicated that the forces at work can be well represented by a ratio of the inflow of new orders to current productive capacity. This device was introduced in the Hart article as a substitute for the more conventional

---

[9] The exploration of these relationships broke off at several points because the equation just obtained was "reasonable," while the next variable to enter was about to do so with a regression coefficient of unacceptable sign. To illustrate, consider equation C–9. The experiment which generated this equation with its adjusted multiple R^2 of 0.868 went on to generate adjusted R^2's of 0.881 and 0.897 by adding to the list of included variables first the stock-price increment (ΔS_{t-5}) and then further (ΔS_{t-4}). But we rejected these results because in both cases the partial regression coefficient for (ΔS_{t-5}) had an unacceptable (negative) sign, and in the final form the positive coefficient for (ΔS_{t-4}) fell short in size of the negative coefficient for (ΔS_{t-5}).

utilization ratio of output to capacity which has proved useful in a number of recent investment studies as a measure of pressure on facilities. Because of gestation lags and the durability of capital goods, it is *future* pressure that should—in theory—be relevant. Since new orders manifestly have more *ex ante* content than output of the same date, the flow of new orders was substituted for output in the numerator of the utilization ratio.[10] Even orders, of course, do not in general have enough futurity to represent activity during more than the very earliest part of the period when new facilities now decided upon will be in use. But it is reasonable to suppose that orders come much closer than output of the same date does to expressing the information by which decision-makers learn about prospective future activity. For these reasons, the orders-capacity variable would seem well adapted to express acceleration forces.

The result of a preliminary experiment, in which all time signatures of the orders-capacity ratio were considered from (t) to $(t-8)$, was that the explanatory value of the ratio with respect to capital appropriations could be exhausted by the relation shown as equation C–7 in

[10] In the Hart article this substitution was managed by multiplying the output-capacity ratio by a second ratio (derived from the new Census series, which happens to carry its revisions back to the beginning of 1953 in suitable detail) of the value of flow of new orders to the value of output; the denominator was obtained by adding to shipments the increment of inventory of goods in process and finished products. Since the article dealt with total manufacturing this procedure was preferred to an attempt to directly deflate orders with a price index into "physical" dimensions. It turns out that the implicit price index obtained by dividing the FRB production index into the value of shipments has an unreasonable look for total manufacturing: in particular, it shows a decline from year to year in every year since 1958. The difficulty would seem to lie in the elements of duplication which exist in orders and shipments but which are netted out in deriving a production index; since these elements of duplication as well as price elements should be expected to alter numerator and denominator of the orders-output ratio proportionally, this procedure seemed preferable to price deflation.

Because the Sachs dissertation aims to provide the foundation for a study disaggregated to the two-digit industry level (for which disaggregation of inventory figures is insufficient and the problem of duplication—because one firm's products are bought by another firm—should recede), Sachs preferred to use a price deflator and his data for durables manufacturers have been carried over into this paper. This procedure enabled Sachs to experiment with orders and capacity as separate explanatory variables (measured, respectively, in 1954 dollars and in points of FRB index of production)—with the result that the ratio designated in the present paper as O_t seems to work in combination with financial variables much the same as do the separate variables orders-flow and capacity. To permit consideration of a rich variety of time lags of the different variables without surpassing the sixty-variable limit of the regression program being used, we preferred to simplify in this paper by using the orders-capacity ratio only.

Table 3 with an adjusted R^2 of 0.823—resting entirely on orders contemporaneous with the appropriation and in the two antecedent quarters. If we had to choose between explanations of the accelerator family and of the financial family, the margin of superiority of equation C–7 over equation C–6 would seem decisive.

Neither the financial-determination model nor the acceleration model of investment decisions, however, can properly be interpreted to exclude all elements of the other, either as a theoretical necessity or in fact. While it would be a convenient simplification if a pure accelerator model left all financial variables without significant partial correlations, or if a reasonably simple financial model left such accelerator variables as the orders-capacity ratio without a partial correlation, the empirical work very definitely shows that eclectic combinations using both financial and accelerator variables are considerably stronger than pure models. Two such eclectic combinations appear as equations C–8 and C–9 in this study. Like the financial and eclectic equations of the Sachs dissertation, these equations suggest that so long as cash flow is included, there is scope for obtaining rather high correlations with widely divergent patterns of the other financial variables. This outcome is somewhat disconcerting in view of the special importance for monetary analysis of the bond-yield variable. It is to be hoped that better research design will yield a more stable pattern of explanation with respect to the financial variables. One more peculiarity of the eclectic equations C–8 and C–9 should be mentioned: with the inclusion of financial variables, it appears uniformly that the rather remote orders-capacity ratio (O_{t-7}) has fairly substantial statistical significance whereas in the pure accelerator equation C–7 only very recent ratios appeared to be significant determinants of capital appropriations. The negative sign of the regression coefficient for (O_{t-7}) in the eclectic formulations presumably implies that decision-makers take into account the *rise* of the orders-capacity ratio over recent quarters as well as its very recent level.[11]

---

[11] In early drafts of the Hart article, there was a good deal of stress on the backlog appropriated but unspent as a *negative* element in the explanation of appropriations, representing the extent to which the needs shown by the orders-capacity ratio have already been provided for. In the present study, both the backlog at the opening of the quarter of appropriation (B_t) and that at the opening of the preceding quarter (B_{t-1}) uniformly have negative partial correlations if incorporated in the equations reported in Table C; but in no equation is either of these variables of statistical significance.

TABLE 4

Regression Coefficients from Equations to Explain Capital Expenditures (Bypassing Appropriations) Directly from Explanatory Variables

(million 1954 dollars per calendar quarter per unit of explanatory variable)

	Financial Explanation				Accelerator Explanation, Ratio of Orders to Capacity, Eq. D-5	Eclectic Explanation, Orders-Capacity with Cash Flow, Eq. D-6
	Cash Flow Only, Eq. D-1	Bond Yield Only, Eq. D-2	Bond Yield with			
			Cash Flow Only, Eq. D-3	Cash Flow with Stock-Price Increment, Eq. D-4		
Adjusted R^2	0.4224	0.4743	0.7515	0.7561	0.9108	0.9305
Intercept	−398±364	2085±236	638±294	736±302	−1137±142	−1280±140
Cash-flow terms:						
F_{t-1}	0.123±0.121		0.203±0.080	0.204±0.080		0.141±0.046
F_{t-3}	0.330±0.134		0.257±0.089	0.252±0.088		
F_{t-4}						−0.077±0.057
F_{t-5}	0.174±0.158		0.111±0.104	0.045±0.116		
F_{t-6}	0.171±0.150		0.184±0.098	0.170±0.098		
Bond-yield term:						
R_{t-8}		−291±61	−268±43	−259±44		
Stock-price increment term:						
ΔS_{t-7}				7.2±5.9		
Orders-capacity terms:						
O_{t-3}					216±72	101±76
O_{t-4}					161±87	271±95
O_{t-6}					230±46	240±42
Adjusted R^2 with B_{t-1} in eq.	0.9306	0.8766	0.9287	0.9341	0.9260	0.9508

D. *Direct Explanations of Expenditures*

The implication of introducing appropriations as an intervening variable between capital expenditures and explanatory variables of the financial or accelerator type is that the explanatory variables in some sense act on expenditures *through* appropriations. Pushed to extremes, this view would suggest a hypothesis that any attempt to bypass appropriations and explain expenditures directly from the variables used to explain investment decisions would in general yield relations weaker than those obtained from using appropriations. A number of regression equations which are useful to test this hypothesis are presented in Table 4.

If we take as baseline the adjusted R^2 of 0.934 obtained in equation A–5 for expenditures as a function of a consecutive series of antecedent appropriations flows, it is evident that we have been unable to find any combination of the explanatory variables used which would outperform appropriations: the best adjusted R^2 we have been able to obtain is 0.931 (equation D–6) for a combination of recent cash flows and somewhat more remote orders-capacity ratios. On the other hand, we might reasonably be suspected of a certain bias toward showing the superiority of the appropriations approach, and one might well be able to improve upon equation D–6 by taking account of variables which did not happen to figure among those used in section C to help explain appropriations. This admittedly limited test, therefore, is to be interpreted as indicating that appropriations are a highly efficient *summary* of the information bearing on the interpretation of capital expenditures rather than that direct explanations are weak in comparison.

Another formulation—a good deal less favorable to the appropriations data—deserves consideration. If in fact the forces represented by the explanatory variables act upon expenditures *only through appropriations,* we can link up the results of Tables 1, 3, and 4 to set ceilings for the correlations to be expected from direct explanations. From Table 1 we know that a consecutive series of appropriations terms together with seasonal dummies can clear up 93.44 per cent of the variance in expenditures (equation A–5) and that the seasonal dummies alone can clear up 12.08 per cent (equation A–1); hence appropriations account for 92.54 per cent of the nonseasonal variance. Multiplying 92.54 per cent by the adjusted R^2's of Table 3, we can infer the maximum percentage of nonseasonal variance which various combinations of explanatory variables ought to be able to clear up *if they acted on expenditures solely through appropriations.* This result can be com-

TABLE 5

Summary of the Relative Ability of Selected Variables to Explain

the Nonseasonal Variance in Capital Expenditures

Combination of Explanatory Variables	Relevant Equations in		Adjusted R^2's of Equations in		Percentages of Nonseasonal Variance Explained		
	Table 3	Table 4	Table 3	Table 4	Expectation Based on Table 3[a]	Table 4 Table 4[b]	Excess
Bond yield	C-4	D-2	0.4788	0.4743	44.3	40.2	-4.1
Bond yield with cash flow	C-5	D-3	0.6882	0.7515	63.7	71.7	8.0
Bond yield with cash flow and Δ (stock price)	C-6	D-4	0.7939	0.7561	73.5	72.3	-1.2
Orders–capacity	C-7	D-5	0.8233	0.9108	76.2	89.8	13.6
Orders–capacity with cash flow	C-8	D-6	0.8563	0.9305	79.2	92.1	12.9

[a]92.54 per cent multiplied by adjusted R^2 from Table 3.

[b]$\dfrac{\text{Adjusted } R^2 \text{ from Table 4 minus } 0.1208}{(1.0000 - 0.1208)} \times 100$ per cent

pared to the percentage of nonseasonal variance in capital expenditures (that is, the partial contribution of the explanatory variables, taking into account that 12.08 per cent of the variance can be "explained" by seasonal dummies) accounted for by the various equations of Table 4. This test is summarized in Table 5.

The purely financial explanations of equations D–2 and D–4 fall short of the expectation so derived as to maximum explanatory power, so that they would leave open the hypothesis that financial variables acted only through appropriations. (The apparently superior explanatory power of equation D–3 does not change this finding, since equation D–3 is dominated by equation D–4, which in turn is dominated by C–6.) But explanations based on the orders-capacity ratio (alone or with cash flow) not only outperform the financial equations, but also exceed the maximum explanatory power consistent with action of the explanatory variables solely through appropriations. Whereas equation C–8 leaves unexplained 20.8 per cent of the nonseasonal variance, equation D–6 leaves unexplained only 7.9 per cent; thus the combination of orders-capacity and cash flow clears up three-fifths of what is left unexplained by equation C–8. It is interesting that a substantial part of the explanatory power of equation D–6 rests on cash flow one quarter before the expenditure.

E. Eclectic Explanation of Expenditures

It is interesting and at the same time somewhat disconcerting that the direct explanation of capital expenditures from the substantive explanatory variables is so powerful. Yet, the over-all results of the best direct explanation are still slightly inferior to those of an explanation of expenditures which takes appropriations as a datum. It follows that we must expect a further eclectic combination of substantive explanatory variables together with appropriations to do considerably better than the direct explanation. That this will be the case is shown by the memorandum at the foot of Table 4 which shows for each equation the effect of incorporating a single appropriations variable: the backlog appropriated but unspent at the opening of the quarter previous to the appropriation. Particularly for the financial equations, but also for the equations including orders-capacity as an explanatory variable, this single addition out of the appropriations data results in a substantial increase in explanatory power. But this is merely illustrative. If we admit more than one appropriations variable and allow the choice of this variable to vary with the content of the direct explanation of capital expenditures, we will be able to improve the relations still further.

Equations which present somewhat more flexible eclectic combinations of appropriations and substantive explanatory variables appear in Table 6.

TABLE 6

Regression Coefficients from Equations to Explain Capital Expenditures

by Composite Functions of Appropriations with Explanatory Variables

(million 1954 dollars per calendar quarter per explanatory variable)

	Appropriations-Finance Explanation		Appropriations-Accelerator Explanation, Appropriations with Orders-Capacity, Eq. E-3
	Appropriations with Cash Flow Only, Eq. E-1	Appropriations with Cash Flow & Stock-Price Increment, Eq. E-2	
Adjusted R^2	0.9565	0.9630	0.9380
Intercept	32 ± 75	-57 ± 81	36 ± 207
Appropriations-flow terms:			
A_{t-2}	0.146 ± 0.044	0.131 ± 0.042	0.098 ± 0.071
A_{t-3}	0.168 ± 0.052	0.153 ± 0.051	0.113 ± 0.065
A_{t-4}	0.090 ± 0.055	0.062 ± 0.052	0.121 ± 0.065
A_{t-5}	0.084 ± 0.062	0.103 ± 0.058	0.028 ± 0.077
A_{t-6}	0.175 ± 0.047	0.187 ± 0.043	0.206 ± 0.071
Cash-flow terms:			
F_{t-1}	0.142 ± 0.037	0.163 ± 0.038	
F_{t-3}		0.041 ± 0.040	
Stock-price increment term:			
ΔS_{t-5}		3.4 ± 1.6	
Orders-capacity terms:			
O_{t-2}			123 ± 64
O_{t-7}			81 ± 79
O_{t-8}			-100 ± 58

Note: Without exception, all bond-yield terms have *positive* partial correlations if added to any of the equations in this table.

Of the composite eclectic equations shown in Table 6, the weakest (equation E–3) is more powerful than any of the direct-explanation equations of Table 4. This equation, however, is only a very small improvement over the original appropriations relationship (equation A–5, with its adjusted R^2 of 0.934). It appears, therefore, that virtually all the relevant information to be found in the orders-capacity ratio is well represented by capital appropriations. By comparison, the two financial equations of Table 6 show more additional information— chiefly by way of the cash-flow term F_{t-1}. This is not an altogether satisfactory outcome, since the cash flow of the quarter just before the actual capital expenditure would seem to come too late to have much scope to influence the expenditure. Our interpretation is that this variable (F_{t-1}) functions as a "surprise variable," influencing last-minute modifications of plans. One possibility is that the cash-flow situation has a strong effect on capital outlays made by division and plant managers under delegated authority, which are for relatively small items and may consist largely of outlays for items which suppliers have in stock and can ship on very short notice.

F. Plan-Image Analysis

If we had fuller information on the expectations of decision-makers about future sales, cash flow, etc., it would be interesting to undertake an adequate analysis of the "realization function"—that is, to treat actual capital expenditures as constituting overfulfillment or underfulfillment of plans—and to seek explanations of these deviations from plans in surprises, i.e., anticipations errors, experiences in sales, cash flow, etc. Unfortunately, we lack the background data on expectations about relevant surprise variables. Therefore, all we can do is to set up equations which represent plans as of a viewpoint date far enough from expenditure to leave scope for making revisions effective and then examine the partial correlations of surprise variables when added to these equations.

A collection of such plan-image equations is presented in Table 7. In order to leave room for effective modifications of plans, we have worked with data in the plan-image function which has a time signature no closer than $(t-3)$ to the date of expenditure. Consequently, there is room for experience which is too late to affect appropriations of date $(t-3)$ and probably even of date $(t-2)$, but long enough ahead of the date of expenditure to be registered and to permit scaling planned capital outlays up or down. We represent the surprise variables by proxies. Cancellations may be taken to be a proxy for adverse news about factors affecting investment. Cash flow of date $(t-1)$, in view of its apparent influence in the eclectic equations of Table 4, may be taken to be a proxy for favorable news. These variables can sensibly be combined, with the stipulation that the regression coefficients for (C_{t-2}) and (C_{t-1}) must both be negative and that for (F_{t-1}) must be positive. An alternative approach would be to suppose that the *partial* relation of the backlog of unspent appropriations at the opening of the current or preceding quarter is a composite proxy for factors leading to alterations of plans. Most of the variance of the appropriations backlog can, of course, be explained by the variables which make up the equations of Table 7 so that to add variable (B_{t-1}) is to add a *residue* of information of later date than the appropriations and other variables which appear in Table 7.

Three of the equations of Table 7 appeared in earlier tables (F–1 is identical to A–1; F–3 to D–3; and F–5 to A–6). They are included here for completeness and because the supplementary relations treated in the memorandum at the end of the table are different from those examined previously. The accelerator plan-image equation (F–3) and the appropriations plan-image equation (F–5) are fairly powerful. The financial variables, when deprived of recent cash flow (F_{t-1}), show a comparatively weak correlation in equation F–2. However, the same variables make a significant contribution when combined with the orders-capacity ratio (equation F–4). But when we combine appropriations with the orders-capacity ratio in equation F–6, none of the financial variables contribute significantly. It should be noted that in setting up these plan-image equations, we were not able to establish any significant contribution for long-term bond yields except in the purely financial variant (equation F–2).

The rather modest residual variance left by the plan-image equations can be appreciably reduced by taking account of our so-called surprise variables, as may be seen from the memorandum in the lowest lines of Table 7. The combined effect of taking account of the two cancellation terms (which have appropriate negative regression coefficients throughout) is clearly visible except for the pure-finance equation. Except in equation F–4, however, we would explain a larger proportion of the residual variance with the cash-flow surprise variable F_{t-1}. The combination of these three variables makes an appreciable improvement over the use of the two cancellation terms alone and a modest improvement over using F_{t-1} alone. The backlog term turns out to contribute considerably less (in several equations essentially zero),

TABLE 7

Regression Coefficients of Equations to Explain
Capital Expenditures by Appropriations and Explanatory
Variables of Dates (t-3) and Earlier

(million 1954 dollars per calendar quarter

per unit of explanatory variable)

	Noncausal Explanation, Pure Seasonal, Eq. F-1 (=A-1)	Financial Explanation, Cash Flow with Bond Yield & Stock-Price Increment, Eq. F-2
Adjusted R^2	0.1208	0.7393
Intercept	1037 ± 87	735 ± 331
Cash-flow terms:		
F_{t-3}		0.352 ± 0.083
F_{t-6}		0.240 ± 0.097
F_{t-7}		
Bond-yield term:		
R_{t-8}		−221 ± 46
Stock-price increment terms:		
ΔS_{t-3}		8.2 ± 4.4
ΔS_{t-4}		
ΔS_{t-7}		9.3 ± 5.4
Orders-capacity terms:		
O_{t-3}		
O_{t-4}		
O_{t-6}		
Appropriations-flow terms:		
A_{t-3}		
A_{t-4}		
A_{t-5}		
A_{t-6}		
Adjusted R^2 with surprise variables in eq.		
C_{t-1} with C_{t-2}	(<0.1208)	(<0.7393)
F_{t-1}		0.7649
C_{t-1} and C_{t-2} with F_{t-1}		0.7513
B_{t-1}	0.8764	0.8978

(continued)

TABLE 7 *(concluded)*

Accelerator Explanation, Orders-Capacity, Eq. F-3	Financial-Accelerator Explanation, Orders-Capacity with Cash Flow & Stock-Price Increment, Eq. F-4	Appropriations Explanation, Consecutive Series of Flows, Eq. F-5(=A-5)	Composite Explanation, Appropriations Flows with Orders-Capacity, Eq. F-6
0.9108	0.9238	0.9040	0.9249
-1037 ± 142	-1337 ± 156	363 ± 62	-116 ± 167
	0.172 ± 0.065		
	3.3 ± 2.7		
2!6 ± 72	229 ± 77		177 ± 60
161 ± 87	199 ± 85		
230 ± 46	149 ± 53		
		0.310 ± 0.058	0.165 ± 0.071
		0.125 ± 0.080	0.099 ± 0.071
		0.102 ± 0.088	0.091 ± 0.078
		0.069 ± 0.063	0.109 ± 0.057
0.9256	0.9432	0.9207	0.9385
0.9267	0.9382	0.9401	0.9501
0.9298	0.9459	0.9422	0.9526
0.9240	0.9278	0.9048	(<0.9249)

CHART 2

Levels of Actual and Plan-Image Capital Expenditures Using
Plan-Image Based on Appropriations, Seasonally Adjusted, 1954-65

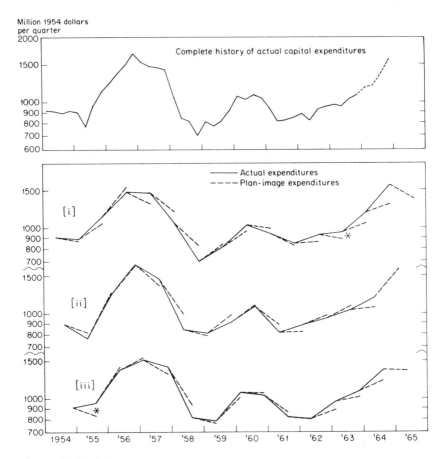

Source: Table A-1.

except that its inclusion clears up some three-fifths of the substantial
residual variance left by the pure-finance equation (F–2).

We may reasonably conclude that if we were able to mobilize suitable data, the realization-function approach would probably offer a
suitable framework for the analysis of capital appropriations and expenditures. But besides the lack of explicit information as to the time shape
of expenditure plans, we suffer (for the present) from a dearth of data

on sales forecasts, etc., so that the only available procedure would be to set up constructs to represent what respondents *could be reasonably expected to anticipate.* This is by no means a hopeless enterprise but it will invariably include several points where we can proceed only by making highly arbitrary assumptions.

RESIDUAL ANALYSIS OF PLAN-IMAGE RELATIONS

Starting from the most interesting of the plan-image equations (F–5, resting purely on appropriations flows), we can form an interesting impression of the time shape of investment planning from Chart 2. Since the time span from the viewpoint date to the date of expenditure is taken as three quarters, we have graphed the actual data (continuous solid curve) with a three-quarters interval between points. Thus we arrive at three curves—one starting with the first quarter of 1955, one with the second quarter of 1955, and one with the third quarter of 1955. The planned level of expenditure implicit in the previous appropriations flows (according to the regression formula F–5) is graphed for each date as a point off the curve. These points are then tied back by broken lines to the actual expenditure of the viewpoint quarter and so each broken line represents a hypothetical extension of the historical record to the left of it. To avoid putting undue emphasis on the ability of decision-makers to visualize seasonal movements, we have adjusted all the points by the seasonal formula yielded by the regression coefficients of the seasonal dummies in equation F–5.

It is visible immediately that the broken lines closely follow the curve of actual movements with a few interesting exceptions to be examined in a moment. That is, the plan image corresponds quite well to the actual course of events. This is as it should be if the plan image is a good proxy for actual plans; for while we have chosen the three-quarter time interval to leave scope for revision of plans, this scope is so narrow that major revisions can be expected only in emergencies.

At the points marked with asterisks on Chart 2, the plan image actually fails to agree in direction with the actual change: this happens only twice (in the changes from the fourth quarter of 1954 to the third quarter of 1955 in set iii and in the changes from the third quarter of 1962 to the second quarter of 1963 in set i). The first of these divergencies (which is much the larger) is readily explained by the dramatic triumph on the market of the 1955 automobile models, which seems to have been an agreeable surprise sharp enough to produce a major change in evaluations of the near future by manufacturers. Note that the presence of a few such divergencies is not pre-

CHART 3

Three-Quarter Increments of Actual and Plan-Image
Capital Expenditures, Using Plan Image Based on Appropriations
(million 1954 dollars)

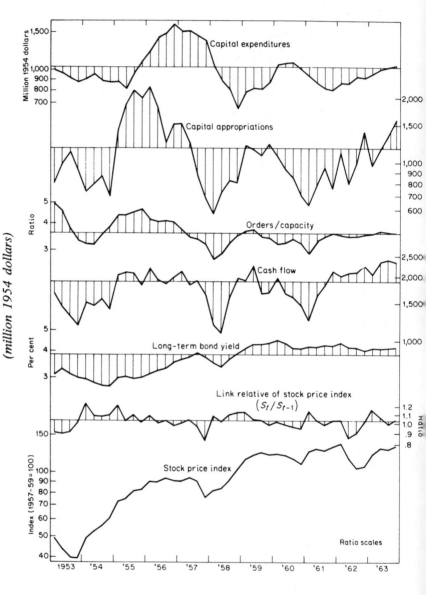

cluded by the concept of plan image: on the contrary, they are required. The basic methodological principle here is that *the same figure can measure both what firms expect and what is actually going to happen only when management is in a position to foretell the course of events.* Even in a field like capital expenditures, where the object of the forecast is something the firm in question will itself participate in, rather than a strictly external phenomenon, some turns of events are so surprising that they must effect deviations from plans of this sort.

The same data may be examined in slightly different perspective in the scatter diagram presented in Chart 3. For the same three sets of dates, we obtain scatter charts whose basic tendency is clearly for roughly proportional variation of plan image and actual.[12] We have dated the points at which the actual change is conspicuously large compared with what the general shape of the scatter would suggest as normal.

The high concentration of recent dates with increments larger than the plan image must be taken to indicate serious shortcomings in the plan image.[13] It must be remembered that while our data book includes a considerable number of calendar quarters, it includes only two and a half business cycles. It is likely that when our experience includes a definite peak for the upswing that started in 1961, more significant results can be obtained by analyses of this type. Furthermore we suspect that somewhat more sophisticated seasonal-adjustment measures will also prove worthwhile.

G. Agenda for Further Research

We hope, with the benefit of criticism, to push this analysis considerably further. The data for two-digit manufacturing industries lend themselves to an analysis of the type undertaken here—though not without some difficulties in applying measures of capacity and the like.

---

[12] Combining all three sets of data into one calculation yields an adjusted R^2 of 0.886 between actual and plan image predicted three-quarter increments, from expenditure dates 1955:1 through 1963:4. The 1964 data (not used in the calculations) are shown with points marked by a dot. Since the high points in the period of observation 1955–63 cluster to the left of the center of gravity, the regression coefficient yielded by the relation (with actual change as dependent variable) is somewhat lower than would be indicated by the consistent tendency of the larger changes to follow closely a 45-degree line.

[13] Inclusion of time as a variable either in the correlation of levels of X with antecedent levels of A or in the correlation of $(X_t - X_{t-3})$ with $(P_t - X_{t-3})$ suggests that mere inclusion of a trend will not clear up the difficulty; for in both cases the regression coefficient for time is nonsignificant, taking a closing date of 1963:4.

Furthermore, it appears that data exist from which sales forecasts can be given a much more appropriate time-shape.[14] As was mentioned above, the present study should probably be viewed as a reconaissance: we have looked at so many relations that the degree to which we can claim to have genuinely tested hypotheses is doubtful. But at the very least, we are in a position to enter upon research at the two-digit industry level with fairly well-defined hypotheses. It may prove practical to experiment also with microdata.

One relatively important shortcoming of the present study should be mentioned at this point, since any further research undertaken in this area will probably face the same difficulty. On the basis of some further work done by one of the authors since the completion of the present paper, we have concluded that our technique of statistical estimation— single-stage least-squares done on the observed, deflated levels of variables—has introduced a systematic bias into our plan-image functions. The difficulty is that, in the plan-image functions based on one or more capital appropriations terms, there is consistently a large and positive intercept. The weights (regression coefficients) of the independent variables in these relations do not sum to unity, which they ought to in theory, but typically sum to approximately 0.65 or so.

The implications of this deficiency of the sum of weights in these plan-image relations became most apparent in some recent work we have done. In attempting to sketch statistically the time shape of the capital expenditure "forecasts" implicit in the antecedent capital appropriations, it became evident that these quasi *ex ante* capital expenditure figures did not perform very well as "forecasters" of the 1964 period. The available evidence suggests that, if we had gotten virtually zero intercepts in the relevant plan-image functions, they would probably have performed better as forecasting relations. As is, our plan-image equations now imply that, if capital appropriations double, capital expenditures will eventually stabilize at a level only approximately two-thirds greater than their previous level. In principle, a conservation of capital appropriations in expenditures is, of course, required.

It should also be noted that the period of observation (1953–63) for the plan-image regression equations exhibited a virtually horizontal time trend in capital appropriations and expenditures. Therefore, because of the bias introduced by our statistical estimation technique,

---

[14] S. Almon, in an unpublished paper, has made a very interesting attempt to reshape McGraw-Hill sales forecasts so as to simulate a moving eight-quarter horizon; we suspect that her approach can profitably be used to backstop alternative methods of estimation, but it contains too many arbitrary elements to be definitive.

although these plan-image functions proved to be highly successful in terms of their "predictive" (explanatory) value, the same relations essentially broke down in terms of their "forecasting" ability, since the forecast period, in distinction to the fit-period, exhibited a very pronounced upward trend.

Two methods of correcting for this bias suggest themselves. One would be to specify an appropriate a priori distribution of lag weights and in this manner constrain the regression coefficients of the plan-image function based on capital appropriations. A conservation of capital expenditures would presumably be established if the intercept of the relation is forced through the origin. A very successful application of such a scheme is illustrated in the recent work of S. Almon, where the lag weights are distributed along a polynomial. A second alternative would be to fit the plan-image equations to variables transformed into some sort of incremental form, working with different increment spans. Our experiments along these latter lines have not yielded any conclusive results.

A crucial problem in this field is the study of the actual institutional content of the lags which students find econometrically in the investment process. It is highly probable that such a study can progress a long way by exploitation of press releases and company reports, which have a great deal to say about major investment projects. The likelihood is high, however, that a *special survey* to deal with the distribution of capital outlays in a current quarter by past quarters when the projects passed the appropriation stage will prove highly illuminating. We hope to promote such an exploratory survey and perhaps to frame recommendations for the more efficient exploitation of the mine of data which existing surveys have been high-grading. The results are sure to be of enough interest to businessmen that they will be willing to continue to generate useful data. With few adaptations, the field of *ex ante* data on investment can probably be restructured to put studies of business investment behavior on a much firmer footing.

Appendix on Data Sources

The several variables used in this study are quarterly, seasonally unadjusted, constant-dollar (except for bond yields and stock prices) series for the period 1953 through 1963. The National Industrial Conference Board (NICB) supplies us with the investment statistics used in the present study. These are generated by way of a survey questionnaire sent by the NICB to 570 of the 1,000 largest manufacturing corporations, including 337 of the largest 627 durable goods producers. The survey data are filed by respondents in the following form:

> Beginning-of-quarter backlog of funds appropriated but unspent
>
> *plus*   Newly authorized appropriations during the quarter
> *minus*   Cancellations of unspent appropriations during the quarter
> *minus*   Capital expenditures during the quarter
> *equals*   End-of-quarter backlog of funds appropriated but unspent.

Revisions occasionally make the new quarter's initial backlog diverge from the previous quarter's initial backlog.

A capital *appropriation* is defined in the survey as the authorization to management by the board of directors or investment committee of a company to incur charges on fixed capital account in order to carry out specific investment projects. Thus, the focus of the NICB capital appropriations survey is on *when* the capital-spending *decision* is actually made final at the company's top management level. The survey figures on investment *expenditures* are, for the panel of 570 companies, identical to those reported by the same firms to the Commerce-SEC survey of capital spending published in the *Survey of Current Business*.

The capital appropriations survey data from the first quarter of 1953 (53:1) to the fourth quarter of 1963 (63:4) was generated from three basic panels. From 53:1 to 54:4, there were 353 reporting companies (reporting retrospectively in 1955); from 55:1 to 57:4, there were 511; and from 58:1 to 63:4, there were 602 reporting companies. The current figure is 570. Splicing of the series to correct for sample changes was done in terms of industry assets. The regression results reported in the present study were all derived from estimating equations in which sampling universe data were used. That is to say, throughout, we worked with investment data estimated for the population of the 1,000 largest U.S. manufacturing corporations. The "blow-up" from reporting company data to estimates for the 1,000 largest firms in manufacturing is done by industry and is simply based on the relationship of the total assets of companies within each industry (universe) to the total assets of companies within each reporting or sample industry.

There are several advantages in using estimated population figures rather than reporting company, i.e., sample data. Significant sample changes have been incorporated into the universe estimates and corrections for changes in company ownership and in the pattern of survey response have been made. As of 64:2, all published NICB investment survey data are population estimates for the 1,000 largest manufacturing companies rather than panel data. The level and time shape of the durables manufacturing subaggregate investment series on a reporting company basis is in part determined by the (varying) representation of the component two-digit industries. On this basis, the component industry weights are essentially response weights and interpretation of the relevant NICB investment series is ambiguous. An industry basis for weighting is achieved and the interpretive problem is thereby lessened, when the panel values of each series for a given two-digit industry are adjusted to estimates of the population of the 1,000 largest firms. For these latter values, each industry contributes a more "realistic" proportion to the corresponding subaggregate series.

The NICB survey population or sampling universe consists of the 1,000 largest U.S. manufacturing corporations. Size is defined here in terms of total assets and the cut-off point is approximately $15 million. These 1,000 companies account for slightly over one-half (55 per cent) of total manufacturing employment, roughly three-quarters of all manufacturing capital outlays, estimated at $18 billion in 1964, and about two-thirds of total manufacturing assets. The individual firms included in the NICB survey universe correspond very closely to those listed in the Federal Trade Commission's *A List of 1,000 Large Manufacturing Companies*. In 1958, the ratio of the total assets of reporting companies in the NICB survey to the total assets of the top 1,000 manufacturing firms was 70 per cent. Reporting companies accounted for more than half of total investment spending in the manufacturing sector, as estimated by the Commerce-SEC survey of capital expenditures. In terms of sample coverage, the NICB and OBE-SEC investment surveys are very similar. For example, the proportion of total capital outlays accounted for by durables and nondurables in the NICB survey is 49.6 and 50.4 per cent, respectively, and the corresponding figures for the OBE-SEC survey are 50.3 and 49.7 per cent. A comparison of the OBE-SEC series on investment spending for the manufacturing aggregate with the corresponding NICB total shows no radical differences in their behavior over time.

The data source for the series on manufacturers' new orders is the U.S. Department of Commerce, Bureau of the Census Publication, *Manufacturers' Shipments, Inventories, and Orders: 1947–1963 (Revised)*. A quarterly new orders series for durable goods manufacturing industries is obtained by simply cumulating the appropriate figures for successive three-month periods. The most recent orders figures were taken from the relevant issues of the *Survey of Current Business*. The sample upon which the Census Bureau's estimates of new orders in durables manufacturing is based has a very strong large-company bias, a helpful distortion for the present study. The number of reporting firms with more than 1,000 employees has been increased from 1,100 in mid-1957 to 1,850 in mid-1962 and such firms are included in the sample with a (probability) weight of 1.0. Moreover, the response rate of small companies is relatively poor. For these and other reasons, the month-to-month changes of the universe estimates reflect primarily the new orders behavior of the larger manufacturing enterprises.

Survey coverage is best in those industries which are characterized by a large scale of production and a correspondingly small number of large firms. Most of the two-digit durable goods manufacturing industries fall into this category. Although this manufacturing sector typically produces to order rather than to stock, in some cases, new orders data is not available and shipments figures are substituted for them. Among the durable goods manufacturing industries at the two-digit level, the percentage of total reported shipments accounted for by companies also reporting unfilled orders backlogs, i.e., really producing to order, ranges from 28 per cent for "stone, clay and glass" to 75 per cent for "total transportation equipment."

The estimates of manufacturing capacity for the durable goods sector used in this study and combined in ratio form with new orders were developed by F. de Leeuw of the Federal Reserve Board (FRB). This capacity index combines three sets of figures: (1) business records on gross investment spending and depreciation, which are used by the Commerce Department to estimate manufacturers' fixed capital stock; (2) the McGraw-Hill manufacturing capacity index which is based on survey questionnaire reports from businesses on the percentage increase in the physical volume of capacity during the year; and (3) the ratio of the seasonally unadjusted December-January average FRB index of the durables manufacturing sector output (1957–59 = 100) to the McGraw-Hill end-of-year estimate of capacity utilization, which is based on survey questionnaire reports from businesses in response to the question: "How much of your capacity were you operating at the end of 19__?"

Both the Commerce Department and McGraw-Hill series exhibit a distinct upward time trend, with the latter series growing at a rate 1.8 per cent faster than the capital stock series for the period 1947–59.

The third component series was assumed to have no drift over time since it is directly linked to actual manufacturing production. However, due to varying response rates, ambiguity in the definition of "end of year," and the alternative use of a seasonally adjusted or unadjusted FRB manufacturing output index, this third series exhibited much sharper short-run fluctuations than did either of the other two. Since the first two component series drifted from the desired capacity measure as a result of the passage of time whereas the third series exhibited fairly random fluctuations with no very pronounced time trend, de Leeuw regressed the ratio of the third series to each of the other two on time and a random disturbance term.

From the estimates of the two regression coefficients, two values of the capacity utilization rate were calculated, one from each regression equation, and the simple average of these was used to derive the final capacity figures. The estimating equations were fitted by de Leeuw on annual time series (converted to logarithms), and the quarterly capacity estimates for durables manufacturers used in the present study represent interpolations which minimize the quarter-to-quarter fluctuations of the index, subject to an annual data constraint.

The source of the cash flow variable, defined as equal to net profits after taxes less dividends plus depreciation allowances, is the *Quarterly Financial Report for Manufacturing Corporations (QFR)* issued jointly by the Federal Trade Commission and the Securities and Exchange Commission. The conventional accounting concept of profits—total net revenues less total costs—is used in the *QFR* income statements. The composite sample (for 62:1, the FTC segment was 100 firms and the SEC segment was 526) from which the *QFR* estimates are generated has an obvious large-company (size) bias. At present, the sample consists of about 2 per cent of all manufacturing corporations with total assets of less than $1 million, 25 per cent of all those firms with total assets between $1 and $5 million, and all manufacturing corporations whose total assets are over $5 million.

Since the *QFR* income statements are estimated from a sample of business enterprises classified as manufacturers and required to file U.S. Corporation Income Tax Form 1120, the asset size distribution of the composite FTC-SEC sample may be compared with the population figures for fiscal year 1960, the latest year for which such information has been published by the Internal Revenue Service in *Statistics of Income*. Of the 156,296 Forms 1120 filed by the active manufacturing corporations with accounting periods from July 1959 to June 1960, some 136,255 were filed by firms whose total assets were between $1 and $5 million, and 3,890 were filed by companies with total assets greater than $5 million.

The long-term bond yield was taken from *Moody's Industrial Manual*. The quarterly series was obtained by taking a simple average of the monthly bond yields on grade Aaa industrial debt securities. Using the Aaa bond yield on industrials rather than some other (lower) rated bond yield is justified in that the rating of the debt securities issued by the largest U.S. manufacturing corporations would typically if not always fall in the Aaa rating category and hence usually exhibit the lowest long-term yield.

The index of common stock prices (1957–59 = 100) used in this study was taken from the Securities and Exchange Commission's *Statistical Bulletin*. The SEC stock price index is an index of the weekly closing prices of some 300 common stocks regularly traded on the New York Stock Exchange (NYSE). The index for the durable goods manufacturing sector includes thirteen two-digit industry categories, four more than the corresponding number included in the same subaggregate of the NICB capital appropriations survey. Since the durables sector stock price index is the weighted average of the last sale price each week of 108 selected common stocks, these weekly indexes were averaged over successive three-month intervals so as to obtain a comparable quarterly index.

The weighting system used by the SEC in calculating the index is to multiply the individual stock price by the corresponding number of common shares outstanding. Companies with common stock traded on the NYSE are initially classified according to their standard industrial classification, i.e., according to their major activity. All of the manufacturing industry groups which individually accounted for more than 1 per cent of the aggregate trading volume on the NYSE during 1958 were selected for inclusion in the SEC index. On this basis, thirteen durable goods manufacturing industries qualified for inclusion and in each of these the most actively traded issues were chosen until a coverage of at least 60 per cent of the trading volume in each of the selected industry groups was accounted for.

For purposes of the present study, it was necessary to construct two price indexes, one for capital goods and the other for manufacturers' new orders. The capital goods price deflator was used to reduce all of the NICB investment statistics as well as the *QFR* cash flow series to constant (1954) dollars. The FRB capacity estimates are, of course, already in "real" terms, the long-term bond yield is expressed in percentage points, and the common stock prices are expressed as the quarter-to-quarter *increments* of an index based on monetary units.

The basic price data used in the construction of the capital goods price index were two component price series of the implicit GNP deflator, namely, for nonfarm, nonresidential construction and for producer durable equipment. These were taken from the U.S. national product accounts as tabulated in the annual issues of *U.S. Income and Output* (Department of Commerce). The most obvious difficulty is that these conventional price indexes are derived from the prices of inputs into the construction and producer durables industries rather than from the prices of their outputs. Aside from the conceptual difficulties which this shortcoming may involve, it probably also results in a significant upward bias in these investment goods price indexes. Moreover, it is clear that the coverage of these two components of the implicit GNP price deflators is much greater than that of the NICB survey data and therefore most certainly include some prices more relevant to commercial, school, and hospital construction as well as to durable goods purchases by such nonmanufacturing enterprises as transportation companies and regulated public utilities.

The most obvious source of weights to be used in combining the above two component price indexes is the annual series given in *U.S. Income and Output* for the purchases of structures and equipment by manufacturers. Alternatively, suitable weights might have been derived from the estimates of investment spending in constant dollars made by the Commerce Department (OBE) in their *Capital Goods Study*. Since both of these sources of the distribution of investment spending would be based on annual time series, an appropriate method of interpolation would have had to have been applied to yield a quarterly capital goods price series. For this reason and because the coverage is more suitably defined, we used the information supplied by the NICB on the quarterly distribution of capital appropriations between plant and equipment for the durable goods manufacturing industries. Since this breakdown is available only from 59:1 on, we experimented with fixed and variable weights for the period 59:1 to 63:4 and determined that the final capital goods price index was relatively insensitive to the weighting system. We, therefore, derived a suitable set of fixed weights and applied these to the GNP price components for the entire forty-four-quarter period under consideration.

The price index used to deflate the Bureau of Census' new orders series was constructed by the National Bureau in a preliminary study by Thor Hultgren. The present writers extended the relevant NBER price series to 63:4 and rebased the entire series from 1947–49 = 100 to 1957–59 = 100 by making direct use of the rebasing factors published by the Bureau of Labor Statistics (BLS).

It is evident that the firms included in the durable goods manufacturing category are engaged in a wide range of production and that a wide variety of commodities are manufactured by these firms and industries. Given this heterogeneous composition of new orders and output as well as the existence of duplication—orders are for final products as well as for inputs of the same products—it is clear that a suitable price deflator will necessarily have to be an index number which *combines* the prices of those commodities manufactured by the durables sector.

The reclassification of the commodity groupings used in the BLS wholesale price index (WPI) is required to conform more nearly to the outputs of the durable goods manufacturing sector. This regrouping is done by two-digit industry, and the weights used in calculating these composite price indexes are the 1947–49 FRB production or value-added weights. These weights are somewhat crude in that they do not incorporate the great diversity of production associated with the two-digit durable goods manufacturing industries. Moreover, the weights are fixed whereas the configuration of an industry's output changes almost continuously. In extending the NBER price series from 61:4, the same base (1947–49 = 100) value-added weights were used since the FRB weights have not really changed significantly in the decade to 1957–59. Weekly BLS wholesale commodity price indexes were simply averaged to obtain quarterly figures.

It is important to emphasize that the composite price indexes were constructed by the NBER so as to be relevant to the products *characteristic* of a given two-digit manufacturing industry and were essentially intended to represent the approximate quarter-to-quarter movements of the prices received by these industries. The resulting new orders price index for the durables sector obviously does not refer to all the commodities produced by the manufacturing enterprises classified in this sector.

The well-known dummy variable technique of seasonal adjustment was used to remove the systematic seasonal variation inherent in most time series analyses done with data taken for a time interval shorter than one year. It should be noted that all of the regression equations discussed in the context of this study contain three seasonal dummy variables. The specification of these three shift variables (Si, where $i = 1, 2, 3$) is 1 in the tth quarter and 0 in all others. Since in the fourth quarter $s_1 = s_2 = s_3 = 0$, the fourth seasonal dummy variable is implicit.

The advantages of this method of correction for seasonal variation are several. We begin with all of our quarterly data on a comparable basis, seasonally unadjusted, rather than with data which have been adjusted by applying a variety of nonparametric methods. Moreover, there is no ambiguity as to the relation of the original data series to the corresponding adjusted series. There is no danger of removing either more or less than the seasonal component. Lastly, this method of adjustment in principle allows part or all of the seasonal variation in the dependent variable (s) to be "explained" by or within the context of our investment model.

There are, of course, some shortcomings in this parametric seasonal adjustment procedure. It implies a fixed additive seasonal or one that is invariant with respect to its pattern over the period 1953–63. Moreover, it implies that the functional relation being statistically estimated undergoes quarter-to-quarter parallel shifts in its position. Only a change in the intercept of the relation is accounted for by the introduction of the dummy variables, whereas it is evident that the effect of seasonal variation (s) may also be to change the slopes as well as the intercepts of the relevant relations. Such a distortion may lead to inaccurate estimates of the regression coefficients and autocorrelation in the residuals.

TABLE A-1

Actual Versus Plan-Image Values of Capital Expenditures Using Plan Image Based on Appropriations:

Levels and Three-Quarter Increments

(million 1954 dollars per calendar quarter)

Year and Quarter	Levels of Capital Expenditures		Seasonally Adjusted Levels of Expenditures						Three-Quarter Increments in Seasonally Adjusted Expenditures					
			Actual :X_t			Plan Image :P_t			Actual :X_t-X_{t-3}			Plan Image :P_t-X_{t-3}		
	Actual	Plan Image	i	ii	iii	i	ii	iii	i	ii	iii	i	ii	iii
1954:1	749				919									
2	964		908											
3	874			891										
4	1043				912									
1955:1	720	702	890			872			-18			-36		
2	823	872		767			816			-124			-75	
*3	946	814			963			831			51			-81
4	1259	1187	1128			1056			238			166		
1956:1	1064	1084		1234			1254			467			487	
2	1422	1463			1366			1407			403			444
3	1466	1532	1483			1556			355			428		
4	1816	1814		1685			1683			451			449	
1957:1	1353	1389			1523			1559			157			193
2	1524	1348	1468			1292			-15			-191		
3	1427	1325		1444			1342			-241			-343	
4	1542	1431			1411			1300			-112			-223

(continued)

TABLE A-1 (continued)

Year and Quarter	Levels of Capital Expenditures		Seasonally Adjusted Levels of Expenditures						Three-Quarter Increments in Seasonally Adjusted Expenditures					
	Actual	Plan Image	Actual :X_t			Plan Image :P_t			Actual :$X_t - X_{t-3}$			Plan Image :$P_t - X_{t-3}$		
			i	ii	iii	i	ii	iii	i	ii	iii	i	ii	iii
1958:1	883	1010	1053			1180			-415			-288		
2	896	1051		840			995			-604			-449	
3	800	912			817			929			-594			-482
4	828	959	697			828			-356			-225		
1959:1	638	620		808			790			-32			-50	
2	828	820			772			764			-45			-53
3	799	826	816			843			119			146		
4	1044	1127		913			996			105			188	
1960:1	895	840	1027			968			211			152		
2	1083	1024		1084			1094			171			181	
3	1067	1074			1065			1010			293			238
4	1169	1195			1038			1064			-27			-1
1961:1	770	815	940			985			-87			-42		
2	873	942		817			886			-267			-198	
3	807	854			824			871			-214			-167
4	974	956	843			825			-97			-115		

(continued)

TABLE A-1 (concluded)

Year and Quarter	Levels of Capital Expenditures: Actual	Levels of Capital Expenditures: Plan Image	Actual X_t : i	Actual X_t : ii	Actual X_t : iii	Plan Image P_t : i	Plan Image P_t : ii	Plan Image P_t : iii	Actual X_t-X_{t-3} : i	Actual X_t-X_{t-3} : ii	Actual X_t-X_{t-3} : iii	Plan Image P_t-X_{t-3} : i	Plan Image P_t-X_{t-3} : ii	Plan Image P_t-X_{t-3} : iii
			Seasonally Adjusted Levels of Expenditures						Three-Quarter Increments in Seasonally Adjusted Expenditures					
1962:1	710	648			817			817			−7			−7
2	873	873		880			818			63			1	
3	914	836	930			852			87			9		
4	1083	1110			968			893			151			76
1963:1	798	723		953			980			73			100	
*2	1009	940	953			884			23			−46		
3	1024	1071			1085			1018			117			50
4	1215	1148		1040			1087			87			134	
Data not used in determining relations														
1964:1	1009	879	1179			1049			226			96		
2	1250	1121			1368			1220			283			135
3	1352	1204		1194			1065			154			25	
4	1715	1420	1585			1290			406			111		
1965:1		1244						1356						−12
2		1412					1610						416	
3		1352				1352						233		

Additive Seasonal Coefficients for Capital Appropriations and Expenditures Equations in Tables 1 – 7

(million 1954 dollars per calendar quarter; to be subtracted from observations or from

calculated values of dependent variables to obtain adjusted figures)

Equation	Dependent and Explanatory Variables	Seasonal-Adjustment Coefficients				Largest Standard Error of Any Coefficient
		January–March	April–June	July–September	October–December	
	Appropriations, explained by:					
C-1	Pure seasonal	143	– 37	-239	133	216
C-2	Autoregression	131	-192	-285	346	135
C-3	Cash flow only	206	-223	-173	190	197
C-4	Bond yield only	99	– 68	-211	180	159
C-5	Cash flow and bond yield	146	-244	-147	240	133
C-6	Cash flow with bond yield and stock-price increment	173	-216	-248	291	112
C-7	Orders–capacity only	143	-100	-208	165	127
C-8	Orders–capacity with cash flow	129	-262	-135	268	107
C-9	Orders–capacity with cash flow and bond yield	280	-216	-255	191	90
	Expenditures, explained by appropriations:					
A-1	Pure seasonal	-167	0	– 10	177	123
A-2	Single appropriations flow	-252	10	109	133	60
A-3	Single appropriations backlog	-150	37	– 34	147	46
A-4	One flow term, one backlog	-113	– 10	– 36	159	42
A-5	Consecutive series of flows	-106	11	– 52	147	52
A-6	Plan image based on flows not more recent than (t-3)	-170	56	– 17	131	59

(continued)

Equation	Dependent and Explanatory Variables	Seasonal-Adjustment Coefficients				Largest Standard Error of Any Coefficient
		January–March	April–June	July–September	October–December	
	Expenditures, explained by autoregression:					
B-1	Latest previous expenditure	-313	146	- 14	181	54
B-2	Practical autoregression	-259	-207	180	286	72
B-3	Strongest autoregression	-387	173	- 19	233	52
	Expenditures, explained by latest previous expenditure with appropriations, with:					
B-4	One backlog					
B-5	One appropriations flow	-224	97	- 53	180	36
B-6	Series of appropriations flows	-201	81	- 50	171	52
	Expenditures, explained by variables used in Table 3, bypassing appropriations:					
D-1	Cash flow only	-169	75	- 55	149	143
D-2	Bond yield only	-198	- 11	6	203	96
D-3	Cash flow with bond yield	-179	62	- 54	170	94
D-4	Cash flow with bond yield and stock-price increment	-197	49	- 24	172	96
D-5(=F-3)	Orders-capacity only	-160	26	- 5	139	45
D-6	Orders-capacity with cash flow	-143	45	- 33	148	41

(continued)

TABLE A-2 (concluded)

Equation	Dependent and Explanatory Variables	Seasonal-Adjustment Coefficients				Largest Standard Error of Any Coefficient
		January–March	April–June	July–September	October–December	
	Expenditures, explained by appropriations with other variables:					
E-1	With cash flow	– 85	17	– 99	167	42
E-2	With cash flow and stock-price increment	– 86	15	–104	175	39
E-3	With orders–capacity	– 92	31	– 72	133	60
	Expenditures, plan-image functions, based on:					
F-1	Appropriations only	–167	0	– 29	177	123
F-2	Bond yield with cash flow and stock-price increment	–246	50	69	127	84
F-3(=D-5)	Orders–capacity only	–160	26	– 5	139	45
F-4	Orders–capacity with cash flow and stock-price increment	–214	45	27	142	44
F-5(=A-5)	Appropriations flows only	–106	11	– 52	147	52
F-6	Appropriations flows with orders–capacity	–168	49	– 22	141	52

TABLE A-3

Data Used in Econometric Operations: Deflated, with
Pure Seasonal Adjustment of Each Series

		Data from NICB Capital Appropriations Survey for 627 Durable Goods Manufacturing Corporations (million 1954 dollars per calendar quarter)			
Year	Quarter	Capital Expenditures X	Flow of New (gross) Capital Appropriations A	Backlog of Unspent Appropriations at Opening of Quarter B	Cancellations of Unspent Capital Appropriations C
1953	1	999	800	4,142	22
	2	962	992	3,860	54
	3	916	1,113	3,807	54
	4	876	913	3,965	68
1954	1	909	727	3,935	76
	2	957	793	3,662	81
	3	888	859	3,406	60
	4	876	691	3,300	51
1955	1	880	1,414	3,058	49
	2	816	1,879	3,513	57
	3	961	2,154	4,471	60
	4	1,092	2,000	5,499	58
1956	1	1,224	2,240	6,266	57
	2	1,415	1,814	7,078	71
	3	1,480	1,244	7,297	80
	4	1,649	1,511	6,814	59
1957	1	1,513	1,514	6,559	50
	2	1,516	1,244	6,427	90
	3	1,441	862	6,004	70
	4	1,375	680	5,320	101
1958	1	1,043	575	4,514	134
	2	888	723	3,893	74
	3	814	821	3,637	45
	4	662	800	3,563	91
1959	1	798	1,199	3,601	49
	2	821	1,151	3,939	48
	3	813	1,073	4,185	61
	4	877	1,220	4,388	18

(continued)

Data from NICB Capital Appropriations Survey for 627
Durable Goods Manufacturing Corporations
(million 1954 dollars per calendar quarter)

Year	Quarter	Capital Expenditures X	Flow of New (gross) Capital Appropriations A	Backlog of Unspent Appropriations at Opening of Quarter B	Cancellations of Unspent Capital Appropriations C
1960	1	1,055	1,073	4,730	71
	2	1,076	926	4,662	49
	3	1,081	850	4,444	55
	4	1,002	701	4,138	58
1961	1	931	632	3,796	63
	2	866	783	3,445	66
	3	821	944	3,284	54
	4	807	753	3,339	61
1962	1	870	1,109	3,245	52
	2	866	797	3,422	46
	3	928	986	3,287	84
	4	916	1,384	3,263	59
1963	1	958	962	3,680	49
	2	1,002	1,141	3,624	36
	3	1,038	1,338	3,703	46
	4	1,048	1,591	3,936	48
1955-63	mean	1,037	1,169	4,445	62

Explanatory Variables Used in Explanations of Capital
Appropriations and in Direct Explanations of Expenditures

Year	Quarter	Ratio of Orders to Capacity O	Cash Flow (million 1954 dollars) F	Long-Term Bond Yield (per cent) R	Stock Prices (1957-59 = 100) S	Increment of Stock Prices ΔS
1953	1	4.94	1,674	3.09	49.0	
	2	4.60	1,443	3.31	43.8	-5.2
	3	3.78	1,301	3.11	39.6	-4.2
	4	3.31	1,186	2.98	39.5	$-.1$
1954	1	3.20	1,508	2.96	48.6	9.1
	2	3.18	1,470	2.85	52.4	3.8
	3	3.55	1,558	2.74	56.1	3.7
	4	3.84	1,401	2.73	60.6	4.5

(continued)

TABLE A-3 (concluded)

Year	Quarter	Ratio of Orders to Capacity O	Cash Flow (million 1954 dollars) F	Long-Term Bond Yield (per cent) R	Stock Prices (1957-59 = 100) S	Increment of Stock Prices ΔS
		Explanatory Variables Used in Explanations of Capital Appropriations and in Direct Explanations of Expenditures				
1955	1	4.36	2,010	3.00	73.3	12.7
	2	4.36	2,099	3.02	75.0	1.7
	3	4.51	2,080	2.97	82.1	7.1
	4	4.68	1,835	2.99	82.9	0.8
1956	1	4.16	2,191	3.13	90.3	7.4
	2	4.08	1,953	3.24	90.2	-0.1
	3	4.10	1,856	3.31	93.6	3.4
	4	4.05	1,981	3.53	91.3	-2.3
1957	1	3.76	2,118	3.66	91.2	-0.1
	2	3.46	1,831	3.72	94.8	3.6
	3	3.38	1,906	3.91	91.7	-3.1
	4	3.21	1,647	3.75	76.1	-15.6
1958	1	2.71	1,192	3.52	82.9	6.8
	2	2.89	1,096	3.39	83.8	.9
	3	3.25	1,599	3.67	91.9	8.1
	4	3.51	1,982	3.88	103.0	11.1
1959	1	3.69	1,914	4.09	115.6	12.6
	2	3.75	2,259	4.31	120.1	4.5
	3	3.48	1,672	4.31	124.5	4.4
	4	3.44	1,676	4.37	121.9	-2.6
1960	1	3.21	1,989	4.51	122.7	0.8
	2	3.24	1,675	4.38	121.0	-1.7
	3	3.39	1,605	4.13	116.3	-4.7
	4	3.22	1,465	4.10	109.6	-6.7
1961	1	2.90	1,246	4.18	125.6	16.0
	2	3.31	1,628	4.17	129.9	4.3
	3	3.47	1,825	4.25	128.5	-1.4
	4	3.60	2,123	4.23	132.6	4.1
1962	1	3.51	2,009	4.38	137.0	4.4
	2	3.48	2,088	4.19	117.1	-19.9
	3	3.49	2,097	4.15	105.3	-11.8
	4	3.57	2,269	4.01	106.4	1.1
1963	1	3.58	2,058	4.13	122.6	16.2
	2	3.68	2,366	4.12	130.4	7.8
	3	3.64	2,409	4.13	129.5	-0.9
	4	3.60	2,342	4.17	134.7	5.2
1955-63	mean	3.60	1,891	3.86	106.8	2.1

Sales Anticipations,
Planned Inventory Investment,
and Realizations

MICHAEL C. LOVELL

CARNEGIE INSTITUTE OF TECHNOLOGY

1. Introduction

The impact upon inventory investment of errors made by firms in anticipating sales volume is an important but hackneyed topic. The topic is significant, because inventory investment—a much more volatile component of private investment spending than either new construction or producer durables—constitutes a critical link in the generation of fluctuations in economic activity. But the topic has constituted the theme of numerous theoretical and empirical studies. The assumption that inventories are drawn down below planned levels when sales volume is underestimated at the start of the production period constitutes the cornerstone of the Lundberg (1955) and Metzler (1941) aggregative inventory cycle models and their multisector generalizations.[1] The empirical problem of explaining how inventory

NOTE: The research reported in this paper was undertaken during the tenure of a Ford Faculty Research Fellowship. Computation time was financed by the Graduate School of Industrial Administration. I am indebted to Theodore Ikola, James Matthews, and Pamela Meyers for programming assistance. I wish to express appreciation to Lawrence Bridge, Murray Foss, and Irving Rottenberg for their cooperation in furnishing the data employed in this study.

[1] The multisector generalizations of Lovell (1962) and Foster (1963) were concerned with the stability properties of dynamic input-output models in which each industry responded to errors made in anticipating sales volume in essentially the same manner as assumed by Lundberg and Metzler for the aggregate. Complete bibliographical references are given at the end of the paper.

investment is related to anticipated sales volume constituted virgin territory when Modigliani and Sauerlander presented their pioneering paper (1955) some ten years ago at an earlier National Bureau Conference. Today we can look back upon a multitude of empirical studies of inventory behavior.[2] In addition, our knowledge is buttressed by numerous studies of anticipatory data, including Robert Ferber's study of the *Railroad Shippers' Forecasts* (1953) and the many notable papers in *The Quality and Economic Significance of Anticipations Data* (1960).

My excuse for revisiting the topic is provided by the new and exciting data now available from the quarterly manufacturers' inventory and sales anticipations survey conducted by the Office of Business Economics, Department of Commerce. In earlier empirical studies of inventory behavior it was necessary either to rely upon grossly imprecise measures of sales anticipations or to resort to surrogative procedures. Furthermore, considerable detective work was necessary in deriving inferences about the nature of the discrepancy between measured inventories and their desired level. The OBE survey now provides us with data on anticipated sales and planned inventory investment for both a three-month and a six-month horizon. In addition, an index of surplus inventories is provided.

The richness of the new OBE data facilitates the investigation of such problems as the structure of sales anticipations and inventory plans and the determinants of desired inventory levels. Research on these topics is currently under way, and this paper is only a preliminary report on one aspect of a larger study. But the results obtained to date, while preliminary, are surprising to say the least. Specifically, the new evidence suggests that the magnitude of the forecasting errors made by firms is not nearly as large as previous empirical studies had suggested. Firms now appear to be much more precise in predicting sales volume than is customarily assumed in theoretical models of the inventory cycle. Equally important, I find that deviations of actual from anticipated sales volume do not generate discrepancies between planned and actual inventory investment in the way that has customarily been assumed in theoretical and empirical investigations.

In the next section of this paper the new data provided by the OBE survey will be discussed. Then, in section 3, the accuracy of these *ex ante* data will be contrasted with the evidence of earlier empirical surveys of anticipations. Section 4 summarizes the basic equations of

---

[2] For an attempt to summarize this literature, see Lovell (1964).

TABLE 1

Industry Code and Variables Utilized in Study

Industry Code

Durables

1. Primary iron and steel
2. Primary nonferrous metals
3. Electrical machinery
4. Machinery except electrical
5. Motor vehicles and equipment
6. Transportation equipment, excluding motor vehicles and equipment
7. Other durable goods

Nondurables

1. Food and beverage
2. Textiles
3. Papers
4. Chemicals
5. Petroleum
6. Rubber
7. Other nondurable goods

Variables (million dollars)

IN	=	actual inventory at end of quarter
ASIN	=	short inventory anticipation (anticipated end-of-quarter inventory)
ALIN	=	long inventory anticipation (anticipated inventory at end of next quarter)
SALE	=	actual sales of quarter t
ASSALE	=	short sales anticipation (sales volume anticipated for current quarter)
ALSALE	=	long sales anticipation (sales volume anticipated for next quarter)
COND	=	condition of inventory (proportion of firms reporting inventories high in relation to total sales and unfilled orders backlog less percentage reporting inventories low)
FIN	=	actual finished goods inventory at end of quarter
PMGIP	=	purchased materials and goods in process
UOR	=	unfilled orders at end of quarter

Note: Approximately half the questionnaires are returned to the OBE by the end of the first month of the quarter. Since the smaller companies generally answer sooner than the larger ones, an average response date weighted by company size is probably the tenth day of the second month of the quarter.

the buffer-stock model of inventory behavior. In sections 5 and 6 the model is used in analyzing finished goods and aggregate inventory behavior. The argument of the paper is summarized in the concluding section.

2. *The New Data*

The manufacturers' inventory and sales expectations survey, initiated by the OBE in the fall of 1957, is currently conducted every quarter. Respondents are asked to report both the expected level of inventories at the end of the current quarter and the level anticipated for the end of the next quarter; in addition, they report on actual inventory at the beginning of the current quarter and the previous quarter.[3] The survey also inquires as to expected sales volume in both the current and the immediately following quarter. Further, information on the discrepancy between desired and actual inventory stocks is provided in terms of the percentage of firms reporting inventories as high, about right, and low relative to total sales and the unfilled orders backlog.

I have been privileged to have access to the data in raw form for the seven durable and seven nondurable industries identified in Table 1. In the present study, data are used for the twenty-one surveys conducted through the second survey of 1963, but there are only eighteen observations on short anticipations for inventories and sales as the first three surveys did not inquire about short-run three-month prospects. The anticipations data used here are adjusted to industry benchmarks by the OBE.[4] But unlike most other anticipatory series, the figures utilized in this study have not been adjusted by the compiling agent in

---

[3] In designing the questionnaire, the OBE benefited from our prior experience with the railroad shippers' survey. By avoiding reference to the corresponding quarter of the previous year, the respondents were in no way encouraged to simply extrapolate from their experience in the same season of last year.

[4] Foss (p. 234) explains that for each industry the firms in the sample are partitioned into two cells on the basis of size. For each size cell of each industry, the anticipated inventory figure is multiplied by a blowup factor. The blowup factor for inventories is simply the ratio of the inventory figure for the regular larger monthly survey to the inventory figure reported by firms in the anticipations survey for the quarter in which the anticipations figure is formulated. A similar procedure is employed for sales. There are certain advantages in employing the benchmark data, for without such an adjustment the observed forecasting error may be distorted as a result of fluctuations in response rates between the survey in which the *ex ante* figures are collected and the subsequent survey in which the *ex post* realizations are reported.

an attempt to eliminate systematic biases or to improve the forecasts.[5] The sample is reasonably large, consisting in 1961 of from 1,250 to 1,400 manufacturing firms, with better than 80 per cent coverage of larger firms with assets over $10,000,000.

Admittedly, quarterly time series covering only five years do not provide as many observations as we would like to have. But the difficulty is mitigated by the breadth of industry coverage. Furthermore, many earlier investigators of expectations behavior, with the notable exception of studies based on the railroad shippers' forecast data, have also had to work with extremely short time series. It would have been useful to have had the inventory figures broken down by stage of fabrication.[6] For the durable and nondurable aggregate, it was possible to utilize the published inventory by stage of fabrication data, but the anticipated inventory figures I utilized were not broken down in this way.[7]

One of the most serious problems involved in collecting *ex ante* data arises from the possibility that the reported figures do not reflect the actual anticipations of individuals making operating decisions for the firm. The questionnaire for the OBE survey is generally submitted by company controllers and treasurers or their assistants, and there exists the distinct possibility that these figures do not correspond to a simple aggregate of expectations of production and purchasing departments. But Murray Foss does report that seven out of every eight respondents reported that the sales anticipations figures "played an important part

[5] The published inventory anticipations figures, in contrast, are adjusted with the aid of the inventory conditions variable in an attempt to eliminate apparent systematic biases. Similar adjustments for systematic biases are made by the OBE-SEC in publishing the results of the survey of business plant and equipment expenditures, and when these data have been used in econometric studies of expectational behavior, the results may have been distorted as a result of the compiling agents' attempt to improve the forecasting ability of the *ex ante* series. Similarly, the raw survey results are subjected to adjustment by some of the regional boards of the American Railway Association in an attempt to improve their accuracy.

[6] The survey does inquire into the condition of inventories (high, low, or about right) by stage of fabrication, and these figures are published for the durable and nondurable aggregates, but this information was not provided to me on an industry basis.

[7] In utilizing the published finished goods aggregates for durables and nondurables, it was necessary to adjust for the fact that the coverage of the individual industries fell short of the published sector totals. The durable and nondurable finished goods aggregates utilized in this study were obtained by multiplying the total inventory figure obtained from summing the component industries by the current ratio of published finished goods to published total inventory. The Department of Commerce now publishes data on industry stage of fabrication, but the new figures are based on a more recent Standard Industrial Classification and are not directly comparable with the industry classification of the anticipations data.

in the company's production and purchasing policies" when this question was raised as a supplemental question on one of the earlier surveys. The proportion was somewhat higher in durables and lower in nondurables; in the food and beverage industry, more than one in three firms answered in the negative. Foss also reports that five out of every six firms reported that they utilized the inventory forecast in production and purchasing policies. Field interviews conducted by the Office of Business Economics confirmed that the sales forecast lies at the heart of most companies' future plans; firms consider the inventory anticipation to be much more difficult to make than the sales projection.[8]

Two questions of ambiguity about the interpretation of the data deserve mention. As with some earlier *ex ante* surveys, there is the question of whether the forecasts are made in terms of current dollars or of the price level anticipated three or six months hence. Fortunately, the period covered by our data has not been marked by sharp inflationary trends. Furthermore, Murray Foss found, early in the history of the survey, that adjusting the inventory data under the assumption that respondents were making the forecast in present prices had only minor effects on the series. The second ambiguity arises from the possibility that the anticipations may have been reported on a seasonally adjusted basis. But when firms were asked, in a supplementary question, to give reasons for the anticipated change, approximately 50 per cent of them indicated "normal seasonal change" as one factor influencing their forecast.[9] The data used in this study have not been seasonally adjusted.

3. On the Accuracy of Sales Anticipations

Early studies of short-term anticipatory data suggested that business firms are remarkably poor forecasters of future sales volume. Ferber (1953) reported in his pioneering study that a simple procedure for extrapolating from the past yielded much more precise forecasts than the anticipated carload shipments data collected by the Regional Ship-

---

[8] See Foss (p. 237) for additional information on the relevance of the forecasts for company planning.

[9] Early in the history of the survey Foss compared the anticipations figures without seasonal adjustment with the seasonally adjusted realizations, but did not find any decisive improvement in the accuracy of the forecasts. Of course, to the extent that the seasonal adjustment procedures are *idempotent,* subjecting a series to repeated seasonal adjustment will have only minor effects upon the series. For inventories, a marked seasonal pattern is observed only in the food and beverage industry, but seasonal movements are somewhat more pronounced in sales volume.

pers' Advisory Board of the American Railway Association. Modigliani and Sauerlander (1955) were also quite pessimistic about the direct forecasting ability of business firms, although they noted that anticipatory data compiled in *Fortune* and in Dun and Bradstreet surveys implied that firms were not quite as unsuccessful at forecasting as the railroad shippers' data suggested. More recently, examination of anticipatory data compiled by the Securities and Exchange Commission and the Office of Business Economics in their annual survey of plant and equipment intentions has suggested that firms are considerably more precise at forecasting annual sales volume than the earlier investigators had concluded.[10] The new data provided by the OBE quarterly survey suggest that businessmen's anticipations of sales volume are much more precise than economists had been led to believe on the basis of the earlier evidence.

ANTICIPATIONS VERSUS NAIVE FORECASTS

A naive forecast is a convenient yardstick by which the accuracy of anticipatory data may be measured. The accuracy of anticipations might be judged by comparing their forecasting accuracy with a naive extrapolation from either the immediately preceding quarter or the corresponding quarter of the preceding year. Ferber (1953) and Modigliani and Sauerlander (1955) used a slightly more complicated naive projection in evaluating their anticipatory data. Specifically, they compared the accuracy of the anticipations forecast with

$$E_t^{**} = A_{t-4}(A_{t-1}/A_{t-5}), \qquad (1)$$

where E_t^{**} is the naive forecast and A_{t-i} is the actual realization i quarters previously. For testing six-month anticipatory data, the Ferber naive forecast may be appropriately modified to

$$E_t^{**} = A_{t-4}(A_{t-2}/A_{t-6}). \qquad (2)$$

In either form, the naive forecast amounts to adjusting the same quarter of the immediately preceding year by recently observed trend. Or to put it another way, the Ferber test elaborates on the simpler naive forecast of "same as current quarter" by adjusting for the change observed last year.[11] Thus it constitutes a crude adjustment for seasonal movements.

---

[10] See Modigliani and Weingartner (1958). On the other hand, Pashigian (1964) suggests that the sales anticipations can be beaten by an artfully designed naive model.

[11] This may be observed by writing (1) as $E_t^{**} = A_{t-1}(A_{t-4}/A_{t-5})$.

TABLE 2

Accuracy of Anticipations Data Relative to Ferber's Naive Test:
Ratios of Average Absolute Errors

(per cent)

	ASSALE	ALSALE	ASIN	ALIN
Durables				
1	8	36	31	46
2	45	54	64	61
3	49	48	77	57
4	66	47	57	57
5	15	29	48	69
6	58	55	93	53
7	96	89	89	73
Aggregate	15	42	60	57
Combined	25	43	58	59
Nondurables				
1	87	115	309	195
2	68	70	206	162
3	70	80	108	187
4	64	65	233	122
5	110	102	151	123
6	83	71	54	57
7	59	60	123	101
Aggregate	59	64	301	196
Combined	73	73	135	101

Ferber computed the average absolute percentage error (AAPE) for both the naive forecast and for the actual railroad anticipatory data.[12] For the most part, the AAPE was considerably larger for the

[12] In other words, AAPE $= 100 \Sigma(E - A)/n$, where n is the number of observations, E the forecast change, and A the realized change. An alternative measure would be the root mean square error, $[\Sigma(E - A)^2/n]^{1/2}$. The root mean square error penalizes extreme errors more severely than the AAPE and is appropriate if the loss function is quadratic. I have computed both measures of accuracy for the OBE quarterly data, but report only the AAPE as these figures are comparable with other studies. In any case, the basic conclusions are quite insensitive to the measure selected.

railroad anticipations data than for the naive forecast. For the prewar period, 1929–41, the naive forecasts were more accurate than observed anticipations for the total nonfarm aggregate and for each of the five component industries that he considered. For the period 1946–50, the forecasts of the nonfarm aggregate had a 23 per cent larger AAPE than the naive forecast, although the anticipatory data were at least marginally superior to the naive forecasts in three industries—iron and steel, flour, and cement.

The accuracy of the new OBE anticipatory data relative to Ferber's naive forecast is shown in Table 2 for individual industries as identified in Table 1, for the durable and nondurable aggregates, and for the individual industries combined. Inspection of the table reveals that in durable manufacturing entrepreneurs are particularly accurate forecasters. For iron and steel, the AAPE for the three-month sales forecast is only 8 per cent of the AAPE of the naive projection; the six-month forecast has an AAPE ratio of 36 per cent. Contrast this with the figure of 79 per cent reported by Ferber for the same industry for the 1946–50 period on the basis of the railroad shippers' forecast data. For only one industry—petroleum—does the ASSALE forecast do worse than the Ferber extrapolation. For two nondurable industries —food and petroleum—the Ferber extrapolation is marginally superior to the ALSALE forecast.[13]

CORRELATION OF ACTUAL WITH ANTICIPATED CHANGE

A second yardstick frequently used in evaluating the precision of expectational data is provided by computing the correlation between the predicted and the actual change. A correlation coefficient that is not significantly different from zero would imply that a naive prediction of a constant percentage change for each period constitutes as good a predictor as the anticipatory series. On the other hand, a high correlation may be obtained with a quite poor predictor, for the correlation test is a weak one in that it automatically corrects for any systematic linear bias between anticipated and actual change; the correlation coefficients measures the potential forecasting ability after correction for systematic bias.

On Table 3, where the correlation coefficients obtained with the OBE data are reported,[14] it may be observed that the coefficients

---

[13] In no case does an alternative to the Ferber naive extrapolation (same as last quarter) do as well as the ASSALE forecast, but for textile and petroleum a naive extrapolation (same as two quarters back) does as well as ALSALE.

[14] The correlation coefficients are adjusted for degrees of freedom.

TABLE 3

Accuracy of Anticipations Data: $\bar{R}^2$ *of Actual with Predicted*
Percentage Change

	ASSALE	ALSALE	ASIN	ALIN
Durables				
1	.9667	.8969	.6444	.5257
2	.7233	.2904	+0	.0439
3	.9225	.4180	.8157	.6732
4	.9185	.7363	.6685	.7149
5	.9812	.8430	.7367	.1891
6	.6834	.3249	.2831	.5571
7	.6558	.5367	.7231	.7738
Aggregate	.9618	.7377	.8267	.7185
Combined	.9396	.8208	.5800	.4479
Nondurables				
1	.7814	.8023	.9115	.8912
2	.2801	+0	.7908	.7529
3	.1540	.4522	.3229	.5646
4	.7173	.5583	.7243	.6860
5	.5962	.2345	.8225	.7579
6	.7050	.3079	.6913	.6909
7	.7988	.6720	.7281	.7068
Aggregate	.6196	.4830	.1009	.0831
Combined	.6304	.3737	.7499	.7264

obtained for sales are higher for short than for long anticipations, as might be expected. Durable sales on the average yield a tighter fit than nondurables. Inventory investment is anticipated with less precision than sales volume.

The evidence of Table 3 reveals that sales anticipations are more precise than had been suggested by earlier studies. When anticipated changes reported in the railroad shippers' survey for the 1927–41 period were correlated with actual changes, the correlation coefficients were negative approximately half the time; this reflects the notorious tendency for anticipatory series to predict short-run movements in the reverse direction from actual developments. In contrast, the correlation coefficients for the OBE quarterly survey are all positive. With the postwar Dun and Bradstreet survey data, Modigliani and Sauerlander obtained correlation coefficients for the postwar period of .03 for durables and .10 for nondurables. The *Fortune* survey did considerably better, Modigliani and Sauerlander reported, with a correlation coefficient of 0.80 for durables, but the OBE data yield a considerably higher figure of R^2 of .96 and .74 for short and long durable sales anticipations, respectively.

While the high correlations between the anticipated and the actual sales and inventory changes reported in Table 3 demonstrate that the OBE *ex ante* data constitute more precise predictors of actual realizations than earlier anticipatory series, they do not suffice to establish that the new *ex ante* series are useful forecasters in their own right. It will be remembered that the Ferber naive test makes a simple allowance for seasonal movements. In contrast, the simple correlation coefficients reported in Table 3 do not reveal the extent to which the suggested forecasting precision of the *ex ante* data arises from the seasonality in the data. In order to investigate the net forecasting ability of the OBE data, over and above seasonal movements, the following regression equation was fitted to the individual industries and the durable and nondurable aggregates:

$$\frac{IN - IN_{-1}}{IN_{-1}} = b_1 + b_2 s_1 + b_3 s_2 + b_4 s_3 + b_5 t + b_6 \left(\frac{ASIN - IN_{-1}}{IN_{-1}} \right) + e. \tag{3}$$

Here the s_i are seasonal dummy variables that equal unity in the ith quarter and zero in all other quarters; the variable t denotes trend.[15] Similar regressions were run for ALIN, ASSALE, and ALSALE.[16] If the forecasters were sufficiently clairvoyant to know the seasonal pattern, the seasonal and trend terms in the regression would be insignificant. In fact, however, the dummy variables are generally large relative to their standard errors, suggesting that there is a consistent seasonal pattern in the discrepancies between actual and anticipated changes. Indeed, the anticipated change variable was insignificant in the majority of the nondurable regressions, suggesting that knowledge of the anticipated change would make a negligible contribution toward predicting

---

[15] This implies a fixed multiplicative seasonal pattern, for equation (3) is equivalent to $IN = (b_1 + b_2 s_1 + b_3 s_2 + b_4 s_3 + b_5 t + 1 - b_6) IN_{-1} + b_6 ASIN + eIN_{-1}$. Seasonality is not marked when represented in additive form.

[16] For the ALIN and ALSALE regressions, a six-month rather than a three-month lag was introduced.

TABLE 4

*Accuracy of Anticipations Data: Partial $\overline{R}^2$ Actual with Predicted
Percentage Change[a]*

	ASSALE	ALSALE	ASIN	ALIN
Durables				
1	.8290	.6735	.4631	.3456
2	.2867	.1015	.0150	–
3	.4588	.2367	.2187	.2945
4	.2958	.1969	.1462	.2813
5	.7566	.5065	.5165	.1244
6	.1858	.2424	.2470	.2975
7	–	–	.2365	.2309
Aggregate	.5517	.4436	.5517	.3932
Nondurables				
1	–	–	.0229	.0928
2	.0221	–	.0026	–
3	.0414	.0931	.1831	.1965
4	.0543	–	.0604	–
5	–	.0350	–	–
6	.0946	–	.2114	.1731
7	.1468	.0967	–	–
Aggregate	.0220	–	–	.1123

Note: Blanks denote negative adjusted partial correlation coefficients.

[a]Partial with respect to seasonality and trend.

the actual change if the seasonal pattern were known.[17] The squared
partial correlation coefficients of actual with anticipated change, net
of the effects of seasonality and trend but adjusted for degrees of freedom, are presented in Table 4. While these partial coefficients are quite
high in a number of durable industries, it is apparent from the table

[17] In the durables, the anticipated change variable appeared with a significant
coefficient in all regressions with the exception of ASSALE and ALSALE for
industry 7 (all other) and ASIN and ALIN for industry 2 (primary nonferrous
metals). For nondurables, on the other hand, ASSALE is significant only for the
industry 6 regression, ALSALE only for industries 3 and 7, ASIN in industries
3 and 6, and ALIN only for 1, 3, and 6.

that the anticipated change makes a negligible contribution toward predicting the seasonally adjusted actual change in most nondurable industries.[18]

CONCLUSION

The new *ex ante* data compiled by OBE constitute a much more precise predictor of actual realization than the quarterly anticipations data analyzed in earlier studies. In terms of the two yardsticks applied in previous investigations of quarterly anticipatory data, the Ferber naive comparison and the correlation of actual with anticipated changes, entrepreneurs seem to be much more precise at predicting short-run sales developments than had been suggested by earlier studies. In terms of a tougher test, however, my analysis of the new data suggests that entrepreneurs in a number of industries are not particularly adept at anticipating seasonal movements in sales and inventory volume. They do considerably better at predicting sales and inventory developments than they would by employing the simple Ferber procedure for roughly adjusting for seasonal effects in projecting from current levels; but in terms of a rather invidious comparison with a seasonal pattern estimated from the whole sample period, we find from Table 4 a rather mixed record of achievement. While entrepreneurs still appear to be quite good at predicting actual changes in a number of durable industries, they are apparently much less adept at predicting developments in the nondurable sector.

Why are the *ex ante* data compiled by the Office of Business Economics more precise predictors of actual realizations than the quarterly sales anticipatory data analyzed in earlier studies? We might expect the ASSALE forecast to be more accurate than the railroad shippers' anticipations because the OBE questionnaire is circulated after the beginning of the quarter while the American Railway Association survey data is gathered during the middle of the preceding quarter. But the lead time on the ALSALE forecast is longer than that of the American Railway Association survey, and yet the ALSALE forecasts are also considerably more accurate than the railroad shippers anticipatory data. It is possible that the greater accuracy of the new survey is in part due to a continued improvement in the ability of firms to forecast demand conditions. Support for this argument is provided by

[18] The partial coefficients of Table 4 are identical to those that would be obtained by correlating seasonally adjusted actual change with seasonally adjusted predicted change if (1) the two series were adjusted separately by a least-squares multiplicative procedure and (2) correct allowances were made for the loss of degrees of freedom resulting from the process of seasonal adjustment.

the fact that the shippers' forecasts were somewhat more accurate after World War II than during the interwar period. But a third and more likely explanation is provided by the fact that the *ex ante* data compiled in the railroad shippers' forecasts are reported in terms of anticipated carload usage by the responding firms traffic manager. Even if the traffic manager is informed about anticipated sales volume, the process of converting forecasted sales into an estimate of carloading requirements may well tend to introduce considerable imprecision. The raw carloading anticipatory data, my earlier research suggested, had a grossly unsatisfactory forecasting record because the errors made by firms with regard to sales anticipations were confounded with additional noise resulting from errors made in converting sales figures into carloading requirements.[19] It may well have been a mistake to interpret the poor forecasting record of the railroad shippers' *ex ante* data on anticipated carloadings as evidence that firms were extremely poor at forecasting sales volume.

4. Buffer-Stock Inventory Behavior

In theoretical models of the inventory cycle it is customarily assumed that inventory investment deviates from its planned level as stocks are run down when entrepreneurs are surprised by a sales volume that exceeds anticipations; in other words,

$$IN = ASIN - (SALE - ASSALE). \tag{4}$$

This elementary version of the realization concept is subject to the obvious objection that no allowance is made for the revision of plans during the quarterly observation period. As errors in anticipating such variables as sales volume become apparent during the quarter, it may be possible for the firm to at least partially revise production schedules and the delivery dates for purchased materials. The possibility of plan revision has received explicit consideration in many empirical studies of inventory behavior, including both the Modigliani and Sauerlander (1955) and the Lovell (1961) papers. A detailed theoretical analysis

[19] See Lovell (1964, pp. 216–220) for a more detailed presentation of this argument. There I showed, for the cement industry data, that if the anticipated carloadings figures are transformed into sales forecasts, the sales forecasts are considerably more accurate predictors of actual sales volume than the *ex ante* carloading figures are predictors of actual carloadings. It is interesting to note that while the Modigliani and Sauerlander study (1955) reported on the inaccuracy of the carloading forecasts, these *ex ante* figures were transformed into sales forecasts, measured in barrels, for purposes of explaining cement inventory behavior; the latter series may have been much more accurate.

of the effects of plan revision on production and inventory levels is to be found in Modigliani and Cohen (1961). I shall briefly summarize the theory in this section and then, in subsequent sections of the paper, evaluate it in the light of the new data provided by the OBE survey.

Let us begin, as has been customary in many studies of inventory behavior, by postulating that the desired level of end-of-quarter inventories, IN^d, is a linear function of current and the next period's sales. Thus we shall assume:

$$IN^d = \beta_1 + \beta_2 SALE + \beta_3 SALE_{+1} + \epsilon_2. \tag{5}$$

Because SALE and $SALE_{+1}$ are unknown at the beginning of the period, the anticipated level of desired inventory is

$$AIN^d = \beta_1 + \beta_2 ASSALE + \beta_3 ALSALE_{+1} + \epsilon_3. \tag{6}$$

Anticipated sales volume as well as the realized volume of sales will be regarded as exogenous. Planned inventory investment may be expected to deviate from the desired level because of costs involved in adjusting stocks. If, as is customary, it is assumed that only a partial adjustment of stocks toward the desired level is attempted, we have for the planned inventory stock

$$ASIN = \delta AIN^d + (1 - \delta)IN_{-1} + \epsilon_4, \tag{7}$$

where δ, the adjustment coefficient, lies between zero and unity. Substituting from equation (6) in order to eliminate the unobserved variable AIN^d yields:

$$ASIN = \delta\beta_1 + \delta\beta_2 ASSALE + \delta\beta_3 ALSALE_{+1} + (1 - \delta)IN_{-1} + \epsilon_5, \tag{8}$$

where $\epsilon_5 = \delta\epsilon_3 + \epsilon_4$.

If no revision of production plans or delivery schedules is feasible, actual inventories will deviate from planned levels by the amount by which actual sales depart from the anticipated level, in accordance with equation (4). On the other hand, in the case of *complete flexibility,* inventory investment would be unaffected by any error in anticipating current sales volume and, in addition, actual inventory would be determined by end- rather than beginning-of-period anticipations of sales in period $t + 1$. In other words, end-of-period knowledge of current sales and end-of-period anticipations of next-quarters sales volume, rather than initial anticipations, would be the relevant determinants of inventory investment. With sufficient flexibility, then, we would have:

$$IN = \delta\beta_1 + \delta\beta_2 SALE + \delta\beta_3 ASSALE_{+1} + (1 - \delta)IN_{-1} + \epsilon_6. \tag{9}$$

In practice, plans may be only partially subject to revision during the three-month observation period. If we are permitted to assume that the effect of plan revision is to cause actual inventory investment to be an average (with weights λ and $1 - \lambda$, respectively) of the extremes suggested by equations (4) and (9), we shall have:[20]

$$IN = \lambda[ASIN + ASSALE - SALE] + (1 - \lambda)\delta\beta_1 + (1 - \lambda)\delta\beta_2 SALE$$
$$+ (1 - \lambda)\delta\beta_3 ASSALE_{+1} + (1 - \lambda)(1 - \delta)IN_{-1} + \epsilon_7. \quad (10)$$

The *realization function* is obtained by a slight modification of equation (10). Specifically, let us add and subtract from the right-hand side of the last equation $(1 - \lambda)ASIN$, as given by equation (8). This yields

$$IN = ASIN + [(1 - \lambda)\delta\beta_2 - \lambda](SALE - ASSALE)$$
$$+ (1 - \lambda)\delta\beta_3(ASSALE_{+1} - ALSALE_{+1}) + \epsilon_8, \quad (11)$$

where $\epsilon_8 = \epsilon_7 - (1 - \lambda)\epsilon_5$.

The realization function explains the discrepancy between actual inventory and its planned level in terms of both the *surprise* effect of errors made in anticipating current sales volume and the *revision* of anticipations of sales volume expected during the following quarter. Observe that if $\beta_3 = 0$, desired inventories being a function of only current rather than the next period's sales, the above equation reduces to (4). A positive effect upon inventories might be generated when sales volume exceeds anticipations, but only if production plans are extremely flexible; i.e., if $\lambda < \delta\beta_2/(\delta\beta_2 + 1)$, the coefficient of the surprise term $SALE - ASSALE$ in equation (11) is positive.

It will be observed that a limitation of the realization function approach is that its application does not yield estimates of the individual parameters of the model. An alternative approach is to work in terms of a reduced-form equation for inventories. It will be observed that, while equations (8) and (10) constitute a system of two simultaneous equations, they are fortunately triangularly recursive. Although the current value of ASIN appears in both equations, actual inventory does not appear in (8). If we use equation (8) to eliminate ASIN from (10), we obtain as the reduced-form equation for inventories[21]

$$IN = \delta\beta_1 + \lambda(1 + \delta\beta_2)ASSALE + \lambda\delta\beta_3 ALSALE_{+1}$$
$$+ (1 - \lambda)\delta\beta_3 ASSALE_{+1} + [\delta\beta_2 - \lambda(\delta\beta_2 + 1)]SALE$$
$$+ (1 - \delta)IN_{-1} + \epsilon_9, \quad (12)$$

[20] If $\lambda = 1$, plans are completely rigid, and this equation reduces to equation (4); with $\lambda = 0$, we again have (9).

[21] Note that since the system is triangular, the structural and reduced-form equations for ASIN are identical.

where $\epsilon_9 = \epsilon_7 + \lambda\epsilon_5$. This reduced-form equation must be employed when observations on planned inventory investment are not available.

5. Finished Goods Inventory Behavior

The distinction between finished goods inventories and purchased materials and goods in process has been stressed in many empirical studies of inventory investment behavior. When anticipations data have been utilized in earlier studies of inventory investment, the primary focus has been upon finished goods. It is possible for us to replicate on the new data models employed by Modigliani and Sauerlander (1958) and Lovell (1964). In addition, it will be possible to exploit the ASSALE versus ALSALE distinction now provided by the new survey. Of course, it will be necessary, as in the earlier studies, to finesse the planned inventory position variable, as data were not available on planned inventory by stage of fabrication. For this reason, we must work with reduced form equation (12). We must also content ourselves with an examination of the durable and nondurable aggregates, for it has not proved convenient to work with stage of fabrication data by individual industries.[22]

First, we will consider the restricted case in which desired inventory depends upon current rather than the next period's anticipated sales volume, i.e., $\beta_3 = 0$. In an earlier study of durable and nondurable finished goods manufacturing inventory data covering the period 1948–55, it was necessary for me to invoke this assumption since the crude measure of anticipated sales that I derived from railroad shippers' forecast data referred only to short anticipations. Equation (12) was tested in the form:

$$\Delta\text{FIN} = \delta\beta_1 + \delta\beta_2\text{SALE} - \lambda(\delta\beta_2 + 1)(\text{SALE} - \text{ASSALE}) - \delta\text{FIN}_{-1} + \epsilon. \quad (13)$$

The coefficient of the surprise term, SALE − ASSALE, was at least three times its estimated standard error in both the durable and the nondurable regressions. The point estimates obtained for λ of .11 for durables and .10 for nondurables were sufficiently large relative to the estimates of δ and β to imply that inventories are reduced when actual sales exceed the anticipated level. I also pointed out that these estimates would be biased toward zero if, as Albert Hart has suggested, there

---

[22] Although the OBE now publishes stage-of-fabrication data by individual industry, the industry classification is not comparable to that of the inventory anticipation survey.

exists a tendency for the railroad shippers' forecast data to systematically exaggerate the errors made by firms in forecasting sales volume. In addition, regressions were run on the cement industry for the
period 1947–56, and here the coefficient of the surprise term was
larger than one-half and more than twice its standard error.[23]

The replication of this same model on the new OBE data yields the
following regressions for finished durable and nondurable goods,
respectively:

$$\Delta\text{FIN} = \begin{array}{c} 53.0 \\ (1089.7) \end{array} + \begin{array}{c} .0799\text{SALE} \\ (.0345) \end{array} - \begin{array}{c} .0474(\text{SALE} - \text{ASSALE}) \\ (.1385) \end{array}$$

$$- \begin{array}{c} .3303\text{FIN}_{-1} + e. \\ (.1655) \end{array} \qquad (14\text{a})$$

$$\bar{R}^2 = .2903,\ d = 1.52,\ \bar{S}_{\text{est}} = 280.85,\ df = 13,$$
$$\delta = .3303,\ \beta_1 = 160.5,\ \beta_2 = .2421,\ \lambda = .0439.$$

$$\Delta\text{FIN} = \begin{array}{c} 449.0 \\ (540.0) \end{array} + \begin{array}{c} .0886\text{SALE} \\ (.0213) \end{array} - \begin{array}{c} .1034(\text{SALE} - \text{ASSALE}) \\ (.0484) \end{array}$$

$$- \begin{array}{c} .4574\text{FIN}_{-1} + e. \\ (.0970) \end{array} \qquad (14\text{b})$$

$$\bar{R}^2 = .5508,\ d = 1.47,\ \bar{S}_{\text{est}} = 104.3,\ df = 13,$$
$$\delta = .4574,\ \beta_1 = 981.6,\ \beta_2 = .1937,\ \lambda = .0950.$$

For the durable regression, the coefficient of the surprise term is less
than half the size of its standard error, but of positive sign. For nondurables, the coefficient is somewhat larger in magnitude and twice
its standard error. The implied values of the adaption coefficient, .044
for durables and .095 for nondurables, are of extremely small magnitude, suggesting that production plans are extremely flexible. It will
be observed that the estimates imply that for nondurable manufacturing an increase in sales above anticipated volume leads to a reduction
in finished goods inventory stocks, while the reverse is true for durables.
It was suggested by Modigliani and Sauerlander (1955), when they
originally tested this model, that the omission of the effect of the revision of expectations with regard to the next period's sales volume (i.e.,
the assumption that $\beta_3 = 0$) may contribute to a downward bias in the
estimation of λ. It will also be noted that the presence of the lagged
endogenous variable means that even if β_3 is in fact zero, the applica-

---

[23] This evidence appears in Lovell (1964, pp. 196–197). My approach was quite
similar to that of Modigliani and Sauerlander (1955), who had already tested with
considerable success on eleven observations on nondurable inventories this same
expression, modified by the assumption that $\beta_1 = 0$, and normalized by dividing
all terms by FIN_{-1}.

tion of least squares yields parameter estimates that are subject to Hurwicz bias, although they will constitute maximum-likelihood estimates if the stochastic disturbance is normally and independently distributed.

With the new data it is possible to elaborate on the approach of earlier studies by using observations on ALSALE as well as ASSALE in working with reduced-form equation (12). It is no longer necessary to suppress the effects of the revision of anticipations of the next period's sales volume. However, a slight complication is introduced in working with the reduced-form equation by the fact that equation (12) is "overidentified." Specifically, the direct application of least squares to equation (12) yields six regression coefficients while there are five parameters to estimate.[24] My approach has been to work with a slight modification of the standard regression procedure that yields maximum-likelihood estimates of the five parameters under the assumption that the stochastic disturbance is normally and independently distributed. This involves finding the values of λ, δ, β_1, β_2, β_3 that minimize the standard error of the estimate of:[25]

$$FIN = \lambda(ASSALE - SALE) + \delta\beta_1 + \delta\beta_2[\lambda ASSALE + (1 - \lambda)SALE] + \delta\beta_3[\lambda ALSALE + (1 - \lambda)ASSALE_{+1}] + (1 - \delta)FIN_{-1} + \epsilon. \quad (15)$$

[24] The direct application of least squares to equation (12) yields six regression coefficients. Adding the coefficient of ASSALE and SALE yields an estimate of $\delta\beta_2$. Dividing the coefficient of ASSALE by this estimate plus unity yields an estimate of λ. But a second estimate of λ may be obtained from the coefficients of $ALSALE_{+1}$ and $ASSALE_{+1}$. Thus, there is no unique way of obtaining estimates of the parameters of the model from the regression coefficients.

[25] The theory of Mann and Wald (1943), summarized by Johnston (1963), for obtaining maximum-likelihood estimates from equations involving lagged dependent variables requires a slight modification because of the restrictions upon the parameters. The problem is to find, given our sample observations, the values of the unknown parameters λ, β_1, β_2, β_3, and δ that maximize the likelihood

$$L = (2\sigma^2\pi)^{-n/2} \exp(-\sigma^{-2}/2) \sum_{t=1}^{T} \epsilon_t^2$$

where T is the number of observations and

$$\epsilon_t = FIN - \delta\beta_1 - \lambda(1 + \delta\beta_2)ASSALE - \lambda\delta\beta_3 ALSALE - (1 - \lambda)ASSALE_{+1} - [\delta\beta_2 - \lambda(\delta\beta_2 + 1)]SALE - (1 - \delta)IN_{-1};$$

IN_0 is regarded as nonstochastic. Taking logarithms reveals that maximizing L with respect to the parameters of interest is equivalent to minimizing

$$\hat{\sigma}^2 = \frac{1}{n} \sum_{t=1}^{T} [FIN - \delta\beta_1 - \lambda(1 + \delta\beta_2)ASSALE - \lambda\delta\beta_3 ALSALE_{+1} - (1 - \lambda)ASSALE_{+1} [\delta\beta_2 - \lambda(\delta\beta_2 + 1)]SALE - (1 - \delta)IN_{-1}]^2$$

The maximum-likelihood estimates of the parameters thus involves the method of least squares.

By the application of a search procedure over λ, we obtain for durable manufacturing.[26]

$$\text{FIN} = .055(\text{ASSALE} - \text{SALE}) - \quad 465.6$$
$$(1083.4)$$
$$+ .0727[.055\text{ASSALE} + .945\text{SALE}] + .0376[.055\text{ALSALE}_{+1}$$
$$(.0246) \qquad\qquad\qquad\qquad (.0273)$$
$$+ .945\text{ASSALE}_{+1}] + .6031\text{FIN}_{-1} + e. \qquad\qquad (16)$$
$$(.1338)$$
$$d = 1.31, \ \bar{S}^2 = 262.47.$$

The maximum-likelihood estimates of the parameters are $\lambda = .055$, $\delta = .397$, $\beta_1 = 1172.8$, $\beta_2 = .183$, and $\beta_3 = .095$. It must be emphasized that these estimates, as indeed those reported earlier for the case in which it was assumed that $\beta_3 = 0$, are subject to Hurwicz bias as a result of the presence of the lagged dependent variable. Furthermore, the standard errors in parentheses and the Durbin-Watson coefficient should be regarded with extreme suspicion. While the parameter estimates themselves, since they are obtained by the method of maximum likelihood, are consistent, this property can provide little solace when dealing as here with an extremely small sample. For nondurable manufacturing, we have:

$$\text{FIN} = .13(\text{ASSALE} - \text{SALE}) + \quad 543.7$$
$$(482.6)$$
$$+ .0476[.13\text{ASSALE} + .87\text{SALE}] + .0459[.13\text{ALSALE}_{+1}$$
$$(.0311) \qquad\qquad\qquad\qquad (.0255)$$
$$+ .87\text{ASSALE}_{+1}] + .507\text{FIN}_{-1} + e. \qquad\qquad (17)$$
$$(.085)$$
$$d = 1.60, \ \bar{S} = 95.5.$$

The maximum-likelihood estimates of the parameters are $\lambda = .13$, $\delta = .493$, $\beta_1 = 1102.8$, $\beta_2 = .0966$, and $\beta_3 = .0931$. It will be noted that the relaxation of the assumptions that $\beta_3 = 0$, permitted by the availability of data on ALSALE, leads to an increase in the maximum likelihood estimate of λ. This is in conformity with the conjecture of Modigliani and Sauerlander. But the increase is quite small, and the parameter estimates still imply that production plans are extremely

---

[26] Although the problem of finding maximum likelihood estimates of the unknown parameters constitutes a least-squares problem (see footnote 25), the computations cannot be performed directly by standard regression procedures unless the value of λ is specified. Since $\min\limits_{\lambda,\delta,\beta_i} \hat{\sigma} = \min\limits_{\lambda}[\min\limits_{\delta,\beta_i} \hat{\sigma}]$, the obvious approach is to search over λ for the value minimizing the standard error of the estimate. At each point in the search procedure, a regression is run for the given valued λ.

flexible. In particular, we again find for durables that an increase in current sales volume above the level anticipated for the quarter leads to an increase in finished goods inventories.

In concluding, it is interesting to contrast the results obtained with the sales anticipatory data provided by the OBE survey with the degree of success that can be obtained utilizing a proxy procedure that has sometimes been employed when anticipations variables have not been observable. By such a comparison, it will be possible to evaluate the suggestion of Modigliani and Sauerlander[27] that whatever the direct forecasting value of anticipatory data, *ex ante* sales observations may be both relevant and useful in explaining short-run inventory movements. Substitution of the actual change in sales for the forecast error in equation (13), under the assumption that errors in forecasting sales volume are proportional to actual changes, yields for durable manufacturing:

$$\Delta FIN = \quad 180.7 \; + \; .0616 SALE + \; .0106(SALE - SALE_{-1})$$
$$ (1133.6) \quad (.0394) \qquad (.0314)$$
$$ - \; .2683 FIN_{-1} + e. \tag{18a}$$
$$ (.1612)$$
$$R^2 = .2901, \; d = 1.58, \; \bar{s} = 280.89, \; df = 13.$$

For nondurables, we have:

$$\Delta FIN = \quad 306.9 \; + \; .0471 SALE + \; .0639(SALE - SALE_{-1})$$
$$ (567.9) \quad (.0300) \qquad (.0412)$$
$$ - \; .2477 FIN_{-1} + e. \tag{18b}$$
$$ (.1318)$$
$$R^2 = .4878, \; d = 1.604, \; \bar{S} = 111.3, \; df = 13.$$

In contrast to my experience with 1948–55 data, the sign of the change in sales term is positive.[28] Comparing the standard errors of the estimates with those obtained utilizing the ASSALE *ex ante* data—equations (14a) and (14b)—we find that there is virtually no effect for durables; with nondurables, on the other hand, information on ASSALE's does lead to a reduction in the standard error of the estimate over what can be achieved with the proxy procedure. The advantages of utilizing *ex ante* data are somewhat more substantial, however, when data on ALSALE are used together with ASSALE, as in regressions (18a) and (18b), for the standard error of the estimate of each

[27] 1955, p. 350.

[28] Equations (18a) and (18b) constitute a replication over a new sample period of the model originally reported in Lovell (1961).

of those equations is considerably below that obtained with the corresponding proxy procedure.[29]

A few additional complications of the basic model were examined. In particular, I considered the effects of production smoothing. This concept, which reflects the effects of costs of adjusting production schedules, is taken into account by adding the change in production as an additional explanatory variable.[30] But, in contrast to my earlier efforts, the coefficient of this term now has an inappropriate sign.

6. Aggregate Inventory Behavior

By focusing attention on the inventory aggregate, rather than partitioning inventories by stage of fabrication, it will be possible to take advantage of the observations provided by the new OBE survey on desired inventory position and anticipated inventory investment. While this approach permits the direct evaluation of a number of the basic equations discussed in section 4, it must be observed that treating inventories as a conglomeration, rather than restricting attention to finished goods inventories, constitutes a refocusing of the theoretical model. When we were considering finished goods inventory behavior, the process of plan revision involved the reorientation of production plans as developments during the quarterly observation period suggested errors in initial sales anticipations. Now that inventories are to be treated in the aggregate, the process of plan revision will concern the rescheduling of deliveries of raw materials. In this section I shall first discuss the determinants of the inventory condition variable, which constitutes an index of desired inventory position. I shall then turn to an evaluation of the planned inventory investment equation and the realization function concept. Since there are, from an econometric point of view, certain disadvantages involved in working separately with these equations, I shall conclude by applying the principle of maximum likelihood to the task of obtaining point estimates of the parameters of the model discussed in section 4. This approach will yield preferred estimates based on a larger number of degrees of freedom, an important consideration given the limited number of observations avail-

---

[29] The significance of the improvement has not been tested. Theil (1961, Ch. 6.2) has suggested that, in deciding between two alternative structures, one is more likely to select the correct one if he chooses that which gives the smallest standard error of the estimate. However, Theil's analysis is based on the assumption that the explanatory variables are nonstochastic.

[30] See Lovell (1964, p. 97).

able for the study. The results of this and earlier sections of the paper will be summarized in section 7.

The inventory condition variable, COND, is derived from the question of how the responding company views its current inventory position. Specifically, it is the excess of the proportion of respondents reporting their end of period inventory as "high" over those who regard them as "low" in relation to "total sales and the unfilled orders backlog." This attitudinal variable constitutes a rough index rather than a precise measure of the excess of actual stocks over desired inventory, discussed in section 4. The wording of the questionnaire presupposes that sales and the order backlog are the determinants of desired inventory. Given current and anticipated sales volume and the order backlog, we would expect COND to be larger the higher the current inventory stock; given the level of current inventories, we would expect COND to be inversely related to sales and orders.

For the durable aggregate, we have:

$$\text{COND} = 32.55 + .000044\text{SALE} - .0028\text{ASSALE}_{+1}$$
$$(54.05) \quad (.000736) \quad\quad (.0007)$$
$$- .0035\text{ALSALE}_{+2} - .00032\text{UOR} + .0090\text{IN} + e.$$
$$(.0009) \quad\quad\quad (.00082) \quad\quad (.0024) \quad\quad\quad (19a)$$
$$\bar{R}^2 = .638, \, d = 1.93, \, \bar{S}_{\text{est}} = 5.66, \, df = 12.$$

With the exception of the SALE variable, which is exceedingly small relative to its standard error, all the coefficients are of the anticipated sign. It is interesting to observe that the coefficient of UOR is quite small relative to its standard error; while this is not consistent with other empirical studies which have suggested that unfilled orders are a critical determinant of inventory investment, it is possible that in earlier studies the important role attributed to unfilled orders actually resulted from its influence upon expectations rather than as a direct determinant of inventory position.[31] When the unfilled orders term is dropped from the regression, the coefficient of SALE assumes the anticipated negative sign. Equations of the same form as (19a), but without the unfilled orders variable, were fitted to the data for the individual component durable industries; practically all the coefficients were of the anticipated sign, although the fits were poorer in several industries than for the aggregate.

---

[31] This point will be elaborated upon in the second part of section 6.

The nondurable regression is unsatisfactory:

$$COND = 82.85 - .0058SALE + .0032ASSALE_{+1}$$
$$(93.81) \quad (.0046) \quad\quad (.0045)$$
$$- .0033ALSALE_{+2} - .0098UOR + .0121IN + e. \quad\quad (19b)$$
$$(.0053) \quad\quad\quad (.0110) \quad\quad (.0154)$$
$$\bar{R}^2 = .0601, d = .5513, \bar{S}_{est} = 7.77, df = 12.$$

The coefficient of multiple determination is exceedingly small; none of the explanatory variables is significant. The component nondurable industry regressions were, for the most part, equally unsatisfactory; even the inventory term had the wrong sign in a number of cases.

How is this evidence to be interpreted? The wording of the questionnaire *presupposes* that sales and unfilled orders are the determinants of desired inventories. Consequently, the success in explaining the COND variable in the durable sector in terms of these variables does not suffice to establish that they in fact are the major determinants of desired inventory position, although the insignificant coefficient for the unfilled order backlog suggests that this variable is not of critical importance. Conversely, given that respondents are asked about the condition of inventories relative to sales and orders, the unsatisfactory results for nondurables do not suffice to demonstrate that desired inventory position is not determined by sales and orders. Perhaps the difficulty stems from working with a variable that is not weighted by size of firm. Nonetheless, it is disappointing to find that the COND variable, the first index that we have of desired inventory position,[32] cannot be explained in nondurables by the variables customarily assumed in many prior empirical studies to be the determinants of desired inventory. Essentially the same results are obtained when the COND variable is regressed upon the ratios of SALE − ASSALE, ALSALE, and UOR to IN, suggesting that the difficulties do not stem from the linear specification of regressions (19a) and (19b).

ANTICIPATED INVENTORY INVESTMENT

In earlier studies of inventory behavior it was not possible to test directly the determinants of planned inventory investment, for that variable had not been observed prior to the new OBE survey. It will be remembered from equation (8) that we argued that planned inventory investment should be a linear function of current anticipations with regard to sales volume expected in the next two quarters and the

---

[32] An indirect measure of surplus inventories for a number of durable industries was presented in Lovell (1961).

lagged inventory stock. But because we are now dealing with total inventories, including purchased materials and goods in process as well as finished goods, the hypothesis that anticipated inventory is also influenced by the backlog of unfilled orders also deserves consideration, for earlier empirical studies have suggested that this variable is an important determinant of inventory investment.

Turning first to planned inventory investment for durable manufacturing, we obtain:

$$ASIN - IN_{-1} = 1639.9 + .0959ASSALE + .0936ALSALE_{+1}$$
$$(2041.8) \quad (.0262) \quad\quad (.0357)$$
$$- .0102UOR - .3320IN_{-1} + e. \quad\quad (20a)$$
$$(.0349) \quad\quad (.0860)$$
$$\bar{R}^2 = .5161, \; dw = 2.38, \; \bar{S} = 215.2, \; df = 13,$$
$$\beta_1 = 4939., \; \beta_2 = .2889, \; \beta_3 = .2819, \; \beta_4 = -.0307, \; \delta = .3320.$$

For nondurables, we have:

$$ASIN - IN_{-1} = 2284.1 + .0679ASSALE + .0012ALSALE_{+1}$$
$$(1093.1) \quad (.0364) \quad\quad (.0494)$$
$$- .0980UOR - .2593IN_{-1} + e. \quad\quad (20b)$$
$$(.1431) \quad\quad (.0983)$$
$$\bar{R}^2 = .3893, \; dw = 2.24, \; \bar{S} = 97.8, \; df = 13,$$
$$\beta_1 = 8809., \; \beta_2 = .2619, \; \beta_3 = .0046, \; \beta_4 = -.3779, \; \delta = .2593.$$

It will be observed that both the short and the long anticipatory sales terms have the anticipated sign; for durables, their regression coefficients are large relative to their standard errors. The estimated values of δ, the speed of adjustment coefficient, suggests that durable manufacturing firms plan to correct approximately one-third of their inventory imbalance, on the average, within the quarter; for nondurables, the coefficient is one-quarter. These coefficients are somewhat larger than those obtained in earlier studies.

The surprising factor is the negative coefficient for unfilled orders. The appropriate test is one-tailed, and the evidence suggests that we should reject the hypothesis that unfilled orders have a direct influence on planned inventory investment. In an earlier study I argued:[33]

If unfilled orders represent an established demand, indeed a possible committal to deliver at some future date, entrepreneurs may well consider it advisable to carry additional stocks when unfilled orders are large as a hedge against possible shortage and price commitments. In addition, a rise in the

[33] 1961, p. 298.

TABLE 5

Durable Manufacturing: Regression Coefficients of Inventory Equations

ASIN on C, ASSALE, ALSALE +1, IN -1	Durables							Aggregate Regression	Pooled Regression	Separate Intercept Regression
	1	2	3	4	5	6	7			
Degrees of freedom	14	14	14	14	14	14	14	14	122	116
R^2 adjusted	0.8142	0.8769	0.9087	0.8944	0.7441	0.8386	0.8188	0.9646	0.9958	0.9961
Standard error	81.74	24.26	91.83	86.90	140.05	79.55	85.75	208.09	96.47	93.22
Durbin-Watson coefficient	1.400	2.270	1.843	1.738	2.064	1.569	1.479	2.297	1.918	1.796
Variable 1	886.166	-25.513	189.167	1455.497	250.897	643.093	412.936	1144.104	21.812	336.505
	363.397	170.092	336.452	466.694	423.031	742.566	274.426	1096.570	21.978	102.648
Variable 2	-0.053	-0.041	0.099	0.031	0.003	0.085	-0.202	0.094	-0.040	-0.024
	0.026	0.113	0.091	0.052	0.040	0.131	0.116	0.024	0.012	0.015
Variable 3	-0.036	0.007	0.121	0.175	0.075	-0.117	-0.048	0.088	0.038	0.045
	0.036	0.099	0.120	0.057	0.037	0.136	0.094	0.028	0.012	0.016
Variable 4	0.806	1.058	0.609	0.473	0.743	0.860	1.168	0.681	0.985	0.845
	0.106	0.104	0.194	0.121	0.198	0.114	0.193	0.071	0.012	0.044

$F = 1.77$ with 24, 98 degrees of freedom if all coefficients are identical.

$F = 1.49$ with 18, 98 degrees of freedom if all coefficients are identical except intercepts.

TABLE 6

Nondurable Manufacturing: Regression Coefficients of Inventory Equations

ASIN on C, ASSALE, ALSALE$_{+1}$, IN$_{-1}$	Nondurables							Aggregate Regression	Pooled Regression	Separate Intercept Regression
	1	2	3	4	5	6	7			
Degrees of freedom	14	14	14	14	14	14	14	14	122	116
R^2 adjusted	0.7163	0.6934	0.9686	0.9483	0.2172	0.7899	0.7284	0.9896	0.9875	0.9893
Standard error	158.24	84.64	19.28	51.32	87.44	30.88	118.69	95.92	140.47	130.35
Durbin-Watson coefficient	2.365	1.629	1.928	2.092	1.401	1.429	1.672	2.079	2.049	1.943
Variable 1	532.318	438.817	119.225	1776.183	1455.869	268.297	635.568	1637.143	57.716	869.959
	809.116	395.389	73.642	285.329	850.984	114.689	442.620	539.879	35.834	201.711
Variable 2	0.522	0.083	-0.133	-0.073	-0.131	-0.277	-0.412	0.077	-0.016	0.029
	0.102	0.153	0.076	0.051	0.097	0.097	0.097	0.033	0.044	0.046
Variable 3	-0.394	-0.342	0.251	0.293	0.125	0.229	0.289	-0.018	0.024	0.046
	0.095	0.175	0.082	0.064	0.069	0.106	0.079	0.040	0.044	0.044
Variable 4	0.519	1.197	0.674	0.164	0.572	0.822	1.067	0.782	0.954	0.535
	0.159	0.211	0.125	0.137	0.309	0.157	0.262	0.077	0.024	0.095

$F = 8.04$ with 24, 98 degrees of freedom if all coefficients are identical.

$F = 7.80$ with 18, 98 degrees of freedom if all coefficients are identical except intercepts.

backlog of unfilled orders may be expected to lead to an acceleration of production that is felt first in terms of an increase of goods in process. . . .

In my earlier investigation with 1948–55 data, and in subsequent studies, the unfilled orders term generally appeared with a highly significant positive coefficient. Because anticipated sales volume was not measured, the question of whether unfilled orders have a direct influence upon desired inventories or only an indirect one through the influence of the order backlog upon anticipated sales volume remained open. It now appears that, if unfilled orders influence inventory investment, it is only indirectly, via their effect upon sales anticipations, rather than as a direct determinant of the desired inventory stock.

Let us now turn to the individual industries. The results of running regression (8) on the seven durable and seven nondurable industries are reported in Tables 5 and 6, respectively. Each column of the tables constitutes a regression. The first seven regressions report results for the individual industries identified in Table 1. The aggregate regression was run on data obtained by summing for each observation over all seven component industries. The pooled regression was obtained by pooling the observations for the component industries under the assumption that there are no interindustry differences in the parameters of the realization function. The separate intercept regression was also run on pooled data, but with industry dummy variables introduced. The standard error of the estimate and the coefficient of multiple determination are adjusted for degrees of freedom. The regression coefficients, with standard errors immediately below, appear in the middle of the table. The two F-statistics provide an approximate test of the hypothesis that there are no interindustry differences in the parameters of the realization function.[34]

The evidence is rather mixed. While they conform with what was expected in certain industries, we find that for several industries the regression coefficients relating planned inventory to short- and longer-run sales anticipations are not both of the expected positive sign; for one durable and two nondurable industries, the negative coefficient is more than twice its standard error in magnitude. Furthermore, the estimated δ coefficients are slightly negative in two durable and two nondurable industries. While the F-statistic is sufficiently low in durable

---

[34] In order for the F-test to be precise, it would be necessary (but not sufficient) for the disturbances to be free of serial and interindustry correlation and that their variance be the same in all industries. The Durbin-Watson statistics for the pooled regression were not computed with precision in that the computer program treated the sequences of observations from successive industries as a single time series.

manufacturing to suggest that the hypothesis of no interindustry differences in the parameter values is tenable, the pooled regressions yield negative point estimates of β_2. It is conceivable, of course, that β_2 should in fact be zero. After all, the inventory planned for the end of the current quarter, ASIN, consists of goods to be available in subsequent periods; so the forward-looking firm may well plan its end-of-quarter inventory with regard to sales anticipated in the succeeding rather than the current quarter, i.e., ALSALE rather than ASSALE. But this rationalization does not serve to explain negative values of β_3.

THE REALIZATION FUNCTION

As explained in section 4, the realization function appears in its most elementary form in theoretical models of the inventory cycle. It is customarily assumed in constructing such cycle models that inventory investment deviates from its planned level as stocks are run down when entrepreneurs are surprised by a sales volume that exceeds anticipations—this is equation (4). For purposes of evaluating this elementary realization function concept, consider the following regression equation:

$$\text{IN} = b_1 + b_2\text{ASIN} - b_3(\text{SALE} - \text{ASSALE}) + \epsilon. \qquad (21)$$

The version of the realization function employed in inventory cycle models requires that b_2 and b_3 equal unity, for no allowance is made for the revision of production plans or delivery schedules within the production planning period. It will be noted that if $b_1 = 0$, equation (21) constitutes a special case of equation (11) in which $\beta_3 = 0$; i.e., desired end-of-period inventory depends only upon current rather than the next period's sales.

The results of fitting equation (21) on individual durable and nondurable industries and the aggregates are presented in Tables 7 and 8. Clearly, they are not in conformity with the elementary formulation of the realization function underlying the theory of the inventory cycle, for while the coefficient of ASIN is always fairly close to unity, the coefficient of the surprise term is of extremely small magnitude and indeed positive in a majority of the regressions. The low values of the F-statistics suggest that pooling the data may not be inappropriate, but the results of the combined regressions yield a negative coefficient for the surprise term only for nondurables, and here the coefficient is statistically insignificant and of such small magnitude as to suggest that errors in anticipating future sales volume have a negligible effect in explaining deviations of inventories from their planned level. Small

TABLE 7

Durable Manufacturing: Regression Coefficients of Realization Functions

IN on C, ASIN, SALE-ASSALE	Durables							Aggregate Regression	Pooled Regression	Separate Intercept Regression
	1	2	3	4	5	6	7			
Degrees of freedom	14	14	14	14	14	14	14	14	116	110
R^2 adjusted	0.7728	0.8410	0.9490	0.8987	0.8697	0.7658	0.9350	0.9632	0.9971	0.9973
Standard error	100.59	22.08	68.39	86.62	89.17	98.86	52.22	200.82	81.56	78.28
Durbin-Watson coefficient	1.343	1.535	1.300	1.221	1.409	1.925	1.920	1.241	1.332	1.473
Variable 1	102.463	387.649	-28.446	428.445	215.668	409.565	18.984	384.263	-6.841	113.005
	346.610	101.841	244.725	525.423	296.709	492.778	184.957	1180.032	19.013	95.997
Variable 2	0.967	0.702	1.028	0.954	0.969	0.908	1.011	1.004	1.022	0.977
	0.129	0.892	0.061	0.083	0.094	0.126	0.067	0.049	0.005	0.034
Variable 3	0.024	-0.141	-0.060	0.329	0.168	0.004	0.011	0.160	0.101	0.084
	0.081	0.890	0.184	0.114	0.117	0.164	0.088	0.070	0.042	0.041

$F = 1.50$ with 18, 98 degrees of freedom if all coefficients are identical.

$F = 0.93$ with 12, 98 degrees of freedom if all coefficients are identical except intercepts.

TABLE 8

Nondurable Manufacturing: Regression Coefficients of Realization Functions

IN on C, ASIN SALE-ASSALE	Nondurables							Aggregate Regression	Pooled Regression	Separate Intercept Regression
	1	2	3	4	5	6	7			
Degrees of freedom	14	14	14	14	14	14	14	14	116	110
R^2 adjusted	0.9216	0.8752	0.9043	0.9348	0.7440	0.8711	0.7823	0.9614	0.9976	0.9976
Standard error	78.94	54.38	33.64	64.00	43.57	27.58	99.59	181.04	63.56	63.53
Durbin-Watson coefficient	1.370	2.085	2.066	1.641	1.658	0.956	2.315	2.874	1.880	1.891
Variable 1	-14.134	400.746	35.683	-545.746	610.794	-127.006	395.888	-1067.945	-26.122	102.144
	414.231	248.189	132.359	319.067	400.111	125.256	358.161	1128.955	15.229	107.400
Variable 2	1.029	0.865	0.991	1.155	0.831	1.126	0.888	1.070	1.028	0.983
	0.083	0.893	0.081	0.077	0.120	0.109	0.116	0.054	0.005	0.035
Variable 3	-0.086	0.200	0.042	0.085	0.015	-0.006	-0.117	0.156	-0.019	-0.017
	0.099	0.102	0.099	0.076	0.062	0.110	0.118	0.080	0.034	0.035

$F = 1.31$ with 18, 98 degrees of freedom if all coefficients are identical.

$F = 1.43$ with 12, 98 degrees of freedom if all coefficients are identical except intercepts.

TABLE 9

Durable Manufacturing: Regression Coefficients of Realization Functions with Anticipation Revision Term

IN on C, ASIN, SALE-ASSALE, ASSALE+1 - ALSALE+1	Durables							Aggregate Regression	Pooled Regression	Separate Intercept Regression
	1	2	3	4	5	6	7			
Degrees of freedom	13	13	13	13	13	13	13	13	115	109
R^2 adjusted	0.8233	0.8537	0.9502	0.8925	0.8707	0.8437	0.9337	0.9662	0.9971	0.9973
Standard error	88.70	21.18	67.64	89.24	88.81	80.77	52.72	192.31	81.92	78.56
Durbin-Watson coefficient	0.898	1.638	1.192	1.278	1.311	1.860	2.072	1.833	1.330	1.462
Variable 1	562.224	287.350	-171.474	380.893	55.212	665.758	-10.308	-1190.155	-6.563	126.446
	368.321	118.038	272.308	552.120	332.251	412.724	189.803	1539.724	19.574	100.967
Variable 2	0.808	0.778	1.063	0.962	1.017	0.844	1.021	1.068	1.022	0.972
	0.134	0.894	0.068	0.087	0.104	0.105	0.069	0.063	0.005	0.036
Variable 3	-0.117	0.836	0.211	0.363	0.199	-0.379	0.115	0.262	0.100	0.072
	0.095	0.147	0.298	0.141	0.120	0.191	0.150	0.096	0.049	0.048
Variable 4	0.096	-0.818	-0.189	-0.045	-0.044	0.416	-0.087	-0.082	0.001	0.010
	0.043	0.146	0.165	0.103	0.041	0.147	0.102	0.055	0.021	0.022

F = 2.12 with 24, 91 degrees of freedom if all coefficients are identical.

F = 1.82 with 18, 91 degrees of freedom if all coefficients are identical except intercepts.

TABLE 10

Nondurable Manufacturing: Regression Coefficients of Realization Functions with Anticipation Revision Term

IN on C, ASIN, SALE-ASSALE, ASSALE +1 − ALSALE +1	Nondurables							Aggregate Regression	Pooled Regression	Separate Intercept Regression
	1	2	3	4	5	6	7			
Degrees of freedom	13	13	13	13	13	13	13	13	115	109
R^2 adjusted	0.9294	0.8637	0.9024	0.9365	0.7857	0.8678	0.7698	0.9596	0.9975	0.9975
Standard error	74.90	56.40	33.97	63.19	39.86	27.92	102.41	185.09	63.82	63.75
Durbin-Watson coefficient	1.181	2.049	2.059	1.941	1.535	0.737	2.543	2.974	1.873	1.872
Variable 1	-13.887	411.257	0.920	-374.713	677.647	-72.980	308.648	-1585.096	-25.733	115.713
	393.072	274.090	139.701	347.438	367.689	143.224	409.427	1417.921	15.382	111.711
Variable 2	1.027	0.862	1.013	1.114	0.811	1.078	0.915	1.095	1.028	0.979
	0.079	0.202	0.086	0.084	0.111	0.125	0.132	0.068	0.005	0.036
Variable 3	-0.278	0.279	0.142	-0.043	0.085	-0.164	-0.066	0.232	-0.027	-0.034
	0.152	0.210	0.154	0.132	0.067	0.225	0.161	0.146	0.050	0.052
Variable 4	0.167	0.023	-0.134	0.116	-0.099	0.111	-0.066	-0.069	0.009	0.019
	0.105	0.196	0.156	0.100	0.051	0.136	0.135	0.111	0.039	0.041

F = 1.31 with 24, 91 degrees of freedom if all coefficients are identical.
F = 1.37 with 18, 91 degrees of freedom if all coefficients are identical except intercepts.

negative values of the coefficient of the surprise term suggest that plans are exceedingly flexible. The positive coefficients, it will be remembered from section 4, imply that plans are so flexible that stocks can actually be increased when the sales volume has been under-estimated. Thus the evidence suggests that firms are exceedingly adept at adjusting schedules for the delivery of raw materials when develop-ments during the quarter reveal errors in initial anticipations of sales volume.[35]

This elementary version of the realization function may also be used to explain the discrepancy between ALIN and actual inventory invest-ment in terms of the discrepancy between SALE and ALSALE. This involves a three-month longer planning horizon, for the ALIN and ALSALE *ex ante* data are collected approximately five months before the end of the quarter to which the actual realizations refer. Essentially the same results were obtained. The sales forecast error term had the anticipated negative sign in only one durable and four nondurable industries. As might be expected, the realization function yields a poorer fit with the longer planning horizon.

Since the OBE survey provides data on longer-run sales anticipa-tions, it is possible to relax the assumption that desired end-of-period inventories depend only upon current sales, that $\beta_3 = 0$ in equation (11). Tables 9 and 10 report the regressions obtained when the anticipation revision term is added to the elementary realization function concept. The results are rather disappointing, for the coeffi-cient of the anticipation revision term, $\text{ASSALE}_{+1} - \text{ALSALE}_{+1}$, has an incorrect negative sign in a number of these regressions. The coeffi-cient has the correct sign for the pooled durable and nondurable regres-sions, but is insignificant. Reasonably satisfactory results are obtained for durable industries 1 and 6 (iron and steel, and transportation equipment) and nondurable industries 1, 2, 4, and 6 (food, textiles, chemicals, and rubber). For the other industries we must argue that $\beta_3 = 0$, on the grounds that a one-tailed test is appropriate.[36]

---

[35] It should be observed that the R^2's are inflated in that if the coefficient of ASIN is constrained to unity, the change in inventory being regressed upon the error in anticipating sales volume, a much lower value of R^2 is obtained; for example, the coefficient of multiple determination for the durable manufacturing aggregate is reduced from .96 to .22; further, the adjusted coefficient of multiple determination is negative for a number of industries.

[36] In order to verify that the difficulties did not stem from the presence of sea-sonality in the data, the equations were refitted with seasonal dummy variables included; the only improvement was to correct the sign of b_3 for other durables and the paper industries, but the coefficients were not significant. This is equivalent to filtering out a constant seasonal pattern in advance of running the regression.

There are, of course, other aspects of the firm's environment in addition to sales volume that may lead to a revision of planned inventory accumulation. In particular, an increase in unfilled orders might well be expected to generate an increase in purchased materials and goods in process inventory. If we postulate that unfilled orders are a factor influencing desired inventory, the change in unfilled orders should be added to equation (11). The following estimates were obtained when this regression was run on the durable aggregates.

$$IN = -1392.4 + 1.0757ASIN + .2735(SALE - ASSALE)$$
$$(1665.5) \quad (.0680) \quad\quad (.1026)$$
$$- .0952(ASSALE_{+1} - ALSALE_{+1}) + .0153(UOR - UOR_{-1}) + e.$$
$$(.0645) \quad\quad\quad\quad (.0374)$$

$$R^2 = .9639, \, dw = 1.79, \, \bar{S}_{est} = 198.8, \, df = 12. \quad\quad (22a)$$

For nondurables, we have:

$$IN = -1735.4 + 1.1024ASIN + .2119(SALE - ASSALE)$$
$$(1424.0) \quad (0.678) \quad\quad (.1474)$$

$$- .0924(ASSALE_{+1} - ALSALE_{+1}) + .2434(UOR - UOR_{-1}).$$
$$(.1128) \quad\quad\quad\quad (.2399)$$

$$R^2 = .9597, \, dw = 2.79, \, \bar{S}_{est} = 184.9, \, df = 12. \quad\quad (22b)$$

While the coefficient of the change in unfilled orders term has the expected sign, it is in both cases small relative to its standard error. Further, the first surprise term, SALE − ASSALE, again has the positive coefficient implying extreme plan revision while the second surprise term has the inappropriate negative sign.

A possible explanation for the limited success with the realization concept is provided by Murray Foss's earlier analysis of the data. He suggested that the anticipated inventory figure may be at least in part a target figure rather than an attempted forecast. When inventory stocks are thought to be excessive, the anticipated inventory figure may be deliberately set at a low level in an effort to discourage purchasing agents and other departments from accumulating stock. If there were a consistent understatement, its effect would be absorbed by the constant term in the regression; in any case, the anticipated inventory figures are not consistently biased downward. It is possible, however, that the magnitude of such an effect hinges upon whether current inventories are regarded as excessive or deficient. Consequently, I fitted the following regression to the data:

$$IN = b_1 + b_2ASIN + b_3(SALE - ASSALE) + b_4COND_{-1}. \quad (23)$$

It will be remembered that the variable COND denotes the excess of the proportion of respondents who report stocks excessive over those who regard them as deficient. Again, b_3, the coefficient of the surprise term, has a positive sign in the majority of cases; contrary to hypothesis, the coefficient of the inventory condition variable was generally negative. Similar results were obtained when the anticipation revision term, $ASSALE_{+1} - ALSALE_{+1}$ was added to equation (23).

MAXIMUM-LIKELIHOOD PARAMETER ESTIMATES

The investigations of the determinants of inventory conditions, of ASIN, and of the realization function have been based on an extremely limited number of observations. Furthermore, the approach has not yielded much information about the magnitude of the parameter λ measuring the extent of plan inflexibility. The anticipated inventory position regressions in the second part of section 6 do not yield any information about the extent to which plans are revised as errors in initial sales anticipations become apparent during the quarter. The realization function construct, examined in the third part of section 6, does not yield a point estimate of λ, although it was possible to infer that plans are subject to quite extensive revision. Of course, it might be possible to use the coefficients obtained from the anticipated inventory regressions in conjunction with the realization function regressions in order to estimate this parameter. But there exists an alternative procedure that yields maximum-likelihood estimates of all the parameters of the inventory model—λ, δ, β_1, β_2, and β_3. An advantage of this method is that the estimates are based on a larger number of degrees of freedom, an important consideration in view of the small number of observations available for the study.

Our strategy, which is analogous to that employed in section 5 when working with finished goods inventories, is easily understood if we first consider a slightly simpler problem. Suppose that the magnitude of the parameter λ were known. We could then proceed to rewrite equation (10) in the form:

$$[IN - \lambda(ASIN + ASSALE - SALE)] = \delta\beta_1[1 - \lambda]$$
$$+ \delta\beta_2[(1 - \lambda)SALE] + \delta\beta_3[(1 - \lambda)ASSALE_{+1}]$$
$$+ (1 - \delta)[(1 - \lambda)IN_{-1}] + \epsilon_7. \quad (24)$$

Given the value of λ, the expressions in brackets could be utilized as the variables in a regression yielding estimates of the other parameters, δ, β_1, β_2, and β_3. But the coefficients of equation (25) are identical to those of equation (8). Thus, it would be possible, knowing λ, to

TABLE 11

Maximum-Likelihood Parameter Estimates

	λ	$\delta\beta_1$	$\delta\beta_2$	$\delta\beta_3$	δ	β_1	β_2	β_3	$\bar{S}_{est}$
Durables									
1	.10	371.9	0	.043	.2054	1810	0	.2093	116.2
2	.08	2.462	.0859*	0	.1061	23.20	.8096	0	24.5
3	.68	171.1	.1581*	.1427*	.5070	337.5	.3118	.2815	102.4
4	0	1709**	.0535	.1514**	.5536	3087	.0966	.2735	131.1
5	0	600.9*	.0200	.0892**	.4117	1460	.0486	.2167	140.0
6	.08	66.15	.0090	.0584	.0946	699.3	.0951	.6173	99.8
7	0	309.6	0	.0520	.1749	1770	0	.2973	97.4
Aggregate	0	2374*	.0975**	.0721**	.3411	6960	.2858	.2114	363.9
Pooled	.11	12.37	0	.0262**	.0421	293.8	0	.6223	120.6
Separate intercept	.06	419.1**	0	.0760**	.2464	1701	0	.3084	111.1
Nondurables									
1	.10	409.8	.2004**	0	.6644	616.8	.3016	0	204.0
2	0	803.8	0	0	.2978	2699	0	0	110.3
3	.05	187.9**	0	.1613**	.4505	417.1	0	.3580	30.9
4	.15	1926**	0	.2428**	.8997	2141	0	.2699	91.3
5	.14	1472**	0	.1251	.8004	1839	0	.1563	80.2
6	.22	229.8**	0	.2237**	.5146	446.6	0	.4347	37.2
7	.11	724.5*	0	.2699**	.8812	822.2	0	.3063	151.0
Aggregate	0	1597	.0666	0	.2257	7076	.2951	0	258.7
Pooled	.29	42.0	0	.0043	.0248	1694	0	.1734	138.8
Separate intercept	.20	865.1**	.0323	.0765**	.5361	1614	.0602	.1427	127.5

Note: The single and double asterisks indicate that the regression procedure yielded coefficients at least two or three times their standard errors in magnitude.

pool the two sets of observations in a single regression.[37] Since there are seventeen observations on the variables entering into equation (10)

[37] This would be difficult if the regression program automatically introduced the intercept. The program utilized introduces an intercept by having the first explanatory variable a column of ones. For this application, then, the first variable consists of ones through the observations on equation (8) and then $[1 - \lambda]$ for the observations on equation (24).

and eighteen on the variables of equation (8), this approach would increase the total number of observations available to thirty-five. Even if we knew λ, of course, pooling the two sets of data might not be appropriate if the disturbances of equations (8) and (10) were not independently distributed. But it is reasonable to assume that this independence condition is satisfied, for the disturbance ϵ_5 of the ASIN equation arises from variables omitted in explaining the generation of beginning-of-period inventory anticipations, while the other disturbance, ϵ_7, results from variables omitted from an equation describing a quite different process, namely, the way in which discrepancies between anticipated and actual inventory are generated by errors in anticipating sales volume. If ϵ_5 and ϵ_7 are independently and normally distributed with equal variances, and λ is known, the application of the straightforward regression approach to the pooled thirty-five observations simultaneously will yield maximum-likelihood estimates of the parameters of the model; such an estimation strategy could be expected to yield more efficient parameter estimates than the regressions reported in the second part of section 6 because of the information provided by the seventeen additional observations.

But how can we proceed when λ is unknown? The application of the maximum-likelihood principle reveals that the appropriate procedure is to search over values of λ, running the pooled regression for each value of λ considered. The value of λ yielding the smallest standard error of the estimate constitutes the maximum-likelihood estimate; maximum-likelihood estimates of the other parameters of the model are provided from the coefficients obtained from that regression.[38] The

[38] Under the assumption that the disturbances of equation (8) are normally and independently distributed, the likelihood of obtaining the n observed values of ASIN is

$$L_5 = \left(\frac{1}{\sigma_{\epsilon_5} \sqrt{2\pi}} \right)^n \exp\left(1 - \frac{1}{2\sigma_{\epsilon_5}^2} \Sigma\epsilon_5^2 \right),$$

where the disturbance ϵ_5 is a function of observed variables and the unknown parameters (except) as given by equation (8). Similarly, the likelihood of obtaining the n' observed values of IN is

$$L_7 = \left(\frac{1}{\sigma_{\epsilon_7} \sqrt{2\pi}} \right)^{n'} \exp\left(- \frac{1}{2\sigma_{\epsilon_7}^2} \Sigma\epsilon_7^2 \right),$$

where the disturbance ϵ_7 is a function of observed variables and the unknown parameters as given by equation (10). The likelihood of obtaining the combined set of observations, assuming as we have that ϵ_5 and ϵ_7 are independently distributed, is simply $L = L_5 L_7$. Taking logarithms, we have

$$\log L = \text{constant} - \frac{1}{2\sigma_{\epsilon_5}^2} \Sigma\epsilon_5^2 - \frac{1}{2\sigma_{\epsilon_7}^2} \Sigma\epsilon_7^2; \text{ consequently,}$$

the values of δ, β_1, β_2, β_3, and λ that maximize L also minimize

$$\sigma = (\Sigma\epsilon_5^2 + \rho\Sigma\epsilon_7^2)/(n + n') \text{ where } \rho = \sigma_{\epsilon_5}^2/\sigma_{\epsilon_7}^2.$$

estimates derived by this procedure, presented in Table 11, were obtained subject to the constraints that β_2 and β_3 be nonnegative and that λ be nonnegative and no greater than unity.[39] These estimates are likely to be subject to Hurwicz bias, because of the presence of the lagged inventory stock in equation (24). They are asymptotically unbiased and consistent; provided the homoscedasticity condition is met, they should be efficient or nearly so.[40] The estimates for the fourteen component industries and the durable and nondurable aggregates are based on thirty-five observations; those obtained by pooling the data over industries are based on 245 observations. I have not applied the likelihood ratio test procedure appropriate for testing hypotheses; the single and double asterisks over the various parameter estimates indicate that the regression procedure yielded coefficients that were at least two or three times, respectively, their standard errors in magnitude, but these should be interpreted with extreme caution.

Examination of the table reveals that the λ coefficient is exceedingly small in most instances, suggesting that plans are subject to extremely rapid revision. Indeed, the parameter is estimated to have a zero value in three durable industries and one nondurable, implying that ASIN is irrelevant in the determination of end-of-quarter inventory position. The evidence suggests that schedules for the delivery of raw materials are, for the most part, subject to extremely sharp revision during the quarterly observation period, when actual sales deviate from their anticipated level. The only notable exception is durable industry 6, electrical machinery, for which $\lambda = .68$. It will be noted that a number of the β_2 coefficients are zero, particularly in nondurables. As may be seen from inspection of equation (4), this implies that desired end-of-period inventories are not affected by current sales volume, a not unreasonable result. The zero values of β_3, on the other hand, do not appear

---

[39] Because of the restriction $0 \leq \lambda \leq 1$ and the unimodal nature of the minimization problem, it was possible to economize on the computations by employing a Fibonacci search procedure. For a description of this procedure, see Wilde (1964).

[40] Inspection of the residuals for the individual industries suggested that this homogeneity assumption was not grossly violated. If it had, the estimates obtained from the residuals of ρ would have been used in an application of the theory of weighted regression in order to obtain maximum-likelihood estimates. It is interesting to observe that *if* the variance of the disturbance term of equation (8) is exceedingly small, relative to that of equation (10), so that ρ is close to zero, the appropriate weighted regression procedure is equivalent to the use of equation (8) to estimate all of the parameters except λ; an estimate of λ is then obtained with a regression based on equation (10), after simplification with the aid of the parameter estimates obtained earlier of the other parameters; this is, in essence, the two-stage procedure used by Gordon R. Sparks in his paper on residential building cycles in this volume. At the other extreme, when ρ is close to infinity, all the parameters would be estimated from equation (10).

reasonable, for they imply that firms do not look to the future in considering what level of inventories is appropriate.

7. Summary and Conclusions

In econometric work we are rarely presented with the opportunity of replicating earlier empirical studies with new data. Given the notorious difficulties involved in attempting to test hypotheses on time series data, the opportunity to replicate prior studies must be welcomed. In this instance, however, the effort has been full of surprises, and in a number of areas we find that points that appeared to be at least tentatively established in earlier work are now open to serious question.

With regard to sales anticipations, the early studies of *ex ante* data had suggested that entrepreneurs' expectations of future sales volume are so imprecise as to yield aggregate anticipations data which are of no direct forecasting value. At the same time, it was concluded that such data might be of considerable use when harnessed with other variables in econometric models involving explicit assumptions about firm behavior. Both of these conclusions now seem questionable. The analysis of the new OBE sales anticipations data presented in section 3 reveals that short-run sales forecasts are considerably more accurate than the earlier studies, based largely on the railroad shippers' forecast data, had suggested. In contrast to the old data, the OBE sales anticipations do considerably better than the Ferber naive model at predicting actual sales volume. The high positive correlations between anticipated and actual changes stand in marked contrast to the negative results of earlier studies. On the other hand, it was found in section 5 that only a marginal improvement could be obtained by using observations on sales anticipations in a model describing the generation of finished goods inventories, rather than resorting to a proxy procedure. Since only a limited number of observations have accumulated for our study, undue pessimism may not be warranted at this time. But the evidence now available suggests that, while sales anticipations are more accurate than the earlier studies had led us to believe, observations on anticipated sales volume may be less useful than we had been led to hope in helping to explain such variables as inventory investment within the context of econometric models.

A second surprise concerns the impact upon inventory position of errors that are made by firms in anticipating sales volume. If firms actually made the substantial errors in forecasting sales volume that the earlier studies suggested, it would doubtless be extremely difficult for them to move far in the direction of error correction within our three-month observation period. But since forecast errors are small in magnitude, error correction is feasible. The evidence suggests that production plans and schedules for the delivery of raw materials are sufficiently flexible to permit considerable adjustment within the quarter to whatever errors are made in forecasting sales volume.

This evidence on the extent of error correction strikes at a basic assumption underlying theoretical models of the inventory cycle. Lloyd Metzler has stated: "The only indispensable assumption in the theory of the inventory cycles is that businessmen do not immediately adapt their production plan to a change in sales."[41] He estimated that the average planning period, the time interval underlying his analysis, has a duration of approximately five months. In examining certain empirical implications of my multisector extension of the Metzler model, I assumed that the average planning period was of three months duration.[42] In contrast, the new evidence suggests that if the planning period is on the order of two or three months duration, then plans must be regarded as being subject to extreme modifications as developments during the quarter reveal errors in anticipating such variables as sales volume. The estimates presented in section 5 suggest that production plans are flexible enough for durable manufacturing to permit an actual *increase* in finished goods inventories when sales volume has been underestimated. Schedules for the delivery of purchased materials, the analysis of section 6 suggests, are so flexible in many industries that terminal inventory stock is virtually unaffected by beginning-of-quarter anticipations of inventories and sales volume.[43] The fact that inventory investment does not lead the cycle must be explained by the willingness of firms to tolerate considerable departures of actual inventory from the desired level, by the flexible accelerator, rather than by errors made by firms in anticipating sales volume.

Can the negative findings with regard to the buffer stock model be attributed to the limitations of the data? As explained in section 2, the OBE inventory and sales anticipations survey constitutes a better source of information than the one available for the earlier studies. For one thing, evidence is provided for the first time on planned inventory investment. In addition, the OBE survey emphasizes a distinction

---

[41] 1947, p. 11.

[42] See Lovell (1962).

[43] These results are consistent with those of Pashigian (1965), who used a simple accelerator model, unencumbered by the buffer stock complication, in using sales anticipations data collected in the OBE plant and equipment survey in explaining manufacturing inventory investment.

between long and short sales anticipations that was not available in earlier investigations. Admittedly, there is a problem created by the fact that the questionnaire's *ex ante* figures may be furnished by individuals remote from the actual decision-making about purchasing and production scheduling. But as indicated in section 2, there exists at least some evidence that the *ex ante* data are relevant to production and inventory decisions. If my difficulties with the buffer-stock concept are to be attributed to bad data, then surely the earlier studies are equally suspect.

A second possible source of error arises from problems of aggregation. Our inability to distinguish stage of fabrication at the industry level may well have constituted a distorting factor; for example, both sales and inventory may fall short of anticipations as a result of delays experienced in obtaining raw materials. Furthermore, to the extent that one firm sells more than anticipated to another firm within the observed aggregate, total inventories will be unaffected by the error made in anticipating sales volume. But the level of disaggregation provided by the OBE survey is at least as fine as that of most other studies of inventory behavior.[44] In earlier investigations more successful empirical results led to the conclusion that the difficulties of aggregation were not critical;[45] this conclusion is shaken if the difficulties reported in this paper are to be attributed to problems of aggregation.

A major qualification of our analysis concerns possible limitations of the accelerator buffer stock framework. It is apparent that at a number of points my empirical results are not in conformity with what was expected on the basis of earlier empirical work and a priori ideas about the signs of certain parameters. In contrast to earlier empirical studies, the unfilled orders backlog was not found to have an important role in determining desired inventory or anticipated inventory investment; this rather surprising result may well be explained by the possibility that in earlier studies unfilled orders served as a proxy for anticipated sales volume, an unobserved variable, rather than as a direct determinant of desired inventory. But it is less easy to reconcile the difficulties encountered in the first part of section 6 in explaining the inventory condition variable. Furthermore, repeated difficulty was

----

[44] The primary exception is Edwin Mills' (1957) study based on individual firm data for the interwar period, but here *ex ante* concepts were not observable and the empirical results were not completely consistent with the theory. The cement studies discussed in section 5 above involved a narrower definition of industry than is available from the OBE.

[45] It will be remembered that Moses Abramovitz (1950) had stressed the importance of the aggregation problem.

encountered in an embarrassing number of industries with the signs of the regression coefficients relating desired inventory to current and anticipated future sales volume. While these difficulties may stem in part from the rather limited number of observations available, they should be regarded as symptomatic of a possible misspecification of the basic model. In order to prevent the statistical analysis from degenerating into an exercise in descriptive statistics, repeated experimentation on the basic format of the model suggested in earlier empirical studies was not attempted in this study. But the difficulties encountered suggest that the basic limitations of the buffer stock theory may be critical. It may well be that revisions of price anticipations belong in the realization function. If firms raise prices when demands conditions are buoyant in order to restrict demand to the available supply, the revaluation of existing inventory may create difficulties for us, as the stocks are not measured in physical units and sales are regarded as exogenous. It may be that a primary source of difficulty stems from the possibility that the firm's total inventory picture is subject to much uncertainty because of difficulties in predicting the arrival of raw materials rather than errors made in anticipating future demand.

BIBLIOGRAPHY

Abramovitz, Moses, *Inventories and Business Cycles, with Special Reference to Manufacturers' Inventories,* New York, NBER, 1950.

Enthoven, Alain, "Studies in the Theory of Inflation," unpublished Ph.D. dissertation, Massachusetts Institute of Technology, 1956.

Ferber, Robert, *The Railroad Shippers' Forecasts,* Urbana, 1953.

Friend, I., and Bronfenbrenner, J., "Business Investment Programs and Their Realization," *Survey of Current Business,* December 1950.

Foss, Murray F., "Manufacturers' Inventory and Sales Anticipations, A New Survey," *American Statistical Association,* Proceedings, Business and Economics Statistics Section, 1961, pp. 234–251.

Foster, Edward, "Sales Forecasts and the Inventory Cycle," *Econometrica,* July 1963, pp. 400–419.

Johnston, Jack, "An Econometric Study of the Production Decision," *Quarterly Journal of Economics,* May 1961, pp. 234–261.

———, *Econometric Methods,* New York, 1963.

Lovell, Michael, "Manufacturers' Inventories, Sales Expectations, and the Acceleration Principle," *Econometrica,* July 1961.

———, "Buffer Stocks, Sales Expectations, and Stability: A Multi-Sector Analysis of the Inventory Cycle," *Econometrica,* April 1962.

———, "Determinants of Inventory Investment," in *Models of Income Determination,* Princeton for NBER, 1964.

Mann, H. B., and Wald, A., "On the Statistical Treatment of Linear Stochastic Difference Equations," *Econometrica*, July-October 1943, pp. 173–220.

Metzler, Lloyd, "The Nature and Stability of Inventory Cycles," *The Review of Economic Statistics*, August 1941, pp. 113–129.

————, "Factors Governing the Length of Inventory Cycles," *The Review of Economic Statistics*, February 1947, pp. 1–14.

Mills, Edwin S., "The Theory of Inventory Decisions," *Econometrica*, April 1957, pp. 222–239.

————, *Prices Output and Inventory Policy*, New York, 1962.

Modigliani, Franco, and Cohen, Kalman J., *The Role of Anticipations and Plans in Economic Behavior and Their Use in Economic Analysis and Forecasting*, Urbana, 1961.

Modigliani, F., and Weingartner, H. M., "Forecasting Uses of Anticipatory Data on Investment and Sales," *Quarterly Journal of Economics*, February 1958, pp. 23–54.

————, and Owen H. Sauerlander, "Economic Expectations and Plans in Relation to Short-Term Economic Forecasting," *Short-Term Economic Forecasting*, Princeton for NBER, 1955, pp. 261–351.

Muth, Jack, "Rational Expectations and the Theory of Price Movements," *Econometrica*, July 1961, pp. 315–335.

Pashigian, Peter B., "The Accuracy of the Commerce-SEC Sales Anticipations," *Review of Economics and Statistics*, November 1964, pp. 398–405.

————, "The Relevance of Sales Anticipatory Data in Explaining Inventory Investment Behavior," *International Economic Review*, January 1965, pp. 65–91.

The Quality and Economic Significance of Anticipations Data, Princeton for NBER, 1960.

Theil, H., *Economic Forecasts and Policy*, Amsterdam, 1961.

Wilde, Douglass J., *Optimum Seeking Methods*, Englewood Cliffs, 1964.

COMMENT

ON SACHS-HART AND LOVELL

BY MILLARD HASTAY, WASHINGTON STATE UNIVERSITY

The proper balance in discussion appears to be about nine parts criticism and one part praise. I think it important that the papers contributed to this session on anticipations and investment behavior receive their full quota of praise. The Sachs-Hart study deals with data on capital appropriations that have been extensively described elsewhere but used relatively little; the Lovell paper describes and analyzes data on sales and inventory anticipations that are essentially new. Both papers are thus highly worthwhile efforts to assess and "prove in" important new bodies of anticipations data. They deal extensively with the uses to which the new data can be put, and they provide illuminating comparisons with the results achieved using different and less satisfactory bodies of data.

For this kind of investigation, a rather free-wheeling attitude in sifting hypotheses is warranted. The problem is one of seeking hypotheses more than of testing them, that is to say, of trying to find unbiased simplifications that relate the new data to information already at hand. Until some experience has been gained, however, a priori information is likely to be insufficient to reduce the possible relationships among variables to models simple enough to be rich in empirical content. In such circumstances, the temptation to seek help in the data themselves is well-nigh irresistible, and sometimes unavoidable.

An exploratory investigation in this spirit is plainly fraught with certain dangers. The rule that the "maintained hypothesis," or model, shall be independent of the data under investigation is a categorical necessity of the strict application of the principles of statistical inference. It is, of course, a rule frequently honored in the breach. This occurs when we incorporate in our maintained hypothesis mathematically convenient assumptions such as linearity, normality, and so forth for which we lack evidence. It occurs more outrageously when we provisionally examine the data to assure ourselves that such convenient assumptions are not patently false, and then proceed as if they were true. When we go further and ask the data which hypotheses are worth investigating, the price is likely to be an inability to make any statements at all about the statistical significance of our findings.

A more serious danger, it seems to me, is the failure to consider a suitably wide range of possibilities. Often this failure is due to the enormous computational burdens involved. Where this is the case, computers can break through the impasse. They offer the possibility of systematic exploration of whole classes of simplified models, they permit the running down of purely formal reservations of uncertain empirical importance, and they foster consideration of the degree of inferiority of unpreferred alternatives. In effect, they liberate the researcher from casual empiricism by permitting him to extend a kind of likelihood technique to hypothesis seeking. The penalties for inadequate imagination remain, but they are no longer aggravated by the crippling limitations of computational economy.

Significantly, the authors of both papers make extensive use of the computer, and the result in each case is a far subtler piece of analysis than would otherwise have been possible. Moreover, the spirit of the Sachs-Hart approach appears to be rather close to that outlined above. They write, ". . . the present study should probably be viewed as a reconnaissance: we have looked at so many relations that the degree to which we can claim to have genuinely tested hypotheses is doubtful. But at the very least, we are in a position to enter upon research at the two-digit industry level with fairly well-defined hypotheses."

I think we must ask, however, what these well defined hypotheses are. At another point, the authors tell us that the results of their study "are perhaps best viewed as hypotheses which should stand confrontation with the corresponding data for the two-digit durable goods manufacturing industries. Time lags and relative weights of variables," they say, "should vary from industry to industry. But if our results are meaningful, the two-digit industries stage of the analysis should yield functions with a strong family resemblance to those presented in this study."

What does this mean in terms of the next research stage? If time lags and relative weights remain open, does not the entire field of hypotheses remain open also? Are we then considering a replication of the whole research program for each two-digit industry? If this is the plan, I submit that the statistical significance of what is learned will still be very much open to question. Perhaps the replicates will coalesce about a very characteristic structure, but suppose they do not. Thus while I agree that the present study provides a very illuminating foundation for subsequent work, I think it does so not by providing hypotheses but by providing constraints on subsequent theorizing. For example, one would be suspicious of any theory that makes capital expenditures at time t a function of a single period's authorizations, that implies a rigid determinism between expenditures and any earlier authorization, that fails to make room for capacity utilization and financial variables in addition to authorizations, and so forth. But these, and other similar constraints derivable from the present paper, are insufficient to specify a theory of the role of authorizations in capital expenditures; and a considerable effort at formal model-building must precede the next stage of the investigation if the findings are to be amenable to the usual apparatus of statistical interpretation.

Quite possibly the authors mean their remarks to be interpreted in this sense. If so, I feel that their research strategy is a defensible one. Perhaps another set of investigators would have been willing to stake more on the adequacy of their prior theory of the expenditures-authorizations nexus, but in the present state of knowledge they could hardly object if others fail to share their confidence. What is important is that any research program provide a place for the maintained-hypothesis approach, and this the Sachs-Hart program appears to do.

Turning next to Michael Lovell's paper, one finds the discipline of prior theorizing a good deal more in evidence. Lovell begins, however, with some purely descriptive findings on the accuracy of manufacturers' anticipations in the new OBE survey. To this end he employs the naive-model approach first used by Ferber in 1953 on the railroad shippers' forecasts. This consists of comparing the accuracy of anticipations about a given variable with a mechanical forecast based on recent actual values of the same variable. The formula employed for the naive forecast is presented in the paper as

$$E_t{}^{**} = A_{t-4}(A_{t-1}/A_{t-5}),$$

which, as Lovell expresses it, "amounts to adjusting the same quarter of the immediately preceding year by the recently observed trend." This provides a one-quarter forecast at the close of period $t - 1$; a two-quarter forecase at the same date is given by

$$E_{t+1}{}^{**} = A_{t-3}(A_{t-1}/A_{t-5}).$$

By and large, Lovell finds that the new anticipations data are substantially more accurate than naive projections. This finding is uniformly true for durable goods manufacturing industries; it is also generally true of the sales anticipations in nondurable goods manufacturing. The exception is provided by inventory anticipations in nondurable goods manufacturing, which are generally inferior to naive projections.

My own feeling, however, is that the Ferber-Modigliani test against a naive model—ingenious and revealing as it has been in characterizing the nature of *ex ante* data—is no longer definitive. We now recognize that the value of anticipations data depends not on how good they are as direct forecasters but rather on what we can do with them in a behavioristic model. One thing that the "realization function" approach shows us is that there is good reason why one- and two-quarter anticipations should not be accurate: their purpose is to initiate correctable action, not to predetermine action. To put the matter metaphorically, business planning is less a matter of sighting a distant target than it is of launching a guided missile on a path that can be adjusted as more information on an approaching target becomes available. Regarded in this light, anticipations data yield valuable information on the planning process, which in turn provides a foundation for describing the process by which realized magnitudes are shaped. Good evidence on the planning process need not be good evidence as forecasts; it undoubtedly helps to be both, but it is not essential.

I pass now to the heart of Lovell's paper, the realization function approach to inventory behavior. In Lovell's notation, the simplest version of this approach states the following relation between realized and planned inventories

$$IN = ASIN - (SALE - ASSALE).$$

This implies complete plan rigidity—an idea appropriate, say, to the "Hicksian week." Lovell considers a slight modification reasonable in time periods long enough for surprises to be recognized and reacted to

$$IN = b_1 + b_2 ASIN - b_3(SALE - ASSALE),$$

where b_2 and b_3 are intrinsically positive. He does not, however, consider a positive coefficient of $(SALE - ASSALE)$ reasonable. Why not?

Let us first see that a positive coefficient is not illogical. Suppose that at the beginning of the current period, it is planned that inventory at the end of the period shall be IN^p. We may suppose that this plan depends in a definite way on the sales anticipated for the same period

$$IN^p = f(ASSALE).$$

Then, with sufficient plan flexibility, we expect to be able to approximate realized inventory at the close of the period by the first terms in Taylor's expansion

$$IN = IN^p + f'(ASSALE)(SALE - ASSALE).$$

In the linear case, this becomes

$$IN^p = \beta_1 + \beta_2 ASSALE, \quad \beta_2 > 0$$
$$IN = IN^p + \beta_2(SALE - ASSALE)$$
$$= \beta_1 + \beta_2 ASSALE + \beta_2(SALE - ASSALE).$$

With moderate plan flexibility, one would expect to find the statistical coefficient of the term (SALE − ASSALE), say, b_3, *less than* β_2; but it need not be negative. Even inverse movements of the ratio IN/SALE with respect to sales, or cyclical alternations of stock shortages and surpluses, need not make b_3 negative.

The truth is that, quite frequently, Lovell does *not* find coefficients of the type b_3 to be negative; and he is much troubled by this outcome. In employing the realization function idea on Dun and Bradstreet data, I got similar results—correction coefficients that were frequently positive and sometimes large. These results were suspect because of the possible influence of inflationary price rises in the period I investigated, 1949–57; but Lovell's data are much less likely to be contaminated in this way.

I therefore recommend that, for total inventories, we steel ourselves to the possibility of having to *accept* this evidence of programming flexibility in manufacturing industry. It begins to have the appearance of an attested fact. I can sympathize with Lovell's concern for the buffer-stock hypothesis; to relax or abandon it threatens some important macrotheories of inventory behavior. But we need to remember that the buffer-stock hypothesis is most plausible for stocks of finished commodities. For stocks of goods in process and even stocks of raw materials, a fairly close correspondence of stocks with sales is to be expected theoretically and has been found statistically by Abramovitz and Stanback. When to these we add finished stocks, the resulting series of total stocks shows at most a short lag behind the turning points of sales; and this phenomenon, as I shall show below, is not incompatible with a positive coefficient for the surprise term (SALE − ASSALE) in Lovell's realization function.

In my initial reaction to Lovell's paper, I was inclined to take a similarly lighthearted view of his dissatisfaction with the coefficients in his equation for investment in finished inventories

$$\Delta\text{FIN} = \delta\beta_1 + \delta\beta_2\text{SALE} + \lambda(\delta\beta_2 + 1)(\text{ASSALE} - \text{SALE}) - \delta\text{FIN}_{-1}.$$

On a closer reading of his paper, however, I am convinced that his concern is warranted. The results he gets are (1) inconsistent with earlier econometric findings of his and others, (2) apparently contrary to the production-smoothing hypothesis, which has strong theoretical and practical support, and (3) difficult to square with Abramovitz' finding, confirmed by Stanback, that finished manufacturers stocks move inversely to sales in short cycles.

Some insight into these difficulties is suggested by a slight transformation of the preceding equation

$$\Delta FIN = \delta\beta_2(SALE - SALE_{-1}) + \lambda(\delta\beta_2 + 1)[(ASSALE - SALE_{-1})$$
$$- (SALE - SALE_{-1})] + \delta\beta_1 + \delta\beta_2 SALE_{-1} - \delta FIN_{-1},$$

or in difference notation

$$\Delta FIN = [\delta\beta_2(1 - \lambda) - \lambda]\Delta SALE + \lambda(\delta\beta_2 + 1)\Delta ASSALE$$
$$+ \delta(FIN_{-1}{}^d - FIN_{-1}),$$

where $(FIN_{-1}{}^d - FIN_{-1})$ is the discrepancy between actual and desired stocks at the close of the preceding period. This version justifies the earlier assertion that Lovell's model of inventory behavior can show a lag of inventories behind sales at turning points, even when the coefficient $[\delta\beta_2(1 - \lambda) - \lambda]$ is positive. For this implies that ΔFIN lags $\Delta SALE$, and this can happen because $\Delta ASSALE$ lags $\Delta SALE$ and the final term, representing stock disequilibrium, also lags $\Delta SALE$.

More significantly, this formulation shows that Lovell's model of inventory behavior implies the same timid planning reaction to an *ex post* stock disequilibrium, $(FIN_{-1}{}^d - FIN_{-1})$, as to an *ex ante* stock disequilibrium, $\beta_2(ASSALE - SALE_{-1})$. This can perhaps be seen more clearly by going back to first principles. We have the anticipated level of desired finished stocks,

$$AFIN^d = \beta_1 + \beta_2 ASSALE + \beta_3 ALSALE_{+1},$$

and the corresponding short-run planned level,

$$ASFIN = \delta AFIN^d + (1 - \delta)FIN_{-1},$$

whence $ASFIN - FIN_{-1} = \delta AFIN^d - \delta FIN_{-1}$, i.e.,

$$\Delta ASFIN = \delta(\beta_1 + \beta_2 ASSALE + \beta_3 ALSALE_{+1}) - \delta FIN_{-1}$$
$$= \delta\beta_2(ASSALE - SALE_{-1}) + \delta\beta_3(ALSALE_{+1} - ASSALE)$$
$$+ \delta(\beta_1 + \beta_2 SALE_{-1} + \beta_3 ASSALE - FIN_{-1}).$$

The final term implies that only a fraction δ of the *ex post* disequilibrium $(FIN_{-1}{}^d - FIN_{-1})$ is planned for correction in the next period.

It seems more reasonable to suppose that this correction will be planned for a single period, thus

$$\Delta ASFIN = \delta\beta_2(ASSALE - SALE_{-1}) + \delta\beta_3(ALSALE_{+1} - ASSALE)$$
$$+ (\beta_1 + \beta_2 SALE_{-1} + \beta_3 ASSALE - FIN_{-1})$$

whence

$$ASFIN = \delta(\beta_1 + \beta_2 ASSALE + \beta_3 ALSALE_{+1}) + (1 - \delta)FIN_{-1}{}^d.$$

The derivation of an equation for realized inventories now proceeds exactly as before, and we arrive at the equation

$$FIN = ASFIN + [(1 - \lambda)\delta\beta_2 - \lambda](SALE - ASSALE)$$
$$+ (1 - \lambda)\delta\beta_3(ASSALE_{+1} - ALSALE_{+1}),$$

which has exactly the same structure as one shown by Lovell for total inventories. The missing anticipations variable ASFIN can be finessed as before by substituting the foregoing expression for it, which gives, after some manipulation,

$$\Delta FIN = FIN - FIN_{-1} = \delta\beta_1 + \delta\beta_2 SALE + \delta\beta_3 ASSALE_{+1}$$
$$- \lambda(1 + \delta\beta_2)(SALE - ASSALE) - \lambda\delta\beta_3(ASSALE_{+1} - ALSALE_{+1})$$
$$+ (1 - \delta)(FIN_{-1}{}^d - FIN_{-1}) - \delta FIN_{-1}.$$

Let us follow Lovell in dropping the long anticipations; then the model becomes

$$\Delta FIN = \delta\beta_1 + \delta\beta_2 SALE - \lambda(1 + \delta\beta_2)(SALE - ASSALE)$$
$$+ (1 - \delta)(FIN_{-1}{}^d - FIN_{-1}) - \delta FIN_{-1},$$

which differs essentially from the equation derived by Lovell.

If, as I believe, the implied handling of *ex post* stock disequilibrium in this model represents a gain in realism, it would appear that part of the trouble with Lovell's finished inventories investment function is inherent in a misspecification of ASFIN. Significantly, this misspecification has no effect on the inventory equations in which inventory anticipations enter explicitly; it thus provides no reason to question the equations for total inventories. But it does lead to the neglect of a relevant term in equations from which inventory anticipations have been finessed, viz., $(1 - \delta)$ $(FIN_{-1}{}^d - FIN_{-1})$. It is thus possible that the variable SALE serves as a proxy for $(FIN_{-1}{}^d - FIN_{-1})$, with which it tends to be positively correlated and which has an intrinsically positive coefficient. In this case $\delta\beta_2$ would tend to be too large, and the derived sum

$$\delta\beta_2 - \lambda(1 + \delta\beta_2) = (1 - \lambda)\delta\beta_2 - \lambda$$

correspondingly too large also.

For estimation purposes, a slight modification of the foregoing equation is convenient

$$\Delta FIN = \delta\beta_2 \Delta SALE - \lambda(1 + \delta\beta_2)(\Delta SALE - \Delta ASSALE)$$
$$+ (\beta_1 + \beta_2 SALE_{-1} - FIN_{-1}).$$

This version shows that the unknown coefficients β_1, β_2, δ, and λ can be estimated uniquely. It also shows that the variable accelerator model, even as modified, depends on surprises—in fact, substantial ones—to generate inverse behavior of finished inventory stocks and sales. Without such surprises, stocks vary directly with sales.

It may be interesting to compare the working of a simple production-smoothing model developed in the same spirit as Lovell's variable accelerator model. Let us introduce the notation PROD for production, APROD^d for desired production in terms of anticipated sales, and ASPROD for short-run planned production. Then we may suppose that desired production equals anticipated sales plus a correction of *ex post* inventory maladjustment

$$\text{APROD}^d = \text{ASSALE} + (\beta_1 + \beta_2 \text{SALE}_{-1} - \text{FIN}_{-1}).$$

But production smoothing implies that the firm will make the desired adjustment of production gradually. One possibility, implying a two stage adjustment to realized sales and a multiple-period correction of inventory stock, is the following:

$$\text{ASPROD} = \text{SALE}_{-1} + \delta(\text{ASSALE} - \text{SALE}_{-1})$$
$$+ \gamma(\beta_1 + \beta_2 \text{SALE}_{-1} - \text{FIN}_{-1}),$$

where both δ and γ are less than unity.

Following Lovell's procedure, we posit two extreme hypotheses about the adjustment of production to surprises: PROD = ASPROD, i.e., complete inflexibility, with weight λ; and PROD = ASPROD + δ(SALE − ASSALE), i.e., two-stage adjustment to sales, with weight $1 - \lambda$. Then over all firms in the industry

$$\text{PROD} = \text{ASPROD} + (1 - \lambda)\delta(\text{SALE} - \text{ASSALE}).$$

Now, evidently we have

$$\text{AFIN} = \text{FIN}_{-1} + (\text{ASPROD} - \text{ASSALE}) \text{ and FIN} = \text{FIN}_{-1}$$
$$+ (\text{PROD} - \text{SALE}).$$

From these we derive

$$\text{FIN} = \text{AFIN} + (\text{PROD} - \text{ASPROD}) - (\text{SALE} - \text{ASSALE})$$

and, substituting from the equation for PROD, we get

$$\text{FIN} = \text{AFIN} - [1 - (1 - \lambda)\delta](\text{SALE} - \text{ASSALE}).$$

Similarly, substituting for ASPROD in the expression for AFIN gives

$$\text{AFIN} = \text{FIN}_{-1} - \text{ASSALE} + \text{SALE}_{-1} + \delta(\text{ASSALE} - \text{SALE}_{-1})$$
$$+ \gamma(\beta_1 + \beta_2 \text{SALE}_{-1} - \text{FIN}_{-1})$$
$$= \text{FIN}_{-1} - (1 - \delta)\Delta\text{ASSALE} + \gamma(\text{FIN}_{-1}{}^d - \text{FIN}_{-1}).$$

Again, by definition, $\Delta\text{FIN} = (\text{FIN} - \text{AFIN}) + (\text{AFIN} - \text{FIN}_{-1})$, whence after substitution from the preceding paragraph

$$\Delta\text{FIN} = -(1 - \delta)\Delta\text{ASSALE} - [1 - (1 - \lambda)\delta](\Delta\text{SALE} - \Delta\text{ASSALE}) + \gamma(\text{FIN}_{-1}{}^d - \text{FIN}_{-1}).$$

In this form we see that, for suitably small γ ($0 < \gamma < 1$), the production-smoothing model yields Abramovitz' findings—inverted behavior of finished stocks in short cycles and conforming behavior with a long lag in major cycles. For in a time of rising sales and sales anticipations, ΔFIN will tend to fall. The only offset to this tendency will be the growth of the discrepancy ($\text{FIN}_{-1}{}^d - \text{FIN}_{-1}$), due both to the rise of $\text{FIN}_{-1}{}^d$ with sales and to the decline of FIN_{-1} with production smoothing. But given that γ is small, this offset will dominate the movement of ΔFIN only with a considerable lag. A parallel argument holds for declining sales and sales anticipations. Finally, the inverse behavior of sales and inventories does not depend on surprises: given that the coefficient of ΔASSALE is negative, even if $\Delta\text{SALE} = \Delta\text{ASSALE}$, inventory change will be inverse to the change in sales until the discrepancy ($\text{FIN}_{-1}{}^d - \text{FIN}_{-1}$) becomes sufficiently large.

As near as I can determine, Lovell's results from fitting his equations for ΔFIN do not yield a test of this model. The above comments suggest that it, or something like it, might be worth investigating.

ON SACHS-HART AND LOVELL

BY ROBERT EISNER, NORTHWESTERN UNIVERSITY

I presume that the role of a discussant is that of a searching critic who offers the most severe scrutiny of possible pitfalls for the unwary on every road traveled. What is more, he should be a kind of backseat driver constantly asking "Why didn't you take that road?" Where the roads traveled are pioneering and ingeniously constructed, as is apparent in the papers under discussion, the challenge to the discussant is all the greater.

To begin with the Sachs-Hart paper, one usually fruitful avenue of criticism—that of asking the authors why they did not try this or that possibility—might seem cut off since Sachs and Hart have tried them all! Indeed they admit quite candidly that they have indulged in "extensive screening" which may raise some questions about the statistical significance of their findings. Well, since I cannot easily suggest that they should have tried other things, I shall *object* to their having tried everything.

None of us is innocent in this regard, and Sachs and Hart are no more guilty than most; but this is, in my opinion, a really serious and growing problem in the modern age of high-speed digital computers. Without specific reference to the Sachs-Hart paper, what indeed are we to make of a relation reported as significant at a .01 probability level if we are told by the authors that they tried 100 different relations and screened out the 99 that did not prove "significant"? I am not prepared to argue that there should be no examination of data during the process of formulating and developing hypotheses. But there are some serious formal and statistical considerations that must be set forth in view of modern technology, and they should be taken quite explicitly into account in our work.

Turning to more substantive matters, the National Industrial Conference Board appropriations data utilized by Sachs and Hart may be of interest for what they reveal about capital expenditure decisions, may be useful per se for forecasting purposes, may be useful for forecasting along with other contemporaneous variables, or may be useful in a realization function along with other variables subsequent in time to the period at which the decisions underlying appropriations are made. They may be meaningful as factors actually influencing investment or they may merely be useful as conveyors of information to the research worker.

I myself am rather inclined to doubt the importance of appropriations as factors determining investment in their own right. I am rather skeptical in general about the significance of financial considerations in determining the rate or even timing of investment. This is not the place to review the growing econometric literature on the subject, but I might relate a high point of one of my interviews of business executives a number of years ago in an effort to find out about the determinants of capital expenditures. One financial officer of a large manufacturing company had just finished assuring me with some passion of the necessity for him to find appropriate ways to "get the money" if capital expenditures were to be made. At this point his superior in the business hierarchy entered the room. I briefed him on the question I had raised and he quickly interjected, "Oh, financial considerations never stop us from making a capital expenditure that we think is profitable. We'll always get the money. That's his job, to get it for us," he said, pointing to the somewhat embarrassed financial officer.

The inference which I would draw from this and other facts is that monetary considerations are important in the timing of monetary arrangements and hence, very likely, important in the timing of appropriations as well. It is hard to believe that either the fact that money could be raised readily or that, as a consequence, appropriations might be made would lead the large firms that do most of our investing to undertake capital expenditures of inappropriate profitability.

Appropriations data may nevertheless contain useful information for forecasting purposes. They may well give a substantial clue to the desired capital stock for some period in the future (but perhaps a period imprecisely defined). A considerable difficulty remains, nevertheless, in moving from information on desired capital stock to information on investment, which will determine the path of capital over time. It is, of course, possible that there may be some stable distribution function that will transform the stock or flow of appropriations data into subsequent capital expenditures. Interesting work has been done on this matter. Proof of the stability of any such relation cannot come, however, from fits of regressions to past data; it must relate to predictions independent of the data from which estimates are made.

The Sachs-Hart results themselves suggest that much information relevant to investment is lost in the appropriations nexus and that a useful, stable relation of investment and appropriations is elusive. For Sachs and Hart note, most interestingly, that a simple or direct function relating investment to such determinants as accelerator and cash flow-type variables offers a better fit, after appropriate adjustment, than does the relation which makes investment a function of the appropriations function based upon these same determinants.

Sachs and Hart suggest that the marked improvement in the fit of the investment-appropriations relation when lagged investment is added to the independent variables may be a result of "random" but serial correlated disturbances in the investment relation. This may in part be true. I should think, however, that lagged investment is particularly important in taking care of not merely random factors but also the critical question of timing of the investment stemming from any given series of past flows of appropriations. The significant role of lagged investment reminds us, therefore, rather of systematic factors lacking in the investment-appropriations relation. Among these systematic factors may be those relating to the supply of capital goods, an element generally ignored in the Sachs-Hart treatment.

A number of questions are suggested by Sachs and Hart or suggest themselves with regard to the role of "cash flow." They wonder themselves at the relevance of cash flow at a period so late as to cast doubt on its real role in determining investment. I suggest that this may be due to the role of cash flow as a proxy for earlier indicators of expected future demands which operate on investment without manifesting themselves fully in the pure appropriations relation.

A further difficulty in accepting the role of cash flow in the "eclectic model" presented by Sachs and Hart lies in the lack of identifiability of the relation they estimate. It would be a brave man who could assert without doubt that a positive association between cash flow and capital expenditures of the same or proximate quarters in a set of time series observations in manufacturing durables establishes that higher cash flow induces a greater rate of investment. One might as easily infer that higher rates of investment expenditures increase the profits and hence the "cash flow" of the manufacturing durable industries which produce capital goods, not to mention other industries which profit indirectly from higher investment expenditures.

Sachs and Hart express surprise that addition of a variable for lagged cancellation of appropriations results in a better fit than was obtained with appropriations themselves. I might hazard the explanation that this result appears because investment realizations are more sensitive to depressing than to exhilarating changes in underlying economic conditions. I have noted some data bearing on this elsewhere. A confirmation with appropriations data might be found by estimating a relation involving separate coefficients for appropriations when appropriations are rising and when they are falling. This might be done, simply enough of course, by adding a set of appropriations variables which would be identical to the actual appropriations series when appropriations are falling but equal to zero when appropriations are rising. Positive coefficients for this additional set of appropriations variables would confirm the hypothesis that appropriations data and, perhaps, the underlying factors influencing them, are associated more sharply with investment in periods of decline than in periods of rise.

In their discussion of "plan image," Sachs and Hart use very recent cancellations data as the additional arguments necessary to convert their anticipatory function involving appropirations data into a realization function, which would presume to explain the difference between anticipations and realized investment. It seems to me that, since cancellations are themselves nothing but more recent anticipatory variables with regard to investment, they are not proper complements in the creation of a realization function. We should rather have real variables which offer corrections of the expectations which underlay the investment anticipations. A realization function involving such real variables would have the advantage of a tie-in for predictive and analytical purposes with the actual or model-generated nonanticipatory variables which might actually determine investment.

The paper by Sachs and Hart is generally scholarly, tentative, and cautious. Yet in the end they seem to be somewhat carried away in their evaluation of the usefulness of the appropriations data for forecasting purposes. For they base their favorable conclusions on the goodness of fit of their regressions of past investment expenditures on appropriations. Surely, however, the test which the appropriations relation must meet is not that of goodness of fit to the data from which it was estimated. It must rather meet the unhappily more exacting test of prediction of capital expenditures in periods other than those in which it was nurtured.

And if the appropriations data are to be compared for accuracy of forecasting with surveys of anticipated capital expenditures by the McGraw-Hill Department of Economics or the Securities and Exchange Commission and Office of Business Economics of the Department of Commerce, it is not appropriate to compare the "errors" in a regression of actual expenditures on past appropriations with the errors in the raw data of the McGraw-Hill and Commerce-SEC surveys. A proper test might then involve regression of actual expenditures on appropriations data, on the one hand, and anticipated expenditures, on the other, with the critical comparisons relating to the errors in *prediction of current or future capital expenditures* on the basis of the relations estimated from *past* data.

In turning to the Lovell paper, I find myself in my more usual role as a critic. Lovell has not tried everything, at least not yet. In fact, Lovell has been brave in presenting to this Conference on short notice the results of still-continuing research. What is more, he presents results which appear to him, prima facie, to contradict the empirical and theoretically well-oriented findings of his own previous important work on inventory investment. We witness a conflict between the presumably well-established earlier Lovell findings and the current Lovell results. I should like to help rescue Lovell from Lovell by explaining away some of Lovell's current findings and thus restoring at least some of the shine of Lovell's earlier accelerator buffer-stock models.

As is certainly clear to the reader of Lovell's paper, Lovell now suffers from a wealth of "better" data in the form of quarterly anticipations of both sales and inventories. In olden times, when he had to improvise to get measures of relatively short-term sales and inventory anticipations, he did better. But now we have two basic problems; the sales anticipations are too good and the buffer-stock role of inventories is too poor. I shall attempt a common explanation of both of these findings.

In regard to sales anticipations, it should be recalled that previous work in this area has taught us to expect generally poor correlations between actual and anticipated sales changes. Lovell's results now are amazingly good, at least in the manufacturing durables industries. Comparing mean absolute errors of anticipations with mean absolute errors from the Ferber naive-model extrapolation, Lovell finds anticipations doing consistently better, and markedly better—no mean feat. And when coefficients of determination are examined for actual and predicted sales changes, these are found to be correspondingly high.

A clue to part of what is going on may be found in the recognition that, even when average absolute errors of anticipations are virtually as high as those from the naive model extrapolation, as in manufacturing durables industry 7 (where the ratio of mean absolute errors of anticipations to mean absolute errors based on naive model projections is .96, or almost 1), the R^2 of actual on anticipated sales *changes* is still a robust .6558. Now the Ferber naive-model test is essentially a seasonally adjusted extrapolation of the past. The fact that, when the short-run sales anticipation variable ASSALE does little better than the naive-model test, it nevertheless produces a high R^2 of actual on anticipated sales changes indicates that a considerable part of the accuracy of sales anticipations stems merely from their property of catching seasonal variations.

But actually I believe that there is something else at work which can be used to explain not only the relative accuracy of sales anticipations as a forecast but the seemingly poor results of the buffer-stock mechanism in the Lovell inventory model. Recall, of course, that this model indicates that desired holdings of inventories are based upon anticipated sales. Actual holdings of inventories are less than desired holdings of inventories to the extent that actual sales exceed anticipated sales and producers are unable or unwilling fully to adjust production within the period of measurement. If producers or sellers can adjust very quickly, the buffer role of inventories will, of course, disappear. It has indeed been suggested that application of modern computers and sophisticated handling of data on sales and distribution has made the length of this period of adjustment virtually infinitesimal. I doubt it.

My explanation is simply that Lovell's theory has been right all along but that his current data are not what they are cracked up to be. My point implies no disrespect to the worthy OBE collectors of these highly useful series. What I want to stress is simply that, from the standpoint of inventory control, the sales anticipations for any given quarter which are made known close to the middle of that quarter, as are the ASSALE series, are as much reflections of actual sales of that quarter as they are of anticipations. I would interpret the difference between this semi-forecast of sales and actual sales as essentially a random error having little to do either with the anticipations on which inventory decisions are made or the realizations of these anticipations. For inventory decisions in a firm facing substantial costs in rapid fluctuations of production may relate to relatively longer-run expectations of future sales.

If my conjecture is correct, the deviation of actual sales from what is reported as ASSALE, rather than reflecting an error in the anticipation of sales on the basis of which desired inventory holdings were determined, is an improvement in the not fully observed measure of those anticipations. We would then expect a substantial component of this deviation, if not all of it, to be *positively* associated with inventory investment. And this, of course, is consistent with Lovell's current findings. It all stems from the fact that presumably short-run sales anticipations, ASSALE, are as much a measure of actual sales as anticipated sales (and indeed may well be used as such by clever analysts in the Department of Commerce faced with the task of estimating actual sales), while the actual sales figures are really in large part, for our purposes, proxies for future sales anticipations.

Although this line of conjecture may appeal to all of us who hate to discard a useful theory at the first hint of derogatory data, we should look for independent confirmation or contradiction. I believe I can see some confirmation in the relation noted by Lovell in the third part of his section 6, where he shows a negative correlation between his variable COND (measuring the proportion of respondents considering inventory holdings too high) and ALSALE of two periods hence. This suggests that, to the extent firms expect sales well into the future to be higher, they are less likely to consider current inventories too high.

Of course, further tests might be attempted. (There usually *are* more things which a discussant can suggest be tried.) In particular I might urge that SALE (actual sales) be introduced in equation (8). If estimates of this modified equation were to yield a positive coefficient for SALE, they would suggest that actual sales *are* proxying for expected future demand along with the presumably short-term sales anticipation variable, ASSALE. In general, I would suggest checks of the relative role of these purported measures of anticipated and actual sales. In pursuance of this, one might try using the change in actual sales as a

measure of surprise or error in anticipation. If, as many of us hypothesize, businessmen tend generally to expect tomorrow to be like today,
unless they have very firm knowledge to the contrary, the change in
actual sales may be one of the better measures of unanticipated sales
that we can find.

ON SACHS-HART AND LOVELL

BY JAMES MORGAN, UNIVERSITY OF MICHIGAN

Early studies of the Commerce-SEC investment plans indicated a
tendency to underestimate investment in the last quarter of good years.[1]
I wonder why we do not investigate the possibility that the accounting
and tax year affects decisions. It is common for businessmen to say
they invest profits before the government gets them. What they mean
is that every dollar of investment in new equipment involves some
amount—say, a quarter, of outlays—that can be counted as installation
expenses for tax purposes. If, as Lovell suggests, the flexibility of
adjustment is more rapid than we thought and if, in such adjustment,
attention is paid to keeping profits from fluctuating too much, then not
only do we have a better chance of explaining fourth-quarter investment, but we may also have to be concerned about the distortion of
reported profits figures.

ON SACHS-HART

BY VICTOR ZARNOWITZ, UNIVERSITY OF CHICAGO AND
NATIONAL BUREAU OF ECONOMIC RESEARCH

Sachs and Hart use two categories of "causal" variables to explain,
first, capital appropriations and, second, capital expenditures (in sections C and D of their paper). The "financial" factors, cash flow and
bond yield, compete in this role with the "accelerator-type explanation"
represented by the ratio of deflated new orders received by durable
goods manufacturers to estimated productive capacity of the durable
goods sector. The competition results in a merger: Sachs and Hart
find that "eclectic combinations using both financial and accelerator
variables are considerably stronger than pure models" (that is, than

[1] See Irwin Friend and Jean Bronfenbrenner, "Plant and Equipment Programs
and Their Realization," in *Short-Term Economic Forecasting,* Studies in Income and
Wealth 17, Princeton for NBER, 1955, pp. 53–96.

either the financial or the accelerator-type explanation alone). However, when combined with capital appropriations, the financial variables (chiefly the cash-flow term) show more additional explanation than the "accelerator": in fact, "it appears . . . that virtually all the relevant information to be found in the orders-capacity ratio is well represented by capital appropriations."

The purpose of this comment is to point out that, in the context of the aggregative data used by Sachs and Hart, the influence of the orders-capacity ratio can be explained without recourse to the accelerator theory—that the interpretation of the ratio as an "accelerator" variable may, indeed, be quite misleading. The reason is simple. Advance orders for durable manufacturers are dominated by orders for machinery and nonautomotive transportation equipment. These orders, which are essentially commitments to buy capital equipment, accounted for about 70 per cent of the total value of outstanding durable goods orders in recent years.[1] As a consequence, new orders for durables and new orders for investment goods are highly correlated.[2] This being so, durable goods orders, taken with a lead, must be highly correlated with the output of capital equipment, simply because these goods are typically produced to order. In other words, new orders for durables may be regarded as a proxy for equipment orders which precede output and shipments of the corresponding items as a matter of prevailing contractual arrangements that have, as such, nothing to do with the accelerator theory or any other "causal" explanation of investment.

There are a few complications which, however, do not invalidate the above argument. The use of expenditures for capital goods instead of output or shipments matters little, since the association between expenditures and output is demonstrably very close in quarterly terms on a simultaneous basis. Expenditures (and appropriations) include a "plant" as well as an "equipment" component. But durable goods orders are nearly as well correlated with the composite of machinery and equipment orders plus industrial and commercial construction contracts as with the equipment part of that aggregate alone.[3] Finally, there is the

[1] Statistical evidence on statements made in this comment comes mainly from my work on the relations between manufacturers' orders and investment in plant and equipment (part of a manuscript in preparation for the National Bureau of Economic Research). Because of space limitations, only a very few short references to this documentation will be made.

[2] See Department of Commerce, *Business Cycle Developments*, series 6 and 24. A mere inspection of these graphs makes it clear that the patterns of change in the two series are very much alike.

[3] The graphs of these series are conveniently grouped in *Business Cycle Developments* (compare items 6, 24, and 10).

fact that durable orders are not used as a separate independent variable in the Sachs-Hart regressions: the relevant term is rather the ratio of these orders to a capacity index (developed by Frank de Leeuw of the Federal Reserve Board). But the capacity index is, as it should be, a fairly stable series with a relatively strong trend and very weak cyclical and irregular components; hence the changes in the ratio are definitely dominated by those in the numerator, that is, in the new orders which are subject to relatively pronounced fluctuations.

Correlations of the SEC-OBE quarterly plant and equipment expenditures with new investment orders and contracts, taken with a lead of either two or three quarters, yield simple r^2 of about .80 for 1949–62. This is for deflated data; in current dollars, the correlations are somewhat higher and they exceed the correlations between expenditures and the new capital appropriations for manufacturing.[4] The R^2 coefficients resulting from the use of distributed instead of simple lags are appreciably higher. Differences in industry and time coverage prevent direct comparisons of these results with those of Sachs and Hart; the point I wish to make here is merely that all these findings are consistent with my interpretation of the orders variables as representing primarily another "anticipatory" factor (like the appropriations data) rather than a "causal" factor in the sense of economic theory.

As already noted, the addition of orders-capacity ratios to the appropriation terms contributed very little to a statistical explanation of capital expenditures (see section E of the Sachs-Hart paper). This is probably largely attributable to the affinity between orders and appropriations, as both variables share the character of anticipatory data relative to capital expenditures. The financial variables, which were found to provide more additional information, cannot be regarded as being also of this "anticipatory" nature. As the results are presented, some readers could infer that the financial variables have more autonomous predictive power than the "accelerator" variables have, but in the light of our argument such conclusion would clearly be unwarranted.

When orders and appropriations are both viewed as anticipatory or symptomatic variables, the question arises which predicts or "anticipates" capital expenditures more effectively. My results suggest that orders-contracts have some advantage, whether taken singly (see footnote 4) or in combination with various "causal" variables. But the

---

[4] For 1954–61, the highest r^2 obtained from regressions of plant and equipment expenditures (I) on new capital appropriations in manufacturing was .793 (for a lag of three quarters); the highest r^2 for the relations between I and new investment orders and contracts was .875 (with a lag of two quarters).

advantage is not large and it may depend on the periods used, the lag distributions chosen, etc.[5]

It is important to note that this argument against an interpretation of the orders-capacity ratio as an accelerator variable is cogent only at the aggregative level. When Sachs and Hart extend their study into the two-digit durable goods industries (and we have every reason to welcome their plan to do so and expect interesting results from it), their use of the ratios will be fully justified. For then they will have correctly used orders received by a particular industry, which cannot be confused with orders for the capital goods that are to serve the investment plans of that industry.

---

[5] The explanatory power of durable goods orders would be expected to be less than that of investment orders-contracts. More importantly, the "deflation" with capacity will reduce the "predictive" efficiency of the orders data. Hence, it is not surprising that the orders-capacity ratios perform weakly alongside appropriations, particularly when several terms of the latter, with different lags, are used simultaneously, as in equation E–3.

Author Index

Subject Index